Revisiting the Liberal Constitutional Features of the European Union

Inês Quadros • Miguel Gorjão-Henriques
Editors

Revisiting the Liberal Constitutional Features of the European Union

Springer

APDE
Associação Portuguesa de Direito Europeu

Editors
Inês Quadros
Universidade Católica Portuguesa
Faculty of Law
Lisbon, Portugal

Miguel Gorjão-Henriques
Univ Coimbra, Faculty of Law
Coimbra, Portugal

ISBN 978-3-031-95716-1 ISBN 978-3-031-95717-8 (eBook)
https://doi.org/10.1007/978-3-031-95717-8

APDE - Associação Portuguesa de Direito Europeu
This work was supported by APDE - Associação Portuguesa de Direito Europeu.

This Springer imprint is published by the registered company Springer Nature Switzerland AG
The registered company address is: Gewerbestrasse 11, 6330 Cham, Switzerland

Preface

Revisiting the Liberal Constitutional Features of the European Union recalls the pillar principles upon which the European Union was conceived—rule of law, democracy, and fundamental rights—and updates their significance taking into account the constitutional drift that has occurred over time and the threats the EU is currently facing.

Constitutionalism is not an innovative framework to describe the legal features of the European Union. Following the early judicial decisions that set the tone for the transformation of the European legal order, and thus for the transformation of Europe (Weiler) from an international organisation into a supranational political actor, the term *Constitution* and its declinations became explicit both in judicial decisions (e.g. the reference to the Treaties as the "Constitutional Charter", in the *Les Verts* judgement, or the "fundamental status" conferred to European citizenship since *Baumbast*) and in political discourse (with the call for a "European sovereignty" by the French EU Presidency in 2022).

Borrowing the semantics and the political conceptualisation of sovereign States was also an early trend in EU Law scholarship, of which this book intends to be part. It aims to revisit the constitutional features of the European Union, by addressing some pressing topics within the framework of what can be considered the pillar upon which the "European way of life" is built—liberal democratic constitutionalism.

The work is split into four sections, each devoted to one dimension of European constitutionalism—political theory; rule of law; public interest; and autonomy of the European legal order.

The first section—*Legal-Political tensions within the European Union*—revisits the legal-political trends currently underpinning the European discourse. One article departs from the 2022 French Presidency proposal of "European sovereignty" to assess the viability of giving that proposal a legal significance (F. de Quadros). Following this, the contribution from former Court of Justice judge J. N. Cunha Rodrigues is devoted to the current illiberal challenges in some member States, which risk undermining the European way of life that was at the basis of the European project. A third contribution analyses the impact of the requirements of European citizenship on national rules on the acquisition and loss of nationality

(R. M. Ramos). The section closes with a chapter about the principle of subsidiarity with a focus on the political mechanisms of control (D. Lopes).

The second section—*Rule of law*—is devoted to the requirements of that principle and the threats that are currently ongoing. The first chapter is dedicated to the role of the Court of Justice in upholding democracy in Member States (M. P. Maduro). The second analyses the declination of the rule of law principle in Competition Law, in particular its implications for competition authorities (S. Pais and M. P. Domingos). A third contribution describes five key aspects of the rule of law crisis in some Member States (A. Silveira). The following chapter proposes a systematisation of the EU procedural and substantive sources of the principle of judicial independence, critically analysing their use by the Court of Justice (I. Quadros). Finally, the last chapter is devoted to the role that the E-Justice project can play in overcoming threats to effective judicial protection (J. C. de Abreu).

The third section—*Contemporary EU policies: Updating public interest*—reviews the state of the art in pressing EU policies and their interplay with national rules. It opens with a contribution that aims to revisit the role of the European Union as a regional bloc in the world economic arena (M. Porto). The chapter that follows deals with the European Data Space and its complex set of rules and governance (G. Enes). The relationship between EU law and national Constitutional law on data protection is the subject of the next contribution (F. P. Coutinho). The last article sets forth the relationship between European and national competition rules regarding merger control in connection with exclusive rights granted by Member States (J. L. Vilaça / R. L. Vasconcelos).

Finally, the last section—*On the verge of autonomy*—revisits the qualities of the EU legal order *vis a vis* the competing claims of authority by Member States. The first chapter analyses one of the latest decisions delivered by a Constitutional court of a Member State that dealt with the primacy principle (P. F. Martins). Another contribution reflects on the possibility of constitutional control of national rules incompatible with the Charter of Fundamental Rights (A. Patrão). The last article aims to strike a balance between, on the one hand, the effectiveness of Union law and the way the Court of Justice perceives the integration process and, on the other hand, the need to soften the application of the principles in order to bring together the European peoples (M. Gorjão-Henriques).

The promoter and sponsor of the book is APDE—Associação Portuguesa de Direito Europeu (Portuguese Association of European Law), a member of the International Federation of European Law (FIDE). APDE aims to promote the study and dissemination of the Law and Institutions of the European Union, of the national law of the Member States and candidate States, and of the system of the European Convention on Human Rights. As such, it ensures that Portuguese legal circles remain connected to the ongoing debate on the most important and current issues of European Law. In accordance with this broad mandate, the book brings together contributions from well-established academics specialising in EU Law. Authors are representative of top-ranked Portuguese Law Schools (Coimbra, University of Lisbon, Universidade Católica Portuguesa, Nova University Lisbon, Minho University, Porto University), and some of them play or have played a role in the national or European Judiciary. The Editors wish to thank APDE for entrusting us with the task of putting in place such a challenging work. We are also thankful to Michelle Wells, who has meticulously revised the English language of all contributions, as well as Brigitte Reschke, from Springer, for embracing the project from the very first moment.

Lisbon, Portugal Inês Quadros
Coimbra, Portugal Miguel Gorjão-Henriques

Contents

Editors and Contributors

About the Editors

Inês Quadros Universidade Católica Portuguesa, Faculty of Law, Católica Research Centre for the Future of Law, Lisbon, Portugal

Miguel Gorjão-Henriques is Professor at Universidade de Coimbra, specialising in European Union Law.

Contributors

Joana Covelo de Abreu University of Minho, School of Law, JusGov - Research Centre for Justice and Governance, Braga, Portugal

Francisco Pereira Coutinho NOVA School of Law, CEDIS – Research & Development Centre on Law and Society, Lisbon, Portugal

José Luís da Cruz Vilaça Antas da Cunha Ecija, Lisbon, Portugal

José Narciso da Cunha Rodrigues Judge (Emeritus) of the Court of Justice of the European Union, Luxembourg, Luxembourg

Marta Prata Domingos Universidade Católica Portuguesa, Faculty of Law, Católica Research Centre for the Future of Law, Oporto, Portugal

Graça Enes University of Porto, Faculty of Law, CIJ - Centre for Interdisciplinary Research on Justice, Oporto, Portugal

Miguel Gorjão-Henriques Univ Coimbra, Faculty of Law, Coimbra, Portugal

Dulce Lopes Univ Coimbra, UCILeR - University of Coimbra Institute for Legal Research, Faculty of Law, Coimbra, Portugal

Miguel Poiares Maduro Católica Global School of Law, Lisbon, Portugal

Patrícia Fragoso Martins Universidade Católica Portuguesa, Faculty of Law, Católica Research Centre for the Future of Law, Lisbon, Portugal

Sofia Oliveira Pais Universidade Católica Portuguesa, Faculty of Law, Católica Research Centre for the Future of Law, Oporto, Portugal

Afonso Patrão Univ Coimbra, UCILeR - University of Coimbra Institute for Legal Research, Faculty of Law, Coimbra, Portugal,

Portuguese Constitutional Court, Lisbon, Portugal

Manuel Lopes Porto Univ Coimbra, Faculty of Law, Coimbra, Portugal

Lusíada University, CEJEIA - Center for Legal, Economic, International and Environmental Studies, Lisbon, Portugal

Fausto de Quadros University of Lisbon, Faculty of Law, Lisbon, Portugal

Inês Quadros Universidade Católica Portuguesa, Faculty of Law, Católica Research Centre for the Future of Law, Lisbon, Portugal

Rui Manuel Moura Ramos Univ Coimbra, UCILeR - University of Coimbra Institute for Legal Research, Faculty of Law, Coimbra, Portugal

Alessandra Silveira University of Minho, School of Law, Braga, Portugal

Rita Leandro Vasconcelos Universidade Católica Portuguesa, Faculty of Law, Lisbon, Portugal

Pérez-Llorca Lisbon, Portugal

Legal-Political Tensions Within the European Union

Reflections on the "European Sovereignty" Proposed by France

Fausto de Quadros

1 Introduction[1]

On 13 September 2017, the President of the European Commission, Jean-Claude Juncker, while delivering his State of the Union speech to the European Parliament, had proposed moving towards "a Europe that protects, a Europe that gives the means to act, a Europe that defends". Taking this proposal as a starting point, a few days later Macron would affirm, while speaking at the Sorbonne University, that the protective capacity of the Union should be an essential component of the "European sovereignty".[2] More recently, Macron reiterated the same idea again while reflecting on the "progress[es] on European sovereignty".[3]

The above-mentioned statements are of the utmost importance from a legal-political standpoint. In the following lines we propose to provide some pointers for the beginning of a serious debate on the meaning and scope of this idea of "European sovereignty." This reflection will, in fact, have the additional advantage of allowing

[1] This chapter complements two other by the same Author: "Subsidiarity and Sovereignty in the European Union", *Zur Verwirklichung eines Vereinten Europas: Festschrift für Rudolf Streinz zum 70 Geburtstag,* Munich, Beck Verlag, 2023, p. 55–62; and "O alargamento da soberania dos Estados-Membros da União Europeia por efeito do princípio da subsidiariedade", in *Estudos em Homenagem a João Caupers*, Coimbra, Gestlegal, 2024. p. 281–298.

[2] The complete speech of 26 September 2017 may be found in Initiative pour l'Europe - Discours d'Emmanuel Macron pour une Europe souveraine, unie, démocratique. | Élysée (elysee.fr) Accessed 4 Oct 2024. See the comments of Eijsbouts and Reestman (2018).

[3] Speech of 25 April 2024 delivered to Sorbonne available in Discours sur l'Europe. | Élysée (elysee.fr).

F. de Quadros (✉)
University of Lisbon, Faculty of Law, Lisbon, Portugal

I. Quadros, M. Gorjão-Henriques (eds.), *Revisiting the Liberal Constitutional Features of the European Union*, https://doi.org/10.1007/978-3-031-95717-8_1

us to revisit concepts and notions that marked the birth of the European integration Legal Order and that are, once again, relevant in this phase of deepening of EU integration and discussion on the future of the European Union.[4]

2 The Concept of Sovereignty Over Time

The concept of sovereignty is a primordial concept of Constitutional Law and Public International Law and, more recently, also of European Union Law. Its importance in Constitutional Law is because it expresses the maximum legal capacity of the State at the domestic level. In International Law, it is because it defines the boundary between State Law and the binding of the State at the international level. Indeed, the concept of sovereignty is, according to certain understandings, the condition of the very existence of International Law. Lastly, in European Union law, sovereignty is a key concept because the entire legal system of the Union develops at the expense of a constant dialogue between the sovereignty of the Member States and the supranational power of the Union. It should be noted that we have not mentioned the relationship between state sovereignty and globalisation. The study of this relationship, in terms of its nature and content, is still in its infancy, although it will be an attractive theme for the Science of Public Law in the near future.[5]

The first expressions of the concept of sovereignty are found in the ancient times, for instance, in Aristotle. However, it was Bodin who, in his classic work *Six Livres de la République,* published in 1576, first gave legal structure to the concept of sovereignty in terms of defining the model of the ideal Republic. For Bodin, sovereignty was an absolute and perpetual power. In other words, sovereignty, which was necessarily linked to the State, took the form of a supreme power in the internal order and an independent power in the external order. That is to say, the concept emerged as "absolute sovereignty, one and indivisible". Unity in the internal order, independence in the outer order.[6]

A century later, Thomas Hobbes, in his *Leviathan*, continued to consider sovereignty an absolute power, and this characterisation would only be challenged later by John Locke, Jeremy Bentham, and Jean-Jacques Rousseau.[7]

However, when the concept of sovereignty was used by the voluntarist theory of law to explain the basis for International Law, it was still regarded as an absolute power. This theory suggested that States would only be bound by International Law if that was their will and within the limits of their will.[8] The theory presented some

[4] de Quadros (1984). Some of the authors that contributed to the work coordinated by de Quadros and Sidjanski (2017) address these matters.

[5] But see our observations on this in de Quadros (2010, 2016). See also Cohen (2012, p. 21) and Medeiros (2015).

[6] Besson (2012, p. 369) and Miranda (2010, p. 177).

[7] Besson (2012, p. 369).

[8] See this matter developed in Pereira and de Quadros (1993, p. 58).

variants, which, however, do not concern us for present purposes. These were based on the Hegelian conception of the State. However, this theory was developed by one great Public Law theorist of the last century, Jellinek,[9] who influenced German legal theory for many years and had many followers in France.[10] One of the main consequences of this theory was that International Law would only be in force in the internal order of the State if it were "transformed" into domestic law and, therefore, was subject to the hierarchy of the domestic law's own sources of law and rules of interpretation. In other words, and in short, this doctrine did not accept the existence of International Law as such, i.e., with autonomy and with its own characteristics.[11]

As we will see below, with the birth of European integration a new conception of sovereignty has appeared in European Union Law. Here the law is supranational rather than merely intergovernmental, as in general it continues to be Public International Law. Hence, the vertical relationship between the Union legal order and State law, even at constitutional level, means that the supremacy of the former over the latter imposes limits to State sovereignty. We will return to this subject in due course.

3 Sovereignty and State

However, from the beginning, sovereignty and State appeared as intrinsically linked notions, i.e., the issue of sovereignty could only be discussed with regard to the State. Sovereignty was exclusive to the State and conferred on it, in the international order, fundamentally three powers: the *ius tractuum*, the *ius legationis*, and the *ius belli*.[12] Nonetheless, from the nineteenth century onwards, the opposite was no longer true: there could be, and are, States without sovereignty, i.e. non-sovereign States, or States with only partial sovereignty, i.e. only semi-sovereign.[13] The best current example of non-sovereign States are federated States, i.e. member States of a federation. Even when, in principle, these have the *ius tractuum*, they can only enter into international treaties (either with other Federal States or with federated States that are members of other federations) when authorised for that purpose by the federal institutions (in the United States, for example, this is what results from Article I (10) of the US Constitution), or only regarding matters that, by virtue of the respective Federal Constitution, do not fall within the competence of the Federation and the Federal Power and over which the federated States have an original right to

[9] Jellinek (1905).

[10] See, for instance, de Malberg (1920, pp. 234, 241).

[11] On the evolution of the concept of sovereignty with reference to the International Law, see Besson (2012, p. 368).

[12] Pereira and de Quadros (1993, p. 331).

[13] Pereira and de Quadros (1993, p. 347).

legislate [this is provided, for example, by the Bonn Fundamental Law, in its Article 32 (3), and by the Swiss Constitution, in its Article 56].[14]

Likewise, there are also semi-sovereign States. These preserve part of their sovereignty. The most important cases are small States and protected States. The small States (of which Monaco is a good example) have the *ius tractuum* and the *ius legationis* and therefore have international legal personality and capacity, but they lack the *ius belli*. Nor would it make sense for them to have this, given their small size, geographically speaking. However, the *ius belli* is a feature of State sovereignty. Protected States also only maintain part of their sovereignty. The actual dimension of sovereignty and international legal capacity that they preserve depends, in each specific case, on the international treaty that establishes the relationship of international protectorate.

Even at the height of the voluntarist theory, a State could only be said to exist if it brought together a people, a territory, and a political power.[15] With regard specifically to the people, it was they who formed and founded the State. In other words, one could only speak of a State if its people held the constituent power and, therefore, gave that State its Constitution. In other words, the people had to have the "competence of competences" (*Kompetenz-Kompetenz*).[16] And this was not dependent on the form of the State, i.e. the State could be simple (i.e. unitary, as is the case, for example, in France) or combined (meaning, with political or autonomous regions, as is the case of Spain and Italy, or a federal state, as is the case, for instance, of Germany or the United States) or hybrid (as is the case of Portugal, where only the archipelagos Azores and Madeira are autonomous regions). These State requirements are maintained in modern Comparative Constitutional Law.

Throughout the twentieth century and in the twenty-first century to date, sovereignty has undergone a great transformation in Constitutional Law and Political Science. Different conceptions of sovereignty have appeared in addition to proposals for alternative dimensions of sovereignty, leading to discussions as to whether it can be limited, whether it is divisible, and, as this chapter will demonstrate, whether it can belong to entities other than, and indeed larger than, States. In other words, sovereignty is today a somewhat controversial and diversified concept, which has suffered the impact of the phenomenon of integration and is also beginning to suffer the effects of globalisation. A good example of the controversial nature of the modern concept of sovereignty appears in the Charter of the United Nations. By stating that the UN is based on the "sovereign equality of States", the Organization remains attached to the theory of absolute and unlimited sovereignty of States. This is, in fact, one of the many symptoms of the United Nations' failure to adapt to modern times.

---

[14] Rudolf (2012, p. 1143). On the specific case of Germany, see Badura (2018, p. 509) and Sauer (2016).

[15] Jellinek (1882).

[16] Pereira and de Quadros (1993, p. 328).

For the purposes of this chapter, we will only deal with this evolution of the concept of sovereignty insofar as it interests us here.[17]

4 The Lack of Sovereignty of the European Union

At this point, it is important to consider whether the European Union has its own sovereignty.

Considering what has been said above, for the Union to have its own sovereignty, it would first have to be a State, since, as noted, it has not yet been possible to separate the concept of sovereignty from the concept of the State. However, the Union cannot be regarded as a State, principally because it does not have a people that holds the constituent power.[18]

In fact, the Union is the sum of the peoples of the Member States, but it does not have its own people, a European people, a people of the Union. This is why the Treaties never refer to a European people, but rather, in the plural, to the peoples of the various Member States—this is the case, for example, in the Preamble of the Treaty on European Union (TEU), in recitals 6, 9, 12 and 13, and then in Article 3 (1 and 5) of the same Treaty. In fact, European citizenship, as results from the Treaties, specifically from Article 20 (1, second sentence) of the Treaty on the Functioning of the European Union (TFEU), is not an autonomous citizenship and different from state citizenship and one that overlaps with it. A person is a citizen of the Union because they have the citizenship of one of the Member States, not because they have a new citizenship, different from the latter. In other words, there is no *dual citizenship* in the Union, which we find in many federal States.

In the absence of a European people, obviously there is no people in the Union with its own constituent power. Despite the flexibility brought by the Treaty of Lisbon to the system of revision of the Treaties with the creation of a simplified revision framework, the truth is that the States continue to revise the Treaties. In other words, to use a very old expression in Union Law, the States continue to be the "owners of the Treaties" ("*maîtres des traités*", "*Herren der Verträge*"). To put it even better, and as we have already noted, the *Kompetenz-Kompetenz*, which is an essential characteristic of the State, remains in the ownership of the Member States and has not yet been transferred to the people of the Union. The Convention method, used in the drafting of the Charter of Fundamental Rights and the failed Constitutional Treaty of 2004, deserves to be revisited and deepened, but, as it was in force, it did not take away the definitive and decisive word from the States in the revision of the Treaties.

---

[17] On the historical evolution that we mention, see Paupério (1958), Guggenheim (1968), Kelsen (1970), Pescatore (2008), Cohen (2010, p. 261), Miranda (2010, p. 179), Besson (2012) and de Quadros (2016).

[18] If it is not a State, much less will it be a "super-State" as some claim. Nor will we consider this hypothesis because Comparative Constitutional Law does not know the concept of a super-State.

Two arguments of the positive Law confirm that the Union does not have State character.

On one hand, nowhere in the long texts of the Treaties, including their Protocols and Declarations, do we find the words "state" or "stateness", or "federal" or "federation".

On the other hand, and this is a decisive argument, Article 5 (1) of the TEU delimits the Union's legal capacity by the principle of conferral or specialty. The combination of this provision with paragraph 2 of the same Article and with Article 4 (1) of the same Treaty means that the Union only has those competences conferred on it by the Treaties and not those that they do not confer, and it is clear that the competences that the States do not confer on the Union through the Treaties continue to belong to the States. Declaration no. 24 annexed to the Treaty of Lisbon emphasises this conclusion, by repeating that the Union's own legal personality "will not in any way authorise the Union to legislate or to act beyond the competences conferred upon it by the Member States in the Treaties". And the first paragraph of Declaration no. 18, on the delimitation of competences, goes in the same direction. The Court of Justice has confirmed this interpretation of the Treaties, even when it has extended it, so that it also encompasses the powers that can be implicitly extracted from the provisions attributing explicit competences to the Union.[19] On the other hand, no different conclusion can be drawn from Articles 4 (3, paragraph 2) of the TEU and Article 352 of the TFEU.

In respect of Article 4 (3, paragraph 2) TEU, it is obvious that all measures that States can take within its scope will have to respect the limits of the Union's competences.[20]

As far as Article 352 TFEU is concerned, it has long been established that it allows the Council to create new powers for the institutions of the Union, but it does not allow it to create new competences for the Union.[21]

Nevertheless, as the German doctrine mainly highlights, the State, on the other hand, has a generic and total capacity, an expansive capacity, i.e. it has an *Allzuständigkeit*. This general capacity stems from the people's sovereignty, enshrined in the Constitution [for instance, Grundgesetz, Art. 20 (2) first sentence,[22] and the Portuguese Constitution, Art. 3(1)]. The principle of conferral or specialty is the denial of that general capacity and, therefore, constitutes an implicit refusal to give State character to the Union.

---

[19] See Opinion 2/94, of 28-3-1996, paras 24, 25 and 30, Judgment of 5-10-2000, C-376/98, *Advertising and sponsorship of tobacco products,* para 43, and Judgment of 3-9-2008, *Kadi*, C-402/05P and C-415/05P, para 203; The interpretation extracted from the provisions mentioned is the same as the one followed by the Commentaries to the Treaties—see, for all, Streinz (2018), annotations 8–19 to Article 4 TEU. See also Louis and Ronse (2005, p. 16), Lenaerts and van Nuffel (2021, p. 112) and Isaac and Blanquet (2012, p. 64).

[20] Streinz (2018), annotations to the Article; Grabitz et al. (2022), annotations to the Article.

[21] Streinz (2018), annotations to the Article; Grabitz et al. (2022), annotations to the Article; de Quadros (2013), p. 397.

[22] Gröschner (2004), p. 369.

It is true that the Union already has federal traits.[23] But it is not yet a State and there can be no complete federalism without a State. Federalism is a method of organising a State and it is in this sense that Comparative Constitutional Law leads us.[24]

The rejection of the stateness of the Union, in addition to the reasoning already mentioned above, has been largely dominant in the doctrine and at different times in the History of Integration. Sixty years ago, Habermas[25] recognised it. A few decades later, this rejection was defended by Jacqué,[26] within the framework of the elaboration of the Constitutional Treaty of 2004. Nowadays, the non-stateness of the Union is analysed in depth by von Bogdandy.[27]

However, this was not the wish of the founding fathers of integration. They wanted the Communities, today the Union, to move towards a federal state model.

In fact, in his Zurich speech of 1947, Churchill proposed the creation of the "United States of Europe", that is, a European State of the federal type. Shortly afterwards, the father of integration, Jean Monnet, commented on the presentation of the Schuman Plan with the following statement: "The United States of Europe has begun".[28] Then, a renowned Professor of Law of the European Communities from Germany and who was the first President of the Commission of the then EEC, Walter Hallstein, defended this path, seeing in the EEC an "unfinished Federal State".[29] More recently, a very important name in the German doctrine of European Law, already mentioned above, von Bogdandy, explains that the Union is late in its project of reaching the stage of the Federal State.[30]

And, as we will see below, the German Federal Constitutional Court has also held for a long time that the Communities and, later, the Union still do not deserve to be called a federal State.

It is true that the federalism of the European Union will have its own features, it will not have to imitate previous federal models which, in turn, do not converge with each other. To reach this conclusion, it will be enough to compare these models,[31] starting, from the outset, by comparing the German and the United States models. And there is one thing that is already known for certain, European federalism will always be strongly decentralised thanks to the principle of subsidiarity, which is in force to a large extent in the Union. And subsidiarity will be the key to cooperative federalism, which, taking the German political and constitutional system as a

[23] de Quadros (2013, p. 431, 2008, p. 301).

[24] Weber (2010, p. 13).

[25] Habermas (1962, p. 40).

[26] Jacqué (2004, p. 554).

[27] von Bogdandy (2021, p. 39).

[28] Monnet (1955, p. 5).

[29] Hallstein (1969, p. 39).

[30] von Bogdandy (2021, p. 39).

[31] Bifulco (2010).

reference, is conceived by the Treaties as a future model for power within the Union.[32] We will return to the principle of subsidiarity later.[33]

5 Characterisation of the Political Power of the Union. The Relationship Between the Sovereignty of Member States and the Political Power of the Union: The "Reconstitution of Sovereignties"

But if the Union does not have its own sovereignty, how is its political power characterised? In other words, if the Union does not have sovereignty, how is its political power formed and how is it defined?

Very early on, Professor, and later Judge of the Court of Justice of the European Communities, Pierre Pescatore characterised the phenomenon of the creation of political power of the Union (formerly of the European Communities) as having at its basis a "reconstitution of sovereignties" ("*réaménagement des souverainetés*").[34] In fact, the creation of this power took place through an original process, hitherto unknown to International Law and Constitutional Law. This process assumed that the sovereignty of Member States was divisible.[35]

We have already referred to the divisibility of the States' sovereignty. The possibility that the sovereignty of the States can be limited was first defended by John Locke in reaction to the absolute character of sovereignty held by Bodin and Hobbes, as we have shown above. Later, this orientation would be deepened by Jeremy Bentham in his model of constitutionalism. However, it would be Jean-Jacques Rousseau who, shortly after Locke, and partly in disagreement with his position, would come to frame State sovereignty in a system of constitutional limitation of sovereignty brought by the value of democracy. Sovereignty and democracy, and, within the latter, the will of the people, become two concepts to be reconciled and, in this way, democracy comes to constitute a limit to the sovereignty of the State. It should be noted, moreover, that in practice the limitations of State sovereignty were not a new phenomenon, as they had also existed in colonial and imperial situations.[36]

The Union power has been characterised since the beginning of integration as a "supranational power." It should be noted that the Treaties never used that expression to characterise the Communities or the Union. It was created by the Treaty establishing the European Coal and Steel Community (ECSC), and only in its

32 Schütze (2009, p. 284), Herwig (2012, p. 67) and von Bogdandy (2003, p. 304).

33 On the underlying issue discussed in the text, see de Quadros (2013, p. 429).

34 Pescatore (1972, p. 31).

35 See Jacqué (2004, p. 551).

36 On these specific aspects of the evolution of the concept of sovereignty, see, especially, Steinberger (2000, p. 501), and Besson (2012, p. 368).

Article 9, to define the roles of the members of its High Authority and not the nature of that Community. However, as it was not known for sure what that word meant and because, therefore, a great controversy was generated around it, it was removed from that Treaty in 1957 by the Treaty of merger of certain institutions of the Communities, known only as the Treaty of Merger, and it never appeared again in any of the founding Treaties of any of the Communities or the Union, given that, due to its novelty in the legal lexicon, it was controversial. Nevertheless, given the way the Treaties shaped, first the Communities and then the Union, and considering the founding fathers of European integration and its legal system, we know how supranationality was intended to be characterised. When we speak of supranational power, we are referring to a vertical power, a power of subordination of the Member States to the Union, in order to make a difference with the horizontal power of coordination of the sovereignties of the States, which has characterised the great framework of Public International Law since Vitória and Suarez, and despite the limitations brought to the sovereignty of States even within the framework of classical International Law after the Second World War.[37]

There are several features of this power of subordination of the States to the Union. We shall consider only the most important here.[38]

Firstly, there is the primacy of Union Law, with all its scope and consequences, as it applies within the Union and in its relationship with the States and as it has been elaborated by the case law of the ECJ with the collaboration of the State courts, namely, the constitutional courts. Today, primacy is no longer a problem for the Member States; it appears in Declaration no. 17 annexed to the Treaty of Lisbon.[39]

The second feature consists of the vast and complex system of applicability and enforcement of Union Law in the internal order of the Member States, from the direct applicability of some acts of secondary law to the coercive competence of the ECJ, to the sanctioning power of the Union over Member States in the event of non-compliance with Union Law, and to the liability framework of the States for violations of Union Law. We can also add, within these most important features, thinking specifically about the Economic and Monetary Union, the powers of the European Central Bank over the financial systems of the Member States.

Despite the Union not being legally able to be deemed a sovereign power, for the reasons mentioned above, the Union's supranational power was created, nonetheless, at the expense of the sovereignty of the States and with their contribution. The reason why many constitutionalists, from different founding States of the Communities, refused or were reluctant to accept European integration at the beginning of the process (i.e. in the 1950s and 60 s) was precisely the fact that for them State sovereignty was indivisible and, as such, it was incompatible with integration

[37] This was the main subject of the academic dissertation of de Quadros (1984).

[38] We addressed this point in a more developed way in de Quadros (2013, p. 431).

[39] de Quadros (2015, p. 672).

and with the creation of a power that was soon to be announced as "supranational" in relation to the Member States.[40]

In fact, in order to accept this supranational power of the Union, the States delegated, or transferred, to the European Communities, and later to the Union, their "sovereign powers," i.e. "powers of authority" included in their sovereignty. The question of whether, from a legal standpoint, this should be considered a delegation or a transfer of sovereign powers became a *vexata quaestio* at the beginning of European integration. The authors of the Treaties were divided on this matter and therefore avoided either expression. We also dedicated many pages of an academic dissertation to this question, where we explained the complexity of this matter.[41] The distinction between the two figures was not irrelevant: if this was a delegation, the Member States could recover the powers that had passed to the Communities (today, the Union), for example, by denouncing the Treaties and leaving the Union; if, on the other hand, it was a transfer, they would forever lose those powers. Today, this dispute has lost its relevance and, without concern for this conceptual accuracy, both the national Constitutions and the jurisprudence of the ECJ have started to use the expression "transfer" of sovereign powers in a generalised way. We say that it is without concern for conceptual accuracy, as it is true that, through subsidiarity, the States, by being given primacy in the exercise of the Union's competences and in the fair measure in which this happens, come to recover the sovereign powers that they passed to the Union.

In fact, and as set forth in the Treaties, the principle of subsidiarity requires that in the pursuit of all the competences conferred on the Union by the Treaties, except in matters falling within its exclusive competence, listed in Article 3 of the TFEU (therefore, within the vast set of shared competence, of Article 4 of the TFEU, and of supporting competence, of Article 6 of the TFEU), the States have preference in their pursuit. In other words, the competences belong to the Union but are preferably fulfilled by the States. This results from Article 5 (3) of the TEU, supplemented by Protocol No. 2 annexed to the Treaty of Lisbon, on the application of the principles of subsidiarity and proportionality, and by the Declaration on the delimitation of competences, also annexed to the Treaty of Lisbon, and already mentioned above. Despite being competences that the States conferred on the Union, and with the great dimension they have, it is the States that, at first instance, will pursue them. As they do so, and insofar as they do so, the States recover, therefore, in the way they exercise these competences, their sovereign powers that have passed to the Union. And they pursue these competences not from a selfish national perspective, but within a broader scope, the scope of the Union. In other words, subsidiarity expands the dimension of sovereign powers delegated or transferred by States to the Union. But the fact that the Member States exercise these powers within the framework of

[40] For example, Badura (1966), who, nonetheless, changed his position over time. On the evolution of the thinking of this author, see de Quadros (2016). On this point, see also Pescatore (1972, p. 35).

[41] de Quadros (1984, p. 200).

the common interest of the Union does not negate that it is they that effectively exercise these powers even though these, at their root, are committed to the Union.[42]

The constitutions of the Member States, in general, see this problem in a complementary perspective. For them, the supranational power of the Union arises from the limitations of sovereignty allowed by States for the benefit of the Union by virtue of their free membership and participation in the Union. These sovereignty limitations result precisely from the transfer of sovereign powers carried out by the States in favour of the Union, in the terms mentioned above.

To understand this phenomenon, we must accept and start from the divisibility of State sovereignty. In other words, we must start from the distinction between qualitative sovereignty and quantitative sovereignty of States. Qualitative sovereignty is the root of sovereignty. The Member States of the Union have not lost it and the proof is that their respective Constitutions continue to treat them as sovereign States. It is, in fact, because they have not lost their sovereignty that States, as we said earlier, can denounce the Treaties, leave the Union, and thereby recover all the sovereign powers they have delegated to the Union. Differently, quantitative sovereignty consists of the sum of sovereign powers, or powers of authority, on which qualitative sovereignty is projected, i.e. the sovereign powers that comprise the content of sovereignty. This is based on the assumption of the divisibility of State sovereignty.

As we said earlier, the State Constitutions expressly accept, though with non-coinciding formal nuances, this orientation, when they intend to confer constitutional legitimacy to the participation of the respective States in the Union. Thus, for example, the Bonn Fundamental Law, in its Article 23 (1, second sentence), authorises Germany to transfer to the European Union, not its sovereignty ("*Souveranität*"), but its "sovereign powers" or "powers of authority" ("*Hoheitsrechte*"), insofar as they are necessary "for the realisation of a united Europe"[43] and which are integrated into its sovereignty.

The French Constitution, in the same sense, sets forth, in its Article 88 (2), that France consents to the transfer of the "necessary powers" for its participation in the European Union.

On the other hand, the Portuguese Constitution, without prejudice to laying down, in its Article 1, that Portugal is a "sovereign Republic", then authorises, in Article 7 (6), the Portuguese State to "agree to the exercise in common, in cooperation or by the institutions of the Union of the powers necessary for the construction and deepening of the European Union".[44]

And the ECJ accepted this orientation very early on. In two of the most famous judgments from the beginning of its case law, the Court made clear that the political power of the then Communities arose from a transfer by the States of their sovereign

[42] Currently, this issue is developed by us in de Quadros (2013, pp. 140 and 247). However, immediately after the inclusion of the subsidiarity principle as a general principle in the Maastricht Treaty, it was discussed by de Quadros (1995).

[43] See Maunz and Dürig (2020), annotations 61–69 to Article 23.

[44] de Quadros (2013, p. 526).

powers to the Communities, which resulted in a limitation, consented to by them, of their sovereignty. Thus, in the Van Gend & Loos case, the Court ruled that the EEC constituted a new legal order "in favour of which the States limited, even if in restricted areas, their sovereign rights".[45] Months later, in Costa v. ENEL, the Court stated that "the transfer, carried out by the States, of their internal legal order in favour of the community legal order, of rights and obligations corresponding to the provisions of the Treaty, implies a definitive limitation of their sovereign rights".[46]

At about the same time, the German Constitutional Court ruled that EEC institutions "exercise sovereign rights which Member States have renounced in favour of the Community." And added: "This Community is not a State itself, much less is it a federal State".[47]

6 "European Sovereignty": A Political Notion Rather Than a Legal One. The Deepening of Integration

From the above, it can be concluded that, in terms of law, it is still not possible to speak of European sovereignty, in the sense of the Union's own sovereignty, as France claims. The expression that is used as an alternative, that of "strategic autonomy," or "European autonomy," in addition to its vacuity, is of no use to European sovereignty. This requires the Union, from the outset, to have the legal characteristics of a State, which we have outlined above. Only in this way can the issue of its sovereignty be discussed, since, if we may reiterate, there is no sovereignty without a State. And, while it is true that the Union has been progressively gaining State and federal traits, as mentioned above, it is also true that it is far from fulfilling the ultimate legal model of a State or federation. Therefore, France's new position must be seen as a political position. It expresses France's desire for greater authority at Union level, but the fulfilment of that wish in the legal field is still far from a reality.

Since it is impossible, for the time being, for the Union to find its own sovereignty in the legal sense of the expression, it can only be given political content in order to satisfy France's ultimate desire, which is, under that expression, to deepen integration.

This deepening will not be possible without revision of the Treaties. It will have to focus on institutional aspects and on aspects connected to the various substantive domains of integration.

At the institutional level, the major change will have to be a substantial reduction in the scope of the unanimity rule and solid replacement of the qualified majority of four-fifths by the normal qualified majority. This is something that the most integrationist academic circles have long been urging for and it should not be delayed

[45] Case 26/62, 5-6-1963, Recueil, IX, p. 23.

[46] Case 6/64, 15-7-1964, Recueil, X, p. 1159.

[47] Judgment 18-10-1967, in Eversen and Sperl (1967), no. 2736.

further. Requiring unanimity for a Council deliberation on important matters in a Union with 27 Member States is tantamount to condemning the Union to paralysis. That is to say, requiring 27 States, with different or very different cultures and historical traditions, to unanimously agree on very sensitive political issues, can very easily lead to the Union taking no decision at all. The Treaties will have to be revised so as to include a list of constitutional matters and to restrict unanimity and a strict qualified majority to those matters.

Neither amendment of the Treaties nor the accession of new States to the Union should be affected by any new rules.

For amendment of the Treaties, ratification by all Member States must continue to be required.[48] It is a strict requirement, we admit, and in the future it will be very difficult to adapt the Treaties to the new circumstances, but the feeling is that no political environment can be envisaged for amending the Treaties by a qualified majority.

The same applies to the accession of new members to the Union. The opposition of current members to the accession of specific candidates and even the opposition of current candidates to accession in relation to other candidates is known. Therefore, unanimity in voting on the entry of new members will make it very difficult for each of the future candidates to join. But, here too, it is unlikely that the Member States will come to an agreement on an amendment to the Treaties to make it possible for a new member to be accepted by a qualified majority.

Let us now look at the case of Article 7 of the TEU. It provides for political sanctions for States in the event of a clear risk of breach (no. 1 of the Article) or serious and persistent breach (no. 2 of the Article) of the values listed in Article 2. These sanctions are very important because they are a way of safeguarding respect for something that became the legal and political heart of the Union after the Treaty of Lisbon, i.e. the values of the Union. The enormous significance of these values in the affirmation of the Union itself and before the world is well reflected in the affirmation of the Union as a "Union of Values," as it was presented to the Member States, their citizens, and the world after the Treaty of Lisbon and following what had already been set forth in the 2004 Constitutional Treaty. Experience shows that the requirement of a four-fifths majority in the Council vote set forth in Article 7(1) and unanimity in the European Council vote to which no. 2 of the same Article refers has the effect of paralysing the two institutions in both cases and, thus, weakening the system for guaranteeing respect for the values provided for in Article 2.

Let us now enter the substantive aspects of integration. It will not be possible to abandon the principle of specialty or conferral regarding the formation of the Union's competences. In other words, the matters allocated to the Union cannot be extended in accordance with the principle of *Allzuständigkeit* in German

[48] It seems clear that Article 48(5) of the TEU does not allow the European Council to go to the extreme of accepting the entry into force of a Treaty without its ratification by all States or negotiating with the State that is reluctant to withdraw from the Union. It no longer seems excluded from this Article that the Council has the power to negotiate with the reluctant State any opting out—see Priollaud and Siritzky (2008, p. 140).

Constitutional law. It is not yet possible to confer State nature on the Union, but it must be possible for the Treaties to create new competences for the Union, which are sorely lacking.

The first competence to be conferred on it will be that of common defence. In this area, the Union is very far behind and the recent war in Ukraine has exposed, to the fullest extent, the Union's dramatic shortcomings in this area if a Member State of the Union were to be the target of aggression similar to that to which Ukraine has been subject. At the time this chapter was concluded, this had not yet happened, but this threat hangs, to begin with, over the three Baltic States, Latvia, Estonia, and Lithuania.

The Treaty on the European Defence Community (EDC) was signed in Paris by the six original Member States on 10 September 1952, i.e., a few weeks after the entry into force of the ECSC Treaty. The only reason it did not enter into force was because the French National Assembly did not approve it for ratification. If this had not been the case, the Communities would have secured a common defence policy as long ago as 1952, though, of course, adapted to the circumstances of the time. It is difficult to imagine how the EDC would have evolved. But the reality is that, to date, the Member States have not yet reached an understanding on the creation of a common defence policy. It has been argued that, to achieve this, the Treaties will need to be revised. This is not the case, however. Recital 11 of the TEU Preamble already provides for a "common defence" by the Union. Building on this idea, Article 42 (2) of the TEU and Article 2 (4) of the TFEU give the Union "competence" to "gradually define a common Union defence policy". And the aforementioned provision of the TEU goes even further, by setting forth that the current common security and defence policy "will lead to a *common defence* as soon as the European Council, acting unanimously, *so decides*".[49] In other words, no revision of the Treaties is necessary for the Union to start defining and creating a common defence policy.

In the meantime, the Treaty of Lisbon was content with the creation of enhanced cooperation in the field of security and defence. This enhanced cooperation was called "permanent structured cooperation," as can be seen from the rules that created it, Article 42 (6) of the TEU, and Protocol No. 10 annexed to the Lisbon Treaty. Paragraph 5 of that Protocol states that the common defence of the States takes place within the framework of NATO. However, it seems that the existence of NATO, despite the fact that the majority of the members of the Union are part of it, does not constitute an obstacle to the creation of this common defence of the Union, for three main reasons. First, NATO itself, at its February 1952 Council meeting, which took place in Lisbon, encouraged the creation of a common defence policy for the Union and, specifically, the creation of the EDC.[50] Second, there may be, and are, States that are members of the Union but not members of NATO. Third, the aforementioned Protocol no. 10 provides, in paragraphs 4 and 5, that the common

[49] Our italics.

[50] de Quadros (2013, p. 45).

defence policy will respect the specific nature of the security and defence policy of the Member States and that NATO will continue to be the "foundation of the collective defence of its members". Finally, one should not forget that NATO is an intergovernmental organisation. Therefore, it will always be a necessary and useful complement to the common defence of the Union but will never be able to replace it. On the other hand, NATO has member States that are not member States of the Union. Hence, its survival does not depend on the specific interest of the Union only.

NATO will continue to depend largely on the United States, and it is true that many Member States of the Union have little confidence in the commitment that the United States will show in the event of aggression by a third State, for example Russia, towards an EU Member State. This distrust dates back to the period of the second World War. And, if one looks at current facts, the recent departure of the United States from Afghanistan in humiliating conditions for itself, and its failure to measure the consequences for security in the region of that withdrawal and to previously agree its decision with its western partners, is a good example of the reasons for this distrust. Nevertheless, without the United States, NATO loses much of its effectiveness. The war in Ukraine shows that the eastern borders of the Union are not secure and that it is paramount and urgent to guarantee conditions of peace and security against a foreign enemy for the EU Member States on the eastern border. This can only be achieved with a common Union defence policy. Russia's imperialist ambitions have become clear, so it is a duty of the Union, through its articulation with NATO, in terms that are yet to be defined, to guarantee these States the necessary conditions to preserve their defence and security.

Another area where the Union needs to deepen integration is energy. This is urgent for two reasons, the energy itself and the defence and security of Europe. Here, too, the aggression against Ukraine serves as a lesson for us. If the Union or its Member States are dependent on third states for energy, this reduces their ability to punish those third states and, therefore, their ability to defend their principles and values. Energy already appears as a shared competence of the Union, in Article 4 (2, i), TFEU, but this has not been exercised in order to guarantee that the Union has "energy autonomy", i.e. is self-sufficient in the field of energy. To remedy this, it may not be necessary to make energy an exclusive competence of the Union, by adding it to the list in Article 3 of the TFEU. But it will be necessary for the Union, together with the Member States under the subsidiarity framework, to define the mechanisms that will lead the States to achieve energy autonomy, by embarking on what is now known as the "energy transition." There is an urgent need for the Union to pay greater attention to this issue and to think quickly about how to diversify energy sources, so that this energy autonomy can be achieved as quickly as possible. Experts say that this is not easy and cannot be done quickly, but the war in Ukraine has brought into sharp relief what was already known, namely that the political autonomy of the Member States and the Union's decision-making power are very conditioned by the absence of autonomy in the field of energy.[51]

[51] On this matter, see the observations, already in the context of war in Ukraine, by Maurice (2022).

Deepening the Union's energy policy is necessarily linked to a commitment the Union must make in the Treaties regarding climate issues. These two areas are intimately linked. The impacts of energy on the climate are now well known, and it is clear that a poorly managed energy policy can have very harmful repercussions for the climate. While, in the field of energy, it is true, as previously stated, that the Union is far from energy autonomy, in the field of climate many Member States do not even have a planned and defined strategy to prevent or deal with climate change. It is urgent for the Union to act with determination in this area, so as not to worsen climate change in its territory. But because the climate can only be protected on a global scale and the actions of a single continent are not sufficient, the Union must also quickly commit to fostering the definition of a coherent, and profound global policy for climate preservation. This policy must be very interventionist, because many of the Member States and candidate States are very far from the minimum standard required for effective climate protection.

Another domain requiring greater intervention from the Union is public health. The fight against the pandemic demonstrated that many States were not prepared to face such a crisis. Besides lacking adequate internal health policies to deal with the situation, they did not know how to react adequately to the pandemic, in terms of both human and material resources, and much less in constitutional, legislative and administrative terms. It is true that the pandemic caught all the Member States by surprise, but the reaction of some was much worse than that of others. Indeed, a global and coordinated response by the Union is necessary in the face of these situations, including a possible resurgence of this pandemic or the emergence of new ones. It is therefore urgent for the Union to commit more to the health policy. The Treaties today promise and guarantee European citizens "a high level of health protection" (Article 168 (1) TFEU). In terms of the Treaties, the Union's action in health matters is today complementary to the action of the Member States and is based on the coordination of national policies, the definition of which is the responsibility of the Member States [Article 168 (1, paragraph 3), (2) and (7), TFUE]. Hence, the "protection and improvement of human health" appears to us to be a supporting competence of the Union (Article 6 (a) of the TFEU). However, the "common security problems in terms of public health", the content of which is unclear due to the vagueness of the expression, appear as a shared competence of the Union in Article 4 (2, k) of the TFEU. In other words, the authors of the Treaties did not have clear ideas on how to deal with health. It seems that the general health policy should become a shared competence of the Union. This would allow the Member States with more structured and better organised health policies, and which were consequently better prepared to fight the recent pandemic, to, through subsidiarity, have a wide margin of autonomy in defining and executing their national health policy, within the scope of the Union.

Lastly, the Union must create a policy in the field of immigration. The number of citizens from Eastern Europe, the Middle East and North Africa entering the European Union area will inevitably increase. In the face of this phenomenon, the Union must find an adequate balance between the acceptance of immigrants, the capacity of each Member State to receive them and the prevention of situations that exploit immigrants or offend their human dignity, and of terrorism. It has also been shown that some Member States have not met these requirements. Therefore, the purposes set out in Articles 77 et seq. of the TFEU, and in the secondary legislation approved based on the foregoing, must be revised, and the immigration policy as a shared policy of the Union must be provided for in Article 4 of that Treaty.

In his address to the European Parliament on 3 May 2022, the then Prime Minister of Italy, Mario Draghi, defended the deepening of integration towards a "pragmatic federalism", covering all areas affected by the changes taking place with the pandemic and the aggression against Ukraine, from the economy to security, also including energy. For him, the sum of the crises that Europe faces today (humanitarian, energy, economic and security), makes it necessary "to accelerate the integration process". Within this pragmatic federalism Draghi includes a more effective decision-making process in the economic, energy, defence, and foreign policy fields. However, Draghi did not make any connection between his proposal and that of Emmanuel Macron on European sovereignty, nor did he provide a concrete explanation of his idea of pragmatic federalism.

7 Conclusion

Creating a "European sovereignty," in the true legal sense of the expression, will be difficult for legal and political reasons, as we believe we have made clear in the preceding lines. But deepening integration within the Union is not only possible but urgently needed. That is the interpretation to be given to the French proposal. At least up until the time of writing, the Union has demonstrated, following Russia's aggression against Ukraine, that it is capable of advancing in integration and, above all, that it is capable of quickly strengthening solidarity and cohesion among its members. As has happened so many times in periods of crisis for Europe since the Schuman Plan, the Member States, faced with the gravity of events in Eastern Europe, decided to put everyone's interests ahead of their own selfish inclinations and give strong hints of a desire to move forward with integration.

This path must be followed, and at the same pace, so that the Union can be a factor of peace, security, and progress on the European continent, as well as a necessary and useful global actor. And the Union's continued pursuit of this path must be coupled with a constant and increasingly intense affirmation of the primacy of the values chosen by it in Article 2 of the TEU, supplemented by Articles 3 and 4 of the same Treaty. These values must be respected in the internal order of the Union and the Member States, as well as in the Union's relationship with the rest of the world, as imposed by Article 3 (5) of the TEU. Within these values, special demands must be made on democracy, freedom, the dignity of the human person and the fundamental rights in which it unfolds, the national identity of the Member States and their territorial integrity.

Within the system of Treaties, States will always play a very important role in the pursuit of these purposes, thanks, first of all, to the principle of subsidiarity, which governs the exercise of most of the Union's competences, as demonstrated once again above.

References

Badura P (1966) Bewahrung und Veränderung demokratischer und rechtsstaatlicher Verfassunsstruktur in den internationalen Gemeinschaften. In: Veröffentlichungen der Vereinigung der Deutschen Staatsrechtslehrer 23. De Gruyter, Berlin, pp 34–104
Badura P (2018) Staatsrecht. C.H. Beck, Munich
Besson S (2012) Sovereignty. In: Wolfrum R (ed) The max Planck Encyclopedia of public international law. Oxford University Press, Oxford, pp 366–391
Bifulco R (2010) Ordinamenti federali comparati. Turim, Turin
Bodin J (1576) Les six livres de la République. Jacques du Puys, Paris
Cohen JL (2010) Sovereignty in the context of globalization: a constitutional pluralist perspective. In: Besson S, Tasioulas J (eds) The philosophy of international law. Academia, Oxford, pp 261–280
Cohen JL (2012) Globalization and sovereignty. Cambridge University Press, New York
De Malberg C (1920) Contribution à la théorie générale de l'État. Tennin, Paris
de Quadros F (1984) Direito das Comunidades Europeias e Direito Internacional Público—contributo para o estudo da natureza jurídica do Direito Comunitário Europeu. Coimbra, Almedina
de Quadros F (1995) O princípio da subsidiariedade no Direito Comunitário após o Tratado da União Europeia. Coimbra, Almedina
de Quadros F (2008) Droit de l'Union européenne. Bruylant, Brussels
de Quadros F (2010) Global law, plural constitutionalism and global administrative law. In: Robalino-Orellana J, Muñoz JRA (eds) Global administrative law—towards a Lex administrativa. Cameron May, London, p 329
de Quadros F (2013) Direito da União Europeia—Direito Constitucional e Administrativo da União Europeia, 3rd edn. Coimbra, Almedina
de Quadros F (2015) La primauté du droit de l'Union européenne sur le droit portugais: un cas particulier. In: Liber amicorum en l'honneur du Professeur Vlad Constantinesco. Bruylant, Brussels, p 667
de Quadros F (2016) Bewahrung und Veränderung demokratischer und rechtsstaatlicher Verfassungsstruktur in den internationalen Gemeinschaften—50 Jahre danach. Arch Öffentl Rechts 141:144
de Quadros F, Sidjanski D (2017) The future of Europe—the reform of the Eurozone and the deepening of political union. AAFDL, Lisboa
Eijsbouts WT, Reestman JH (2018) European sovereignty. Eur Const Law Rev 14:1
Eversen HJ, Sperl H (1967) Répertoire de la jurisprudence relative aux traités instituant les Communautés. Cambridge University Press, Paris
Grabitz E, Hilf M, Nettesheim M (2022) Das Recht der europäischen Union (EUV/AEUV). Beck Verlag, Munich
Gröschner R (2004) Die Republik. In: Isensee J, Kirchhof P (eds) Handbuch des Staatsrechts der Bundesrepublik Deutschland, II, 3rd edn. Müller, Heidelberg, pp 369–428
Guggenheim P (1968) La souveraineté dans l'histoire du droit des gens. De Vitoria à Vattel. In: Ibler V (ed) Mélanges offerts À Juraj Andrassy. Springer, Cham, pp 111–121
Habermas J (1962) Strukturwandel der Öffentlichkeit. Untersuchungen zu einer Kategorie der bürgerlichen Gesellschaft. Luchterhand, Berlin
Hallstein W (1969) Der unvollendete Bundesstaat. Econ Verlag, Dusseldorf

Herwig A (2012) Federalism, the EU and international law. In: Cloots E, Baere G, Sottiaux S (eds) Federalism in the European Union. Hart Publishing, Oxford, p 83
Isaac G, Blanquet M (2012) Droit général de l'Union Européenne. Cours Dalloz, Paris
Jacqué JP (2004) Der Vertrag über eine verfassung für Europa. Europäische Grundrechte Zeitschrift. Engel Verlag, Kegel, pp 551–554
Jellinek G (1882) Die Lehre von der Staatenverbindungen. A. Hölder, Wein
Jellinek G (1905) Allgemeine Staatslehre. Verlag Von Julius Springer, Berlin
Kelsen H (1970) Der Wandel des Souveränitätsbegriffes. In: Kurz H (ed) Volkssouveränität uns Staatssouveränität. Wissenschaftliche Buchgesellschaft, Darmstadt, p 164
Lenaerts K, van Nuffel P (2021) European Union law. Thomson Reuters, Sweet & Maxwell, London
Louis JV, Ronse T (2005) L'ordre juridique de l'Union européenne. Bruylant, Brussels
Macron E (2024) Discours sur l'Europe. https://www.elysee.fr/emmanuel-macron/2024/04/24/discours-sur-leurope Accessed 23 Sept 2024
Maunz T, Dürig G (2020) Grundgesetz Kommentar. Beck Verlag, Munich
Maurice E (2022) Les dépendances stratégiques, une question de souveraineté. Schuman Papers, n° 630, Brussels. https://www.robert-schuman.eu/fr/doc/questions-d-europe/qe-630-fr.pdf. Accessed 23 Sept 2024
Medeiros R (2015) A Constituição Portuguesa num contexto global. Universidade Católica Editora, Lisboa
Miranda J (2010) Manual de Direito Constitucional. Coimbra Editora, Coimbra
Monnet J (1955) Les États Unis d'Europe ont commencé. Robert Laffort, Paris
Paupério AM (1958) O conceito polémico de soberania. Forense, Rio de Janeiro
Pereira AG, Quadros F (1993) Manual de Direito Internacional Público. Coimbra, Almedina
Pescatore P (1972) Le droit de l'intégration. Sijthoff, Leyden
Pescatore P (2008) La souveraineté dans une societé d'inégaux, pouvoir suprême coalisable, partageable, divisible, intégrale responsable? Justiciable? In: L'État souverain dans le monde d'aujourd'hui, Mélanges en honneur de J-P Puissochet. Pedone, Paris, p 231
Priollaud FX, Siritzky D (2008) Le Traité de Lisbonne. La documentation française, Paris
Rudolf W (2012) Federal States. In: Wolfrum R (ed) The max Planck Encyclopedia of public international law. Oxford University Press, Oxford, pp 1143–1146
Sauer H (2016) Staatsrecht III: Auswärtige gewalt, Bezüge des Grundgesetzes zu Völker- und Europarecht. C.H. Beck, München
Schütze R (2009) From dual to cooperative federalism: the changing structure of European law. Oxford University PressOxford, Oxford
Steinberger H (2000) Sovereignty. In: Bernhardt R (ed) Max Planck Encyclopedia of public international law. Oxford University Press, NorthHolland Elsevier, pp 500–512
Streinz R (2018) EUV/AEUV. C.H. Beck, Munich
von Bogdandy A (2003) Europäisches Verfassungsrecht. Springer, Berlin Heidelberg
von Bogdandy A (2021) Strukturwandel des Öffentliches Rechts—Entstehung und Demokratisierung der europäischen Gesellschaft. Suhrkamp Verlag, Heidelberg
Weber A (2010) Europäische Verfassungsvergleichung. C. H. Beck, Munich

Fausto de Quadros University of Lisbon, School of Law, Portugal. Jean Monnet Chair *ad personam*.

Liberalism and Illiberalism in the European Construction

José Narciso da Cunha Rodrigues

1 The Faces of Freedom

The antagonism between *liberalism/illiberalism* went viral when Fareed Zacaria first referred to it in 1998.

It is an issue that warrants an ideological discussion.

However, the purpose of this article is rather to describe how the European decision-makers reflected social movements and particularly the path that the Court of Justice has taken to interpret and apply the legislation.

The changes that have occurred in the last decades have shown that conceptions that appeared to be stable are no longer applicable to postmodern styles of living and to the emergence of disruptive beliefs.

Europe has entered a new era.

The matter at issue is not only an unbalanced relationship between nation states; it is also the sensation of no-future, given the increasing number of deadlocks that are appearing.

Economic models have changed. And even more critically, governments have revealed their inability to find credible solutions in sensitive areas, such as the threat of war or of scarcity.

At the same time, populisms have erupted, modifying the rules of the game and using simplistic constructions based on the idea that the solutions reside in the opposition between "us and them".

Former Attorney General of the Portuguese Republic, Former Judge at the Court of Justice of the European Union.

J. N. da Cunha Rodrigues (✉)
Judge (Emeritus) of the Court of Justice of the European Union, Luxembourg, Luxembourg

I. Quadros, M. Gorjão-Henriques (eds.), *Revisiting the Liberal Constitutional Features of the European Union*, https://doi.org/10.1007/978-3-031-95717-8_2

Such a reality renders any analysis precarious and paves the way for unreasonable alternatives.

The question of liberty is at the heart of these problems.

After centuries of revolutionary and liberal declarations, a broad notion of liberty has not yet been achieved.

History proves that liberty cannot be seen as an abstract concept. One must consider specific individuals to observe the role of the State and the reciprocal relationships between individuals, and between individuals and the State.

It is true that the European Communities have achieved great results in economic and legal integration.

The Community founders sought to create, in the fragmented continent of Europe, an integrated economic market that would afford the benefits of harmonisation and generate economies of scale, while bringing a higher standard of living to the population (Bermann et al. 2002).

Given the democratic commitment to the rule of law, it is not surprising that the European Communities have evolved into a highly structured and principled legal environment.

The Preamble of the Treaty of Rome announced ambitious aims: to lay the foundations of an ever-closer union among the peoples of Europe; to ensure the economic and social progress of their countries by common action to eliminate the barriers which divide Europe; to improve the living and working conditions of their peoples; to guarantee steady expansion, balanced trade and fair competition; to strengthen the unity of their economies and to ensure their harmonious development by reducing the differences existing between the various regions and the backwardness of the less favoured regions; to contribute, by means of a common commercial policy, to the progressive abolition of restrictions on international trade; to confirm the solidarity which binds Europe and the overseas countries to ensure the development of their prosperity, in accordance with the principles of the Charter of the United Nations; to pool their resources to preserve and strengthen peace and liberty, to establish this combination of resources; and to call upon the other peoples of Europe who share their ideal to join in their efforts.

Giving concrete expression to these objectives, Article 2 of the Treaty stated:

> It shall be the aim of the Community, by establishing a Common Market and progressively approximating the economic policies of Member States, to promote throughout the Community a harmonious development of economic activities, a continuous and balanced expansion, an increased stability, an accelerated raising of the standard of living and closer relations between its Member States.

These provisions recognised the need for fast and strong development, in a Europe scourged by the war, yet with an economic perspective.

Liberty was certainly a consensual collective desire as a means of counteracting the tragedies of the war and feeding hope.

However, the concept of liberty was quite strict. It predominantly contained negative elements which imposed a duty on the State not to invade the sphere of individuals.

The text "The liberty of the Ancients compared with that of the Moderns", in which Benjamin Constant reproduced the lecture he had given in Paris in 1819, provides us with an important tool to evaluate the evolution of the concept of liberty (Constant 2015).

Benjamin Constant explained how the ancients' notion of freedom, even inspiring philosophers, was different from that of the moderns and how the enlargement of the concept opened the door to fundamental rights and to a liberal idea of democracy.

He highlighted the difference between two kinds of liberty: liberty valued by ancient peoples and liberty adopted by modern nations.

After a critical analysis of several ancient institutions and regimes, Constant noted the difference between the freedom they granted and the freedom offered by representative governments.

The liberty of the ancients—he compared—consisted of carrying out collectively but directly many parts of the over-all functions of government, coming together in the public square to discuss and make decisions about war and peace; forming alliances with foreign governments; voting on new laws; pronouncing judgments; examining the accounts, acts, and stewardship of the magistrates; calling the magistrates to appear in front of the assembled people; accusing the magistrates and then condemning or acquitting them.

This kind of direct democracy was possible because, while the citizens gathered in the squares to philosophise and decide, the slaves ensured the day-to-day business.

The ancients had no notion of individual rights.

Constant argued that a strict notion of freedom was not sufficient to support a larger notion that could empower a human being as holder of his essential dignity.

One could say that such conditions persisted for a long time and influenced political and social perceptions, particularly about slavery and colonialism.

I will focus my attention on the post-war period.

The notion of freedom remains a key issue for philosophers and social scientists.

Raymond Aron elaborated on it in his comparison of intellectual movements such as Marxism, liberalism and libertarianism. This latter reflected a view of American tendencies which addressed the role of government, the role of intellectuals in government and the nature of intellectuals themselves. *Libertarians* believed that the primary function of the government is to secure the rights of the individual, with an emphasis on political rights and property rights, which are closely connected.

It should be noted that Raymond Aron employed the word *freedom* in a dual sense: singular and plural. For him, there are *freedoms*, not *freedom*. He took Tocqueville and Marx as a starting point and the distinction they made between *formal* freedoms and *real* freedoms. Raymond Aron explained that the word *freedom* is to be applied to a relationship between one and more individuals, while recognising that freedoms which are threatened are those for which liberals plead (Aron 1970).

For him, the institutions of representative democracy do not seem to constitute, in our age, the expression of the universal desire for freedom. Those who comment on the crisis of liberal democracy wonder precisely what contribution is made to political freedom by institutions inherited from the age of Enlightenment and from the bourgeoisie, transformed and impoverished in the context of mass society.

This approach, based on historical movements, is useful to understand the evolution and the nature of certain principles but it did not contribute to a clear concept of freedom.

Indeed, the implications of the welfare state changed the conditions that governed these movements and determined the current situation in which mixed and sometimes contradictory elements cohabit with historically established principles.

Antagonisms such as *formal/real freedoms* or *freedom/freedoms* end up weakening the value of freedom in today's troubled societies. The word *freedoms,* rather than *freedom,* is generally used by Marxists based on discrimination that must be rejected and on tactical ideological reasons.

The work of Karl Popper also constitutes an important source of our understanding of liberalism. Liberalism—he wrote—is based on individualism. Individualism is a positive power allowing people to determine their destiny as an individual. It leads to self-respect, self-fulfilment, self-development and emancipation from traditional relations and groups.

For Popper, it is correct that individualism goes hand in hand with self-interest. However, individualism is more than self-interest. It is a never-ending process towards increasing liberty and self-reliance. For the citizen it is also a process of adaptation to social behaviour. Individualism is not an obstacle, but a condition for true solidarity.

He continues: Liberals fought against nationalists, communists, fascists, and religious fanatics. And the fight was successful. With the boost of the liberal aspiration for freedom and justice, universal human rights were accepted, abuses condemned, dictatorships eliminated.

Popper warns that we may neither accept dogmas nor have a blind belief in absolute freedom, absolute property rights and the absolute free market.[1]

Since the fall of the Berlin Wall and the theory expressed by Fukuyama (2020) in *The End of History and the Last Man,* neoliberals and libertarians have considered the free market as a kind of scientific certainty.

Liberals have never followed this dogmatic concept because they understand that not only is freedom necessary for a better society, but also justice. Liberals do not like absolute freedom because they know that absolute freedom frequently leads to negative effects for individuals and society as a whole. They refuse to subject themselves to blind capitalism because money and extreme selfishness are frequently poor advisors and can harm society and freedom, and hamper opportunities for fellow humans. Liberals support the idea of the open society as defended by Karl Popper.

[1] Edgar Morin is one of the philosophers who better approached the question of the truth and limits of science. Following the idea of Adorno, he stated that "totality is untruth". For him, the purpose of knowledge is not to discover the secret of the world in an owner and master equation that would be equivalent to magic word of the great magicians, but rather it is to dialogue with the mystery of the world. See Morin (1994, p. 180; 1996, p. 98).

In his book *The Open Society and Its Enemies,* Karl Popper became a persuasive advocate for a liberal and democratic open society; a society of free civilians who are able to assess policy and inspire transformations. According to Popper, progress and knowledge are based on free discussion and a gradual reform of society.

Popper's moderation is not free of criticism as he states that while the totalitarian state is not good, neither is unlimited freedom for every individual. His reasoning is that freedom means being free to do whatever you want. Those who are free to do whatever they want, are free to take away the freedom of others. Unlimited freedom results in slavery.[2]

Popper turned against every form of dogmatism and thus against absolute statements such as 'truth' and 'certainty'. For him, a thesis is a hypothesis. A thesis stands firm as long as it is not countered by evidence against it. The thesis that all swans are white stands firm until a black one appears. This is the basis for his falsification theory, which also applies to political philosophy. This is the reason why Popper is suspicious of people who claim they are convinced of anything "beyond all doubt".

Popper rejected every political and philosophical thought that started from its own infallibility. The basis of a democratic constitutional state contains both freedom and justice.

The notion of *liberty* has also been developed by liberal thinkers such as John Rawls, Amartya Sen, Martha Nussbaum and Shoshana Zuboff.

With a special meaning at present, Zuboff (2019) concludes that *Surveillance capitalism* departs from the history of market capitalism in surprising ways, demanding both unimpeded freedom and total knowledge, abandoning capitalism's reciprocities with people and society, and imposing a totalizing collectivist vision of life in the hive, with surveillance capitalists and their data priesthood in charge of oversight and control. *Surveillance capitalism* and its rapidly accumulating *instrumentarian* power exceed the historical norms of capitalist ambitions, claiming dominion over human, societal, and political territories that range far beyond the conventional institutional terrain of the private firm or the market. (…) Only "we the people" can reverse this course, first by naming the unprecedented, then by mobilizing new forms of collaborative action: the crucial friction that reasserts the primacy of a flourishing human future as the foundation of our information civilization. If the digital future is to be our home, then it is we who must make it so."[3] The reality

---

[2] In his work *All Life is Problem Solving*, he stated: "To protect freedom, freedom should be restrained".

[3] Shoshana Zuboff clarified: "we have backed ourselves into an untenable social framework, where a few giant companies own and operate the Internet. The companies are black boxes, outside of societal influence and democratic control. Their surveillance economics compel them to extract data from our lives at a massive scale. They simply claimed the right to treat our private lives as raw material for their profit. The data come from us, but they are not for us. The more they track us and engage us, the more data they gather, the better they can target, manipulate, and predict future behavior — insights that they sell to lucrative markets of business customers. Algorithms are engineered to amplify the most extreme, angry, toxic content, drawing people in to maximize data extraction. These operations undermine human autonomy and create huge societal asymmetries of

of *surveillance capitalism* degrades human dignity. The future of this narrative depends on the understanding that efficacy without autonomy is not effective, consensus induced by dependency is not a social contract, and liberty without uncertainty is not liberty.

Some have stated that the nature and the future of democracy have become a questionable issue in postmodernity for those who are surprised by the change in the political-party landscape and the new movements that indicate the erosion of representative democracy, evoking the inability or the weariness of the political regimes that appeared after the second war. They fear that mainstream centre-right parties are being captured by tendencies that are indifferent or even hostile to liberal democracy. For them, features such as the rule of law and the freedoms of speech, assembly, religion, and the press, though more properly categorised as liberal, are often regarded as hallmarks of democracy. A lack of theorising is the source of much confusion, in particular the difference between the categories of liberalism and conservatism and the use of the term neo-liberalism to refer to power and deregulation of the markets (Plattner 2019, pp. 5–19).

The idea appears to be sufficiently functional to give rise to a historical and prospective examination and assessment of governance models.

2 A New Political Landscape

These thoughts remain valid and are essential to understand the European construction.

The transformations that have occurred in recent times have been ambiguous and complex.

They demand a holistic reading of numerous and sometimes contradictory segments of the organisation of modern States.

For this reason, many authors prefer to focus their observations on concrete situations rather than developing general theories.

In relation to the Hungarian situation, the following has been written:

> Populism, after all, is an outlook that emphatically claims to be democratic and that relies for its legitimacy on elections as expressions of the popular will. Yet when populists come to power, they tend to infringe upon the rule of law, the independence of the courts and the media, and the rights of individuals and minorities.

knowledge and power—a whole new dimension of inequality. We are learning the hard way about their destructive effects on society and democracy. These systems can be regulated, but the fact is that we've barely even tried so far. Important new legislative proposals in the E.U. and the U.K. would for the first time insist that the largest tech platforms are accountable to audit and oversight, the rule of law and the established rights of citizens. The message is that democracy is finally on the move after two decades of surveillance capitalism having all the power". *Time*, interview on 22/1/2021.

This criticism was levelled particularly at the argument of the Hungarian Prime Minister when he suggested "Christian democracy" was as an alternative to "liberal democracy" (Plattner 2019, pp. 5–19).

It is worth noting how Viktor Orbán's suggestion manipulates Christian principles: liberal democracy favours multiculturalism while Christian democracy gives priority to Christian culture; liberal democracy is pro-immigration, while Christian democracy is anti-immigration; liberal democracy sides with adaptable family models rather than the Christian family model.

Órban almost certainly did not read the Pope's encyclicals.

What has been the reaction of the European Union?

In September 2018, Órban's programme suffered an apparent setback when the European Parliament achieved the two-thirds majority needed to initiate the so-called Article 7 proceedings against Hungary. These proceedings are intended to trigger disciplinary action against a Member State when it has been found to present "a clear risk of a serious breach" of EU values. The Parliament report referred to the independence of the judiciary and the freedoms of expression and religion. Some analysts alluded to "social conservatism" and "authoritarianism".

A similar movement occurred in Poland.

Since coming to power in 2015, the Law and Justice (PiS) government has introduced a series of changes to the judicial system that have ignited nationwide street protests, have put Poland at loggerheads with the European Commission over breaches of EU law, and have been met with remarkable resistance from judges in Poland.

The Court of Justice of the European Union issued a judgment related to some of the key elements of Poland's judicial reform: the new National Council of the Judiciary (NCJ) and the new Disciplinary Chamber of the Supreme Court.

A closer reading of that judgment shows that the Court of Justice reconfirmed at length that EU law implies the independence of the judiciary, which therefore is not only an internal matter for each EU Member State.

The Court also provided all necessary elements for it to crush the key elements of judiciary "reforms" in the future.

Paragraph 75 of the Decision reads:

> *The Court has previously held that, although the organisation of justice in the Member States falls within the competence of those Member States, the fact remains that, when exercising that competence, the Member States are required to comply with their obligations deriving from EU law. (Judgment of 24 June 2019, Commission v Poland (Independence of the Supreme Court), C-619/18, EU:C:2019:531, paragraph 52 and the case-law cited).*

In that judgment, the Court of Justice of the European Union included a comprehensive, broad and very detailed list of criteria that must be considered when deciding on the independence of a court under the EU law. The Court highlighted that independence *"requires that the court concerned exercise its functions wholly autonomously, without being subject to any hierarchical constraint or subordinated to any other body and without taking orders or instructions from any source whatsoever, thus being protected against external interventions or pressure liable to impair the independent judgment of its members and to influence their decisions*".

This judgment represented an important development of the idea of the Rule of Law and revealed how particular forms of organisation of the State can influence the guarantees accorded to the citizens and the trust in the institutions, as elements for a liberal society.

This judgment was confirmed by the judgment issued on 15 July 2021.

Regarding the application of Article 7 to the situations created by the Hungarian and Polish governments, we may note that there are circumstances where the violation of the EU's basic principles is obvious and there are others that warrant a deeper analysis.

It is necessary to find a breeding ground within which different movements classified as illiberalism may operate.

One theory that merits our special interest has been put forward by András Sajó.

Sajó (2021, p. 1), a prominent scholar and former vice-president of the European Court of Human Rights, writes that the prevailing understanding of illiberal regimes, particularly those that emerge from popular movements, indicates that we are facing a general democratic backlash.

Sajó refers to certain philosophers, saying that illiberal democracies belong to the democratic family in the Rousseauist understanding of democracy, where the notion of liberalism has a totalitarian potential. He adds that the mirror of illiberalism reflects the weaknesses of the liberal (Sajó 2021, pp. 3 and 4).

Populist illiberal democracy relies upon and brings to light the authoritarian elements of Western constitutional systems.

The following comment made by András Sajó is particularly impressive:

> Illiberal democracy is viable because it can rely on the totalitarian potential of democracy. In the real world, constitutional arrangements, liberal and illiberal (authoritarian) constitutive elements cohabit, and illiberalism and authoritarianism are built into the liberal constitutional order and its institutions (Sajó 2021, p. 37).

It is not always easy to classify certain movements; yet we feel sometimes that those illiberal conceptions are within our midst. For example, one expression of illiberal conceptions is the trend, in many countries, to over-criminalise and to toughen security policies. The lack of independence and effectiveness of justice is another example which represents not just a failure of liberal conceptions but the implementation of illiberal policies and practices.

In more radical terms, one may ponder that, while liberal constitutionalism and early declarations of rights centred on freedom, today they no longer hold the same importance for a majority that takes liberty for granted, one that is not concerned with liberation from specific forms of despotic oppression. Such a vision can be applied to simple fragments of the law or to practices that imply unjustified harm to individual rights and interests.

If we observe the positions of today's far-right thinkers, we will conclude that they are engaged in a contradictory exercise. On the one hand, they fight for recognition and respect, affirming some of the core elements of liberal democracy. On the other hand, they criticise politics based on so-called *artificial principles*. For them the ideas of individual autonomy, universal human rights, and absolute equality have no real connection with the human experience (McAdams and Castrillon 2022, p. 7).

In the twenty-first century, far right *identitarian* politics increased in Europe as a reaction to mass immigration and to multicultural models of society (Zúquete 2018, p. 207).

Thomas Piketty speaks of the emergence of *social nativism* as a product of a world that is simultaneously post-communist and post-colonial (Piketty 2019, p. 993).

Identitarian movements have also grown in Europe due to internal factors or as a reaction to the European construction. We may recall the Catalan case, *Brexit* and the recent events in Poland (Piketty 2019, p. 1056).

International policies have contributed to this situation.

As Robert Kagan wrote, a new configuration of power is reformulating the international order (Kagan 2008, p. 12).

Even within liberal conceptions, rights proliferation runs the risk of turning human rights into something banal and far from essential values (Sajó 2021, p. 214). An example that could be quoted as a case study is the reform in Portugal that included judicial secrecy in the Constitution as a fundamental right. Sometime later, the legislator established that criminal proceedings are, in principle, public. No one reported the legal contradiction or acted to obtain a declaration of unconstitutionality of the provisions.

During crises, this trivialisation has resulted in a kind of "abundance of rights". The term *abundance* is used to express the idea that there is an enormous gap between the rights themselves and their effectiveness (Rodrigues 2013). This situation has produced movements to deconstruct the law, particularly in social and tax matters.

The terms liberalism and illiberalism brought with them new ideas about democracy. One of these was the concept of the "good society". In my opinion, this notion is not functional. On the contrary, it might suggest moral elements which do not help the features of an ordered society in the sense of active citizenship and collective solidarity.

In my view, different visions of post-war capitalism explain the situation in Europe.

The beginning of this century heralded a period of more profound and faster transformation.

These shifts resulted, in part, from the new international geostrategic balances, but mainly from internal political and social changes that eroded the representative model of governance and inspired subcultures and countercultures.

The tensions created by the weakening of liberal principles and practices have been heightened by national populism, a movement that is increasingly challenging the political mainstream.

National populism claims to prioritise the culture and interests of the nation, and promises to give voice to a people who feel that they have been neglected, even held in contempt, by distant and often corrupt elites (Eatwell and Goodwin 2018, p. IX et seq).

This movement needs to be understood as a whole, due to its international character.

Although most national populists in Europe do not hold office, they are subjected to much the same treatment. They are dismissed as extremists whose authoritarian and racist politics pose a serious threat to liberal democracy and minorities.

Roger Eatwell and Matthew Goodwin provide a very opportune summary illustrating these movements, in which they speak of four historic shifts: the "Four Ds".

The first one is how the natural elites of liberal democracy have promoted distrust of politicians and institutions and fuelled a sense among large numbers of citizens that they no longer have a voice in their national conversation.

The second is how immigration and hyper ethnic change are cultivating strong fears about the possible destruction of the national group's historic identity and established ways of life. These fears are wrapped up in a belief that culturally liberal politicians, transnational organisations and global finance are eroding the nation by encouraging mass immigration, while "politically correct" agendas seek to silent any opposition.

The third shift is the way in which neoliberal globalised economics has stoked strong feelings about what psychologists call "relative deprivation", referring to inequalities of income and wealth, and a loss of faith in a better future.

The Authors explain what is at issue: people's deeper desire to bring a broader set of values back onto the agenda and to regain their voice, to reassert the primacy of the nation over distant and unaccountable international organisations, to reassert cherished and rooted national identities over rootless and diffuse transnational ones, to reassert the importance of stability and conformity over the never-ending and disruptive instability that flows from globalisation and rapid ethnic change, and to reassert the will of the people over those of elitist liberal democrats who appear increasingly detached from the life experiences and outlooks of the average citizen.

The financial crisis in fact created more room for national populism.

It is important to note that the narrative of national populists focuses less on the detail of policies and far more on claims about national decline and destruction, as a result of incompatible immigrant cultures.

One point that warrants further attention is the idea that populists are not merely protesting, but are choosing new forms of democracy.

Many critics reject the idea that populism is a serious ideology with a body of principles and views about politics and society. In their view, it should rather be regarded as a way of competing for power, a way of doing politics.[4] This consideration is perhaps valid, but its worth is negligible given that these movements compete on the same stage as real ideologies.

Populists' actions are described with an acute sense of reality:

---

[4] *Ibidem*, 39. See also, Longart (2021).

"National-populist leaders are routinely presented as lacking any programme beyond diatribes against immigrants, minorities, established politicians, the media and miscellaneous other "enemies of the people". Populist leaders often use common and even coarse language to demonstrate their affinity with the "true", "pure" or "real" people; they seek to cement their bond with them and reinforce their status as outsiders through "us versus them" or "good versus evil" terminology".

Populists routinely criticise more culturally liberal politicians and opinion formers, whom they regard as having neglected or opposed public concerns about the nation and the national identity.[5]

The European Union's construction and functioning has contributed, at the same time, to controlling and exacerbating these movements.

In fact, people have realised that decisions over key issues have moved up to the European level, creating longer and less transparent chains and reducing the accountability of those who are making the decisions.

We shall return to this topic.

3 A Liberal Paradox

According to Article 2 of the European Union Treaty, "The Union is founded on the values of respect for human dignity, freedom, democracy, equality, the rule of law and respect for human rights, including the rights of persons belonging to minorities. These values are common to the Member States in a society in which pluralism, non-discrimination, tolerance, justice, solidarity and equality between women and men prevail."

To better understand the evolution of the European law and jurisprudence we might revisit the treaties of the European Communities and consider the notion of economic freedoms that characterised the early days.

The economic tension that inspired the founding treaties could be seen as an application of illiberal conceptions if we do not consider that, parallel to this, the Council of Europe initiated a model of protection that included civil, political, social and cultural rights incorporated in the European Convention of Human Rights and in its successive Protocols.

The dialogue between the European Communities and the Council of Europe was not always easy but has been essential to expand the initial notion of freedom.

The combination of economic openness and political closure that characterised the first Treaties has been defined by certain authors as a "liberal paradox".

Restrictions imposed on migration and the many continuing forms of discrimination revealed a concept of *exclusionary openness* that was inconsistent with the modern demands of an *open society*.

---

[5] *Ibidem*, p. 53.

In any case, the European leaders were aware of the need for a gradual transformation.

The Court of Justice anticipated this evolution (Rodrigues 2010, p. 89).

Some judgments announced that the economic priority of the treaties was not in itself sufficient. The question of human rights should not be evaded.

One of the first cases in which the question of fundamental rights was raised was an annulment action against the High Authority of the European Coal and Steel Community.[6]

The applicant argued that, in the contested decisions of the High Authority, the rights of the individual, protected under almost all the constitutions of the Member States, had remained a dead letter.

Starting from a dichotomy between community law and national law, the Court decided in three steps: first, it stated that the High Authority was only required to apply Community law and consequently the Court was not competent to apply the national law of the Member States. Secondly, it confirmed that, under Article 31 of the ECSC Treaty, the Court was only required to ensure that the law was observed in the interpretation and application of the Treaty and of rules laid down for the implementation thereof. Thirdly, it held that, since it was not normally required to rule on provisions of national law, the High Authority was not empowered to examine a complaint that it had infringed principles of German constitutional law when it adopted its decision.

The Court's concern was to mark out the boundaries between the ECSC and the Member States.

That judgment opened a long controversy about the supremacy of Community law (Weiler 1991, p. 576).

In joined cases 36, 37, 38 and 40/59, *Geitling v High Authority of the ECSC,*[7] the applicants relied on German case-law relating to the interpretation of Article 14 of the German Basic Law guaranteeing private property.

The Court insisted that it was not its function to ensure the observance of rules of internal law, even constitutional rules. Moreover, it held that Community law, as it arises under the European Coal and Steel Community Treaty, did not contain any general principle, express or otherwise, guaranteeing the maintenance of vested rights.

The case 40/64 *Sgarlata v Commission*[8] was an annulment action in the field of the common agricultural policy.

The applicants argued that the Commission's interpretation of *locus standi* did not give growers of citrus fruit in the Community sufficient legal protection, either at national or at Community level. More precisely, they alleged that, if recourse to Article 173 of the EEC Treaty was to be refused as a result of a restrictive interpretation of its wording, individuals would be deprived of all protection by the courts,

---

[6] Case *Stork*, 1/58, ECR 1959, p. 17.

[7] ECR 1960, p. 423.

[8] ECR 1965, p. 215.

both under Community law and under national law, which would be contrary to the fundamental principles governing all the Member States.

Holding the case inadmissible, the Court took a narrow view of that allegation, merely stating that those considerations "would not be discussed here".

The first judgment in which the Court applied a general principle of law which can be regarded as a fundamental right appears to be joined cases 18 and 35/65 *Max Gutmann v Commission.*[9]

This was an action for the annulment of a decision by the Commission of the European Atomic Energy Authority rejecting a complaint by the applicant official against two earlier decisions suspending him and transferring him.

The applicant had alleged a breach of the rule "*ne bis in idem*".

The Court considered that that rule prohibited not only the imposition of two disciplinary measures for a single offence but also the holding of disciplinary proceedings more than once with regard to a single set of facts (Rodrigues 2003).

This was back when the concept of supremacy, and the creation, within a body of law based on economic freedoms, of methods corresponding to those built up in the different national laws, was not yet stabilised.[10]

The preliminary ruling delivered in case 11/70 *Internationale Handelsgesellschaft*[11] appeared then as a foreseeable development.

The spirit of the time can be discerned in the order of reference itself.

The national court had made the following observations:

> Although Community regulations 120/67 and 473/67 are not German laws, but legal rules pertaining to the European Economic Community which belong neither to public international law nor to the internal law of the Member States [...], in accordance with Article 24, paragraph 1, of the Basic Law, by rectifying the EEC Treaty, the Federal Republic did not give up the application of elementary fundamental rights laid down in the Basic Law within the European Economic Community.

That order of reference went on:

> It is necessary to start from the idea that the German legislature agreed to enter the European Economic Community only because it supposed that the law of the Community of States would be of the same nature as German constitutional law, that is to say that the essential structural principles of internal law would be protected in Community law.

The defendant in the main action made the point in a more indirect way when it submitted that the Court of Justice could not assess the validity of measures taken by Community institutions by reference to rules of national law, even constitutional law, or to the fundamental rights enshrined therein. It argued that the fundamental right to free expression and free choice in commercial decisions, prescribed by the

---

[9] ECR 1966, p. 103 and 1967 p.1961.

[10] Case 29/69 *Stauder v* Ulm, ECR 1969, p. 419 carried out the first review in terms of fundamental rights but did not find that they had been breached. The Court stated that, interpreted in a certain way, the provision at issue contained "nothing capable of prejudicing the fundamental human rights enshrined in the general principles of Community law and protected by the Court".

[11] ECR 1970, p. 1125.

German Basic Law, constituted an element of that common fund of fundamental values which formed part of Community law.

The Court of Justice replied to those arguments in a passage entitled "The protection of fundamental rights in the Community legal system".

The "rhetorical" character of that title announced the importance of the passage that was to follow.

It included several findings of major interpretative significance.

Firstly, the Court reaffirmed the supremacy of Community law and its rank as an autonomous source of law. It gave two reasons for this: on the one hand, because recourse to the legal rules or concepts of national law in order to judge the validity of measures adopted by the institutions of the Community would have an adverse effect on the uniformity and efficacy of Community law. On the other hand, because the law stemming from the Treaty, an independent source of law, could not because of its very nature be overridden by rules of national law, however framed, without being deprived of its character as Community law and without the legal basis of the Community itself being called in question.

Secondly, the Court considered that an examination should be made as to whether any analogous guarantee inherent in Community law had been disregarded. As a result, the Court held that respect for fundamental rights forms an integral part of the general principles of law protected by the Court of Justice and that the protection of such rights, whilst inspired by the constitutional traditions common to the Member States, must be ensured within the framework of the structure and objectives of the Community.

Those findings mark a break with the process by which the Court had been declining to analyse the question of fundamental rights.

The approach in *Internationale Handelsgesellschaft* was also that the autonomy of Community law required the inspiration from the constitutional traditions common to the Member States to be carried out "within the framework of the structure and objectives of the Community".

However, as certain authors have pointed out (Weiler 1991, p. 583), the accent was placed less on fundamental rights as subjective rights than on fundamental rights as instruments of integration.

In Case 4/73 *Nold v Commission,*[12] a coal wholesaler sought the annulment of a Commission decision authorising new terms of business by Ruhrkohle AG.

The claimant claimed that the terms of business of Ruhrkohle and the way they were applied infringed certain fundamental rights enshrined in the national constitutions and received into Community law. This was alleged to be the case in respect of the right of property ownership, the protection of which was ensured particularly by Article 14 of the German Basic Law and by the constitution of the Land of Hesse.

The claimant relied on the Constitutions of other Member States and various international treaties, including the European Convention for the Protection of

[12] ECR 1974, p. 491; followed in later decisions, in particular Case 136/79 *National Panasonic,* ECR 1980, p. 2033.

Human Rights and Fundamental Freedoms of 4 November 1950 (ECHR) and the Protocol to that Convention of 20 March 1952.

The defendant answered that it was not for the Court of Justice to interpret and apply rules of domestic law of a Member State, even those appertaining to the Constitution. Moreover, it argued, the ECSC Treaty contained no general principle of law, written or unwritten, guaranteeing the maintenance of acquired positions.

In its judgment of 14 May 1974, the Court of Justice held that, as it had already stated, "fundamental rights form an integral part of the general principles of law, the observance of which it ensures" and that "in safeguarding these rights, the Court is bound to draw inspiration from the constitutional traditions common to the Member States".

From those considerations the Court drew the inference that it could not "uphold measures which are incompatible with fundamental rights recognized and protected by the constitutions of those States".

That postulate, inserted in the specific context of a complaint (i.e. the terms of business applied by a company and approved by the Commission in breach of fundamental rights) raises interesting theoretical questions. Although it cannot be read as laying down a principle, at the very least it was the beginning of a line of case-law, consolidated later, whereby the Court extended the review of compliance with fundamental rights to national measures when these were adopted in implementation of Community law.[13]

Likewise, for the first time, the Court referred to international instruments.

The *Internationale Handelsgesellschaft* and *Nold* cases were inspired by a pan-European vision which clearly contained a liberal dimension.

Those judgments are typical of a period when, after the autonomous and supranational framework of the Community law had been established, it had to be endowed with the principles inherent to the rule of law, understood in conformity with international instruments of fundamental rights.

Tracing the presence of fundamental rights in the case-law of the Court of Justice over the years, one can find that, before 1969, fundamental rights were considered to be outside the jurisdiction of the Court or otherwise not necessary to resolve the dispute. From 1969 onwards, fundamental rights were analysed as being included in the general principles of Community law, the observance of which the Court ensures. From 1974/1975, the Court refers explicitly to the ECHR.[14] From 1989, the

[13] That case-law has been confirmed in Joined Cases 60 and 61/84 *Cinéthèque* ECR 1985, p. 2605, and in Case 5/88 *Wachau*, ECR 1989, p. 2609.

[14] Case 36/75 *Rutili,* ECR 1975, p. 1219. See also Case 136/79 *National Panasonic v Commission*, ECR 1980, p. 203.

ECHR is cited as having a "particular significance".[15] From 1990 onwards, the Court of Justice cites actual decisions of the European Court of Human Rights.[16]

The Court of Justice designed a system that comprised its standards, its own areas of competence,[17] a capacity of dialogue with the constitutional traditions common to the Member States, observance of the established body of Community law in the field of human rights, as supplied by the ECHR, and the ability to be developed within its specific theoretical context.

It must be highlighted that those judgments represented a dialogue with German jurisdictions.

It is understandable that the rulings had come from a country devastated by the war and anxious to empower citizens with fundamental rights.

This evolution meant that the initial context of economic liberalism progressed towards a liberal conception in which liberty would be endowed with positive elements, in order to assure respect for human dignity and protection of individuals as social and political actors.

4 The Inequalities

There is a certain consensus on fundamental principles of social justice.

Modern theories of social justice have expressed the idea that fair society must maximise the minimal opportunities and living conditions offered by the social system, a principle formally introduced by Christophe Koln and John Rawls (Piketty 2015, p. 2).

Most scholars agree that inequalities in Western countries began to increase again in the 1980s. An EDCO report published in 2015 stated that, for the past half century, the average income of the richest 10% of the population was about nine times that of the poorest 10%. A report published in November 2021, concerning public perceptions about income notes that, while in 2015 the lowest-paid workers thought that the highest-paid workers earned five times as much as they did, they now think that the highest-paid earn eight times as much as they do.

One of the most sensitive points of the judicial and administrative work relating to fundamental rights is the principle of equality.

---

[15] Joined Cases 46/87 and 227/88 *Hoechst v Commission*, ECR 1989, p. 2859, paragraph 13, and Case C-260/89 *ERT*, ECR 1991, p. I-2925, paragraph 41.

[16] See for example Case C-7/98 *Krombach,* ECR 2000, p. I-1935, paragraph 39.

After hesitations due to a certain reading of the Court's Opinion 2/94, ECR 1996, p. I-1759, the accession of the European Union to the ECHR appears to be a settled aim: see Article I-9 of the draft European Constitution. In this regard, it may be said that the Intergovernmental Conference went further than the preparatory Convention, in whose view the Union should only "endeavour" to proceed to accession.

[17] These areas of competence refer to the Community as a whole and may thus be complemented by the courts of the Member States.

This principle figures in the Treaties and is a constant reference in the jurisprudence of the Court of Justice.

It is opportune to recall that it was considered necessary to establish a kind of *memorandum* on this matter.

This movement was later followed by the Declaration of Principles on Equality and activities of the Council of Europe (Resolution adopted by the Standing Committee on behalf of the Parliamentary Assembly 1844 (2011), of 25 November 2011). Signed initially by 128 prominent legal practitioners, academics and human rights activists from 44 countries, including the Council of Europe Commissioner for Human Rights, the Declaration has subsequently been endorsed by hundreds of signatories (individuals and organisations).

The Parliamentary Assembly reiterated the crucial importance of the principle of equality and non-discrimination, as an essential part of the international protection of human rights, already enshrined in the 1948 Universal Declaration of Human Rights and the 1966 International Covenant on Civil and Political Rights.

The Assembly highlighted the path followed in combating all forms of inequality and discrimination of different persons and groups, including vulnerable groups such as national minorities or persons with disabilities. In particular, in its Resolution 1547 (2007) on the state of human rights and democracy in Europe, it called upon all member States of the Council of Europe to combat effectively all forms of discrimination based on racial, ethnic or religious origin, gender or sexual orientation, and to better protect the rights of persons belonging to national and other minorities.

Notwithstanding, one might say that inequalities have persisted as the main obstacle to the development of modern liberal societies.

Thomas Piketty explains the social success of neoliberalism in the United States of America: in 1980, 1% of the wealthiest owned 50% of the incomes of the poorest; now, 1% of the wealthiest own twice the incomes of the poorest.

Many scholars argue that liberalism excludes matters of social justice from the responsibility of the State, thus rejecting the legitimacy of income redistribution policies aimed at reducing inequalities and seeking greater equity, more social justice and more real equality.[18]

In Europe, a considerable part of the population of many countries continues to live in poverty.

On this matter, the minimum that can be said is that the issue at stake is freedom of choice, a basic condition to act in the society and to be a citizen.

The European Union, as a whole, can hardly be said to comprise liberal societies.

[18] See, for example, Nunes (2003, p. 49).

5 The Saga of European Citizenship

Naturally following on from the above, European citizenship, enshrined in the Treaty of Maastricht, and the inherent declaration of the right to move and reside freely in the European Community irrespective of socio-economic criteria, was in itself a decisive goal.

The Union lacked a broad definition of the position of Members States' nationals vis-à-vis the European Communities.

European citizenship was the answer to this problem.

The notion of European citizenship was, however, a controversial matter (Rodrigues 2012, p. 201).

European citizenship was said to genetically be a superposed citizenship and to endure as an imbalanced asymmetric notion in favour of economic factors.

From the beginning, the difficulties were understood as, on the one hand, legal questions, and on the other, questions concerning other matters such as *belonging* and *identity*.

Legally, one can say that what emerged from an initial reading of the notion of European citizenship was the secondary nature of its link and the completeness of the rights explicitly conferred, going beyond the economic functionalisation.

The constitutional dimension of European citizenship, based on a new legal and political reality oriented towards the recognition of "special rights", has marked the transition from the status of the society, owner of fundamental freedoms, to the individual, owner of fundamental rights.

The Community legislator itself took this route, annexing to Article 8 TEU an evolutionary or progressive clause in line with the "plastic" and "dynamic" character of the status of citizenship, which can be adapted as the process develops.

In the beginning, European citizenship was associated with a functional logic and tried to compensate for the "democratic deficit" of which the process of European construction had been accused.

In a certain sense, the origins and the common destinies of citizenship and fundamental rights constituted the values on which the Union should be based.

These conditions have been reflected in the jurisprudence of the Court.

The judgments illustrate the expansion of the notion of citizenship, despite revealing a certain argumentative discontinuity. Among the most relevant we can recall are *Grzelczyk*,[19] *Baumbast and R.*,[20] *Zhu and Chen*,[21] *Rottmann*,[22] *Zambrano*,[23] *McCarthy*,[24] *Rendón Marin*,[25] *CS*,[26] Chavez Vilchez[27] and *KA*.[28]

It is worth highlighting three of these judgments, *Grzelczyk*, *Zambrano* and *McCarthy*, given their particular significance:.

In the *Grzelczyk* case, the Court appears to have made a proclamation on the status of European citizenship. It stated that Union citizenship is destined to be the fundamental status of nationals of the Member States.

Zambrano (ruled by the Grand Chamber) developed this jurisprudence and was the object of an extensive debate in the scientific mainstream, being welcomed by some as timely and fair, and criticised by others for being the product of a certain activism.

McCarthy (handed down by a Chamber of five judges) was regarded by some as having the objective of limiting the effects of *Zambrano*; others saw it as a way of substantiating the essential content of the rights derived from European citizenship, in a case that did not refer to parental protection but to protection of spouses.[29]

A few judgments followed the restrictive approach adopted in *McCarthy*.[30]

However, the Grand Chamber of the Court of Justice did not take long to confirm and expand the jurisprudence in Zambrano. This clarification was particularly welcomed in a situation "where Zambrano's and Rottmann's potential seemed hopelessly gagged" (Silveira 2017, pp. 48–62).

The Charter of Human Rights of the European Union represented a substantial change, but only in the axiological plan defined by the rules.

It intervened in the new context of the Treaty of Lisbon, which contained overlapping dynamics: that of further integration, produced by the abolition of pillars and the strengthening of the scope of fundamental rights (i.e. by the adhesion of the Union to the Convention of Human Rights and Fundamental Freedoms) and that of the greater participation of Member States, in particular within the framework of the principle of subsidiarity.

---

[19] Case C-184/99, ECR 2001, p. I-6193.

[20] Case-413/99, ECR 2002, p. I-7091.

[21] Case C-200/02, ECR 2004, p. I-7091.

[22] Case C-135/08, ECLI:EU:C:2010:104.

[23] Case -C.-34/09, ECR 2012, p. I-1232.

[24] Case 434/09, ECR 2012, p. 3393.

[25] Case C-165/14, ECLI:EU:C:2016:675.

[26] Case-304/14, ECLI:EU:C:2016:674.

[27] Case 133/14, ECLI:EU:C:2017:354.

[28] Case C-82/16, ECLI:EU:C:2018:308.

[29] The Court stressed that no element of McCarthy's situation, as described by the national court, revealed that the national measure at issue in the main proceedings had the effect of depriving the wife of the genuine enjoyment of the substance of the rights associated with the status as a Union citizen.

[30] See Haag (2017). The commentator considered that the Court "swiftly backtracked" from *Zambrano*.

6 Media Pluralism

With European citizenship and the Charter, we could conclude that the European Union had reached a high standard of liberalism.

However, these standards promised new and serious obstacles.

Among the most complex challenges were the implications of the information society and particularly the role of the media.

We cannot ignore the media when we speak of democracy and liberalism.

Nevertheless, experience quickly shows that many elements of mass communications are ambivalent.

One of these, naturally, is Television. Due to its impressive effects and its power of dissemination, television has enjoyed increasing influence in the formation of public opinion. Similarly, the economic potential of audio-visual was very soon recognised by businesses and gave rise to a sector dominated by market rules.

With an understandable sense of reality, certain Authors have dared to write that television is a danger for democracy (Popper and Condry 1995).

Popper (1994) also added that public opinion, without a powerful liberal tradition, is a threat to liberty.

Maintaining the quality and pluralism of the media is a major issue which intensified during the crisis.

Several phenomena lead us to the conclusion that media pluralism is under threat. Among these are the extinction of companies, weakened working conditions, movements to concentrate undertakings and the multiplication of controlling positions.

The debate on the concentration of undertakings was contaminated by the effects of the crisis, which reduced the advertising market and consequently the economic conditions that guaranteed technological standards, quality of information and consistency of sources.

Since media pluralism is at the heart of democracy, we can only wonder why the Union's instruments remain precarious, and the political institutions seem to assume an attitude of mere observation, even when, through the action of the technological revolution, the clock is ticking to resolve instant problems.

The need to create inclusive societies is increasing.

However, quality and pluralism are not facilitated by means of the simple guarantee of non-intrusion by political powers. On the contrary, these powers are called on to ensure an approach that enhances those values, which implies the existence of an adequate platform for individual expression, consistent access to information and the possibility of debate in the name of each social group.

These objectives cover a range of areas, in particular the existence of pluralism among newsmakers, the dissemination of media headlines to the periphery, protection of sources and the offer of cultural goods.

Moreover, the technical revolution, with digital and the creation and convergence of new platforms, such as the Internet, has changed the notion of "resource scarcity" that inspired the legislation (Rodrigues 2021, p. 29).

These new realities have questioned the law in different ways (Rodrigues 2014, p. 289 et seq).

The common understanding seems to be captured by the idea that the European Union lacks competence to act on this matter.

The European Parliament approved several resolutions appealing for direct intervention of the European Commission in the context of the *Green Paper on Services of General Interests* (2003).

For its part, the Commission recognised that the debate had evolved. It noted the Protocol on the system of public broadcasting, which stressed that broadcasting was directly related to the democratic, social and cultural needs of each society and to the need to preserve media pluralism,

The Court of Justice entered this subject matter with the *Sacchi* case.

This case dates back to 1974 and signals a first interrogation into the relationship between economic freedoms and the media.

The questions submitted to the Court referred to the free provision of services and the free movement of goods.

That judgment quoted freedom of expression, as protected by Article 10 of the European Convention on Human Rights and Fundamental Freedoms, as one of the fundamental rights guaranteed by the Community legal order, while observing that there is no necessary connection between a cultural policy and the conditions relating to the structure of foreign broadcasting bodies.

It was not yet the time to be more explicit, but the Court of Justice alluded to the need for pluralism in the audio-visual sector.

The judgment was based on the general interest.

This jurisprudence was also referred to in the *Green Paper* of 1984 and in the Directive of 1989, which was revised in 1997 and 2007.

Underlying the timid nature of these initiatives was the idea that issues raised in economic activities should be resolved within the framework of competition law. This claim clearly denied the role of the media in a liberal society.

In fact, according to Article 2 of the European Union Treaty, "the Union is founded on the values of respect for human dignity, freedom, democracy, equality, the rule of law and respect for human rights, including the rights of persons belonging to minorities. These values are common to the Member States in a society in which pluralism, non-discrimination, tolerance, justice, solidarity and equality between women and men prevail".

On the other hand, Article 11(2) of the EU Charter of Fundamental Rights states that "The freedom and pluralism of the media shall be respected".

One can argue that the latter provision has negative content in establishing an obligation of no interference of the Member States in the implementation of media pluralism.

Addressing this argument, it may be stated that paragraph 2 follows a provision that grants everyone the right to freedom of expression. This right "shall include freedom to hold opinions and to receive and impart information and ideas without interference by public authority and regardless of frontiers."

The distinction between rights with positive content and rights with negative content will be diluted if the provision is articulated with Article 2 of the European Union Treaty.

The Court of Justice case-law was quick to follow this route, giving considerable relevance to the need for pluralism in the field of justifications. In the *Gouda*[31] case, it was stated that a cultural policy understood in that sense may constitute an overriding requirement relating to the general interest which justifies a restriction on the freedom to provide services. The Court added that maintaining pluralism is connected with freedom of expression, as protected by Article 10 of the European Convention on Human Rights and Fundamental Freedoms, which is one of the fundamental rights guaranteed by Community law.

The centrality of audio-visual pluralism was reiterated in several Court of Justice rulings, namely in *Veronika,*[32] *TV10*[33] and *Vereinigle Familiapress*.[34]

The European Court of Human Rights followed the same path, when referring to Article 10(2) of the European Convention of Human Rights, stating that pluralism, tolerance and broadmindedness are essential for a democratic society.[35] The considerations expressed in the judgment in *Manole v* Moldova of 17 September 2009 are particularly revealing:

> There can be no democracy without pluralism. One of the principal characteristics of democracy is the possibility it offers of resolving a country's problems through dialogue, without recourse to violence, even when they are irksome. Democracy thrives on freedom of expression. It is of the essence of democracy to allow diverse political programmes to be proposed and debated, even those that call into question the way a State is currently organised, provided that they do not harm democracy itself. Freedom of expression, as secured in Article 10 § 1, constitutes one of the essential foundations of a democratic society and one of the basic conditions for its progress. Freedom of the press and other news media afford the public one of the best means of discovering and forming an opinion of the ideas and attitudes of political leaders. It is incumbent on the press to impart information and ideas on political issues and on other subjects of public interest. Not only does the press have the task of imparting such information and ideas: the public also has a right to receive them. The audiovisual media, such as radio and television, have a particularly important role in this respect. Because of their power to convey messages through sound and images, such media have a more immediate and powerful effect than print.

These questions have been the subject of growing debate in recent years. There has been an increase in technological potential and substantial modifications in the functioning of the State with new formulations to restore important losses in the structure of representative democracies.

At the same time, the crisis brought broadcasters closer to the owners of economic groups, in some cases as a matter of economic rationality, and in other cases,

---

[31] C-288/89, ECR, I-4007.

[32] C-148/91, ECR 1993, p. I-487.

[33] C-23/93, ECR 1994, p. I-4795.

[34] C-368/95, ECR 1997, p. I-3689.

[35] *Handyside v UK, 5493/72, Informationsverein Lentia and others v. Austria 1993* e *Manole v Moldova, 13,936/02.*

by the mere power of influence that they can exercise over political institutions and over the society in general.

Increasing competition within the advertising market and the consequent austerity within the media had the effect of compromising the offer of products and the actual working environment, leading to expressions of self-censorship that do not favour pluralism.

The European Parliament continued to be the most consequential forum of debate. In a Resolution of 2004, the Parliament recalled that the Union already had competences in a significant number of policy areas with repercussions for media pluralism.

A European Parliament Resolution of 25 September 2008 on media concentration and pluralism stated that the European Union confirmed its commitment to protecting and promoting media pluralism, as an essential pillar of the right to information and freedom of expression enshrined in Article 11 of the Charter of Fundamental Rights of the European Union, which remain fundamental principles for preserving democracy, civic pluralism and cultural diversity. The Resolution also mentioned that the European Union had no intrinsic competence to regulate media concentration, nevertheless its competence in various policy fields enabled it to play an active role in safeguarding and promoting media pluralism.

The Audio-visual policy in the EU is now governed by Articles 167 and 173 of the Treaty on the Functioning of the European Union (TFEU). The key piece of legislation in this field is the Audio-visual Media Services Directive, revised in 2018. The European Union highlighted the need to construct policies in this regard derived from the nature of media goods and services, which can be defined neither solely as cultural goods nor simply as economic goods. We can cite the following steps: the so-called Television without Frontiers Directive of 1989, revised in 1997 and 2007, which was subsequently codified in 2010 and renamed the Audio-visual Media Services Directive, and the Commission's *Green Papers* of 2013 and 2018; the Commission guidelines to help Member States to transpose the Directive; many other instruments adopted by different entities, such as the media strand of the Creative Europe programme, the action plan for the media and audio-visual sectors and the initiatives concerning media literacy and media pluralism.

While it must be acknowledged that the Commission's management of this issue experienced certain fluctuations, it is encouraging that the debate happened at the European level, stemming from the European Parliament's initiative on media pluralism, with a proposal to the Commission for a new directive aimed at partial harmonisation of the national rules on media ownership.

In the absence of explicit competences, Article 167(4) of the TFEU provided the grounds for the Commission to use competition law to draw up an appropriate framework of principles and provisions on media pluralism, and to pursue this objective through the Fundamental Rights Agency. This Agency cooperates with the Union institutions and the Member States, assisting them in close cooperation with the Council of Europe.

Although this approach was not sufficient, it merits applause.

The jurisprudence of the Court of Justice also developed in the same direction.

A prudent attitude developed that recognised media pluralism as a fundamental issue. This status went beyond the idea of a general principle and placed media pluralism at the same level as the economic freedoms and other similar principles.

These objectives were fundamental in a situation of political emergency in which the media was being taken over by economic groups.

As previously stated, the European Parliament played an important role in the implementation of media pluralism.

In fact, neither the Treaty of Rome nor the Treaty on European Union provided for any direct powers in the field of audio-visual and media policy.

7 National Identity, Nationalisms and *Identitarian* Movements

Another important challenge is the confrontation between *national identity, nationalisms* and *identitarian* movements.

The Treaty of Lisbon reiterated and densified the principle of respect for *national identity*.

In accordance with Article 4(2) of the Treaty on European Union, "The Union shall respect the equality of Member States before the treaties as well as their national identities, inherent in their fundamental structures, political and constitutional, inclusive of regional and local self-government. It shall respect their essential State functions, including ensuring the territorial integrity of the State, maintaining law and order and safeguarding national security. National security remains the sole responsibility of each Member State".

It is generally recognised that the Treaty of Lisbon sought to compensate the advances that were being made in the integration process. In a spirit of vigilant integration, the Treaty extended the rights of the European Parliament to the detriment of the rights of the Council and reduced the number of cases in which a unanimous vote was required. It also established the need for ratification by Member States of any changes which extended the competences of the Union. Moreover, it explicitly acknowledged the right of any Member State to withdraw from the Union (Article 50) (Konstadinides 2013).

The understanding of much of the case-law is that respect for *national identity* may be invoked by Member States as a procedural means to scrutinise the legality of the Union's legislative acts.

The German Constitutional Court once again challenged this jurisprudence.

In certain judgments, this Court ruled that constitutional control enables national actors to examine whether their Constitutions are compatible with the competences exercised by the Institutions of the Union.

The judgment of that Court in the *Lissabon-Urteil* case (30 June 2009) emerged in this respect as a doctrine that develops the Solange II and Maastricht cases according to a formula that appeals to the idea of *constitutional identity*.[36] At the same time, it confirms the need for the intervention of Parliaments in the case of a transfer of sovereignty to the supranational level.

The essence of this judgment lies in the so-called *eternity clause*, contained in Article 79 § 3 of the German Constitution that, according to the generally agreed interpretation, enforces the intangibility of democracy, the rule of law, the welfare state, the Republic, the Federal State and fundamental rights.

The German Constitutional Court refers to a "responsibility for integration" which would have as agents, in particular, national parliaments and governments. The process of integration would have to be drawn up in terms of an integration *secundum constitutionem* and not by way of a customary model, so to speak, as hitherto had happened.[37]

The relationship between *national identity* and Union Law would be based on a multilevel (national and supranational) structure.

With this jurisprudence, the German Constitutional Court went from a reactive constitutional pluralism to a proactive constitutional pluralism.

The control of the principle of *national identity* has an important symbolic value, albeit sometimes erratic. Very often, one may question which principle (*national identity* or *constitutional identity)* is at issue.

The epistemological arena within which the debate has progressed shows that the subject of dialogue between the German Constitutional Court and the legal order of the Union still has a long future.

What should we say?

For some scholars, the Court of Justice would be moving towards a form of *constitutionalism* in which Member States would be accorded a monopoly over the definition of the interests inherent to *national identity*, with the Court retaining the power to determine the compatibility with obligations relating to the European Union.[38]

Other authors have noted that the discourse on constitutionalism has a significant symbolic burden in terms of material and procedural legitimacy.

For these authors, the way the Court has been deciding is "a creative adjustment" (Wilkinson 2003, p. 458).

---

[36] The provision refers to Articles 1 and 20.

[37] In the *Honeywell* judgment of 6 July 2010, the German Constitutional Court included in its supervisory powers a test of *constitutional identity*.

[38] Regarding the draft of a European Constitution, it was said that, at the moment when the Community legal order evolves into more consolidated forms of constitutionalism, it is the Court's own position to be "constitutionalised". See Tizzano (2003, p. 456).

The first decision, after the Lisbon Treaty, in which the Court directly examined the principle of respect for *national identity* was the *Fürstin von Sayn-Wittgenstein* case.[39,40]

In this Decision, the principle of respect for *national identity* was considered a justification for restriction of an economic freedom.

The existence of a triangular relationship in which the primacy of Union law, *constitutional identity* and fundamental rights interact is an immovable axis within the values, and the principles establish the scope of the essential content that must be respected. The difficulties stem from the fact that each of the components of that relationship has a historical and specific nature.

The way the Court has chosen to resolve the conflict between *national identity* and economic freedoms confirms that we are facing a new area of speculation which, as such, requires legal construction (Rodrigues 2006, p. 675 et seq).

The Court should perhaps base its reading of *national citizenship* on social principles, given that the content of the notion is indeterminate (Cloots 2016).

But the relationship between *national identity* and fundamental rights has other possible implications.

Does *national identity* have the importance attached to it? Or, regardless of the existence of a supranational law, is it only gaining visibility as a result of the globalisation and integration processes?

There is a natural and foreseeable ambiguity in the possible answers.

National identity is increasingly an internationalised identity.

The interdependence of the States has reached areas as diverse as the economy, finances, internal and external security, technology and science, telecommunications, energy, environment protection, food production, agriculture and even social security insofar as it is closely linked to growth. With globalisation, there has been an acceleration in processes of change. The technological revolution and mass communication have boosted the exchange of ideas, knowledge and values and influenced the cultural environment, modifying conceptions and lifestyles and dissolving or weakening key aspects of national identities.

The new cultural expressions are now characterised by specificity, difference, diversity and multiplicity of discourses (Sandoval 2009, pp. 7–16).

---

[39] Judgment C-208/09 (22 December 2010), ECLI:EU:C:2010:806, reported by Judge Allan Rosas. Referring, in different contexts, to *national identity*, see cases C-156/13, *Digibet et Albers* (12 June 2014, ECLI:EU:C:2014:1756) and C-15/15, *Remondis GmbH & Co. KG Region Nord* (21 December 2016, ECLI:EU:C:2016:985). See also Case C-105/2014, *Taricco* (8 September 2015, ECLI:EU:C:2015:555, wherein the question of *constitutional id*entity was invoked in the ruling but not dealt with by the Court.

[40] See also cases C-391/09 *Malgozata Runevic-Vardyn* (12 May 2011) ECLI:EU:C:2011:291 and C-393/10, *Dermod Patrick O'Brien v. Ministry of Justice* (first March 2012) *ECLI:EU:C:2012:110*. In the first, the Court stated that, according to the fourth subparagraph of Article 3 (3) EU and Article 22 of the Charter of Fundamental Rights of the European Union, the Union must respect its rich cultural and linguistic diversity and Article 4 (2) provides that the Union must also respect the national identity of its Member States, which includes protection of a State's official language.

It is generally recognised that identity movements are encouraged by phenomena such as (Sandoval 2009, pp. 13–14):

- the emergence of social spaces in which alternative cultural practices are increasing.
- the promotion of diversity and the claim for rights by minorities.
- the dynamics of micro-worlds in the political conception of the State.
- the political pressure coming from international bodies on human rights.
- the plurality of cultural expressions expressed by symbols, fashions, values.

Bauman (2000) used the term "liquid modernity" to define the present situation in which social systems and institutions no longer have time and knowledge to solidify their ideas and cannot consequently serve as frames of reference for human actions and long-term life plans.

Individuals must discover their ways, although they are less and less able to choose.

8 On the Future

To be productive, the dialogue between the Member States and the European Union needs a new framework.

Europe is facing crucial challenges which derive from its own institutional architecture but also from the changes in the geostrategic balances.

On the other hand, national populisms and *identitarian* movements will hinder internal governance, namely by creating neuralgic points of tension in relation to the application of the treaties.

Internally, influences susceptible of transforming the will of individuals and collective aspirations are increasing. Examples of this are the erosion of representative democracy, the situation of the media, the role of social networks and the phenomena of meta globalisation.

The characteristics of mass communication have probably acted as an insurmountable obstacle.

Radical movements are not only drifts of liberalism but also expressions of illiberal conceptions. For this reason, we are likely to be at risk of a reversal of the trend towards generalisation of liberal societies.

The European Union is empowered with dense and complex codes and provisions that seek to respond to the complex societies of the modern world. However, as several Authors have noted, complexity generates complexity.

The reforms need to find models that facilitate dialogue and respect for national identities. Not fake identities used to feed populisms and justify revendications, but those able to protect the genuineness and the diversity of the societies.

The European jurisprudence has taken a prudent route in this regard.

It can be observed that the Court, in certain issues, has adopted an approach of self-restraint, which should be read as corresponding to a prudential method explained by the uncertainty and the complexity of the matters in question. It is now time to see some themes not only as values but also as ways towards reform of the Union. I allude to the need to develop the political dimension of the Union with regard to global geostrategic balances, simplification of the decision-making process and achievement of the economic dimension by implementing a coherent budgetary system.

Nationalisms require a multi-level answer. They are very often mere epiphenomena of illiberal tendencies. Nevertheless, they may correspond to internal social and political fractures. It is understandable that the European Union should look for a neutral analysis. However, we must explore the possibility of an intervention that is able to reinforce common values.

Nationalisms and *identitarian* movements are true challenges to the Union's cohesion. Greater attention to the national identity could operate as a means of affirming respect for *diversity* as part of the Union values.

These times demand a new approach to the future.

There are, today, four unavoidable threats: *poverty*, *climate change*, *migrations and scarcity*. All of these are linked to globalisation and consequently depend on a multiplicity of factors and agents. The European Union should assume its role by creating adequate instruments, where necessary.

Indeed, it is up to the European Union to recognise its historical responsibilities in the global world, as an unprecedented model of cooperation between nation States aimed at the construction of a liberal Community.

Given that the European Union already has a charter of freedoms and rights, the reforms should particularly evolve to a European synthesis of the *acquis*, in order to strengthen the capacity of the Union as a Community of Law and to promote liberty, equality, pluralism and progress.

References

Aron R (1970) An essay on freedom. World Publishing Company, New Yok
Bauman S (2000) Liquid modernity. Polity Press, Cambridge
Bermann G, Goebl R, Davey W, Fox E (2002) Cases and materials on European Union, 2nd edn. West Group, Eagan
Cloots E (2016) National identity, constitutional identity, and sovereignty in the EU. Neth J Leg Philos 45:82–98
Constant B (2015) The liberty of ancients compared with that of moderns. Laissez Faire Books, Agora Inc., Baltimore
Eatwell R, Goodwin M (2018) National populism: the revolt against liberal democracy. Pelikan Books, London
Fukuyama F (2020) The end of history and the last man. Penguin Books Ltd, London
Haag M (2017) Case C-133/15 Chávez-Vílchez and Others—Taking EU Children's Rights Seriously. https://europeanlawblog.eu/2017/05/30/case-c-13315-chavez-vilchez-and-others-taking-eu-childrens-rights-seriously/. Accessed 12 Mar 2024
Kagan R (2008) The return of history and the end of dreams. Alfred A. Knopf, New York

Konstadinides T (2013) The constitutionalisation of national identity in EU law and its implications. https://ssrn.com/abstract=2318972. Accessed 30 Sept 2024
Longart J (2021) El populismo como elemento de transición política hacia una democracia illiberal. Madrid
McAdams J, Castrillon A (2022) Contemporary far-right thinkers and the future of liberal democracy. Routledge, London
Morin E (1994) Ciência com consciência. Europa-América, Lisboa
Morin E (1996) O problema epistemológico da complexidade. Europa-América, Lisboa
Nunes A (2003) Neoliberalismo e direitos humanos. Caminho, Lisboa
Piketty T (2015) The economics of inequality. Harvard University Press, Cambridge
Piketty T (2019) Capital et idéologie. Seuil, Paris
Plattner MF (2019) Illiberal democracy and the struggle on the right. J Democr 30:5–19
Popper K (1994) In search of a better world. Routledge, London
Popper K, Condry J (1995) Télévision, un danger pour la démocratie. Anatolia, France
Rodrigues C (2003) A propos du principe « ne bis in idem» - Un regard sur la jurisprudence de la Cour de justice des Communautés européennes. In: Colneric N, Edward D, Puisso-chet J-P, Colomer DR-J (eds) Une Communauté de droit. Festschrift fur Gil Carlos Rodriguez Iglesias. BWV Berliner Wissenshafts, Berlin, p 165
Rodrigues C (2006) Entre a Europa das liberdades e a Europa dos cidadãos. In: Estudos jurídicos e económicos em homenagem ao Professor Doutor António de Sousa Franco. Coimbra Editora, Coimbra, pp 675–707
Rodrigues C (2010) The incorporation of fundamental rights in the community legal order. In: Maduro M, Azoulai L (eds) The past and future of EU law: the classics of EU law revisited on the 50th anniversary of the Rome treaty. Hart Publishing, Oxford, pp 89–97
Rodrigues C (2012) *A propos* European citizenship: the right to move and reside freely. In: Cardonnel P, Rosas A, Wahl N (eds) Constitutionalising the EU judicial system - essays in honour of Pernilla Lindh. Hart Publishing, Oxford, pp 201–211
Rodrigues C (2013) De l'abondance de droits en temps de crise. In: L'Europe des Droits Fondamentaux - Mélanges en hommage à Albert Weitzel. Pedone, Paris, pp 29–57
Rodrigues C (2014) Direito da União Europeia e comunicação social. Media, Direito e Democracia. Almedina, Coimbra
Rodrigues C (2021) Está disponível para ser julgado por algoritmos?, Jornal de Letras, July 28 2021
Sajó A (2021) Ruling by cheating: governance in illiberal democracy. Cambridge University Press, New York
Sandoval LA (2009) La identidad nacional en tiempos de globalización. Rev Electron Educ 13:7–16
Silveira A (2017) On the CJEU'S post-Brexit case-law on European citizenship: the recovery of the identity Ariadne's thread? UNIO EU Law J 3:48–62
Tizzano A (2003) La "Costituzione Europea" e il sistema giurisdizionale comunitario. Il Diritto dell'Unione Europea. Giuffré Editore, Milano, pp 455–479
Weiler J (1991) Methods of protection: towards a second and third generation of protection. In: Cassese A et al (eds) Human rights and the European Community: methods of protection. Nomos, Baden-Baden, p 555
Wilkinson M (2003) Civil society and the re-imagination of European constitutionalism. Eur Law J 9:451–472
Zuboff S (2019) The age of surveillance capitalism. Profile Books Ltd., London
Zuboff S (2021) Interview, Time, January 22, 2021
Zúquete JP (2018) The Identitarians. The movement against globalism and Islam in Europe. University of Notre Dame, Notre Dame

José Narciso da Cunha Rodrigues Former Judge at the CJEU. Former Attorney-General of the Republic, Portugal.

Member States Nationality and European Union Citizenship: The Reinforcement of Interdependence in the Recent Court of Justice Case-Law

Rui Manuel Moura Ramos

1 Introduction

Just over three decades ago, I was honoured to receive an invitation from Dr. Carlos Botelho Moniz, on behalf of the Board of the Portuguese Association of European Law (APDE), to be one of the general rapporteurs at the XV Congress of the International Federation of European Law (FIDE), which was due to take place for the first time in Portugal in 1992. I was asked to select one of three topics which had been chosen for the Congress: *La prestation des services financiers au sein de la CEE et avec les pays tiers, La sanction des infractions au droit communautaire*, or *Les aspects nouveaux de la libre circulation des personnes: vers une citoyenneté européenne*. After some brief hesitation, I decided to focus on the last of these three, and the version of the report that was distributed prior to the Congress[1] was able to take into account the provisions that were incorporated into the Treaty on European Union (TEU), which was signed in Maastricht[2] on 7 February 1992.

[1] See Ramos (1992, pp. 393–453). In addition to the general report, this publication also includes the questionnaire sent (on 9 August 1991) to the various national rapporteurs and the reports received in the meantime (German, Austrian, Belgian, Danish, Spanish, Dutch, English, Irish, Italian, Luxembourgish, Norwegian and Portuguese). As is well known, within the FIDE, the issue would be revisited later at the XXVI Congress in Copenhagen. Cf. Shuibhne and Shaw (2014).

[2] The new Part (which would become Part II, entitled Citizenship of the Union) of what was then called the Treaty on the European Community (which includes Articles 8 to 8E), added to by Article G, paragraph C, of Title II (Provisions amending the Treaty establishing the European Economic Community with a view to establishing the European Community) of the TEU. Regarding

R. M. M. Ramos (✉)
Univ Coimbra, UCILeR - University of Coimbra Institute for Legal Research, Faculty of Law, Coimbra, Portugal
e-mail: rmmramos@fd.uc.pt

I. Quadros, M. Gorjão-Henriques (eds.), *Revisiting the Liberal Constitutional Features of the European Union*, https://doi.org/10.1007/978-3-031-95717-8_3

Over the years since then, this topic has gained my attention on numerous occasions (in particular, Ramos (1994, pp. 93–129, 2005–2006, pp. 352–368, 2008, pp. 67–77)), and I wish to return to it once again now, particularly with regard to one aspect that has been raised in some recent Court of Justice case-law. I am speaking of a (core) aspect of the new status that was established at that time, which was defined in that report with reference to its "beneficiaries".[3] In this regard, it is a well-known fact that, in wording that has remained unchanged to date,[4] the Treaty specified that "every person holding the nationality of a Member State shall be a citizen of the Union".[5]

Several issues were raised by the use of the classical notion of nationality (understood as the reflection of the legal-political bond connecting an individual to a State), with reference to the Member States, to define the group of persons who would be afforded the new status of "citizen of the Union".[6] On the one hand, firstly, and at least apparently, as we wrote at the time, we find ourselves in a situation in which "*l'entité politique à l'égard de laquelle ce statut prend un sens – l'Union Européenne – n'intervient pas, au moins d'une façon directe et à titre essentiel, dans la determination de l'ensemble de ceux qui en jouissent*".[7] Secondly, the result of using this criterion was that another option was excluded, and this latter would have allowed for a distinct (and autonomous) definition of this concept[8] rather than fixing its content by reference to another notion.[9] Finally, by making Member State nationality "*la circonstance de rattachement dont la vérification appelle l'application*

---

the concept, basis, content, development and limits of this new institutional reality, cf., for example, the contributions included in La Torre (1998), Philip and Soldatos (2000), Calliess (2013, pp. 425–441), Tobler (2013, pp. 443–469), Barnard (2013, pp. 505–522), and in Portugal, the studies collected in Pais (2015).

[3] *Sup. cit.*, note 2, p. 417.

[4] But the Amsterdam Treaty (of 2 October 1997) added the note that "Citizenship of the Union shall complement and not replace national citizenship". Cf. Article 2(9) of this Treaty.

[5] Cf., today, Article 9 TEU and Article 20(1) TFEU.

[6] The Court of Justice considered, from the judgment of 20 September 2001 (*Grzelczyk*, C-184/99, *ECR*, pp. I-6229–I-6249, paragraph 31), that "Union citizenship is destined to be the fundamental status of nationals of the Member States, enabling those who find themselves in the same situation to enjoy the same treatment in law irrespective of their nationality, subject to such exceptions as are expressly provided for".

[7] Cf. the general Report *sup. Cit.*, in note 2, p. 419. This would result from the fact that, as was also noted therein, we find ourselves "*dans un stade où l'Union reconnait des droits à des personnes sans pouvoir intervenir dans la définition des situations qui sont determinantes pour l'acquisition et la jouissance de ces droits*".

[8] In particular, using the concept of residence. Cf., in this regard, for example, the contributions of Marin (1998, pp. 201–227), and Garot (1998, pp. 229–248). Arguing in favour of maintaining the current situation (the *linkage* or *derivation* criterion), cf., however, more recently, Van Den Brink (2020b-II, pp. 177–202).

[9] This option, as also noted, would not be "*sans inconvenients, dans la mesure où d'abord l'Union n'aura pas de moyens pour contrecarrer tout acte d'un État-Membre qui voudrait élargir ou rétrécir le nombre de leur nationaux*".

du statut inhérent á la citoyenneté européenne", it became essential to reconsider the relationship between these two concepts.[10]

We will devote the following brief considerations to the contribution that the Court of Justice case-law has made to this reconsideration.

2 The *Micheletti* Decision

Although nationality is one area that has always been considered to fall within a State's reserved domain, this has not stopped the Court of Justice from expressing an opinion on the matter, and indeed ruling out the application of State rules in this area of law, even when they derive from international law. Hence, in the *Micheletti*[11] case, the Court stated what would become its fundamental line of action in this regard, by making it clear that "Under international law, it is for each Member State, having due regard to Community law, to lay down the conditions for the acquisition and loss of nationality. However, it is not permissible for the legislation of a Member State to restrict the effects of the grant of the nationality of another Member State by imposing an additional condition for recognition of that nationality with a view to the exercise of the fundamental freedoms provided for in the Treaty".[12] In this way, without directly calling into question the substance of the rule on the positive conflict of nationalities, the Court neutralised the effects of its application to the disputed situation by stressing, in response to the national court, that "The provisions of Community law on freedom of establishment preclude a Member State from denying a national of another Member State who possesses at the same time the nationality of a non-member country entitlement to that freedom on the ground that the law of the host State[13] deems him to be a national of the non-member country".[14]

What is specific, therefore, about this decision is that it does not even take into account the substance of the national rule[15] but purely its effect, which is to disregard the person in question's status of national of a Member State. This condition,

---

[10] This has been undertaken to some extent in the legal commentary. See, for example, Evans and D'Oliveira (1991, pp. 299–350), Guiguet (1998, pp. 95–111, 1997), Castro and Escudero (2003, pp. 105–153), Colas (2004), and Schnapper (2017, pp. 61–71). Setting the issue within the context that interests us, cf. De Groot (1998, pp. 115–147), D'Oliveira (2018), and, recently, Lepoutre (2024, pp. 12–18).

[11] Judgment of 7 July 1992, Case 390/90, *ECR*, pp. I-4258–I-4264. Regarding this decision, cf. in Portuguese legal commentary, Dos Santos (1998, pp. 306–309), Ramos (2001–2002, pp. 146–160), and Morais (2003, pp. 269–348).

[12] Paragraph 10.

[13] By virtue of the aforementioned rule on the positive conflict of nationalities.

[14] Paragraph 15.

[15] Contained at the time in Article 9 of the Spanish Civil Code, according to which, in the case of dual nationality and when neither of the nationalities is Spanish, the habitual residence prior to the person's arrival in Spain is the one that prevails.

in so far as it forms the basis of a particular set of rights arising from the Community legal system,[16] is in itself sufficient to ensure the enjoyment of these rights in any of the Member States, regardless of the fact that the legal system of the State to which the referring court belongs (the Kingdom of Spain) does not regard it as significant in the specific situation, since the person concerned holds another nationality with a stronger bond, and Spain thus considers them to be a national of the State which granted them that other nationality. As the Court rightly pointed out, respecting this requirement would be tantamount to making the exercise of one of the Community freedoms subject (in addition to that established by the Community legal system itself) to conditions imposed by the law of the Member States[17]; this would mean that "recognition of the status of Community citizen" would be subject to such conditions.

3 The *Rottmann* Decision

We can thus see that, even before the entry into force of the TEU (and, therefore, the institutionalisation of Union citizenship),[18] application of the nationality law rules of the Member States had to take into account a person's status of Community citizen, i.e. the status that would thereafter be called Union citizenship. And, since this was already the case at that time, this trend would only be confirmed by the passage of time.

It is not surprising then, given the derivative nature of Union citizenship,[19] that developments in case-law have essentially been concerned with the rules relating to the loss of nationality and the repercussions of this for the status of citizen of the Union. In fact, while, as has always been said since the Maastricht Treaty, to be a citizen of the Union, one must be a national of one of the Member States, it is equally true that it is necessary to "reconcile the Community's lack of competence to determine nationality with its natural competence to define the conditions for granting the rights it grants through its own system".[20]

The issue first arose in relation to loss of nationality with a particularly specific situation. The question to be answered was whether if one Member State revoked a

---

[16] Those associated with the free movement of persons, which is based on the simple "Member State nationality".

[17] And, therefore, they might vary from one Member State to another. Cf. paragraphs 11 and 12 of the decision.

[18] This only took place on 1 November 1993, as we know. It should be noted that with this treaty the Member States sought to "establish a citizenship common to nationals of their countries" (Preamble), which would help to achieve one of the Union's objectives: "to strengthen the protection of the rights and interests of the nationals of its Member States" (Article B, third indent).

[19] Stressing the lack of separation of the group of beneficiaries of "Union citizenship from nationals of Member States", cf. Ramos (1994, pp. 109–115 and 127–128.

[20] See Ramos (1994, p. 112).

person's naturalisation (the granting of which had led to him losing his citizenship of another Member State), on the grounds that that naturalisation had been acquired fraudulently,[21] so that the person, having thus been rendered stateless, was therefore deprived of their status of Union citizen, and the corresponding rights, could this be said to be in line with Union law. In the proceedings in which the preliminary[22] question was raised, the Court of Justice reaffirmed its previous position that the fact that "under international law, it is for each Member State, having due regard to Community law, to lay down the conditions for the acquisition and loss of nationality" did not negate that "in situations covered by European Union law, the national rules concerned must have due regard to the latter",[23] which included those rules relating to nationality, when, since they include the possibility of someone losing the status of citizen of the Union and the corresponding rights, they are covered by Union law by their very nature and consequences.[24] The Court concluded by stating that it is not contrary to European Union law "for a Member State to withdraw from a citizen of the Union the nationality of that State acquired by naturalisation when that nationality has been obtained by deception, on condition that the decision to withdraw observes the principle of proportionality".[25]

When analysing the question, the Court considered that, since the decision to revoke naturalisation was motivated by the fraudulent conduct of the person concerned in the process of acquiring nationality, that decision could be regarded as complying with Union law, because it corresponded to a reason relating to the public interest. It is legitimate for "a Member State to wish to protect the special relationship of solidarity and good faith between it and its nationals and also the reciprocity of rights and duties, which form the bedrock of the bond of nationality".[26] The Court expressly accepted that this conclusion would also be valid, in principle, in a situation where the act in question resulted not only in the loss of Member State nationality, but also in the loss of Union citizenship, although the referring court would be required to assess compliance with the principle of proportionality as regards the consequences that the decision would have for the person concerned, in the light of Union law. The Court also specified that, in view of the importance attached to the status of citizen of the Union, observance of this principle would mean taking into account, when examining a decision to revoke naturalisation, any possible consequences that the decision would have for the person concerned and, possibly, for their family members, as regards the loss of the rights enjoyed by every

[21] "Wilful, malicious and fraudulent", in the terminology used by the referring jurisdiction.

[22] Judgment of 2 March 2010, *Rottmann*, Case C-135/08, *ECR*, 2010, p. 104. On this decision, cf. the comments of Shaw (2010, pp. 612–618, 2011), D'Oliveira (2011, pp. 139–149), De Groot and Seling (2011, pp. 150–160), and Hernandez (2012, pp. 1405–1417). And for the purposes of analysing its influence on the case-law of Member States in the matter concerning us, cf. Nuñez and De Groot (2015, pp. 329–585).

[23] Paragraphs 39 and 41 of the decision.

[24] Paragraphs 42 to 45.

[25] Paragraph 59.

[26] Paragraph 51.

Union citizen. It is essential to ascertain, in particular, whether such loss is justified in relation to the seriousness of the offence committed by the person in question, the time that has elapsed between the naturalisation decision and the revocation decision and the potential for the person concerned to reacquire their original nationality.[27]

4 The *Tjebbes* Decision

Having formulated the general principle, the Court would specify, almost a decade later,[28] the conditions for its application, when called on to consider the application of the grounds for loss of nationality by operation of law provided for in Dutch law, in situations where the persons concerned held only the nationality of one Member State.[29]

In the proceedings that gave rise to the *Tjebbes* decision, the issues discussed related, in fact, to whether it could be deemed proportional, under the terms and for the purposes of the *Rottmann* case-law, for a person to lose their nationality[30] due to having their principal residence, for an uninterrupted period of 10 years, abroad and outside the Union,[31] and, in the case of a minor, for that minor to lose their nationality by virtue of their parent having lost their nationality.[32] Since the citizens concerned were only nationals of one Member State (the Netherlands), loss of that nationality under the aforementioned conditions would mean loss of the associated status of citizen of the Union, and so the question of meeting the conditions laid down in the *Rottmann* case-law was entirely relevant. In any case, the Court stressed

[27] Paragraph 56. With regard to the latter aspect, the Court stated that a Member State whose nationality has been fraudulently acquired cannot be considered obliged to refrain from revoking naturalisation for the simple reason that the person concerned has not reacquired the nationality of the State of origin. It is for the referring court to assess whether, in view of all relevant circumstances, compliance with the principle of proportionality requires that, before such a decision to revoke naturalisation takes effect, the person concerned is granted a reasonable period of time in order to try to reacquire the nationality of their Member State of origin (paragraphs 57 and 58).

[28] In the judgment of 12 March 2019, *Tjebbes*, C-221/17, *ECR*, p. 189. On this decision, cf., Van Eijken (2019, pp. 714–730), Vlieks (2019, pp. 142–146), Kochenov (2019b, pp. 319–336), Ramos (2020, pp. 412–433), Swider (2020, pp. 1163–1182), Gotti (2020, pp. 350–365), and Pataut (2021, pp. 768–771).

[29] Precisely the one the loss of which the administrative and judicial bodies of the Kingdom of the Netherlands were seeking to confirm.

[30] This also corresponded to a loss of Union citizenship, since the persons concerned, while holding third-country nationality (and consequently not having run the risk of becoming stateless persons), were not nationals of any other Member State. Regarding the country's position on multiple nationalities, cf. Peters and Vink (2021, pp. 121–140).

[31] Cf. Article 15(1)(c) of the Dutch Nationality Law in force at the time. On this law (of 1984, amended in 2000), cf. Van Loon (1986, pp. 182–192), De Groot and Bollen (1996, pp. 580–582), Struycken (1988, pp. 3–19), and Groenendijk and Heijs (1999, pp. 145–175).

[32] Cf. Article 16(1)(d) of the law mentioned in the previous note.

that since Article 20 TFEU "confers on every individual who is a national of a Member State citizenship of the Union, which (...) is intended to be the fundamental status of nationals of the Member States...",[33] the situation of Union citizens who "are nationals of one Member State only and who, by losing that nationality, are faced with losing the status conferred by Article 20 TFEU and the rights attaching thereto falls, by reason of its nature and its consequences, within the ambit of EU law".[34] Accordingly, the Member States "must, when exercising their powers in the sphere of nationality, have due regard to EU law".

The Court then began its assessment of the situation by recalling the key statement in the *Rottmann* decision, that "it is legitimate for a Member State to wish to protect the special relationship of solidarity and good faith between it and its nationals and also the reciprocity of rights and duties, which form the bedrock of the bond of nationality".[35] It then went on to consider whether the reasons for loss of nationality by operation of law in question were justified, and concluded that the aim of one of them[36] was to "introduce a system to avoid, *inter* alia, the undesirable consequences of one person having multiple nationalities", and, additionally, "preclude persons from obtaining or retaining Netherlands nationality where they do not, or no longer have, any link with the Kingdom of the Netherlands", while the other[37] aimed to "restore unity of nationality within the family".[38]

The Court was entirely clear in its understanding that it is legitimate for Member States, when exercising their competence to establish the conditions for acquisition and loss of nationality, to consider that nationality is the expression of a genuine link between the State and its nationals (principle of effective nationality[39]) and, consequently, to attribute loss of nationality to the absence or termination of such a genuine link.[40] It went on to state that a criterion such as that laid down in Article 15(1)(c) of the Nationality Law of the Kingdom of the Netherlands, based on the habitual residence of nationals of that country for an uninterrupted period of 10 years outside that Member State and the territories to which the TEU applies, reflects the absence of such a genuine link.[41]

---

[33] Paragraph 31 of the decision under analysis. The assertion is also settled case-law, at least since the *Grzelczyk* decision (referred to above in note 8).

[34] See paragraph 32 of the decision being commented.

[35] Paragraph 33 of the same decision.

[36] As established in Article 15(1)(c) of the Nationality Law. Cf. paragraph 10 of the decision.

[37] As contained in Article 16(1)(d) of the Nationality Law. Cf. above, n.° 2, and paragraph 11 of the decision.

[38] Also paragraph 34 of the decision.

[39] On the understanding of this principle, cf. the decision of the International Court of Justice in the Nottebohm case (*Liechtenstein v. Guatemala*), of 1955, De Burlet (1976, pp. 75–89), Dolinger (2000, pp. 141–186), Sloane (2009, pp. 1–60), Wautelet (2015, pp. 537–557), Thwaites (2018), Pataut (2021, pp. 747–771), and, in Portugal, Dos Santos (1998), and Gil (2010, pp. 727–741). And for its application in the context that interests us here, cf. Van Der Brink (2020a-I).

[40] Paragraph 35.

[41] Paragraph 36, first sentence.

The Court also considered it legitimate for a Member State to protect the unity of nationality within the same family (principle of unity of family nationality.[42])[43] It accepted that the absence of a genuine link between the parents of a minor and the Kingdom of the Netherlands implies, in principle, that this is also the case for the relationship between the minor and that Member State, which would also legitimise the criterion laid down in Article 16(1)(d) of that law.[44]

Having concluded that the reasons for loss of nationality by operation of law in question were, in principle, legitimate, it was then up to the Court to consider the specific application of those rules, in order to determine whether, due to the consequences they might have for the person concerned,[45] their application would be disproportionate. Given that these are cases of loss of nationality by operation of law, this examination would require individual consideration of the situation of a person deprived of Union citizenship, which led the Court to state that "The loss of the nationality of a Member State by operation of law would be inconsistent with the principle of proportionality if the relevant national rules did not permit at any time an individual examination of the consequences of that loss for the persons concerned from the point of view of EU law".[46] In view of the foregoing, in a situation where the loss of nationality of a Member State occurs *ope legis* and implies the loss of the status of citizen of the Union, the competent national authorities and courts should be able to assess, separately, the consequences of this loss of nationality and, where appropriate, to ensure that the person concerned recovers the

[42] On this principle, cf. Dutoit (1984, pp. 445–474), and Lagarde (1984, pp. 475–508).

[43] Paragraph 35.

[44] Paragraph 36, second sentence.

[45] And, as specified in this decision, for their family members.

[46] Cf. paragraph 41 of the decision being commented.

On this point, the Court has provided some additional guidance in its subsequent case law. Thus, it ruled that «a person must have a reasonable period in which to make a request to the competent authorities for an examination of the proportionality of the consequences of that loss and, where appropriate, the retention or recovery *ex tunc* of that nationality. That period must then extend, for a reasonable length of time, beyond the date on which that person reaches that age». Cf. paragraph 50 of judgement of 5 september 2023, *X v Udlændinge- og Integrationsministeriet*, C-689/21, *ELR*, p. 626, Ramos (2023, pp. 23–42) and Rodríguez (2024). And later it added that «EU law does not preclude, as a matter of principle, a Member State from providing that the individual examination, in the light of the principle of proportionality, of the consequences of the loss of the nationality of a Member State in the light of EU law for the persons concerned is to be carried out in the specific context of an advance permission procedure» since «in order to ensure observance of the rights that Union citizens derive from Article 20 TFEU, that procedure must actually allow that individual examination of proportionality to take place in accordance with the requirements of that article as interpreted by the Court in its case-law» and that it is for the referring court to determine that the persons concerned were duly informed of such procedure (cf. judgement of 25 april 2024, *S.Ö. v Stadt Duisburg*, joined cases C-684/22 to 686/22, *ELR*, p. 345, paragraphs 46, 47 and 57, and Ramos (2024, pp. 360–380) thus emphasizing the need of effectiveness of the individual examination of the proportionality of the consequences of loss of nationality.

nationality *ex tunc* when they apply for a travel document or any other document proving their nationality.[47]

The decision adds that, in this regard, the national court states that under national law both the decision-making bodies at national level and the competent judicial review bodies are required to examine the possibility of retaining Dutch nationality in the context of the procedure governing applications for passport renewal, by conducting a thorough assessment in the light of the principle of proportionality enshrined in Union law.[48] It goes on to stress that such an analysis "requires an individual assessment of the situation of the person concerned and that of his or her family in order to determine whether the consequences of losing the nationality of the Member State concerned, when it entails the loss of his or her citizenship of the Union, might, with regard to the objective pursued by the national legislature, disproportionately affect the normal development of his or her family and professional life from the point of view of EU law".[49]

Further detailing the context in which the assessment of proportionality takes place, the Court added that it is the responsibility, in particular, of the competent national authorities and, possibly, the national courts "to ensure that the loss of nationality is consistent with the fundamental rights guaranteed by the Charter […], and specifically the right to respect for family life as stated in Article 7 of the Charter, that article requiring to be read in conjunction with the obligation to take into consideration the best interests of the child, recognised in Article 24(2) of the Charter".[50]

Regarding the circumstances of the individual situation of the person concerned which are likely to be relevant in the assessment to be carried out by the competent national authorities and national courts in this case, the Court notes, in particular, that, following the loss of Dutch nationality by operation of law and the loss of the status of citizen of the Union, the person concerned would be exposed to limitations when exercising their right to move and reside freely within the territory of the Member States, including, depending on the circumstances, particular difficulties in continuing to travel to the Netherlands or to another Member State in order to maintain genuine and regular links with members of their family, to pursue their professional activities or to take the steps necessary to pursue such activities there. The Court also considers relevant, firstly, the fact that the person concerned might not have been able to renounce the nationality of a third country, and for this reason falls

[47] Paragraph 42.

[48] Paragraph 43.

[49] Paragraph 44. The Court added that such consequences cannot be hypothetical or merely a possibility.

[50] Paragraph 45. It should be noted that [as is also noted in the analysis by Van Eijken (2019, pp. 727–728)] the introduction of the provisions of the Charter into the reasoning of the decision being discussed constitutes a novelty in relation to what happened in the *Rottmann* decision, thus explicitly situating the issue under analysis in the context of protecting fundamental rights. It should be remembered, in fact, that the operative part of the decision begins by stating: "Article 20 TFEU, read in the light of Articles 7 and 24 of the Charter...").

within the scope of Article 15(1)(c) of the Nationality Law and, secondly, the serious risk to which the person concerned would be exposed of a substantial deterioration in their safety or freedom of movement due to the impossibility of their benefiting from consular protection under Article 20(2)(c) TFEU in the territory of the third country in which they reside.[51]

In the case of minors, the Court adds that the competent administrative or judicial authorities should also take into account, in their individual assessment, whether there are any circumstances where the loss of Dutch nationality of the minor concerned, which the national legislature has attached to one of their parents losing their Dutch nationality in order to preserve unity of nationality within the family, is not in the best interests of the child, as enshrined in Article 24 of the Charter, given the consequences of that loss for the minor with regard to Union law.[52]

Reflecting on the issues it has addressed, the Court concludes that, in answer to the question referred to it, Article 20 TFEU, read in the light of Articles 7 and 24 of the Charter, must be interpreted as not precluding Member State legislation which provides, under certain conditions, for the loss, by operation of law, of the nationality of that Member State, involving, in the case of persons who do not also hold the nationality of another Member State, the loss of their status of citizen of the Union and the associated rights, provided that the competent national authorities, including, where appropriate, the national courts, are in a position to assess, separately, the consequences of this loss of nationality and, where appropriate, to allow the person concerned to recover their nationality *ex tunc* when they apply for a travel document or any other document proving their nationality. It should also be added that, in the context of this assessment, these authorities and courts must ascertain whether the loss of nationality of the Member State concerned, when it implies the loss of the status of citizen of the Union, respects the principle of proportionality as regards its consequences for the situation of each person concerned and, where appropriate, for their family members with regard to Union law.[53]

5 The *JY* Decision

Having clarified to some extent what is meant by the principle of proportionality, it is also worth recalling the more recent judgment of 18 January 2022.[54] This relates to a case where, once again, the referring court[55] had doubts, this time during proceedings related to an application for Austrian nationality made by an Estonian

---

[51] Paragraph 46.

[52] Paragraph 47.

[53] Paragraph 48.

[54] Case C-118/20, *JY*, *ECR*, p. 34. On this decision, cf. Ramos (2022, pp. 257–280), Gambardella (2022, pp. 399–408), Hyltén-Cavallius (2022, pp. 1–16), Loconi (2022, pp. 1297–1306), and Bariatti (2022).

[55] The *Verwaltungsgerichthof* (Supreme Administrative Court) in Vienna.

national resident in that country (*JY*). Having made the application, *JY* received a reply containing an assurance that Austrian nationality would be granted if she could prove that she had renounced her Estonian nationality.[56] After reporting to the Austrian authorities the Estonian Government's Decision[57] that confirmed her loss of Estonian nationality (meaning that she was stateless), *JY* was informed that the authorities had revoked[58] the decision of the Government of the Province of Lower Austria assuring her that she would be granted Austrian nationality and had rejected her nationality application.[59] The reason given for this decision was that, after 11 March 2014 (when she was given the assurance that she would be granted Austrian nationality), *JY* had committed two serious administrative offences (failing to display a vehicle inspection disc and driving a motor vehicle while under the influence of alcohol), and that she had also committed eight administrative offences between 2007 and 2013, before that assurance was given. She would therefore not satisfy the conditions for granting Austrian nationality as laid down by law.[60]

The appeal against that decision was dismissed, on the grounds that an assurance for granting Austrian nationality can be revoked,[61] in particular when, as in the case in question, grounds for refusal arise after the proof of renouncing the previous nationality has been provided. In this regard, the court[62] pointed out that the first serious administrative offence committed by *JY* after the assurance was issued was likely to jeopardise road safety and the second would jeopardise the safety of other road users. Thus, for that court, firstly, those two serious administrative offences, considered together with the eight administrative offences committed between 2007 and 2013, meant it was no longer possible, with regard to *JY*, to give a favourable prognosis for the future,[63] and, secondly, *JY*'s long period of residence in Austria, and her professional and personal integration into that Member State were unlikely to alter that conclusion. The court considered not only that the decision given in the main proceedings was proportionate in light of the Convention on the Reduction of Statelessness, but also that the case was not covered by Union law.

This decision was also challenged,[64] however, and during the proceedings the Court of Justice was asked to rule on whether the matter *sub judice* was covered by

[56] This is a common mechanism for states seeking to combat situations of multiple nationality. Regarding the opposite perspective, cf. Ramos (1983, pp. 181–211, 1990–1993, pp. 577–605, 1996, pp. 96–119), and, more recently, Haller (2021, pp. 33–58), Baubock (2021, pp. 59–79), Spiro (2021, pp. 81–95), and Harpaz (2021, pp. 97–117).

[57] Of 27 August 2015 (judgment issued after *JY* renounced that nationality).

[58] Pursuant to § 20(2) of the Nationality Law (the *Staatsburgerschaftsgezetz*, 1985). On this law, cf. Brandel (1996, pp. 60–93), Baubock and Cinar (1999, pp. 265–280), and Baubock and Valchars (2021, pp. 207–227).

[59] By application of § 10(1)(6) of that law.

[60] In particular, in the provision cited in the previous note.

[61] As results from paragraph 20(2) of the Nationality Law.

[62] The *Verwaltungsgericht Wien* (Vienna Administrative Court).

[63] Within the meaning of § 10(1)(6) of the Nationality Law.

[64] Now before the *Verwaltungsgerichthof*.

Union law and, if so, whether the withdrawal of the assurance in respect of granting the nationality in question, which prevents citizenship of the Union from being regained, is consistent, from the perspective of Union law, with the principle of proportionality, taking into account the consequences of that decision on the situation of the person concerned.

The Court of Justice considered that the first question it had to consider was "whether the situation of a person who, having the nationality of one Member State only, renounces that nationality and loses, as a result, his or her status of citizen of the Union, with a view to obtaining the nationality of another Member State, following the assurance given by the authorities of the latter Member State that he or she will be granted that nationality, falls, by reason of its nature and its consequences, within the scope of EU law where that assurance is revoked with the effect of preventing that person from recovering the status of citizen of the Union",[65] and it had no difficulty in finding that it did, in fact, fall within the scope of that law. In fact, *JY*'s loss of the status of citizen of the Union[66] was a direct consequence of the fact that she had requested the Estonian Government to dissolve the bond of nationality connecting her to that State,[67] and the Austrian decision to revoke the assurance that Austrian nationality would be granted merely rendered the loss of that status permanent.[68] Although the loss of the status of citizen of the Union arises from the fact that the person's Member State of origin has, at their request, dissolved the bond of nationality with them, the fact of the matter is that the request was made in the context of a naturalisation process aimed at acquiring Austrian nationality and was a consequence of that person, relying on the assurance given to them that they would be granted that nationality, complying with the requirements both of the Nationality Law and of the decision granting that assurance.[69] This allowed the Court of Justice to conclude that a person such as *JY* cannot be regarded as having voluntarily renounced their status of citizen of the Union. Having been assured by the host Member State that they would be granted nationality, the purpose of the request to terminate the bond of nationality with the Member State of which they were a national was to enable them to satisfy a condition for acquiring that new nationality and, once this had been obtained, to continue to enjoy the status of citizen of the Union and the rights associated with that. Therefore, the procedure in question, taken as a whole, even if it involves an administrative decision of a Member State other than the one nationality of which is sought,[70] affects the status conferred by Article 20 TFEU on nationals of the Member States, since it may mean that a person in a situation such as that of *JY* is deprived of all the rights associated with that

[65] Paragraph 29 of the decision referred to above in note 55.

[66] It should be noted that the person in question only held the nationality of their home Member State (Estonia).

[67] As the Court recalls in paragraph 31.

[68] Paragraph 32 of the decision.

[69] Paragraph 35.

[70] In this case, the Estonian Government Decision of 27 August 2015.

status, even though, at the time when the naturalisation procedure began, they held the nationality of a Member State and thus had the status of citizen of the Union.[71]

Turning to the application of the proportionality test, the Court of Justice pointed out that Article 20(2)(a) TFEU provides that citizens of the Union shall enjoy the rights and be subject to the duties provided for in the Treaties, and shall have, among others, the right to move and reside freely within the territory of the Member States. Consequently, in the Court's opinion, when, in the context of a naturalisation procedure brought in a Member State, the latter, under the competence it holds to lay down the conditions for the acquisition and loss of nationality, requires a Union citizen to renounce the nationality of their Member State of origin, the exercise and useful effect of the rights which Article 20 TFEU confers on that citizen of the Union mean that that person should not at any time be liable to lose that status solely due to that procedure.[72] In fact, any loss of that status, even if only temporary, means that the person concerned is deprived, for an indefinite period, of the possibility of enjoying all the rights conferred by it.[73]

In this context, the Court pointed out that the principles deriving from Union law with regard to the competence of Member States in matters of nationality (as well as their obligation to exercise that competence in compliance with Union law) apply both to the host Member State and to the Member State of the original nationality.[74] This means that when a national of a Member State renounces their nationality in order to be able to obtain the nationality of another Member State and thus continue to enjoy their status of citizen of the Union, the Member State of origin shall not adopt, on the basis of an assurance given by that other Member State that the latter nationality will be granted to the person concerned, a final decision on the loss of nationality without ensuring that this decision will only enter into force after the new nationality has actually been acquired.[75] However, in a situation in which the status of citizen of the Union has already been temporarily lost,[76] the obligation to ensure the useful effect of Article 20 TFEU rests primarily with the host Member State. This is particularly necessary when the Member State concerned decides to revoke the assurance previously given to that person that the nationality will be granted, since that decision could have the effect of rendering the loss of the status of citizen of the Union permanent. Such a decision can therefore only be taken for legitimate reasons and in line with the principle of proportionality.[77]

[71] Paragraph 40.

[72] Paragraph 47.

[73] Paragraph 48.

[74] Paragraph 49.

[75] Paragraph 50.

[76] On the grounds that, within a naturalisation procedure, the Member State of origin has withdrawn its nationality from the person concerned before they have actually acquired the nationality of the host Member State.

[77] Paragraph 51.

The Court of Justice did not depart from its previous case-law, which expressly accepted that States could maintain grounds for loss of nationality,[78] now expressly accepting that those grounds may include the avoidance of one person having multiple nationalities and that a decision to revoke an assurance as to the grant of nationality on the ground that the person concerned does not have a positive attitude towards the Member State of which they intend to acquire the nationality, and that their conduct is liable to represent a danger to public order and security of that Member State, is based on a reason relating to the public interest. However, it considered that, in view of the nature and seriousness of the two administrative offences committed after the granting of the assurance, and also the requirement that the concepts of "public policy" and "public safety" be understood in the strict sense, it did not appear that *JY* represented a real, current and sufficiently serious threat affecting a fundamental interest of society or a threat to public security in the Republic of Austria. The Court recognised that the offences committed were an infringement of the provisions of the Highway Code and were detrimental to road safety. However, it noted that neither of the two administrative offences, which, moreover, had only resulted in relatively minor fines,[79] were capable of leading to the withdrawal of *JY*'s driving licence and therefore prohibiting her from driving a motor vehicle on the public highway.

Hence, the Court considered that such offences, punishable by simple administrative fines, could not be regarded as demonstrating that the person who committed them was a threat to public policy and security that could justify the permanent loss of their status of citizen of the Union. It therefore considered that, due to the significance of the consequences for *JY's* situation, in particular as regards the normal development of her family and professional life, the decision to revoke the assurance for granting Austrian nationality, which had the effect of rendering the loss of her status of citizen of the Union permanent, was not proportionate to the seriousness of the offences she had committed.[80]

6 The *EP* Decision

While the latest developments in case-law can be considered to confirm the key foundations of the line of reasoning that began with the *Rottmann* decision,[81] in which protection of the status of citizen of the Union has occupied a particularly significant position, it should also be noted that this conclusion is equally valid for cases where the limits of the autonomy of this status are present. This is particularly

[78] Cf. *supra*, paragraphs 3 and 4.

[79] EUR 112 and EUR 300 respectively.

[80] Paragraph 73.

[81] Cf. also the analysis of Oosterom-Staples (2018, pp. 442–445).

the case with a recent judgment of 9 June 2022,[82] in which it is stated that "as of the withdrawal of the United Kingdom from the European Union, on 1 February 2020, nationals of that State who exercised their right to reside in a Member State before the end of the transition period, no longer enjoy the status of citizen of the Union, nor, more specifically, by virtue of Article 20(2)(b) TFEU and Article 22 TFEU, the right to vote and to stand as a candidate in municipal elections in their Member State of residence, including where they are also deprived, by virtue of the law of the State of which they are nationals, of the right to vote in elections held by that State".[83]

The Court noted, in particular, that "citizenship of the Union requires possession of the nationality of a Member State",[84] and therefore there is "an inseparable and exclusive link between possession of the nationality of a Member State and not only the acquisition, but also the retention, of the status of citizen of the Union".[85] As a result, UK nationals became nationals of a third country as from 1 February 2020,[86] since the Treaties establishing the Union ceased to apply to that country on that date.[87] They therefore no longer enjoy, under Article 20(2)(b) and Article 22 TFEU, the right to vote and to stand as a candidate in municipal elections in their host Member State,[88] or any of the other rights granted by that status.

7 Conclusion

This brief review of recent Court of Justice case-law concerning the relationship between being a national of a Member State and being a citizen of the Union clearly confirms the close connection between these two concepts, given that the latter cannot be considered without reference to the former. Despite this dependence of one concept on the other, which was also expressly confirmed in the last decision

---

[82] *EP v. Préfet du Gers*, C-673/20, *ECR*, p. 449. On this decision cf. Faggiani (2022), Gomes (2022), and Shuibhne (2023); and regarding the issue that is discussed, cf. also Worster (2021, pp. 95–134).

For an analysis of a number of decisions after the referendum that led to Brexit, cf. Silveira (2017, pp. 49–64).

[83] Paragraph 83.

[84] Paragraph 46.

[85] Paragraph 48. In view of the fact that "The loss of nationality of a Member State therefore entails, for the person concerned, the automatic loss of his or her status as a citizen of the Union" (paragraph 57).

[86] Regarding the position of the latter vis-à-vis Union citizenship, cf. Oliveira (1998, pp. 185–199), and Ziemele (2013, pp. 471–483).

[87] Paragraphs 55 and 56.

[88] Paragraph 58. And it is irrelevant, as the decision adds, "that UK nationals have previously exercised their right to reside in a Member State". Regarding the fact that this right has not been maintained for such persons by the Withdrawal Agreement, see the explanation in paragraphs 64 to 81 of the decision.

referred to in this work,[89] the relationship between the two, each from a different legal system,[90] is not quite as clear cut as one might imagine. In fact, the position of the Court of Justice was, as noted, that while "under international law, it is for each Member State, having due regard to Community law, to lay down the conditions for the acquisition and loss of nationality", this does not negate that "in situations covered by European Union law,[91] the national rules concerned must have due regard to the latter".[92] In addition, it does not mean that Member States should be powerless to implement loss of nationality, even in cases where this entails loss of the status of citizen of the Union,[93] since "it is legitimate for a Member State to wish to protect the special relationship of solidarity and good faith between it and its nationals and also the reciprocity of rights and duties, which form the bedrock of the bond of nationality".[94] To put it simply, and here lies the interdependence between the two legal situations, due to the fact that the protection of Union citizenship is at stake, when examining a decision that triggers loss of nationality[95] we must take into account "the consequences that the decision entails for the person concerned and, if relevant, for the members of his family with regard to the loss of the rights enjoyed by every citizen of the Union", and it is "necessary to establish, in particular, whether that loss is justified in relation to the gravity of the offence committed by that person, to the lapse of time between the naturalisation decision and the withdrawal decision and to whether it is possible for that person to recover his original nationality".[96] The Court subsequently reiterated these requirements for situations where loss of nationality by operation of law was at issue[97] or complex procedures in the context of which loss of nationality would occur,[98] issuing decisions that elaborated on the terms in which the national courts ought to apply the proportionality test.[99]

It now remains to be seen whether the Court of Justice will draw any consequences, and if so which, from this interdependence,[100] in relation to the acquisition

---

[89] *Sup. cit.*, paragraph 6.

[90] Those of the Member States and that of the European Union.

[91] As we must consider those that lead to the loss of a status conferred by the latter (that of citizenship of the Union), and which, moreover, is defined by the Court, in consistent case-law, as "the fundamental status of Member State nationals"; cf. for example, the judgment of 8 May 2018, *K.A. and Others (Family reunification in Belgium)*, C-82/16, *ECR*, 2018, p. 308, paragraph 47.

[92] Paragraphs 39 and 41 of the *Rottmann* decision and paragraph 3 above.

[93] Paragraph 54 of the *Rottmann* decision and paragraph 3 above.

[94] Paragraph 51 of the *Rottmann* decision and paragraph 3 above.

[95] As is the case with a decision revoking a naturalisation.

[96] Paragraph 56 of the *Rottmann* decision and paragraph 3 above. This naturally leads to an assessment of proportionality (cf. also, *ibidem*, paragraph 55).

[97] Cf. the *Tjebbes* decision and paragraph 4 above.

[98] Cf. the *JY* decision and paragraph 5 above.

[99] Cf. the *Tjebbes* and *JY* decisions and paragraphs 4 and 5 above, respectively.

[100] For a global consideration of the problem, cf. Worster (2020, pp. 767–818).

of nationality, in the analysis it will be called on to undertake as part of the infringement procedure concerning the Maltese "golden passport" scheme.[101]

References

Bariatti S (2022) A new CJEU judgment on the loss of the nationality of a Member State. https://gedip-egpil.eu/en/2022/a-new-cjeu-judgment-on-the-loss-of-the-nationality-of-a-member-state/. Accessed 30 Sept 2024

Barnard C (2013) Citizenship of the union and the area of justice: (almost) the court's moment of glory. In: Court of Justice of the European Union (ed) The court of justice and the construction of Europe: analyses and perspectives on sixty years of case-law. T.M.C. Asser Press, The Hague, pp 505–522

Baubcock R (2018) Debating transformations of national citizenship [part I - should citizenship be for sale?]. European University Institute, San Domenico di Fiesole

Baubock R (2021) The toleration of dual citizenship: global trend and its limits. In: Baubock R, Haller M (eds) Dual citizenship and naturalisation: global, comparative and Austrian perspectives. Austrian Academy of Sciences Press, Vienna, pp 59–79

Bauböck R, Çinar D (1999) La législation sur la nationalité et la naturalisation en Autriche. In: Weil P, Hansen R (eds) Nationalité et citoyenneté en Europe. La Découverte, Paris, pp 265–280

Baubock R, Valchars G (2021) Non-toleration of dual citizenship in Austria. In: Baubock R, Haller M (eds) Dual citizenship and naturalisation: global, comparative and Austrian perspectives. Austrian Academy of Sciences Press, Vienna, pp 207–227

Brandel U (1996) Austrian nationality law. In: Bruno N (ed) Nationality laws in the European Union. Giuffrè, Milan, pp 60–93

Calliess C (2013) The dynamics of european citizenship: from bourgeois to citoyen. In: Court of Justice of the European Union (ed) The court of justice and the construction of Europe: analyses and perspectives on sixty years of case-law. T.M.C. Asser Press, The Hague, pp 425–441

Castro AR, Escudero MM (2003) Nacionalidad y ciudadanía: una relación a debate. An Cátedra Fr Suárez 37:105–153

Colas D (2004) Citoyenneté et nationalité. Éditions Gallimard, Paris

De Burlet J (1976) Effective et nationalite des personnes physiques. Rev Belge Droit Int 12:75–89

De Groot GR (1998) The relationship between the nationality legislation of the member states of the European Union and European citizenship. In: La Torre M (ed) European citizenship: an institutional challenge: European forum. Kluwer Law International, The Hague, pp 115–147

De Groot GR, Bollen C (1996) Netherlands nationality law. In: Bruno N (ed) Nationality laws in the European Union. Giuffrè, Milan, pp 545–589

De Groot GR, Seling A (2011) The consequences of the Rottmann judgment on member state autonomy-the European court of justice's avant-gardism in nationality matters. Eur Const Law Rev 7:150–160

[101] On this issue, cf. the Commission Report on *Investor Citizenship and Residence Schemes in the European Union* [COM(2019) 12 final] of 23 January 2019 [analysed by Kochenov (2019a), which, following a general recommendation on 28 March 2020, led to the non-compliance notices sent on 20 November 2020 against Malta, in infringement of the principle of loyal cooperation and the status of Union citizenship, and Cyprus, and more recently on 29 September 2022, the infringement proceedings against Malta, brought in accordance with Article 258(2) TFEU. For a discussion of this issue, see Dzankic (2012), the contributions gathered by Shachar and Baubock (2014), and Baubcock (2018, pp. 3–70), Oosterom-Staples (2018, pp. 447–450), D'Oliveira (2023), Lepoutre (2024, pp. 18–23) and, in Portugal, Jardim (2017, pp. 197–259).

Dolinger J (2000) Nottebohm revisited. In: Borba P, Coordenador C (eds) Dimensão internacional do direito. Estudos em homenagem a G.E. do Nascimento e Silva. LTr, São Paulo, pp 141–186
D'Oliveira JHU (2011) Decoupling nationality and European citizenship? Eur Const Law Rev 7(139–149):150–160
D'Oliveira JHU (2018) Union citizenship and beyond, EUI Working Paper, RCAS 2018/15
D'Oliveira JHU (2023) Golden passports. European Commission and European Parliament Reports built on quicksand. January 2023,Working Paper n.° 162, The Centre on Migration, Policy & Society, University of Oxford
Dos Santos AM (1998) Estudos de direito da nacionalidade. Almedina, Coimbra, pp 279–310
Dutoit B (1984) Nationalité et mariage: leur interaction dans le droit comparé de la nationalité. In: De Michel V (ed) Nationalité et statute personnel. Leur interaction dans les traités internationaux et dans les législations nationales. Bruylant, Brussels, pp 445–474
Dzankic J (2012) The pros and cons of ius pecuniae. Investor citizenship in comparative perspective, EUI Working Paper, RCAS 2012/14
Evans A, D'Oliveira JHU (1991) Nationality and citizenship. In: Cassese A, Clapham A, Weiler J (eds) Human rights and the European community. Nomos, Baden-Baden, pp 299–350
Faggiani V (2022) Ciudadania Sustantiva y Derechos de Participación Politica en la UE: Limites del Sistema e Necessidad de una mayor inclusion. RevDerComunEur 73(915):949
Gambardella I (2022) JY v wiener landesregierung: adding another stone to the case law built up by the CJEU on nationality and EU citizenship. Eur Pap J Law Integr 2022:399–408
Garot MJ (1998) A new basis for European citizenship: residence? In: La Torre M (ed) European citizenship: an institutional challenge. Kluwer Law International, The Hague, pp 229–248
Gil AR (2010) Princípios de direito da nacionalidade–sua consagração no ordenamento jurídico Português. O Direito 142:723–760
Gomes JG (2022) "Brexit means Brexit" for the EU citizenship rights of British nationals—The Court of Justice conclusions in Préfet du Gers, UNIO EU Law Journal Blog, 27 October 2022
Gotti G (2020) Cittadinanza dell'Unione e residenza: quali prospettive dopo Tjebbes? Forum Quad Cost Rass 2020:350–366
Groenendijk CA, Heijs E (1999) Immigration, immigrés et législation sur la nationalité aux Pays-Bas (1945–1998). In: Weil P, Hansen R (eds) Nationalité et citoyenneté en Europe. La Découverte, Paris, pp 145–175
Guiguet B (1997) Citoyennete et nationalite: limites de la rupture d'un lien. Institut Universitaire Européen, Florence
Guiguet B (1998) Citizenship and nationality: tracing the French roots of the distinction. In: La Torre M (ed) European citizenship. An institutional challenge. Kluwer Law International, The Hague, pp 95–111
Haller M (2021) (Dual) citizenship and national identity in a globalised world: sociological perspectives. In: Baubcock R, Haller M (eds) Dual citizenship and naturalisation: global, comparative and Austrian perspectives. Austrian Academy of Sciences Press, Vienna, pp 33–58
Harpaz Y (2021) Strategic dual citizenship: global dynamics of supply and demand. In: Baubcock R, Haller M (eds) Dual citizenship and naturalisation: global, comparative and Austrian perspectives. Austrian Academy of Sciences Press, Vienna, pp 97–117
Hernández FJC (2012) El ámbito de aplicación personal de la libre ciruculación de personas a examen: el asunto" Rottmann" y la pérdida del estatuto de ciudadano de la Unión Europea. In: Estudios de derecho internacional y de derecho Europeo: en homenaje al profesor Manuel Pérez González. Tirant lo Blanch, Valencia, pp 1405–1417
Hyltén-Cavallius K (2022) Stateless union citizens in a nationality conundrum: EU safeguarding against broken promises. Eur Const Law Rev 18:556–571
Jardim RM (2017) A Dessacralização e reconceptualização da cidadania e os regimes de naturalização e residência dourados. In: A economia social e civil. Estudos de doutoramento II. SPES I Instituto Jurídico I Faculdade de Direito I Universidade de Coimbra, Coimbra, pp 197–259
Kochenov D (2019a) Investor citizenship and residence: the EU commission's incompetent case for blood and soil. Verfassungsblog Matters Const. https://doi.org/10.17176/20190211-220929-0

Kochenov D (2019b) The Tjebbes fail. Eur Pap 1:319–336
La Torre M (1998) European citizenship. An institutional challenge. Kluwer Law International, The Hague
Laconi A (2022) La corte di giustizia dell'Unione Europea sulla perdita della cittadinanza Europea: davvero è sufficiente rispettare il solo principio di proporzionalità? Dirit Pubblico Comp Eur 52:1297–1306
Lagarde P (1984) Nationalité et filiation: leur interaction dans le droit comparé de la nationalité. In: Verwilghen M (ed) Nationalité et statut personnel. Leur interaction dans les traités internationaux et dans les législations nationales. Bruylant, Brussels, pp 475–508
Lepoutre J (2024) Citoyenneté de l'Union et nationalités des Etats membres. Entre romantisme et réalisme RTDEur 2024:9–32
Marin RR (1998) Equal citizenship and the difference that residence makes. In: La Torre M (ed) European citizenship. An institutional challenge. Kluwer Law International, The Hague, pp 201–227
Morais DDBR (2003) O acordáo" Micheletti" e as suas repercussóes em matéria de direito da nacionalidade dos estados-membros. Rev Fac Direito Univ Lisb 44:269–348
Nuñez SC, De Groot GR (2015) European citizenship at the crossroads. The role of the European Union on loss and acquisition of nationality. Wolf Legal Publishers, Oisterwijk
Oliveira AC (1998) The position of resident third country nationals: is it too early to grant them union citizenship? In: La Torre M (ed) European citizenship. An institutional challenge. Kluwer Law International, The Hague, pp 185–199
Oosterom-Staples H (2018) The triangular relationship between nationality, EU citizenship and migration in EU law: a tale of competing competences. Neth Int Law Rev 65:431–461
Pais SO (2015) EU citizenship. Challenges and opportunities. Universidade Católica Editora, Porto
Pataut E (2021) Contrôle de l'État ou protection de l'individu? Remarques sur l'effectivité de la nationalité. Rev Crit Droit Int Privé 4:747–771
Peters F, Vink MP (2021) Dual citizenship acceptance and immigrant naturalisation propensity in The Netherlands: the relevance of origin-and destination-country rules. In: Baubcock R, Haller M (eds) Dual citizenship and naturalisation: global, comparative and Austrian perspectives. Austrian Academy of Science Press, Vienna, pp 121–140
Philip C, Soldatos P (2000) La Citoyenneté Européenne. Université de Montréal, Montréal
Ramos RMGM (1983) La double nationalité d'après le droit Portugais. Bol Fac Direito U Coimbra 59:181–211
Ramos RMM (1990–1993) La double nationalité et les liens spéciaux avec d'autres pays, les développements et les perspectives au Portugal. Rev Direito Econ 16–19:577–605
Ramos RMM (1992) FIDE XV congrès, III les aspects nouveaux de la libre circulation des personnes: vers une citoyenneté Européenne. Rapport général. Portuguese Association of European Law, Lisbon
Ramos RMM (1994) Maastricht e os direitos do cidadão Europeu. In: A União Europeia. Faculdade de direito—Curso de Estudos Europeus, Coimbra, pp 93–129
Ramos RMM (1996) Nationalité, plurinationalité et supranationalité en droit Portugais. Arch Völkerr 34:96–119
Ramos RMM (2001–2002) Conflitos positivos (concursos) de nacionalidade e direito comunitário (Anotação ao acórdão do tribunal de justiça de 11 de Novembro de 1999). Rev Legis Jurisprud 134:146–160
Ramos RMM (2005–2006) A cidadania da união: caracterização, conteúdo e desenvolvimento. Rev Legis Jurisprud 135:352–368
Ramos RMM (2008) Da livre circulação de pessoas à cidadania Europeia. In: De Almeida MT, Piçarra N (eds) 50 anos tratado de Roma 1957–2007. Âncora Editora, Lisbon, pp 67–77
Ramos RMM (2020) Perda automática da nacionalidade de um Estado-membro e perda do estatuto de cidadão da união Europeia. Anotação ao acórdão do tribunal de justiça (grande secção) de 12 de Março de 2019. Rev Legis Jurisprud 149:412–433

Ramos RMM (2022) Cidadania da união e revogação de garantia de concessão da nacionalidade a um nacional de outro estado-membro que renunciara a esta nacionalidade no âmbito do processo de naturalização. Anotação ao acórdão do tribunal de justiça (grande secção) de 18 de Janeiro de 2022. Rev Legis Jurisprud 151:257–280
Ramos RMM (2023) Condições procedimentais em que deve decorrer a apreciação da proporcionalidade em caso de perda da nacionalidade de um Estado-Membro susceptível de desencadear a perda da cidadania da União. Anotação ao acórdão do tribunal de justiça (grande secção) de 5 de setembro de 2023. RevLegis Jurisprud 153:23–42
Ramos RMM (2024) Necessidade e Termos do Exame Individual da Proporciona lidade das Consequências da Perda da Cidadania da União desencadeada pela Perda (Automática) da Nacionalidade de um Estado-Membro por Aquisição da Nacionalidade de um País Terceiro. Anotação ao Acórdão do tribunal de justiça (quarta secção) de 25 de abril de 2024. RevLegis Jurisprud 154:360–380
Rodriguez BV (2024) Una nueva aportación del Tribunal de Luxemburgo en matéria de adquisición y perdida de nacionalidadd a la luz del derecho de la Unión Europea: El asunto C-689/21, Udlændinge og Integrationsministeriet. RevDerComEurop 77:211–231
Schnapper D (2017) Nationalité et citoyenneté. Pouvoirs 160:61–71
Shachar A, Baubock R (2014) Should citizenship be for sale? EUI Working Paper, RCAS 2014/01
Shaw J (2010) La corte Europea di giustizia di fronte al diritto di cittadinanza: una sfida alla sovranità nazionale dei Paesi membri? Quad Cost Riv Ital Dirit Cost 30:612–617
Shaw J (2011) Has the European court of justice challenged member state sovereignty in nationality law? EUI Working Papers, RSCAS 2011/62
Shuibhne NN (2023) Protecting the legal heritage of former union citizens. ComMar Law Rev 60:475–516
Shuibhne NN, Shaw J (2014) General report: union citizenship: development, impact and challenges. In: Neergaard U, Jacqueson C, Holst-Christensen N (eds) Union citizenship: development, impact and challenges, the XXVI FIDE congress in Copenhagen, 2014 congress publications. DJØF Publishing, Copenhagen
Silveira A (2017) Da jurisprudência do TJUE pós-Brexit sobre cidadania europeia. A recuperação do fio de Ariadne identitário? Unio-EU Law J 3:49–64
Sloane RD (2009) Breaking the genuine link: the contemporary international legal regulation of nationality. Harv Int Law J 50:1–60
Spiro PJ (2021) The past and (post-COVID) future of dual citizenship. In: Baubcock R, Haller M (eds) Dual citizenship and naturalisation: global, comparative and Austrian perspectives. Austrian Academy of Sciences Press, Vienna, pp 81–95
Struycken AVM (1988) Acquisition et perte de la nationalité néerlandaise. In: La condition juridique de l'étranger, hier et aujourd'hui. Actes du colloque organisé à Nimègue les 9-11 Mai 1988 par les facultés de droit de poitiers et de Nimègue. Faculteit der Rechtsgeleerdheid Katholieke, Nimègue, pp 3–19
Swider K (2020) Legitimizing precarity of EU citizenship: Tjebbes. Common Mark Law Rev 57:1163–1182
Thwaites R (2018) The life and times of the genuine link. VictUnivWellLawRev 49:645–670
Tobler C (2013) The prohibition of discrimination in the union's layered system of equality law: from early staff cases to the mangold approach. In: Court of Justice of the European Union (ed) The court of justice and the construction of Europe: analyses and perspectives on sixty years of case-law. T.M.C. Asser Press, The Hague, pp 443–469
Van Den Brink M (2020a-I) Revising citizenship within the European Union: is a genuine link requirement the way forward? RSCAS 2020/76, EUI Working Papers
Van Den Brink M (2020b-II) A qualified defence of the primacy of nationality over European Union citizenship. Int Comp Law Q 69:177–202
Van Eijken H (2019) Tjebbes in wonderland: on European citizenship, nationality and fundamental rights: ECJ 12 march 2019, case C-221/17, *M.G. Tjebbes and others v minister van Buitenlandse Zaken*, ECLI: EU: C: 2019: 189. Eur Const Law Rev 15:714–730

Van Loon H (1986) Pays Bas - nationalité. Rev Crit Droit Int Privé 75:182–192
Vlieks C (2019) Tjebbes and others v minister van Buitenlandse Zaken: a next step in European Union case law on nationality matters? Tilburg Law Rev 24:142–146
Wautelet P (2015) A propos de effectivite et nationalite des personnes physiques de Jacques de Burlet. Rev Belge Droit Int 48:537–557
Worster WT (2020) European Union citizenship and the unlawful denial of member state nationality. Fordham Int Law J 43:767–818
Worster WT (2021) Brexit as an arbitrary withdrawal of European Union citizenship. Fordham Int Law J 33:95–134
Ziemele I (2013) Nationality and third country nationals. In: Court of Justice of the European Union (ed) The court of justice and the construction of Europe: analyses and perspectives on sixty years of case-law. T.M.C. Asser Press, The Hague, pp 471–483

Rui Manuel Moura Ramos Universidade de Coimbra, Faculty of Law, Coimbra, Portugal. Former Judge at the Court of First Instance of European Communities. Former President of Portuguese Constitutional Court.

Subsidiarity: Quo Vadis?

Dulce Lopes

1 Introduction

The principle of subsidiarity is viewed as an essential principle within the European Union framework and in the Union's relationship with the Member States. The ability of this principle to regulate "shared spaces" where both the European Union and the Member States have legislative competence makes it a pivotal point of intersection between policies and legislation with different origins, purposes, and content. The principle is able to capture and manage plurality and may lead to the design of a common framework or to the understanding that this is not the best route to follow. Regardless of the outcome, the principle of subsidiarity will always have an important contribution to make as it opens up the possibility for dialogue, which is the essence of the European Union construction. Nonetheless, the process of building up the subsidiarity principle has not been a simple one and has had many critics. This chapter aims to show some of the difficulties, the promises offered by subsidiarity, and the path that lies ahead.

We will begin with a short introduction to the principles that govern the distribution of competences within the European Union (Part 2.). Part 3 will then provide further detail on the principle of subsidiarity within the European Union. Part 4 will summarise the mechanisms that enable the implementation of this principle and Part 5 will refer to the use of subsidiarity by the Portuguese Parliament ("Assembleia da República"). Lastly, we will conclude with an appraisal of the trends that have emerged from the application of the principle of subsidiarity to date (Part 6).

D. Lopes (✉)
Univ Coimbra, UCILeR - University of Coimbra Institute for Legal Research, Faculty of Law, Coimbra, Portugal
e-mail: dulcel@fd.uc.pt

I. Quadros, M. Gorjão-Henriques (eds.), *Revisiting the Liberal Constitutional Features of the European Union*, https://doi.org/10.1007/978-3-031-95717-8_4

2 Brief Introduction to the Principles Governing Competence Within the European Union

To gain a full understanding of the role the principle of subsidiarity plays within the European Union, it is important to consider how it relates to other principles governing the allocation of competences between the European Union and its Member States, the exercise of these, and, in general terms, their delimitation.[1]

The principle of conferral is emblematically assumed in the Treaty of the European Union, which mentions and emphasises that "competences not conferred upon the Union in the Treaties remain with the Member States" (Article 4(1) and Article 5(2), *in fine*). It follows from this principle, primarily, that Member States have general competence in matters which are not exclusive to the Union so that the actual assertion of the Union's competence always depends on the implementation of other principles of division of competences.[2]

Indeed, over time shared competences have been a testing ground for interrelations between the European Union and the Member States, demonstrating the dynamic nature of the construction of the European Union, which, as in other fields (such as primacy and direct effect), was anchored in structuring principles that underpin and reinforce those relations.

Among these is the principle of pre-emption, by means of which the Member States are not prevented from exercising shared competences and can exercise them to the extent that the Union does not do so. In short, this aims to avoid positive or negative conflicts in the exercise of competences and is linked to a traditional view of vertical distribution of powers. Ultimately, as a result of this principle, it would be possible for state competences to be so eroded that, from initially being shared competences, they would become exclusive competences due to the exhaustiveness of Community regulations.[3] However, this principle does not prevent, and indeed includes, a possible "retreat" from the space occupied by European Union law, although this normative dimension of the principle of pre-emption has not so far been prioritised.

The principle of pre-emption is now enshrined in Article 2(2) TFEU, in the Protocol (No 25) on the exercise of shared competence, and is explained in

[1] For a fuller overview, cf. Lopes (2008, pp. 91–114).

[2] The Treaty of Lisbon attempted to stabilise competences held by the European Union by establishing an exhaustive list of exclusive competences and defining a non-exhaustive list of shared competences and competences with special characteristics, such as support competences (Articles 3 to 6 of the Treaty on the Functioning of the European Union). Nonetheless, as general lists, they do not anticipate or solve in themselves all conflicting positions in particular cases.

[3] This can lead to a metamorphosis of shared competences, as illustrated by Soares (1996, p.139 et seq). On the intimate link between the principle of pre-emption and the primacy principle (although the first concerns the possibility of intervention, in some cases in a merely potential way, and the second deals with the resolution of concrete legal conflicts), cf. Martins (2005, p. 23 et seq).

Declaration No 18 concerning the delimitation of competences, so that it is no longer an "institution formally unknown" in European Union law.[4]

If the principle of pre-emption operates in the sense of recognising a conditional competence of the States, which the European Union may block at any time through its actions,[5] this raises the question of whether there are material limits to the European Union's competences and powers. The answer to this comes from the combined intervention of other principles, some showing an inclination towards increasing the European Union playing field (as is the case of the principles of implied powers and competences), others pointing to the limitation of such competences and powers (such as the principles of sincere cooperation and proportionality), and a final and decisive one that may lean either way (the principle of subsidiarity).

The first set of principles includes the so-called doctrine of implied powers,[6] which aims to provide the Union with all means of action for the fulfilment of the competences recognised in its founding acts [Article 3(6) of the TFEU], and, in a broader sense, the principle of implied competences, which also allows the expansion of the Union's competences beyond what results explicitly from the founding Treaties but may still be attributed to it (given its aims and objectives).[7] One inference from this is the principle of parallel powers, of essentially jurisprudential construction, according to which the European Union enjoys, both internally[8] and externally,[9] powers of action to implement the competences resulting from the Treaties, even though these are not explicitly and directly provided for in the Treaties. This specific principle, in its external dimension, is now also expressly provided for in Article 3(2) TFEU, which states that "The Union shall also have exclusive competence for the conclusion of an international agreement when its conclusion is provided for in a legislative act of the Union or is necessary to enable the Union to exercise its internal competence, or in so far as its conclusion may affect common rules or alter their scope". Also closely linked to the principle of implicit competences, Article 352 of the TFEU (previously Article 235 of the Treaty of Rome) allows competences to be derived from the very objectives laid down in the Treaty, forming a flexible but genuine rule of allocation of competence, which is

---

[4] Soares (1996, p. 206).

[5] This is a competence "rule of blocking effect" according to Timmermans (2014, p. 162).

[6] A principle recognised in the international arena in the Advisory Opinion on Reparation for Injuries Suffered in the Service of the United Nations of 11 April 1949.

[7] Cf., in the Portuguese doctrine, Duarte (1997) and Martins (1995).

[8] Cf. the Judgment of the Court of 9 July 1987, *Federal Republic of Germany and others v Commission of the European Communities*, cases 281, 283–285,287/85, ECLI:EU:C:1987:351, on the interaction between social and migration policies of the European Union.

[9] Cf. the seminal judgment of the Court of 31 March 1971, Commission of the European Communities v Council of the European Communities, European Agreement on Road Transport (EART), case 22/70, ECLI:EU:C:1971:32, followed by other relevant case law as tracked by Schütze (2004).

understandably less used nowadays than it initially was, given the more extensive regulation of European Union competences.

In the second set of principles, we include the principle of sincere cooperation enshrined in Article 4(3) TEU. By creating mutual obligations of loyal behaviour, this express normative provision, on the one hand, requires States to refrain from acting when this could jeopardise the effect of European Union measures (already adopted or to be adopted). On the other hand, it also binds the European Union to act in cooperation and potentially to re-examine the instruments it uses to determine whether or not its action should yield to the intervention of the Member States.[10] However, it is the proportionality principle that is the crux when it comes to limiting European Union competences. Proportionality permeates both exclusive and concurrent Union action since it entails an imperative of minimum intervention. It requires the Union, in its relations with the Member States, to adopt means which are materially and formally the least arduous, thus restricting European Union intervention to the measures that are adequate, necessary and proportional *stricto sensu*. This principle, which both opens and closes Article 5 of the TEU and is enshrined in the Protocol on applying the principles of subsidiarity and proportionality, has a clear methodological dimension and broad application in European Union Law, both in an active and in a controlling sense.

As for the principle of subsidiarity, it deserves a classification of its own given that it has no predefined intent, and may point either to the extension of European Union competences or to their restriction, depending on the fulfilment of two conditions: one negative (the inadequacy of action by the Member States) and another positive (the added value of the European Union action).[11]

Included in Article 5(3) of the TEU, the principle of subsidiarity has long been the focus of attempts to restrict its scope, make its criteria more straightforward and render its application more operational. Furthermore, if the first conquest—the integration of the principle of subsidiarity into the Treaties (in the environmental field within the Single European Act and, as a general principle of law, within the Treaty of Maastricht[12])—was no easy chore, the affirmation of its relevance within the

[10] Klammert (2014, p. 25), refers to this as reverse vertical loyalty, although it is less used in practice than the "usual" vertical dimension: from Member States to the European Union. This principle also has horizontal dimensions, guiding the relations between the European institutions (Article 13(2) TEU) and also between Member States, as stems particularly from the principle of mutual recognition.

[11] Oxana Pimenova sees it as a regulatory principle that balances the claim for regulatory powers between the European Union and its Member States (Pimenova 2016, pp. 382–383).

[12] It is worth mentioning, given their importance to the characterisation of the subsidiarity principle, almost from its inception within the European Legal Framework, the "Overall Approach to the Application by the Council of the Subsidiarity Principle and Article 3b of the Treaty on European Union" adopted at the Edinburgh European Council of 11 and 12 December 1992, and the "Interinstitutional Declaration on Democracy, Transparency and Subsidiarity" including an "Interinstitutional Agreement between the European Parliament, the Council and the Commission on procedures for implementing the principle of subsidiarity" adopted on 25 October 1993 by the Interinstitutional Conference of Parliament, the Commission and the Council.

European Union framework has proven to be an even more arduous task. In fact, after the inclusion of subsidiarity as a primary law principle in the Treaty of Maastricht (1993) and until the changes brought about by the Treaty of Lisbon (2009), the major advance made is credited to the Amsterdam Treaty (1999), with the inclusion of a Protocol annexed to the EC Treaty on the application of the principles of subsidiarity and proportionality. Ten years had elapsed with little to show for it, which seemed at the time to have turned subsidiarity into a failed promise.[13]

However, with the Treaty of Lisbon, and in particular with the new Protocol No. 2 on the principles of subsidiarity and proportionality (in close connection with Protocol No. 1 on the role of national parliaments in the European Union), additional mechanisms were established to reinforce compliance with the subsidiarity principle. An early warning system related to legislative procedures was introduced,[14] strengthened judicial scrutiny of the principle of subsidiarity was affirmed,[15] and the principle's regional and local dimensions were explicitly valued.[16]

The principle of subsidiarity, legally established as the *punctum crucis* of the task of delimiting the competences of the European Union in relation to its Member States, seemed to have found a new spark. The reference to this principle is pervasive in all types of European texts, even if only with a prospective nature,[17] and its practical use seems to have grown stronger—although not always at the same pace—as shown by the Annual Reports delivered by the Commission on its application.

Nonetheless, before considering the various developments and trends related to the principle of subsidiarity, it is important to highlight its characteristics.

---

[13] As already noted in the Laeken Declaration on the Future of Europe of 15 December 2001. This stagnation was in part "to blame" for the failure to adopt the draft Treaty establishing a Constitution for Europe, which included a set of rules on the subsidiarity principle that were, however, recovered in the Treaty of Lisbon.

[14] Under this mechanism—particularly relevant because of its preventive rather than reactive nature—national parliaments, the representatives of the main interests which could be harmed by an infringement of the principle of subsidiarity, may integrate their concerns into proposed legislative procedures, as will be detailed further.

[15] Protocol No. 2 states that the Court of Justice shall have jurisdiction in actions brought by Member States for annulment on grounds of infringement of the principle of subsidiarity. In this respect, the Protocol ensures that national parliaments or any of their chambers shall have the possibility, in accordance with their internal constitutional organisation, to request their governments to initiate such actions for annulment.

[16] The regional dimension of the principle of subsidiarity is accentuated by the fact that the Committee of the Regions, generally considered to be only an interested party for procedural purposes, will also be legitimately entitled to raise the infringement of the principle of subsidiarity where the Treaty provides for its mandatory consultation. For an analysis on the regional dimension on the principle of subsidiarity, cf. Borońska-Hryniewiecka (2013b, pp. 1–23).

[17] Cf. more recently, the Communication from the Commission to the European Parliament, the European Council, the Council, the European Economic and Social Council and the Committee of the Regions—Conference on the Future of Europe—Putting Vision into Concrete Action, COM (2022) 404 final.

3 Principle of Subsidiarity: Main Features

In line with the principle of subsidiarity, before the European Union can exercise a shared competence it must pass two tests. The first is a negative or sufficiency test, which allows the European Union to "act only if and in so far as the objectives of the proposed action cannot be sufficiently achieved by the Member States, either at central level or at a regional and local level". The second test is a positive or value-added test, which considers whether "by reason of the scale or effects of the proposed action", that action would be "better achieved at Union level".

Looking first at the negative test, several elements need to be considered, such as the lack, insufficiency or ineffectiveness of regulation at a national or lower level, and financial, economic and social factors are taken into account, as well as the existence of intergovernmental cooperation and not merely the individual capacity of some Member States to achieve the objective being pursued. As for the test to establish whether Union action would provide added value, this involves consideration of the comparative efficiency of that action (even if the alternative—the absence of intervention—is theoretically construed),[18] which may exist if the issue in question has transnational aspects which action by Member States cannot satisfactorily resolve. Union action may also be more efficient if action taken by the Member States alone is contrary to the provisions of the Treaties or would cause significant damage to the interests of the Member States and the Union, or if existing European Union measures have not yet been sufficient to achieve the goals which have been set and need to be strengthened.

The principle is complex and it will be helpful to provide further clarification regarding its nature and functions.

3.1 A Legal or Political Principle?

One of the most commonly raised questions regarding the subsidiarity principle is whether it is a political or legal principle.[19] The complexity of this principle, in all its multifaceted dimensions,[20] and the fact that it aims to regulate areas of overlapping or intersecting public powers, naturally make it an embedded political

---

[18] The potential added value of European action and the cost of not acting (cost of non-Europe) are closely related concepts.

Cf. https://www.europarl.europa.eu/thinktank/en/document/EPRS_STU(2017)603239.

[19] Fausto de Quadros sees it as a principle with a double nature (legal and political), which requires particular care in its application and control (de Quadros 1997, p. 29). See also De Búrca (2000, p. 3).

[20] Evans (2013, p. 63). According to Rute Saraiva, the principle of subsidiarity is linked to three fundamental criteria of the European institutions: effectiveness, proximity and democracy (Saraiva 2001, p. 105). For more developments on this principle, cf. Martins (2003).

principle, which is understood in different ways depending on the political and legitimacy models in force.

However, while it is political in terms of its origin and function, the principle of subsidiarity can equally be classified as a legal principle within the European Union, since it has been introduced and regulated as a legally binding tool to (re)allocate shared competences. Indeed, it is the legal construction of the subsidiarity principle that affords it its definitive position in the European arena and enables its criteria to be understood, applied and scrutinised.

As Silvia Mangerona puts it, "this principle is for many an undesirable and ambiguous concept, but recognizable with less difficulty in the area of law".[21] Therefore, through the law, the principle of subsidiarity is rendered operational and may (or must) impact the decision-making and control tasks of the authorities bound to apply it.

Of course, in the case of structuring principles, such as the principle of subsidiarity, the law cannot be seen in its "pure form" (if this even exists) as an application of rules to a concrete situation in an all-or-nothing fashion.[22] Indeed, the legal relevance of principles is closely connected to a set of other references—political, administrative, managerial—that are mediated and condensed by law. The fact that the principle of subsidiarity requires political-economic assessments does not mean, however, that it is not a legal principle. In fact, the principles (and their control mechanisms) have progressively evolved, so that they are no longer predominantly the preserve of politics but now have significant—or even essential—dimensions with legal relevance.[23]

Indeed, while the principle is open to political and public debate regarding the fulfilment of its criteria, which entails a wide margin of discretion, legal mechanisms of an administrative, judicial and legislative nature have been set in motion to allow for its proper application and control, so that the scenario behind subsidiarity is primarily one of legal regulation.

This regulation is not exclusive, however, and leaves room for political intervention or for subsidiarity to be used as a strategic tool[24] through formal or informal fora, but, even here, subsidiarity has a slight legal angle (although less visible and controllable), since public authorities are bound to take into consideration, and include in their decision-making procedures all interests that may be affected by their standpoints.

In fact, while "the use of legal instruments is often a political decision" (Marauhn and Mengeler 2021, p. 39), it is important to note that, within the European Union, legal regulation of the principle of subsidiarity was seen as increasingly

[21] Mangerona (2021, p. 99). Cf., also, Gorjão-Henriques (2019, p. 343).

[22] Schilling, though looking at the subsidiarity principle in part as a rule, concludes that it is not a "well-defined or clear-cut rule" (Schilling 1994, p. 214).

[23] According to Raimundo (2019, p. 134), this movement should come as no surprise: the entire history of public law is a history of the retraction of the zones of immunity of power from legal control.

[24] Developing subsidiarity as strategy within the European Union, cf. Fonseca (2020, pp. 39–61).

necessary—in particular by the Member States—to compensate for centralising tendencies of the European Union and to increase its legitimacy[25] and, on another level, to ensure the legality of European Union measures. Hence, in our view, law has played a decisive role in the evolution of the principle of subsidiarity and in its consolidation in the European Union area, to a point that would not have been possible were it not for the legal developments that took place. Without law and its application in administrative, judicial and legislative procedures, subsidiarity would still be a mere case for political debate and not an effective tool to manage plurality, legitimacy and the requirements of multi-level governance.

3.2 A Neutral or Committed Principle?

Another question frequently asked is whether the principle of subsidiarity is a mechanism for politically safeguarding the Member States or an instrument of cooperation between them and the European Union.[26]

If we regard the principle as having the purpose of defending the periphery against the centre (preference for decision-making at the level closest to the citizens, as established in Article 2(1) TEU), it will essentially be a principle with a value attached to it, operating as a safeguard against the European Union assuming excessive powers.

On the other hand, if we regard it as a neutral principle (aimed at defining the most appropriate level of regulation for the measures to be adopted), it will be considered a mechanism of an essentially collaborative nature.

While the preamble of the Treaty on European Union suggests the first position ("Resolved to continue the process of creating an ever closer union among the peoples of Europe, in which decisions are taken as closely as possible to the citizen under the principle of subsidiarity"), the Treaty itself [Article 5(3) of the TEU] and the annexed Protocol go in a different direction, by establishing the best level of

[25] The subsidiarity mechanism comprises each of the three alternative concepts of legitimacy identified in the White Paper on European Governance: input legitimacy, output legitimacy and vertical inter-level legitimacy, according to Popelier and Vandenbruwaene (2011, p. 207). According to Borońska-Hryniewiecka (2013a, p. 75), "the principle of subsidiarity links the input and output dimensions of legitimacy inasmuch as it regulates the allocation and the use of authority within a political decision-making process according to democracy - and efficiency- related arguments".

[26] In general, three positions can be traced, the less prominent integrationist position (that places the focus on subsidiarity as a motor for integration), the devolutionist position (that places the focus on subsidiarity as an obstacle to centripetal forces within the European Union) and the neutral position that tends towards variable and flexible results. Cf. Saraiva (2001, pp. 111–120). According to Paul Craig, this principle serves a multiplicity of functions, some more neutral, such as a mechanism for alleviating disputes concerning the division of competence between the European Union and the Member States, others less, such as avoiding excessive centralisation and enhancing pluralism and the diversity of national values (Craig 2012).

action as the key purpose behind subsidiarity.[27] This duality is confirmed in other important documents, among which we may highlight the Conclusions of the Presidency of the Edinburgh European Council, 11/12 December 1992 (which was the basis for the Protocol to the Amsterdam Treaty). The Conclusions state that "This principle contributes to the respect for the national identities of Member States and safeguards their powers" but also go on to state that "Subsidiarity is a dynamic concept and should be applied in the light of the objectives set out in the Treaty. It allows Community action to be expanded where circumstances so require, and conversely, to be restricted or discontinued where it is no longer justified".

This apparent contradiction, seen by Andrea Biondi as an "underlying bipolar ethos" (Biondi 2012, p. 220), can be dispelled if we consider subsidiarity as neutral in results but not in process. Indeed, although the results of this principle are variable and are not founded in any bias or categorical position (indeed, no explicit presumption in favour of Member States' regulation is established), the process in itself is embedded with several elements that point to a *desideratum* or *meaning*: the safeguarding of Member States' scope of action.[28] In fact, the criteria established demonstrate that it is up to the European Union Institutions to prove not only that Member States do not satisfy the required level of action, but that, rather, this is better satisfied by the European Union. As a result, if either of these requirements is not met, the competence remains at Member-State level.

3.3 A Multi-Level Principle

The more complex the public arena becomes, the greater the importance of the principle of subsidiarity. Seen as a principle that "at a legal level was born federalist",[29] it is now relevant regardless of the form public organisation takes. This principle decisively shapes how public entities relate to each other in federal, regional or even unitary states (regarding local administrations mostly), since in all these there are—and with increasing frequency—multiple centres of competences which need to be integrated into a coherent whole.

As Paulo Otero states, traditional state monolithism has given way to the tendencies that are, in a way, overwhelming and this has determined the multiplication of

[27] The Communication from the Commission to the European Parliament, the European Council, the Council, the European Economic and Social Committee and the Committee of the Regions, COM (2018) 703 Final, p. 3, concludes that "subsidiarity is about identifying the best level of governance to make and implement policies".

[28] According to Peter Rinderle, "To put it in a nutshell, subsidiarity speaks—in a conditional and pragmatic manner—in favour of decentralisation for the allocation and use of authority. Thus, subsidiarity does not take any categorical or principled stance and cannot be used to justify a decentralised or federal distribution of political power" (Rinderle 2021, p. 21).

[29] Though at a federal level it has a more centralising slant than in other forms of administration (Morais 1998, pp. 782–783).

"law-creating centres" (Otero 2007, pp. 147–152), both internally and internationally. It is, therefore, in a pluralistic and complex environment that the principle of subsidiarity comes into play, making an *a priori* and generic distribution of competences more flexible and adequate (Martinico 2011, p. 651).

We may note that subsidiarity does not exist solely at European Union level, since Member States' legal orders also include it as one of their internal principles (in Portugal this is by means of Article 7(6) of the Portuguese Constitution). The Portuguese principle is said to operate as a constitutional principle that binds the legislator while dividing competences and exercising existing competences (Correia 2000, p. 242). Moreover, although it is greatly influenced by the principle of subsidiarity developed at European Union level,[30] it brings to the table the particular *ethos* behind the Portuguese legal order, with its own perception of the need for regulation and the sufficiency of national public action.

Therefore, an analysis of subsidiarity mostly within the early warning system established by the Treaty of Lisbon will bring together several closely related conceptions of that principle that may not be coincidental, and hence the need for control and adjustment mechanisms within the European Union framework.

Subsidiarity is not only relevant at European Union and national levels. As a result of the progressive globalisation and sharing of interests, the articulation between the international legal order and its organisations and the European and national legal orders has also been analysed from the point of view of the principle of subsidiarity. The increasingly close relations between these levels of regulation have allowed subsidiarity concerns to be included in their reciprocal relationship, and it has been highlighted that, following the application of this principle, the most appropriate level of the decision is not necessarily always the European Union or State level. Here too, in matters of a transnational nature, such as the environment, climate change and nuclear threats, if the interests underlying subsidiarity are considered, this may point to a preference for regulation of an international nature.[31]

Lastly, the principle of subsidiarity is not only meant to underlie "high-end" decisions, but all measures that may impact the balance of competences within the European Union. Indeed, although the focus of the early warning system within the European Union is on legislative acts—given their primordial importance in setting the framework for European Union intervention—it should be highlighted that non-legislative acts (for instance, delegated and implementing acts) should also be subject to subsidiarity considerations and administrative and judicial control. Even in the case of implementing acts for which Member States, in principle, have competence (Article 291 of TFEU), if this competence is conferred upon the Commission

[30] Rute Saraiva noted that this principle has a double nature—constitutional and community—although this causes uncertainty in its application and possible conflict between levels of jurisdiction (Saraiva 2001, p. 146).

[31] Cf. Paulus (2008, pp. 197–198), Jachtenfuchs and Krisch (2016) and Follesdal (2013). Article 191(4) TFEU explicitly specifies that, taking into account the division of competences, the Union and the Member States "shall cooperate with third countries and with the competent international organisations".

or, in duly justified cases, the Council, a subsidiarity evaluation must be made to ascertain whether uniform conditions for the implementation of the Union acts in question are needed (Lanceiro 2018, p. 83; Lopes 2018).

Furthermore, there may be a case for applying subsidiarity to the intra-European Union movement proposed by Horsley (2012, pp. 277–282). Within the European Union itself, the multiplication or proliferation of EU bodies and agencies with extensive competences in administrative and regulatory fields should likewise be justified on the basis of subsidiarity assessments, not only from an internal perspective, but also from an external point of view, since this impacts the broader governance arrangements reflected in the Treaties (Sorace 2013, pp. 194–195).

Consequently, no area appears to be beyond the reach of the principle of subsidiarity, although its criteria must meet the requirements of each specific field of action and the nature and reciprocal relationship of the public entities or bodies involved.

3.4 An Open-Ended Principle

Subsidiarity, as a principle, must be constantly satisfied and this is why it is said to assume a variable geometry, adjusting to specific regulation demands (Trachtman 1992, p. 469). However, this satisfaction must be structured and reasoned, in order to avoid this principle being effortlessly rebutted.[32]

Furthermore, although, at European Union level, there is a definition of the (negative and positive) criteria on which the principle rests, these being essential for a full understanding of it, these criteria are also open-ended and need to be considered and applied on a case-by-case basis.

Naturally, there have been efforts to define more precisely what those criteria entail and how they should be understood, for example in Recital 5 of the Protocol on applying the principles of subsidiarity and proportionality to the Treaty of Amsterdam. This stated that the following guidelines should be used when examining whether those conditions are met:

> - the issue under consideration has transnational aspects which cannot be satisfactorily regulated by action by Member States;
> - actions by Member States alone or lack of Community action would conflict with the requirements of the Treaty (such as the need to correct distortion of competition or avoid disguised restrictions on trade or strengthen economic and social cohesion) or would otherwise significantly damage Member States' interests;
> - action at Community level would produce clear benefits by reason of its scale or effects compared with action at the level of the Member States.

[32] For a methodological proposal for applying the principle of subsidiarity, cf. Pelkmans (2006, pp. 8–11). For allocative criteria according to the relevant features of the regulated activity, in environmental law cf. Van Zeben (2014, p. 438).

Interestingly, these illustrative criteria were not retained in the Protocol to the Treaty of Lisbon, which preferred to regulate the mechanisms of control rather than the principle as such. Instead, Article 5 of the current protocol emphasises financial and regulatory impacts and the need for substantiation of qualitative and, whenever possible, quantitative indicators.

More recently, the European Commission's Taskforce on subsidiarity, proportionality and "doing less more efficiently", among other recommendations, presented a subsidiarity grid that aims to provide a shared and consistent approach to assess conformity of a given proposal or initiative with the Treaty-based principles of subsidiarity and proportionality. In this grid the questions address both subsidiarity tests, with targeted questions. For the sufficiency test, the questions posed are: (a) Are there significant/appreciable transnational/cross-border aspects to the problems being tackled? Have these been quantified?; (b) Would national action or the absence of EU level action conflict with core objectives of the Treaty or significantly damage the interests of other Member States?; (c) To what extent do Member States have the ability or possibility to enact appropriate measures? (d) How does the problem and its causes (e.g. negative externalities, spill over effects) vary across the national, regional and local levels of the EU?; (e) Is the problem widespread across the EU or limited to a few Member States?; (f) Are Member States overstretched in achieving the objectives of the planned measure?; (g) How do the views/preferred courses of action of national, regional and local authorities differ across the EU?

For the added-value test, the questions are as follows: (a) Are there clear benefits from EU level action?; (b) Are there economies of scale? Can the objectives be met more efficiently at EU level (larger benefits per unit cost)? Will the functioning of the internal market be improved?; (c) What are the benefits in replacing different national policies and rules with a more homogenous policy approach?; (d) Do the benefits of EU-level action outweigh the loss of competence of the Member States and the local and regional authorities (beyond the costs and benefits of acting at national, local and regional levels?; (e) Will there be improved legal clarity for those having to implement the legislation?[33]

We are therefore very far from the often quoted Commission Report to the European Council on the Adaptation of Community Legislation to the Subsidiarity Principle, COM(93) 545, when it states that subsidiarity would be "first and foremost a political principle", given its progressive grounding in legal terms.

However, in each specific case the principle of subsidiarity will be able to reach its full potential and suggest a defined direction, despite the difficulties that may be faced along the way. These difficulties are not only related to the criteria for fulfilling the principle of subsidiarity itself, since the dividing lines between it and the conferral and proportionality principles are blurred in many situations. Indeed, it is common to find, within the reasoned opinions issued by Parliaments or in opinions

[33] https://portal.cor.europa.eu/subsidiarity/news/Pages/subsidiarity-assessment-grid.aspx.

delivered under the political dialogue procedure, a mix of arguments that clearly intersect. Conferral that, at the point where subsidiarity is debated, should be a given, is discussed when, for instance, particular issues have been reserved to States or highly impact national interests. On the other hand, proportionality has been discussed when the intended measures have too great an impact, which makes it particularly difficult to assess subsidiarity in a specific case, as a review of the measure based on its adequacy, necessity and proportionality *stricto sensu* is required and may also affect the possibility for Member States to comply with it adequately.[34]

There is no clear-cut solution in these cases. However, claims that subsidiarity has been violated may involve additional and related arguments as long as these reinforce the lack of fulfilment of one or both legal criteria (for instance, the argument that the area being partially regulated is largely reserved for States, which might lead to the conclusion that a European level regulation will not present sufficient added value, or that the measure is so disproportionate that the European Union itself will face severe difficulties in enforcing it).[35]

3.5 A Dynamic Principle

From a time-based point of view, another characteristic of the principle of subsidiarity is its flexibility, since both the needs to be addressed and the means to achieve them (the means available to the public entities potentially involved) may vary.

Similarly, it may be concluded that the exercise of powers was misallocated, in the light of inefficiencies that arise. A rethink of the proper place to exercise competences may be required, involving efforts to assess and update the fulfilment of the assumptions of the principle of subsidiarity. Therefore, from time to time, what may have been seen as an infringement of the subsidiarity principle may be justified under a different light; and, conversely, what might have been seen as a welcome European Union measure may stop being so, either because national intervention (that may in many cases go beyond community provisions) became sufficient or because European Union measures stopped presenting sufficient added value. This latter situation is hard to imagine. It could, however, be the case if Member States

[34] Indeed, the assessment of proportionality is clearly linked to the assessment of subsidiarity and the need to match the nature and intensity of a given measure to the identified problem, as stated on p. 35 of the Commission Staff Working Document—Better Regulation Guidelines, Brussels, 3.11.2021, SWD (2021) 305 final. This link is also highlighted in legal doctrine. Cf., among many others, Machado (2018, pp. 97–98), Piedrafita (2013), and Schütze (2009, pp. 525–526). Davies goes on to argue that subsidiarity is not in need, since it does not provide a method to balance between Member State and European Union interests, as does proportionality (Davies 2006, pp. 63–84). However, Bermann defends both criteria, stating that, if taken seriously, they may lead to different directions, even though some trade-offs may be required between the two (Bermann 1994, pp. 386–390).

[35] With a similar approach, Kiiver (2012, p. 98).

wished to be bound by conventional international instruments that went beyond the demands of European Union Law; yet, the broad competences of the European Union in the external field and the fact that enhanced cooperation is also dealt with within the scope of the European Union make it particularly difficult, although not impossible, to reach such a conclusion.

This dynamism also means that subsidiarity should be a concern in all policy cycles. Since periodical reporting and evaluation of measures is a widespread feature of European Union secondary legislation, subsidiarity (re)analysis should be taken seriously.

4 Principle of Subsidiarity: Application and Control Mechanisms

An essential element of subsidiarity as a legal principle is the existence of mechanisms that allow for its appropriate application and control from all "parties concerned". Without a high level of legal debate and reasoning this principle would be just a chapter in European Union history and not one of its main features.

As for these mechanisms, although the latest annual reports on the application of the Principles of Subsidiarity and Proportionality and on relations with National Parliaments divide its application by the Institutions (Commission, European Parliament, Council, Committee of the Regions and the Court of Justice), and then by National and Regional Parliaments, we prefer to highlight the existing types of implementation mechanisms organised according to their scope and nature. Indeed, the operational character of the subsidiarity principle depends on the combined effect of the application and control mechanisms it entails, which may have predominantly administrative, judicial and legislative dimensions.

4.1 Administrative Dimension

From the point of view of the "internal life" of the European Union institutions, bodies, offices or agencies, subsidiarity is an ever-present concern. Respect for the principle of subsidiarity must figure in all their actions and procedures.

This is particularly relevant for the European Commission—given its almost exclusive initiative role. Under its own better regulation agenda and more recently, under its "Fit for Future platform" the Commission has developed a set of robust guidelines and methods to better insert subsidiarity into its proposals. Moreover, it analyses the principle of subsidiarity in all impact assessments prepared for policy proposals and conducts consultations, evaluations and fitness checks to support a claim for a European regulation on a specific area, as well as organising the annual report on the application of the principles of subsidiarity and proportionality (Article 9 of Protocol no. 2).

The Committee of the Regions is also a key player in the subsidiarity field, as is well recognised by the Treaty of Lisbon. The Committee has issued opinions (both on request and *ex officio* and in close cooperation with the Subsidiarity Monitoring Network) that have been particularly important in shaping how subsidiarity should be understood and indicating whether proposals presented comply with the principle.

Nevertheless, it is the European Parliament that has long been a constant advocate regarding the adoption and strengthening of the principle of subsidiarity and that has never given up in this respect, concluding interinstitutional agreements[36] and passing several Resolutions in this field[37] that have decisively helped shape how the principle of subsidiarity is applied.

This work of assessing compliance with the subsidiarity principle, which is shared by all the institutions and bodies, is particularly relevant within the European Union, as all draft legislative acts must be justified in accordance with the principle of subsidiarity (Articles 1 and 5 of the Protocol) and this justification must be solid enough to support the measure until its adoption and beyond. The *onus probandi* of respect for the principle of subsidiarity, as a requirement for the intervention of the European Union, lies with the Union, and the effort put into this must be robust and well substantiated.[38]

4.2 Judicial Dimension

At this level, the principle of subsidiarity has been less frequently invoked and used than the principle of proportionality, although both incorporate validity requirements regarding European Union acts of a binding nature, are open-ended principles and involve judgements rooted in comparative arguments. In fact, even before it was explicitly enshrined in the Treaties, the principle of proportionality was used as a control parameter (Emiliou 1996, p. 115). In contrast, the virtues of the principle of subsidiarity have not been extensively exploited in the Court of Justice case law and, in some cases, even rebutted based on the principle's temporal and material scope (Duarte 2006, p. 75 et seq).

[36] Cf., for an illustration, the interinstitutional agreement of 13 April 2016 between the European Parliament, the Council of the European Union and the European Commission on Better Law-Making.

[37] Cf. the European Parliament resolution of 13 February 2019 on the state of the debate on the future of Europe (2018/2094(INI)) and the European Parliament resolution of 24 June 2021 on European Union regulatory fitness and subsidiarity and proportionality—report on Better Law Making covering the years 2017, 2018 and 2019 (2020/2262(INI)).

[38] As results from the Decision of the then Court of First Instance (CFI) of 7 November 2007, *Federal Republic of Germany v Commission of the European Communities*, case T-374/04, ECLI:EU:T:2007:332, para. 79.

In its decision of 21 February 1995, the then Court of First Instance (now General Court) held that "The principle of subsidiarity did not, before the entry into force of the Treaty on European Union, constitute a general principle of law by reference to which the legality of Community acts should be reviewed".[39] In the decision of 31 January 2007, the same Court, held that the principle of subsidiarity could not be invoked in the sphere of application of economic sanctions against third countries and persons, given that "it is plain that the uniform implementation in the Member States of Security Council resolutions, which are binding on all members of the United Nations without distinction, can be better achieved at Community level than at national level".[40]

The subsidiarity principle was analysed in other early cases, although in connection with the obligation to state reasons or borderline situations of manifest error. This was, for instance, the case of the Court of Justice decision of 13 May 1997, in which it stated that "it is apparent that, on any view, the Parliament and the Council did explain why they considered that their action conformed with the principle of subsidiarity and, accordingly, that they complied with the obligation to give reasons" and that "An express reference to that principle cannot be required".[41] On the other hand, in the Decision of 12 November 1996, the Court simply emphasised the need for Community action, without any accurate analysis of the subsidiarity question, and limited its appraisal—although directly regarding the proportionality principle—to situations vitiated by manifest error or misuse of powers, or where the institution concerned has manifestly exceeded the limits of its discretion.[42]

These decisions fell short, given the growing importance and elaboration of the principle of subsidiarity. Since then, the Court of Justice has been called on to engage more with the subsidiarity principle over the years, and does now carry out a scrutiny of subsidiarity (Panara 2016, pp. 305–331), although it has not yet, until the cutting line of this article, found reasons to invalidate European Union acts on this basis.[43]

Let us look at one example in which the case law of the Court of Justice has been most plentiful: the case of tobacco regulation.[44]

---

[39] CFI decision of 21 February 1995, Vereniging van Samenwerkende Prijsregelende Organisaties in de Bouwnijverheid and others v Commission of the European Communities, Case T-29/92, ECLI:EU:T:1995:34, para. 12.

[40] CFI decision of 31 January 2007, *Leonid Minin v Commission of the European Communities*, Case T-362/04, ECLI:EU:T:2007:25, para. 89.

[41] Court of Justice of the European Union (CJEU) decision of 13 May 1997, *Federal Republic of Germany v European Parliament and Council of the European Union*, Case C-233/94, ECLI:EU:C:1997:231, para. 28.

[42] ECJ decision of 12 November 1996, United Kingdom of Great Britain and Northern Ireland v Council of the European Union, Case C-84/94, ECLI:EU:C:1996:431, para. 55.

[43] We do not believe that this necessarily means a "failure of subsidiarity as a judicial principle to guard against centralisation in the European Union" (Evans 2013, p. 72), since, as stated, this principle does not need to point—as a result—to a preference for national level regulation.

[44] Gernat (2013, pp. 203–207). More generally, on the interplay of the early warning system and judicial control regarding lifestyle risk policy of the European Union, cf. Maletic (2015).

In the first set of cases, although the departure point in the Decision of the Court of Justice of 5 October 2000 set limits on the regulatory competences of the European Union (never mentioning subsidiarity as such),[45] soon the Court, on 10 December 2002, found that Directive 2001/37/EC did not infringe the principle of subsidiarity, mainly because the Directive's objective was to eliminate the barriers raised by the differences which still exist between the Member States' laws, regulations and administrative provisions on the manufacture, presentation and sale of tobacco products, while ensuring a high level of health protection, and it was considered that that objective "cannot be sufficiently achieved by the Member States individually and calls for action at the Community level, as demonstrated by the multifarious development of national laws in this case".[46] This case is, indeed, an example of a "perfunctory scrutiny" that brings little more to the table than the application by the Court of the general wording of the subsidiarity principle, and deprives "judicial inspection of the use of subsidiarity of all meaningful purpose" (Biondi 2012, p. 217).

However, in its decision of 4 May 2016, the Court went further when asked to assess the validity of Article 7 of Directive 2014/40 in the light of the principle of subsidiarity, in so far as that article prohibits the placing on the EU market of tobacco products containing menthol as a characterising flavour. In this case, when asked if using a "standard formula" to confirm compliance with the principle of subsidiarity (para. 214) was sufficient for the purposes of the subsidiarity principle, the Court went on to justify the measure in formal and substantive terms. In formal terms, not only is the wording of the contested act relevant, but also its context and the circumstances of the individual case, which show that the Commission proposal and its impact assessment have allowed for all interested parties (European Union legislature, national parliaments and individuals) to be able to understand the reasons behind the subsidiarity appraisal (para. 225 to 227). However, in substantive terms, even if the Directive's second objective—ensuring a high level of protection of human health, especially for young people—could have been better achieved at Member-State level, this would run "completely counter to the first objective of [...] improvement of the functioning of the internal market for tobacco and related products" and to the interdependence between both legislative objectives (para. 221).[47]

On 22 November 2018, the Court confirmed this view, stating that Directive 2014/40's twofold objective of facilitating the smooth functioning of the internal

[45] ECJ decision of 5 October 2000, Federal Republic of Germany v European Parliament and Council of the European Union, Case C-376/98, ECLI:EU:C:2000:544.

[46] ECJ decision of 10 December 2002, *The Queen v Secretary of State for Health, ex parte British American Tobacco (Investments) Ltd and Imperial Tobacco Ltd.*, Case C-491/01, ECLI:EU:C:2002:741, para. 182. In the area of food supplements but also focusing on the fact subsidiarity was complied with, because the uncoordinated development of national rules would create obstacles to trade between Member States and distortions of competition, vide ECJ decision of 12 July 2005, *The Queen v Secretary of State for Health and National Assembly for Wales*, Joined cases C-154/04 and C-155/04, ECLI:EU:C:2005:449, para. 106.

[47] ECJ decision of 4 May 2016, Philip Morris Brands SARL and Others v Secretary of State for Health, Case C-547/14, ECLI:EU:C:2016:325

market for tobacco, while ensuring a high level of protection of human health, could best be achieved at European level.[48]

An analysis of the case law shows that the Court of Justice of the European Union, after asserting the type of competence at hand, details the objective (or interdependence of objectives) of the measure adopted, without discussing the measure itself in length, separating conferral and subsidiarity and appraising only the latter. Within this framework it goes on to analyse the justification provided for compliance with the subsidiarity principle (based on its wording, but also its context, including the specific procedures followed and participations received, and the circumstances of the case) and the sufficiency of this justification from a formal and substantive point of view. It is at this point that the technical but also legal complexity of the measure and the areas of discretion come into place, given that the Court's review is made strictly within its role as a gatekeeper, without showing particular activism in this area as it has been accused of showing in others.[49]

However, even in that role, it is apparent that the Court does not, as a rule, perform a two-tiered analysis of the subsidiarity principle since its criteria are read altogether, which does not contribute to methodological stability in the assessment of the principle of subsidiarity. Of course, it can be argued that those criteria, both negative and positive, are enormously intertwined and that it is difficult to analyse them separately. However, this is also the case of the tests involved in the proportionality principle and, in this regard, case law has played a significant role in establishing the methodological soundness of this principle.

However, in the ECJ decision of 6 June 2019, *P. M. and Others v Ministerraad*, Case C-264/18, ECLI:EU:C:2019:472, the Court was called upon to analyse, under the principles of equality and subsidiarity, the exclusion of legal services from the scope of the public procurement directive. The Court considered, in this situation, that it was legitimate to adopt the view that national legislatures are best able to determine whether those services should be subject to the public procurement rules, given their specific *intuit personae* nature which renders them incomparable with other services, and therefore to decide not to include such services in the scope of the Directive (para. 21 and 38). Given these considerations, the Court did not consider that a European Union regulation would provide added value.

---

[48] ECJ decision of 22 November 2018, *Swedish Match AB v Secretary of State for Health*, Case C-151/17, ECLI:EU:C:2018:938, para. 64 to 76. In an example pertaining to roaming regulations, the interdependence between retail and wholesale charges for roaming services was also seen as a factor that led to the view that this twofold regulation was legitimate from a subsidiarity point of view (ECJ decision of 8 June 2010, *The Queen, on the application of Vodafone Ltd and Others v Secretary of State for Business, Enterprise and Regulatory Reform*, Case C-58/08, ECLI:EU:C:2010:321, para 78 to 79). This case is particularly interesting with regard to the conclusions of the Advocate General Poiares Maduro, who, despite considering that due to the transnational character of the economic activity in question (roaming), the European Union would be in a better position to balance all the costs and benefits of the intended action for the internal market, rebutted some of the arguments by the Council to support such a measure, related to price fixing.

[49] Or maybe showing a different type of activism, given the excessive deference to political powers, according to Moens and Trone (2015, p. 81).

More generally, in the cases it has been called upon to decide on subsidiarity issues, the Court of Justice of the European Union has played its part—although somewhat timidly so far—in establishing some features of this principle. For instance, in addition to the clarification of probatory issues incumbent upon the European Union (in Case T-374/04, mentioned above), the Court of Justice decision of 18 June 2015 defined that this principle cannot have the effect of rendering a European Union measure invalid because of the particular situation of a Member State, but involves a more global analysis (para 54 and 55) and that it is not necessary to require a specific statement of reasons for each of the technical choices made by the institution, as long as the contested measure clearly discloses the essential objective pursued (para 60).[50]

In any event, although the Court has, in our opinion, shown some promise in addressing the principle of subsidiarity, the quality of its case law is mostly dependent on the pronouncements on subsidiarity previously made at the administrative and legislative stages and if, indeed, reasons of economic, social or environmental nature were sufficiently addressed and specified, there, this will not allow for an "appropriate" level of scrutiny to be performed.[51]

4.3 Legislative Dimension

The legislative dimension[52] of control of the principle of subsidiarity has been centred, after the Treaty of Lisbon, on the innovative early warning system that allows for scrutiny of the principle of subsidiarity by national parliaments under Protocol no. 2.[53]

[50] ECJ decision of 18 June 2015, Judgment of the Court (Second Chamber) of 18 June 2015, Republic of Estonia v European Parliament and Council of the European Union, Case C-508/13, ECLI:EU:C:2015:403.

[51] The judicial principle of subsidiarity is neither a placebo nor a panacea (differently, Moens and Trone (2014, p. 163); and Moens and Trone (2015, pp. 65–80)), it is a challenging form of scrutiny that still needs to be entrenched into the European Union institutional system, in order to be an "appropriate judicial response" to particularly complex cases (De Búrca 1998, p. 234).

[52] We refer to a legislative dimension, given that this is included as a pre-legislative process in the procedures established in the Treaties. Indeed, before continuing with legislative procedures, the draft legislative acts must first be forwarded to the national parliaments.

[53] However, subsidiarity control goes far beyond the early warning system. As Bermann puts it, since "subsidiarity addresses issues that are ordinarily relegated to the political realm, then subsidiarity's central function must be its legislative one". "Subsidiarity thus essentially describes a method of policy analysis that each participant in the Community's legislative process should follow in deciding whether to propose, endorse, or enact a given measure" (Bermann 1994, pp. 378–382).

Essentially, national parliaments are informed of draft legislative acts by, in most cases, the Commission (Article 4 of Protocol no. 2)[54] and may express their opinion on the draft, in principle within 8 weeks,[55] employing a reasoned opinion stating why they consider that the draft in question does not comply with the principle of subsidiarity (Article 6 idem).

National parliaments have two votes, so that in the case of bicameral parliaments each chamber can be allocated one vote, to enable potential voting in a different sense by the different chambers [Article 7(1) ibidem].[56] In Portugal, both votes are allocated to the single chamber.

These opinions, provided they meet the legal requirements,[57] must always be taken into consideration [Article 7 (1) ibidem]. However, when reasoned opinions on a draft legislative act's non-compliance with the principle of subsidiarity represent at least one third of the total votes allocated to the national parliaments, or a quarter of these votes within the area of freedom, security and justice (Article 76 of the TFEU), the draft must be re-examined and the Commission (in most cases), or another institution which produced the draft legislative act, may maintain, amend or withdraw it, stating its reasons [Article 7 (2) ibidem]. This is usually described as a "yellow card" for the proposal in question.

If reasoned opinions on non-compliance with the principle of subsidiarity represent at least a simple majority of the total votes allocated to the national parliaments (this is described as an "orange card" being given), the Commission must re-examine the proposal. If the Commission chooses to maintain the proposal, it must specify in a reasoned opinion why it considers that it complies with the principle of subsidiarity. This opinion, together with the reasoned opinions of the national parliaments, must be submitted to the Union legislator for consideration during the ordinary legislative procedure. This takes place in two stages: the first, broader stage, before the conclusion of the first reading, in which the legislator (European Parliament and Council) considers the compatibility of the legislative proposal with the principle of subsidiarity; the second, stricter, where, if the legislator considers that the proposal is not compatible with the principle of subsidiarity (a majority of 55% of the members of the Council or a majority of the votes cast in the European

[54] Nonetheless, such draft legislative acts may come from other entities, as established in this article. For the sake of simplicity, we will refer only to the dominant situation (the Commission's initiative) across the text.

[55] Article 4 of Protocol no. 1 on the Role of National Parliaments in the European Union allows for exceptions in cases of urgency but does not allow for an extension of the eight-week delay.

[56] In order to reach a compromise between the need for intervention at the national level as part of assessment and the intention of not further complicating European Union decision-making procedures, regional parliaments with legislative powers are not directly involved, but only via the national parliaments, in accordance with the internal constitutional rules. Also, the hearing of private dimensions affected by the principle of subsidiarity are not formally encompassed in the Protocol. Nonetheless, this does not mean that national parliaments cannot set up those consultations as they see fit.

[57] They should originate from a national parliament or a chamber, relate to a draft European legislative act, be sent in time, and allege a reasoned violation of the principle of subsidiarity.

Parliament is required), the proposal will not be examined further and its adoption will be ruled out [Article 7 (3) ibidem]. Thus, the "orange card" may trigger a decision by the Union legislator to block the adoption of the measure in question, due to its lack of compatibility with the principle of subsidiarity.[58]

The opinions of national parliaments, therefore, have varying degrees of consequences, but these are essentially dependent on three main factors:

- the actual intervention of national parliaments;
- the degree of consensus reached globally by them on a particular draft legislative act and;
- the justification (compelling force) of the opinions issued.

However, these factors do not always coincide, which means that the effectiveness, legitimacy and democratisation sought from this mechanism are not always achieved to their fullest potential. Indeed, the activity of national parliaments has not been as prolific as one might think, due not only to the short timeline for issuing an opinion (which is a dissuasive factor, given that the internal organisation and functioning of parliaments are usually complex), but also to the practical need to prioritise domestic or European Union issues in the parliament's agenda (which is also related to the type of measures coming from the European level i.e. if they are more or less invasive).

The numbers speak for themselves. Looking back over the last 6 years, before the cut-off date of this article, thirty-seven reasoned opinions were received by the Commission in 2018, none in 2019, nine in 2020, sixteen in 2021, thirty-two in 2022 and twenty-two in 2023.[59]

Although the number of reasoned opinions was higher in the early years, the level of consensus reached between national parliaments or chambers on the same legislative draft was insufficient to reach the full potential of the early warning mechanism. Besides individual action, this mechanism, to be fruitful, requires joint or concerted interparliamentary action—so that besides "gatekeepers", the parliaments also become "networkers" (Sprungk 2013, pp. 551–552). Unfortunately, to date this has not led to significant results, despite the existence of several networking tools, for instance, the COSAC—Conference of Parliamentary Committees for Union Affairs of Parliaments of the European Union, and the permanent representatives of national parliaments in Brussels. This could be because to achieve this "horizontal dynamic" required from parliaments under the early warning system, national bureaucracies will need to adapt and to make their work transnational, and not all parliaments may be ready for this or be working at the same pace (Christiansen et al. 2014).

---

[58] A red card at the hands of the national parliaments was not established; indeed, not continuing with a measure that has given rise to questions regarding its subsidiarity implications is a matter for the Commission and the Parliament and the Council under the above-mentioned yellow and orange card procedures.

[59] For figures up until 2018 with analysis, cf. Matei and Dumitru (2020, pp. 1–15).

Indeed, to date, the 'orange card' procedure has never been triggered and the 'yellow card' procedure has only been triggered three times. In two of those cases, in 2013 and 2016, the Commission decided to maintain its proposal, after analysing the reasoned opinions received and explaining further the non-infringement of the principle of subsidiarity.[60] In one of the cases—and, indeed, the first one, in 2012—the Commission decided not to pursue its proposal for a regulation concerning the exercise of the right to take collective action within the context of the freedom of establishment and the freedom to provide services ('Monti II'), anticipating the troubles ahead when trying to regulate delicate issues such as the interconnections between fundamental freedoms and collective rights of workers, in particular the right to strike, that touch on essential features of the constitutional legal orders.[61]

Lastly, the opinions have not always been sufficiently or convincingly reasoned. Simply stating that there is an incompatibility with the principle of subsidiarity on political grounds, without giving compelling technical, economic and legal grounds for this opinion, provides little basis for reflection on the subsequent examination/consideration by the Commission, Parliament and Council, and ultimately the Court of Justice.[62] In fact, one of the reasons behind this legislative pre-procedure is to gather the data and arguments to confirm/infirm compliance with the principle under consideration. Therefore, another crucial element for the success of the early warning system is related with the willingness and capacity to conduct sound domestic subsidiarity checks, which requires motivation, involvement, time and knowledge and, of course, the enhancement of national parliaments' powers and means to review proposals, especially in troubled times such as those we are facing.[63]

These considerations show, at first glance, that the intended results of this early warning system have not been as overwhelming as expected. This is due, however,

---

[60] Respectively, Communication from the Commission to the European Parliament, the Council and the National Parliaments on the review of the proposal for a Council Regulation on the establishment of the European Public Prosecutor's Office with regard to the principle of subsidiarity, in accordance with Protocol No 2—**COM/2013/0851 final and** Communication from the Commission to the European Parliament, the Council and the National Parliaments on the proposal for a Directive amending the Posting of Workers Directive, with regard to the principle of subsidiarity, in accordance with Protocol No 2—COM/2016/0505 final. The first of those measures was adopted nonetheless under an enhanced cooperation framework which shows the longstanding impact of the objections raised (Council Regulation (EU) 2017/1939 of 12 October 2017 implementing enhanced cooperation on the establishment of the European Public Prosecutor's Office ('the EPPO')).

[61] On this decision cf. Barrett (2012, pp. 595–600), Goldoni (2014), and Fabbrini and Granat (2013).

[62] In many cases, however, "national parliaments, which are conventionally called political institutions, in fact engage in what can be best described as legal review. Parliaments thus behave in a court-like manner, accepting or at least attempting to use subsidiarity as a legal principle" and not only dealing with political statements (Kiiver 2012, p. 76).

[63] Donatella Viola considers that further Europeanisation of national parliaments and parliamentarisation of the European Union could be an antidote for the alienation regarding European politics (Viola 2021, p. 52).

not only to the shortcomings in the design and implementation of this mechanism[64] but also to the establishment by the Commission, in 2006, of the so-called "political dialogue" mechanism (under the "Barroso initiative"), which includes written exchanges on any Commission initiative that national Parliaments wish to give input or comment on and oral political dialogue. We will develop this issue further when analysing the role of the Portuguese Parliament, but to support our argument it is interesting to note, by way of comparison, that in 2023 22 reasoned opinions were received, whereas 402 political dialogue opinions were forwarded to the Commission.

In fact, the early warning system is not the only communication channel between the European Union law-making institutions and national parliaments. Although these other channels do not have the same legal strength, they tend to serve the same purpose, i.e. dialogue and cooperation between the European Union and national parliaments, but with the advantages of not being bound by strict deadlines, not requiring a "definitive" position on the subsidiarity principle, so that other public and private entities may be consulted in parallel and also so that other arguments (related to proportionality and conferral, for instance) may be brought to the table without having necessarily to define their limits, thus breaking out of the "straight-jacket" imposed by the early warning system (Jancic 2015, pp. 952–953).

5 The Contribution of the Portuguese Parliament to the Control and Application of the Principle of Subsidiarity

Turning now to the Portuguese legal system, merely by way of an example, Law no. 43/2006, 25 August 2006 (amended by Laws nos. 21/2012, 18/2018, 64/2020 and 44/2023) set out the forms of participation of the Portuguese Parliament (*Assembleia da República*) in monitoring the principle of subsidiarity and, in general, the activity of the European Union. This is the most significant institutional context, at the internal level, according to which the European political discussion should be focused and developed. The hope was that this framework would promote the involvement of citizens through their national representatives and not only through their representatives at European Parliament level, and also that it would prompt a change in how European politics was seen and discussed in the Portuguese parliament. Indeed, from a "system of informal influence" (Fraga 2001) where the Parliament's participation in European Union affairs was infrequent and indirect (exercised through the Government) the Parliament "has undergone a tacit renaissance in its engagement with EU policy and decision making", as a consequence of two factors: internal scrutiny reforms and the Barroso initiative, both dated 2006 (Jancic 2011, pp. 94–103).

---

[64] For a summary of the literature on these shortcomings and empirical evidence, cf. Gattermann and Hefftler (2015).

Jumping forward to the debate in the Portuguese Parliament prior to the approval of the 2012 legislation to amend Law no. 43/2006 and in the aftermath of the Lisbon Treaty,[65] one of the principal questions posed was, in the words of the member of the Parliament, Vitalino Canas, whether the "principle of non-binding intervention of the Portuguese Parliament" should be changed or at least tempered with greater respect from the Government for guidelines issued by the Portuguese Parliament. Vitalino Canas stressed that, from then on, the Portuguese Parliament would have "two sources of legitimacy to pronounce on themes related to European issues: one is the legitimacy that derives from the Portuguese Constitution; the other is the legitimacy innovatively recognised by the Treaty of Lisbon. On the strength of the former, the Parliament supervises the government and its action in the European context. On the strength of the latter, the Parliament scrutinises, controls and analyses acts of European Institutions that were previously out of its reach".

From a legislative point of view, Law no. 43/2006 provides that the Parliament will monitor and assess the Portuguese participation in the process of building the European Union, for instance by holding debates in plenary sessions with the participation of the Government, debates in the Committee on European Affairs (the Committee mainly dedicated to analysis of themes with European relevance, according to Articles 6 and 7), joint meetings between this Committee and the member of the Government with responsibility for European Affairs, and other parliamentary committees and hearings of persons nominated or appointed by the Government to European Union positions. In addition, the Parliament may also initiate debate on all matters and positions under discussion in the European institutions that involve matters within its competence (cf. Article 4). The Law also requires the Government to inform Parliament on all matters of relevance to European construction, and to present an annual report on the subject (Article 5). These provisions acknowledge the importance of debate and reflection on the European Union within the sovereign body, allowing for greater participation, and publicity and visibility of European issues. The Parliament, which is directly and centrally committed to the construction, deepening and consolidation of this process, is required to play a more active and critical role in it and in influencing the actions of the Portuguese Government.

As might be expected, this legislation also lays down the general rules on intervention of the Portuguese Parliament with regard to control of the application of the principle of subsidiarity (Article 3). The Committee on European Affairs, without prejudice to the competence of the plenary and other parliamentary committees, is primarily responsible for such action. Article 3(4) also states that "where the opinion concerns a matter that falls within the competence of the Legislative Assemblies of the autonomous regions, those Assemblies shall be consulted in a timely manner", which is in line with what is required by the Treaties but does not go beyond them.

[65] Official Journal of the Portuguese Parliament (Diário da Assembleia da República), I Series, No. 47/XII/1, 9 December 2011, pp. 55–63. Cf., also, Martins (2010) and Resende and Paulo (2017).

The specific rules governing this extremely important parliamentary intervention are not defined globally and it is left to the Committee on European Affairs to define a method, which has changed over the years (Article 6(3)).

The first point to make regarding Portugal's application of the early warning system is that Portuguese participation has not been extensive and the number of negative opinions (claiming non-compliance with the principle of subsidiarity, in the form of Parliamentary Resolutions) has been limited, with only four so far.

Nevertheless, rather than focusing on the quantity, the quality of these opinions on the principle of subsidiarity should be studied, because they are demonstrative of the technical and argumentative capacity of national parliaments.

Taking these examples as a basis for our analysis, the first reasoned opinion was issued in 2011 (Parliament Resolution no. 147/2011, of 11 November),[66] in relation to COM(2011)560.[67] Regarding the proposed community procedures for temporary reintroduction of border control at internal borders in exceptional circumstances (at the request of the member states, on the initiative of the Commission, and on the initiative of the Member States, though only in absolutely exceptional cases and limited to a period of 5 days), the Resolution considered that the subsidiarity principle was not respected given that Member States are the entities best placed to decide on issues of threats to public order and internal security. Therefore, each Member State can achieve the regulation objectives better *per se*. The Resolution expressed the view that these questions are reserved for national sovereignty and, therefore, should not be regulated at European Union level. In this case, the interconnection between the conferral and subsidiarity principles was visible and difficult to separate in the opinion issued.

It should also be stressed that, in 2013, on the proposed tobacco regulation (contained in COM(2012)788[68]), several tobacco companies and the Regional Parliament of Azores were heard, raising questions of subsidiarity that were followed up in the draft resolution. In the reasoned opinion, both subsidiarity and proportionality aspects were considered. The fact that public health is only a support competence of the European Union was addressed, as was the fact that some of the proposed regulations are imprecise and indefinite and this prevents the development of national strategies regarding the consumption of tobacco. In addition, it was argued that the proposal did not clearly show the benefits arising from the transfer of regulatory powers to the European Union.[69]

[66] Parliament Reference RPE-UE_39/XII/1.

[67] Proposal for a Regulation of the European Parliament and of the Council amending Regulation (EC) No 562/2006 in order to provide for common rules on the temporary reintroduction of border control at internal borders in exceptional circumstances.

[68] Proposal for a Directive of the European Parliament and of the Council on the approximation of the laws, regulations and administrative provisions of the Member States concerning the manufacture, presentation and sale of tobacco and related products.

[69] Parliament Reference RPE-EU_349XII-2, followed by the Portuguese Parliament Resolution no. 38/2013, of 26 March.

In the case of the reasoned opinion on non-compliance with the principle of subsidiarity of the Proposal for a Council Regulation on the exercise of the right to take collective action within the context of the freedom of establishment and the freedom to provide services [COM(2012)130], the scrutiny of the Committee on European Affairs was deeper and the assessments more convincing, despite going beyond the relevance of the principle of subsidiarity. The opinion discussed the constitutionality of the proposed measure, since it regulates collective action, and the limits of the European Union's own competences. It relied on the unnecessary change in the jurisdictional procedures regarding the definition and adjudication of these issues, as well as the nature and function of the flexibility clause provided for in Article 352 TFEU.[70] The conclusion reached was that the Proposal's objective would not be more effectively achieved by Union action, and, therefore, there was no need for a shift in the balance of competences. It should be noted that the Committee on Constitutional Affairs, Rights, Freedoms and Guarantees and the Committee on Social Security were both of the opinion, contrary to that which was finally concluded, that there was no incompatibility with the subsidiarity principle.

Lastly, in Portugal's reasoned opinion on the Proposal for a Decision of the European Parliament and of the Council on establishing an information exchange mechanism concerning intergovernmental agreements and non-binding instruments in the field of energy [COM(2016) 53 final], the Parliament noted the lack of added value of European Union intervention resulting from the proposed shift of competences.[71] Despite recognising the growing importance of the construction of an Energy Union, the opinion stated that, at that time, the Member States were still in a better position to guarantee those objectives. It also took the view that the course of action to be taken by the European Union should have been the one analysed as option 2 in the impact assessment presented, i.e. the introduction of model clauses in those agreements, which would better satisfy the principles of subsidiarity and proportionality.

This very limited intervention by the Portuguese Parliament has one main explanation, which has already been mentioned. In addition to the Parliament predefining a list of European initiatives that are considered to be a priority for scrutiny (which significantly limits the type and number of initiatives under the Parliament's radar),[72] it also began to give preference to the use of more informal political mechanisms of intervention, still analysing compliance with the principle of subsidiarity, but through political dialogue either with the European institutions, mostly the European Commission, or internally with the Portuguese Government, in order for the Government to forward Parliament's views to the competent European institutions.[73]

---

[70] Parliament Reference RPE-EU 226/XII/1, followed by the Portuguese Parliament Resolution no. 76/2012, of 18 May.

[71] Portuguese Parliament Resolution no. 89/2016, of 24 May.

[72] For 2023, the list is defined in Portuguese Parliament Resolution no. 45/2023, of 11 May.

[73] As happened under Resolution no. 53/2022, of 8 August, of the Portuguese Parliament on COM/2022/0245 and COM/2022/0247, and under Resolution no. 55/2002, of 10 August, on the

The numbers contained in the Commission's annual reports provide evidence of this situation. The Portuguese Parliament has been particularly active in the realm of political dialogue, being one of the ten most active Parliaments or chambers usually mentioned in those reports. In 2021, national Parliaments sent 360 opinions to the Commission, 54 of these came from the Portuguese Parliament (this number was only exceeded by the 57 opinions from the Spanish *Cortes Generales*). In 2022, the total number of opinions was of 355 from which Portugal sent 19 (sixth place) and in 2023, from 402 opinions 41 came from the Portuguese Parliament (first place *ex aequo* with the Czech Senát).

This is illustrative of the path chosen by the Portuguese Parliament, which prefers to use political dialogue rather than the more structured legal procedure set out in Protocol 2. This also seems to be the case with the Parliaments of some other Member States.[74]

We should also note that the Portuguese Parliament's participation is not limited to issuing resolutions within the scope of legislative acts but also extends to appreciation and intervention within the scope of non-legislative procedures or non-binding acts, such as European Commission Communications. Furthermore, opinions are sometimes issued in support of the Commission's proposal for a legislative decision, stating that the principle of subsidiarity has been complied with, although comments are presented on the limits of Community intervention.

Although these latter opinions demonstrate the position of the Portuguese Parliament, they do not have well-defined legal consequences, other than those resulting from the duty of sincere cooperation, which also places duties on the European Union institutions to dialogue fruitfully with national institutions and to consider their views.[75] The Commission is currently developing this practice, as we shall see.

6 Subsidiarity Principle: Where to Go from Here?

Due to its importance as a structuring principle, subsidiarity is and will remain a hot topic within European Union Law. The questions surrounding it, however, are being reshaped. On one hand, while in the past the justiciability of the principle was called into question (Toth 1994, p. 268 et seq), the Court of Justice is now showing some promise when addressing subsidiarity. On the other hand, the pledged early warning system has come to a stalemate, and it is possible, responding to Kiiver (2006, p. 6),

European Parliament Legislative Resolution of 3 May 2022 on the proposal for a Council Regulation on the election of the members of the European Parliament by direct universal suffrage, of 3 May 2022.

[74] António Gameiro states that political dialogue has become a daily practice in most national parliaments and is an integral part of the European system of governance (Gameiro 2012, p. 497).

[75] Martinico highlights the intimate link between subsidiarity and sincere cooperation (Martinico 2011, pp. 658–660).

that the parliaments have not lived up to the expectations raised by the introduction of this type of legislative control. However, this does not mean that the national parliaments are no longer the main entrusted "watchdogs" (Cooper 2006) or "gate-keepers" (Raunio 2011) of the subsidiarity principle; they are simply adopting more flexible formats to perform these roles.[76]

From a political point of view that has been ever present, the various forms of political dialogue within the European Union have prompted a qualitative change due to their widespread use. In the Communication from the Commission to the European Parliament, the European Council, the Council, the European Economic and Social Committee and the Committee of the Regions COM(2018) 703 Final, p. 8, the Commission states that it "intends to prepare an aggregated response where a significant number of national parliaments have raised similar concerns even where the threshold for a "yellow card" is not attained", adding that "opinions of regional Parliaments with legislative powers sent directly to the Commission could also be reflected". This means that the Commission has drawn some legal effects from political participation in the principle of subsidiarity, committing itself to a "qualified" balancing and response in cases where the appraisal of subsidiarity is under check.

Given this, it can no longer be said that the "principle of subsidiarity has remained a subsidiary principle of European constitutionalism" (Schütze 2009, p. 526). On the contrary, its conceptual contours are now better defined, mostly with the recently introduced subsidiarity grid, and are applied at an administrative level with more care and competence. Moreover, this seems to be the structural level to which a discretional principle such as the principle of subsidiarity should be tied to: it is in the administrative sphere that studies and assessments are carried out and that the fulfillment of the negative and positive criteria of subsidiarity are justified, allowing for their subsequent (legislative or judicial) control.

Furthermore, different approaches to subsidiarity are now being tested, as is shown by the concept of active subsidiarity,[77] highly regarded by the Committee of the Regions and the Commission, especially in the aftermath of the Conference on the Future of Europe and the Recovery and Resilience Mechanism, as a way to involve multi-governance levels and also other actors and networks in the discussion of subsidiarity. Thus, elements that appeared to be absent from the analysis of subsidiarity have been added to it, such as partnership and coordination between all levels of government and society.

A question remains: Will this be enough? The answer is probably never—as nothing ever seems to be sufficient in the European Union area, but we believe that the principle of subsidiarity has reached an age of maturity and can be regarded as a well-established and fundamental principle of law that will continue to run its

[76] Jancic proposes a fundamental reform of both the early warning system and the political dialogue, in order for national parliaments to play a more active role as policy shapers and not merely policy commentators, for instance through the introduction of so-called "green cards", similar to the European citizens' initiative (Jancic 2015).

[77] For a general conceptual approach cf. Calame (1996).

course, and, along the way, respond to its main critics. Indeed, if we trace Marquardt's summary of the main criticisms of subsidiarity—"the multiple meanings of the word, its incomplete application to EU institutions to date, the difficulty of conducting the required analyses, and its unenforceability" (Marquardt 1994, p. 628)—all of them seem to have been dealt with in time, through the development of *ex ante, ex post* and *ad intra* mechanisms to ensure better application of the principle and the development of real control possibilities. And these developments are still taking place as we finish this chapter.

References

Barrett G (2012) Monti II: the subsidiary review process comes of age or then again maybe it doesn't. Maastricht J Eur Comp Law 19:595

Bermann GA (1994) Taking subsidiarity seriously: federalism in the European Community and the United States. Columbia Law Rev 94:331–456

Biondi A (2012) Subsidiarity in the courtroom. In: Biondi A, Eeckhout P, Ripley S (eds) EU law after Lisbon. Oxford University Press, Oxford, pp 213–227

Borońska-Hryniewiecka K (2013a) Legitimacy through subsidiarity? The parliamentary control of EU policy-making. Pol Political Sci Rev 1:73–86

Borońska-Hryniewiecka K (2013b) Regions and subsidiarity after Lisbon: overcoming the" regional blindness"? Working paper series of the LUISS school of government, SOG-WP3/2013. LUISS School of Government, Via di Villa Emiliani

Calame P (1996) The principle of active subsidiarity - reconciling unity and diversity. FPH, Rte de Praz Véguey

Christiansen T, Högenauer AL, Neuhold C (2014) National parliaments in the post-Lisbon European Union: bureaucratization rather than democratization? Comp Eur Politics 12:121–140

Cooper IAN (2006) The watchdogs of subsidiarity: national parliaments and the logic of arguing in the EU. JCMS J Common Mark Stud 44:281–304

Correia JS (2000) Portugal. In: Andersen R, Déom D (eds) Droit administratif et subsidiarité. Bruylant, Brussels

Craig P (2012) Subsidiarity: a political and legal analysis. JCMS J Common Mark Stud 50:72–87

Davies G (2006) Subsidiarity: the wrong idea, in the wrong place, at the wrong time. Common Mark Law Rev 43:63–84

De Búrca G (1998) The principle of subsidiarity and the court of justice as an institutional actor. JCMS J Common Mark Stud 36:217–235

De Búrca G (2000) Reappraising subsidiarity's significance after Amsterdam, Jean Monnet working paper 7/99. Harvard Law School, Harvard

de Quadros F (1997) O princípio da subsidiariedade no Tratado da União Europeia, Em torno da revisão do Tratado da União Europeia, Almedina. In: de Quadros F (ed) Em torno da revisão do Tratado da União Europeia. Almedina, Coimbra, pp 231–247

Duarte ML (1997) A teoria dos poderes implícitos e a delimitação de competências entre a União Europeia e os Estados-membros. Lex, Lisbon

Duarte ML (2006) A aplicação jurisdicional do princípio da subsidiariedade no direito comunitário pressupostos e limites, estudos de direito da união e das comunidades Europeias. Coimbra Editora, Coimbra

Emiliou N (1996) The principle of proportionality in European law: a comparative study. Kluwer Law International, The Hague

Evans M (2013) The principle of subsidiarity in European Union law: some comparisons with Catholic social teaching. Solidar J Cathol Soc Thought Secul Ethics 3:5

Fabbrini F, Granat K (2013) Yellow card, but no foul: the role of the national parliaments under the subsidiarity protocol and the commission proposal for an EU regulation on the right to strike. Common Mark Law Rev 50:115–143
Follesdal A (2013) The principle of subsidiarity as a constitutional principle in international law. Glob Const 2:37–62
Fonseca MR (2020) Subsidiariedade como Instituição na Europa: dos pequenos passos ao futuro comum. Principia, Cascais
Fraga A (2001) The parliament of Portugal: loyal scrutiny and informal influence. In: Wessels AM (ed) National parliaments on their ways to Europe: losers or latecomers? Nomos Verlagsgesellschaft, Baden-Baden, pp 359–375
Gameiro A (2012) O papel dos parlamentos nacionais na União Europeia. Coimbra Editora, Coimbra
Gattermann K, Hefftler C (2015) Beyond institutional capacity: political motivation and parliamentary behaviour in the early warning system. West Eur Politics 38:305–334
Gernat S (2013) Interpreting subsidiarity–how to develop into a constitutional principle? MaRBLe 4:187–237
Goldoni M (2014) The early warning system and the Monti II regulation: the case for a political interpretation. Eur Const Law Rev 10:90–108
Gorjão-Henriques M (2019) Direito da união-história, direito, cidadania, mercado interno e concorrência. Livraria Almedina, Coimbra
Horsley T (2012) Subsidiarity and the European court of justice: missing pieces in the subsidiarity jigsaw? JCMS J Common Mark Stud 50:267–282
Jachtenfuchs M, Krisch N (2016) Subsidiarity in global governance. Law Contemp Probl 79:1–26
Jancic D (2011) The Portuguese parliament: blazing the trail to the European scrutiny trophy? Interdiscip Political Stud 1:93–108
Jancic D (2015) The game of cards: national parliaments in the EU and the future of the early warning mechanism and the political dialogue. Common Mark Law Rev 52:939–975
Kiiver P (2006) The national parliaments in the European Union: a critical view on EU constitution-building. Kluwer Law International, The Hague
Kiiver P (2012) The early warning system for the principle of subsidiarity—constitutional theory and empirical reality. Routledge, Oxford
Klammert M (2014) The principle of loyalty in EU law. Oxford University Press, Oxford
Lanceiro RT (2018) The implementation of EU law by national administrations: executive federalism and the principle of sincere cooperation. Perspect Fed 10:71–102
Lopes D (2008) A articulação de competências entre união e estados-membros no Tratado de Lisboa. Gráfica de Coimbra, Almedina
Lopes D (2018) O princípio da subsidiariedade: o seu contributo para a organização administrative. In: Gomes CA, Neves AF, Tiago S (eds) Organização administrativa: novos actores, novos modelos. AAFDL, Lisboa, pp 129–152
Machado JEM (2018) Direito da união Europeia. Gestlegal, Coimbra
Maletic I (2015) The role of the principle of subsidiarity in the EU'S lifestyle risk policy. In: Allemano A, Garde A (eds) Regulating lifestyles: Europe, tobacco, alcohol and unhealthy diets. Cambridge University Press, Cambridge, pp 197–214
Mangerona STGLG (2021) A subsidiariedade: doutrina política e modelo de estado. Principia, Cascais
Marauhn T, Mengeler D (2021) The subsidiarity principle at the interface of law and politics. In: Walzenbach G, Alleweldt R (eds) Varieties of European subsidiarity: a multidisciplinary approach. E-International Relations, pp 1–6
Marquardt PD (1994) Subsidiary and sovereignty in the European Union. Fordham Int Law J 18:616–639
Martinico G (2011) Dating Cinderella: on subsidiarity as a political safeguard of federalism in the European Union. Eur Public Law 17:649–660

Martins AMG (1995) O artigo 235.° do Tratado da Comunidade Europeia: cláusula de alargamento das competências dos órgãos comunitários. Lex, Lisbon
Martins MSO (2003) O princípio da subsidiariedade em perspectiva jurídico-política. Coimbra Editora, Coimbra
Martins PF (2005) O princípio do primado do direito comunitário sobre as normas constitucionais dos estados-membros dos tratados ao projecto de constituição Europeia. Principia, Cascais
Martins MSDO (2010) O Tratado de Lisboa e o novo regime do princípio da subsidiariedade e o papel reforçado dos parlamentos nacionais. Cad Direito 5:131–148
Matei A, Dumitru AS (2020) The subsidiarity principle and national parliament's role: from formal need to real use of powers. Adm Sci 10:24
Moens GA, Trone J (2014) Subsidiarity as judicial and legislative review principles in the European Union. In: Evans M, Zimmermann A (eds) Global perspectives on subsidiarity. Springer, Dordrecht, pp 157–183
Moens GA, Trone J (2015) The principle of subsidarity in EU judicial and legislative practice: panacea or placebo. J Legis 41:65–102
Morais CB (1998) A dimensão interna do princípio da subsidiariedade no ordenamento português. Rev Ordem Advog 58:779–821
Otero P (2007) Legalidade e administração pública—o sentido da vinculação administrativa à juridicidade. Almedina, Coimbra
Panara C (2016) The enforceability of subsidiarity in the EU and the ethos of cooperative federalism: a comparative law perspective. Eur Public Law 22:1–27
Paulus AL (2008) Subsidiarity, fragmentation and democracy: towards the demise of general international law? In: Braude T, Shani Y (eds) The shifting allocation of authority in international law: considering sovereignty, supremacy and subsidiarity. Hart Publishing, Portland, pp 193–213
Pelkmans J (2006) Testing for subsidiarity. Bruges European economic policy (BEEP) briefing 13/2006. College of Europe, Bruges
Piedrafita S (2013) EU democratic legitimacy and national parliaments, CEPS essays no. 7. CEPS, Brussels
Pimenova O (2016) Subsidiarity as a 'regulation principle' in the EU. Theory Pract Legis 4:381–398
Popelier P, Vandenbruwaene W (2011) The subsidiarity mechanism as a tool for inter-level dialogue in Belgium: on 'regional blindness' and cooperative flaws. Eur Const Law Rev 7:204–228
Raimundo MA (2019) Novos desafios da legalidade administrativa: o caso da eficiência como princípio jurídico. In: Gomes CA, Neves AF, Neto EB, Motta F (eds) O direito administrativo nos 30 anos da constituição Brasileira de 1988. FDL, London, pp 130–143
Raunio T (2011) The gatekeepers of European integration? The functions of national parliaments in the EU political system. J Eur Integr 33:303–321
Resende MM, Paulo MT (2017) A implementação do Tratado de Lisboa: o parlamento português enquanto ator na esfera legislativa europeia. In: Teixeira NS, Pinto AC (eds) A Europeização da Democracia Portuguesa. Imprensa de Ciências Sociais (ICS), Lisboa, pp 59–86
Rinderle P (2021) The political philosophy of European subsidiarity. In: Walzenbach G, Alleweldt R (eds) Varieties of European subsidiarity: a multidisciplinary approach. E-International Relations, pp 1–9
Saraiva R (2001) Sobre o princípio da subsidiariedade (Génese, evolução, interpretação e aplicação). AAFDL, Lisboa
Schilling T (1994) A new dimension of subsidiarity: subsidiarity as a rule and a principle. Yearb Eur Law 14:203–255
Schütze R (2004) Parallel external powers in the European community: from'cubist'perspectives towards' naturalist'constitutional principles? Yearb Eur Law 23:225–274
Schütze R (2009) Subsidiarity after Lisbon: reinforcing the safeguards of federalism? Camb Law J 68:525–536
Soares AG (1996) Repartição de competências e preempção no direito comunitário. Edições Cosmos, Lisbon

Sorace D (2013) L'amministrazione europea secondo il Trattato di Lisbona. Dirit Pubblico 19:167–238
Sprungk C (2013) A new type of representative democracy? Reconsidering the role of national parliaments in the European Union. J Eur Integr 35:547–563
Timmermans C (2014) ECJ doctrines on competences. In: Azoulai L (ed) The question of competence in the European Union. Oxford University Press, Oxford, pp 155–167
Toth AG (1994) Is subsidiarity justiciable? Eur Law Rev 19:268–285
Trachtman JP (1992) L'etat, C'est nous: sovereignty, economic integration and subsidiarity. Harv Int Law J 33:459
Van Zeben J (2014) Subsidiarity in European environmental law: a competence allocation approach. Harv Environ Law Rev 38:415–464
Viola DM (2021) National parliaments in the EU: synergy under the subsidiarity principle? In: Walzenbach G, Alleweldt R (eds) Varieties of European subsidiarity: a multidisciplinary approach. E-International Relations, pp 1–8

Dulce Lopes Univ Coimbra, University of Coimbra Institute for Legal Research, Faculty of Law, Coimbra, Portugal.

Rule of Law

Courts and the Protection of Democracy

Miguel Poiares Maduro

1 Democracy and Human Rights

There are growing concerns about the state of democracy in Europe and the world. The Secretary-General of the Council of Europe has talked of a democratic decline. These concerns reflect what many perceive as growing challenges to democracy. In this text, I will consider the role of courts, and in particular transnational courts, in the face of these challenges.

The protection of democracy has always been at the core of the judicial role. This is particularly the case for courts entrusted with the application and protection of a Constitution or human rights charter. This is so even though constitutionalism and the protection of human rights have also, at times, been misleadingly presented as a limit to democracy. In this light, constitutionalism established the borders of political action, i.e. the limits that power, including democratic power, needed to respect in order to protect human rights. This limited vision still has a considerable influence in how the role of courts is presented regarding the protection of human rights and constitutionalism. Often, the role of human rights and constitutional courts is presented as being focused on protecting fundamental rights from potential abuses of the democratic process. However, this conveys a limited and wrong understanding of democracy, constitutionalism and fundamental rights and, as a consequence, of the courts themselves.

This text was the basis for a Speech given at the Judicial Seminar Opening the Judicial Year of the European Court of Human Rights, in January 2023.

M. P. Maduro (✉)
Católica Global School of Law, Lisbon, Portugal
e-mail: lmaduro@ucp.pt

I. Quadros, M. Gorjão-Henriques (eds.), *Revisiting the Liberal Constitutional Features of the European Union*, https://doi.org/10.1007/978-3-031-95717-8_5

This vision is based, in the first place, on an understanding of democracy that tends to reduce it to majority voting. Democracy, and the idea of self-government, is based on the equal political dignity of all citizens. This requires both an equal voice in the political process and equal consideration of the interests of all citizens by that political process (hence, taking into account how they may be disparately affected). Protecting these two dimensions of democracy requires much more than free elections. It requires those elections to take place in a manner that allows all views to be expressed and to be compared with each other. It also requires citizens' political preferences to be formed, as far as possible, on the basis of rational and honest cognitive and epistemological processes. Without rationality and truth, there is no genuine democracy as the preferences expressed by citizens will be false. The difference with other processes is that in democracy truth is itself the product of pluralism and not hierarchically imposed. In addition, the broader conception of democracy also requires checks and balances and fundamental rights, in order to prevent any occasional majority from entrenching itself in power or abusing its power against the interests of those in the minority (ignoring, therefore, the democratic requirement to take all citizens' interests into equal account).

This understanding of democracy has increasingly become mainstream in the scholarship and in the case-law of the courts. It regards human rights and the rule of law as inextricably linked to (if not part of) democracy and vice versa. It is often referred to as the concept of liberal democracy. It includes free and fair elections, fundamental rights, separation of powers, judicial independence and certain general principles of law, such as legal certainty, legal clarity, transparency and effective judicial protection.

This bond between democracy and human rights is recognised in the preamble to the European Convention of Human Rights, which states that human rights and freedoms are best maintained by an effective political democracy. It is also enshrined in the case-law of the European Court of Human Rights. The Court has stated that "the Convention was designed to maintain and promote the ideals and values of a democratic society" and, furthermore that "democracy thus appears to be the only political model contemplated by the Convention and, accordingly, the only one compatible with it."[1]

This assumes that, on one hand, without democracy there can be no effective protection of human rights since there will be no effective recognition and protection of many of those rights and no political institutions embedded with the necessary culture to respect such rights. Equally, on the other hand, without human rights there can be no real democracy. In fact, as I expressed before, the deliberative, cognitive and epistemological conditions necessary for genuine democracy are predicated on certain human rights. Without the protection of those rights there can be no democracy. In addition, the equal political dignity of citizens, which is the

[1] United Communist Party of Turkey and Others v. Turkey, 30 January 1998, Reports of Judgments and Decisions 1998-I.

core of democracy, requires protection of the equal consideration of their interests, including by imposing certain limits on the political process.

2 The Role of Courts in Protecting Democracy

In this way, it is possible to connect the human rights case-law of the courts with democracy beyond the political rights and freedoms and the checks and balances that the courts often protect. It is the latter, however, that take centre stage in the judicial protection of democracy.

This is visible in the case-law of the European Court of Human Rights. The Court protects rights, such as the freedom of expression or of association, that are the backbone of the open and discursive sphere required by democracy. The Court has made it clear that the protection of these rights, in connection with democracy, extends, beyond mere free speech, to the protection and promotion of media and political pluralism and, even further, of a rich and diverse civil society.[2] It follows from the case-law of the court that protecting democracy requires more than the protection of political speech and political organisations. It requires the protection of other forms of discourse and association that are part of the public sphere and that are necessary for a rich and genuine democracy. At the same time, the Court has demonstrated its sensitivity to the quality and integrity of such discourse. This is so when it protects the independence and integrity of journalism or of public broadcasters, but also regarding how it addresses the risks of disinformation, including in the new digital public sphere.

Following Article 3 of Protocol 1 the Court also protects electoral democracy. This includes the right to vote and stand for election. However, to effectively protect these rights it is also necessary to protect the democratic character of the institutions and processes upon which they depend. This includes a variety of issues, from reviewing electoral procedures to protecting political actors, such as parliamentarians.

As happens with many national constitutions, the European Court of Human Rights has made it clear that democracy is not a suicide pact and that democracy is entitled to defend itself against anti-democratic forces. In this respect, it appears to me that the Court's case-law on militant democracy is very much in line with that of national constitutional courts. It is not enough for certain social movements or political parties to expose ideas that may be contrary to democracy. It is necessary that they constitute an actual threat to democracy by acting to undermine democracy or advocating violence in the pursuit of those ideas. It is not necessary to wait until such organisations come to power. But the risk needs to be, in the words of the Court, "sufficiently imminent".[3]

---

[2] See, in particular, Ecodefence and Others v. Russia, 14 June 2022.

[3] Judgment in Refah Partisi (the Welfare Party) and Others v. Turkey [GC], ECHR 2003-II.

Unlike the European Court of Human Rights, the European Court of Justice is not a human rights court. However, it has increasingly become involved in human rights and democratic issues by virtue of two, seemingly contradictory, trends. One of these limits EU powers, while the other expands them. The first is a consequence of the introduction of a fundamental rights review of the powers granted to the EU institutions. As certain powers moved from the state to the European level, it became necessary to accompany that transfer with instruments and standards of fundamental rights review similar to those applicable in the national legal orders of the EU Member States. This is the well-known, if not always consensual, story of the "Pretorian" introduction of fundamental rights review by the European Court of Justice, in dialogue with the national constitutional courts, followed by its recognition and enshrinement in the Treaties and, later, complemented by the Charter of Fundamental Rights. The European Convention of Human Rights, together with the case-law of the Court, played a leading role in this story, as the most important instrument in determining the constitutional traditions common to all EU Member States upon which the development of EU fundamental rights took off.

The second European Union fundamental rights trend is more recent and is bound to be more controversial. It initially emerged in a piecemeal manner as the application of other EU rules, such as those on free movement, had the potential to raise fundamental rights issues, some of them deeply connected to democracy. A public broadcasting monopoly was challenged as restricting both the provision of services and the freedom of information. The lack of media pluralism in a particular Member State was also at the heart of a challenge under EU rules aimed at protecting competition and access to that State's media market. EU legislation seeking to prohibit discrimination on the basis of age was also used to try to prevent national legislation aimed at packing the judiciary in a particular Member State. This indirect application of EU fundamental rights to address national democracy issues has been progressively complemented by rules aimed at directly tackling such issues. Some of these rules are embodied in legislation adopted under existing EU competences. A primary example, in the area of fundamental rights, is the legislation adopted in the field of non-discrimination. But of particular interest for the protection of democracy are the recent general regime of conditionality for the protection of the Union budget and the pending proposed Regulation on Media Freedom and Pluralism. This trend has also been furthered by Treaty developments, notably Article 7 of the Treaty on European Union, which created a political instrument aimed at monitoring, and sanctioning, possible breaches by the Member States of the values set out in Article 2 of the same Treaty, notably democracy, the rule of law and respect for human rights. As mentioned, this provision is, however, a political instrument that has proved ineffective in the face of increased challenges to these values in certain EU Member States.

In this context, the European Commission and litigants have explored other avenues for bringing potential violations of fundamental rights and the rule of law in EU Member States before the European Court of Justice. Unfortunately, time constraints prevent me from describing in detail the debate that has taken place, in that respect, in both the legal and political spheres.

The extent to which EU fundamental rights can be used to review the acts of Member States can be seen as an issue of the incorporation of EU fundamental rights into national legal orders. This brings to mind the process through which the American Supreme Court incorporated the Bill of Rights of the American Constitution[4] (which initially was only directed at the federal government) into the due process clause directed at the individual states. This process made the Bill of Rights applicable to the individual states even within their purely domestic arenas. No such fully fledged incorporation has yet occurred in EU law. The European Court of Justice (CJEU) has extended the initial reach of EU fundamental rights to also cover Member State's actions but only when they fall within the scope of application of EU law, notably when they either implement EU law or derogate from it.[5]

3 Upholding the Rule of Law in EU Member States

More recently, however, the European Court of Justice, in the context of a series of cases involving challenges to judicial independence, has applied a treaty-based provision not limited by the traditional scope of application of EU fundamental rights under Article 51(1) of the Charter, in order to effectively address rule of law issues in Member States. That provision is Article 19(1) TEU, which requires the Court to guarantee that the law is observed and requires Member States to ensure effective legal protection in the fields covered by EU law. The Court concluded that Article 19 TEU gives 'concrete expression to the value of the rule of law stated in Article 2 TEU', and ensures mutual trust between Member States, in particular with regard to the common values on which the European Union was founded.[6] Furthermore, the Court stated that 'the very existence of effective judicial review designed to ensure compliance with EU law is of the essence of the rule of law'.[7] The latter includes the right to a fair trial which, in turn (and in a similar way to the European Court of Human Rights), requires the protection of judicial independence.[8]

In my view, there is nothing surprising in this case-law. In fact, as Advocate General I argued in favour of a similar approach in the Centro Europa 7 case. As I stated then, "that type of review flows logically from the nature of the process of European integration. It serves to guarantee that the basic conditions are in place for the proper functioning of the EU legal order and for the effective exercise of many of the rights granted to European citizens".[9]

---

[4] The Bill of Rights corresponds to the first ten amendments of the American Constitution.

[5] See Case 5/88 Wachauf v Germany [1989] ECR 2609; and Case C-260/89 Elliniki Radiophonia Tileorassi AE v Domitiki Etairia Pliroforissis and Sotiris Kouvelas [1991] ECR I-2925.

[6] Ibid., Paras 30 and 32.

[7] Ibid., Para 36 and Case C-72/15, *Rosneft* [2017] EU:C:2017:236 [2017] 3 CMLR 23, Para 73.

[8] C-216/18 PPU, *LM* (n 28) Para 48.

[9] Ibid., Para 20.

I believe this approach is bound to be tested in other fields, in particular with regard to issues of democracy. Consider the requirements, enshrined in Articles 10 and 14 TEU, that the Union must be based on representative democracy and that elections for the European Parliament must be free. The protection of free and fair elections and a democratically elected and functioning European Parliament requires certain minimum conditions to be guaranteed in all Member States. It is not possible to distinguish between compliance with these conditions for the purposes of national elections and democracy or for the purposes of European ones. Sooner or later, the European Court of Justice is going to be called on to assess whether or not these conditions are being respected in a particular Member State in the context of a challenge to the outcome of the European Parliament elections in that State.

As a consequence, the European Court of Justice will increasingly be involved in protecting democracy in EU Member States. How the EU court performs this role, however, is bound to be shaped by the particular direction of its own case-law, rather than that of the European Court of Human Rights. Any review undertaken by the Court of Justice concerning Member States' national issues of democracy is instrumental in protecting the EU political democracy and the legal order itself. This leads to a more systemic approach. In other words, the Court of Justice is focused on whether the cases before it expose a systemic problem capable of spilling over to the EU itself. This provides ground for both convergence and a complementarity between the role of the European Court of Human Rights and that of the ECJ. To understand the reasons for this, it is also important to understand the various reasons behind the roles played by these two transnational or supranational courts.

There are three possible normative reasons for a transnational court to be given a role in protecting democracy (including fundamental rights) in a State's domestic sphere.

The first reason is, paradoxically, purely internal to the States themselves. It consists of adding an external layer of constitutional discipline 'on top of' the domestic constitution. It amounts to a form of collective self-discipline that Member States have imposed upon themselves because past experience has shown that domestic constitutional mechanisms are not always effective in protecting fundamental rights and democracy.

The second reason is based on the moral and political externalities that such breaches of democracy and human rights may cause in other States. Of course, the concept of moral and political externalities is controversial, in particular in the absence of a consensus about the concept of an international community. However, when Member States make a commitment to share a certain political and economic space (that can be embodied in a Treaty such as the European Convention or the EU Treaties) it is legitimate to argue that underlying that commitment is an assumption that they all share a certain common set of fundamental values and that any breach of those values would call into question the entire collective transnational endeavour.

There is a third possible reason, which is particularly relevant in the case of the European Union. EU Member States have entered a form of integration that increases their interdependence to such an extent that breaches of the rule of law, democracy, and fundamental rights by one Member State can directly impact the other Member States. This may be so either because the latter are called on to give effect to decisions of the former taken in breach of those values, or because breaches of those values by one or more Member States call into question whether EU actions themselves comply with those values. In other words, problems with fundamental rights and democracy in one Member State become problems in complying with fundamental rights and democracy by the EU itself.

As I have mentioned, this explains the most recent developments in the European Court of Justice case-law.

While the role the European Court of Human Rights will play in protecting democracy will be predicated largely on the first two reasons mentioned above, the role of the European Court of Justice has largely been driven by the third. This is explained by the differences in the scope of their jurisdiction and focus of analysis, in particular with the Court of Justice undertaking more systemic review. The two roles are not contradictory, however. There are no significant differences in the analysis of the substantive issues. Moreover, the broader jurisdiction and case-law of the ECtHR will be extremely useful for the Court of Justice as it will increasingly be called upon to carry out a systemic review of democracy issues in EU Member States. Each court should see the other as complementing it rather than competing with it.

4 Current Challenges

The problems both courts will face are the same. The current challenges to democracy are particularly difficult for courts to address because, at least in part, they involve some questioning of the role of the courts (and particularly transnational courts) in democracies.

These current challenges to democracy are linked to the increasing dissatisfaction with democracies, as expressed by citizens in a number of surveys in Europe. This dissatisfaction is, in turn, linked to two factors: (1) the fact that people increasingly do not feel represented by the political establishment; (2) the fact that the correlation between democracy and better economic and social outcomes has been called into question by the growth rates of certain authoritarian regimes while many democracies have stagnated and are witnessing rising levels of inequality.

These two factors can, in turn, be related to three transformations taking place in politics. The first of these is an increased asymmetry between the policy arena (increasingly linked to transnational interdependence) and the political arena (which remains profoundly national).

The second transformation relates to changes in the means and methods of engaging in politics as a consequence of the digital revolution. This includes changes in how information is constructed and disseminated, how political and policy preferences are formed and how collective decisions are taken in the public sphere.

The third and last transformation relates to the timescale of politics, which is becoming increasingly short-term.

A more detailed look at this transformation of politics will have to be left for another occasion, but suffice it to say that it is having a profound impact on the cognitive, epistemological and deliberative foundations of democracy.

This brings with it new democratic challenges that the courts are required to address but, at the same time, it challenges the conditions under which courts can do so.

The most obvious of these challenges comes from populist forces and their proto-authoritarian conception of power. This challenge does not only entail an escalation of the number of cases involving alleged human rights violations. In many instances there is also a downgrading of the prevailing democratic culture and a systemic taking over of democratic institutions. Courts are less well equipped to deal with issues falling within the scope of democratic institutions. They are also less likely to be effective as the remedies they can provide are rarely of a systemic nature. Additionally, as recent events in Europe have demonstrated, the courts themselves can also become the object of this 'takeover' of democracy. At the same time, in this context, intervention by the courts is becoming ever more necessary and is often the only alternative available. This is particularly true for transnational courts, which may end up being the last resort when democratic challenges become embedded in a political culture that is increasingly distancing itself from democracy. Yet this will not be an easy role as the populist narrative often presents the judiciary as members of the elite opposed to the democratic will of the people. This will require transnational courts to develop both judicial remedies that encourage democratic change and a form of legal argumentation that extends beyond the legal community, into the broader political community.

A second challenge is emerging even where populists are not a dominant force. Democracy is increasingly fragmented and polarised. This makes it harder for it to fulfil its function of reconciling and arbitrating the preferences of different groups and citizens in a way that is acceptable to all. As democracy struggles, the role of the courts as a rationalising force of politics comes to the fore. What is sometimes referred to as the judicialisation of political life is a consequence of an implicit delegation from the political process to the courts of certain disagreements, transforming them from political disputes into legal arguments to be arbitrated by courts on the basis of universally agreed principles.

This role is linked to a conception of democratic constitutionalism that is not limited to taming politics and entrenching certain values so as to protect them from the ordinary course of politics. Rather, it is also about making politics possible and productive. The task is not only to limit disagreement, but also to allow, regulate and accommodate such disagreement. This conception of democratic constitutionalism has important consequences for the role of the courts. Their function becomes more one of framing the search for meaning in a political community than of revealing a meaning that has been previously set in the rules.

A third challenge is also visible in light of the new characterisation of the public sphere. As the virtual public sphere gains ground, the courts will be equally involved in securing freedom of expression and pluralism and in guaranteeing the quality and integrity of that public sphere and speech within it. This is not a new role but one that the European Court of Human Rights is very familiar with, for example in cases such as Delfi, Hoiness or Magiar Jetty. Its importance is bound to increase, however, and, more importantly, it will increasingly be connected with the growing role of transnational forms of power that evade the control of national democracies but shape their policies and politics. This is the case of social networks but also of other forms of transnational private power, such as the long standing public role of sports organisations.

The transnational character of these entities makes effective judicial and democratic scrutiny of them very difficult at the national level. Both the European Court of Human Rights and the European Court of Justice have rightly demonstrated that *prima facie* jurisdictional limits on the application of the Convention or certain EU rules to private powers do not constitute an obstacle to their judicial role in this area. They have not, however, fully embraced the extent of the challenges that these organisations pose in terms of democratic accountability and the importance of approaching them in light of those challenges. At the same time, this constitutes an opportunity for these courts, since they can play their part in reintroducing democratic accountability where national democracies can no longer act alone.

These three challenges have two main consequences for the courts. First, they will necessarily become involved in framing and designing the political space. Secondly, whether they like it or not, they will be placed at the centre of many political disputes. All this creates a paradox. As I previously stated, the political centrality of courts is often a consequence of politics and not of the courts themselves. But this same phenomena will increase the contestability of judicial decisions. The only way to deal with this paradox is to improve our understanding of the role of the courts in a democratic political community. The courts themselves will have to change the nature of their legal reasoning and their understanding of their role in judicial review.

Miguel Poiares Maduro Dean, Católica Global School of Law, Universidade Católica Portuguesa, Portugal. European University Institute. Former Advocate-General at the CJEU.

The Rule of Law and EU Competition Law: The *Sped-Pro* Case

Sofia Oliveira Pais and Marta Prata Domingos

1 Introduction

The value of the rule of law is enshrined in Article 2 of the Treaty on European Union as one of the core values on which the Union is founded and which are commonly shared by the Member States.

For some authors, the concept of the rule of law can be translated into the idea of "supremacy of law" (Henley 1999, p. 765), according to which no person is above the defined set of legal rules and principles, including the heads of Government and State. As such, besides being an equalising factor, the rule of law also works as a guarantee of legal certainty against the arbitrary use of political powers. The exercise of public prerogatives will always be constrained by constitutional boundaries that every single member of society knows in advance (Allan 2005, p. 922).

The central role of the rule of law in society's legal construction and regulation becomes remarkably clear. Nevertheless, the crucial role it plays in today's idea of State and Government is the product of an evolution and discussion process that has been ongoing throughout history. At each moment in time, the idea of the rule of law is itself an accurate representation of how societies perceive their political organisation and the different roles that each member needs to play. As such, the concept of the rule of law, its definitions and its boundaries provide a window to history and to political development.

S. O. Pais (✉) · M. Prata Domingos
Universidade Católica Portuguesa, Faculty of Law, Católica Research Centre for the Future of Law, Oporto, Portugal
e-mail: spais@ucp.pt; mardomingos@ucp.pt

I. Quadros, M. Gorjão-Henriques (eds.), *Revisiting the Liberal Constitutional Features of the European Union*, https://doi.org/10.1007/978-3-031-95717-8_6

1.1 From Ancient Greece to the Magna Carta

Although the most recognisable use of the expression "rule of law" is usually attributed to Albert Venn Dicey in 1885 (Dicey 1885), the discussion about the functioning of law has been at the centre of legal thinking since Socrates reflected on the role of law, namely when discussing the law in the dialogue portrayed by Plato in *Crito*. Socrates presented the law as a conforming force of the *polis*, as an organisational system to which citizens adhere by agreeing to a common set of rules. As such, as long as they belong to the *polis*, to the society, citizens are obliged to comply with its laws. Later, Plato would write his own account of the law and the rule of law, giving special emphasis to the natural acceptance of rules designed by "wise men/legislators" (Lisi 2013, p. 88). However, this notion was still far from our modern understanding of the rule of law, given that it uses the natural hierarchy of society as a basis that individual citizens accept (Lisi 2013, p. 88).

Later on, Aristotle regards the rule of law as more suitable for regulating societies than the rule of men (Aristóteles 1998, p. 1286a). As opposed to the rule of men, the law was considered an impartial regulator as it provided "an impersonal answer to questions where personal interests are involved" (Letwin 2005, p. 23). When debating the objections to an absolute monarchy, Aristotle highlights the role of law as a guarantee for the subjects due to its "rationality, stability, and impartiality" (Horn 2013, p. 242). According to Aristotle, the fact that laws are enacted after long deliberation experience and are drafted after careful consideration for a universal and future scenario means that they act as a guarantee of justice (Aristóteles 2005, p. 1354b). Consequently, they serve as a reassurance factor, given that those who hold positions of power could be tempted to use that power in their own favour. The philosopher affirms the distinction between governing and being above the law, since even if some individuals are entrusted with the role of governing "they must be appointed as guardians of the laws and in subordination to them" (Aristóteles 1998, pp. 1287a20–1287a25).

Aristotle considered that the constitution to which the individual members of the society adhere is the factor that binds them together as a whole (Letwin 2005, p. 22). However, differently from the idea of unity put forward by Plato, Aristotle believed that the constitution did not entail a loss of identity for different individuals. Each of them preserved their differences and roles.

Nevertheless, and connecting this with the idea mentioned above, Aristotle concluded that within the *polis*, the best form of government was one based on laws and not on the rule of men. As such, the different identities that compose the community have a relevant role in defining the course of governance. Only by doing so, by taking into account the valuable contribution of the whole as opposed to the individual, is the *polis* not at the mercy of being governed by rules defined by passion, with a tendency towards tyranny (Aristóteles 1998, pp. 1286a15–1286a1535). Aristotle illustrates the idea by saying that "the multitude is more incorruptible—just as the larger stream of water is purer, so the mass of citizens is less corruptible than the few" (Aristóteles 1998, p. 1286a35).

Several authors developed their own concepts and understanding of the rule of law from the work of Aristotle. The Christian perspective on legal thought was mostly established by St. Augustine and St. Thomas Aquinas, the latter reconciling the ideas developed by Aristotle with the concept of a Creator. Aquinas acknowledges that all elements are subject to limits when enacting new laws. As such, he recognises that if an individual legislates in excess of the power invested in him, this will constitute an act of violence, not a law (Letwin 2005, p. 82). Nevertheless, Aquinas grants a special position to the sovereign, rejecting the idea of the equal subjection to the law. If the sovereign disrespects the law, the only possible judgement comes from God. The sovereign can only be subject to the law if it is of his own free will (Tamanaha 2004, p. 19).

This last point was demonstrated 10 years before the birth of St. Thomas Aquinas by the events surrounding the Magna Carta. Signed in 1215, it is seen by many as one of the first legal instruments to codify limits to the sovereign's activity. Nevertheless, the document, which was drawn up by the Barons to impose limits on King John's power, initially had a short lifetime. The Charter was repudiated almost immediately by King John himself (Elkins et al. 2016, p. 4). However, it was later confirmed by Henry III, and its content is often associated with the modern concept of the Rule of Law, it being claimed that "the ancient Magna Carta and modern Rule of Law jurisprudence were (…) cut from the same cloth or animated by the same intellectual DNA" (Johnson 2015, p. 10). Clause 39 of the Charter remains in place today and establishes the right to due process of law, namely by basing legal decisions on law rather than on the will of the King.

1.2 From the Magna Carta to the French Revolution

In his defence of the King's absolute power, Thomas Hobbes builds the idea of an implicit contract between subjects and the sovereign according to which the former agree to obey the rules dictated by the latter. According to Hobbes, the only valid positive law emerges from the King's will (Harvey 1961, p. 489). For Hobbes, the monarchy, and in particular the one that concentrates all power in a single sovereign—the absolute monarchy—is the most perfect form of government, compared to its alternatives, such as democracy or aristocracy (Gauthier 2000, p. 108). In its representation of every single individual, the ruler's power is not subject to any kind of limitation as that would necessarily lead to chaos and to the questioning of the sovereign's authority (Tamanaha 2004, pp. 47–48). Hobbes rejects the idea of the separation of powers, and the sovereign, who assumes the role of legislator, is not subject to civil law. He is merely subject to the commands of natural law that are only transposed into law by himself (Newey 2008, p. 131).

Hobbes establishes that some freedoms are out of the reach of the people. They are entitled to private freedom—to make personal choices that govern their individual lives—but not to public freedom, to interfere with public decisions (Badgy

2007, p. 46). There is a clear separation between the sovereign's governance of the public sphere and the interference of individual subjects.

According to Hobbes, it is essential for the law to be written and published. This is the case, he claims, not only because the people must have knowledge of the law, but also because this demonstrates that the rules stem from the will of the sovereign (Letwin 2005, pp. 96–97). The central notion for Hobbes is the use of law as a political tool of power—the sovereign exercises his power through the enactment of the law that binds the people. For this reason, Hobbes is considered to be the founder of the rule by law school of thought, according to which the "law is the commands of the sovereign, the sovereign is identified by seeing who in the political community is habitually obeyed by the bulk of the population and (…) is legally unlimited, and the motivation for obedience is the fear of the sanctions that attach to each command" (Dyzenhaus 2021, p. 266).

In opposition to this concept of rule by law, in which the norms enacted by the sovereign are merely means of exercising power (Dyzenhaus 2021, p. 263), years later, John Locke and Charles Montesquieu came up with different theories of law.

The concept developed by John Locke comes much closer to the modern idea of the State. Although Locke agrees with Hobbes on the existence of a state of nature where humankind exists without any form of political organisation, the features defined by Locke in Chapter II of his book *Second Treatise of Government* are very different. According to Locke, natural laws required human beings to preserve themselves and "to preserve the rest of mankind". As such, individuals lived in perfect equity (Locke 1982, chapter II, sections 6 to 8). However, in a state where everyone holds executive power, evident problems arise from the absence of structures. Locke identifies three main challenges (Locke 1982, chapter IX, sections 124–126). First of all, in a society guided by abstract natural commands, everyone can decide on the content and limits of the law for their own benefit, whether driven by their interests or by their ignorance. Secondly, the instincts that motivate human actions, be they of passion or revenge, would lead human beings too far as they would be "both the judge and the executioner of the law of nature" (Locke 1982, chapter IX, section 125). This creates the need for an impartial judge. The third obstacle Locke identified in this sequence relates to the difficulty in enforcing punishment decisions.

These three hurdles create the need for a social contract that produces "the political structures of society" (White 2012, p. 272). In the design of this political order, Locke disagrees once again with Hobbes, rejecting the idea of an absolute sovereign with unlimited power. For Locke, this construction is based on the idea that individuals would delegate some form of power to the government for defined purposes and with clear limits. The notion of accountability also comes into play, given that civil society would revoke this mandate if there was a failure by the government to meet its obligations (Tamanaha 2004, p. 49).

Locke introduces the idea of a separation of powers between the legislative and the executive power. However, he subordinates the executive power (that can even be held by a constitutional monarch) to the legislative power that must be its only source. On the legislative power, Locke imposes the limit of certainty, as its exercise should not be arbitrary and must be oriented towards the public good of the society (Locke 1982, Chapter XI, Section 135). He also recognises that in order to promote this certainty, the law must be written so it is known by every citizen (as opposed to the law of nature) and must be applied by "known authorized judges" (Locke 1982, Chapter XI, Section 136–137).

Despite acknowledging the importance of impartial judges to settle conflicts that arise in civil society, Locke does not mention the separation of powers with regard to the power of the judiciary. That aspect was better developed by Montesquieu, for whom the separation between the executive, legislative and judicial power was the only way to avoid despotism.

Although views on Montesquieu's concept of the separation of powers have differed among scholars, the majority seems to agree that the author introduces the term "power of judging" into the trilogy of powers and attributes it to the courts (Vile 1998, pp. 94–97). It is worth noting that Montesquieu uses the term 'distribution of powers' to denote that there should not be an absolute barrier between powers. Instead, there should be communication between them in order to allow a balance. However, to guarantee its independence, the judicial power is removed from this system of checks and balances and "there remain only two powers that must be made to check each other" (Krause 2000, p. 236)—the legislative and the executive. Montesquieu emphasises the importance of removing the judicial power from the government's prerogatives in order to ensure that it works as a proper "barrier against lawless government actions", as the judicial sector needs to function as the citizen's ultimate protector (Tamanaha 2004, p. 52). Hence, Montesquieu identifies the need to access an independent judicial system and have a fair and equitable trial as an essential guarantee against despotic forms of government.

At the end of the eighteenth century, the French Revolution serves as a historical milestone that asserts the principles of freedom, equality, and fraternity as core values, not only of French society but also of the modern world. It brought to continental Europe the concept of the rule of law that had already played an essential part in the British legal system, admired by authors like Montesquieu (Costa 2018, pp. 142–143). From that point onwards, every legal theorist would, to a lesser or greater extent, reflect those ideals in their work, regardless of their political orientation.

1.3 The Modern Concept of the Rule of Law

Although under construction since Aristotle's time and always mirroring political and societal developments, the concept of the 'rule of law' was popularised through the work of A.V. Dicey in the second half of the nineteenth century. More than simply popularising the term, some authors have claimed that Dicey formally shaped the rule of law in the constitutional landscape (Allison 2018, pp. 170–172). His concept of the rule of law is anchored in three essential aspects. The first one is the need for public decisions to be based on ordinary law rather than being a pure exercise of discretionary power. Governance should use legal norms and established procedures as its compass. The same applies to courts that must decide cases in light of pre-existing law. Secondly, Dicey draws attention to the need for every individual to be considered formally equal before the law, regardless of social class. The third part of his definition of the rule of law has been seen as highlighting the role of judicial rulings in the establishment of individual rights (Lino 2018, p. 741).

Writing from a common law perspective, Dicey centred most of his definition of the rule of law and consequent limitations on the central role of the courts (Walters 2021, pp. 154–156). In addition, Dicey and his follower Friedrich Hayek defended, and were criticised for defending, the strict elimination of any kind of discretionary interpretation of legal norms (Harvey 1961, p. 493).[1]

Later, Lon Fuller would further develop the catalogue of components that a legal system needs to successfully implement the concept of the rule of law. His list was composed of eight purely formal principles that should be interpreted as the content of the rule of law. Accordingly, (1) the law should be general; (2) rules must be publicly promulgated; (3) law must be applied prospectively; (4) the content of law should be understandable; (5) norms should be coherent with one another; (6) laws should not impose duties or obligations that are impossible to fulfil; (7) rules should be constant and stable through time; (8) there should be coherence between the enacted norm and its actual administration (Rundle 2021, p. 189). According to Fuller, the fulfilment of these requisites is an essential requirement for the existence of a legal system, although the degree to which they are accomplished can vary according to the type of legal regime in question (Kramer 2004, p. 74).

1.4 The Rule of Law in the European Union

Much of the result of the evolution of the rule of law concept that we have witnessed throughout time has brought us to the remarkable moment when it is championed as one of the foundational values of the European Union.

The concept of the rule of law was intrinsically reflected in the essential pillars that served as the foundations for the then European Coal and Steel Community, although not explicitly referred to in the text of the founding Treaty. Indeed, Article 31 of the European Coal and Steel Community Treaty (1951) assigned the task of ensuring "*le respect du droit*" to the Court. Later, the first explicit recognition of the rule of law as a fundamental basis of the then European Economic Community (EEC) came from the Court itself in 1986. When deciding the *Les Verts* case, the Court clearly stated that the EEC was a "Community based on the rule of law, inasmuch as neither its Member States nor its institutions can avoid a review of the question whether the measures adopted by them are in conformity with the basic

[1] They were strong voices warning against the decadence of the rule of law announced by the development of social welfare policies (Tamanaha 2004, p. 72).

constitutional charter, the Treaty".[2] As such, besides declaring the rule of law as a basis for the EEC, the Court went further and gave concrete expression to this in the subordination "of all EU actors' conduct (both EU institutions and Member States) to judicial review" (Konstadinides 2017, p. 114).

The echoes of the Court's decision made their way to the European legal instruments in 1992 with the Maastricht Treaty, reflecting the concerns of a post-Cold War era (Pech 2021, pp. 313–314). The Treaty's preamble spoke about the "attachment to the principles of liberty, democracy and respect for human rights and fundamental freedoms and of the rule of law". However, the allusions in the Treaty's text only referred to the Common Foreign and Security Policy and development cooperation.

The rule of law only gained a prominent place in 1997 with the Treaty of Amsterdam, when the reference that had been confined to the preamble in the Maastricht Treaty became part of the main treaty provisions. Besides establishing the rule of law as one of the cornerstones of the European Union, alongside respect for human rights and democracy (Article 6), the Treaty of Amsterdam makes the admission to EU membership conditional on the respect for these principles (Article 49) (Craig and De Búrca 2015, p. 14).

The position of the rule of law within the Treaties would undergo a final change with the Treaty of Lisbon (2007), leaving it in its current place in Article 2 TEU. It is worth mentioning that, apart from stating that the EU is founded on these values, Article 2 extends them as shared values of the Member States. As such, this Article is paired with Article 7, which establishes a preventive and a sanctioning mechanism to guarantee compliance by the Member States with the foundational values enshrined in Article 2.

However, the changes introduced by the Treaty of Lisbon to the role played by the rule of law did not relate merely to the internal dimension of the European Union, but also affected the external dimension. Article 21 reflects the intention of orienting "the Union's action on the international scene [according to] the principles which have inspired its own creation, development and enlargement",[3] namely the rule of law.

The configuration of the rule of law principle continues to undergo constant change, driven by the demands of modern society. As we will see below, the case-law of the European Court of Justice continues to be a propelling factor for these developments that take the role of the rule of law further. This is especially true if we consider some of the features that are unique to the European Union, such as the prominent role played by an internal market comprised of 27 different economies that constantly interact with each other and in which the role played by public institutions is paramount to guarantee its correct functioning, as we will see below.

---

[2] Judgment of 23 April 1986, *Les Verts v. Parliament,* 294/83, EU:C:1986:166, §23.

[3] Article 21 TEU.

1.5 The Mechanisms Surrounding the Rule of Law in the European Union

In 2014, when launching a new framework designed to tackle the frequent breaches of the rule of law, the Commission expanded on the concept. The communication, entitled "A new EU Framework to strengthen the Rule of Law",[4] presented a set of new steps that should precede the use of the mechanism contained in Article 7. This initiative aimed to "address and resolve a situation where there is a systemic threat to the rule of law",[5] allowing the Commission to initiate a dialogue comprising different stages designed to enable the breaching Member State to rectify its actions. In the initial stage, the Commission leads an assessment of the national legal situation and informs the Member State of its concerns related to the deterioration of the rule of law within that country's legal system. If no new measures are adopted, the Commission will then issue a recommendation with clear steps and deadlines for resolving the issue. The third stage of the process aims to monitor the implementation of those recommended steps. After this follow-up period, and if no satisfactory measures have been adopted, the Commission will then decide on the possibility of activating the mechanism laid down in Article 7.

At this juncture, there are two different options within the text of Article 7, and they may or may not be used as subsequent steps. At a starting point, the essential difference between them relates to whether there has been an actual breach of the values established in Article 2 TEU or whether there is only a risk of this occurring. As such, Article 7(1) can be activated by one-third of the Member States, by the European Parliament or by the Commission in cases in which there is only a "clear risk of a serious breach", and Article 7(2) is meant to be triggered by one-third of the Member States or by the Commission in situations where the existence of that breach has already been confirmed. Naturally, each of these options will produce different consequences. Since the first is limited to preventing an actual breach, it will have the effect of compelling the Member State to initiate a discussion with EU representatives with a view to adopting appropriate measures to guarantee the preservation of the rule of law (Kochenov 2021, p. 138). This limited reach of Article 7(1) means that "the existence of a serious and persistent breach" under the second paragraph of Article 7 must be confirmed in order to apply the sanctioning measures envisioned by Article 7(3). According to this paragraph, the sanctions imposed may include the suspension of rights deriving from the Treaties, namely voting rights. Besides that, the Article leaves room for manoeuvre to include other types of sanctions.

To complement the tools presented by Article 7 and by the possibility of initiating an infringement procedure against a breaching Member State, in December

[4] Communication from the Commission to the European Parliament and the Council, *A new EU Framework to strengthen the Rule of Law*, COM(2014)158, 2014.

[5] Communication from the Commission to the European Parliament and the Council, *A new EU Framework to strengthen the Rule of Law*, COM(2014)158, 2014. P. 3.

2020 the Parliament and the Council launched a conditionality mechanism for the protection of the Union budget "against breaches of the principles of the rule of law affecting its sound financial management or the protection of the financial interests of the Union".[6] In fact, the legislator took the opportunity to connect and protect two areas—the rule of law and the integrity of the Union budget (Łacny 2021, p. 84). In response to a breach of the rule of law, a Member State can be sanctioned with measures that range from a suspension of payments to a prohibition on entering into new legal commitments (Article 5 Regulation 2020/2092).[7]

Article 3 of Regulation 2020/2092 sets out the conduct which may be indicative of a breach of the principles of the rule of law for the purposes of that legal instrument. In fact, although the rule of law is frequently invoked in legal instruments and public speeches, its specific content and that of the 'EU rule of law' is usually left out in the open. In a political construction where 27 Member States may give different meanings and contours to this principle, establishing common ground becomes of the utmost importance.

While recognising that the content of principles that arise from the rule of law may vary in accordance with the constitutional system of each Member State (Craig and De Búrca 2015, pp. 388–389), the Commission relies upon the case-law of the European Court of Justice (hereinafter the Court) and of the European Court of Human Rights and on the work of the Council of Europe through the Venice Commission. In doing so, the Commission has been able to provide us with a "non-exhaustive list of (…) principles and hence define the core meaning of the rule of law as a common value of the EU in accordance with Article 2".[8] The configuration defined by the Commission has since found its way back to the Court and it has been included in its annual report to provide a clear description of the concept.[9]

Accordingly, these principles are: (1) legality, which means that the legislative process must be marked by transparency and accountability and that it should be democratic and pluralistic; (2) legal certainty, which entails that besides being clear and predictable, encapsulating the principle of legitimate expectations, legal rules should suffer alterations *a posteriori*[10]; (3) the executive power must be totally distanced from any form of arbitrariness, which means that "any intervention by the public authorities in the sphere of private activities of any person (…) must have a

[6] Regulation (EU, Euratom) 2020/2092 of the European Parliament and of the Council of 16 December 2020 on a general regime of conditionality for the protection of the Union budget. §14.

[7] The validity of such mechanism was recognised by the Court in the actions brought by Poland and Hungary against the Parliament and the Council. (Judgment of the Court of 16 February 2022, *Hungary v. Parliament and Council,* C-156/21, EU:C:2022:97; Judgment of the Court of 16 of February 2022, *Poland v. Parliament and Council,* C-157/21, EU:C:2022:98).

[8] Communication from the Commission to the European Parliament and the Council, *A new EU Framework to strengthen the Rule of Law,* COM(2014)158, 2014. P. 4.

[9] Court of Justice of the European Union—*Annual Report 2022: The Year in Review,* p. 46. Each year the Court has devoted a special section of its annual report to the most important cases on the rule of law.

[10] Annexes to the Communication from the Commission to the European Parliament and the Council—Annex 1, p. 1.

legal basis and be justified on the grounds laid down by law"[11]; (4) courts must be impartial and independent, which constitutes an expression of the principle of the separation of powers, although subject, at national level, to different configurations in accordance with the national systems of governance; (5) the acts of the institutions and the Member States are subject to "effective judicial review including respect for fundamental rights". The case-law of the Court has consolidated this right since the *Johnston*[12] case in 1986, when it affirmed that the requirement for judicial control stems not only from the "constitutional traditions common to the Member States", but also from Articles 6 and 13 of the European Convention on Human Rights (ECHR).[13] In 1977, the then European Communities had already given special significance to the ECHR in matters related to the protection of fundamental rights[14]; (6) "equality before the law".[15]

It is doubtless recognisable that almost all the principles catalogued by the Commission were already part of the legal thinking of the scholars we considered at the beginning of this discussion. Nevertheless, being a *suis generis* construction, one might say that the European Union has been following its own path as regards the rule of law, sometimes taking requirements that were already part of the rule of law construction in the eighteenth century to a new extreme. The independence and impartiality of the courts was advocated by Montesquieu as far back as 1748, but it acquires a whole new level of importance when we speak about the European Union.

In a system marked by the direct effect of a supranational legal order on national legal systems, producing obligations and rights for individual citizens[16] and attending to the primacy of EU law over conflicting national laws,[17] the role of the Court and the national courts and their correct functioning is paramount. The EU Courts and the national courts have established a cooperation designed to uphold EU law, where "it is for the Court of Justice to say what the law is and for national courts (…) to apply that law" (Lenaerts 2020, p. 30).

Bearing this vital role in mind, we should not be surprised by the increasing number of cases involving the independence and impartiality of national courts. In fact, the launch of the above-mentioned "Framework to strengthen the Rule of Law" sought to provide an answer for the many cases where the rule of law appeared to

---

[11] Judgment of 21 September 1989, *Hoechst AG*, joined cases 46/87 and 227/88, EU:C:1989:337. §19.

[12] Judgment of 15 May 1986, *Johnston v. Chief Constable of the RUC*, C-222/84, EU:C:1986:206.

[13] Judgment of 15 May 1986, *Johnston v. Chief Constable of the RUC*, C-222/84, EU:C:1986:206. §17 and 18.

[14] Joint Declaration by the European Parliament, the Council and the Commission concerning the Protection of Fundamental Rights and the European Convention for the Protection of Human Rights and Fundamental Freedoms, Official Journal C 103, 27 April 1977. Since 1997 with the Amsterdam Treaty, the Treaty on the European Union has expressly incorporated the Convention into the EU's legal realm (Article 6 TEU).

[15] Communication from the Commission to the European Parliament and the Council, *A new EU Framework to strengthen the Rule of Law*, COM(2014)158, 2014. P. 4.

[16] Judgment of 5 February 1963, *Van Gend & Loos*, C-26/62, EU:C:1985:104. P. 12.

[17] Judgment of 15 July 1964, *Costa v. ENEL*, C-6/64, EU:C:1964:66. P. 594.

be in danger.[18] This mechanism is seen as an "early warning tool" (Kochenov and Pech 2016, p. 1066) designed to allow the Commission and the Member State to initiate dialogue and negotiate before the threat of a rule of law 'disruption' becomes real. If these efforts do not succeed, the Commission can then activate the Article 7 procedure.

The framework was first used in the case of Poland in an issue related precisely to judicial independence. In January 2016, the First Vice-President of the European Commission, Frans Timmermans, announced that the situation surrounding the recent developments in the Polish national legal system would be assessed under the Rule of Law Framework.[19] After four different recommendations, the Commission decided, in December 2017, to activate Article 7(1) for the first time. Nevertheless, the Polish government has not complied with the demands of the principle of the rule of law, and since 2018 multiple infringement procedures have been initiated, with some of them culminating with the referencing to the Court.[20] The main concern regarding the Polish legal system relates to the independence of the judicial system. In 2018, the Court had already provided an answer to this matter and took the opportunity presented by the case involving Portuguese judges to clarify that national courts need to remain independent, namely from hierarchical constraints, "external interventions or pressure liable to impair the independent judgment of its members and to influence their decisions".[21] Only in this way will national courts be able to fulfil the principle of effective judicial protection as enshrined in Article 19(1) TEU and guarantee the "proper working of the judicial cooperation system",[22] securing coherence between national judicial decisions.[23]

---

[18] Cf., the speech by the Vice President of the European Commission and EU Justice Commissioner, "The EU and the Rule of Law: What next?", delivered on 4 September 2013. Available at: https://ec.europa.eu/commission/presscorner/detail/en/SPEECH_13_677.

[19] Cf. the speech by the First Vice-President Timmermans following the College Meeting of 13 January 2016. Available at: https://ec.europa.eu/commission/presscorner/detail/en/SPEECH_16_71.

[20] Judgment of 24 June 2019, C-619/18 R, *Commission v. Poland*, EU:C:2018:1021. Judgment of 5 November 2019, C-192/18, *Commission v. Poland,* EU:C:2019:924. Judgment of 15 July 2021, C-791/19, *Commission v. Poland,* EU:C:2021:59. Judgment of 5 June 2023, *Commission v. Poland,* C-204/21, EU:C:2023:442. On 15 February 2023 the Commission announced the decision to, once again, refer Poland to the Court as a consequence of another infringement procedure.

[21] Judgment of 27 February 2018, *Associação Sindical dos Juízes Portugueses,* C-64/16, EU:C:2018:117. §44.

[22] Judgment of 27 February 2018, *Associação Sindical dos Juízes Portugueses,* C-64/16, EU:C:2018:117. §43.

[23] The independence of the members of the judiciary, in particular as regards their appointment procedures, was again examined by the Court in 2021 in two important cases. The first concerned the appointment of judges to the Polish Supreme Court and the need to ensure an effective judicial review of this procedure in order to safeguard it from undue interference which would consequently jeopardise the independence of the nominees. (Judgment of the Court of 2 of March 2021, *A.B and others,* C-824/18, EU:C:2021:153) Later that year, the Court ruled on the role of the Maltese Prime Minister in the appointment of judges. It held that the impartiality of judge was not

1.6 The Rule of Law and EU Competition Law

The rule of law penetrates all areas of EU law and its influence in the enforcement of competition law cannot be underestimated. Any limitation of the independence of the courts[24] when reviewing competition decisions would preclude effective judicial protection (considered the "essence" (Bernatt 2019, p. 349) of the rule of law) and would jeopardise the effectiveness of the decentralised system of EU competition law enforcement.

The Court of Justice has ruled, in the context of the European Arrest Warrant, that if there are generalised deficiencies concerning the independence of the judiciary (and, therefore the rule of law), the executing judicial authority can refuse to execute the warrant.[25] In the *Minister for Justice and Equality* case, an individual challenged the European Arrest Warrants issued against him for several drug trafficking offences, arguing that recent reforms of the Polish judicial system would preclude his rights to a fair trial under Article 6 ECHR and Article 47 of the Charter of Fundamental Rights of the EU. The Court of Justice decided to apply the two-step test developed in *Aranyosi and Caldararu*[26] and concluded that the authorities could refuse to execute the warrant after assessing that there was a real risk of fundamental rights' infringement and confirming that the individual concerned would be exposed to that risk. This means that the principle of mutual trust between national authorities, based on the presumption of equivalent protection of fundamental rights in all the Member States of the Union, is not absolute. It can be rebutted in exceptional circumstances.

Recently, in the *Sped-Pro*[27] case, the Court of Justice went a step further and applied a similar reasoning to the alleged lack of independence of national competition authorities.

---

compromised as long as an independent body responsible for assessing candidates was involved. (Judgment of the Court of 20 of April 2021, *Repubblika*, C-896/19, EU:C:2021:311).

[24] Independence of the judiciary, as the Court explained in the above-mentioned *Associação Sindical de Juízes* case, §44 and 52, must be external, which presupposes that the court exercises its functions autonomously "without being subject to any hierarchical constraint or subordinated to any other body and without taking orders or instructions from any source whatsoever", and also internal (this means that it should be linked to impartiality, requires objectivity and absence of interest in the outcome of the procedures, and seeks "to ensure that an equal distance is maintained from the parties to the proceedings and their respective interests with regard to the subject matter of those proceedings". Cf. Judgment of 19 September 2006, *Wilson*, C-506/04, EU:C:2006:587, §52).

[25] Judgment of 25 July 2018, *Minister for Justice and Equality (Deficiencies in the system of justice)*, C-216/18 PPU, EU:C:2018:586, § 60–72.

[26] Judgment of 5 April 2016, *Aranyosi and Caldararu,* joined cases C-404/15 and C-659/15 PPU, EU:C:2016:198.

[27] Judgment of the General Court of 9 February 2022, *Sped-Pro v Commission*, T-791/19, EU:T:2022:67.

1.7 The Sped-Pro *Case*

On 9 February 2022, in the *Sped-Pro* case, the General Court examined, for the first time, the impact of systemic deficiencies in the rule of law concerning the lack of independence of national competition authorities.

This case concerned a company, Sped-Pro S.A., established in Warsaw, that used rail freight transport services supplied by PKP Cargo S.A. (a company controlled by the Polish State). Sped-Pro complained to the European Commission that PKP Cargo had abused its dominant position when it refused to conclude a multi-annual cooperation agreement with the applicant, on market conditions. On 12 August 2019, the European Commission rejected the complaint on the grounds that the Polish competition authority was best placed to examine the case as the market involved *in casu* was the Polish one (the companies operated in Poland and the dominant position was held there),[28] stating that a single National Competition Authority is usually well placed to deal with agreements or practices that substantially affect competition mainly within its territory.[29]

The applicant's main argument was that the European Commission was best placed to examine the complaint, given the systemic or generalised deficiencies in the rule of law in Poland and, in particular, the lack of independence of the Polish competition authority and the national courts with jurisdiction in the field. And, as the Court of Justice pointed out, the fundamental right to a fair trial before an independent tribunal enshrined in the second paragraph of Article 47 of the Charter of Fundamental Rights is of paramount importance for the effective application of competition rules.[30]

The European Commission rejected the complaint, but the General Court annulled the decision and held that the Commission should take into account the lack of independence of the Polish competition authority and the national courts with jurisdiction in the field. Such deficiencies should prevent the European Commission from rejecting the complaint.

In addition, the Court also clarified that the European Commission was entitled to apply, by *analogy*, the two-stage analysis required in the context of execution of European arrest warrants in order to safeguard the fundamental right to a fair trial, in accordance with the judgment in *Minister for Justice and Equality (Deficiencies in the system of justice)*[31]: the first step was to assess whether there was a real risk of a breach of that right connected with a lack of independence of the courts of the Member State in question, on account of systemic deficiencies, and the second step

[28] Notice from 27.4.2004 (2004/C 101/03).

[29] Para. 10; and para. 14 adds that the "[t]he Commission is particularly well placed if one or several agreement(s) or practice(s), including networks of similar agreements or practices, have effects on competition in more than three Member States (cross-border markets covering more than three Member States or several national markets)".

[30] *Sped-Pro* case, §91.

[31] Case C- 216/18 PPU.

was to assess whether the person concerned would actually run a real risk, having regard to the particular circumstances of the case. The argument of the Republic of Poland that the *Minister for Justice and Equality* case could not be applied by analogy, as it concerned the principle of effective judicial protection enshrined in Article 19 TEU and the right to a fair trial before an independent tribunal laid down in Article 47 of the Charter, provisions that do not apply to administrative bodies, was rejected.[32] The Court held that the analogy was justified because in both cases the principle of mutual trust between competent authorities could not be ignored, and it concluded that the Commission could not reject a complaint for lack of an EU interest, if national authorities were not in a position to adequately safeguard the complainant's rights.[33]

In casu, the General Court considered that the Commission had failed to examine the evidence presented by the applicant, in particular the possible control exercised by the State over PKP Cargo, the dependence of the president of the Polish competition authority vis-à-vis the executive, the potential leniency of the Polish competition authority towards PKP Cargo, and the Public Prosecutor General's opposition to a decision of the Polish competition authority that penalised PKP Cargo for anticompetitive conduct, and the inability of national courts to remedy these deficiencies given their lack of independence.

It is worth noting that the Court had already decided, in relation to national courts—in the *Automec*, *Au Liz de France* and *Associazione 'Giùlemanidallajuve'* cases—that where the effects of the infringements are essentially nationwide, the Commission is entitled to reject the complaint for lack of an EU interest, provided that the rights of the complainant can be adequately safeguarded by the national courts, "which presupposes that the latter are in a position to gather the factual information necessary in order to determine whether the practices at issue constitute an infringement".[34]

In the *Sped-Pro* case, the Court extended this argument to national competition authorities. It explicitly decided that the principle of "mutual recognition, mutual trust, and loyal cooperation",[35] supporting cooperation between all competition authorities, may be limited in exceptional circumstances: the European Commission has to assess whether the rights of the complainant can be adequately safeguarded by the national authorities before rejecting the complaint. In other words, the trust in institutional cooperation "should not be blind so as not to allow the non-noticing of irregularities occurred in other Member States or before the European Commission" (Kozak 2020, p. 132). The main goal of mutual trust is the effective and uniform enforcement of EU competition law, assuming that national systems

[32] §75.

[33] §89.

[34] Judgment of 18 September 1992, *Automec v Commission*, T-24/90, EU:T:1992:97, §89 to 96, and Judgment of 3 July 2007, *Au Lys de France* v *Commission*, T-458/04, EU:T:2007:195, §83, and Order of 19 March 2012, *Associazione 'Giùlemanidallajuve' v Commission*, T-273/09, EU:T:2012:129, § 68.

[35] § 88.

are equivalent. This presumption of trust may, however, be rebutted, if there is a breach of the rule of law.

1.8 The Presumption of Mutual Trust Can Be Limited in Exceptional Circumstances

In the *Sped-Pro* case, the General Court decided that the principle of mutual trust, supporting cooperation between all competition authorities, may be limited if the rule of law is not protected.

The principle of mutual trust mentioned by the Court in the *Sped-Pro* case is not written in the Treaty but is anchored in other principles, such as the principle of sincere cooperation and the principle of equality.

Some authors claim that the constitutional basis for the close cooperation between competition authorities flows from the principle of sincere cooperation, established in Article 4(3) TEU: Member States and the Union will comply with the obligations of the Treaty with mutual respect (Kozak 2020, p. 134).[36] This means that, in the competition context, the standards of one of the Member States will, usually, be accepted by the others and by the Union.[37] This mutual recognition of decisions, which limits the autonomy of Member States, is grounded on the mutual trust of the Member States, which is based on the premise that all the Member States share the values stated in Article 2 of the TEU, on which the Union is founded. As we mentioned above, one of those core values that should be shared by all Member States and by the Union itself is respect for the rule of law with all its different components and dimensions. As such, the rule of law principle functions as a guarantee that fosters mutual trust between Member States and their respective competition authorities.

Other authors explain that the basis of mutual trust, afforded constitutional status by Opinion of the Court 2/13, is the principle of equality as mentioned in Article 4(2) of the TEU, which precludes the Union from favouring some citizens or Member States over others and means that "all Member States are equally committed to upholding the rule of law within the EU, of which fundamental rights are part and parcel" (Lenaerts 2017, p. 809).[38]

In the competition context, the principle of mutual trust is embedded in Council Regulation (EC) No. 1/2003, of 16 December 2002, on the implementation of the

[36] The Author explains that the principle of sincere cooperation claims for positive actions "warrants cooperation, mutual respect, and assistance", and considers that "mutual trust constitutes *lex specialis* to the principle of sincere cooperation" (Kozak 2020, p. 135).

[37] European Commission, Council, Joint Statement by the Council and the Commission on the functioning of the network of competition authorities, entered in the Council minutes (doc. 15,435/02 ADD 1 of 10 December 2002), 6–8.

[38] According to the Author, "the principle of equality is thus both a fundamental right, when applied to individuals, and a principle of governance, when applied to the Member States", cf. p. 808.

rules on competition laid down in Articles 101 and 102 of the Treaty,[39] and in Directive (EU) 2019/1 of the European Parliament and of the Council of 11 December 2018 to empower the competition authorities of the Member States to be more effective enforcers and to ensure the proper functioning of the internal market.[40]

Regulation 1/2003 establishes a system of parallel competences between the European Commission, National Competition Authorities (NCA), and national courts. This process of decentralisation puts the decision closer to the citizens and has improved the democratic nature of the system. Competition authorities have, therefore, to trust each other, and also national courts, although national competition authorities may have different experiences at the political and institutional levels, increasing the risk of re-nationalisation of EU competition rules. In fact, National Competition Authorities could be tempted to promote national champions. Regulation 1/2003 does not establish any requirements concerning the independence of NCA; it was left up to the Member States to design the enforcement system. If independence of NCA is not ensured, the effective enforcement of competition rules could be jeopardised.

The ECN+ Directive (Directive 2019/1) establishes minimum safeguards concerning the independence and accountability of National Competition Authorities, hence addressing some of the previous concerns. Article 4 of the Directive requires that NCA act independently from political pressure or external intervention.[41] The independence of NCA is, therefore, considered essential to effective enforcement of competition rules.[42] In addition, Article 3 of the Directive requires that proceedings concerning infringement of European antitrust rules must comply with the general principles of Union law and the Charter of Fundamental Rights of the European Union. The Directive does not take into account, however, the multilevel nature of the European Competition Network (Kozak 2020, p. 139).[43] It does not provide any solutions or remedies to allow competition authorities to check each other's actions to ensure the effective enforcement of competition rules. The *Sped-Pro* case may

---

[39] OJ L 1, 4.1.2003, p. 1–25.

[40] OJ L 11, 14.1.2019, p. 3–33.

[41] Although some literature argues that independence of regulatory agencies is only possible from market players (cf. da Silva 2019), EU law requires regulators to be independent from political actors and other external influences, It does not, however, lay down specific criteria to be fulfilled.

[42] Kati Cseres criticises the Directive because its implementation may not produce "any significant impact on more effective enforcement" in countries where "the overall institutional capacity of administrative authorities has been deteriorating for the past years, where the competition authority has been several times constrained directly by the government in its enforcement work" (Cseres 2019, p. 87).

[43] As the Author explained, the scope and content of the principle of mutual trust was developed by the Court with the publication of *Opinion 2/13* on the accession of the European Union to the European Convention of Human Rights (ECHR); the Court explained that the EU and Member States share the values of Article 2 of the TEU, which justifies the mutual trust between them and will lead to the mutual recognition of the different standards of enforcement between them (Kozak 2020, p. 141).

close some of these gaps, as it allows the European Commission to take into account the lack of independence of the national competition authorities when deciding whether to reject a complaint or not. The Court's judgment falls a little short of expectations, however; it leaves unresolved the breach of trust between national competition authorities, if one of them lacks independence. In addition, it does not address the problem of the allocation of the case; the European Commission stills maintains its discretion to assess whether national authorities are in a position to ensure the rights of the complainant. The European institution cannot reject a complaint without assessing the evidence presented by the complainant regarding the independence of national authorities. But it also cannot be forced to open an antitrust investigation, as the Court explained in the *Agria Polska* judgment: "it is for the Member States to provide remedies sufficient to ensure effective judicial protection for individual parties in the fields covered by EU law (...) and not for the Commission to make up for any shortcomings in judicial protection at national level by opening an investigation requiring considerable resources where the likelihood of finding an infringement of Articles 101 and 102 TFEU is low".[44] In other words, the solution provided in the *Sped-Pro* case is only another small step to address the problems of lack of independence of national authorities. Other legal remedies, mentioned above, such as Article 7 of the TEU or the Conditionality Regulation, still need to be called upon to protect the rule of law.

1.9 Competition as an Institution of a (Democratic) Union Essential to the Advance of the Rule of Law

The *Sped-Pro* case is also particularly relevant because it illustrates that the effective enforcement of competition law is essential in improving the rule of law. The link between competition law and democratic societies has been extensively debated in the legal and economic literature, no consensus has been reached.

Not everyone believes that competition law can contribute to non-economic goals, namely fostering democracy. Public choice literature, for instance, has argued that State intervention via competition laws can be inefficient. Breaking away from the theory that "antitrust decision makers are benign seekers of the public interest" (Tollison 1985, p. 907), the public choice perspective claimed that the government should not always get a "green light in antitrust" (Tollison 1985, p. 915).

The ordoliberals, on the other hand, believed that competition was the best mechanism to prevent excessive concentration of economic power and to guarantee political freedom. Developed by Walter Eucken at Freiburg University, this school of economic thought was a response to the cartelisation and monopolisation of the

[44] Judgment of the Court (Ninth Chamber) of 20 September 2018, *Agria Polska sp. z o.o. and Others v European Commission*, C-373/17 P, EU:C:2018:756, §87. As Van Rompuy (2022, p. 415) has pointed out, this case breaks new ground but it "will not force the Commission's hand".

German economy and the incapability of the Weimar Republic to control the concentration of private economic power that destroyed competition and jeopardised the social and political preconditions of democracy, facilitating the rise of totalitarian regimes. As a consequence of this concentration of economic and political power, the rule of law was flawed, and individuals' freedom was eliminated (Behrens 2014, p. 3).[45]

The ordoliberals highlighted that the State should intervene to create the conditions for fair competition, and that there was a *nexus* between competition and democracy (Deutscher and Makris 2016, p. 186). For this reason, the ordoliberals acknowledge competition not only as maximising welfare, but also for its "deontological dimension", claiming that "competition should be protected as such, since it sets the boundaries of economic power and creates the preconditions for economic freedom and equality of opportunity", ensuring that the functioning of the market is conducive to a democratic society (Deutscher and Makris 2016, p. 181). On one hand, economic freedom is a "precondition and counterpart" of other political rights, such as the right to vote, freedom of speech, or freedom of assembly; on the other hand, economic freedom is not an absolute unrestricted right, as it cannot restrict other citizens' economic freedom (Deutscher and Makris 2016, pp. 189–190).

The link between competition and democratic society has also been discussed on the other side of the Atlantic. Although the Sherman Act does not provide an answer to this conundrum, the Supreme Court stated in 1958 that antitrust laws are concerned with "the preservation of our democratic political and social institutions".[46] And more recently, scholars and policymakers identified as Neo-Brandeisians (as they are inspired by the work of Louis Brandeis, a United States Supreme Court Justice) explained that monopolies and concentrated private power may harm the economic and social conditions of a democratic society (Khan 2018, p. 131; Wu 2018, p. 33). As economic power may interfere with political power, antitrust law should shift its focus on efficiency and consumer welfare to combat economic and political domination and protect the competitive process (Wu 2018, p. 33). It remains unclear, however, which methods Neo-Brandeisians propose to distinguish between pro- and anticompetitive practices. Some suggest that the reform needed and highlighted by this movement can be achieved by the elastic consumer welfare standard (Beaton-Wells 2020, pp. 173, 176–177, 193), while others call for other workable criteria (Wu 2018, p. 791).[47]

---

[45] In this article the Author explains the impact of German ordoliberal thought on EU competition law and policy and its core elements: "the crucial role attributed to consumers' choice as the driving force behind producers' rivalry, the dependence of consumers' freedom of choice upon an open market structure, efficiency (consumer welfare) as the result of competition rather than an entrepreneurial market strategy".

[46] As the Supreme Court decided in the Northern Pacific R. Co. v. United States case, 356 U.S. 1, 4 (1958).

[47] On the other hand, Khan proposed the introduction of presumptions and formalistic rules (Khan 2018, p. 131).

In the EU, Articles 101 and 102 of the Treaty on the Functioning of the European Union also do not clarify the goals of European competition rules. As a framework Treaty, it entrusts this task to the European institutions (the Court and the European Commission), which should fulfil it taking into account the fundamental objectives of the European Union. Article 3(1) of the Treaty of the European Union provides that the Union's aim is to "promote peace, its values and the well-being of its peoples", and Article 3(2) of the same Treaty explains that the Union "shall offer its citizens an area of freedom, security and justice without internal frontiers", and "shall establish an internal market". A coherent reading of the Treaty's provisions, including its general goals, suggests that European competition law has several goals, both economic and non-economic, which need to be achieved in a balanced way.[48]

This legislative holistic view is, however, not followed by the European Commission. This European institution has, since the 1990s,[49] identified the protection of consumers as the main goal of EU competition law.[50] Consumer welfare (a *proxy* for economic efficiency)[51] should be the standard embraced in the Union, according to the Commission. The goal of competition law should be to satisfy the

[48] Significant literature reflects upon the insertion of non-economic goals under EU competition law, namely democratic objectives. Among many authors, Witt (2012), Lianos (2013), Iacovides and Vrettos (2022). Some scholars propose, therefore, new theories of harm based on the violation of certain public policy values and objectives such as environmental protection or incorporating democratic values into competition analyses. See, for instance, Robertson (2022). Others advocate the replacement of the consumer welfare standard by the capabilities approach, cf. Gerbrandy (2019, p. 138).

[49] Contributing to this were the adoption of a more economic approach, following the lessons of the Chicago school of thought, and the adoption, in the EU, of Council Regulation (EEC) No 4064/89 of 21 December 1989 on the control of concentrations between undertakings (replaced by the Council Regulation (EC) No 139/2004 of 20 January 2004, the EC Merger Regulation) and Commission Regulation (EC) No 2790/1999 of 22 December 1999 on the application of Article 101(3) of the Treaty to categories of vertical agreements and concerted practices (replaced by the Commission Regulation (EU) No 330/2010 of 20 April 2010 and more recently by Commission Regulation (EU) 2022/720 of 10 May 2022).

[50] Commission Guidelines on the application of Article 81(3) of the Treaty [2004] OJ C 101/97, § 84 explains that "the concept of 'consumers' encompasses all direct or indirect users of the products covered by the agreement, including producers that use the products as an input, wholesalers, retailers and final consumers, i.e., natural persons who are acting for purposes which can be regarded as outside their trade or profession". In other words, consumers in EU competition law includes end-users but also intermediate customers (that may be competitors of the supplier in the downstream market).

[51] The Kaldor-Hicks efficiency (or potential Pareto efficiency) means that a change in a competition situation will increase welfare if those that win compensate the losers and distribution concerns are not relevant. In the EU, some literature argues that consumer surplus is more important than producer surplus, as Article 101(3) TFEU suggests. However, the Court held in *GlaxoSmithKline*, C-501/06 P, that EU competition law aims to protect the structure of the market, and competition as such, and not only the final consumers, suggesting a total welfare standard approach. Zimmer argues that this is the best solution to protect consumers and producers: "producers have the same rights as anyone else in a market economy. In particular, they enjoy property rights. If we wish, and this seems to be the most important point, to encourage people to commit themselves to an activity on a market, we ought to protect them from expropriation" (Zimmer 2007).

revealed preferences[52] of the consumers (final consumers or intermediaries), avoiding consumer harm "in the form of higher price levels than would have otherwise prevailed or in some other form such as limiting quality or reducing consumer choice".[53] This view is supported by significant literature that invokes legal texts (Article 101(3) TFEU, which requires that the benefits are passed to the consumers), as well as the need to limit competition law to its function (solving market failures caused by market power) and to avoid overburdening competition authorities with the assessment of non-economic interests.[54]

The Court of Justice, however, has been more flexible and has acknowledged that European competition rules have promoted economic and non-economic objectives since their inception.[55]

In the *Continental Can* case, the Court ruled that "it is only on the basis of a process of exegesis with due regard to the fundamental objectives" of the EU that the content and scope of European competition rules can be established, and it highlighted that it was clear from Article 2 of the Treaty that "the Community has as its task inter alia, by establishing the Common Market, to promote throughout the Community a harmonious development of economic activities and an accelerated raising of the standard of living in the Member States".[56] The Court used, therefore, a systematic and teleological interpretation of competition rules and, on the one

[52] The problem is that preferences are not always an exogenous process as assumed by this criterion; preferences are also endogenous. They depend on the individual's history and the respective context. Hausman (2000) argues, therefore, that revealed preference theory is unclear and should be abandoned. Others suggest a different criterion: instead of revealed preferences, an objective list of preferences (capabilities) may be constructed to promote well-being, cf. Gerbrandy (2019, p. 138), and Claassen and Gerbrandy (2016, p. 8).

[53] Communication from the Commission — Guidance on the Commission's enforcement priorities in applying Article 82 of the EC Treaty to abusive exclusionary conduct by dominant undertakings, [2009] OJ C 45/7, § 19.

[54] Although the adoption of a broader consumer welfare might be a way to take into account some of the distributive justice effects and concerns of anticompetitive practices, some literature argues that it is not enough and there should be a shift in the paradigm to the capabilities criteria, cf. Rutger Claassen, Anna Gerbrandy, op. cit., loc. Cit. In addition, Rutger Claassen and Anna Gerbrandy have pointed out it is worse to exclude non-economic goals than to include them, claiming that the consumer welfare approach should be replaced by the capability approach: "only a democratic process which includes all interests at stake can gain legitimacy", and law-making authorities "still have the last word in the matter if they want to" Claassen and Gerbrandy (2016, pp. 8–10).

[55] The Court acknowledges in its case-law that European competition rules promote several non-economic objectives, namely: the achievement of the internal market—Judgment of 13 July 1966, Consten and Grundig v. Commission of the EEC, C-56/64, EU:C:1966:41; economic freedom—Judgment of 17 February 2011, *TeliaSenora Sverge AB,* C-52/09, EU:C:2011:83; fairness—Judgment of 14 February 1978, *United Brands,* C-27/76, EU:C:1978:22; and equality of opportunities—Judgment of 1 July 2008, *Motosykletistiki Omospondia Ellados NPID (MOTOE) v Elliniko Dimosio,* C-49/07, ECR I-4863, § 51; Judgment of 14 October 2010, *Deutsche Telekom v. European Commission,* C-280/08, ECR I-9555.

[56] Judgment of 21 February 1973, *Europemballage Corporation and Continental Can Company Inc. v Commission of the European Communities,* C-6/72, EU:C:1973:22. p. 226.

hand, linked competition law to the promotion of the internal market and other objectives of the EU, deciding that competition rules should be read in relation to other provisions of the Treaty. On the other hand, it held that the establishment of a system ensuring undistorted competition in the internal market was indispensable for the achievement of the 'Community's' tasks.[57]

The *nexus* between competition law and the internal market was confirmed with the Lisbon Treaty, which, nevertheless, eliminated the reference, included in the draft Constitutional Treaty, to competition as an objective of the Union.[58] Article 3(3) of the TEU provides that the Union shall establish an internal market with the goal of achieving "a highly competitive social market economy", replacing the expression "open market economy with free competition" in Article 4(1) of the former Treaty. And Article 3(1) (g) of the EC Treaty regarding the commitment of the Union to 'undistorted competition' was moved to Protocol No. 27, annexed to the Treaties. The constitutional dimension of EU competition law and its nature as a fundamental right may, according to some authors, have been "downgraded" by the legal reform.[59]

Some literature argues that competition law was transformed from a fundamental goal of the EU (under the draft Constitutional Treaty) to a "means" of achieving other EU objectives. They argue that the concept of social market economy operates more as an "interpretive principle" than as an "objective" of the EU, transforming "the Union [in]to some form of holistic polity with competence to act, or at least to consider, all aspects of the welfare of its citizens" (Lianos 2013, p. 43).

Others consider that Protocol No. 27 does not represent a substantive change in the law. The Court of Justice would not abandon its previous case-law according to which European competition rules protect the competitive structure of the market and, indirectly, consumers. Competition should be considered an objective (or general principle), meaning that competition rules are "fundamental constitutional provisions of the EU legal order" (Van Rompuy 2011).

The Court of Justice has also clarified the issue and held that the protocol has the same interpretative status as the preamble and former Article 3(1) (g) of the EC Treaty. In Commission v. Italy,[60] the Court held that the "vital nature" of the Treaty rules on competition "is apparent from Article 3(3) TEU, namely the establishment of an internal market, and from Protocol No. 27 on the internal market and competition, which forms an integral part of the Treaties in accordance with Article 51 TEU, and states that the internal market includes a system ensuring that competition is not distorted".[61]

---

[57] Case cit., loc. cit.

[58] It was the French delegation that insisted on deleting the reference to 'undistorted competition' in the Lisbon Treaty, insisting that competition should no longer be considered an objective of the EU, but just a means to achieve the internal market (Van Rompuy 2011, p. 2).

[59] Discussing the legal reform, see Lianos (2013, p. 41).

[60] Judgment of 17 November 2011, *European Commission v. Italy*, C-496/09, EU:C:2011:740.

[61] § 60.

The idea that the protection of competition as such should be an objective of EU competition rules was also defended by Advocate General Kokott in *British Airways*: "[Article 102] forms part of a system designed to protect competition within the internal market from distortions (...) like the other competition rules of the Treaty, [it] is not designed only or primarily to protect the immediate interests of individual competitors or consumers, but to protect the *structure of the market* and thus *competition as such* (*as an institution*), which has already been weakened by the presence of the dominant undertaking on the market. In this way, consumers are also indirectly protected".[62] The main objective of EU competition law is not to protect the final consumer (as the General Court alleged in the *Glaxosmithkline* case[63]) but to preserve the competitive process, from abuse of economic power, and indirectly benefit final consumers.[64]

The Court of Justice followed the same reasoning in the *T-Mobile* case.[65] It ruled that competition rules are designed "to protect not only the immediate interests of individual competitors or consumers but also to protect the structure of the market and thus competition as such",[66] and it "is a matter of public policy, essential for the accomplishment of the tasks entrusted to the Community".[67]

In conclusion, competition should be protected as a public interest objective, an essential institution of a democratic Union, a fundamental value shared between the Member States and the Union, contributing to the achievement of the European values of freedom, democracy and respect for the rule of law.

2 Conclusion

The rule of law penetrates all areas of EU law and its influence in the enforcement of competition law was highlighted by the Court in the *Sped-Pro* case. The Court held that the European Commission could not reject a complaint for lack of an EU interest, if national authorities were not in a position to adequately safeguard the complainant's rights. Independence of the judiciary, as well as independence of national competition authorities, is essential to guarantee the fundamental rights of complainants and the effective enforcement of competition rules. The European Commission must, therefore, scrutinise the evidence presented by the complainants regarding the breach of the rule of law.

---

[62] Opinion of Advocate General Kokott delivered on 23 February 2006, *British Airways plc v Commission of the European Communities*, C-95/04 P, EU:C:2006:133 §68.

[63] *GlaxoSmithKline Services*, T-168/01, cit.

[64] Joined cases C-501/06 P, C-513/06 P, C-515/06 P and C-519/06 P., cit.

[65] Judgment of 4 June 2009, *T-Mobile Netherlands BV, KPN Mobile NV, Orange Nederland NV and Vodafone Libertel NV v Raad van bestuur van de Nederlandse Mededingingsautoriteit*, C-8/08, EU:C:2009:343.

[66] § 38.

[67] § 49.

On one hand, this case breaks new ground as, for the first time, the Court extended its reasoning on breach of the rule of law, in the light of systemic deficiencies regarding the independence of judiciary, to include the independence of National Competition Authorities. In addition, the case confirms the lesson from the ordoliberals that competition is an objective of the EU and is essential to guarantee a democratic Union.

On the other hand, the judgment falls a little short of expectations as the Court did not address the issue of the breach of trust between national competition authorities, regarding the lack of independence of one of them, and neither did it resolve the problem of the allocation of the case, as the European Commission cannot be forced to open an antitrust investigation.

Altogether, the *Sped-Pro* case can be seen as a critical step in an important journey that the European Union's legal order is continuing to make. As the Union and its internal market evolve, the importance of ensuring the proper functioning of national competition authorities and their independence will become even more apparent. It is for the Court and the legislators to ensure that the legal vacuum is filled with appropriate interpretations and provisions designed to ensure the protection of fundamental rights to their fullest extent.

References

Allan TRS (2005) Rule of law (rechtsstaat). In: Craig E (ed) The shorter Routledge encyclopedia of philosophy. Routledge, London, pp 388–391

Allison JWF (2018) Turning the rule of law into an English constitutional idea. In: May C, Winchester A (eds) Handbook on the rule of law. Edward Elgar, Cheltenham, pp 167–183

Aristóteles (1998) Política. Vega Editora, Lisboa

Aristóteles (2005) Retórica, obras completas de Aristóteles, translated by Júnior, MA. Imprensa Nacional Casa da Moeda, Lisboa

Badgy LMJ (2007) Hobbes's leviathan: reader's guide. Continuum International Publishing Group, New York

Beaton-Wells C (2020) Antitrust's neglected question: who is "the consumer"? Antitrust Bull 65:173–193

Behrens P (2014) The consumer choice paradigm in German Ordoliberalism and its impact upon EU competition law, discussion paper 1/40, Europea-Kolleg Hanburg, Institute for European Integration. https://www.econstor.eu/bitstream/10419/95925/1/780714202.pdf. Accessed 30 Sept 2023

Bernatt M (2019) Rule of law crisis, judiciary and competition law. Leg Issues Econ Integr 46:345–362

Claassen R, Gerbrandy A (2016) Rethinking European competition law: from a consumer welfare to a capability approach. Utrecht L Rev 12:1

Costa P (2018) The rule of law: an outline of its historical foundations. In: May C, Winchester A (eds) Handbook on the rule of law. Edward Elgar, Cheltenham, pp 135–148

Craig P, De Búrca G (2015) EU law: text, cases and materials, 6th edn. Oxford University Press, Oxford

Cseres KJ (2019) The implementation of the ECN+ directive in Hungary and lessons beyond. YARS 12:55–90

da Silva JNC (2019) Agências de Regulação da União Europeia. Gestlegal, Coimbra

Deutscher E, Makris S (2016) Exploring the ordoliberal paradigm: the competition-democracy nexus. Compet Law Rev 11:181–214
Dicey AV (1885) An introduction to the study of law of the constitution. Macmillan, London
Dyzenhaus D (2021) Thomas Hobbes and the rule by law tradition. In: Meierhenrich J, Loughlin M (eds) The Cambridge companion to the rule of law. Cambridge University Press, Cambridge, pp 261–277
Elkins Z, Ginsburg T, Melton J (2016) On the influence of magna carta and other cultural relics. Int Rev Law Econ 47:3–9
Gauthier DP (2000) The logic of leviathan: the moral and political theory of Thomas Hobbes. Oxford University Press, Oxford
Gerbrandy A (2019) Rethinking competition law within the European economic constitution. J Common Mark Stud 57:127–142
Harvey WB (1961) The rule of law in historical perspective. Mich Law Rev 59:487–500
Hausman DM (2000) Revealed preference, belief, and game theory. Econ Philos 16:99–115
Henley K (1999) Rule of law. In: Gray B (ed) The philosophy of law: an encyclopedia. Taylor and Francis, Milton Park, pp 765–767
Horn C (2013) Law, governance, and political obligation. In: Deslauriers M, Destrées P (eds) The Cambridge companion to Aristotle's politics. Cambridge University Press, Cambridge, pp 223–246
Iacovides MC, Vrettos C (2022) Falling through the cracks no more? Article 102 TFEU and sustainability: the relation between dominance, environmental degradation, and social injustice. J Antitrust Enforc 10:32–62
Johnson VR (2015) The ancient magna carta and the modern rule of law: 1215 to 2015. St Mary's Law J 47:1–62
Khan L (2018) The new Brandeis movement: America's antimonopoly debate. J Eur Compet Law Pract 9:131–132
Kochenov D (2021) Article 7: a commentary on a much talked-about 'dead' provision. In: von Bogdandy A, Bogdanowicz P, Canor I, Grabenwarter C, Taborowski M, Schmidt M (eds) Defending checks and balances in EU member states. Springer, Berlin, pp 127–154
Kochenov D, Pech L (2016) Better late than never? On the European Commission's rule of law framework and its first activation. J Common Mark Stud 54:1062–1074
Konstadinides T (2017) The rule of law in the European Union: the internal dimension. Hart Publishing, Oxford
Kozak M (2020) Mutual trust as a backbone of EU antitrust law. Market Compet Law Rev 4:127
Kramer MH (2004) On the moral status of the rule of law. Camb Law J 63:65–97
Krause S (2000) The spirit of separate powers in Montesquieu. Rev Politics 62:231–265
Łacny J (2021) The rule of law conditionality under regulation no 2092/2020—is it all about the money? Hague J Rule Law 13:79–105
Lenaerts K (2017) La vie après l'avis: exploring the principle of mutual (yet not blind) trust. Common Mark Law Rev 54:805–840
Lenaerts K (2020) New horizons for the rule of law within the EU. Ger Law J 21:29–34
Letwin SR (2005) On the history of the idea of law. Cambridge University Press, Cambridge
Lianos I (2013) Some reflections on the question of the goals of EU competition law. CLES research paper series 3/2013. Centre for Law, Economics and Society, UCL Faculty of Laws, London
Lino D (2018) The rule of law and the rule of empire: AV Dicey in imperial context. Mod Law Rev 81:739–764
Lisi F (2013) Plato and the rule of law. Méthexis 26:83–102
Locke J (1982) In: Cox RH (ed) Second treatise of government. Harlan Davidson, Inc, Wheeling
Newey G (2008) Routledge philosophy guidebook to Hobbes and Leviathan. Routledge, New York
Pech L (2021) The rule of law. In: Craig P, De Búrca G (eds) The evolution of EU law, 3rd edn. Oxford University Press, Oxford, pp 307–338
Robertson VH (2022) Antitrust, big tech, and democracy: a research agenda. Antitrust Bull 67:259–279

Rundle K (2021) The morality of the rule of law: Lon L. fuller. In: Meierhenrich J, Loughlin M (eds) The Cambridge companion to the rule of law. Cambridge University Press, Cambridge, pp 186–201
Tamanaha BZ (2004) On the rule of law: history, politics, theory. Cambridge University Press, Cambridge
Tollison RD (1985) Public choice and antitrust. Cato J 4:905–932
Van Rompuy B (2011) The impact of the Lisbon treaty on EU competition law: a review of recent case law of the EU courts. CPI Antitrust Chron 1:1–9
Van Rompuy B (2022) Independence as a prerequisite for mutual trust between EU competition enforcers: case T-791/19, Sped-pro v commission. J Eur Compet Law Pract 13:413–415
Vile MJC (1998) Constitutionalism and the separation of powers, 2nd edn. Liberty Fund, Indianapolis
Walters MD (2021) A.V. Dicey and the common law constitutional tradition: a legal turn of mind. Cambridge University Press, Cambridge
White MJ (2012) Political philosophy: a historical introduction, 2nd edn. Oxford University Press, Oxford
Witt AC (2012) Public policy goals under EU competition law—now is the time to set the house in order. Eur Compet J 8:443–471
Wu T (2018) The curse of bigness: antitrust in the new gilded age, Columbia global reports, 33. Columbia Global Reports, New York
Zimmer D (2007) On fairness and welfare: the objectives of competition policy. In: Ehlermann CD, Marquis M (eds) European competition annual 2007. Hart Publications, Oxford, pp 103–108

Judicial Independence in a Union Based on the Rule of Law: A Play in Five Acts

Alessandra Silveira

1 First Act

European integration emerged as an anti-fascist response to the collapse of the rule of law in the period between the two World Wars. Since then, the entire European legal-constitutional construction is based on the idea that democracy, in the absence of the rule of law, becomes the "tyranny of the majority" (Alexis de Tocqueville). [For further developments on the idea of the rule of law in the European Union, see Canotilho (2017), Silveira (2022, 2023)]. In fact, since the beginning of European integration, the mission of impartial and independent courts has never been as important as it is today, given the current war in Ukraine. Therefore, it is important to consider that "*It is when the cannons roar that we especially need the laws...Every struggle of the state – against terrorism or any other enemy – is conducted according to rules and law. There is always law which the state must comply with*", as stated by the Advocate General Poiares Maduro in his Opinion in the *Kadi* case, quoting Aharon Barak, the former President of the Supreme Court of Israel.[1]

In a recent action for annulment of the rules of Regulation 2020/2092 (on the general regime of conditionality for the protection of the European Union (EU)

[1] *Kadi*, C-402/05 P, ECLI:EU:C:2008:11, recital 45.

Director of Master's Degree in EU Law. Jean Monnet (JM) Chair Holder in EU Law. Director of the JM Centre of Excellence "Digital citizenship and technological sustainability" (CitDig), Erasmus+ (https://citdig.direito.uminho.pt)

A. Silveira (✉)
University of Minho, School of Law, Braga, Portugal
e-mail: asilveira@direito.uminho.pt

I. Quadros, M. Gorjão-Henriques (eds.), *Revisiting the Liberal Constitutional Features of the European Union*, https://doi.org/10.1007/978-3-031-95717-8_7

budget in the case of breaches of the principles of the rule of law in the Member States), the Court of Justice of the EU (CJEU) had to examine the arguments put forward by Hungary (supported by the Republic of Poland) in support of its plea alleging infringement of the principle of legal certainty: (i) the arguments according to which the concept of the rule of law cannot be precisely defined and cannot be given a uniform interpretation, because of the obligation to 'protect' the national identity of each of the Member States; (ii) the arguments according to which the concept of the rule of law, defined in Article 2(a) of the contested regulation includes other values contained in Article 2 TEU, all of which are political and not legal in nature, and (iii) the arguments according to which Article 2(a) of the contested regulation undermines the interpretation of the concept of the rule of law as a common value of the EU.

The CJEU clarified that the principles of the rule of law, as developed in the case-law of the Court on the basis of the EU Treaties, are thus recognised and specified in the legal order of the EU, and have their source in common values which are also recognised and applied by the Member States in their own legal system.[2] Accordingly, and considering the particular features of the legal system of the Member State in question, as well as the discretion which that Member State enjoys in implementing the principles of the rule of law, that requirement is in no way incompatible with the application of uniform assessment criteria.[3] In those circumstances, Hungary cannot maintain that the Member States are not in a position to determine with sufficient precision the essential content and the requirements flowing from each of the principles listed in Article 2(a) of the contested regulation—nor that those principles are of a purely political nature and that an assessment of whether they have been respected cannot be the subject of a strictly legal analysis.[4]

In any event, one should recall the meaning of the rule of law. The expression "rule of law" means that the exercise of public power is subject to legal norms and procedures—legislative, executive and judicial procedures—which allow citizens to monitor and potentially challenge the legitimacy of decisions taken by the public power. The core idea of the value of the rule of law is to submit power to law, restraining the natural tendency of power to expand and operate in an arbitrary manner—be it the traditional power of the State, the power of novel political structures such as the EU, or the power of private organisational complexes—such as market forces, internet forces, sports forces, etc.

Although there is no definition of the rule of law in the European constitutive treaties, it follows from the case-law of the CJEU that this is a fundamental norm which guides and conditions the exercise of public powers. The rule of law is the source of the principles in force in the Union's legal system, such as the principle of

[2] *Hungary v European Parliament/Council of the European Union*, C-156/21, ECLI:EU:C:2022:97, recital 237.

[3] *Hungary v European Parliament/Council of the European Union*, C-156/21, ECLI:EU:C:2022:97, recital 235.

[4] *Hungary v European Parliament/Council of the European Union*, C-156/21, ECLI:EU:C:2022:97, recital 240.

legality, the principle of legal certainty, the principle of the protection of legitimate expectations, prohibition of arbitrariness by the public authorities, the principle of the balance of power, the principle of equality before the law, the principle of effective judicial protection, etc. It is a core norm that requires all citizens to be treated in a dignified and equitable manner by all decision-makers, in accordance with the law, giving them the opportunity to challenge such decisions before independent and impartial courts.

The principle of the rule of law essentially implies a transparent, accountable, democratic, and pluralistic process for enacting laws; legal certainty; prohibition of arbitrariness of the executive powers; independent and impartial courts; effective judicial review; and equality before the law. Both the CJEU and the European Court of Human Rights (ECtHR) have confirmed that these principles are not purely formal and procedural requirements. They are the vehicle for ensuring compliance with and respect for democracy and human rights.

The rule of law is therefore a constitutional principle with both formal and substantive components. This means that respect for the rule of law is intrinsically linked to respect for democracy and for fundamental rights: there can be no democracy and respect for fundamental rights without respect for the rule of law and vice-versa. Thus, in formal terms, the rule of law points to an idea of a government functioning in legal conformity. However, this basic lawfulness—i.e., specific norms of coherence, generality, clarity, stability, non-retroactivity, etc.—is not in itself an opening for a material conception of justice of the rule of law.

This is particularly important today, because there is no longer any doubt that we are facing a wave of intentionally cohesive and highly coordinated right-wing authoritarian politics that is taking over global affairs. Although such movements have a short-sighted and materially anti-democratic cosmovision, the fact is that they have gained force and are increasingly coming to power precisely through the instruments of formal democracy. They are phenomena that are potentially threatening to democracy, and yet generated in democracy, based on the fundamental rights that define it, such as freedom of association and freedom of speech.

The rule of law has been under increasing pressure in Europe. Indeed, the rule of law has not been immune to the crises that the EU has gone through and continues to go through, from the European debt crisis and the migrant crisis to the constitutional crisis with Brexit and the populist drift, and more recently, the health emergency due to the COVID-19 pandemic. The rule of law is threatened when a significant number of actors, in different sectors and different Member States, fail to guarantee normative expectations to the point of creating a lack in confidence in the law and in public institutions.

However, public confidence in the legal systems of all Member States is crucial for the functioning of the EU as a whole. It follows that compliance by a Member State with the values contained in Article 2 TEU is a condition for the enjoyment of all the rights deriving from the application of the Treaties to that Member State.[5]

[5] *Repubblika,* C-896/19, EU:C:2021:311, recital 63.

Compliance with those values cannot be reduced to an obligation which a candidate State must meet in order to accede to the EU and which it may disregard after its accession.[6]

The values contained in Article 2 TEU have been identified and are shared by the Member States. They define the very identity of the EU as a common legal order. Thus, the EU must be able to defend those values, within the limits of its powers as laid down by the Treaties.[7] For this reason, proclaiming the value of the rule of law must be interpreted as an attempt by Western legal-political culture to recover its most recognised and precious heritage.

2 Second Act

A "Union based on the rule of law" (or simply a "Union of law", such as the EU) implies the exercise of a jurisdictional function separate and distinct from the governmental function. Based on the criteria of judicial independence, the case-law of the CJEU has broadened the scope of protection of the principle of the Union of law (what does it protect? what does it prohibit?), enforced since the *Les Verts* judgment as a norm that (i) imposes limits on the action of the European institutions and Member States in areas covered by EU law, and (ii) provides guarantees for the rights of individuals affected by European provisions.[8]

Although it is true that the organisation of justice in the Member States falls within the competence of those Member States, in the exercise of that competence they are required to comply with their obligations deriving from EU law. This is the case, in particular, with national rules on the adoption of decisions appointing judges and, where applicable, rules relating to the judicial review pursuant to such appointment procedures, and rules governing the disciplinary regime applicable to judges.[9]

Such developments began with the "*Portuguese Judges*" judgment,[10] in which the CJEU was asked to determine whether there is a general principle of EU law according to which the authorities of the Member States are obliged to respect the independence of national judges as functionally European judges. [On this judgment, see Silveira et al. (2018)]. In its response in the "*Portuguese Judges*"

[6] *Hungary v European Parliament/Council of the European Union*, C-156/21, ECLI:EU:C:2022:97, recital 126.

[7] *Hungary v European Parliament/Council of the European Union*, C-156/21, ECLI:EU:C:2022:97, recital 127.

[8] *Les Verts*, 294/83, EU:C:1986:166.

[9] *Commission v Poland - Disciplinary regime for judges*, C-791/19, EU:C:2021:596, recitals 56 and 61; *Prokuratura Rejonowa w Mińsku Mazowieckim and Others*, C-748/19 to C-754/19, EU:C:2021:931, recital 36.

[10] *Associação Sindical dos Juízes Portugueses ("Portuguese Judges")*, C-64/16, ECLI:EU:C:2018:117.

judgment, the CJEU defined judicial independence within the meaning of EU law, establishing criteria and guarantees for its proper exercise. This is the central idea in the "*Portuguese Judges*" judgment: the very existence of effective judicial review designed to ensure compliance with EU law is of the essence of the rule of law.

It follows that every Member State must ensure that the bodies which, as courts or tribunals within the meaning of EU law, come within its judicial system in the fields covered by that law, meet the requirements of effective judicial protection.[11] This embodies the value of the rule of law stated in Article 2 TEU and recognises the integrated nature of the EU's judicial system, as national courts play a role which is jointly assigned to them with the CJEU in order to ensure respect for the law in the interpretation and application of the Treaties.

Due to its relevance for effective judicial protection and the rule of law in the EU, the *"Portuguese Judges"* judgment is compared with the *Les Verts* judgment, according to which the EU is a "Union based on the rule of law", inasmuch as neither its Member States nor its institutions can avoid a review of the question whether the measures adopted by them are in conformity with the basic constitutional charter, the Treaty.[12] It is worth recalling the circumstances of this case-law to understand the subsequent CJEU steps on judicial independence, so that Article 19 TEU gives tangible expression to the value of the rule of law asserted in Article 2 TEU.

At the origin of the request for a preliminary ruling in the "*Portuguese Judges*" case is a special administrative action brought before the "Supremo Tribunal Administrativo" (Supreme Administrative Court, Portugal) seeking the annulment of (administrative) measures reducing the salary of the judges of the "Tribunal de Contas" (Court of Auditors, Portugal). These measures were adopted on the basis of a 2014 Portuguese law that puts in place mechanisms for the temporary reduction of remuneration (and the conditions governing its reversibility) of a series of office holders and employees performing duties in the public sector, including members of the judiciary. As the Advocate General Saugmandsgaard Øe pointed out, the CJEU was in essence asked to "*determine whether there is a general principle of EU law that the authorities of the Member States are required to respect the independence of the national judges and, more particularly – in the light of the circumstances of the main proceedings – to maintain their remuneration at a constant level that is sufficient for them to be able to perform their duties freely*".[13]

The legal action brought before the Portuguese Supreme Administrative Court (STA) was accompanied by an Opinion which I had the honour of writing with my colleague Pedro Froufe. That Opinion intended to clarify the extent to which the subject matter fell within the scope of application of EU law, triggering the need to refer to the CJEU for a preliminary ruling. It was important to convince the Portuguese STA to interact with the CJEU because the latter Court had already

[11] *Associação Sindical dos Juízes Portugueses ("Portuguese Judges")*, C-64/16, ECLI:EU:C:2018:117, recitals 36 and 37.

[12] *Les Verts*, 294/83, EU:C:1986:166, recital 23.

[13] *Associação Sindical dos Juízes Portugueses* ("*Portuguese Judges*"), C-64/16, ECLI:EU:C:2017:395, recital 55.

decided that the austerity measures adopted by the Portuguese Government were not applying EU law under Article 51(1) of the Charter of Fundamental Rights of the EU (CFREU).[14] According to that provision, the requirements flowing from the protection of fundamental rights are binding on Member States whenever they implement EU law. Given that, according to the CJEU, the order for reference in *Sindicato dos Bancários do Norte* did not contain any specific information to show that the austerity measures were implementing EU law—or would be connected in any other way with that law[15]–, the jurisdiction of the CJEU to rule on that reference for a preliminary ruling was not established, and the CJEU understood that it had no jurisdiction to answer the questions referred to it.

In light of this, the Portuguese STA eventually referred a question to the CJEU focusing on judicial independence as a requirement for effective judicial protection within EU law with a view to ascertaining the compatibility of the austerity measures in question with that principle: "*In view of the mandatory requirements of eliminating the excessive budget deficit and of financial assistance regulated by (…) rules [of EU law], must the principle of judicial independence, enshrined in the second subparagraph of Article 19(1) TEU, in Article 47 of the [Charter] and in the case-law of the Court of Justice, be interpreted as meaning that it precludes the measures to reduce remuneration that are applied to the judiciary in Portugal, where they are imposed unilaterally and on an ongoing basis by other constitutional authorities and bodies, as is the consequence of Article 2 of Law [No. 75/2014]?*"

In turn, the CJEU seized the opportunity provided by this somewhat technical issue to deliver a judgment with far-reaching consequences for effective judicial protection and the rule of law within the EU and, arguably, for the construction of the legal-constitutional model that supports the European integration process.

The reasoning of the CJUE is based on a combined reading of Article 2 TEU (values of the EU), Article 4(3) TEU (principle of loyal cooperation) and Article 19(1) TEU (principle of effective judicial protection of individuals' rights under EU law) (recitals 29–36). In particular, the CJEU especially emphasises that Article 19 TEU "*gives concrete expression to the value of the rule of law stated in Article 2 TEU*" and acknowledges the integrated nature of the EU judiciary system, as "*national courts and tribunals, in collaboration with the Court of Justice, fulfil a duty entrusted to them jointly of ensuring that in the interpretation and application of the Treaties the law is observed*". The principle of effective judicial protection of individuals' rights under EU law as "*now reaffirmed by Article 47 of the Charter*" is also mentioned, but in what could almost be considered a side note.

The main argument is clearly that based on the principle of effective judicial protection as a concrete expression of the value of the rule of law on which the EU is founded as "*the very existence of effective judicial review designed to ensure compliance with EU law is of the essence of the rule of law.*" Also, by placing the principle of effective judicial protection as a fundamental right on the sidelines, the

[14] *Sindicato dos Bancários do Norte*, ECLI:EU:C:2013:149, recitals 10–14.

[15] *Asparuhov*, ECLI:EU:C:2010:680, recital 14.

CJEU unshackles the principle from the constraints of Article 51(1) CFREU. The CJEU expressly states that "*as regards the material scope of the second subparagraph of Article 19(1) TEU, that provision relates to 'the fields covered by Union law', irrespective of whether the Member States are implementing Union law, within the meaning of Article 51(1) of the Charter.*"

The difference between "*the fields covered by EU law*" [Article 19(1) TEU] and "*situations that come within the scope of EU law*" [Article 51(1) CFREU, as interpreted in *Fransson,* ECLI:EU:C:2013:105, recital 21] remains to be clearly ascertained, because there should be no situations which are covered by EU law without fundamental rights being applicable. Nevertheless, following the "*Portuguese Judges*" judgment, it seems fair to state that the scope of application of Article 19(1) TEU is broader than the scope of EU law for the purposes of Article 47 CFREU. While an effective and sufficient link with EU law is necessary to trigger Article 47 CFREU by virtue of Article 51(1) CFREU, the mere possibility of applying EU law appears to be enough to trigger Article 19(1) TEU. Therefore, Member States must ensure that the bodies which, as '*courts or tribunals*' within the meaning of EU law, come within their judicial system in the fields covered by EU law, meet the requirements of effective judicial protection, irrespective of whether they are implementing EU law within the meaning of Article 51(1) CFREU.

This state of affairs has far-reaching consequences within the constitutionalism model emerging from the European integration. Bringing to light the legal-operational force of the values on which the EU is founded, the judgment given in "*Portuguese Judges*" does not ignore the challenges that the rule of law is facing today in the Europe. At the same time, however, the judgment discretely acknowledges and seeks to overcome the methodical difficulties posed by Article 51(1) CFREU within the EU system of protection of fundamental rights.

Moreover, the CJEU clarifies that the requirement of independence is an essential requirement for effective judicial protection under Article 19(1) TEU (recitals 40–45). After pointing out its inherent character in the task of adjudication and its essential role in the proper working of the judicial cooperation system embodied by the preliminary ruling mechanism (Article 267 TFEU), the CJEU interprets the concept of judicial independence as presupposing that "*the body concerned exercises its judicial functions wholly autonomously, without being subject to any hierarchical constraint or subordinated to any other body and without taking orders or instructions from any source whatsoever, and that it is thus protected against external interventions or pressure liable to impair the independent judgment of its members and to influence their decisions.*" In particular, both the "*protection against removal from office of the members of the body concerned*" and the "*receipt by those members of a level of remuneration commensurate with the importance of the functions they carry out*" are mentioned as constituting guarantees essential to judicial independence.

In the case at hand, and unsurprisingly, the CJEU did not consider that the salary reduction measures at issue undermined the independence of the judges of the Portuguese Court of Auditors (recitals 46–52). The limited and variable reduction of remuneration at issue (up to a percentage varying in accordance with the level of remuneration), the temporary nature of the salary-reduction measures (which were brought to an end on 1 October 2016), and their general nature, insofar as the measures were part of a collective austerity effort affecting several agents of the executive, the legislature, and the judiciary, were all important considerations in reaching this conclusion.

The answer given by the CJEU cannot, however, divert attention from the fact that a question of judicial independence was assessed without any relevance being given to the question of whether or not the austerity measures in question were covered by EU law. According to the Portuguese STA, the measures for the temporary reduction in the amount of public sector remuneration, also applied to the members of the judiciary, were based on mandatory requirements for reducing the Portuguese State's excessive budget deficit during the year 2011. The referring court therefore considered those measures to be measures adopted within the framework of EU law or, at least, as being European in origin, on the ground that those requirements were imposed on the Portuguese Government by EU decisions granting financial assistance (recital 14). However, the CJEU bypassed the issue, putting into practice the reasoning set out above that, as a concrete expression of the value of the rule of law on which the EU is founded, the principle of effective judicial protection and its requirements are to be ensured by every Member State in the fields covered by EU law, irrespective of whether they are implementing EU law.

3 Third Act

In the "*Portuguese Judges*" judgment, the CJEU highlighted that what is at stake is not (or is not only) a question on fundamental rights. With its judgment of 24 June 2019,[16] the CJEU seems to have recovered the "jus-fundamental" dimension of the question and decided that the second subparagraph of Article 19(1) TEU requires Member States to provide remedies that are sufficient to ensure effective legal protection, within the meaning in particular of Article 47 CFREU, in the fields covered by EU law. To a certain extent, the CJEU is reassessing the "jus-fundamentality" of situations which are covered by EU law.

Relying on the "*Portuguese Judges*"[17] and *Minister for Justice and Equality*[18] judgments, in *Commission v Poland*[19] the European Commission was seeking, in essence, a declaration that the second subparagraph of Article 19(1) TEU, read in the light of Article 47 CFREU, had been infringed. According to the Commission, the concept of effective legal protection referred to in the second subparagraph of Article 19(1) TEU must be interpreted having regard to the content of Article 47

[16] *Commission v Poland*, C-619/18, ECLI:EU:C:2019:531.

[17] *Associação Sindical dos Juízes Portugueses* ("*Portuguese Judges*"), C-64/16, EU:C:2018:117.

[18] *Minister for Justice and Equality*, C-216/18 PPU, EU:C:2018:586.

[19] *Commission v Poland*, C-619/18, ECLI:EU:C:2019:531.

CFREU and, in particular, the guarantees essential to the right to an effective remedy laid down in that latter provision, and accordingly the first of those provisions entails that the preservation of the independence of a body such as the Polish Supreme Court, which is entrusted, inter alia, with the task of interpreting and applying EU law, must be guaranteed.

The Commission argued that the Member States are required, *inter alia*, to ensure that the national bodies which may rule on issues in relation to the application or interpretation of EU law meet the requirement in respect of judicial independence, that requirement being a key part of the fundamental right to a fair trial as guaranteed by the second paragraph of Article 47 CFREU. Since the Polish Supreme Court constitutes such a body, the national provisions governing the composition, the organisational structure and the working method of that court should ensure that it meets that independence requirement. That requirement concerns not only the way in which an individual case is conducted, but also the way in which the justice system is organised. The consequence of a national measure affecting, in general, the independence of the national courts is that an effective legal remedy is no longer guaranteed, *inter alia* when those courts apply or interpret EU law.

The Republic of Poland, supported in this connection by Hungary, argued that those provisions of EU law do not include any derogation from the principle of conferral which governs the competences of the EU and which follows from Article 4(1) and Article 5(1) and (2) and Article 13(2) TEU. Therefore, the organisation of the national justice system constitutes a competence reserved exclusively to the Member States, so that the EU cannot arrogate competences in that domain. Moreover, the second subparagraph of Article 19(1) TEU and Article 47 CFREU, like general principles of EU law such as the principle of judicial independence, are applicable only in situations governed under EU law.

According to the Republic of Poland, the national rules called into question by the Commission have no link with EU law and in this respect can be distinguished from the national legislation which was the subject matter of the "*Portuguese Judges*" judgment—legislation which, for its part, was connected with the grant of financial assistance by the EU to a Member State in the context of combatting excessive budget deficits and which was therefore adopted pursuant to EU law.

However, according to the CJEU, although the organisation of justice in the Member States falls within the competence of those Member States, the fact remains that, when exercising that competence, the Member States are required to comply with their obligations deriving from EU law. Moreover, by requiring the Member States to comply with those obligations, the EU is not in any way claiming to exercise that competence itself and nor is it therefore, contrary to that alleged by the Republic of Poland, arrogating that competence to itself.

As regards the material scope of the second subparagraph of Article 19(1) TEU, the CJEU expanded it on its "*Portuguese Judges*" judgment. As mentioned above, and contrary to what the Republic of Poland and Hungary claim in this regard, the fact that the national salary reduction measures at issue in "*Portuguese Judges*" were adopted due to requirements linked to the elimination of the excessive budget deficit, as part of an EU financial assistance programme for Portugal, played no role in the interpretation which led the CJEU to conclude that the second subparagraph of Article 19(1) TEU was applicable in the case in question. That conclusion was reached on the basis that the national body to which that case related, i.e., the Court of Auditors, may, subject to a review by the referring court in that case, rule, as a court or tribunal, on questions concerning the application or interpretation of EU law and which therefore fall within the areas covered by EU law.

According to the CJEU, the same occurs with the Polish Supreme Court in the *Commission v Poland* case—thus, to ensure that a body such as the Supreme Court is in a position to offer effective judicial protection, maintaining its independence is essential, as confirmed by the second paragraph of Article 47 CFREU, which refers to access to an 'independent' tribunal as one of the requirements linked to the fundamental right to an effective remedy. That requirement that courts be independent, which is inherent in the task of adjudication, is part of the essence of the right to effective judicial protection and the fundamental right to a fair trial, which is of cardinal importance as a guarantee that all the rights which individuals derive from EU law will be protected and that the values common to the Member States set out in Article 2 TEU, in particular the value of the rule of law, will be safeguarded.

4 Fourth Act

The expression "rule of law" means that the exercise of public power is subject to legal norms and procedures—legislative, executive and judicial procedures—which allow citizens to monitor and potentially challenge the legitimacy of decisions taken by the public power. The core idea of the value of the rule of law is to submit power to law, restraining the natural tendency of power to expand and operate in an arbitrary manner—be it the traditional power of the State, the power of novel political structures such as the EU, or the power of private organisational complexes—such as market forces, internet forces, sports forces, etc.

The procedure provided by Article 7 TEU is the most emblematic political instrument to defend the rule of law in the EU. Article 7(1) TEU constitutes the initial phase in the procedure in the event of a clear risk of a serious breach by a Member State of the common values enshrined in Article 2 TEU. Article 7(2) TEU governs the next stage in which a serious and persistent breach by a Member State of the values laid down in Article 2 TEU can be established. Article 7(3) TEU ultimately provides for the issuing of sanctions against the Member State concerned.

Article 7(1) TEU provides that on a reasoned proposal by the European Parliament, the Council acting by a majority of 4/5 of its members may determine that there is a clear risk of a serious breach by a Member State of the common values of the Union referred to in Article 2 TEU. Moreover, Article 7(5) TUE provides that the voting arrangements applicable to the European Parliament are laid down in Article 354 TFEU—which provides that the European Parliament shall act by a 2/3 majority of the votes cast, representing the majority of its component Members.

On 12 September 2018, the European Parliament adopted a resolution on a proposal calling on the Council to determine, pursuant to Article 7(1) TEU, the existence of a clear risk of a serious breach by Hungary of the values on which the Union is founded. There were 448 votes cast in favour of the resolution, 197 cast against, and 48 abstentions. Hungary asked the CJEU to annul that resolution under Article 263 TFEU.[20]

As explained by the Advocate General Michael Bobek in his Opinion delivered on 3 December 2020, that action for annulment raises two key legal issues: (i) first, would the reasoned proposals adopted under Article 7(1) TEU be amenable to judicial review under Article 263 TFEU, in particular, in view of Article 269 TFEU? (by virtue of Article 269 TFEU, the Court of Justice shall have jurisdiction to decide on the legality of an act adopted by the Council pursuant to Article 7 TEU solely at the request of the Member State concerned by a determination of the Council and in respect solely of the procedural stipulations contained in that Article); (ii) second, should that indeed be the case, how would the abstentions be counted in the European Parliament for the purpose of determining whether the 2/3 majority of the votes cast, as required by Article 354 TFEU, has been reached? (Hungary argued that the contested resolution would not have been adopted if abstentions had been considered properly).

On 3 June 2021, the CJEU dismissed the action, closely following the Advocate General's Opinion. The Court decided that resolutions of the Parliament, adopted under Article 7(1) TEU, do not fall under Article 269. Thus, the authors of the Treaties did not intend to exclude an act such as the contested resolution from the general jurisdiction conferred on the Court of Justice by Article 263 TFEU. Furthermore, when calculating the votes cast when that resolution was adopted, the Parliament was right not to take abstentions into account. Thus, the rule laid down in the fourth paragraph of Article 354 TFEU, which requires a majority of votes cast, must be interpreted as precluding the consideration of abstentions.

It is important to focus on the first key legal issue raised by the action for annulment, since the Court's interpretation contributes to the observance of the principle that the EU is a Union based on the rule of law, which has established a complete system of legal remedies and procedures designed to enable the CJEU to review the legality of acts of the EU institutions.

According to the European Parliament, the action for annulment against the contested resolution was inadmissible. It argued that Article 269 TFEU—which is a *lex specialis* with regard to Article 263 TFEU, the *lex generalis*—was applicable in that case. Article 269 TFEU, the Parliament claimed, was one of a number of other provisions limiting the Court's jurisdiction in special domains. It precluded judicial review by the Court of the contested resolution. According to the European Parliament, the authors of the Treaties did not intend to have a broad scope of judicial review for acts pertaining to the Article 7 TEU procedure. The procedure under Article 7 TEU constituted an extraordinary political safeguard which is largely

---

[20] *Hungary v European Parliament*, C-650/18.

insulated from the Court's jurisdiction. Among the different acts that may be adopted under Article 7 TEU, only the determination made by the European Council or the Council could be subject to judicial review under Article 269 TFEU.

In particular, the European Parliament argued that it would be illogical to have full judicial review of preparatory acts under Article 263 TFEU while determinations are subject to a limited review under Article 269 TFEU. This would mean that the political debate which ought to take place within the Council would then take place in the courtroom. The Court could examine alleged procedural irregularities committed during the adoption of an act, such as the contested resolution, but at a later stage during the judicial review of the determination made by the Council or the European Council.

Should the Court embrace a different approach, the European Parliament remained of the view that the contested resolution was not challengeable due to its lack of legal effects. The resolution did not entail any change in the applicant's legal situation. The Council was entirely free to follow the Parliament's proposal or to choose not to do so. The contested resolution was an intermediary measure immune from judicial challenge. It did contain the final position of the Parliament, since the latter would have to approve the determination made by the Council pursuant to Article 7 TEU at a later stage of the procedure.

However, the CJEU considered that it is established case-law that the EU is a Union based on the rule of law, in which all acts of its institutions are subject to review of their compatibility with the Treaties, the general principles of EU law and fundamental rights. As explained by the Advocate General in his Opinion, since the Treaty of Lisbon entered into force, the Court enjoys jurisdiction by default regarding all acts adopted by EU institutions, at least those which are intended to have legal effects. However, even in those scenarios, the Court has insisted on the fact that Article 19 TEU has conferred general jurisdiction on the Court to ensure that, with regard to the interpretation and application of the Treaties, the law is observed. Accordingly, any derogation from that rule of general jurisdiction must be interpreted narrowly. In short, under the Treaty of Lisbon, the default rule is uncompromisingly simple: unless the Treaty clearly and expressly excludes it, the Court has jurisdiction over all EU acts. Moreover, any such express exclusion is to be interpreted narrowly.

So, how did Article 269 TFEU—which, along with Article 263 TFEU, is at the core of that action for annulment—fit within the Union's complete system of legal remedies with regard to the specific procedure under Article 7 TEU? Was it, as argued by the European Parliament, a *lex specialis* which applies across the entire Article 7 TEU procedure and excludes judicial review of any act adopted within that procedure, except for the acts expressly set out in Article 269 TFEU?

The CJEU concluded that Article 269 TFEU is not in fact a jurisdiction exclusion clause. As stated by the Advocate General in his Opinion, within the system and the reasoning for standing under Article 263 TFEU, especially in view of the exclusion of preparatory acts from judicial review, the effect of Article 269 TFEU is to expressly confirm and thus to attribute (albeit indeed limited) jurisdiction to the Court with regard to specific types of act (determinations made by the European

Council or the Council) that could be, if normal rules were applicable, excluded. Thus, Article 269 TFEU does not govern—nor, consequently, preclude—the initiation of actions for annulment against other acts under Article 7 TEU, those not referred to in Article 269 TFEU, including the reasoned proposal of the Parliament under Article 7(1) TEU.

The CJEU decided that, in the light of Article 269 TFEU, an action for annulment under Article 263 TFEU against a reasoned proposal adopted by the Parliament under Article 7 TEU may be brought only by the Member State which is the subject of that proposal within 2 months of its adoption. However, the grounds for annulment relied on in support of such an action can only be based on infringement of the procedural rules referred to in Article 7 TEU.

One may ask: for what reason? Because to accept that, on the basis of Article 263 TFEU, an action for annulment against a reasoned proposal of the Parliament, adopted under Article 7(1) TEU, may be brought by an applicant other than the Member State which is the subject of that proposal, and that, in support of that action, any ground referred to in the second paragraph of Article 263 TFEU may be relied on, would, to a large extent, deprive of their practical effect the specific conditions, laid down in Article 269 TFEU, relating to the bringing of an action for annulment against the determination of the Council referred to in Article 7(1) TEU, which could be adopted as a result of that proposal.

Therefore, as mentioned by the Advocate General in his Opinion, Article 269 TFEU is indeed a type of *lex specialis*, but a very different one from that suggested by the European Parliament. It is not, and logically cannot be, a straightforward, across the board exclusion from judicial review of any acts not expressly mentioned therein but adopted nonetheless under Article 7 TEU. It is a special confirmation or attribution of jurisdiction *vis-à-vis* specific types of acts mentioned therein that were likely to be excluded.

Article 7 TEU has set up a procedure that is specifically dedicated to ensuring compliance with the rule of law by the Member States—and judicial protection is one of the most important principles of the rule of law. Since the "*Portuguese Judges*" judgment[21] the CJEU has stressed that Article 19 TEU obliges Member States to ensure effective judicial protection in areas covered by EU law, recognising the integrated nature of the Union's judicial system. As recently recalled by the Court on the basis of Article 2 TEU, the very existence of effective judicial review designed to ensure compliance with provisions of EU law is inherent in the existence of the rule of law,[22] which upheld the Court's jurisdiction despite the first paragraph of Article 275 TFEU.

Therefore, the CJEU decided that effective judicial protection requires that reasoned proposals may be subject to review pursuant to Article 263 TFEU, provided they produce binding legal effects. The contested resolution did not constitute an

---

[21] *Associação Sindical dos Juízes Portugueses* ("*Portuguese Judges*"), C-64/16, EU:C:2018:117.

[22] *H v Council and Others*, C-455/14 P, EU:C:2016:569, recital 41; *Rosneft*, C-72/15, EU:C:2017:236, recitals 72 and 73.

intermediate measure the legality of which can be challenged only in the event of a dispute concerning the definitive act for which it represents a preparatory step. As mentioned by the Advocate General in his Opinion, it would be positively Kafkaesque to make access to judicial review dependent on the existence, potentially 1 day, of a final decision of an unknown nature, while in the meantime the reasoned proposal remains effective for an indefinite period of time. Such a scenario would hardly fit the description of a Union of law where the very existence of effective judicial review designed to ensure compliance with provisions of EU law is inherent in the existence of the rule of law.

5 Fifth Act

Recently the CJUE added a further piece to the puzzle of a Union based on the rule of law—and it did so once again from the judicial independence in which the effective judicial protection of individuals' rights under EU law is rooted. More precisely, on 22 March 2022, in the case *M. F.*[23] the CJEU claimed that the second subparagraph of Article 19(1) TEU—according to which "Member States shall provide remedies sufficient to ensure effective legal protection in the fields covered by Union law"—, must be regarded as having direct effect.

What novelty does the *M. F.* judgment bring with it? In January 2019, disciplinary proceedings were initiated against M.F., a judge at a Regional Court of Poland, for alleged delays in handling the cases on which she was called upon to rule. J.M., in his capacity as President of the Supreme Court, responsible for the work of the disciplinary chamber of the latter court, designated the disciplinary court competent to hear that case at first instance. However, M.F. claimed that the proceedings against her could not be continued because J.M. was not a judge of the Supreme Court, arguing that J.M.'s appointment in the Supreme Court's disciplinary chamber was vitiated by several irregularities. One of the chambers of the Supreme Court, the Labour and Social Insurance Chamber, was then instructed to examine those claims.

On 22 March 2022, the CJEU declared inadmissible the request for a preliminary ruling made by that chamber of the Polish Supreme Court. The referring court had asked whether EU law confers on it the power, which is not conferred on it by Polish law, to declare that a judge's service relationship does not exist because of irregularities vitiating the instrument of his appointment. The questions referred to the CJEU were related intrinsically to a dispute other than that in the main proceedings, to which the latter was merely incidental.[24] The referring court itself observed that when a civil action is brought for a declaration of the non-existence of a legal relationship, that court lacks, under national law, the jurisdiction which would enable it

[23] *M. F.*, C-508/19, ECLI:EU:C:2022:201.

[24] *M. F.*, C-508/19, ECLI:EU:C:2022:201, recital 71.

to rule on the lawfulness of the instrument of appointment at issue.[25] It is the case, however, that Article 267 TFEU presupposes that the referring court has jurisdiction to rule on the dispute in the main proceedings, so that the issue cannot be regarded as purely hypothetical. Thus, the CJEU decided that the questions referred do not meet an objective need for the purpose of settling the dispute brought before it.

Anyway, the CJEU notes that, in the absence of a direct right of action (i) against J.M.'s appointment as President of the disciplinary chamber of the Supreme Court or (ii) against J.M.'s decision designating the disciplinary court in charge of examining that dispute, M.F. could have raised before that court an objection alleging a possible infringement, arising from the decision at issue, of her right to have the said dispute determined by an independent and impartial tribunal previously established by law.[26]

What is relevant in this *M. F.* case for the principle of effective judicial protection? In recital 73 the CJEU recalled that the rules on the ordinary courts—inasmuch as they confer on the President of the disciplinary chamber of the Supreme Court the discretionary power to designate the disciplinary tribunal with territorial jurisdiction to hear disciplinary proceedings in respect of judges of the ordinary courts—do not meet the requirement derived from the second subparagraph of Article 19(1) TEU that such cases must be examined by a tribunal "established by law".[27]

The novelty in the *M. F.* case is the CJEU's claim that the second subparagraph of Article 19(1) TEU must be regarded as having direct effect, with the result that the principle of primacy of EU law requires a disciplinary court thus designated not to apply the national provisions pursuant to which that designation was made and, consequently, declare that it has no jurisdiction to hear the dispute before it.[28] The effects of the principle of the primacy of EU law are binding on all the bodies of a Member State, without the provisions of domestic law relating to the attribution of jurisdiction, including constitutional provisions, being able to prevent that. In accordance with settled case-law, rules of national law, even constitutional provisions, cannot be allowed to undermine the unity and effectiveness of EU law.[29]

Where it is not possible to interpret national law in compliance with the requirements of EU law—because this is the first exercise that judges must to do –, the national court which is called upon within the exercise of its jurisdiction to apply provisions of EU law is under a duty to give full effect to those provisions, if necessary refusing of its own motion to apply any conflicting provision of national legislation, even if adopted subsequently, and it is not necessary for that court to request or await the prior setting aside of such provision by legislative or other

[25] *M. F.*, C-508/19, ECLI:EU:C:2022:201, recital 67.

[26] *M. F.*, C-508/19, ECLI:EU:C:2022:201, recital 72.

[27] *European Commission v Republic of Poland*, C-791/19, ECLI:EU:C:2021:596, recital 176.

[28] *M. F.*, C-508/19, ECLI:EU:C:2022:201, recital 74.

[29] *A.B. and o.*, C-824/18, ECLI:EU:C:2021:153, recital 148.

constitutional means.[30] On the other hand, a provision of EU law which does not have direct effect may not be relied on, as such, in a dispute covered by EU law, to exclude the application of a provision of national law that conflicts with it.[31]

Why is the direct effect of the second subparagraph of Article 19(1) TEU so relevant, especially to protect EU fundamental rights in times of war? The CJEU had already stated that this norm imposes on the Member States a clear and precise obligation as to the result to be achieved—and that obligation is not subject to any condition as regards the independence which must characterise the courts called upon to interpret and apply EU law.[32] But now the direct effect of the second subparagraph of Article 19(1) TEU is expressly recognised—and this allows the holder of the right to invoke that norm in order to ask the competent judge not to apply incompatible national rules.

One should not forget that the *Van Gend & Loos* judgment, in which the rules of the direct effect principle were established, is considered the most important of the CJUE's judgments regarding European citizenship. Following this judgment, it became clear that when a provision is interpreted as producing direct effect, the consequence is the creation of individual rights, which national courts must protect. Independently of the legislation of the Member States, EU law not only imposes obligations on individuals but is also intended to confer upon them rights which become part of their legal heritage. These rights arise not only where they are expressly granted by the Treaties, but also by reason of obligations which those Treaties impose in a clearly defined way upon individuals as well as upon the Member States and upon the EU Institutions.[33]

References

Canotilho JJG (2017) Dislocations on understanding the rule of law. UNIO—EU Law J 3:4–9. https://revistas.uminho.pt/index.php/unio/article/view/313. Accessed 7 Oct 2024

Silveira A (2022) Horizontal integration and union based on the rule of law. In: Rodrigues AM, Machado J, Albuquerque PP (eds) The rule of law in the European Union. Instituto Jurídico, Faculdade de Direito, Universidade de Coimbra, Coimbra, pp 1–12. https://estudogeral.sib.uc.pt/bitstream/10316/104159/1/RuleOfLaw_Livro.pdf Accessed 7 Oct 2024

Silveira A (2023) Is there a threat to the rule of law in the EU as a consequence of the government agreement in Spain and the institutional crisis in Portugal? https://officialblogofunio.com/2023/12/09/editorial-of-december-2023/. Accessed 7 Oct 2024

Silveira A, Froufe P, Perez S, Abreu J (2018) União de direito para além do direito da União—as garantias de independência judicial no acórdão Associação Sindical dos Juízes Portugueses. http://julgar.pt/uniao-de-direito-para-alem-do-direito-da-uniao-as-garantias-de-independencia-judicial-no-acordao-associacao-sindical-dos-juizes-portugueses/. Accessed 7 Oct 2024

[30] *M. F.*, C-508/19, ECLI:EU:C:2022:201, recital 79.

[31] *Popławski*, C-573/17, ECLI:EU:C:2019:530, recitals 58 and 62.

[32] *A.B. and o.*, C-824/18, ECLI:EU:C:2021:153, recital 146.

[33] *Van Gend & Loos*, 26–62, ECLI:EU:C:1963:1.

Alessandra Silveira School of Law at University of Minho (UMinho), Portugal. Director of the master's degree in European Union Law at UMinho. Holder of the Jean Monnet Chair in European Union Law at UMinho. Academic Coordinator of the Jean Monnet Centre of Excellence "Digital Citizenship and Technological Sustainability" (CitDig) at UMinho. Director of "UNIO—EU Law Journal" and the blog "Thinking & Debating Europe."

The Court of Justice of the EU and the Independence of the Judiciary

Inês Quadros

1 Introduction

As is widely known, the Court of Justice has been particularly active in addressing the rule of law crisis in Europe, taking on the role of guarantor of the values of the EU, which are being jeopardised in some Member States.

There is no question about the primary role of States in protecting the rule of law. Despite the progressive transference of powers to the Union, the Member States remain—and are expected to be—the main guarantors of the principle, and theoretically have adequate political and legal tools to enforce it. This is also true with regard to one particular dimension of the rule of law principle—the independence of the judiciary—since national courts, besides adjudicating within domestic law, are required to solve a significant portion of cases involving EU law, and, hence, responsibility for shaping the judicial function to meet independence requirements mostly lies with the States.

Notwithstanding, the principle's substance is not defined only at the national level. On the contrary, there is a shared understanding among the Member States—which comes as no surprise, given their common (legal, political, and cultural) foundations—that has allowed the principle to form part of what is known as the *European way of life*.[1] That is why—more than due to any instrumental importance

[1] The CJEU considers that the fundamental values of Article 2 TEU "define the very identity of the European Union as a common legal order": CJEU judgement of 16 February 2022, *Hungary v Parliament and Council—conditionality mechanism*, C-156/21, EU:C:2022:97, para 127.

I. Quadros (✉)
Universidade Católica Portuguesa, Faculty of Law, Católica Research Centre for the Future of Law, Lisbon, Portugal
e-mail: miquadros@ucp.pt

I. Quadros, M. Gorjão-Henriques (eds.), *Revisiting the Liberal Constitutional Features of the European Union*, https://doi.org/10.1007/978-3-031-95717-8_8

of the principle in view of the effective application of EU law—the principle was included in the very first Articles of the EU treaties.

In the last few years, the European Union has taken on the role of overseeing and promoting the independence of the judiciary in the Member States, in view of violations that have occurred at the national level and the inability—or lack of will—of some States to carry out this task. Promoting the rule of law with EU law is not, however, an easy task, given the limited instruments available to the Union for this purpose. Von Bogdandy et al. (2018, p. 984) even suggest that we might be witnessing a "constitutional moment" at the EU. Some points deserve consideration.

Firstly, the fact is that national laws that impair the rule of law principle are—at least formally[2]—supported by democratic majorities and are adopted by means of competences reserved for Member States, namely the organisation of the judiciary. As on many other occasions, but on a more sensitive scale, the Court is faced with the need to balance European Union Law effectiveness with Member States' autonomy and different understandings of the principle.

Secondly, the idea that every principle enshrined in the Treaties should be justiciable and capable of being used as a parameter of judicial control of Member States' (or even the Union's) activity is not without controversy. Some of those principles may be said to be mere statements or goals of a political nature. The fact that the Treaty provides a specific political mechanism (in Article 7 TEU) to censure Member States' activity regarding the values on which the Union is based may reinforce the political status of those values, as opposed to granting them a legal status.

Lastly, and with regard to the current crisis, one must not forget that one counter-argument used by Member States whose legislation is being contested relates to the Court of Justice's known activism. By relying on provisions not originally intended to protect the principle of the rule of law in order to ensure greater protection for that principle, the Court may be at risk of competence creep[3]—for which the Court has a prodigal track record—and this may exacerbate the difficult relationship between the EU and the Member States concerned. The Court thus seems to be walking on thin ice.

For these reasons, it is more crucial than ever that the competence of the Court is established beyond any doubt and with clearly defined boundaries. Hence, this contribution concerns the sources of Union law which establish the principle of the rule of law, and from which the Court of Justice derives its competence to control the activity of the Member States. Our purpose is to critically analyse the use of those sources by the Court of Justice, questioning their limits as to the role they are expected to play.

In Sect. 2 we will identify the normative sources the Court of Justice uses to exercise control over Member States' respect for the independence of the judiciary.

[2] Doubts on whether there is substantive democracy—freedom of expression and free elections—are, of course, relevant but will not be considered here.

[3] Bonelli and Claes (2018), pp. 632, 640–641; Pech and Platon (2018), p. 1841.

We will not be dealing with the entire 'toolbox'[4] available at EU level, but only with the tools that stem from primary sources of EU law (the Treaties and the Charter), even if some reference to case-law concerning secondary sources (*e.g.* the conditionality mechanism regulation) might be needed. Section 3 will analyse the protection of the rule of law in conjunction with the fundamental right to judicial protection under Article 47 of the Charter, while Sect. 4 will deal with the specific case of the execution of European Arrest Warrants issued by courts located in Member States involved in the rule of law saga. Section 5 will analyse the use of Article 267 and its concept of "court and tribunal" as a means of filtering preliminary questions referred to the Court of Justice by dubiously independent bodies. Finally, Sect. 6 will deal with Article 19 TEU, which, in our view, is the most controversial tool for dealing with rule of law conundrums.

2 EU Law Substantive and Procedural Sources of Control of Respect for the Independence of the Judiciary

There is a notable widening and deepening of the rule of law principle running through the various historical versions of the Treaties[5]. This evolution has been accompanied by a consistent line of judicial decisions that confirm the legal nature of the principle and of its ramifications, including the independence of courts. Pech describes extensively how the principle has been shaped from the converging of national, Council of Europe/ECtHR and EU traits, notwithstanding the controversies surrounding its boundaries, which should be considered natural in every constitutional system[6].

It is not evident, however, that every substantive provision from which one can derive an affirmation of the independence of the judiciary is guaranteed by a corresponding legal mechanism to enforce it. It is thus of utmost importance to distinguish between substantial sources of the principle and procedural mechanisms able to protect them. International treaties very often include statements that are non-justiciable, and which are there first and foremost for the legislature to take them seriously and incorporate them into legal acts, and which, ultimately, are to be enforced through political means or diplomatic efforts or controlled by democratic elections in the light of the steps that have been taken towards those objectives. It is plausible that the *masters of the Treaties* were convinced that this was the case with some of the Treaties' provisions, and that therefore the core values of the Union were only subject to specific political guarantees—as is the case of Article 7

[4] Pech (2021), p. 318; Ladenburger et al. (2023), p. 95.

[5] Pech (2022), pp. 110 et seq.

[6] Pech (2022), p. 120.

TEU—or to mechanisms to be created by secondary legislation—such as the conditionality mechanism.[7]

However, the Court of Justice has, ever since *Les Verts,* acknowledged that, since the (now) Union is based on the rule of law, "neither its Member States nor its institutions can avoid review of the conformity of their acts with the basic constitutional charter, the EC Treaty".[8] The growing importance of the rule of law, at a time when threats do not seem to be overcome through the primary national means, has led to the identification of denser norms that affirm that principle as well as the means to safeguard it. Furthermore, this concern for conformity has arisen at the same time as the constitutional nature of the Treaties is increasingly upheld, which strengthens its legal superior significance and calls for positive efforts towards its enforcement. In this chapter, we will deal with substantive sources of the principle of the independence of judges, in connection with procedural mechanisms used to protect them. Among these, we will only consider those that allow for judicial control by the Court of Justice. Hence, Article 7 TEU will not be contemplated, as the Court cannot assess the substance of the decisions taken on the basis of that provision (see Article 269 TFEU).

The substantive sources of the general principle of the rule of law correspond to the legal provisions that shape the principle, bring it to the realm of the European Union, and give it substantive meaning. Article 2 TEU lists the "values" that are common to the Member States and thus elevated to EU values. Article 47 of the CFR (that translates the principle into the fundamental right of judicial protection) and Article 19 (1), second subparagraph TEU (which sets out the duty of Member States to provide effective remedies that ensure legal protection "in the fields covered by EU law") give effectiveness to particular expressions of those values.

The procedural sources are the provisions that allow the Court to exercise control over compliance with those principles by the Member States. These have been the infringement proceedings (Articles 258–260 TFEU) and the preliminary rulings procedure (Article 267 TFEU). In fact, Article 267 plays a special role in this respect since it acts both as a substantial ground for evaluating the status of the independence of judges (as a result of the case-law of the Court of Justice regarding the interpretation of that provision as to the concept of a "court or tribunal" that is entitled to refer questions), and as a formal mechanism to enforce it, since it empowers national courts to indirectly subject the compatibility of national legislation with the rule of law principle to CJEU control.

---

[7] Regulation (EU, EURATOM) 2020/2092 of the European Parliament and of the Council of 16 December 2020 on a general regime of conditionality for the protection of the Union budget. There are, of course, many other secondary rules that grant rights to individuals and, accordingly, prescribe guarantees for their protection, among which the principle of independence can be included (e.g. Articles 7(1) and (2) of Council Directive 93/13/EEC of 5 April 1993 on unfair terms in consumer contracts). See CJEU judgment (Grand Chamber) of 29 March 2022, *Getin Noble Bank*, C-132/20, EU:C:2022:235.

[8] ECJ Judgment of 23 April 1986, *Parti écologiste "Les Verts" v European Parliament*, 294/83, EU:C:1986:166, para 23.

As Bobek has rightly pointed out, "this 'multiplication' of legal bases with respect to the principle of judicial independence reflects its constitutional significance and its transversal nature in a community based on the rule of law. However, it may also be the source of some confusion. One may wonder whether those provisions lay down different types of 'judicial independence', with the consequence being that, for example, a national court may be independent for the purposes of one of those provisions, while not independent enough for another".[9] Therefore, a deeper look into each of these sources is needed and will be undertaken in the following chapters.

3 Article 47 of the Charter of Fundamental Rights

3.1 Stretching the Scope of the Charter

A first substantial ground for review of Member States' activity can be found in Article 47 of the Charter, which enunciates a dimension of the rule of law principle that corresponds to a fundamental right. Paragraph 3 of that provision states that "everyone is entitled to a fair and public hearing within a reasonable time by an independent and impartial tribunal previously established by law".

Interpretation of the provision has benefited from extensive case-law that can be traced back to *Johnston*[10] and has been built on Member States' traditions and the ECHR system.[11] There is little doubt that it includes not only the right of access to courts, but also the judicial guarantees attached to the exercise of the judicial function. Among these, the independence of the courts and the right to a tribunal that is established by law play a starring role. The latter requires that the tribunal is set up according to legal rules, that it complies with the rules concerning its jurisdiction

[9] See AG Bobek's opinion of 8 July 2021, *Getin Noble Bank S.A.*, C-132/20, EU:C:2021:557, para 35.

[10] ECJ judgment of 15 May 1986, *Johnston*, C-222/84, EU:C:1986:206.

[11] The Court has consistently found that Article 47 must be defined in accordance with the European Convention on Human Rights (hereinafter, ECHR). See CJEU judgment (Grand Chamber) of 19 November 2019, *AK*, C-585/18, EU:C:2019:982, paras 116, 126 seq. and CJEU judgment (Grand Chamber) of 6 October 2021, *W.Ż.*, C-487/19, EU:C:2021:798, para 123. The ECtHR judgment of 7 May 2021, *Xero Flor v. Poland*, 4907/18, sheds light on the content of the right to a fair hearing and to a tribunal established by law (Article 6 para 1 of the Convention). The decision was mentioned in AG Rantos' opinion of 16 December 2021, *X and Y v Openbaar Ministerie*, joined cases C-562/21 PPU and C-563/21 PPU, EU:C:2021:1019, fn. 62; AG Collins' opinion of 15 December 2022, *Commission v. Poland (Disciplinary regime applicable to judges)*, C-204/21, EU:C:2022:991, fn. 45; and AG Bobek's opinion of 8 July 2021, *Getin Noble Bank S.A.*, C-132/20, EU:C:2021:557, fn 27. Despite the influence of the ECtHR case-law in shaping the principle of effective judicial protection within EU law, it is argued that the CJEU now has more effective mechanisms to deal with breaches of the principle. See María (2021), pp. 184–185.

and composition when it issues rules[12], and that the appointment of judges is governed by a procedure established by law.[13] The former, the independence of the judiciary, adds a substantive requirement to the performance of the judicial function, requiring those rules to guarantee independence from other branches of power. Moreover, the Court has more than once stressed the link between effective judicial protection and judicial independence: in *X and Y*, for instance, it recalled that there can be a "breach, in the issuing Member State, of the fundamental right to a fair trial guaranteed by that provision, on account of systemic or generalised deficiencies so far as concerns the independence of that Member State's judiciary".[14] Furthermore, it added that the access to a tribunal established by law is "inextricably linked to the guarantees of independence and impartiality", in the light of "the need to maintain public confidence in the judiciary".[15]

In the last few years the Court of Justice's case-law has given us plenty of indications of the importance that the Court of Justice affords to the principle and the connection with the right to effective judicial protection. In the *LM* case, for instance, the Court stated that "it must be pointed out that the requirement of judicial independence forms part of the essence of the fundamental right to a fair trial, a right which is of cardinal importance as a guarantee that all the rights which individuals derive from EU law will be protected and that the values common to the Member States set out in Article 2 TEU, in particular the value of the rule of law, will be safeguarded".[16] Finally, to set aside any doubts, the Court has stressed that Article 47 of the Charter "is sufficient in itself and does not need to be made more specific by provisions of EU or national law in order to confer on individuals a right which they may rely on as such"[17]— in other words, the provision is directly effective.

---

[12] Leloup (2020), p. 1149.

[13] CJEU judgment (Grand Chamber) of 6 October 2021, *W.Ż.*, C-487/19, EU:C:2021:798, para 117–130.

[14] CJEU judgment (Grand Chamber) of 22 February 2022, *X and Y v Openbaar Ministerie*, joined cases C-562/21 PPU and C-563/21 PPU, EU:C:2022:100, para 52.

[15] Ib., para 56. See, in relation to allegations of breaches of the rule of law principle in the Court of Justice itself, the CJEU judgment (Grand Chamber) of 26 March 2020, *Erik Simpson*, C-542/18, EU:C:2020:232, in which the Court stated that: "an irregularity committed during the appointment of judges within the judicial system concerned entails an infringement of the first sentence of the second paragraph of Article 47 of the Charter, particularly when that irregularity is of such a kind and of such gravity as to create a real risk that other branches of the State, in particular the executive, could exercise undue discretion undermining the integrity of the outcome of the appointment process and thus give rise to a reasonable doubt in the minds of individuals as to the independence and the impartiality of the judge or judges concerned, which is the case when what is at issue are fundamental rules forming an integral part of the establishment and functioning of that judicial system" (para 75).

[16] CJEU judgment (Grand Chamber) of 25 July 2018, *LM*, C-216/18 PPU, EU:C:2018:586, para 48.

[17] CJEU judgment (Grand Chamber) of 2 March 2021, *A.B. and Others*, C-824/18, EU:C:2021:153, para 145.

Solid as it may seem, the most important limitation to Article 47 of the Charter comes from Article 51 of the same instrument, which defines, in a rather limited fashion, that "the provisions of this Charter are addressed (…) to the Member States only when they are implementing Union law (…)" and that the Charter "does not establish any new power or task for the Community or the Union, or modify powers and tasks defined by the Treaties". It seemed indisputable at the outset that this provision reflected an attempt to avoid overapplication of the Charter in regard to Member States' actions[18].

However, far from erecting a Berlin wall that would clearly separate an area with enhanced fundamental rights protection through the Charter, from a "State's land" where such protection would be strictly dependent on national authorities, Article 51, as interpreted by the Court, draws a thin line between both areas, which interact like communicating vessels. In fact, the Court has always struggled with the limitation of Article 51, having progressively stretched the limits of the Charter[19] by interpreting rather generously the situations in which it considers that the Member States are "implementing Union law".

Several doctrinal proposals have offered a systematisation of the Court's case-law in this respect.[20] To mention only one, von Bogdandy identifies three constellations of situations that the Court considers fall within the notion of "implementation of EU law", as stated in Article 51 of the Charter, and hence that are subject to compliance with the Charter and to the Court's control. The first constellation comprises situations in which Member States execute "outright obligations stemming from Union law"[21], while the second relates to situations where Member States implement Union law, "including directives which only lay down minimum harmonization or grant a margin of discretion"[22]. The difficulties start at this point, with von Bogdandy drawing attention to the fact that the Court has further extended this second constellation to include national "legislation that is not intended to implement a directive in a strict sense but otherwise touches upon fields regulated by that act".[23] Lastly, and most controversially, the third constellation relates to matters that come within the "scope of EU law", merely because they are related to market freedoms or—as von Bogdandy proposes, as part of his argument—citizenship[24].

---

[18] Snell (2015), p. 220.

[19] Von Bogdandy et al. (2012), p. 497.

[20] See, for instance, Snell (2015), p. 292 or Silveira (2014), p. 180 et seq. Pirker (2018), pp. 135–136 offers a revision of the literature that attempted to categorize the case law of the CJEU on the Charter's scope of application.

[21] Von Bogdandy et al. (2012), pp. 497–498.

[22] Von Bogdandy et al. (2012), pp. 498–499.

[23] *Idem*. A proposal that suggests application of the Charter in this last constellation of cases can be found in AG Sharpston's Opinion of 30 September 2010, *Ruiz Zambrano*, C-34/09, EU:C:2010:560, para 163.

[24] Von Bogdandy et al. (2012), pp. 499–500.

The *Fransson* decision[25] is a good example of how blurred these boundaries have become, because in it the Court allowed the Charter to also be triggered "where national legislation falls within the scope of European Union law".[26] The conflict at hand dealt with procedural guarantees related to tax fraud, which, despite falling under Member States' competence, constituted the procedural dimension of European directives on VAT. One could say, borrowing von Bogdandy's classification, that this case corresponds to the extension of the second constellation, because, even though it was related to a matter governed by domestic law, it was closely connected with an area extensively harmonised by EU law. Nevertheless, the wide expression used by the Court—"within the scope of EU law"—was enough to instigate further incursions into the Member State's realm, thus removing another brick from the wall.[27]

This extension does not appear to be unlimited, however, as becomes apparent from certain cases relating to the rule of law crisis. In the *Miasto Łowicz*[28] case, for instance, the Court of Justice expressly distinguished the scope of application of Article 47 of the Charter from that of Article 19 TEU: "As regards the scope of the second subparagraph of Article 19(1) TEU, it follows, moreover, from the Court's case-law that that provision refers to the 'fields covered by Union law', irrespective of whether the Member States are implementing Union law within the meaning of Article 51(1) of the Charter of Fundamental Rights of the European Union".[29] That means that, according to the CJEU, the Charter should be triggered only by a substantive connection—a "sufficient link"[30]—to EU law. Defining the exact terms of that connection seems a difficult task, however.

3.2 *Applying the Charter to Situations Where There Is Lack of Independence of Judges*

Following this expansive case-law, a question arose as to the possibility of invoking the Charter to deal with national laws that impair the independence of judges.

---

25 CJEU judgment (Grand Chamber) of 26 February 2013, *Åkerberg Fransson*, C-617/10, EU:C:2013:105.

26 Para 21.

27 In a similar vein, CJEU judgment of 16 May 2017, *Berlioz Investment Fund*, C-682/15, EU:C:2017:373, where the Court considered that the Charter was applicable in relation to a sanction enacted by a Member State to guarantee an obligation stemming from a European directive. The Court clarified that "the fact that Directive 2011/16 does not make express provision for penalties to be imposed does not mean that penalties cannot be regarded as involving the implementation of that Directive and, consequently, falling within the scope of EU law" (para 39).

28 CJEU judgment (Grand Chamber) of 26 March 2020, *Miasto Łowicz*, joined cases C-558/18 and C-563/18, EU:C:2020:234.

29 Paras 33 and 34.

30 Leloup (2020), p. 1153.

Jakab explicitly proposed that Article 51 should be "creatively reinterpreted"[31]—*rectius*, expanded—with the purpose of allowing the Charter to be applied in all matters, even if only of domestic concern. Jakab recognises the disruptive potential effect of such a suggestion—comparable to the constitutional *momentum* of *Costa-ENEL*—but considers it necessary in order to preserve the values of European integration[32].

The Court was called upon to rule on a national law relating to that matter in the *AK* case[33]—at stake was the Polish law that set non-transparent conditions for judges to remain in office after having reached 65 years of age. A section of the Polish Supreme Court, the referring body, asked the Court whether that law breached Article 47 of the Charter and should therefore be disapplied. The Court, in a Grand Chamber judgment, agreed with the complainants in the national proceedings in that the link with EU law could be found in Directive 2000/78,[34] which aimed at establishing a general framework for equal treatment in employment and occupation, and that forbids discrimination on grounds of age and requires that Member States guarantee access of all persons to judicial procedures necessary for the enforcement of obligations stemming from the directive.[35] It is necessary to bear in mind that the organisation of the judiciary is a matter reserved for the Member States, and that the directive had been adopted on the basis of what is now Article 19 TFEU, which allows European institutions to "take appropriate action to combat discrimination based on (…) age (…)", but only "within the limits of the powers conferred by [the Treaties] upon the Union".[36] Furthermore, EU law does not guarantee access to the profession of judge by EU citizens, since Article 45 (4) TFEU (like Article 51 TFEU, applicable to services *ex vi* Article 62) exempts those activities from free movement rights. Nevertheless, the situation was considered by the Court to be substantively ruled by the Directive, which the Court found applicable to every kind of employment or occupation, and hence was brought within the scope of application of the Charter in accordance with its Article 51.

On another occasion, in *Ministertwo Sprawiedliwości,*[37] the Court considered that "a decision of the State authority ordering removal from the register of the Bar Association constitutes, in principle, a 'withdrawal of an authorisation' within the meaning of Article 10(6) of Directive 2006/123" (Services Directive), that would, accordingly, be subject to compliance with Article 47 of the Charter—hence, the bodies competent to judge on that removal decision would have to be independent.

---

[31] Jakab (2016), p. 187.

[32] Jakab (2016), pp. 200 et seq.

[33] CJEU judgment (Grand Chamber) of 19 November 2019, *AK*, Joined cases C-585/18, C-624/18 and C-626/18 EU:C:2019:982.

[34] Council Directive 2000/78/EC of 27 November 2000.

[35] Article 9 of the Directive.

[36] When the Directive was adopted, the corresponding provision was Article 13 TEC (Amsterdam version).

[37] CJEU judgment of 13 January 2022, *Minister Sprawiedliwości*, case C-55/20, EU:C:2022:6, para 88 et seq.

However, since in the proceedings pending before the referring court that removal was not yet at stake—the national body was deciding on a case between the Disciplinary Agent, on the one side, and the National Prosecutor and the Minister for Justice, on the other side, and the individual subject to disciplinary proceedings was not yet a party to the case—the Directive was, conversely, not applicable, and, consequently, neither was the Charter. It is interesting to note that in relation to this last finding, Advocate General Bobek (whose conclusions, read together, form a doctrinal approach to judicial independence) had proposed a different answer, by noting that "the normative scope of an EU law instrument cannot be defined *ex post facto* in an outcome-dependent way, with the case falling either within or out of the scope of EU law depending on whether a person is eventually convicted or acquitted. In general, the fact that certain proceedings fall within the scope of an EU law instrument *rationae materiae* is sufficient for the entirety of those proceedings, irrespective of the ultimate outcome or stage at which they close, also to fall within the scope of EU law".[38] The Advocate General's argument was weak, though, as became clear in the subsequent paragraphs of his conclusions—with Bobek showing difficulties in identifying "which exact individual right deriving from EU law could specifically be at issue in the case pending before the referring court", because, "while the prospective outcome of the main proceedings may eventually have detrimental effects on the legal position of R.G. (by being made subject to disciplinary proceedings as a result), it has been pointed out that R.G. is not yet a party in the main proceedings".[39] Accordingly, the Advocate General had to suggest the Court leave the question from the national court unanswered.

From these decisions, one can infer the rule the Court is applying: if the matter is materially (substantially) connected to EU law, the Charter can be triggered.[40] That happens when the national bodies whose independence is being challenged are part of the system of guarantees of substantive rights granted by EU law (such as the right not to be discriminated against on grounds of age, or the right to provide services) or of rights directly connected to EU law (which may happen if the situation is linked to, even if not directly regulated by, an extensively harmonised area, such as VAT, or, more controversially, if it is connected to a EU competence that has not yet been exercised).[41] However, the rulings stand on the edge of the Union's competences. The broader the rights and principles that the Court considers shape the scope of EU law, the easier it will be for these to impact on matters that still fall under the Member States' reserved powers.

If, on the other hand, the subject at hand is not EU-related, the Charter will not be applicable—and this is where Article 19 TEU may come into play, as we will see in Sect. 6.

---

[38] AG Bobek's opinion of 17 June 2021, *Ministerstwo Sprawiedliwości*, C-55/20, EU:C:2021:500, para 97.

[39] Para 102.

[40] AG Tanchev's opinion of 27 June 2019, *AK*, C-585/18, EU:C:2019:551.

[41] AG Sharpston's opinion of 30 September 2010, *Zambrano*, C-34/09, EU:C:2010:560, para 163. See von Bogdandy et al. (2012), p. 500.

While recognising the risk of competence creep[42], the rule is, in our view, reasonable, in that it intends to take the limitation set out in Article 51 of the Charter seriously. Further control in the light of the Charter could only be exercised through a revision of the Treaties, allowing for wider control by the Union of fundamental rights' protection at the national level.[43]

4 A Particular Case Concerning the Application of the Charter: Execution of European Arrest Warrants

4.1 The Importance of Being Trustworthy

The European Arrest Warrant (EAW) plays a vital role in securing the success of the European free movement area, where persons circulate freely and hence where criminality can easily have a transnational impact. Additionally, because it requires a "high level of trust"[44] and close collaboration between the judicial authorities of Member States, it is also a useful barometer of Member States' compliance with the rule of law.

Sharing a common language for fundamental rights and fair institutions is the basis of this mutual trust between Member States[45] and a crucial element for the mechanism to work. Among these, criminal guarantees play a significant role in upholding the rule of law in Member States. That is why, in support of the EAW mechanism, several common rules regarding criminal law and criminal procedure were enacted by the EU institutions in order to guarantee a common ground of compliance with the principle of judicial protection.

Voluntary adherence to those common principles, derived either from Member States' shared values or from European rules, has made it possible to consider only exceptional grounds for refusing the execution of an arrest warrant. In fact, the balancing exercise between the duty to recognise decisions of, or execute requests from, courts of another Member State, and the duty to protect individuals from illegal decisions and guarantee they are subject to due process, has leaned towards the former in the Court's case-law. The Court made it clear, in its Opinion 2/13, *a propos* accession to the ECHR, that "the Member States may, under EU law, be required to presume that fundamental rights have been observed by the other Member States, so that not only may they not demand a higher level of national

---

[42] Snell (2018), p. 476.

[43] Snell adopts a cautious approach similar to the one presented here, although he warns against possible State behaviours that could undermine the trust between the EU and Member States. Writing before the rule of law crisis, it is unclear whether that situation would favour the Author's more expansive use of the Charter. Snell (2015), pp. 304 et seq.

[44] CJEU judgment (Grand Chamber) of 25 July 2018, *LM*, C-216/18 PPU, EU:C:2018:586, para 58.

[45] CJEU judgment (Grand Chamber) of 25 July 2018, *LM*, C-216/18 PPU, EU:C:2018:586, para 35. See Closa (2016), p. 16.

protection of fundamental rights from another Member State than that provided by EU law, but, save in exceptional cases, they may not check whether that other Member State has actually, in a specific case, observed the fundamental rights guaranteed by the EU".[46]

The reference to the protection of fundamental rights in the area of freedom, security and justice (AFSJ) stems from Article 67 TFEU and Article 1 (3) of Framework Decision 2002/584/JHA.[47] While the latter seems to safeguard fundamental rights concerns of Member States in the Arrest Warrant procedure—in particular effective judicial protection (which should include the guarantee of independent courts)[48]—the Court has insisted on a narrow interpretation of the circumstances under which the executing authorities may perform such control.

4.2 *Consistent Case-Law of the CJEU*

In fact, the principle of mutual trust, which underpins all matters covered by the AFSJ, is clearly incorporated into criminal cooperation. Since *Aranyosi* and *Căldăraru*[49] (regarding the conditions of criminal detention in the issuing Member State) the case-law of the Court has been steady on this principle, which was later adopted in relation to the independence of judges' crisis in *LM*[50] and later reaffirmed by a Grand Chamber decision in *Openbaar Ministerie.*[51]

Aranyosi and *Căldăraru*[52] paved the way, delivering a clear-cut rule: an EAW may only in exceptional circumstances be refused on grounds other that those stated in Articles 3 and 4 of the Framework Decision, particularly when there is a serious risk of breaching a fundamental right protected by the Charter.[53] For that purpose, the executing court should perform a two-step analysis: first, it must analyse whether there is a systemic violation of fundamental rights (in the case at hand, the risk was

---

[46] CJEU Opinion of 18 December 2014, C-2/13, *Accession of the EU to the ECHR*, EU:C:2014:2454, para 192.

[47] Council Framework Decision 2002/584/JHA of 13 June 2002 on the European arrest warrant and the surrender procedures between Member States, amended by Council Framework Decision 2009/299/JHA of 26 February 2009.

[48] CJEU judgment (Grand Chamber) of 25 July 2018, *LM*, C-216/18 PPU, EU:C:2018:586, para 56. See Martufi (2022), pp. 1392–1395.

[49] CJEU judgment (Grand Chamber) of 5 April 2016, *Aranyosi and Căldăraru,* joined cases C-404/15 and C-659/15 PPU, EU:C:2016:198.

[50] CJEU judgment (Grand Chamber) of 25 July 2018, *LM*, C-216/18 PPU, EU:C:2018:586, para 35–36. See Wahl (2020), p. 322.

[51] CJEU judgment (Grand Chamber) of 22 February 2022, *X and Y v Openbaar Ministerie*, joined cases C-562/21 PPU and C-563/21 PPU, EU:C:2022:100, para 40.

[52] CJEU judgment (Grand Chamber) of 5 April 2016, *Aranyosi and Căldăraru,* joined cases C-404/15 and C-659/15 PPU, EU:C:2016:198.

[53] In the case at hand, the fundamental right was of an absolute nature—the prohibition of torture (Article 4 of the Charter).

related to conditions of detention); and secondly, it should consider whether the specific situation of the individual would be impacted by those systemic deficiencies. In fact, the Court warned that "the mere existence of evidence that there are deficiencies, which may be systemic or generalised, or which may affect certain groups of people, or which may affect certain places of detention, with respect to detention conditions in the issuing Member State does not necessarily imply that, in a specific case, the individual concerned will be subject to inhuman or degrading treatment in the event that he is surrendered to the authorities of that Member State".[54] Only when the answer to both questions is affirmative can the executing court refuse the execution of an arrest warrant.

This reasoning has been adopted in relation to lack of independence of the judiciary in the Member States of issuing courts since *LM*, in which the Court confirmed that the fact that there are issues affecting the independence of judges in the requesting court's Member State is not enough for the execution court to refuse the execution of an EAW; it is only when there is a real and effective risk of subjecting the individual concerned to a non-impartial or non-independent court that the executing court may refuse it.[55] In *LM* the Court went a step further in relation to *Aranyosi* and *Căldăraru*, by clarifying that the rule therein defined remains the same even when the systemic deficiencies in the rule of law of a Member State have already given rise to political proceedings, such as the one foreseen in Article 7(1) TEU.

This rule could not be clearer. The double-step analysis that executing courts have to perform when deciding on the execution of an EAW—comprising, first, an assessment of the risk, and, second, an assessment of the specific exposure of the individual concerned to that risk—is the result of the balancing procedure previously identified, which affords priority to the effectiveness of the EAW and puts mutual trust between Member States at the apex of their relationship.

However, a later decision of the Court in the *OG (Parquet de Lübeck)* case[56] cast doubt on the resilience of the rule for some time. The Court was called upon to decide whether the public prosecutor's office of a German *Land* could be considered a "judiciary authority" for the purposes of issuing an EAW. The Court gave a negative answer on the grounds that that body carried the risk of being subject to instructions from the executive branch. It is noteworthy that the Court was convinced of that decision even if the risk of pressure from the government was merely potential, considering the safeguards prescribed by law. In fact, it held that "it is clear that such safeguards, assuming that their existence were to be established, cannot wholly rule out the possibility, in all circumstances, that a decision of a public prosecutor's office, such as those at issue in the cases in the main proceedings, to issue a European arrest warrant may, in a given case, be subject to an instruction

[54] CJEU judgment (Grand Chamber) of 5 April 2016, *Aranyosi and Căldăraru*, joined cases C-404/15 and C-659/15 PPU, EU:C:2016:198, para 93.

[55] CJEU judgment (Grand Chamber) of 25 July 2018, *LM*, C-216/18 PPU, EU:C:2018:586, para 37–44.

[56] CJEU judgment (Grand Chamber), *OG (Parquet de Lübeck)*, joined cases C-508/18 and C-82/19 PPU, EU:C:2019:456.

from the minister for justice (…)".[57] But even more, the Court found that, in relation to the case at hand, "it is, in that regard, irrelevant (…) that, in connection with the issuing of the European arrest warrants at issue in the main proceedings, no instruction in a specific case was issued to the public prosecutor's office".[58] That is to say, it is enough that the 'issuing judicial authority' is "exposed to the risk that its decision-making power be subject to external directions or instructions, in particular from the executive", in such a way that it is not "beyond doubt that the decision to issue a European arrest warrant lies with that authority and not, ultimately, with the executive".[59]

The dismissal here of an assessment of risk in the individual case is puzzling, bearing in mind the previous case-law. However, later developments show that this was an isolated decision. In fact, the Court had the opportunity to confirm the *LM* rule in a judgment delivered by the Grand Chamber in the midst of the rule of law storm, in February 2022. In *Openbaar Ministerie,*[60] the Court answered a preliminary ruling request from a Dutch court, which was deciding on the execution of an EAW issued by a Polish court. The question formulated by the national court was unambiguous: should the two-step approach be applicable even when there is such strong evidence of a systemic deficiency in compliance with the rule of law principle, which would probably affect the issuing authority, and when the Court itself has already so clearly stated, in previous infringement rulings, that the judiciary reforms in that Member State were liable to affect the application of EU Law?

The Court relied on its previous case-law in *LM* and confirmed the need to perform a two-step assessment: executing courts should first "make a general assessment of whether there is a real risk of breach of the fundamental right to a fair trial, connected in particular with a lack of independence of the courts of the issuing Member State or a failure to comply with the requirement for a tribunal established by law, on account of systemic or generalised deficiencies in that Member State".[61] For that purpose, contextual analysis including previous decisions of the Court of Justice, the case-law of the ECtHR, and the constitutional case law of the issuing Member State could be valuable. However, a finding, by the national executing court, that there are systemic deficiencies, does not allow it to refuse to execute a European arrest warrant without proceeding to the second step of the examination, since it "cannot (…) presume that there are substantial grounds for believing that that person runs a real risk of breach of his or her fundamental right to a fair trial if surrendered to that Member State, without carrying out a specific and precise verification which takes account of, inter alia, that person's personal situation, the nature of the offence in question and the factual context in which that warrant was issued,

---

[57] Para 80.

[58] Para 89.

[59] Para 73.

[60] CJEU judgment (Grand Chamber) of 22 February 2022, *X and Y v Openbaar Ministerie*, joined cases C-562/21 PPU and C-563/21 PPU, EU:C:2022:100.

[61] CJEU judgment (Grand Chamber) of 22 February 2022, *X and Y v Openbaar Ministerie*, joined cases C-562/21 PPU and C-563/21 PPU, EU:C:2022:100, para 67.

such as statements or acts by public authorities which are liable to interfere with how an individual case is handled". Accordingly, the second step checks whether the "systemic or generalised deficiencies found in the first step of that examination are likely to materialise if the person concerned is surrendered to the issuing Member State and whether, in the particular circumstances of the case, that person thus runs a real risk of breach of his or her fundamental right to a fair trial before a tribunal previously established by law, enshrined in the second paragraph of Article 47 of the Charter".[62]

Bearing in mind this case-law, the matter seems to have been settled for now, with the Court continuing to maintain a high threshold for Member States to derogate from the mutual recognition principle.[63]

4.3 Analysis

There may be two reasons why the Court did not use the decision in *OG (Parquet de Lübeck)* as a turning point, preferring instead, in *Openbaar Ministerie*, to confirm the two-step test performed in *LM*.

The first explanation may be found in the fact that in *OG (Parquet de Lübeck)* the issuing body was not a "judge or a court", as the Court explicitly highlighted,[64] but rather a public prosecutor's office. Although that was considered not to affect the power to issue a warrant—since it was nevertheless considered to be a "judicial authority",[65]—an extra look into the ability of the body to perform judicial functions seemed prudent. Notably, the Court enunciated the characteristics of a "judicial authority" for the sake of the Framework Decision, in a manner which is not unfamiliar to those that follow the case-law around Article 267.[66]

A second explanation relates to the fact that in *OG (Parquet de Lübeck)* there was no issue of a systemic deficiency in the rule of law; the point which was being discussed was merely the statutory characteristic of the issuing body, which raised no concerns regarding the overall situation of the independence of the judicial function in Germany. By contrast, the discussion underpinning the situation in certain Eastern Member States stems from a structural deficiency in judicial organisation—a much more sensitive issue to deal with. Now, a factor that surely played a role in the different outcomes in both cases relates to the countries that were involved in each of them: in *OG (Parquet de Lübeck)* the issuing body was Germany, where no known general issues of lack of judicial independence are currently ongoing. Conversely,

[62] *Idem*, para 82.

[63] See, more recently, CJEU judgment (Grand Chamber) of 31 January 2023, *Puig Gordi and Others*, C-158/21, EU:C:2023:57, para 122.

[64] Para 47–51.

[65] For the purpose of Article 6(1) of Framework Decision 2002/584.

[66] Para 60 *et seq*. See, below, Sect. 5.

in *X* and *Y* the decision was taken in regard to Polish courts; if the Court had said that a general assessment of the rule of law situation would suffice, this would probably have had a spill-over effect and given rise to a total ban on execution of arrest warrants issued by Polish courts, with tremendous implications for the fight against crime in that State.

This leads to the next explanation of why the Court is so insistent on this cautious approach in relation to the execution of EAWs, despite every ruling that has so far been delivered confirming the existence of generalised breaches of the principle of the independence of judges in some Member States. The Court has to strike a difficult balance between upholding the rule of law and ensuring effective pursuit of criminals. Systematic or generalised refusal to execute EAWs could ultimately undermine the area of freedom, security and justice, where effective cooperation on criminal matters is essential, by creating safe havens for criminals.

Moreover, the EAW is specific in that it relies on a horizontal relationship between the courts of different Member States. So, a refusal to execute a warrant amounts to horizontal control by one court of another court—that is to say, control between equals. This is very different from vertical—top-down—enforcement, which requires some sort of authority. If generalised, it could ultimately undermine mutual trust between courts of different Member States.

Finally, the caution of the Court is also wise, in our view, in that it correctly understands the task of courts: courts are called on to decide individual cases and are not entrusted with the task of overall evaluation of systemic deficiencies in the judiciary of Member States. What they are competent to assess is how, in the particular case at hand, the individual will be impacted by the issuing Member States' legislation.

These considerations may lead us to conclude that the approach of the Court seems, after all, to be the only plausible way to tackle rule of law deficiencies in Member States while ensuring the fight against transnational threats to security.

5 Article 267 TFEU

5.1 The Case-Law of the CJEU Regarding Which Bodies Can Refer Questions Under the Article 267 TFEU Procedure

Article 267 plays an important procedural role in enforcing the rule of law principle, because it allows the Court—while interpreting EU law—to indirectly check how the Member States comply with the principle.[67] We have seen how that comes into play in the previous sections, in which we saw how the Court promoted the rule of

[67] Pescatore (2010), p. 10 referred to the preliminary rulings' procedure as the "infringement procedure for the European citizen".

law in the context of cases that were brought to it through the preliminary rulings' procedure.

However, there has also been growing interest in how the interpretation of Article 267 can help the Court to perform that task, by being used itself as a substantive ground for review of the independence of judges. Among the questions that were submitted to the Court in this respect, some led to decisions that warrant a mention. For example, it was ruled that Article 267 "preclude[s] disciplinary proceedings from being brought against a national judge on the ground that he or she has made a reference for a preliminary ruling to the Court of Justice under that provision",[68] that the decision to refer a preliminary question to the Court cannot be subject to review by a superior court on the ground that the questions referred are not relevant or necessary,[69] and that it is also contrary to Article 267 to amend national legislation the specific effects of which are to "prevent requests for a preliminary ruling addressed to the Court from being maintained after they have been made, and thus to prevent the latter from giving judgment on such requests, and to preclude any possibility of a national court repeating similar requests in the future".[70] These decisions were taken in relation to national rules, supposedly adopted in line with national procedural autonomy, but which, nonetheless, had an impact on the referring court's decision to send a question to the CJEU. The decisions echo the early case-law of the Court of Justice regarding the preliminary rulings' procedure, in which it empowered national courts with the task of adjudicating in European law, thereby bearing the sole responsibility for engaging in dialogue with the CJEU.[71]

We would, however, like to focus on one aspect of the CJEU case-law relating to Article 267 that has gained new light as a result of a series of cases connected with the independence of courts. That aspect is related to the very notion of "court or tribunal" enshrined in Article 267.

As is widely known, the Court developed consistent case-law regarding who its national interlocutors should be within the Article 267 procedure. As with many other Treaty concepts, the Court was convinced that the expression "court or tribunal", as used in Articles 267(2) and (3), should be given a European meaning, so as to guarantee its uniform application throughout the judicial network of the Member States.[72] Hence, beginning with the *Vaassen Göbbels* case,[73] and continuing in *Dorsch*[74] and *Umweltanwalt von Kärnten,*[75] the Court identified the features that

[68] CJEU judgment (Grand Chamber) of 23 November 2021, *IS*, C-564/19, EU:C:2021:949, para 93.

[69] CJEU judgment (Grand Chamber) of 23 November 2021, *IS*, C-564/19, EU:C:2021:949, para 72.

[70] CJEU judgment (Grand Chamber) of 2 March 2021, *A.B. and Others*, C-824/18, EU:C:2021:153, para 95.

[71] ECJ judgment of 9 March 1978, *Amministrazione delle finanze dello Stato v Simmenthal*, C-106/77, EU:C:1978:49, para 24 and ECJ judgment of 6 October 1982, *Cilfit*, C-283/81, EU:C:1982:335, para 7.

[72] ECJ judgment of 6 October 1981, *Bröckmülen*, C-246/80, EU:C:1981:218.

[73] ECJ judgment of 30 June 1966, *Vaassen Göbbels*, C-61/65, EU:C:1966:39.

[74] ECJ judgment of 17 September 1997, *Dorsch Consult*, C-54/96, EU:C:1997:413.

[75] ECJ judgment of 10 December 2009, *Umweltanwalt von Kärnten*, C-205/08, EU:C:2009:767.

usually characterise an ordinary court of law (Campos 2018, pp. 186–188). The conclusion reached was that the Court can only accept preliminary requests from a body that is established by law, has permanent character, has compulsory jurisdiction, uses an *inter partes* procedure, decides on the basis of legal rules, can issue decisions of a judicial nature, has competence to settle disputes within which the preliminary question arose (Broberg and Fenger 2021, pp. 43 et seq.), and is *independent.* The presence of all these criteria is not required in every case; rather, the Court clearly checks whether, overall, the body resembles a judicial court.[76]

As regards independence, the case-law of the Court had, first and foremost, conceived it as a criterion to distinguish judicial courts from administrative bodies, which could be institutionally linked to one of the parties, in cases where private parties and the Administration were on opposing sides.[77] In that sense, the notion of independence was held to involve two dimensions: the first dimension, internal, "is linked to impartiality and seeks to ensure a level playing field for the parties to the proceedings and their respective interests with regard to the subject matter of those proceedings";[78] the second dimension is external and requires that "the body is protected against external intervention or pressure liable to jeopardise the independent judgment of its members as regards proceedings before them".[79] For these conditions to be met, independence requires clear rules on, for instance, appointment and dismissal of the members of the body in question, as well as procedural rules that make it clear that the body is a third party to the conflict.[80]

In *Corbiau,* for instance, the Court refused a preliminary ruling request, within tax litigation, that came from the Director of Taxation, who, in the Court's words, "has a clear organizational link with the departments which made the disputed tax assessment"[81] and hence was not a third party to the dispute. In other cases, the ability of certain administrative bodies to request preliminary rulings from the Court was successfully contested. This was the case of the Danish "Telecommunications Complaints Board"[82] and the Greek[83] and Spanish[84] Competition Authorities, all of which were deemed not to be covered by the concept of "court or tribunal".

[76] Wahl and Prete (2018), pp. 523–524.

[77] For instance, CJEU judgment of 9 October 2014, *TDC*, C-222/13, EU:C:2014:2265, para 37. Broberg and Fenger (2021), p. 47.

[78] CJEU judgment of 9 October 2014, *TDC*, C-222/13, EU:C:2014:2265, para 31.

[79] CJEU judgment of 9 October 2014, *TDC*, C-222/13, EU:C:2014:2265, para 30.

[80] In *TDC,* one crucial point that led the Court to refuse jurisdiction was the fact that, should an appeal against a decision of the referring body be made before the ordinary courts, the referring body itself would be the defendant (para 37).

[81] ECJ judgment of 30 March 1993, *Corbiau v Administration des contributions*, C-24/92, EU:C:1993:118, para 16.

[82] CJEU judgment of 9 October 2014, *TDC*, C-222/13, EU:C:2014:2265.

[83] ECJ judgment (Grand Chamber) of 31 May 2005, *Syfait and Others,* C-53/03, EU:C:2005:333.

[84] CJEU judgment of 16 September 2020, *Asociación Nacional de Empresas Estibadoras y Consignatarios de Buques (Anesco) and Others*, C-462/19, EU:C:2020:715.

The issue began to be less clear-cut when, in a number of cases, the Court had to decide whether administrative bodies that were somewhat misleadingly called "tribunals" should be able to refer questions to the CJEU.

The first time the Court was called upon to rule on this issue was in the *Gabalfrisa* case, in which the nature of "court or tribunal" regarding the Spanish "*Tribunales Económico-Administrativos*" was contested.[85] At that time, although the members of these bodies were appointed and removed from office by a decision of the Minister for Economic Affairs and Finance, the Court found that the safeguards surrounding the exercise of competence were enough to affirm "the character of a third party in relation to the departments which adopted the decision forming the subject matter of the complaint and the independence necessary for them to be regarded as courts or tribunals for the purposes of Article [267] of the Treaty".[86] A similar finding was reached regarding the "*Tribunal Català de Contractes del Sector Públic*".[87] Two decisive elements for that decision were the fact that the *Tribunal* was not in a "hierarchical or subordinate position in relation to any other body",[88] and that "the members of the Tribunal are appointed on a permanent basis and cease to hold office only in the circumstances expressly set out"[89] in the legislation.

More recently, however, in *Banco de Santander*, S.A., the Court felt the need to "re-examine" its previous case-law, "notably in the light of the most recent case-law of the Court concerning, in particular, the criterion of independence which any national body must meet in order to be categorised as a 'court or tribunal' for the purposes of Article 267 TFEU".[90] One can only imagine that the state of judicial power in some Eastern European Member States played a role in the mind of the Court, which was conscious of the pressure that it had put on the criterion of independence in the aftermath of the *Associação Sindical dos Juízes Portugueses*[91] case. Once again confronted with a request from a "*Tribunal Económico-Administrativo*", the Court added more detail to the requirements of the *external meaning* of independence, affording greater importance to the guarantee of the irremovability of judges, which "requires that dismissals of members of that body should be determined by specific rules, by means of express legislative provisions offering safeguards that go beyond those provided for by the general rules of administrative law and

[85] ECJ judgment of 21 March 2000, *Gabalfrisa and Others*, joined cases C-110-147/98, EU:C:2000:145.

[86] Para 40.

[87] CJEU judgment (Grand Chamber) of 6 October 2015, *Consorci Sanitari del Maresm*, C-203/14, EU:C:2015:664, paras 17–21.

[88] Para 19.

[89] Para 20.

[90] CJEU judgment (Grand Chamber) of 21 January 2020, *Banco de Santander*, C-274/14, EU:C:2020:17, para 55.

[91] CJEU judgment (Grand Chamber) of 27 February 2018, *Associação Sindical dos Juízes Portugueses*, C-64/16, EU:C:2018:117.

employment law which apply in the event of an unlawful dismissal".[92] In the Court's view, that guarantee was not safeguarded in the case at hand, since the removal of the members of the TEAC was not determined by any specific rules beyond the general rules of administrative law, and therefore they were not "protected against direct or indirect external pressures that are liable to cast doubt on their independence".[93] Additionally, the fact that the Director-General of Taxation could lodge an extraordinary appeal against decisions of the *Tribunal* and then be part himself of the panel that heard that appeal "cast doubt on its independence as well as its impartiality".[94] Moreover, the Court indicated, in a remark that should not go unnoticed, that the law provided for subsequent judicial appeals to the National High Court and the Supreme Court—and therefore, the opportunity for a preliminary ruling request could effectively arise at a later stage.

One must concede, however, that, despite the name given to these bodies, the Court was not really dealing with ordinary courts. They were administrative bodies, the main tasks of which were not of a judicial nature, or the judicial functions of which were incidental or represented only part of the tasks they performed. As a matter of fact, in many cases, the decisions of those bodies were themselves subject to judicial review, and that may have played a role in the Court's decisions.

5.2 Should the CJEU Refuse a Request for a Preliminary Ruling on the Grounds That It Has Been Submitted by a Non-Independent Judicial Court?

A situation that was likely inconceivable in the early cases, but is inevitably on the table now, is the possibility of ordinary judicial courts being prevented from submitting questions to the Court, on the ground that they are not independent bodies, following the passing of contested national legislation that enables governmental interference in the judicial branch. The question to be dealt with now, then, is the following: should the CJEU refuse a preliminary ruling request from an ordinary court on the grounds that it is not a "court or tribunal" because it lacks independence, as a result of national regulations that, *inter alia,* subject judges to disciplinary proceedings on account of their decisions,[95] or that give government officials power to influence the composition of courts through a procedure of secondment of

[92] CJEU judgment (Grand Chamber) of 21 January 2020, *Banco de Santander*, C-274/14, EU:C:2020:17, para 60.

[93] CJEU judgment (Grand Chamber) of 21 January 2020, *Banco de Santander*, C-274/14, EU:C:2020:17, para 68.

[94] CJEU judgment (Grand Chamber) of 21 January 2020, *Banco de Santander*, C-274/14, EU:C:2020:17, para 75.

[95] CJEU judgment (Grand Chamber) of 23 November 2021, *IS*, C-564/19, EU:C:2021:949.

judges,[96] or that subject retirement of judges to a discretionary decision of the President?[97] What criteria should be taken into consideration to assess the independence of the referring court in question? Does Article 267 have a role to play as a substantive ground for control of the respect for the rule of law in individual cases?

Since judicial courts are the model example of a "court or tribunal" for the sake of Article 267, the question is hence much trickier, because these courts were considered to be the natural interlocutors of the Court of Justice. In fact, given that they are the ordinary courts of EU law, with the competence to adjudicate in all sorts of matters, denying them access to the CJEU can risk undermining the uniformity of EU law, which is surely not the most effective way to deal with rebellious Member States.

One must remember that the CJEU does not require every referring body to display all the paradigmatic features of a "tribunal or court". Nor does it consider the list of characteristics to be exhaustive, as it has, on occasion, made use of other criteria besides those that have consistently appeared in decisions since *Vaassen-Göbbels*[98] and *Dorsch.*[99] As previously mentioned, the Court is only concerned that the body in question resembles an ordinary court. Up until now, the Court has accepted questions from very different bodies, sometimes ignoring some of the characteristics that it had previously listed, as is the case with the principle *audi alteram partem.*[100] However, be that as it may, the fact remains that the Court has never, to our knowledge, dispensed with independence as a feature of a "tribunal or court". It is only natural for this to be so, because independence is inherent to the adjudication task, and not only an incidental feature of judicial courts. A court that is not independent is not capable of adjudicating fairly and hence uniformity of EU law is not guaranteed.

The fact is that the Court has been very cautious when dealing with the issue and, in particular, when applying the independence criterion to judicial courts.

Firstly, for the CJEU, classifying a body as a "court or tribunal" will depend on its statutory nature, rather than on the political context[101]. The Court considers, first and foremost, the legal characteristics of the body and the legal context in which those characteristics are established (whether they are required to comply with fundamental principles, or if they ought to be interpreted according to some other rules, etc.). In a case where the independence of the *Landesvergabeamt of Tyrol* was con-

---

[96] CJEU judgment (Grand Chamber) of 16 November 2021, *Prokuratura Rejonowa w Mińsku Mazowieckim*, joined cases C-748/19 to C-754/19, EU:C:2021:931.

[97] CJEU judgment (Grand Chamber) of 24 June 2019, *Commission v Poland (Independence of the Supreme Court)*, C-619/18, EU:C:2019:531, para 113 et seq.

[98] ECJ judgment of 30 June 1966, *Vaassen-Goebbels*, 61/65, EU:C:1966:39.

[99] ECJ judgment of 17 September 1997, *Dorsch Consult*, C-54/96, EU:C:1997:413; Wahl and Prete (2018), p. 523.

[100] In ECJ judgment of 17 September 1997, *Dorsch Consult*, C-54/96, EU:C:1997:413, the Court stated that "it must be reiterated that the requirement that the procedure before the hearing body concerned must be *inter partes* is not an absolute criterion" (para 31).

[101] Wahl and Prete (2018), p. 527.

tested, the Court drew attention to the legal and constitutional guarantees surrounding its activity, and concluded that, as long as the legal provisions forbid political interference with members of the body, then "it is not for the Court to infer that such a provision is applied in a manner contrary to the Austrian constitution and the principles of a State governed by the rule of law".[102] The mere fear of judicial pressure, or interference from non-independent high courts, if not expressed in a legal provision, should not be taken as a reason for the CJEU to deny a preliminary decision request.

This may not be enough to rule out CJEU control over the independence of courts, though, since some of the current rule of law issues arose in the context of legislative reforms in some Member States, and the reasons to suspect that the courts are not fully independent stem from the legislation itself. In those cases, it may be difficult to argue that the suspicions regarding the independence of courts are only political assumptions or based on personal conduct.

In recent years, the Court had given many warnings regarding the possibility of rejecting preliminary requests from national judicial courts subject to laws that impair the independence of judges. One suggestive case is *Getin Noble Bank S.A.*[103] The Court received a preliminary request from a judge (of the Polish Supreme Court) who was suspected of having been appointed through a procedure that did not guarantee his independence. Moreover, the question that he had submitted concerned the very concept of "independent court" under EU law, regarding the possibility of using this classification for a body that included a person appointed through a non-transparent procedure.

Advocate General Bobek argued against the possibility of refusing preliminary questions from a national court on the ground that the judge was not independent because he had been appointed by the Polish President. Bobek recalled that "Article 267 TFEU sets up a dialogue between judicial institutions, not between the individuals of which those institutions are composed."[104] The rationale behind Bobek's opinion was that the Article 267 concept of "court or tribunal" required the identification of an institutional interlocutor of the Court,[105] and that reinterpreting that provision in such a way as to "require the Court to examine the specific situation of the individuals who form part of those national bodies would be at odds with both the nature and purpose of the preliminary ruling procedure".[106] The scope of control

[102] ECJ judgment of 4 February 1999, *Köllensperger and Atzwanger*, C-103/97, EU:C:1999:52, para 24. Wahl and Prete (2018), pp. 527–528.

[103] CJEU judgment (Grand Chamber) of 29 March 2022, *Getin Noble Bank*, C-132/20, EU:C:2022:235.

[104] AG Bobek's opinion of 8 July 2021, *Getin Noble Bank S.A.*, C-132/20, EU:C:2021:557, para 66.

[105] AG Bobek's opinion of 8 July 2021, *Getin Noble Bank S.A.*, C-132/20, EU:C:2021:557, paras 51–52.

[106] AG Bobek's opinion of 8 July 2021, Getin Noble Bank S.A., C-132/20, EU:C:2021:557, para 65. This finding is entirely consistent with other opinions rendered by the same Advocate General, which stress the objective character of the preliminary rulings' procedure. In case C-561/19, Bobek had proposed the Court revisit the criterion set out by the Court in *Cilfit* that dispensed the

was thus very different from that under Article 47 of the Charter, which allowed the Court to "detect (…) breaches of the lawful composition of the bench in each individual case in order to protect individual EU law-based rights".[107] Notwithstanding, Bobek had already suggested that the answer could be different if the "accumulation of the issues relating to, for example, appointments to that (formally judicial) institution, [or] the political influence being exercised over its decision-making" was such that the referring body could no longer be considered a 'court or tribunal'.[108] In any case, that would still amount to an assessment of the institution, and not of the judge itself.

The Court decided in the same way, accepting the referral, and pointing (rather summarily) to the fact that it was undisputed that the Supreme Court satisfied the conditions of a "court or tribunal",[109] from which it followed that a question emanating from it presumably satisfies those conditions, irrespective of the actual composition of the court. It agreed with the Advocate General that a different answer could arise if the functioning of the referring court was affected by circumstances that transcended the individual situation of a judge.[110] On the other hand, it also accepted that a national or international judicial decision leading to the conclusion that the referring court was not independent could lead to a different finding.[111]

A recent decision, in *Krajowa Rada Sądownictwa* case,[112] changed the course of events.

In late 2021, the Chamber of Extraordinary Control and Public Affairs, part of the Polish Supreme Court, submitted a request for a preliminary ruling. The request concerned the interpretation of Article 19 TEU, in respect of a refusal to authorise a national judge to continue to carry out his duties beyond the normal retirement age. Once again, during the written proceedings, doubts were raised regarding the independence of the referring court, forcing the Court to decide on the admissibility of

---

national court of the last instance from submitting a preliminary question to the CJEU. The argumentation of the Advocate General (that led him to propose granting more discretion to the national court, softening the obligation to refer) was based on the assumption that the purpose of the preliminary rulings' obligation was to guarantee the uniform application of EU Law, and, only to a lesser extent, to assist the individual judge in his adjudication task. See AG Bobek's opinion of 15 April 2021, *Consorzio Italian Management*, C-561/19, EU:C:2021:291, paras 49–56, 131–133.

[107] AG Bobek's opinion of 8 July 2021, *Getin Noble Bank S.A.*, C-132/20, EU:C:2021:557, para 60.

[108] AG Bobek's opinion of 8 July 2021, *Getin Noble Bank S.A.*, C-132/20, EU:C:2021:557, para 78.

[109] CJEU judgment (Grand Chamber) of 29 March 2022, *Getin Noble Bank*, C-132/20, EU:C:2022:235, para 68. See also CJEU judgment of 13 October 2022, *Gmina Wieliszew*, C-698/20, EU:C:2022:787, para 57.

[110] CJEU judgment (Grand Chamber) of 29 March 2022, *Getin Noble Bank*, C-132/20, EU:C:2022:235, para 75.

[111] CJEU judgment (Grand Chamber) of 29 March 2022, *Getin Noble Bank*, C-132/20, EU:C:2022:235, para 72. CJEU judgment of 13 October 2022, *Gmina Wieliszew*, C-698/20, EU:C:2022:787, para 52–63, C-644/20, paras 44–52.

[112] CJEU judgment (Grand Chamber) of 21 December 2023, *Krajowa Rada Sądownictwa*, C-718/21, EU:C:2023:1015.

the request. The Opinion of Advocate General Rantos[113] followed the previous line of reasoning. He reaffirmed the need to interpret the independence criterion solely in the light of Article 267, which, he recalled, had a different function to those of Articles 19 TEU and 47 of the Charter. Even recognising that the doubts concerning independence were now of a higher degree (considering the increasing number of judges in office appointed according to the contested legislation), the Advocate General did not depart from the principle established in *Getín Noble*, considering that the presumption of independence, if not absolute, should anyway not be rebutted in the case at hand, given the risk that "the Polish judiciary would be *de facto* removed from the European Union's judicial system".[114]

The Court did not agree. Following an extensive consideration of "factors, both systemic and circumstantial",[115] which included analysis of the composition of the panel of national judges that had submitted the request for a preliminary rulings, as well as decisions of both the Polish Supreme Administrative Court and the European Court of Human Rights that had addressed the national provisions under which they had been appointed, the Court considered it necessary to rebut the presumption of independence and stated that that panel of judges "does not constitute a 'court or tribunal' within the meaning of Article 267 TFEU".[116] Accordingly, it considered the request for a preliminary ruling inadmissible.

One cannot say that this decision came as a surprise, given that in *Getín Noble* the Court had already anticipated such a possible result. Actually, in that decision, the Court had expressly mentioned the fact that the relevant date for determining the applicable law should be that of the closing of the oral part of the procedure, which in that case had occurred in March 2021, prior to both of the important external decisions that could have influenced the Court in the case: the judgment of the Polish Supreme Administrative Court and the judgment of the ECtHR in case *Dloinska-Ficek and Ozimek v Poland* (which were delivered respectively, in September and November 2021). Unable to use them *ratione temporis* in *Getín Noble,* the Court had now, in *Krajowa Rada Sądownictwa*, the big opportunity. The Court grabbed it, taking those decisions as the decisive factor—after proving their pertinence to the facts at hand—just at it had promised in *Getín Noble*, where it had stated that "the presumption (…) may nevertheless be rebutted where a final judicial decision *handed down by a national or international court or tribunal* leads to the conclusion that the judge constituting the referring court is not an independent and impartial tribunal previously established by law".[117]

[113] AG Ranto's opinion of 2 March 2023, *Krajowa Rada Sądownictwa*, C-718/21, EU:C:2023:150.

[114] AG Ranto's opinion of 2 March 2023, *Krajowa Rada Sądownictwa*, C-718/21, EU:C:2023:150 para 25.

[115] CJEU judgment (Grand Chamber) of 21 December 2023, *Krajowa Rada Sądownictwa*, C-718/21, EU:C:2023:1015, para 77.

[116] CJEU judgment (Grand Chamber) of 21 December 2023, *Krajowa Rada Sądownictwa*, C-718/21, EU:C:2023:1015, para 58.

[117] CJEU judgment (Grand Chamber) of 29 March 2022, *Getin Noble Bank*, C-132/20, EU:C:2022:235, para 72. Emphasis added.

It looks, for now, as if the matter is settled with the presumption that a judicial court can raise preliminary questions to the Court, regardless of the situation of a particular judge who participates in the case. That presumption will be rebutted if there is a systemic disregard of the principle of independence, confirmed by national decisions or, more dramatically, other international decisions.

Another argument remains strong in favour of relatively lenient scrutiny by the CJEU of the independence of the referring court, leading to a decision of inadmissibility only in exceptional circumstances. As was previously recalled, many of the cases in which, prior to the rule of law crisis, the Court refused preliminary requests, on the ground that they were not submitted by a "court or tribunal" for the purposes of Article 267, were comforted by the fact that those bodies' decisions were, according to national law, still subject to subsequent appeals to judicial courts. Hence, "the effectiveness of the mechanism of the request for a preliminary ruling provided for in Article 267 TFEU and the uniform interpretation of EU law"[118] would be guaranteed at a later stage. Undoubtedly, this may not be the case when it comes to common judicial bodies. Considering that the judicial reforms affect every instance of judicial courts, it may well happen that the national court's decision becomes final without being subject to a truly independent court. However, at the moment of the referral, the CJEU may not have sufficient information to consider which national judicial courts are independent and which are not, and therefore to ascertain what the situation of its current interlocutor is regarding independence. In the suggestive words of Advocate General Bobek in *Minister Sprawiedliwości v. Prokurator Krajowy,*[119] "It is not the role of this Court to second-guess the ulterior motives of a national court. It is even far less appropriate to imply bad faith on the part of a national court and, on the basis of that conjecture, refuse to provide an answer to a question referred". Accordingly, to avoid the risk of having a final mandatory national decision that is not in conformity with EU law, or of having genuinely independent judges unable to refer questions or to count on the CJEU to deliver EU Law-consistent decisions, the Court is right in not being too strict on its judgment of admissibility. In particular, a general perception of the lack of independence of a given Member State's judiciary should not be the basis for a general refusal of preliminary rulings requests. In this regard, one can only hope that the fact that the national court decides to refer a question to the CJEU may be in itself an indication of its independence,[120] or at least of its commitment to accept the contribution of the Court to the case at hand.

One cannot ignore the tremendous empowering effect that access to EU courts through the preliminary rulings' procedure has on national jurisdictions *vis-à-vis* national authorities, and the role it has played over the years in favour of European

[118] CJEU judgment (Grand Chamber) of 21 January 2020, *Banco de Santander SA*, case C-274/14, EU:C:2020:17, para 79.

[119] CJEU judgment of 13 January 2022, *Minister Sprawiedliwości*, case C-55/20, EU:C:2022:6.

[120] See, for instance, CJEU judgment (Grand Chamber) of 23 November 2021, *IS*, C-564/19, EU:C:2021:949, paras 47–50, in which the referring judge was very clear on the effect that the submission of a question to the CJEU might have on his specific situation.

integration.[121] Even in a difficult environment, there are still courts that strive to be independent and are counting on the Court of Justice to deliver their rulings, and the Court should uphold this relationship of trust that is inherent in the preliminary rulings' procedure.

This does not mean that the Court should ignore situations in which violation of the principle is clear in the case at hand, as was the case in *Krajowa Rada Sądownictwa*. However, this should only be on the basis of an objective situation, acknowledged by a judicial decision that declared the national court to be non-independent, and by the recognition of an overall failure of the judicial system.

It is worth noting that this solution is not in line with the Court's case-law on the refusal of EAWs—as the Court itself acknowledges, when stressing that this mere "institutional assessment" is to be performed only in relation to Article 267.[122] In fact, whenever a situation falls within the scope of the Charter and can be confronted with Article 47, the analysis is one of fundamental rights, and the purpose is to check whether there has been a breach of the right of access to a court. In that case, consideration of the personal capacity of judges dealing with the case can and should be considered. As we have seen, the Court is very conscious of the impact that a non-independent court issuing an EAW may have on the judicial protection of individuals, let alone their freedom. In that case, the individual situation should be considered and, if indicative of judicial malfunctions in the issuing court, the executing court should be exempted from executing the warrant.

The combination of the findings of this section—that an evaluation of the independence of the referring body for the purpose of considering it a "court or tribunal" able to refer preliminary questions should be strictly institutional, and that an individual assessment should only come into play whenever the question is one of fundamental rights—is in line with the ECtHR case-law in relation to the preliminary rulings' procedure. In fact, over the years, the Strasbourg Court has developed consistent case-law that has helped reinforce the duty to refer questions to the CJEU under Article 267, by considering that the procedure contributes to the judicial protection of individuals and that, consequently, it can control the Member State's compliance with that duty under Article 6 of the ECHR.[123] Accordingly, an analysis of the institutional independence of referring bodies, instead of a case-by-case assessment, leads, in general, to greater acceptance of preliminary questions, and therefore can better contribute to the judicial protection of the parties. That is why an institutional approach such as the one favoured by the Court of Justice is not at odds with the recognition that the preliminary rulings procedure is also part of the judicial guarantees of individuals (in the sense that they have a legitimate expectation regarding the correct application of the law): they will still be better off if the Court of Justice accepts the preliminary question, rather than if it refuses it on the ground

[121] Whether that has always been uncontroversial is yet another story, which would require us to engage in the never-ending debate about the Court's activism.

[122] CJEU judgment of 13 October 2022, *Gmina Wieliszew*, C-698/20, EU:C:2022:787, para 61.

[123] *E.g.* ECtHR judgment of 8 July 2014, *Dhahbi v. Italy*, 17120/09, para 32–34; ECtHR judgment of 13 July 2021, *Bio Farmland Betriebs S.R.L. v. Romania*, 43639/17, para 55.

that the referring body is not a "court or tribunal" due to its lack of independence. Punishing the interlocutor of the Court would not do any good for the uniformity of EU law or the legitimate expectations of the parties.

6 Article 19 TEU

6.1 The Court's Case Law on Article 19 TEU

Article 19 TEU has been playing a central role in judging whether Member States are complying with the rule of law principle. *Portuguese Judges*[124] was the landmark decision in this respect, since it opened the gateway door to considering Article 19 TEU a normative basis for control of compliance with the principle of judicial independence. Rather than considering it a merely political principle, more specific than Article 2 TEU but with the same (lack of) legal force,[125] the Court upgraded the provision, and the principle of effective judicial protection set out in it, to the status of a standard of control of national rules concerning the organisation of the judiciary. In this case, setting aside the Charter and focusing exclusively on Article 19 TEU,[126] the Court stated that the fact that national courts are the ultimate

[124] CJEU judgment (Grand Chamber) of 27 February 2018, *Associação Sindical dos Juízes Portugueses,* C-64/16, EU:C:2018:117.

[125] The question about whether Article 2 should have legal force and be justiciable has reached the Court in 2022, when the Commission brought proceedings against Hungary on the ground that it had violated the fundamental principles of the European Union. At the time of writing, the decision is still pending, but AG Ćapeta delivered his Opinion proposing that values mentioned in Article 2 be considered justiciable, and admitting a self-standing finding of breach of the provision: Opinion delivered on 5 June 2025 in case *Commission v. Hungary,* C-769/22. In contrast, Hillion (2018), p. 74 considered it only "possible to invoke a failure of Article 2 alongside other, more specific failures" (such as non-compliance with a directive).

[126] The Court implied that the Charter was not applicable to the case at hand. Actually, the national measure at stake in *Portuguese Judges*, prescribing a temporary reduction in the remuneration paid to the Court of Auditors' judges, was a consequence of the economic and financial assistance that Portugal was undergoing. Already in *Sindicato dos Bancários*, in which a similar national budgetary measure was analysed regarding the public sector, the Court had considered the question to be inadmissible, because there was no indication that the said law was intended to apply Union law (CJEU order of 7 March 2013, *Sindicato dos Bancários do Norte*, Case C-128/12, EU:C:2013:149, para 12). Against these cases, however, in a more recent decision, the Court considered that the Memorandum of Understanding between Portugal on one side, and the Commission, the IMF and the ECB on the other side (and from which the budgetary measures of the two previously mentioned cases derived), should be considered an integral part of EU law (CJEU judgment of 5 May 2022, *BPC Lux 2 and Others*, C-83/20, EU:C:2022:346, para 28–29), and therefore, national measures that were adopted to give effect to it should be compatible with the Charter. Pech and Platon (2018), p. 1834, had already referred to the *Florescu* case (CJEU judgment (Grand Chamber) of 13 June 2017, *Eugenia Florescu and Others*, C-258/14, EU:C:2017:448, para 48), which could have been used by the Court as a precedent for applying the Charter to national measures adopted to meet the conditions attached to the financial assistance granted by the EU to a Member State.

appliers of EU law should be enough to trigger that provision and allow for European control in cases where they lacked independence.[127] Accordingly, the Court took Article 19 TEU as a self-standing ground for review of national measures, allowing more general control over those impairing judges' independence, even in cases where States were not implementing EU law.

The Court adopted a strategy that was not new—offering a ground-breaking formula with no consequences for the case at hand, and thus softening its impact by postponing its practical effects to a later stage.[128] In fact, although Article 19 TEU was accepted for the first time as an independent ground of review, the Court considered that the national measure at stake was compatible with it since it was associated with imperative budgetary requirements, was temporary, and was not discriminatory.[129]

The first step had been taken, however subsequent decisions provided the pretext for developing and applying the principle to different situations. The Court later stated that not only does Article 19 TEU have legal value, but it also has direct effect[130] and can therefore be invoked by individuals with respect for it being controlled by national courts. In parallel, the provision was also used by the Commission in direct infringement actions as a ground for reviewing Member States' actions.[131] As to the substantive requirements of Article 19, the Court has emphasised that they should be read alongside Article 47 of the Charter, very often making cross-references to cases decided under both provisions.[132]

The Court's use of Article 19 TEU is based on a number of assumptions. The first is that compliance with the rule of law is a requirement for membership of the EU, and that it should be so not only upon accession (as required by Article 49 TEU) but also after accession, on an ongoing basis.[133] The value of the rule of law is presumed to be shared by Member States and forms part of the common civilisational core that

[127] CJEU judgment (Grand Chamber) of 27 February 2018, *Associação Sindical dos Juízes Portugueses*, C-64/16, EU:C:2018:117, para 40.

[128] Jakab (2016), p. 203.

[129] CJEU judgment (Grand Chamber) of 27 February 2018, *Associação Sindical dos Juízes Portugueses*, C-64/16, EU:C:2018:117 paras 46–52.

[130] CJEU judgment (Grand Chamber) of 22 March 2022, *Prokurator Generalny*, C-508/19, EU:C:2022:201, para 74.

[131] CJEU judgment (Grand Chamber) of 24 June 2019, *Commission v Poland (Independence of the Supreme Court)*, C-619/18, EU:C:2019:531; CJEU judgment (Grand Chamber) of 5 November 2019, *Commission v Poland (Independence of ordinary courts)*, C-192/18, EU:C:2019:924; CJEU judgment (Grand Chamber) of 15 July 2021, *Commission v Poland (Disciplinary regime applicable to judges)*, C-791/19, EU:C:2021:596.

[132] See, for instance, CJEU judgment (Grand Chamber) of 20 April 2021, *Repubblika*, C-896/19, EU:C:2021:311, para 45, and CJEU judgment (Grand Chamber) of 15 July 2021, *Commission v Poland (Disciplinary regime applicable to judges)*, C-791/19, EU:C:2021:596, para 57.

[133] CJEU judgment (Grand Chamber) of 24 June 2019, *Commission v Poland (Independence of the Supreme Court)*, C-619/18, EU:C:2019:531, para 42 and CJEU judgment (Grand Chamber) of 20 April 2021, *Repubblika*, C-896/19, EU:C:2021:311, para 63. Hillion (2018), pp. 60 et seq.; Schmidt and Bogdanowicz (2018), p. 1071.

made European integration possible and that is outlined at the very beginning of the treaties, in Article 2 TEU. The second assumption is that compliance with the rule of law, in particular with the independence of the judiciary, is crucial to ensure the effectiveness of EU law in Member States. Finally, Article 19 TEU is also said to have a role in protecting individuals' rights, since, without independent courts, they cannot be assured that the rights they derive from EU law will be recognised and given full effect by the Member States—especially when those rights constitute a burden (*e.g.* financial) for States, and hence the supervision of courts is especially needed.[134]

Having stated that Article 19 TEU is a substantive source of the principle of independence of the judiciary, with direct effect, the Court gave us a first indication of a procedural means that allows it to perform such control over Member States' activity: the preliminary rulings procedure under Article 267 TFEU. Although not directly intended to sanction Member States, the procedure inevitably leads the Court to assess their activity in the light of the requirements of the European principle, with the advantage of the control being performed within a specific case, thus contributing, with the help of the principle of primacy and the collaboration of national judges, to softening the individual impact of national rules contrary to that principle. *Portuguese Judges,*[135] *A.B. and Others,*[136] *Repubblika,*[137] *W.Ż.,*[138] *Prokuratura Krajowa,*[139] *R.I.,*[140] are all examples of cases in which Article 19 TEU was used as the control parameter by means of the preliminary rulings' procedure.

A path towards allowing infringement proceedings on the same ground was thus forged. In 2019 the Court accepted a case against Poland, on the ground that it had failed to observe the obligations stemming from Article 19 TEU by adopting legislation that impaired the independence of judges.[141] It is now settled that rule of law issues can be addressed via direct actions pursuant to Article 258 TFEU.

[134] Although requirements of effectiveness of EU law and effective judicial protection sometimes overlap, we acknowledge the difference between the two principles. See Prechal and Widdershoven (2011), p. 38.

[135] CJEU judgment (Grand Chamber) of 27 February 2018, *Associação Sindical dos Juízes Portugueses,* C-64/16, EU:C:2018:117.

[136] CJEU judgment (Grand Chamber) of 2 March 2021, *A.B. and Others*, C-824/18, EU:C:2021:153.

[137] CJEU judgment (Grand Chamber) of 20 April 2021, *Repubblika*, C-896/19, EU:C:2021:311.

[138] CJEU judgment (Grand Chamber) of 6 October 2021, *W.Ż.*, C-487/19, EU:C:2021:798.

[139] CJEU judgment (Grand Chamber) of 16 November 2021, *Prokuratura Rejonowa w Mińsku Mazowieckim*, joined cases C-748/19 to C-754/19, EU:C:2021:931.

[140] CJEU judgment of 11 May 2023, *R.I. v Inspecţia Judiciară*, C-817/21, ECLI:EU:C:2023:391.

[141] CJEU judgment (Grand Chamber) of 24 June 2019, *Commission v Poland (Independence of the Supreme Court)*, C-619/18, EU:C:2019:531.

6.2 Analysis

Although the case-law on Article 19 TEU is now settled, it is not without controversy. In fact, having been accepted that compliance with the rule of law is necessary, the key question now is whether, under the current status of EU law, European judicial control over Member States' activity in that respect should take place[142]. The main objections to that possibility come from the existence of a specific procedure, in Article 7 TEU, to address violations of the values on which the Union is based, and from the limitation established in Article 51 of the Charter, or, to put it in more general terms, from the division of competences between the EU and the Member States.

The first objection is based on the political procedure contained in Article 7 TEU and whether this should be considered as precluding the judicial competence of the CJEU to control Member States' compliance with the rule of law.

The argument deserves consideration. Some literature,[143] and the Court itself, has justified the possibility of judicial control, recalling the fact that, within the accession procedure, candidate States must show respect for the rule of law principle; accordingly, the principle of no regression[144] should require that control continues even after accession. However, this finding is not bulletproof. One cannot ignore that the *ex ante* control (upon accession) of respect for the values of Article 49 TEU is of a political, rather than a legal, nature. It is for the European institutions and the existing Member States (the actors within Article 49 TEU) to check whether the candidate State complies with those principles. Therefore, from that provision one cannot immediately infer that there can be judicial control to be exercised after accession. In fact, if it was necessary to establish a continuum of control before and after accession, the most appropriate match would be between Articles 49 and 7 TEU, both corresponding to political procedures. Given the sensitive nature of the assessment, it is plausible that Member States wanted to continue addressing violations of EU values through a strictly political mechanism. The fact that Article 269 TFEU limits the Court's jurisdiction over Article 7 TEU to procedural aspects, excluding control over the political findings of the Council, may favour this line of argumentation. In fact, if the Member States had wished for stronger, judicial, control, they would not have left so many political imprints in the Treaties.

And yet, the controversy remains.[145] It is possible to counterargue that, within the fields covered by EU law, the rule should be that the Court has competence to control Member States' activity. The infringement proceedings of Articles 258–260 TFEU are intended to control Member States' failure "to fulfil an obligation under

[142] Quadros (2020), p. 104.

[143] Van Elsuwege and Gremmelprez (2020), p. 19.

[144] CJEU judgment (Grand Chamber) of 15 July 2021, Commission v Poland (*Disciplinary regime applicable to judges*), C-791/19, EU:C:2021:596, para 51.

[145] Hillion (2018), p. 66. Similarly, AG Tanchev's opinion of 11 April 2019, *Commission v Poland (Independence of the Supreme Court)*, C-619/18, EU:C:2019:325.

the Treaties", thus including obligations under the TEU. Therefore, the exceptions to the CJEU's control should be only those clearly identified in the Treaty—*e.g.* Article 24 TEU in relation to the Common Foreign and Security Policy (CFSP)—and should not be extended any further.

However, there is still room left for a rejoinder argument: the need for express exclusion of the Court's competence in the CFSP results from the fact that it corresponds to an area of competence that belongs to the Union (even if with an intergovernmental facet). If institutions are authorised to adopt legal acts—or at least acts with legal implications—the assumption is that these would be subject to judicial review; if that is not intended, the exclusion would need to be, as it is, clearly expressed. Yet, we cannot infer from this that all exclusion of competence of the Court of Justice needs to be expressly stated. Regarding areas that do not fall under the positive competence of the Union in the first place, it is not necessary for the Treaty to exclude the competence, because the principle of conferral would naturally lead us to presume that the competence does not exist.[146]

The debate inevitably leads to the ongoing discussion surrounding the EU competence creep. The truth is that judicial control and the political procedure of Article 7 are essentially different in their scope. While the former is specifically aimed at judicial malfunctions and is mostly designed to evaluate their effect on EU law effectiveness (and on the rights of individuals that are dependent on that effectiveness), the latter is more general in nature, and designed as a means of institutionalised peer pressure.

In fact, the Court did not feel constrained in deciding on matters that were already the object of the Commission's "Reasoned Proposal for a Council decision on the determination of a clear risk of a serious breach by Poland of the rule of law", adopted under Article 7(1) TEU.[147] The question had been addressed and dismissed by Advocate General Tanchev, who stated that "the fact that the Article 7(1) TEU mechanism has been engaged does not preclude" the Commission from initiating judicial proceedings against a Member State under Article 258 TFEU.[148]

Once it is accepted that Article 19 TEU is justiciable, a second objection to the Court's control arises from the fact that the independence of the judiciary, which the

[146] We do not mean to ignore the challenges that the EU imposes on the principle of conferral, nor to suggest that it should be read as strictly it is required in regard to International Organisations, given the breadth of the EU Treaties. However, despite its several shades and declinations, it seems undisputed that, as long as it is enshrined in the Treaties, the principle should be given a material content and constitute a criterion for the action of the European institutions.

[147] See CJEU judgment of 24 June 2019, *Commission v Poland (Independence of the Supreme Court)*, C-619/18, EU:C:2019:531.

[148] See AG Tanchev's opinion of 11 April 2019, *Commission v Poland (Independence of the Supreme Court)*, C-619/18, EU:C:2019:325, para 51. Tanchev proposed the same approach on the second infringement action against Poland: AG Tanchev's opinion of 20 June 2019, *Commission v Poland (Independence of ordinary courts)*, C-192/18, EU:C:2019:529, para 73. The same difference in nature was found between Article 7 TEU and Article 322 TFEU (which was the basis for the adoption of the new conditionality mechanism): CJEU judgment of 16 February 2022, *Hungary v Parliament and Council—conditionality mechanism*, C-156/21, EU:C:2022:97, paras 195–218.

Court acknowledges as "inherent in the task of adjudication"[149] is required also by the right to effective judicial protection included in the Charter. The question is, then, how to reconcile both sources.

There are three possible approaches to this (see Figs. 1, 2, and 3).

The first approach, presented by Poland in infringement proceedings against it,[150] considers that Article 19 TEU does not add to obligations already arising from the application of the Charter. Considering the progressive widening of the scope of the latter, through a generous interpretation of the situations in which States are "implementing Union law",[151] there has been in practice an approximation to the wording of Article 19 TEU, which requires effective judicial protection "in the fields covered by Union law". If this is the case, a material link to a European provision is required in order for both Article 47 of the Charter and Article 19 TEU to be triggered. The consequence would be that Article 19 TEU should be subject to the same limitations of the Charter, with Article 51 thereof setting the limit for EU supervision which should only be put into place "in situations governed under EU law".[152]

This argument is often combined with references to national procedural autonomy.[153] In fact, competence to decide on the organisation of the judiciary lies with the

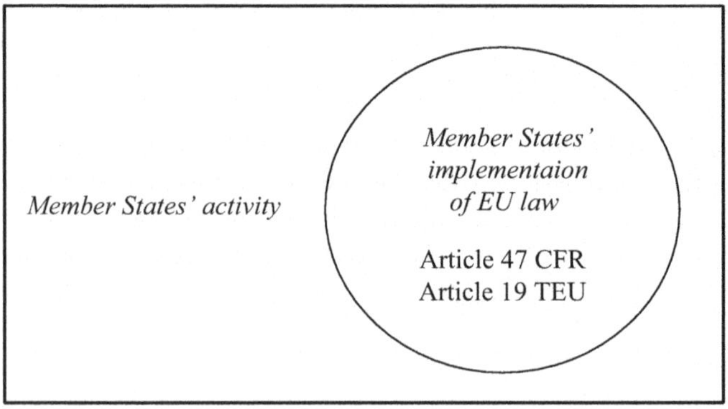

Fig. 1 First approach—Article 19 TEU equivalent to Article 47 CFR, subject to the scope of application of the Charter as defined in Article 51 thereof

[149] CJEU judgment (Grand Chamber) of 27 February 2018, *Associação Sindical dos Juízes Portugueses*, C-64/16, EU:C:2018:117, para 48.

[150] See CJEU judgment of 24 June 2019, *Commission v Poland (Independence of the Supreme Court)*, C-619/18, EU:C:2019:531, paras 37–39, and AG Tanchev's opinion of 11 April 2019 in the same case, paras 52–60.

[151] See above, Sect. 3.1. CJEU judgment (Grand Chamber) of 26 February 2013, *Åkerberg Fransson*, C-617/10, EU:C:2013:105, and CJEU judgment of 14 June 2017, *Online Games*, C-685/15, EU:C:2017:452, para 55.

[152] See CJEU judgment of 24 June 2019, *Commission v Poland (Independence of the Supreme Court)*, C-619/18, EU:C:2019:531, para 39.

[153] See CJEU judgment of 24 June 2019, *Commission v Poland (Independence of the Supreme Court)*, C-619/18, EU:C:2019:531, para 38.

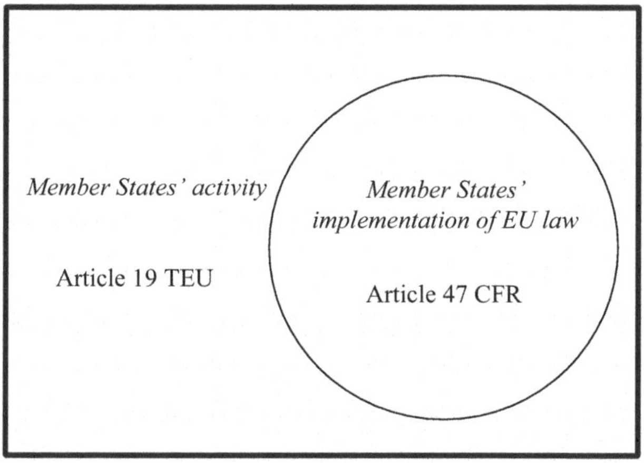

Fig. 2 Second approach—Article 19 covering all Member States' activity

Member States, and this rule has always been recognised by the Court.[154] Thus, it comes as no surprise that this has become a counterargument used by the Eastern European Member States to resist EU control. They also rely on national identity to argue against a single definition of the rule of law principle. According to this reasoning, the values expressed in Article 2 TEU are broad and flexible enough to allow different solutions stemming from national traditions and legal culture. Therefore, subjecting national action to the European parameter of such principles would violate the division of competences and Article 4 (2) TEU.

One advantage of this first proposal is that it avoids the conundrum of distinguishing between "implementation of EU law" and "fields covered by Union law", paying serious heed to the limitations set out in Article 51 of the Charter and in the second paragraph of Article 19 TEU, as true limitations on EU intervention. The rule is clear: there are boundaries to the realm of EU law, and neither the Charter nor Article 19 TEU can overcome those barriers. However, the proposal fails to provide Article 19 TEU with an autonomous meaning, rendering the provision useless. Given that it was introduced in the Lisbon Treaty, at the same time as the Charter was incorporated in it and acquired legal force, it would be odd for the Member States to want the provisions to be redundant and without an articulated purpose.

The second approach lies at the opposite extreme and considers that Article 19 TEU can be applied to every situation the Charter does not cover, so that "it is not necessary, for the purposes of alleging violation of the second subparagraph of Article 19(1) TEU, to demonstrate that the contested measures implement EU law within the meaning of Article 51(1) of the Charter".[155] The mere fact that national

[154] See CJEU judgment of 24 June 2019, *Commission v Poland (Independence of the Supreme Court)*, C-619/18, EU:C:2019:531, para 52.

[155] AG Tanchev's opinion of 11 April 2019, *Commission v Poland (Independence of the Supreme Court)*, C-619/18, EU:C:2019:325, para 53.

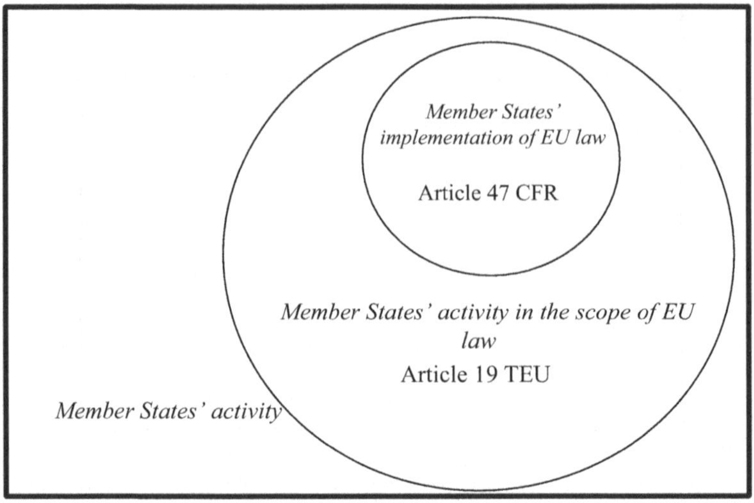

Fig. 3 Third (intermediate) approach—Article 19 TEU broader that Article 47, but not covering all States' activity

courts can apply EU law should be enough to subject the entire national organisation of the judiciary to compatibility with Article 19 TEU. In other words, the limitation in the second subparagraph of Article 19(1) TEU should not be taken literally, since nearly every aspect of the judicial organisation has a potential effect on EU law and should therefore be preserved from interference and ultimately subject to the Court of Justice's surveillance.

The virtues and vices of this proposal are the opposite of those of the previous one. The greatest difficulty in using Article 19 TEU as a basis for direct control of Member States' actions outside EU law implementation lies in the limitation found in Article 51 of the Charter. Why would States have included such a clear limitation if they wanted the control to take place by another means? The paradox is further amplified since the Court itself stated in *Prokuratura* that there is some correspondence between the criteria for interpreting both Article 19 TEU and Article 47 of the Charter,[156] that is, the content of the judicial protection included in Article 19 TEU should be read in the light of the Court's case-law in relation to Article 47 of the Charter. It is hard to take the Article 51 limitation seriously if control through Article 19 TEU under the same standards would always be possible.[157]

[156] CJEU judgment (Grand Chamber) of 16 November 2021, *Prokuratura Rejonowa w Mińsku Mazowieckim*, joined cases C-748/19 to C-754/19, EU:C:2021:931, para 61. That was also the Commission's view in case C-619/18 (*Commission v. Poland*) expressed at the audience, according to the Advocate General: see AG Tanchev's opinion of 11 April 2019, *Commission v Poland (Independence of the Supreme Court)*, C-619/18, EU:C:2019:325, para 26.

[157] See AG Tanchev's opinion of 11 April 2019, *Commission v Poland (Independence of the Supreme Court)*, C-619/18 EU:C:2019:325, para 57. Van Elsuwege and Gremmelprez (2020), p. 28; Spieker (2022), pp. 781–782.

Lastly, the intermediate proposal provides Article 19 TEU with a scope of application separate from that of the Charter, while still trying to make sense of the different wording of the respective limitations: Article 51 of the Charter acknowledges that States are bound by it "only when they are implementing EU law", whilst Article 19 TEU extends the control to all "fields covered by Union law" which, after all, still suggests a limited scope of control.

A trial of this proposal was defended by Advocate General Tanchev, who suggested, in *Miasto Łowicz,*[158] that control under Article 19 TEU should come into play only when there is a generalised breach of the rule of law principle. This would be different from granting the provision a more general scope by considering it to be applicable whenever the Charter was not, while avoiding gaps in the surveillance of compliance with the rule of law principle in cases where the application of EU law would, in fact, be at risk.

Notwithstanding, the difficulty of placing limits on the scope of EU law could give a potential all-encompassing power to Article 19 TEU. If all that there is to trigger Article 19 is the fact that the judicial bodies may potentially apply EU law, it is difficult to think of situations in which that provision could not be applied as a standard of review of national legislation.[159]

The Court has apparently taken the second route, by stating that "as regards the material scope of the second subparagraph of Article 19(1) TEU, that provision moreover refers to 'the fields covered by Union law', irrespective of whether the Member States are implementing Union law within the meaning of Article 51(1) of the Charter".[160]

That seems to suggest, first of all, that Article 19 TEU can be used alongside Article 47 of the Charter as a substantive ground of review in cases that also fall under the Charter. In *Getin Noble* the material situation involved Council Directive 93/13/EEC of 5 April 1993 on unfair terms in consumer contracts, thus it unequivocally implied the application of the Charter, and the Court did not shy away from also referring to Article 19 TEU as a supplementary argument.[161] It becomes apparent that the CJEU is concerned not only with the effect of national laws on the fundamental right to judicial protection, but also with the impact they have in relation to the effectiveness of the EU legal order.

However, the most important outcome of the Court's case-law, since *Portuguese Judges,* is that Article 19 TEU can come into play autonomously in situations where States are not "implementing Union law" (within the meaning of Article 51 (2) of the Charter), but which still relate to "fields covered by Union law" (by dint of

[158] CJEU judgment (Grand Chamber) of 26 March 2020, *Miasto Łowicz*, joined Cases C-558/18 and C-563/18, EU:C:2020:234, para 125.

[159] Pech and Platon (2018), p. 1840.

[160] CJEU judgment (Grand Chamber) of 24 June 2019, *Commission v Poland (Independence of the Supreme Court)*, C-619/18, EU:C:2019:531, para 50. CJEU judgment of 2 March 2021, *A.B. et al. (Appointment of judges to the Supreme Court)*, C-824/18, EU:C:2021:153.

[161] CJEU judgment (Grand Chamber) of 29 March 2022, *Getin Noble Bank*, C-132/20, EU:C:2022:235, para 93–99.

Article 19 (2) TEU).[162] As to the exact meaning of the expression, the question can be tricky, given that situations are complex and multifaceted. At first sight, one would think that the expression relates to European competences that were not yet exercised, but in *Fransson* the Court made it clear that this category still falls within the scope of application of the Charter.[163] Therefore, the favoured understanding is that Article 19 TEU allows for the Court's control even outside of the conferred powers and the areas in which the State's activity is directly involved with the implementation of EU law. As the Court recalled in *Commission v. Poland*, the fact that Member States remain competent to regulate some fields does not exempt them from complying with EU Law.[164]

In keeping the expression "fields covered by EU law" the Court seems to be paying lip service to the principle of conferral, while in fact allowing control to be performed in a general way. The truth is that the CJEU was never convinced by the proposals to restrict control based on procedural autonomy, pointing to the fact that the rule of law is an "obligation as to the result to be achieved", which cannot vary from State to State. What can vary is the specific way in which that obligation is implemented, which corresponds to the discretion States enjoy under Article 4 (2) TEU.[165] However, early in its case-law, the Court held that procedural autonomy is not unlimited, but rather is subject to the principles of equivalence and effectiveness.[166] This rule is still in force and the Court has brought it to the rule of law crisis, reminding the Member States that they need to exercise their, so-called, reserved powers, without impacting on EU law. The seriousness of the violations must certainly have played a role in determining the Court's mind, leading it to act as a guarantor of the fundamental values upon which the EU, *rectius,* the European project, is founded.[167]

Therefore, even when there is no *substantial link* with the EU legal order, the mere fact that a national court can be called to rule on cases involving EU law creates a *procedural link* with it, which is enough to bring the rules on its organisation within the scope of EU law, and hence to require them to comply with Article 19 TEU. In leaving aside the calls for procedural autonomy, the Court placed emphasis

---

[162] CJEU judgment (Grand Chamber) of 16 November 2021, *Prokuratura Rejonowa w Mińsku Mazowieckim*, joined cases C-748/19 to C-754/19, EU:C:2021:931, para 62.

[163] CJEU judgment (Grand Chamber) of 26 February 2013, *Åkerberg Fransson*, C-617/10, EU:C:2013:105, paras 20–30.

[164] CJEU judgment (Grand Chamber) of 24 June 2019, *Commission v Poland (Independence of the Supreme Court)*, C-619/18, EU:C:2019:531, para 52.

[165] CJEU judgment of 16 February 2022, *Hungary v Parliament and Council—conditionality mechanism*, C-156/21, EU:C:2022:97 paras. 231–233.

[166] ECJ judgment of 16 December 1976, *Rewe-Zentralfinanz eG and Rewe-Zentral AG v Landwirtschaftskammer für das Saarland*, 33/76, EU:C:1976:188.

[167] See another manifestation of this in AG Bobek's opinion of 29 July 2019, Case C-556/17, *Alekszij Torubarov*, EU: C:2019:339, para 55. Van Elsuwege and Gremmelprez (2020), p. 28; Spieker (2022), p. 27.

on the need for EU law to be effective, and, more importantly, enhanced the principle of judicial protection as a criterion for judging national law.[168]

6.3 Lines for Future Action

We hope that any doubts surrounding the use of Article 19 TEU in infringement proceedings have now been clearly identified. Given the "potentially highly intrusive" character of Article 19,[169] we should keep in mind the exceptional circumstances that led to its use, so as not to trivialise it in the future. In fact, while Article 47 of the Charter is understood from an individual rights' perspective and is safeguarded by a clear mandate of Member States as to the application of the Charter (either through the preliminary rulings procedure or through the infringement procedure), Article 19 TEU contains an objective obligation[170] that hovers over the actions of Member States in general and requires their compliance.

Accordingly, there have been some calls for cautious recourse to Article 19 TEU, even from within the Court itself. The idea that it should only be applied whenever there is a systemic violation of the principle can be found, for instance, in Advocate General Tanchev's opinions, together with harsh criticism of the judicial reforms in Eastern European Member States. In his words, Article 19 TEU "is concerned predominantly with objective independence and national measures having a generalised impact on the overall system established by the Member States for ensuring effective judicial protection and the essential requirements thereof".[171] Only in a "context of a structural failing" should EU control take place outside the scope of the Charter.[172] Bobek agrees with this proposal, admitting that "the threshold for a breach of [Article 19] is rather high" and that it "contains an extraordinary remedy for extraordinary situations";[173] therefore, Article 19(1) TEU is infringed only by "breaches of a certain seriousness and/or of a systemic nature",[174] "likely to threaten the proper functioning of the national judicial system, thereby jeopardizing the

[168] On the relationship between the principle of effectiveness and judicial protection, see Prechal and Widdershoven (2011), pp. 292–296.

[169] Editorial comments (2021), p. 1643.

[170] Roeben (2020), pp. 38–40.

[171] AG Tanchev's opinion of 11 April 2019, *Commission v Republic of Poland*, C-619/18, EU:C:2019:325, note 41.

[172] AG Tanchev's opinion of 20 June 2019, *Commission v Poland (Independence of ordinary courts)*, C-192/18, EU:C:2019:529, para 101.

[173] AG Bobek's opinion of 8 July 2021, *Getin Noble Bank S.A.*, C-132/20, EU:C:2021:557, paras 38–39.

[174] *Idem.*

capacity of the Member States in question to provide sufficient remedies to the individuals".[175]

The concept of "systemic violations" can be traced back to that of *systemic deficiencies in the rule of law* developed by von Bogdandy and Ioannidis, borrowing from the expression used by the European institutions to address problems arising at the time[176]. Their contribution aimed to give substance to the concept as a trigger for the Article 7 TEU procedure as well as other mechanisms, offering criteria to identify systemic deficiencies. They argued that EU control should intervene whenever citizens have lost their subjective trust in the power of the law to fulfil legitimate expectations[177]. We can find a clear acceptance of this criterion in the CJEU's decision in the *Prokurator Generalny* case, in which we read that "*infringements of the second subparagraph of Article 19(1) TEU may arise in circumstances in which all the relevant factors (…) appear to be such as to give rise to systemic doubts in the minds of subjects of the law as to the independence and impartiality of the judges appointed at the end of that process*".[178]

On a more serious scale, where national governments are supported by majorities, Schmidt/Bogdanowicz consider that systemic deficiencies may be found when there is a spill-over effect to other Member States, that is when the deficiencies affect their decision to act (Schmidt and Bogdanowicz 2018, pp. 1082–1084)—which is, in their view, what was at stake in the *LM*[179] case*: a* "spill-over" of the deficiency (in Poland) to the Irish legal system.[180]

If this interpretation of Article 19 TEU is to be taken seriously, then it should affect not only the control exercised by the Court in infringement proceedings but also the control exercised by national courts.

7 Conclusion

Whenever there is a suspicion that a Member State's judicial system is not functioning adequately, alarms sound as to the impact of that situation on the effectiveness of EU law. But along with that practical concern, there is also the fear that the shared foundations of values on which the EU was built may be eroded in some Member States in such a way that the "European way of life" becomes impossible and the relationship of trust between Member States is undermined. Addressing these difficulties may be hard because it requires European principles to be

[175] AG Bobek's opinion of 20 May 2021, *Prokuratura Rejonowa w Mińsku Mazowieckim*, joined cases C-748/19 to C-754/19, EU:C:2021:403, para 148.

[176] Von Bogdandy and Ioannidis (2014), pp. 65–67.

[177] Von Bogdandy and Ioannidis (2014), p. 73.

[178] CJEU judgment (Grand Chamber) of 22 March 2022, *Prokurator Generalny*, C-508/19, EU:C:2022:201, para. 80.

[179] CJEU judgment (Grand Chamber) of 25 July 2018, LM, C-216/18 PPU, EU:C:2018:586.

[180] Schmidt and Bogdanowicz (2018), p. 1084.

balanced with national decisions that may be democratically supported. That is why judicial control by the CJEU should be particularly consistent, so as to remove any doubts and strengthen its authority.

In this contribution, we have attempted to identify the sources of judicial control and their limits. Our research has demonstrated that there is a preference for solutions that carry a fundamental rights concern, capable of triggering the application of the Charter, in particular Article 47 which grants the right to effective judicial protection, of which the independence of the judiciary is a corollary. The case-law on the execution of EAWs offers goods examples in this regard, showing the Court's concern regarding guarantees of a fair trial by the issuing court, although only with regard to each specific case. Conversely, Article 267 TFEU is not such a useful filter to tackle rule of law issues from referring courts, since the mere submission of a question by a referring court may indicate that court's intention to cooperate and, moreover, may provide an opportunity for the Court to address those questions, engaging in a culture of dialogue with national courts and acting as a partner to them. It has, nonetheless, been argued that this would not be the case if there was evidence that the referring court was merely setting the procedure in motion (*e.g.* to avoid being censured for not complying with the Article 267 obligation), although with no intention of deciding in accordance with the Court's decision. Apart from that, only in extreme situations, clarified by relevant national or international courts will the Court refuse a preliminary ruling from a judicial court on grounds of lack of independence of the referring judge.

Finally, we have identified Article 19 TEU and addressed the difficulties surrounding the use of that provision, namely the difficulty in defining its precise scope as a stand-alone source for judging rule of law violations in Member States. Given that it involves a significant expansion of the jurisdiction of the Court, we have favoured a restrictive approach that limits the use of infringement proceedings to systemic violations of the rule of law principle.

It is undeniable that a holistic concern for respect for the fundamental values of the European Union requires analysis of compliance with the rule of law by the European institutions themselves. Some commentators have urged the Court to undertake self-examination.[181] It seems clear, however, that there is still much to be done in this respect, beginning with the accession of the European Union to the ECHR.

References

Bonelli M, Claes M (2018) Judicial serendipity: how Portuguese judges came to the rescue of the Polish judiciary. Eur Const Law Rev 14:622–643

Broberg M, Fenger N (2021) Broberg and Fenger on preliminary references to the European Court of Justice. Oxford University Press, Oxford

[181] Kochenov (2018), pp. 300–301.

Campos MF (2018) Acórdão do tribunal de justiça de 30 de junho de 1996 – Processo 61/65 Viúva G. Vaassen-Göbbels c. Direção do Beambtenfonds voor het Mijmbedrijf. In: Pais SO (ed) Princípios fundamentais de direito da união Europeia. Almedina, Coimbra, pp 179–198
Closa C (2016) Reinforcing EU monitoring of the rule of law. In: Closa C, Kochenov D (eds) Reinforcing rule of law oversight in the European Union. Cambridge University Press, Cambridge, pp 15–35
Editorial comments: clear and present danger: Poland, the rule of law & primacy (2021) Common Mark Law Rev 58:1635–1648. https://doi.org/10.54648/COLA2021107
Hillion C (2018) Overseeing the rule of law in the EU. In: Closa C, Kochenov D (eds) Reinforcing rule of law oversight in the European Union. Cambridge University Press, Cambridge, pp 59–81
Jakab A (2016) The EU charter of fundamental rights as the most promising way of enforcing the rule of law against EU member states. In: Closa C, Kochenov D (eds) Reinforcing rule of law oversight in the European Union. Cambridge University Press, Cambridge, pp 187–205
Kochenov D (2018) The missing EU rule of law? In: Closa C, Kochenov D (eds) Reinforcing rule of law oversight in the European Union. Cambridge University Press, Cambridge, pp 290–312
Ladenburger C, Marinova Y, Tomkin J (2023) Institutional report. In: Kornezov A (ed) The XXX FIDE congress in Sofia. Congress Publications, Sofia, pp 67–154
Leloup M (2020) The appointment of judges and the right to a tribunal established by law: the ECJ tightens its grip on issues of domestic judicial organization: review Simpson. Common Mark Law Rev 57:1139–1162
María PASDS (2021) Rule of law and judicial independence in the light of CJEU and ECtHR case law. In: Izquierdo-Sans C, Martínez-Capdevila C, Nogueira-Guastavino M (eds) Fundamental rights challenges: horizontal effectiveness, rule of law and margin of national appreciation. Springer International Publishing, Cham, pp 167–187
Martufi A (2022) Effective judicial protection and the European arrest warrant: navigating between procedural autonomy and mutual trust. Common Mark Law Rev 59:1371–1406
Pech L (2021) The rule of law. In: Craig P, Búrca G (eds) The evolution of EU Law. Oxford University Press, Oxford, pp 307–338
Pech L (2022) The rule of law as a well-established and well-defined principle of EU law. Hague J Rule Law 14:107–138
Pech L, Platon S (2018) Judicial independence under threat: the Court of Justice to the rescue in the ASJP case. Common Mark Law Rev 55:1827–1854
Pescatore P (2010) Van Gend en Loos, 3 February 1963 – a view from within. In: Maduro MP, Azoulai L (eds) The past and future of EU Law: the classics of EU law revisited on the 50th anniversary of the Rome Treaty. Hart, Oxford, pp 3–8
Pirker B (2018) Mapping the scope of application of EU fundamental rights: a typology. Eur Papers 3:133–156
Prechal S, Widdershoven R (2011) Redefining the relationship between 'Rewe-effectiveness' and effective judicial protection. Rev Eur Adm Law 4:31–50
Quadros I (2020) O Tribunal de Justiça e a questão da possibilidade do controlo judicial das ameaças ao Estado de Direito – Comentário ao acórdão do TJUE de 5.11.2019, Comissão c. Polónia (C-192/18). Catól Law Rev 4:99
Roeben V (2020) Judicial protection as the meta-norm in the EU judicial architecture. Hague J Rule Law 12:29–62
Schmidt M, Bogdanowicz P (2018) The infringement procedure in the rule of law crisis: how to make effective use of Article 258 TFEU. Common Mark Law Rev 55:1061–1100
Silveira A (2014) Do âmbito de aplicação da Carta dos Direitos Fundamentais da União Europeia: recai ou não recai? — eis a questão! Julgar 22:179–209
Snell J (2015) Fundamental rights review of national measures: nothing new under the charter? Eur Public Law 21:285–308
Snell J (2018) Do fundamental rights determine the scope of EU law? Eur Law Rev 43:475–476

Spieker LD (2022) The conflict over the Polish disciplinary regime for judges – an acid test for judicial independence, Union values and the primacy of EU law: commission v. Poland. Common Mark Law Rev 59:777–812

Van Elsuwege P, Gremmelprez F (2020) Protecting the rule of law in the EU legal order: a constitutional role for the court of justice. Eur Const Law Rev 16:8–32

Von Bogdandy A, Ioannidis M (2014) Systemic deficiency in the rule of law: what it is, what has been done, what can be done. Common Mark Law Rev 51:59–96

Von Bogdandy A, Smrkolj M, Kottmann M, Antpöhler C, Dickschen J, Hentrei S (2012) Reverse solange-protecting the essence of fundamental rights against EU member states. Common Mark Law Rev 49:489–519

Von Bogdandy A, Bogdanowicz P, Canor I, Schmidt M, Taborowski M (2018) Guest editorial – a potential constitutional moment for the European rule of law – the importance of red lines. Common Mark Law Rev 55:983–995

Wahl T (2020) Refusal of European arrest warrants due to fair trial infringements - review of the CJEU's judgment in 'LM' by national courts in Europe. Eur Crim Law Assoc Forum:321–330. https://doi.org/10.30709/eucrim-2020-026

Wahl N, Prete L (2018) The gatekeepers of article 267 TFEU: on jurisdiction and admissibility of references for preliminary rulings. Common Mark Law Rev 55:511–547

Inês Quadros is Professor at Universidade Católica Portuguesa, specializing in European Union Law and Public International Law.

Current Challenges to the Rule of Law and European e-Justice as an Original Tool to Answer Effective Judicial Protection Demands

Joana Covelo de Abreu

1 The Union of Law and the Challenges It Faces from the Perspective of Effective Judicial Protection: Some Constitutional Considerations

In recent years, we have witnessed a certain urgency to reaffirm the Union of law in the judicial context of the European Union. In fact, the European Commission has reflected on the state of this Union of law and reached the conclusion that the main challenges expressed revolve around the obstacles raised, in several Member States, to one of its driving forces: that which relates, at the heart of effective judicial protection, to the independence and impartiality of the courts, and which has also gained the attention of the Court of Justice. In the light of these concerns, this reflection aims at determining whether European e-justice can act as a catalyst, specifically when viewed as a means of promoting digital articulation between the European courts as a whole, to serve the objective of effective judicial protection, given that the European Commission has been focusing its attention on devising new methods to safeguard and affirm this Union of law.

In April 2019, the European Commission recalled the fundamental nature of the rule of law as a value of the Union and a reflection of the common identity and

This contribution corresponds, in essence, to the intervention made in the Webinar "A tutela do estado de direito na União Europeia", promoted by JusGov (Research Centre for Justice and Governance—University of Minho) and APDE (Portuguese Association of European Law), on 28 May 2021.

J. C. de Abreu (✉)
University of Minho, School of Law, JusGov - Research Centre for Justice and Governance, Braga, Portugal
e-mail: jabreu@direito.uminho.pt

I. Quadros, M. Gorjão-Henriques (eds.), *Revisiting the Liberal Constitutional Features of the European Union*, https://doi.org/10.1007/978-3-031-95717-8_9

constitutional traditions, given that it forms the basis of the democratic systems of all the Member States and is indispensable in effectively guaranteeing the protection of fundamental rights (Court of Justice of the European Union e-Curia: User guide n.d.). In fact, the European Union must continue to be a place "where laws apply effectively and uniformly" and where "trust in public institutions, including in the justice system, is crucial for the smooth functioning of democratic societies" (European Commission, Communication to the European Parliament, The European Council and the Council 2019, p. 1) since "[u]nder the rule of law, all public powers always act within the constraints set out by law, in accordance with the values of democracy and fundamental rights, and under the control of independent and impartial courts" (European Commission, Communication to the European Parliament, The European Council and the Council 2019, p. 1). Therefore, effective judicial protection emerges as an indispensable instrument for the Union of law that is intended, in particular with regard to the independence and impartiality of the judiciary. At the heart of an integrated juridical and jurisdictional system lies the idea of a strengthening mutual recognition (For further developments, Mattera 2016), the fruit of long decades of a tendency to trust in other Member States' judicial systems and their reflexive interactions—through the preliminary ruling procedure—with the Court of Justice, founded on a gradual but steady increase in trust in the procedural solutions and decisions adopted in other Member States. In fact, "[i]f the rule of law is not properly protected in all Member States, the Union's foundation stone of solidarity, cohesion, and the trust necessary for mutual recognition of national decisions [...] is damaged" (European Commission, Communication to the European Parliament, The European Council and the Council 2019, p. 2).

In the Foreword to the *2019 EU Justice Scoreboard*, which is described as "a key tool of the European Union's rule of law toolbox" (European Commission 2019a), Věra Jourová noted that "challenges to the rule of law continue to mount", a feeling that remained unchanged in the *2021 EU Justice Scoreboard*, where Didier Reynders wrote "[t]he ninth edition of the EU Justice Scoreboard comes at a time of increased attention on the rule of law across the European Union" because, in "a year marked by a profound global health crisis, EU justice systems have been put to the test and the importance of effective judicial systems for the rule of law and the protection of fundamental rights has been clearly demonstrated" (European Commission 2019b). In 2019, in a context where the Union of law was facing several challenges in several Member States, the Commission considered it pertinent to engage in "an additional reflection process to further strengthen the rule of law", believing that "[w]e all should share the same objective of improving our European judiciary, as without independent and efficient justice systems, there can be no rule of law, no trust from citizens, and no business and investment-friendly environment" (European Commission 2019a, p. 2).

The term "Union of law" is used in this chapter to refer, in the European context, to the dynamics associated with the rule of law,[1] in alignment with the legal theory

[1] The option results from a direct translation of the similar expression used in the Portuguese version (the language of the proceedings) of Judgment ECJ Associação Sindical dos Juízes Portugueses

that has adopted this term as being more consistent with the reality to which it relates and in order to avoid legal and constitutional confusions: the Union of law develops as a general principle of EU law[2] from the establishment of the idea that the activity (legislative, executive and judicial) of the European Union must be subject to the law, which is its foundation, limit and teleology, because it operates through its own "autonomous" (Moreira 2014, p. 25) legal order (Judgments Costa vs. ENEL[3] and Les Verts[4]).

In this sense, the Union recognises that it is based, among others, on the rule of law, "in a society in which pluralism, non-discrimination, tolerance, justice, solidarity and equality between women and men prevail" (Article 2 of the Treaty of the European Union—TEU). Therefore, the constitutional law construction of the Union of law requires the observance, in a given political order, of a pre-existing judicial arrangement that is constantly evolving—i.e., one that, in its essence, reverts back to the idea of a State that guarantees fair treatment to its citizens (Canotilho 2010, p. 172). In the same sense, "[t]he European Union [...] is not a State (in the modern understanding), but it creates law as if it were, i.e., it creates legal rules that are binding on Member States and their citizens" (Silveira 2011, p. 28) and, also, their institutions, bodies and agencies. Moreover, in an autonomous legal order, the production of legislation will not suffice; it must also have its own institutions, and appropriate procedures for adopting and interpreting rules, as well as mechanisms for reacting in the event of any violation of the existing legal order. Therefore, "the European Union acts as a Union of law (alluding to the expression Rule of law)" (Silveira 2011, p. 28) insofar as, being the holder of public power (that the Member States have voluntarily transferred to it), this has to be limited, by being subject to the law.

In order to achieve this, the Union, through its Treaties—and implementing the objectives and values set out in Article 2 TEU—adopted (1) its own institutions that are organised according to the principle of institutional balance, (2) a system of juridical and normative acts, adopted according to a specific procedure, which have impact in the legal sphere of individuals, and (3) a procedural system, both through the adoption of *sui generis* jurisdictional mechanisms,[5] and also through the innovative recognition of a jurisdictional and organisational framework that simultaneously includes European courts in the organic sense (those based on the Treaties and the functioning, organisation and composition of which are established in the

(ASJP), 27.2.2018, case C-64/16, ECLI:EU:C:2018:117, recital 31. In the same sense (Silveira 2011, pp. 19–38).

[2] Concerning general principles of EU law in the European Union legal order (Duarte 2006, pp. 79 et seq.).

[3] Judgment ECJ Costa vs. ENEL, 15.7.1964, case 6/64, ECLI:EU:C:1964:66.

[4] Judgment ECJ Les Verts, 23.4.1986, case C-294/83, ECLI:EU:C:1986:166.

[5] The adopted expression is related to the preliminary ruling procedure (Article 267 TFEU) since it was designed to be developed jointly by the courts—national courts and the Court of Justice—so uniform application of EU law could be achieved through the *prima facie* intervention of national courts, as European functioning courts.

Union's legislative framework—European organic courts) and European courts in the functional sense (the national courts that, when called on to apply EU law, will function as "common courts" of the Union[6] or European functioning courts), practically implementing one of the dimensions of the principle of Member States' procedural autonomy. This option was mostly due to the need to promote a European local justice, so that Union citizens would be able to exercise their rights before courts (and using procedural solutions) with which they were familiar.

Concerns regarding the Union of law in the jurisdictional context have now begun to appear in the case law of the Court of Justice. This trend began with the Associação Sindical dos Juízes Portugueses (ASJP) judgment. In the main proceedings, the issue raised was whether effective judicial protection in the Union precluded the imposition, on the judges of the Portuguese Court of Auditors (Tribunal de Contas), of general salary-reduction measures established to eliminate the Portuguese State's excessive budget deficit and linked to a financial assistance programme. Although the Court of Justice considered that EU law did not preclude those circumstances—since those salary-reduction measures were applicable to "all members of the national public administration", were "temporary in nature",[7] and, in the meanwhile, were eliminated—it ultimately established the scope, meaning and reach of effective judicial protection as a general principle of EU law. The Court of Justice began by recognising effective judicial protection essential instrumentality [under Article 19 (1) (2) TEU] in the Union's common values "such as the rule of law, which are common to the Member States in a society in which, inter alia, justice prevails".[8] In fact, "Article 19 TEU, which gives concrete expression to the value of the rule of law stated in Article 2 TEU, entrusts the responsibility for ensuring judicial review in the EU legal order not only to the Court of Justice but also to national courts and tribunals",[9] which, together with that Court, exercise the jurisdictional function in the European Union, it being the responsibility of the Member States to create adequate appeals procedures to enable the pursuit of effective judicial protection, which is regarded as "a general principle of EU law stemming from the constitutional traditions common to the Member States" and from its proclamation, as a human right, in international rules on the protection of human rights.[10] Regarding the guarantee of independence of the courts, the Court of Justice highlights that this is "inherent in the task of adjudication", and is required "not only at EU level as regards the Judges of the Union and the Advocates-General of the Court of Justice, [...] but also at the level of the Member States as regards national courts",[11] presupposing "that the body concerned exercises its judicial functions wholly autonomously, without being subject

[6] On the use of a similar expression (Piçarra and Coutinho 2011, p. 158; de Mesquita 2018, p. 13).

[7] Judgment ECJ ASJP, §49 and 50.

[8] Judgment ECJ ASJP, §30.

[9] Judgment ECJ ASJP, §32.

[10] Judgment ECJ ASJP, §35.

[11] Judgment ECJ ASJP, §42.

to any hierarchical constraint or subordinated to any other body and without taking orders or instructions from any source whatsoever, and that it is thus protected against external interventions or pressure liable to impair the independent judgment of its members and to influence their decisions".[12] The Court of Justice, in this line of thought, acknowledges that effective judicial protection plays a vital role as a general principle within a Union of law.

In turn, in the LM judgment,[13] a symbiotic relationship is established between effective judicial protection as a general principle [Article 19 (1) (2) TEU] and as a fundamental right (Article 47 Charter of Fundamental Rights of the European Union—CFREU). The purpose of this preliminary ruling was to ascertain whether a rule in the European arrest warrant legal regime allows the executing judicial authority not to give effect to the arrest warrant because "there are substantial grounds to believe that the individual concerned will be exposed to a risk of breach of his right to a fair trial"[14] under Article 47 (2) CFREU.

As introductory remarks, the Court of Justice clarified that "EU law is based on the fundamental premiss that each Member State shares with all the other Member States, and recognises that they share with it, a set of common values on which the European Union is founded", which "implies and justifies the existence of mutual trust between the Member States that those values will be recognised, and therefore that the EU law that implements them will be respected",[15] observing those fundamental rights that are protected in this context. Thus, the Court of Justice explained that "when implementing EU law, the Member States may, under EU law, be required to presume that fundamental rights have been observed by other Member States";[16] by reason of the principle of mutual recognition, a body executing a European arrest warrant cannot refuse to give effect to it, as refusal must be regarded as an exception, and interpretation of its scope must be strictly limited.[17] Notwithstanding, the Court of Justice did provide clarification regarding exceptional situations—namely those associated with the right to a fair trial before an independent court. If one of those exceptional situations is observed, refusal may be possible, through approaches implementing effective judicial protection as a fundamental right. The Court stated that "judicial independence forms part of the essence of the fundamental right to a fair trial, a right which is of cardinal importance as a guarantee that all the rights which individuals derive from EU law will be protected and that the values common to the Member States set out in Article 2 TEU, in particular the value of the rule of law, will be safeguarded".[18]

Therefore, the Court of Justice concluded that where there is a real risk that the fundamental right to a fair trial before an independent court (as guaranteed in Article

[12] Judgment ECJ ASJP, §44.

[13] Judgment ECJ LM, 25.7.2018, case C-216/18 PPU, ECLI:EU:C:2018:586.

[14] Judgment ECJ LM, §24.

[15] Judgment ECJ LM, §35.

[16] Judgment ECJ LM, §37.

[17] Judgment ECJ LM, §41.

[18] Judgment ECJ LM, §48.

47, § 2 CFREU), of the person in respect of whom a warrant has been issued, will not be protected by the issuing judicial authority, this can be deemed an exceptional reason for an executing authority to refuse to give effect to the European arrest warrant.[19]

It follows then that the general principle of EU law and the fundamental right to effective judicial protection are opposite sides of the same coin. The case law of the Court of Justice, thus, took into account the "dual nature of judicial independence in the EU legal order – it seeks to take proper advantage from it in terms of systemic complementarity" (Silveira et al. 2022), anticipating the desire to enhance the fundamental right dimension of the right to an independent court departing from its guise as a general principle of EU law. Therefore, if the purpose of the arrest warrant is to simplify the system of surrender between judicial authorities in criminal proceedings, an essential condition of this is that all related authorities are independent,[20] "having regard to the standard of protection of the fundamental right that is guaranteed by the second paragraph of Article 47 of the Charter".[21]

In an infringement procedure (under Articles 258–260 of the Treaty on the Functioning of the European Union—TFEU), dated 24 June 2019,[22] the Court of Justice was called to rule on a potential infringement by Poland based on the adoption of internal legislation that could violate effective judicial protection as it is promoted under the EU law, specifically regarding the irremovability of judges and judicial independence.

In the pre-litigation phase, the European Commission issued a letter of formal notice addressed to that Member State where it mentioned that the adoption of the New Law on the Supreme Court infringed Poland's obligations under Articles 19 TEU and 47 CFREU. This was disputed by the Member State. Following this, the Commission issued a reasoned opinion in which it maintained that the said legislation was infringing Union law and invited Poland to take the necessary measures to comply with the reasoned opinion within one month of receiving it.[23] Once again, Poland replied, stating it had not breached EU law.

The facts inherent to the infringements that the European Commission claimed Poland had committed were: (1) on one hand, the New Law on the Supreme Court, in lowering the retirement age of judges only for those judges appointed before its entry into force, compromised the principle of judicial independence based on their irremovability; (2) on the other hand, Poland was violating judicial independence when it granted the President of the Republic the discretion to extend twice, each time for a 3-year term, the period of judicial activity of Supreme Court judges beyond the newly established retirement age.

---

[19] Judgment ECJ LM, §59.

[20] Judgment ECJ LM, §56.

[21] Judgment ECJ LM, §62.

[22] Judgment ECJ Commission vs. Poland, 24.6.2019, case C-619/18, ECLI:EU:C:2019:531.

[23] Judgment ECJ Commission vs. Poland, §16.

Taking the case law of ASJP and LM as a starting point, the Court of Justice clarified that the Union is based on a commitment freely and voluntarily undertaken by all Member States on joining the Union, focusing on the common values enshrined in Article 2 TEU. Accordingly, "EU law [is] based on the fundamental premiss that each Member State shares with all the other Member States, and recognises that those Member States share with it, those same values".[24] Only by accepting this has it been possible to create an environment where effective judicial integration (For further development, de Abreu 2019b) could develop, based on mutual recognition and reciprocal trust between Member States and, specifically, between their courts.[25] That said, the ECJ reaffirms the importance of effective judicial protection for a Union of law "in which individuals have the right to challenge before the courts the legality of any decision or other national measure concerning the application to them of an EU act",[26] recalling that "Article 19 TEU, which gives concrete expression to the value of the rule of law [...], entrusts the responsibility for ensuring the full application of EU law in all Member States and judicial protection of the rights of individuals under the law to national courts and tribunals and to the Court of Justice".[27] Hence, explaining the dynamics connected with the procedural autonomy of Member States (For further development, and among others, Christianos 2007–2008; Couronne 2010), namely those that determine their autonomy with regard to the organisation of their national judicial system, the Court recalls that such competence has to be exercised with respect for Member States' obligations stemming from EU law. If this were not the case, the test principles of equivalence and effectiveness—that aim to confirm whether national solutions (1) are less favourable when applicable to disputes arising from EU law in comparison with purely internal disputes; and (2) make it excessively difficult or impossible, in practice, to exercise rights derived from the European legal order—would be void of content. This means that Member States' procedural autonomy is not an absolute general principle, and national procedural solutions must be scrutinised in the light of equivalence and effectiveness. Stating the opposite would go against European integration, effectiveness and the primacy of EU law, allowing Member States to hide behind national procedural solutions to escape the obligations incumbent on them under EU law.

Beginning with the premiss that "every Member State must [...] ensure that bodies which, as 'courts or tribunals' within the meaning of EU law, come within its judicial systems in the fields covered by EU law meet the requirements of effective judicial protection",[28] the Court of Justice concluded, with regard to the guarantees of independence and impartiality, that both measures could constitute a breach of EU law, in particular the general principle of effective judicial protection stemming

[24] Judgment ECJ Commission vs. Poland, §42.

[25] Judgment ECJ Commission vs. Poland, §43.

[26] Judgment ECJ Commission vs. Poland, §46.

[27] Judgment ECJ Commission vs. Poland, §47.

[28] Judgment ECJ Commission vs. Poland, §55.

from Article 19 (1) (2) TEU, since this principle requires that the exercise of the judicial function and the actual judicial architecture of a Member State are able to "ensure that the substantive conditions and detailed procedural rules governing the adoption of such decisions are such that they cannot give rise to reasonable doubts, in the minds of individuals, as to the imperviousness of the judges concerned to external factors and as to their neutrality with respect to the interests before them".[29] This excludes, in particular, any kind of possibility of "direct influence, in the form of instructions" or "types of influence which are more indirect and which are liable to have an effect on the decisions of the judges concerned".[30]

With this judgment, the Court of Justice once again enhances the systemic complementary relationship between the general principle of EU law and the fundamental right to effective judicial protection. In fact, through its analysis of these violations, in Poland, in the light of the general principle of Article 19 (1) (2) TEU, the Court was able to promote enforcement of the related fundamental right, stemming from Article 47 CFREU, without being limited by the scope of application of the Charter, "discretely acknowledg[ing] and seek[ing] to overcome the methodical difficulties posed by Article 51 (1) CFREU within the EU system of protection of fundamental rights". Even so, "the ECJ seems to recover the "jus-fundamental" dimension of the question and decided that the second subparagraph of Article 19 (1) TEU requires Member States to provide remedies that are sufficient to ensure effective legal protection, within the meaning in particular of Article 47 CFREU, in the fields covered by EU law" (Silveira 2019).

And here lies the particular complementary and systemic relationship that primarily serves the purpose of a Union of law: through this judgment, the Court of Justice enhanced that symbiotic relationship with its ability to demonstrate how independence of the courts is a broader principle-based and fundamental right-related concept that should—and must—cover not only the actual conditions for exercising the judicial function (as derived from the ASJP and LM judgments) but also the way Member States' judicial architecture is reflected in giving effect to this dimension. Therefore, even if all the conditions are provided, within proceedings, for a judge to decide independently, if s/he is placed within that organisational and judicial layer with any influence, the exercise of her/his powers may never be effectively independent, and this may harm individuals' trust in justice and affect the mutual recognition and reciprocal trust in the administration of justice between Member States, which may lead to decades of effective judicial integration being undermined.

In the light of this, the most pressing concerns for the European Commission regarding the challenges to the Union of law are based, above all, on finding new mechanisms and revitalising existing ones in order to ensure that effective judicial protection is observed uniformly across the different Member States. On this matter, the Commission has noted that "[a]t the core of the rule of law is the necessity of all

[29] Judgment ECJ Commission vs. Poland, §111.

[30] Judgment ECJ Commission vs. Poland, §112.

public powers to be subject at all times to established values, rules and procedures", especially when "many recent cases with resonance at EU level have centred on the independence of the judicial process" (European Commission, Communication to the European Parliament, The European Council and the Council 2019, p. 9). Therefore, as "[t]he judiciary is at the heart of the rule of law", the Commission invites all those involved to find a solution that overcomes "attempts by political actors to undermine [...] independence and the binding force of [...] decisions" (European Commission, Communication to the European Parliament, The European Council and the Council 2019, p. 9),[31] in an effort to unravel new paths to strengthen effective judicial protection.

Having established that effective judicial protection is both instrumental to and indispensable for a Union of law, it is important to analyse, in these times of worrying challenges, which solutions can be found in more recent European models, such as the European e-Justice paramount.

2 European e-Justice at the Service of Effective Judicial Protection: Enhancing the Role of Electronic Tools

The European Union has predicted that economic growth within its space could be enabled through the use of new information and communication technologies, making it more attractive both to those working in these areas and to those that use these services and products and are looking for a more protected environment. In fact, "[t]he global economy is rapidly becoming digital" and "Information and Communications Technology (ICT)" has become "the foundation of all modern innovative economic systems" (European Commission et al. 2019a, p. 3). The digital strategy for Europe involved the establishment of a Digital Single Market (For further development, de Abreu 2017), the enhancement of which was based on an inclusive information society in which "citizens and businesses have the necessary skills and can benefit from interlinked and multi-lingual e-services, from e-government, e-justice, e-health, e-energy or e-transport" (European Commission et al. 2019a, p. 18).

In the Digital Single Market, European e-Justice began to appear as a secondary public interest that received particular attention as such, alongside European e-Government: it was through the e-Government Action Plan that European e-Justice began to appear in the field of digitalisation of public services (which also included judicial services). Hence, beginning with e-Government—and its aim of promoting "quality of the services" and "internal public sector efficiency" (European Commission et al. 2019b, p. 2)—the Commission began to set out the

[31] In the same sense, the Commission also refers to the witnessing of a weakening of constitutional courts, which again highlights current issues related to effective judicial protection (European Commission, Communication to the European Parliament, The European Council and the Council 2019, p. 9).

modernisation efforts that would be made, at EU level, with an impact on justice, through digitalisation. Therefore, for politicians, e-Justice was primarily related to the creation of ICT systems to promote the organisation of massive quantities of information and legal questions, that could be understood as a competitive advantage within the global economy (Kengyel and Nemessányi 2012, p. ix). In fact, e-Justice was considered within the European Union, for the first time, when the Council established the first Working Group on the matter (For further development, Storskrubb 2017, p. 276). Following this, in 2008 the Commission adopted a Communication (Commission of the European Communities et al. 2008) and, in the same year, the European Parliament, in a plenary session, approved a resolution on e-Justice (European Parliament 2008). In their initial approaches, the two institutions concluded that new technologies could make a significant contribution to the promotion and accessibility of judicial systems, especially bearing in mind the need to promote the proper functioning of the Internal Market and, considering that cross-border litigation would tend to increase exponentially, the need to adopt measures that could facilitate reflexive articulation between Member States and between their courts and the Court of Justice.

The third Council Action Plan (2019–2023) on European e-Justice (Council 2019a) is currently being implemented. With the aim of promoting the development of e-Justice, the Council also presented a Strategy (Council 2019b), in which it establishes that this model "aims at improving access to justice in a pan-European context and is developing and integrating information and communication technologies into access to legal information and the workings of judicial systems" (Council 2019b, p. §1).

The Council recalls that "[t]he development of electronic tools for e-Justice has been exponential, as they now allow for digital judicial proceedings using secure electronic channels, secure communication between judicial authorities, easier information for citizens on legal provisions and access to certain national registers" (Council 2019b, p. §5).

As previously stated, the e-Justice and e-Government paradigms have been connected since the establishment of the Digital Single Market and this synergetic relationship was also enshrined in this Strategy, insofar as "European e-Justice initiatives should strive for further consistency within the eGovernment framework, having regard to the constitutional provisions concerning the judiciary in Member States (judicial independence and separation of powers)", following what already resulted from the e-Government Action Plan (Council 2019b, p. §9).

For this purpose, e-Justice requires that, in addition to the applicable general principles of EU law (as is the case of effective judicial protection), others must be added that seek to pursue digital aims: (1) the digital-by-default principle, which means interaction between individuals and judicial authorities should be through digital platforms, both for the submission of procedural documents and other procedural interactions between the parties and the court, and also for the provision of the information required for those lawsuits (Council 2019b, p. §11 (1)); (2) the once-only principle, which seeks to avoid redundant procedures, focusing on data reuse, provided that the Union's high standard of personal data protection is met (Council

2019b, p. §11 (2)); (3) the user-focused principle that, based on a user-centric vision, envisages the adoption of platforms and applications that facilitate users' experiences (Council 2019b, p. §11 (3)); and (4) the interoperability-by-default principle which aims at promoting digital articulation of databases and operative systems and of data sharing, in a cross-border context and articulated with European institutions in order to facilitate "free movement of data and digital services in the European Union".[32] It is important to highlight that interoperability, besides being a method and a general principle of EU law, also appears, in terms of e-Justice, as an objective to be achieved by 2023.

In fact, the objectives of access to justice and better functioning of judicial systems can only be achieved "by simplifying and digitising communications, access to procedures and legal information and connection to and between national systems in a cross-border context" (Council 2019b, p. §12). Accordingly, in relation to access to information, the Council explains that this involves providing more information on citizens' rights and on EU legislation that can be mobilised to raise awareness of their importance and effects; adopting simplified procedures based on the use of interactive forms and tools that help to identify the authorities with competence to deal with a request; and providing research tools for legal practitioners. In this area, the Council highlights the European e-Justice and Eur-Lex Portals: the former because it operates as a "one-stop-shop for justice, offering access to e-services or e-solutions" (Council 2019b, p. §15); and the latter because it "should be develop[ed] to further meet the needs of citizens and allow them to easily find all relevant information on EU law" in the same way that it is already possible to access national solutions on directives' transposition (Council 2019b, p. §16). Interoperable platforms also have an important role to play here, since they enable access to compiled information, with cross-border relevance, that is important both for the economic activities of individuals and for the proper administration of justice.

On the other hand, the importance of interaction with legal practitioners is acknowledged, since they "have a dual role – both as users of the information provided by projects concerning the interconnection of registers or databases and, in some cases, as those responsible for the implementation and operation of such registers and databases" (Council 2019b, p. §18).

Regarding the development of electronic communication in the field of justice, the Council highlighted (1) the role of e-CODEX (For further development, de Abreu 2018), as a means for "dematerialisation of judicial and extrajudicial procedures [...] through the use of electronic communications' tools that are secure in cross border situations"; (2) the importance of videoconferencing developments (For further development, de Abreu 2019a); (3) the promotion of means of "secure access with specific access rights and a uniform or interoperable authentication method, based on eIDAS-compliant systems" (Council 2019b, p. §21); and (4) the enhancement of the role played by networks, such as the European Judicial Networks

[32] Although this term is not used to refer to it here, we have availed ourselves, for this matter, of the 2016–2020 European Action Plan on eGovernment and the concept adopted there (European Commission et al. 2019b, chapter 2). Vision and underlying principles, §6.

in civil and commercial matters or in criminal matters, for which "the possibilities offered by the European e-Justice system and the Portal could be further employed" (Council 2019b, p. §23).

Looking ahead, the Council outlines the need to consider the role of artificial intelligence in the field of e-Justice, and recognises its potential positive impact in terms of increasing "efficiency and trust". However, it points to the need to assess the "risks and challenges" involved with this technology, "in particular in relation to data protection and ethics" (Council 2019b, p. §31). Hence, given that e-Justice developments are able to place "litigants in a position of collaboration and change the formal adversary system into a cooperative and permanent dialogue" (Storme 2012) and that, as early as 2010, significant steps were being taken so that this evolution in e-Justice could take place ["we do not have to look for new codes of procedural law. In the cybersociety we have to draft a new code for the actors of Justice (Attorneys and Judges): a code of conduct"] (Storme 2012), the reality is that, promoting the anthropocentric perspective of law in the field of e-Justice, e-Justice—supported by information technologies, and especially artificial intelligence—will be capable of contributing significantly to overcoming the difficulties that have been arising with regard to effective judicial protection and, specifically, judicial independence. To this end, it is important to encourage greater digital literacy among all legal practitioners, so they can understand the procedures involved in the use of artificial intelligence that will contribute to the decision in a case, allowing them, using critical thinking, to determine which results might be useful for a good outcome in the case.

Furthermore, and although this is not expressly dealt with in the Action Plan or in the Strategy on e-Justice, we must also consider digital developments in proceedings before the Court of Justice of the European Union. In fact, as Eva Storskrubb has rightly indicated, "[i]n general terms, e-justice can be defined as the use of information and communication technologies (ICT) in the area of justice" (Storskrubb 2017, p. 271). In this context, there is a methodological explanation based on the fact that EU law presupposes judicial interaction between the national courts and the Court of Justice, which, together, establish a broad functional notion of EU Procedure (de Abreu 2019b, p. 497).[33] This seems to suggest that technological developments are not limited only to courts and to the judicial systems of the Member States, but also have an impact on the functioning of the Court of Justice of the European Union.

[33] The author argues that "functionally, European Union jurisdictional structure embraces not only the Court of Justice of the European Union, as the organic capsule of European courts, but also national courts, when they apply EU law, as common courts or European functioning courts". In this sense, the definition of e-Justice is sufficiently elastic to include all technological and digital developments in the field of justice, making it possible to reflect on advances in the national courts, but also in the European organic courts and, especially, how digital components are able to facilitate the interaction between national courts and the Court of Justice when preliminary references are made to the latter.

In light of this, on 11 July 2018, the General Court adopted a Decision on the lodging and service of procedural documents by means of e-Curia (General Court 2018), and on 16 October 2018, the Court of Justice did the same (Court of Justice 2018). In both of these Decisions, it was stated that "[i]n order to take account of developments in communication technology, an information technology application has been developed to allow the lodging and service of procedural documents by electronic means" (Court of Justice 2018; General Court 2018, p. §1), based "on an electronic authentication system using a combination of a user identification and a password" (Court of Justice 2018; General Court 2018, p. §2). Given the improvements on electronic protocol, the Court of Justice considered that it was essential, "notably in terms of the rapidity with which documents are exchanged, […] to widen the circle of its beneficiaries and to give the courts and tribunals of the Member States the opportunity to lodge or to receive procedural documents using this application when the Court is dealing with requests for a preliminary ruling" (Court of Justice 2018, p. §3)—i.e., it was noted that this platform could enhance judicial relations between the national courts and the Court of Justice related to preliminary references. On the other hand, and to safeguard the proper administration of justice, it sought to offer "the same opportunity […] to persons who are not agents or lawyers but who are nevertheless authorised, under national procedural rules, to represent a party before the courts or tribunals of their own State" (Court of Justice 2018, p. §4).

By reason of Articles 8 and 9 of the Decisions of the Court of Justice and of the General Court, the conditions of use of e-Curia were amended on 1 December 2018 (Court of Justice of the European Union 2018). Through this system, it is possible for the European courts, in the organic sense, to exchange with parties in the proceedings before them using a reliable and trustworthy system that promotes the general principles of e-Justice. On one hand, it promotes the digital-by-default principle since it offers an application that allows judicial interactions by electronic means. On the other hand, it promotes the interoperability-by-default principle since it is a common platform used by all parties in the proceedings that allows them to interact and upload and access judicial proceedings brought before the Court of Justice of the European Union. It is also capable of enhancing the user-focused principle since it promotes engagement between users and the system administrator, through an intuitive platform with conditions of use that are easy to understand and the adoption of a users' guide (Court of Justice of the European Union). Lastly, e-Curia supports the once-only principle since any procedural documents lodged will be deemed to be the original of that document (Article 3 of the Decision of the Court of Justice).

Therefore, although e-Curia was previously a platform where the full impact of digitalisation was not yet evident for preliminary rulings, the need for greater, faster and more effective reflexive interaction between courts led to its scope of application being widened, demonstrating that developments in e-Justice are not limited to the national courts and relations between them and with the parties and participants in cross-border actions, but are fundamental in EU Procedure and, in particular, can introduce new dynamics in the articulation between national courts and the Court of Justice, within the field of preliminary references.

3 From the Original Contribution of European e-Justice to Strengthening of the Union of Law

In its Communication on the state of the Union of law, the Commission stressed that efforts have been made to observe it as a fundamental value of the Union, giving the impression that measures have gone beyond the instruments deriving from Article 7 TEU and Articles 258–260 TFEU. In fact, there is a suggestion that it is necessary "to mount an effective common response when a problem of sufficient significance has been identified" (European Commission, Communication to the European Parliament, The European Council and the Council 2019, p. 10). More recent understandings of the scope of the Digital Single Market would seem to point to the significant role played by e-Justice as a model and, from this perspective, it may be regarded as an original path—even if not expressly stated as such—for the promotion and lateral (but constant) protection of this Union of law, given that it places all the potential of the digital world at the disposal of justice and the courts and promotes increased trust and proximity of judicial activities within the scope of application of EU law.

In this sense, "[t]he Commission has already proposed to boost funding and support for a thriving civil society, the promotion of media pluralism and networking among stakeholders in the rule of law area, as well as supporting Union-wide organisations, bodies and entities pursuing a general European interest in the field of justice and rule of law" (European Commission, Communication to the European Parliament, The European Council and the Council 2019, p. 10), namely through the adoption of a Regulation establishing the Justice Programme,[34] in which the European legislator stressed that it is crucial that core values and rights stemming from Articles 2 and 3 TEU "continue to be actively cultivated, protected, promoted, enforced and shared among the citizens and peoples and that they remain at the heart of the Union project" since "[a]t a time when European societies are confronted with extremism, radicalism and divisions, […], it is more important than ever to promote, strengthen and defend justice, rights and the Union values". The aim of this Regulation is to support the further development "of a Union area of justice based on the rule of law, the independence and impartiality of the judiciary, mutual recognition and mutual trust, access to justice and cross-border cooperation" (Recital 2).

Hence, some authors consider that there are "normative arguments [that] justify the involvement of the European Union in a reinforced monitoring of compliance of

[34] Regulation (EU) 2021/693 of the European Parliament and of the Council, of 28 April 2021, establishing the Justice programme and repealing Regulation (EU) No 1382/2013.

the Rule of Law requirement by its Member States" since, firstly, the EU acts as "a community of law [,] depends on mutual recognition and mutual trust". Secondly, "breach of the principle of the Rule of Law affects all the members of this community", which could lead to an "all affected principle". Lastly, there is a need to promote "consistency between EU's own proclaimed values and policies" (Closa 2016, pp. 15 and 16).

Bearing in mind these considerations, the path to be taken must involve the adoption of proper mechanisms to react to and prevent breaches of Union values, particularly the Union of law, but parallel paths must also be mapped out, which are not as intrusive and can produce a solution to guarantee effective judicial protection and, as such, enable greater compliance with the principle of a Union of law. The Commission itself forecast that this path would involve promoting equal treatment between Member States since the "EU's role [...] must be objective and treat all Member States alike" (European Commission, Communication to the European Parliament, The European Council and the Council 2019, p. 7). Digital solutions that are being adopted under the Digital Single Market can be reproduced, in the same terms, in all Member States, thereby achieving that aimed equality.

Furthermore, in the chapter on "Enforcement at Union level when national mechanisms falter", the Commission clarified that "[w]hen national rule of law safeguards do not seem capable of addressing threats to the rule of law in a Member State, it is a common responsibility of the EU institutions and the Member States to take action to remedy the situation" since "there is a common interest in tackling issues such as threats to Constitutional Courts or judicial independence before they can compromise the implementation of EU law, policies or funding" (European Commission, Communication to the European Parliament, The European Council and the Council 2019, p. 15). However, on this topic, the Commission also explains that "[d]ifferent approaches may also be appropriate in specific policy areas" (European Commission, Communication to the European Parliament, The European Council and the Council 2019, p. 15), attaching to this a question for further reflection: "Are there other areas [...] where the EU should develop specific mechanisms (including rule of law-related conditionalities) to avoid or remedy specific risks to the implementation of EU law or policies?" (European Commission, Communication to the European Parliament, The European Council and the Council 2019, pp. 15 e 16). In light of this challenge, it would seem useful to consider the role European e-Justice might play as a catalyst, particularly when it is regarded as a means of digital articulation between the European courts, as a whole, and a mechanism at the service of effective judicial protection.

In fact, the Structural Reform Support Service of the European Commission, acknowledging that "[e]ffective judicial systems play a crucial role in upholding the rule of law and the Union's fundamental values" (European Commission, p. 22), deemed it appropriate to promote wider "efficiency", "quality" and "independence of the judicial system" (European Commission, p. 17), supporting, with regard to the digitalisation of public services, the "[d]esign and implementation of an e-Government system" and the "[d]evelopment of an IT strategy and action plan" (European Commission, p. 17).

In this wider sense of e-Justice, the Council also established that electronic tools play a significant role in the proper administration of justice, "as they allow for digital judicial proceedings using secure electronic channels, secure communication between judicial authorities, easier information for citizens on legal provisions and access to certain national registers under the responsibility of Member States" (Council 2019b, p. §5). These considerations serve to reinforce the conviction that e-Justice improvements are not only those that enable articulation between national courts in cross-border disputes, but also those applicable when they address the Court of Justice and, also, those that can be seen in cases brought before European courts in the organic sense. In fact, the underlying argument cannot exclude digital advances occurring in any context or before any judicial order.

In light of the above, it would seem appropriate to suggest three complementary strategies, in order for European e-Justice to be the original solution to overcome certain issues facing effective judicial protection and, therefore, a solution for observance of the principle of a Union of law. These will be outlined below:

1. Enhancement of a technical, semantic and organisational interoperability to stabilise mutual recognition, since this would put the courts of several Member States in a position to review their action based on the actions of other Member States, leading to a scale effect among peers;
2. Express recognition that electronic and digital developments linked to proceedings before the European courts (in the organic sense) are also included within the scope of European e-Justice;
3. Commitment to promoting the proper literacy of legal practitioners and college students (active literacy) and individuals (passive literacy) in order to demonstrate the positive effects of this paradigm in reaffirming a Union of law.

Concerning the first strategy, it is necessary for all dimensions of interoperability to take place. As has been demonstrated in the legal theory, almost all definitions distinguish between three types or dimensions of interoperability: (1) technical interoperability that requires the existence of characteristics and technological elements that connect information systems; (2) semantic interoperability that assures the precise meaning of the exchanged information is understood and preserved along the exchanges between organisations, aiming at facilitating "communication between systems by aligning terms used" (Council 2019a, p. §19); and (3) organisational interoperability that relates to achieving mutually settled objectives through the adoption of common rules in the organisation (Gascó-Hernández 2017, p. 160). If these dimensions are implemented, there is a significant increase in mutual recognition and reciprocal trust between Member States. On one hand, these developments will enable national courts acting in a cross-border context to understand whether or not the equivalent entity of another Member State is observing the same requirements in terms of effective judicial protection, making it easier to adopt measures to prevent deviation away from Union values and eventually promoting more uniform application of EU law. On the other hand, semantic interoperability, in particular, can help to reinforce individuals' trust in justice, since, even though they may not be familiar with the judicial system of another Member State, they will be able to discover which entity will have jurisdiction and which powers it will have to solve the specific dispute they are involved in. Lastly, these different types of interoperability will also allow persons, particularly lawyers, to resort to EU law with greater confidence, in the disputes they are part of, since they will be more comfortable with the established interoperable solutions, and this will increase their level of trust as the way the proceedings will run will be more intuitive, the procedural timescales will be more predictable, and they will also know who they must address their written observations to or which judicial fee is applicable.

In terms of the second strategy, it is important to note that the Council's institutional positions (its Action Plan and Strategy) on e-Justice do not expressly mention the implementation of digital solutions in the Court of Justice of the European Union; however, it seems undeniable that the e-Curia developments are part of a larger plan for the digitalisation of justice *lato sensu*, which will also include proceedings brought before the European organic courts. In fact, those amendments were introduced almost at the same time as the Council's e-Justice Action Plan was adopted, so that, systematically, it makes sense for those developments to also be explained in the light of the e-Justice paradigm. Furthermore, in a context that promotes, first hand, the application of EU law by national courts, importance should be given to the fact that digital means may be used in the proceedings of preliminary references. This demonstrates the effective pursuit of the objectives established for e-Justice, which propose improved access to justice in a pan-European context: the choice of the term "pan-European" also seems to suggest that digital advances extend beyond cross-border disputes. The preliminary ruling procedure is, in fact, the one with the capacity to be the most "pan-European"—since it requires interaction between national courts and the Court of Justice in order to establish binding jurisprudence. Therefore, the literal argument is essential, starting with a wider notion of EU Procedure in functional terms (that studies the judicial architecture of the Court of Justice of the European Union and the role of national courts),[35] in order to demonstrate that only the European e-Justice appears to explain the instrumentalisation of digital solutions in the field of justice, both before the European functional courts and before the European organic courts.

Lastly, literacy presupposes a preliminary path and an ultimate impact. Significant changes to the administration of justice brought about by technological tools require legal practitioners to be digitally informed and aware. This means that digital literacy must be geared to those practitioners, in the first place, in order for the principle of under user control to be observed. The legal practitioner must be able to see the intended legal solutions and be able to master the technological operations available to achieve them, without becoming a hostage of technology. Although referring to

[35] de Mesquita, using a different term, considers that "European Union Procedure, in a material sense, can be understood as the study of the application of EU law by the Court of Justice of the European Union – and, therefore, the courts that integrate that Union's institution – and by national courts, as common courts of Union law and, still, by other courts that can be called to make that application – to give resolution to litigations that involve the application of European Union law" (de Mesquita 2018, pp. 13 and 14).

the use of artificial intelligence in the field of justice, the Council of Europe's European Commission for the Efficiency of Justice (CEPEJ) identified the need for users to be "informed actors and in control of their choices", stressing the importance of their increasing autonomy, especially in the case of professionals in the justice system (Council of Europe – European Commission for the Efficiency of Justice (CEPEJ) 2018, p. 12). Employing these dynamics is only possible if a training framework is used that is designed and applied at source, with *curricula* being updated to include these new realities.

Hence, there is a need to revisit the purpose of digital literacy, established in the Digital Single Market Strategy. In fact, at that time, the Commission, referring to "[d]igital skills and expertise", established that "[t]he EU has seen improvements in the basic digital skills of its citizens [...], but still has a long way to go", and considered that "[d]igital skill levels need [...] to be raised among employees in all economic sectors and among job seekers to improve their employability" (European Commission et al. 2019a, p. 18). This has also been also acknowledged in the 2030 Digital Compass: the European way for the Digital Decade (European Commission et al. 2021) and in the Digital Economy and Society Index (DESI) 2021, concerning Human Capital (European Commission). To achieve this, "[c]hange is needed in the way education and training systems adapt to digital revolution", and Member States are entrusted with the responsibility of producing *curricula* that "need urgently to address the lack of essential digital skills" (European Commission et al. 2019a, p. 18). Regarding European e-Justice, it is up to academia to increase awareness among students and legal practitioners, with training activities focused on this, of the new challenges this model might raise, not only as a public interest, but also as a tool of legal work and of an original empirical increment to the Union of law. Adopting this approach, active literacy would be encouraged so that legal practitioners would be able to perform their roles in a more effective way, guaranteeing effective judicial protection of individuals' rights.

Passive literacy—of individuals, especially those that come into contact with courts—is essential in order for citizens to regain trust in justice systems, when they understand the developments that are brought about by digitalisation. In fact, if the belief is created that the courts' application of EU law, using digital tools, is faster and better able to deliver material justice, citizens recover their "trust in public institutions, including in the judicial system" (European Commission, Communication to the European Parliament, The European Council and the Council 2019, p. 1). Indeed, if a paramount is presented that increases individuals' trust in justice, in Member States' judicial systems and in the Court of Justice's judicial apparatus, the problems that the Union of law is purported to be suffering will necessarily occupy a more modest position.

Lastly, only a broad understanding of European e-Justice is consistent with the developments in interpretation arising from the Court of Justice case law on effective judicial protection: with these judgments, the Court of Justice established that the fundamental right-related achievement of effective judicial protection is through the construction of principles, and is not limited by the literal terms of Article 51 CFREU. Since the Court of Justice has given a broader scope to effective judicial protection, it cannot be limited with regard to European e-Justice, if read in a strict sense.

This is the only way that the Union of law, particularly the part that requires effective judicial protection to be observed and enhanced, can be strengthened by a model which, in an original approach, contributes to it.

References

Canotilho JJG (2010) Estado de direito e internormatividade. In: Silveira A (ed) Direito da União Europeia e transnacionalidade. Quid Juris, Lisboa, pp 171–185

Christianos V (2007–2008) Le mécanisme de l'harmonization procédurale dans l'Union Européenne. Revue des affaires Européennes, Année 16(3):589–600

Closa C (2016) Reinforcing EU monitoring of the rule of law: normative arguments, institutional proposals and the procedural limitations. In: Closa C, Kochenov D (eds) Reinforcing rule of law oversight in the European Union. Cambridge University Press, Cambridge, pp 15–35

Commission of the European Communities, Communication to the Council, The European Parliament, The European Economic and Social Committee (2008) Towards a European e-Justice strategy, COM(2008) 329 final. European Commission, Brussels

Council (2019a) 2019-2023 action plan European e-Justice, 13.3.2019, 2019/C 96/05

Council (2019b) 2019-2023 strategy on e-Justice, 13.3.2019, 2019/C 96/04

Council of Europe – European Commission for the Efficiency of Justice (CEPEJ) (2018) European Ethical Charter on the use of artificial intelligence in judicial systems and their environment. CEPEJ, Strasbourg

Couronne V (2010) L'autonomie procédurale des États Membres del'Union Européenne à l'épreuve du temps. Cahiers de droit européen, No 3/4, XLVI (46), pp 273–309

Court of Justice (2018) Decision on the lodging and service of procedural documents by means of e-Curia

Court of Justice of the European Union (2018) Conditions of use of e-Curia. European Union, Brussels

Court of Justice of the European Union e-Curia: User guide (n.d.) https://curia.europa.eu/jcms/upload/docs/application/pdf/2018-11/e-curia_guide_en.pdf. Accessed 29 Sept 2024

de Abreu JC (2017) Digital single market under EU political and constitutional calling: European electronic agenda's impact on interoperability solutions. UNIO EU Law J 3:130–150

de Abreu JC (2018) Judicial interoperability in the e-Justice paradigm: perceiving e-Codex as the proper answer? A synchronic melody for a judicial integration. Port Law Rev 2:31–48

de Abreu JC (2019a) A justiça eletrónica europeia e a modernização do espaço de liberdade, segurança e justiça: a videoconferência no Regulamento n.° 1206/2001 ao serviço de uma integração judiciária. In: Carvalho MM-G, Messa AF, Nohara IP (eds) Democracia económica e responsabilidade social nas sociedades tecnológicas. Escola de Direito da Universidade do Minho, pp 93–116

de Abreu JC (2019b) Tribunais nacionais e tutela jurisdicional efetiva. Da cooperação à integração judiciária no Contencioso da União Europeia. Almedina, Coimbra

de Mesquita MJR (2018) Introdução ao contencioso da União Europeia. Lições, 3rd edn. Almedina, Coimbra

Duarte ML (2006) União Europeia e direitos fundamentais – no espaço da internormatividade. AAFDL, Lisboa

European Commission (2019a) The 2019 EU justice scoreboard – communication to the European Parliament, the Council, the European Central Bank, the Economic and Social Committee and the Committee of the Regions, COM(2019) 198/2. European Commission, Luxembourg

European Commission (2019b) The 2021 EU justice scoreboard – communication to the European Parliament, the Council, the European Central Bank, the European Economic and Social Committee and the Committee of the Regions, COM(2021) 389. European Commission, Luxembourg

European Commission, Communication to the European Parliament, The Council, The European Economic and Social Committee, The Committee of the Regions (2019a) A digital single market strategy for Europe, COM(2015) 192 final. European Commission, Brussels

European Commission, Communication to the European Parliament, The Council, The European Economic and Social Committee, The Committee of the Regions (2019b) EU eGovernment Action Plan 2016-2020. Accelerating the digital trans-formation of government, COM(2016) 179 final. European Commission, Brussels

European Commission, Communication to the European Parliament, The Council, The European Economic and Social Committee, The Committee of the Regions (2021) 2030 Digital compass: the European way for the digital decade, COM(2021) 118 final. European Commission, Brussels

European Commission, Communication to the European Parliament, The European Council and the Council (2019) Further strengthening the rule of law within the Union. State of play and possible next steps, COM(2019) 163 final. European Commission, Brussels

European Commission Digital Economy and Society Index (DESI) 2021 – Human capital. European Commission, Brussels

European Parliament (2008) Resolution with recommendations to the commission on e-Justice, 2008/2125(INI). European Parliament

Gascó-Hernández M (2017) Chapter 8: digitalizing police requirements: open-ing up justice through collaborative initiatives. In: Jiménez-Gómez CE, Gascó-Hernández M (eds) Achieving open justice through citizen participation and transparency. IGI Global, Hershey, pp 157–172

General Court (2018) Decision on the lodging and service of procedural documents by means of e-Curia

Kengyel M, Nemessányi Z (2012) Electronic technology and civil procedure: new paths to justice from around the world. Springer, Netherlands

Mattera A (2016) La reconnaissance mutuelle: une valeur historique ancienne, um principe juridique intégrationniste, l'assise politique d'um modele de société humaniste. Revue du droit d l'Union Europeénne 3:457–490

Moreira V (2014) "Respublica" Europeia: estudos de direito constitucional da União Europeia. Coimbra Editora, Coimbra

Piçarra N, Coutinho FP (2011) The "Europeanization" of the Portuguese courts. In: Rev de Direito Público, Instituto de Direito Público, Year II, January/June 2011, No 5. Almedina, pp 157–181

Silveira A (2011) Princípios de Direito da União Europeia. Doutrina e Jurisprudência, 2nd edn. Quid Juris, Lisboa

Silveira A (2019) Building the ECJ puzzle on judicial independence in a Union based on the rule of law (Commission vs. Poland in the light of ASJP). In: Silveira A (ed) The official blog of UNIO – EU Law Journal "Thinking & Debating Europe", Reviews Building the ECJ puzzle on judicial independence in a Union based on the rule of law (Commission v Poland in the light of ASJP) – Official Blog of UNIO. Accessed 29 Sept 2024

Silveira A, de Abreu JC, Perez S, Froufe P (2022) Judicial independence as a general principle and a fundamental right – Yin and Yang in the ECJ's jurisprudence concerning a union based on the rule of law. In: de Castro PC (ed) 60 years after the Treaties of Rome: what is the future for the European Union? University of Macau, Macau

Storme M (2012) Intervention of honorary president Marcel Storme at the colloquium on e-justice in Pécs (September 2010). In: Kengyel M, Nemessányi Z (eds) Electronic technology and civil procedure new paths to justice from around the world. Springer, p xv

Storskrubb E (2017) E-justice, innovation and the EU. In: Hess B, Kramer XE (eds) From common rules to best practices in European civil procedure. Hart, Nomos, Max Planck Institute of Luxembourg for Procedural Law, pp 271–302

Joana Covelo de Abreu School of Law of the University of Minho, Portugal. Scientific coordinator of the Jean Monnet Module eUjust "EU Procedure and credits' claims: approaching electronic solutions under e-Justice paradigm" (611662-EPP-1-2019-1-PTEPPJMO-MODULE). Member of the Directive Committee of JusGov (Research Centre for Justice and Governance) and integrated researcher of the Centre.

Contemporary EU Policies: Updating Public Interest

Regional Blocs and World Challenges. The Role of the European Union

Manuel Lopes Porto

When we consider the purposes and achievements of the World Trade Organization (WTO) and other global organisations, a question naturally arises concerning what can or should be expected of movements of regional integration.

This is because experience and theory clearly demonstrate that much better results are achieved with international trade and openness of economies.[1] Most of the justifications of regional blocs point out, following the same arguments, that

[1] As concluded by major research by prestigious economists and institutions, over a number of decades, including the OECD (with a summary in Little et al. 1970), the National Bureau of Economic Research, NBER (summary in Bhagwati 1978; Krueger 1978), or the World Bank (summary in Papageorgiou et al. 1990), with the research on the Portuguese experience by Macedo, Corado and Porto). Impressive results are presented by Maddison (2001; mentioned in Porto 2017, p. 31), comparing the period between the two world wars, with closed economies, with the periods before and after that time, with open economies. It is clear that the impressive growth of China and India in more recent decades is largely due to the opening of their economies (externally and internally).

It is worth stressing that the benefits of openness are not only or mainly for richer countries and people. According to a study of 27 European and 13 other countries, the real income loss from closing off trade would be 63 per cent for the poorest households and 28 per cent for the richest ones, because the poor spend a larger portion of their income on consumption (Fajgelbaum and Khandelwal 2015; European Commission 2017b, p. 14).

It is important to quote these and previous figures nowadays, given that protectionist measures were taken by President Trump and would have been tried by Marine le Pen if she had been elected President of France (probably without success, as France is a member of the EU, a customs union).

M. L. Porto (✉)
Univ Coimbra, Faculty of Law, Coimbra, Portugal

Lusíada University, CEJEIA - Center for Legal, Economic, International and Environmental Studies, Lisbon, Portugal
e-mail: mporto@fd.uc.pt

I. Quadros, M. Gorjão-Henriques (eds.), *Revisiting the Liberal Constitutional Features of the European Union*, https://doi.org/10.1007/978-3-031-95717-8_10

rather than having regional integration, it is better to have broader free trade and greater competition, so as to increase the opportunities available.

Creating regional blocs may, however, provide the possibility of introducing initiatives and policies for improvement which would not otherwise occur. In fact, in some cases it may be the only mean of doing so. Moreover, the resulting benefits may extend to other countries outside the region itself.

The European Union (EU) is a case in point, with policies that are advantageous to EU countries, but which also benefit countries in other areas of the world.

It is also possible to demonstrate that such blocs are more likely to attain better results when they follow strategies based on a spirit of openness, rather than protectionist policies. The EU is generally a good example, once again (with the exception of the Common Agricultural Policy, in the early decades), and recent documents suggest that this strategy will continue to be followed in the future.

Indeed, this strategy ought to be followed in all continents, *e.g.* within the framework of the World Trade Organization, with broad responsibilities for all regional blocs, in all continents.

1 GATT (1947) on the Creation of Regional Blocs

According to Article XXIV of GATT (the General Agreement on Tariffs and Trade), member countries can and should create free-trade areas or customs unions in their geographical regions.

The article states that "the contracting parties recognize the desirability of increasing freedom of trade by the development, through voluntary agreements, of closer integration between the economies of the countries parties to such agreements. They also recognize that the purpose of a customs union or of a free-trade area should be to facilitate trade between the constituent territories and not to raise barriers to trade of other contracting parties with such territories".

Hence, the provisions of GATT, rather than preventing the formation of customs unions or free-trade areas between the territories of some of the contracting parties, actually encourage this, and of course the adoption of interim agreements necessary for the formation of such unions or areas.

Article XXIV was and continues to be necessary, however, to avoid the application of the 'most-favoured-nation' clause, contained in Article I of GATT, according to which "any advantage, favour, privilege or immunity granted by any contracting party to any product originating in or destined for any other country shall be accorded immediately and unconditionally to the like product originating in or destined for the territories of all other contracting parties".

Were it not for Article XXIV, since for some years after the Agreement had been signed there were no restrictions at all (i.e. no duties or quantitative restrictions) between some GATT members (e.g. the founding members of the EEC and the founding members of the EFTA), it would be necessary to eliminate all tariffs or restrictions between all GATT countries(nowadays, WTO countries).

Another interesting point to note is that the politicians who were responsible for the Agreement did, in fact, recognise that it would make sense for certain member countries covered by it to have greater openness and proximity, without tariffs or other kinds of trade restrictions between them.

2 Arguments Justifying the Creation of Regional Blocs, Even Though 'Second Best' Arguments

We should note that most of the arguments presented to justify the creation of regional blocs (*e.g.* customs unions or free-trade areas) state that regional integration is better for countries than their remaining isolated, without opening their economies. However, the same arguments show that nothing is lost and more advantages are obtained if this openness is at the global level.

This is highlighted by the static theory of customs unions,[2] which demonstrates that while regional blocs produce positive effects, including trade creation effects, they also have negative consequences, with trade deviation effects. The formation of a customs union is justified if the trade creation effects are greater than the trade deviation effects. Yet, with world free trade there are no trade deviation effects, only trade creation effects. We therefore have a 'first best' policy, which is clearly advantageous, as it is possible to import with the lowest global price.

Another reason that is pointed out for establishing regional blocs is the possibility of gaining international trade benefits, taking advantage of different specialisations. Theories of international trade explain the phenomenon of different countries specialising in different goods, with larger amounts of goods being produced with the same characteristics, or similar amounts with fewer production factors. However, global free trade increases this possibility even further, with more opportunities for specialisation.

A further argument put forward is that regional blocs will benefit certain types of production that require or will gain advantages from increasing their size. i.e. productions requiring large economies of scale (see Corden 1972). However, with global free trade, the whole world becomes our market, rather than only the market of the countries belonging to the regional bloc; hence, the scale is greater and there is a greater possibility of reducing costs.

If we take dynamic circumstances into account, there are two arguments in favour of the creation of regional blocs.

The first is that regional blocs may bring an end to national monopolies. What was once a monopoly must now compete, across borders, with firms of other member countries, which may also have previously been national monopolies. Such

[2]Going back to Viner (1950), considering the effects on production, and to Meade (1956, 1968), Gehrels (1956/7) and Lipsey (1957, 1960, 1970), considering also the effects on consumption (see for example Calvete 1999–2001, pp. 229–374; Porto 2017, pp. 198–208).

competition naturally entails lower prices (for consumers). Yet, there is also the possibility that, within a single regional bloc, free-trade area or customs union, there will also be a monopoly, with only one firm serving the whole area. The way to avoid this situation is to have more extensive free trade, involving the need to compete with firms from other areas of the world.

Even in situations where there is no market monopoly, it can be argued that competition within a regional bloc leads all companies, including small and medium-sized enterprises, to be more efficient, ultimately benefiting consumers and other stakeholders. The so-called 'cold shower effect',[3] involving a requirement of greater efficiency in production, was highlighted in the run-up to the 1975 referendum in the UK in discussions surrounding the benefits of joining the EEC. When countries open up to other areas of the world, this need to maximise efficiency is even greater, as companies are required to compete not only with firms in their regional bloc, but also with those from all other areas, in all continents.

From a dynamic point of view, it is also worth noting the effects that a trade bloc can have on rising incomes, both in the initial period after their creation and subsequently, as a consequence of the multiplier effects of external trade. Once again, however, these effects are more pronounced on a worldwide scale than in relation to a regional bloc.

The creation of a trade bloc may also be an attractive means of achieving the required dimension to promote terms of trade (following a 'strategic trade policy'), which a small or even a large country may not be able to achieve on its own. However, experience has clearly demonstrated the general harm that can be caused by a deterioration in the terms of trade of other countries, potentially leading to retaliations and trade wars, or at the very least to negative income multiplier effects, which ultimately harm all the countries concerned.

Considering the limitations of all these arguments, one might question the rationale behind forming regional blocs (of course including the costs and difficulties in their activity). The preferred route would seem to be to move to global free trade as quickly as possible, within the framework of the World Trade Organization, which currently already has 166 member countries.

3 Reasons Justifying the Creation of Regional Blocs

The underlying reason behind the creation of regional blocs may be more than simply economic. This was clearly the case of the European Communities, the creation of which was initially regarded as a mean of preventing conditions that might open the way to a third world war.[4]

[3] The argument was heavily emphasised at the time, with this term being coined by the former British Prime Minister Harold Macmillan (see Porto 2020a).

[4] In the words of Moreira (s.d.), "both wars, of 1914–1918 and of 1939–1945, were classified as world wars, although people usually forget to add that they were world wars in their effects, but exclusively European in their causes".

Yet, from their inception the European Communities also had an economic purpose, which was achieved with steps that also had a great impact in other areas of the world.

Examples of this are certain policies contained in the Treaty of Rome of 1957 (and, even before that, in 1950 with the European Coal and Steel Community). The competition policy and transport policy are cases in point.[5]

These are both good examples of policies which, despite having the main purpose of benefiting European entrepreneurs and citizens in general, also benefited people, and especially entrepreneurs, in other areas of the world.

In this text we are, however, more concerned with more recent initiatives and policies, all of them with global implications.

3.1 Necessary Conditions for the Initiation and Success of Large-Scale Projects

The movement towards European integration has been enhanced by the development of the principle of subsidiarity. According to this principle, "in areas which do not fall within its exclusive competence, the Union shall act only if and in so far as the objectives of the proposed action cannot be sufficiently achieved by the Member States, either at central level or at regional and local level, but can rather, by reason of the scale or effects of the proposed action, be better achieved at Union level" (Article 5 of The Treaty of EU; cf. Quadros 2012/20).

In fact, there are cases where one country alone, regardless of how large it may be, cannot be expected to assume the risk of an initiative, due to the costs involved and uncertainty as to whether the benefits resulting from the initiative will be exclusively or mainly for that country, thereby justifying the costs.

A good example of this is the Airbus project.[6] This was not a 'Community project', i.e. one initiating within the Union, but rather a joint initiative of a group of companies from five (later four) countries, which probably would not have taken place if the firms and countries of this 'consortium' had not 'felt' that they were members of the European Union and had not had the financial support of the Union budget (approval of which, incidentally, the author of this article took part in, as a member of the European Parliament at the time).

---

[5] The Agricultural Policy was also in the original text of the Treaty of Rome. However, since it was a protectionist policy, Community consumers and entrepreneurs using agricultural products as raw materials were also penalised with higher prices, in addition to the agricultural producers of countries of other areas of the world (thereby making it difficult or even impossible to enter into agreements with these countries that could have been advantageous for the European economy).

[6] Justifying the attention it has received in the economic literature (among others Pomfret 1991; Golich 1992; Hill and Hult 2019, pp. 193, 335; Parkin 2019, pp. 381, 393, 697; Guillochon et al. 2020, p. 152).

For two or three decades the countries of Europe did not compete in the production of large commercial aircraft. The global market was completely dominated at the time by three US companies, Boeing, McDonnell Douglas and Lockhead.

Recognising that Europe would, however, have a comparative advantage in the production of this kind of airplanes, a consortium was formed with firms from four important countries in Europe: the United Kingdom, France, Germany and Spain.

Intervention at 'regional bloc' level was justified in this case owing to the cost of the investment and of its externalities. These two reasons meant that one individual country, or one firm of a single country, could not be expected to take the initiative, as this would entail a huge budget burden and the risk that others would benefit equally from the investment (*e.g.* with the research carried out) without bearing any of the original cost or risk.

It is worth noting here that the success of the Airbus project is benefiting not only Europe, but the whole world, including the United States. Currently, the only two companies producing large commercial aircraft are Airbus and Boeing (some years ago Lockhead restricted its activity to the production of military aircraft and McDonnell Douglas merged with Boeing). Consequently, if Airbus was not producing this kind of airplanes, United States carriers would have no option but to buy Boeings for their service (obviously at higher prices, as Boeing would have a global monopoly).

A recent success case is the European response to the COVID crisis. As was well recognised by the Commission (European Commission 2021a), "drawing on the pool of excellence in life sciences, [European industry] has been at the forefront of global COVID 19 vaccine development and production, notably thanks to the EU Vaccine Strategy and the EU support to ramp up industry capacity" (demonstrating "the resilience of our Single Market").

This was clearly a benefit for the whole world, with the production of good quality European vaccines.

3.2 Structural Policies, as is the Case of Regional Policy

Regional policy was not considered in the original text of the Treaty of Rome and did not, therefore, begin in 1957. Part of the reason for this is that the six founding members of the EEC were rich countries, generally speaking, and there was no great disparity between the different regions within them (Mezzogiorno, in Italy, being an exception, to some extent). Moreover, at that time the political leaders were unaware of both the scale and drawbacks of regional imbalance and the overall benefits of regional promotion.

As more countries joined the Communities, many of them not so rich and with greater regional disparities, and as knowledge grew, from the 1960s onwards, of the benefits of regional promotion, important steps began to be taken to promote an active regional policy.[7]

---

[7] Leading at that time to the beginning of a new area of economics research and teaching, with 'regional economics'.

These first steps included the creation within the European Commission of a Directorate-General concerned with regional development (DG XVI, now known as Regio) and the subsequent creation of a regional fund (ERDF), in 1975. These changes were not merely institutional, over the years the ERDF has benefited from an impressive increase in its share of the EU budget, nowadays accounting for approximately 40 per cent of the total (see, for example, Porto 2019, 2020b, 2021).

Hence, there are now resources to promote less developed regions which the Member States might not have had if they had not joined the Union.

For the regions concerned, this represents a very important effect of being a member of a regional bloc. It is important to note, however, that the benefits of this can also be seen in richer areas. Firstly, migration flows, often characterised by poor integration of migrants and increased social problems, are generally lower. Secondly, as previously less developed areas become more prosperous, people and companies within them have more disposable income to spend on imports from other regions (Germany is a prime example of a richer country that has benefited in this way).

3.3 *The Single Market, with the Removal of Physical and Technical Barriers*

In the last decades of the twentieth century two particularly important developments occurred which were only possible due to the existence of a regional bloc, with its own institutions.

One of these developments was the creation of the single market, following the passing of the Single European Act.

This was a necessary response to the so-called 'Eurosclerosis' and 'Europessimism' that the European Community was suffering in the seventies.

Eurosclerosis, resulting from the need for unanimity in the Council to pass acts such as regulations or directives, was overcome with the Single European Act, as most acts no longer required unanimity, only a majority vote in favour.[8]

Efforts to counteract Europessimism about the European situation, and the future of the European community, involved removing physical, technical and fiscal barriers in order to achieve the purpose of the single market.

This initiative took place following the Cockfield Report, which proposed 286 decrees to remove these obstacles (resulting in 267 decrees being approved).

Another report, produced by a commission chaired by Checchini (1988), evaluated the 'cost of non-Europe', i.e. the cost of not having this market. And more recent data shows that 'single market' integration, opening market opportunities and increasing the mobility of production factors, besides producing other benefits, led to higher income in both 'old' Member States (+3.4%) and 'new' ones (+7.5%) (see, with other references, Porto and Guincho 2012/20; Felbermayr et al. 2018).

---

[8] With some exceptions, for example in the taxation area, thus explaining why less progress has been made in tax harmonisation.

It should, however, be stressed that the creation of this single market, the direct purpose of which was to benefit the countries, citizens and companies of the EU, also benefited countries, citizens and companies right across the globe.

The free flow of people and vehicles (including freight) across borders where it had previously been necessary to undergo border checks presented advantages to citizens and companies from all areas of the globe.

In addition, harmonisation of technical standards across the EU had an even greater economic impact, with benefits for EU companies and for companies in all other areas of the world. Once these standards were approved all companies could gain access to buyers from any of the EU countries, which amounted to a market of about 450 million citizens.

Of course, these benefits could only be achieved because Europe had become a heavily institutionalised regional bloc. It is very difficult to imagine the countries entering into bilateral or multilateral agreements on an individual basis, in order to remove physical barriers and establish common positions concerning safety in that common area, or to remove technical barriers, given the many difficult aspects that would need to be taken into account. In other words, it is hard to imagine the countries individually taking the steps taken by the Commission, the European Parliament and the Council to produce the same rules across the entire EU area.

3.4 The Euro, Adopted by a Significant Number of Countries

Another achievement which of course could take place only in an institutionalised regional bloc was the creation of a single currency, the euro. The process was set in motion in 1992, with the Treaty of Maastricht, with the currency originally being adopted by 12 Member States, this number subsequently increasing up to 20.

The main rationale behind the introduction of the euro was the benefits it would bring to the participating countries, including savings in microeconomic costs (transaction costs, uncertainty costs and information and calculation costs), and macroeconomic gains, with lower prices and fewer oscillations (although it would entail the loss of one means of intervening in the economy, albeit not the best means). A further advantage would be less need for reserves available for emission by the national central banks.

Besides these advantages, which are mainly felt at national level, the euro avoids the situation of there being only one important currency in the world: the US dollar (in earlier times, the British pound).

Nowadays the euro is clearly the second most important currency in the world, after the US dollar, and well ahead of the Japanese yen. 29.4 per cent of world global payments are made in euro (compared to 43.0 per cent in dollars and 3.1 per cent in yen). Moreover, the euro accounts for 19.9 per cent of foreign exchange reserves (64.1 per cent in dollars and 4.1 percent in yen) and 21.9 per cent of international loans (57.7 per cent in dollars and 3.9 percent in yen).

The existence of other important currencies in the world (soon to be joined by the Chinese yuan) is also good for the United States, as it forces the country to have a sensible monetary policy, so as to be able to compete with other currencies.

In addition, the microeconomic benefits noted above (i.e. the avoidance of transaction, uncertainty, and information and calculation costs) are also benefits for firms from all over the world that do business in the euro area, which will always be a very important market (not to mention the benefits for tourists who visit this popular area and are able to use the same currency in 20 different countries).

4 Difficulties Versus Benefits of Promoting and Deepening Regional Integration in Other Areas of the World

The creation of regional blocs is taking place in all continents, but the integration achieved in the European Union is much deeper than in any other case. For example, in no other case is there a single market (akin to the European single market) or a common currency in use in such a significant number of different countries.

These developments can more easily occur, and in some cases can only occur, when there are common institutions that can take certain steps and approve the necessary measures, for example, to remove borders (with security requirements) or to harmonise technical standards.

We must, however, acknowledge that the creation of similar possibilities in other blocs could prove difficult, mainly due to the great differences in the populations of the member countries. One example is the former NAFTA, now replaced by the USMCA, with the United States having more population than Mexico and Canada together. Another is MERCOSUL, where Brazil is in a similar situation compared to the other members, with four times more population than the three other countries (Argentina, Paraguay and Uruguay) together. Lastly, we have the Asian example of the SAARC (South Asia Association for Regional Cooperation), which includes, at opposite ends of the scale, Bhutan with 200,000 inhabitants and India currently with more than 1.4 billion inhabitants.

While the populations of the EU countries are certainly not uniform in size, the difference is that no one country has more population than all of the other countries together. Moreover, it is important to note that the most populated countries of the European Union accept that their citizens are under-represented in the institutions, e.g. in the Council and the Parliament (not to mention the Courts and the European Central Bank). For example, each German MEP currently represents around 900,000 citizens, while the figure for Luxembourg and Malta is closer to 100,000 citizens, the latter therefore being over-represented.

This situation being accepted, the EU institutions are able to introduce quite relevant measures, such as those creating and regulating the single market and the euro.

In other blocs the necessary steps must therefore be taken at the inter-state level. However, many steps can indeed be taken, and we should look forward to more steps being taken in this direction.

Moreover, greater integration in other blocs produces advantages not only for their economies and citizens, but also for the companies and citizens of other areas in the world. Considering the benefits already mentioned, if, for example, technical barriers are removed in MERCOSUL or in USMCA, with the same standards being established for the production of manufactured goods, this will benefit not only the entrepreneurs of those areas, but also the entrepreneurs of Europe or of Japan who produce or sell goods there. And if borders are removed, free movement with no border checks will also apply to lorries transporting goods from one country to another and to citizens from other continents who wish to do business there or to visit more than one of those countries.

Hence, there are two main arguments for trying to convince the authorities of other regional blocs to deepen their integration: the first to promote their economies and the conditions of their citizens, and the second to create better opportunities for the companies and for citizens of other areas of the world (e.g. Europe), since by promoting the economies of these areas, there will be an overall increase in demand, with more opportunities for European firms.

5 The Role of Regional Blocs When It Is Difficult to Go Forward with the WTO

Establishing and strengthening regional blocs has always been a worthy target to pursue, but in the current climate it has a special relevance.

It has become clear that it is now more difficult to move forward in the WTO via the traditional routes, which played a very important role some decades ago.

The situation now is quite different, with the Doha Agenda of 2004, and the initiatives taken since then, not having been as successful as expected.

In addition to other reasons,[9] it is difficult to achieve great success due to the large number of members (166 countries), each of them with specific conditions and requirements.

Given this situation, one alternative is the creation and strengthening of regional blocs, with all the benefits mentioned, in other areas of the world besides Europe.

Moreover, the existence of blocs can also help to facilitate global negotiations. The customs union established in the EU, for example, means that several countries can be represented by a single voice in negotiations with the World Trade

[9] Highlighting some reasons for this difficulty, some of them quite recent, see Cunha (2019a).

Organization. This is a benefit that other groups of countries could gain, following the establishment of a regional bloc.[10]

Nowadays there are also an increasing number of agreements between regional blocs (see Cunha (2008, 2019b) and Mota (2020, 2022)), in some cases between blocs in the same continent and in many cases between blocs and countries from different continents.

These developments often produce a positive outcome of greater proximity between nations and more open economies.

The open policies produced often help to guard against the risk of protectionism, which will be discussed in the next section.

6 The Strategy to Be Followed

The formation of large-scale blocs, for example of a size similar to the European Union, can carry with it the risk of the practice of protectionism in relation to other areas of the world.

This is a real risk nowadays, in the light of the new map of the world, in particular with the astonishing rise of the economies of China and India. These countries not only have lower labour costs, but also important and growing stocks of capital and successful technologies.

In response to this, it could undoubtedly be tempting for Europe and in particular for the European Union to adopt a protectionist stance, as a means of preserving European companies and jobs. The same could be true for other regional blocs, or for very large nations.

Even though the lessons of history and experience have shown very clearly that the best results come from openness,[11] strategies involving protectionism should still be feared. This is because history has also shown that in society there are forces, in particular forces of organised groups, that frequently lead to protectionist policies (see for example Porto 2017, p. 152).

For its part, the European Union has not taken that route, and in principle will not do so, given that all the documents that define its strategy highlight the benefits of an open external policy, with progressive improvements of the single market.

---

[10] Questions may arise as to whether the interests of the countries are better defended in this way than if they were participating individually.

In the case of Portugal, it is clear that they are better defended in this way, given our relevant weight in the EU institutions; and the voice of the EU is of course strongly taken into account in an institution such as the WTO, much more than the voice of Portugal, if we participated individually.

In our opinion, this was also the case for the UK, despite its larger size, while a member of the EU. We disagree with those who argued, in the campaign in favour of the Brexit, that the country would have greater influence participating individually in the WTO (and in other organisations) than as a member of the EU (see again Porto 2020a).

[11] Noted in footnote 1, with the lessons of economic theory pointing in the same direction.

6.1 A Single Market for the Twenty-first Century

This is the title of Section 1 of "Strategy Europe 2020" (European Commission 2010). And the initial words of the section could not be clearer, stating that "a stronger, deeper, extended single market is vital for growth and job creation".

In this document, the Commission states that it is well aware, however, that much is still to be done. Referring to the crisis at that time, it goes on to highlight that "the crisis has added temptations of economic nationalism". And bearing in mind this risk, it is keen to stress that "a new momentum – a genuine political commitment – is needed to relaunch the single market".[12]

The Commission acknowledges that this is so because "often, businesses and citizens still need to deal with 27 legal systems for one and the same transaction. Whilst our companies are still confronted with the day-to-day reality of fragmentation and diverging rules, their competitors from China, the US or Japan can draw full strength from their large home markets".

Following this perspective, and bearing in mind the important effects already obtained with the 1993 single market, other steps have been taken over the years. Examples include an initiative of the Commission in 1997 entitled the "Action Plan for the Single Market", the "Lisbon Strategy" in 2000,[13] and the Monti Report, "A New Strategy for the Single Market" in 2010. In his mission letter to Mario Monti, President Barroso stated that the "Single Market has been, and remains, the cornerstone of Europe's integration and sustainable growth".

With the same purpose in mind, in March of the same year the document "The Economic Impact of a European Digital Market, was published. This was followed by COM (2010) 608 final, of 27.10.2010, entitled "Towards a Single Market Act. For a highly competitive social market economy. 50 proposals for improving our work, business and exchanges with one another".

Some years later "The Five Presidents Report, Completing Europe's Economic and Monetary Union",[14] of 11 June 2015, was published. The report recognises that steps still need to be taken, highlighting in particular that "completing and fully exploiting the Single Market in goods and services, digital, energy and capital markets, should be part of a stronger boost towards economic union, as well as more jobs and higher growth".

The same idea was emphasised in subsequent documents, one of them being the "White Paper on the Future of Europe; with Reflections and Scenarios for the EU 27 by 2025" (COM (2017)2025, of 1.3.2017: European Commission 2017a). Five scenarios are considered here, all of them stressing the role of the single market.

---

[12] In particular, it is added that "such political commitment will require a combination of measures to fill the gaps in the single market".

[13] On this strategy, see Kok (2004), Rodrigues (2004), Lopes (2007), Rodrigues et al. (2009), Ardy (2011), Barthe (2011, pp. 97–105) and Costa (2000).

[14] Report by Jean Claude Junker, "in close cooperation with Donald Tusk, Jeroen Dijsselbloem, Mario Draghi and Martin Schultz".

More recently, we can refer to the following documents: "A New Industrial Strategy for Europe", COM (2020) 102 final, of 10.3.2020 (European Commission 2020), the Update to this, COM (2021) 350 final, of 5.5.2021 (European Commission 2021b), the "Annual Single Market Report 2021", SWD(2021) 351 final, of 5.5.2021 (European Commission 2021c); "The Single Market at 30", COM 162 (2023) final, the Single Market Programme, adopted under Regulation (EU) 2021/690, and secondary legislation (such as, *inter alia*, Commission delegated regulations, such as 2023/2445); on the same line, we have now the Letta Report, "Much more than a market" (April 2024) and the Draghi Report on the future of European competitiveness (September 2024).

At the beginning of section 3 of the "Update", entitled "Strengthening Single Market Resilience", it is stated emphatically that "the Single Market is the EU's most important asset, offering certainty, scale and a global springboard for our companies, and wide availability of quality products for consumers".

6.2 An External Strategy

The "Strategy Europe 2020" was also already quite clear about the strategy to follow externally, considered in section 3.3 of COM (2010) 2020 (European Commission 2010).

The situation, mentioned above, of difficult competition mainly with the new emerging and re-emerging countries, could indeed have given rise to protectionist temptations and measures.

The response of the Strategy Europe 2020 was totally different, however, with globalisation being seen not as a threat, but as a means of gaining access to larger opportunities.

The beginning of section 3.3 (p. 22) is quite clear, stating that "global growth will open up new opportunities for Europe's exporters and competitive access to vital imports".

Earlier in the document (p. 8), after mentioning the emerging countries, it was also noted that "every threat is also an opportunity", and then again (p. 14) that "the EU has prospered through trade, exporting round the world and importing inputs as well as finished goods. Faced with intense pressure on export markets and for a growing range of inputs we must improve our competitiveness vis-à-vis our main trading partners through higher productivity".

In the same vein, the authors of the strategy state (p. 22) that "all instruments of external economic policy need to be deployed to foster European growth through our participation in open and fair markets worldwide".

This idea is reinforced three lines later, with the statement that "an open Europe, operating within a rules-based international framework, is the best route to exploit the benefits of globalisation that will boost growth and employment".

The text could not be clearer; globalisation is seen as an opportunity much more than as a threat. Whereas very often we consider the growth of emerging economies to be a risk, with negative consequences for our firms, destroying our jobs, COM

(2010) 2020 (p. 22) states that "a part of the growth that Europe needs to generate over the next decade will need to come from the emerging economies as their middle classes develop and import goods and services in which the European Union has a comparative advantage. As the biggest trading bloc in the world, the EU prospers by being open to the world and paying close attention to what other developed or emerging economies are doing to anticipate or adapt to future trends".

This idea about the opportunities of globalisation, subject however to the right rules, was also highlighted in COM (2017) 240 final, of 10.5.2017, entitled "Harnessing Globalisation" (European Commission 2017b).

And more recently particular attention should be given to the "Trade Policy Review – An Open, Sustainable and Assertive Trade Policy", defined in COM (2021) 66 final, of 18.2.2021 (European Commission 2021a).

The introductory words of this document are very clear, stating that "trade is one of the EU's most powerful tools. It is at the centre of Europe's economic prosperity and competitiveness, supporting a vibrant internal market and assertive external action. As a result of the openness of our trade regime, the EU is the world's larger trader of agricultural and manufactured goods and services and ranks first in both inbound and outbound international investments. Thanks to the common commercial policy, the EU speaks with one voice on the global scene. This is a unique lever".

The strategy of openness is reflected in the average level of import duties of the European Union following the Uruguay Round, of 3.6 per cent, with 38 per cent of imports not being taxed (figures similar to those of the United States, but much more favourable to trade than the figures in most countries of the world, in the different continents (see Porto 2017, p. 542). There was indeed a wrong protectionist policy with the Common Agricultural Policy, but improvements have been made in recent decades (mainly since 1992, with the reform made during the Portuguese presidency (see Seia 1994; Cunha 1998, 2004, 2019a, b)).

Despite the challenges of openness, the EU, in particular the euro area, has by far the greatest surplus of the world in the current account balance.

And this is so despite it having some difficult conditions for competition, for example high labour costs, in countries with a demanding social model (with free trade unions, deciding frequently to take strike action) and open democracies.

So, Europe has had the important task, which it has successfully accomplished, of showing that it is possible to compete at the world level while also fulfilling difficult but important social (and political) requirements. This was highlighted in a recent Council (in 2020) which took place in Porto, during the Portuguese presidency of the Union.

7 Conclusions

We must be realistic when we look at the future characteristics of the world, with new or renewed great economic (and political) powers.

And this applies especially to those politicians with responsibilities in Europe, in particular in the European Union, which will have no more than 5 per cent of the world's population and a diminishing percentage in the world economy.

Given that the advantage of open economies is well recognised, it could perhaps be thought that the way forward should be only or mainly through world institutions, in particular through the World Trade Organization.

Yet, nowadays, it is also clear that taking steps at this level is not so easy, with so many different countries with vastly differing circumstances. It is also evident that only among a much smaller number of countries, with common institutions, is it possible to take the steps required for deeper economic integration.

No other examples in the world can compete with the example of the European Union, which has taken important initiatives, broadly promoting territorial and social cohesion and establishing a space with many fewer barriers (in particular physical and technical barriers) and where a significant number of countries use the same currency.

Besides favouring the citizens, and namely the entrepreneurs, of the EU, these steps also benefit the citizens and entrepreneurs of other parts of the world, as there are no restrictions to movement between member states, in addition to better market conditions with the same rules applying to the whole area, not to mention the advantages of a single currency being accepted in several countries.

The success of the European Union, which has low levels of trade protection and remains competitive with an open political, economic and social model, with high wages, is a good example for other areas of the world to follow, motivating them to adopt the same strategy and the same model, and thereby improve the quality of their citizens' lives.

References

Ardy B (2011) Industrial and competitiveness policy: the Lisbon strategy. In: El-Agraa AM (ed) The European Union. Economics and policies. Cambridge University Press, Cambridge, pp 214–228

Barthe MA (2011) Économie de l'Union Européenne. Economica, Paris

Bhagwati JN (1978) Anatomy and consequences of exchange control regimes. National Bureau of Economic Research (NBER), Ballinger Publishing Company, New York

Calvete V (1999–2001) Sobre a teoria das uniões aduaneiras. In: Boletim de Ciências Económicas. Volumes XLII-XLIII-XLIV (1999-2000-2001) Faculdade de Direito da Universidade de Coimbra, Coimbra

Checchini P (1988) The economics of 1992: an assessment of the potential economic effects of completing the internal market of the European Community. European Economy/Économie Européenne, Perspectivas e Realidades, Lisboa

Corden WM (1972) Economies of scale and customs union theory. J Polit Econ 80:465–475

Costa FSD (2000) A segunda presidência Portuguesa. A agenda de Lisboa. In: Cunha A, Lã JR, Nunes PS (eds) (2019) As Décadas da Europa. Bookbuilders, Santa Cruz, pp 297–313

Cunha A (1998) A PAC e o futuro da agricultura europeia. Temas Integração 6:101–114

Cunha A (2004) A política agrícola comum na era da globalização. Almedina, Coimbra

Cunha LP (2008) O sistema comercial multilateral e os espaços de integração. Coimbra Editora, Coimbra

Cunha A (2019) A evolução das políticas comuns de agricultura e das pescas e sua aplicação em Portugal na primeira década da adesão à CEE. In: Cunha A, Lã JR, Nunes PS (eds) As Décadas da Europa. Bookbuilders, Santa Cruz, pp 81–102
Cunha LP (2019a) A OMC e o seu impasse: exposição de motivos. In: Boletim de Ciências Económicas n.° 27. Faculdade de Direito, Universidade de Coimbra, Coimbra
Cunha LP (2019b) A União Europeia e os acordos de integração regionais. Problemas e situação atual. Boletim da Faculdade de Direito da Universidade de Coimbra, 95(2):1131–1160
Draghi M (2024) The future of European Competitiveness. https://commission.europa.eu/topics/strengthening-european-competitiveness/eu-competitiveness-looking-ahead_en#paragraph_47059. Accessed 7 Oct 2024
European Commission (2010) Strategy Europe 2020, A strategy for smart, sustainable and inclusive growth, COM 2020. European Commission, Brussels
European Commission (2017a) White paper on the future of Europe. European Commission, Brussels
European Commission (2017b) Reflection paper in harnessing globalization, COM 240. European Commission, Brussels
European Commission (2020) A new industrial strategy for Europe, COM 102. European Commission, Brussels
European Commission (2021a) Trade policy review – An open, sustainable and assertive trade policy, COM 66. European Commission, Brussels
European Commission (2021b) Updating the 2020 new industrial strategy: building a stronger single market for Europe's recovery, COM 350. European Commission, Brussels
European Commission (2021c) Annual single market report 2021, updating the 2020 new industrial strategy, COM 351. European Commission, Brussels
European Commission (2023) The Single Market at 30, COM 162, European Commission, Brussels
Fajgelbaum PD, Khandelwal AK (2015) Measuring the unequal gains from trade. Working paper. National Bureau of Economic Research (NBER), New York
Felbermayr G, Gröschl JK, Heiland I (2018) Undoing Europe in a new quantitative trade model. Ifo Working Paper no. 250
Gehrels F (1956) Customs union from a single-country viewpoint. Rev Econ Stud 24:61–64
Golich VL (1992) From competition to collaboration: the challenge of commercial-class aircraft manufacturing. Int Organ 46:899–934
Guillochon B, Peltrault F, Venet B (2020) Économie internationale. Dunod, Paris
Hill CW, Hult GT (2019) International business. Competing in the global marketplace. McGraw Hill, New York
Kok W (2004) Facing the challenge: the Lisbon strategy for growth and employment. OOPEC, Luxembourg
Krueger AO (1978) Foreign trade regimes and economic development. Liberalization attempts and consequences. National Bureau of Economic Research, Ballinger Publishing Company, New York
LETTA Report (2024) Much more than a market
Lipsey RG (1957) The theory of customs unions: trade diversion and welfare. Economica 24:40–46
Lipsey RG (1960) The theory of customs unions: a general survey. Econ J 70:496–513
Lipsey R (1970) The theory of customs unions: a general equilibrium analysis. Weidenfeld and Nicolson, London
Little IM, Scitovsky T, Scott MF (1970) Industry and trade in some developing countries. Oxford University Press, OECD Development Center, London
Lopes AC (2007) A estratégia de Lisboa e a modernização da economia europeia. Instituto Nacional de Administração (INA), Oeiras
Maddison A (2001) The World Economy: a millennial perspective. In: Historical statistics, OECD
Meade J (1956) The theory of customs unions. Amsterdam, North Holland
Meade J (1968) The pure theory of customs unions. Amsterdam, North Holland

Monti M (2010) A new strategy for the single market. At the service of Europe's economy and society. (Study commissioned by the President of the European Commission J.M. Durão Barroso)
Moreira A (1989) A lei da complexidade crescente na vida internacional. Comentários. Lisboa: Academia Internacional da Cultura Portuguesa, pp 11–20
Mota PI (2020) Os acordos mega-regionais: uma nova ordem comercial mundial? In: Boletim de Ciências Económicas, Coimbra, v.63 (2020), pp 37–187
Mota PI (2022) Acordos comerciais preferenciais. Almedina, Coimbra
Papageorgiou D, Choksi AM, Michaely M (1990) Liberalizing foreign trade in developing countries. The lessons of experience, 1990, World Bank, Washington (summary published by Basil Blackwell, Oxford, 1990-1; and the research on Portugal, conducted by Macedo, Jorge Braga de, Corado, Cristina and Porto, Manuel, published as Working Paper no. 114 of Faculdade de Economia da Universidade Nova de Lisboa)
Parkin M (2019) Economics. Pearson, Harlow
Pelkmans J (2011) The case for more single market. CEPS Policy Brief, No. 234/February 2011
Pomfret R (1991) The trade theories, rent-snatching and jet aircraft. World Econ 14:269–277
Porto M (2017) Teoria da integração e políticas da União Europeia: face aos desafios da globalização. Almedina, Coimbra
Porto M (2019) O que pode e deve ser esperado da política orçamental da União Europeia. In: Caetano JM, Sousa M (eds) Desafios e Oportunidades na Governança da Zona Euro (Challenges and Opportunities for Eurozone Governance, Nova Science Publishers, New York, pp 147–161). Sílabo, Lisboa, pp 203–227
Porto M (2020a) O brexit face à globalização. In: Correia JDM, Pinto RL (eds) Estudos em homenagem ao professor António Martins da Cruz. Universidade Lusíada Editora, Lisboa, pp 649–667
Porto M (2020b) A coesão territorial e o novo quadro financeiro da União Europeia. In: Molina DP, Pablo C (eds) Derecho da la union Europeia e integracion regional, liber amicorum al Prof. Dr. Carlos Francisco Molina del Pozo. Tirant lo Blanche, Valencia, pp 1589–1614
Porto M (2021) O novo quadro financeiro plurianual e os desafios da União Europeia. In: Basto JGXD, Ferreira EP, Palma CC, Lopes CMM (eds) Estudos em homenagem ao professor doutor António Carlos dos Santos. Almedina, Coimbra, pp 757–779
Porto M (2022) União Europeia: que futuro no novo quadro global? In: González J, Venes N, Alves RP (coords) União Europeia: que futuro?, Lusíada Editora, Lisboa, pp 139–160
Porto M, Guincho L (2012/20) Comment on Article 26 of TFEU. In: Porto M, Anastácio G (eds) Tratado de Lisboa - Anotado e Comentado. Coimbra, Almedina, 2012
Quadros F (2012/20) Comment on Article 5 of TEU. In: Porto M, Anastácio G (eds) Tratado de Lisboa - Anotado e Comentado. Coimbra, Almedina, 2012
Rodrigues MJ (2004) A agenda económica e social da União Europeia. A agenda de Lisboa. Dom Quixote, Lisboa
Rodrigues MJ, Troglic JF, Ehrenkrona O, Centre d'Analyse Stratégique, Herzog P, Sapir A (2009) Europe. Globalization and the Lisbon agenda. Edward Elgar, Cheltenham and Nottingham
Seia MCDA (1994) A reforma da política agrícola comum. Almedina, Coimbra
Viner J (1950) The customs union issue. Stevens and Sons, New York

Manuel Lopes Porto Universidade de Coimbra, Faculty of Law, Coimbra, Portugal.

Building a European Data Space

Graça Enes

Data is shaping the future of Humanity—United Nations Secretariat (2019)

1 Introduction[1]

The above quote reminds us of the crucial importance of data for the economy, society, and indeed humankind.

Data is information (European Commission 2011, p. 2, fnt. 1), and the collection and processing of data is as old as mankind. Yet, the digital revolution and the digitisation of every activity has increased the amount of data created/collected and aggregated by people and corporations, including public bodies. Today, data is created/owned/held by individuals, public bodies and companies (among the latter, "big tech" companies are the ones that profit the most from data monetisation).

This plethora of data is the driving force behind the 4th industrial revolution, as the raw material for the creation and improvement of products and services, including government and public services. The IoT (Internet of Things), soon to be the IoE (Internet of Everything), exponentiates machine and sensor-generated data and its production is almost costless. Objects such as vehicles, home appliances and other items are connected and exchange data. Data information is everywhere,

[1] This chapter analyses the "Open Data Directive", the "Free Flow Regulation", and the "Data Governance Act".

G. Enes (✉)
University of Porto, Faculty of Law, CIJ - Centre for Interdisciplinary Research on Justice, Oporto, Portugal
e-mail: gef@direito.up.pt

I. Quadros, M. Gorjão-Henriques (eds.), *Revisiting the Liberal Constitutional Features of the European Union*, https://doi.org/10.1007/978-3-031-95717-8_11

permanently, and this, coupled with supercomputers, AI capabilities and automated production, is pushing the horizon of knowledge and production to an unimagined frontier.[2] A data-based society is not the future, it is here and now. The ordinary day-to-day life of any person generates huge amounts and diverse types of both personal and non-personal data. The collection of this data by so many different agents and for different purposes completely absorbs human existence, while at the same time and paradoxically it fragments it (Cantazariti 2021, p. 83) by decoupling the data from its origin.

In 2018, the volume of data in the world was 33 zettabytes. In 2025, it is expected to reach 175 zettabytes (European Commission 2020a, p. 2). This explosion of data feeds a flourishing data economy. Even though it is still in its infancy (European Commission 2018a, p. 175), with only 6.3% of European companies being intensive data users in 2018, the digital sector is the most dynamic and high-value job creator, leading data-driven innovation in this new phase of capitalism, already labelled as "information capitalism" (Cohen 2020). This data economy is overwhelmingly dominated by non-European companies, and Europe "is falling behind in growing sectors as well as in areas of innovation (…) where it is being outpaced by the United States and China" (Bughin et al. 2022, p. 2).

Besides its economic value, data is a tool for developing R&D, improving science and addressing specific challenges and problems in society, for instance in the fields of health or the environment (European Commission 2011, p. 3). Moreover, access to data means access to information and, therefore, it is a fundamental right *per se* (Directive 2019/1024, Preamble, Recital 5).

Data access has been receiving increasing attention at international level and "open data" is on the agenda of policymakers around the world (European Commission/European Data Portal 2015, pp. 24–25): the OECD Recommendation of the Council on Enhancing Access to and Sharing of Data (OECD 2022), the 2013 G8's *Open Data Charter* (G8 2013), the UN's *Cape Town Global Action Plan for Sustainable Development Data* (UN Statistical Commission 2017), the United Nations Development Group's *Data privacy, Ethics and Protection. Guidance note on big data for achievement of the 2030 Agenda* (United Nations Development Group 2017), to mention just a few.

Regulation of data is a sensitive and complex issue. Because data is an "emerging market", any intervention must be cautious so as not to stifle innovation, but, at the same time, the EU considers that regulation is a necessary part of the development of the EU data market (European Commission 2018, p. 176).[3] The Union's regulatory approach has been limited and incremental. In 2018, the EU was accused of lacking "[a] common vision and [a] widely accepted approach to create open data markets that would benefit big and small companies" (Demchenko et al. 2018, p. 3).

---

[2]The McKinsey Report, in 2011, offered a broad view on the potential of data (Manyika et al. 2011). In 2020, the "European Strategy for Data" highlighted some examples of the innovative potential of data (European Commission 2020a).

[3]This study conducts a sectoral and Member States analysis, and the results show relevant differences.

That same year, it announced its "Data Package initiative". The progressive opening of data for re-use across the Union without discrimination or restrictions (unless justified by legitimate reasons), starting with public sector data, became a policy objective. An open data policy seeking to unlock the full potential of data cannot ignore data held by private bodies or the need for "European data spaces" and a European governance framework for data. A broad framework for data governance, composed of "soft" and "hard" law and a multi-level institutional network, is in the making.[4]

The importance of data for society and the protection of fundamental values and liberties require a European data policy that follows a "European way", adopting a "constitutional approach" that balances "the flow and wide use of data, while preserving high privacy, security, safety and ethical standards" (European Commission 2020a, p. 3) with the human being at the centre. Technological transformations have an impact on constitutional values, "as the state formulates its legal response to new technologies based on constitutional principles which meet market dynamics, and as it considers its own use of technologies in light of the limitation imposed by constitutional safeguards" (Pollicino and De Gregorio 2021, p. 5). Only a "constitutional" approach can prevent the risks of a "surveillance capitalism" (Zuboff 2019). Data must be recognised not as the "new oil" but as the "new water", a general interest resource to nourish the progress of a free society and all its citizens, overcoming the "digital divide" that leaves large categories of citizens behind in this new "digital world" (women, the elderly, the less educated, etc.). The sovereign relevance of data (Hummel et al. 2018; Woods 2018) has also gained attention.

The most important acts enacted by the EU to promote "open data" and "EU data governance" will be analysed.

2 Open Data, Related Concepts and Principles

According to ISO/IEC 2382-1, data is "a reinterpretable representation of information in a formalized manner, suitable for communication, interpretation or processing". Article 2 (1) of Regulation (EU) 2022/868 defines 'data' as "any digital representation of acts, facts or information and any compilation of such acts, facts or information, including in the form of sound, visual or audiovisual recording". EU law also refers to "documents" as being synonymous with data.[5] Data encompasses content in any medium (written on paper, sound, visual or audio-visual recordings, or in electronic format). The increasing digitisation of every sector of the economy and society means that the vast majority of data is "digital".

[4] The Commission also proposed a programme to support digital innovation in the EU (European Commission 2021).

[5] In fact, a document is a container of data.

Data can be created by a human or produced by machines, and it is often a "by-product" of an economic activity (*e.g.* flight schedules). Data produced and collected by individuals and the private sector has increased exponentially in recent years. States and public bodies own large amounts of data and datasets collected through their activities. Much of this is dynamic data, i.e. information subject to frequent or real-time updates because of its volatility or rapid obsolescence[6] (*e.g.* meteorological data, city traffic data, environmental data, and the increasing amount of sensor-generated data, collected from vehicles, industry, commerce, domestic appliances, etc.), and its economic value depends on its real-time availability. Bulk download[7] and APIs[8] are fundamental for this. APIs enable automatic searches and bulk download, both of which are crucial in achieving rapid accessibility which is paramount to ensure economic value.[9] In fact, this move away from static data represents a fundamental change towards "data as service". Some datasets are high-value and are important for the creation of high-value goods and services or for society (*e.g.* education, transport, health or justice).

The legal nature of data is difficult to appraise.[10] Regardless of that nature, it is, however, a valuable asset.[11] One obvious feature of data is that it is an intangible, almost completely non rivalrous good, which can be shared and re-used without losing its intrinsic value.[12] Sometimes it is confused with the devices that store or process data, and intellectual property law is applied to non-personal data through the rights over the devices that store it (software rights). Some human-created data is subject to copyright law (*e.g.* photos posted on social media). Personal data (identification or IP address) is governed by the legal regime of the General Data Protection Regulation (GDPR). Most data consist of raw assets, which are not valu-

[6] Directive 2019/1024, Article 2 (8).

[7] Eurostat allows the bulk download of its datasets with updates twice a day, at 11:00 and 23:00 (https://ec.europa.eu/eurostat/data/bulkdownload).

[8] Application Programming Interfaces (a set of functions, procedures, definitions and technical protocols for machine-to-machine communication by means of which one software asks another programme to perform a service, namely granting access to data, making exchange of data automatic and seamless).

[9] Directive 2019/1024, Preamble, Recital 32.

[10] There can be overlapping statutory regimes (Benhamou 2020).

[11] To value data D. Moody and P. Walsh propose a specific approach that reflects its unique characteristics (Moody and Walsh 1999). The authors describe "7 laws" to define information as an economic good (infinitely shareable, increasing returns to re-use, perishability, value increases with accuracy, value increases with comparison and combination with other information, more is not necessarily better, information is not depletable). One of its most distinguishable features is that it can have use value and market value simultaneously (p. 13) and its value is normally dependent on its use (information with no use has no value, only costs, namely with storage). On 27 February 2010, *The Economist* stated "[d]ata are becoming the new raw material of business: an economic input almost on a par with capital and labour" (Cukier 2020, p. 5). For an assessment of the value of different types of data, see European Parliament (2017, p. 10).

[12] This means data is not a "consumable good" (Demchenko et al. 2018, p. 1). Paradoxically, some data may lose value if it is widely known and at the same time its re-use multiplies the value created.

able *per se*, and to reach its full potential it must be processed and aggregated to extract/build relevant information for data-driven innovation for services and goods (SIIA Policy 2013).[13] This is why the focus is moving towards processing or aggregating services, involving a new "data as service" approach. One example of this move is the protection of datasets that derive from an intellectual effort using a *sui generis* right. Machine-generated data, on the other hand, does not fall within the scope of intellectual property or similar rights because it is not a human creation,[14] but it can be protected under the legal regime for trade secrets and subject to contract arrangements.

One of the most prominent features of digital data is that there is a disconnection between storage and accessibility (Daskal 2015, p. 369). This new information space builds on the interaction between public and private actors, regardless of territorial borders (Cantazariti 2021, p. 82). Among other issues, such as privacy, fundamental rights, or economic value, this new un-territorial data space raises concerns related to public security and claims of state sovereignty (Cantazariti 2021, p. 88).[15]

Law on data has evolved with a binary logic of personal and non-personal data (Somaini 2020). "Personal data" is a broad concept and means any information relating to an identified or identifiable natural person ("data subject").[16] Non-personal data is defined by exclusion: that data which is not covered by the broad concept of personal data provided for in the GDPR. The first brick laid in the "European data space" was the protection of personal data. Strict rules on the use and re-use of personal data, in particular requiring the consent of the data subject, were implemented alongside the free movement of that data. In reality, the two categories are often mixed (mixed datasets)[17] and, more significantly, most data flows are of non-personal data or mixed data.[18]

The exponential increase in data has led to "big-data", i.e. "extensive datasets—primarily in the characteristics of volume, variety, velocity, and/or variability—that require a scalable architecture for efficient storage, manipulation, and analysis"

---

[13] A good example is the value extracted from data posted on social media platforms.

[14] Results of data integration, analytics, etc. can be indirectly protected by the protection given to the intellectual effort put into the design of the data integration process or the analytics algorithm (software).

[15] The "Microsoft case" in the US is remarkable in this respect (Woods 2018).

[16] Article 4(1) GDPR. An identifiable natural person is "one who can be identified, directly or indirectly, in particular by reference to an identifier such as a name, an identification number, location data, an online identifier or to one or more factors specific to the physical, physiological, genetic, mental, economic, cultural or social identity of that natural person" (European Commission 2019, pp. 4–5). Article 29 Working Party group has densified this concept in that broad sense and, for instance, pseudonymised information remains personal data if it can be attributed to a person using additional information.

[17] IoT has increased the importance and number of mixed datasets (some examples are in European Commission 2019, p. 8).

[18] In 2019, the Commission published practical guidelines regarding the interaction between the free flow of non-personal data and personal data (European Commission 2019).

(National Institute of Standards and Technology 2015, p. 5). Access to "big data" is necessary to harness the potential of AI technology.

More generally, to foster innovation it is necessary to promote access to and sharing of data, especially for SMEs. "Data access" and "data sharing" are different concepts. "Data sharing" is a broader concept and covers "the provision of data by a data subject or a data holder to a data user for the purpose of the joint or individual use of such data, based on voluntary agreements or Union or national law, directly or through an intermediary, for example under open or commercial licences subject to a fee or free of charge".[19] "Data access" does not necessarily imply the transmission or downloading of data[20] and it can take place in a "controlled environment".[21]

The pressure to develop an "open data" policy increased. "Open data" is data that is freely available for re-use for commercial and non-commercial purposes without restrictions of copyright, patents or other mechanisms of control.[22] Open data offers direct and indirect benefits, including the creation of new products and services and an increase in employment that will foster economic growth, knowledge and cost savings (European Commission 2015a, p. 8).

Acknowledgement of the value of data to society, especially data resulting from publicly funded research and science, led to the formulation of principles for scientific data management and stewardship—the FAIR principles[23]—Findable, Accessible, Interoperable, Reusable (Wilkinson et al. 2016). These principles are being transposed to industry (DAMA International 2017).[24]

Commoditisation of data requires the addition of new principles—the STREAM principles[25]—and a few other properties.[26] "Sovereignty" means that data owners maintain control over their data, and its use or re-use by third parties is subject to consent. This principle has not been set aside by the legal framework laid down in the European Union. "Trust" means all aspects of data production and origin must

[19] Article 2 (10) of Regulation 2022/1724.

[20] Article 2 (13) of Regulation 2022/1724.

[21] Article 2 (20) of Regulation 2022/1724 refers to a "secure processing environment" as "the physical or virtual environment and organisational means to ensure compliance with Union law, such as Regulation (EU) 2016/679, in particular with regard to data subjects' rights, intellectual property rights, and commercial and statistical confidentiality, integrity and accessibility, as well as with applicable national law, and to allow the entity providing the secure processing environment to determine and supervise all data processing actions, including the display, storage, download and export of data and the calculation of derivative data through computational algorithms".

[22] According to Recital 16 of the Preamble of Directive 2019/1024 "open data means data in an open format that can be freely used, re-used and shared by anyone for any purpose". It can be subject, at most, to measures that preserve provenance and openness (Open Knowledge Foundation n.d.).

[23] Recently, the 41st General Conference of UNESCO approved, in November 2021, a recommendation on science data (UNESCO 2021).

[24] Other principles are being formulated, namely the "CARE Principles for Indigenous Data Governance" (Carroll et al. 2020).

[25] Sovereign, Trusted, Reusable, Exchangeable, Actionable, Measurable.

[26] Quality, value, auditability/traceability, branding, authenticity (Demchenko et al. 2018, p. 4).

be verifiable and auditable. "Reusability" means that it should be possible to use data for purposes other than those for which it was created, and it requires well-defined metadata and well-documented data collection processes (Demchenko et al. 2018, p. 5). "Exchangeability", on one hand, means that there should be no technical obstacles to re-use by other users than the producer/owner of data and stresses the importance of data format and platform and APIs compatibility; on the other hand, it means that data can be subject to economic transactions. "Actionability" means usefulness, i.e. data must be suitable for a purpose and able to achieve a result and inform a decision in a business or activity.[27] Finally, "measurability" is important for economic valuation and for managing, processing, and storage devices and facilities. It is not easy to combine different and sometimes competing values and purposes, namely re-use and open access and data ownership and sovereignty (Demchenko et al. 2018, p. 4).[28]

Data markets have emerged over the last two decades to exchange data and data services. Commoditisation of data has occurred, and the European Union considered that data is covered by the internal market freedoms, regardless of its status as a good or a service. Yet, Member States often impose localisation requirements for data storage, invoking public policy reasons or the need to control compliance with the rules on personal data. Restrictions may also result from commercial practices (e.g. the lock-in effects of the big platform practices, even if these are not intended but result from interoperability shortcomings). General internal market principles apply, although subject to the necessary adaptations. Borders should not be reinstated through Member States' localisation rules or through private geo-blocking.[29] Data markets were among the priorities of the Horizon 2020 Work Programme 2018–2020. Despite, or because of, its ambiguous nature, perhaps a fifth freedom should be envisaged for this valuable asset.

3 A Legal Framework for Open Public Data in the EU

3.1 From the "PSI Directive" to the "Open Data Directive"

Public bodies are in possession of huge and very diverse sets of data: weather data, trade and services data, education data, traffic data, general health data, etc. Opening that data for re-use, while safeguarding personal data protection and privacy, would have a significant effect on the economy and on society, in matters such as

[27] Otherwise, data is meaningless and not "smart data". Nowadays, the continuous flow of data from IoT demands real-time streaming analytics.

[28] The authors also note technical shortcomings regarding storage and processing sensitive/proprietary data in the cloud.

[29] Regulation 2018/302 on addressing unjustified geo-blocking and other forms of discrimination based on customers' nationality, place of residence or place of establishment within the internal market.

navigation systems, weather forecasts, banking and insurance, tourism services, health treatments and products such as health devices, etc. Yet, different practices regarding access and re-use among Member States limit these possibilities. This hinders the development of new and innovative goods and services and affects the internal market.

General principles and rules (free movement, non-discrimination, competition rules) apply to data (Capgemini 2020, p. 10), but the overwhelming digitisation demands for regulation to overcome restrictions, uncertainty and lack of transparency, and to ensure respect for fundamental rights.

A proactive data policy to dismantle and harmonise the conditions for re-use of public sector data began in 1999 (European Commission 1998). The Public Sector Information Group (the "PSI Group") (European Commission 2013) was created and, in 2003, Directive 2003/98 on the re-use of public sector information (the "PSI Directive") was enacted.[30] It was the first step towards building a data policy in the EU, albeit cautious and limited, mostly "encouraging" Member States to allow the re-use of data held by public sector bodies, since it did not impose any obligation on Member States to provide access to public sector information or to grant permission for re-use. Though it mentioned the right to knowledge as a democratic right (Preamble, § 16), and it applied across all sectors to all public bodies or publicly funded or controlled bodies, its scope was limited, as it excluded commercial companies and public service broadcasters, cultural and educational establishments and public enterprises.

Meanwhile, several legislative and non-legislative initiatives with an impact on data access and re-use have been enforced in specific sectors, including: 1) on environmental information: Directive 2003/4/EC (the "Aarhus Directive") and Directive 2007/2/EC (the "INSPIRE Directive"); 2) on human health and the environment: Regulation 1907/2006; 3) on chemical substances: Regulation 1907/2006 (the "REACH Regulation").[31]

Directive 2013/37 amended Directive 2003/98/EC. Its keyword could be "enhancement". The approach continues to be incremental, expanding the bodies covered by the directive. The rules on access to documents continue to be outside the scope of the Directive and Member States continue to be responsible for deciding which documents are to be available for access and may place restrictions on access. The major change was the obligation to allow the re-use of generally accessible documents, with some exceptions laid down in the directive.

After the *Mid-Term Review of the Digital Single Market (DSM) Strategy* (European Commission 2017a), the Communication *Building a European Data Economy* (European Commission 2017b) and the *Evaluation Report* (European Commission 2018b), in 2018, the European Commission presented the proposal for

[30] Following the example of the US federal administration policy of open access to data, charging only the marginal costs for its reproduction and dissemination (European Commission 2015a, p. 24).

[31] For a more extensive list, see Capgemini (2020, pp. 11–12).

a new directive on the re-use of public sector information (European Commission 2018c).

The impact assessment document accompanying that proposal (European Commission 2018d) offered a thorough analysis of the needs and challenges, and the options available. It included an Evaluation report on the implementation of Directive 2013/37 and a comparison with other major international players (Annex 7). The document concluded that new legislation was necessary (European Commission 2018d, pp. 24–25).

It was found that some former barriers remained, and new ones had emerged.

Rapid technological progress makes the remaining fragmentation, heterogeneity and limits[32] more burdensome, especially for SMEs. The production and collection of data, namely from "smart" interconnected devices, has increased exponentially but it must be available for re-use. "Big data" analytics and AI solutions depend heavily on public data (European Commission 2018c, p. 2). Member States were legislating at different speeds and that increased the risk of divergences.[33] There was an increase in accessibility and re-use of public data in the EU (European Commission 2018d, p. 2) but insufficiencies were evident and were summed up in four "problem areas": 1) Insufficient use of methods for access and re-use of dynamic data by machines; 2) Market entry barriers and fragmentation; 3) Insufficient availability of public and publicly funded data for re-use; 4) Distortion of competition in the internal market (European Commission 2018d, p. 9). The complaints presented were many: the need to build consistency with other legislation, copyright law or the "Database Directive", with legitimate commercial interests and confidentiality, public procurement law or data protection rules, was acknowledged in accordance with the principle "as open as possible, as closed as necessary"; the exclusion of public undertakings and the utilities sector was considered an important shortcoming; problems existed regarding dynamic data and the lack of APIs, as public sector bodies were finding it difficult to make dynamic data available in real time, which reduced its usefulness; the use of contractual arrangements with private parties to perform this task raised competition objections when these conferred exclusivity or produced a "lock-in effect"; difficulties arose with regard to access and re-use of research data, despite the "open science policy" promoted at European and Member State level (European Commission 2018d, pp. 10–18).

The new directive was expected to have a significant economic and social impact. The direct economic benefits, by 2027/2028, were estimated to be EUR 44 billion, while the indirect economic benefits, by 2030, were estimated to be EUR 214 billion. Regarding employment, it was estimated that 19,000 new jobs would be created (European Commission 2018d, p. 75). Beyond the evident economic benefits of open access to data, other aims were paramount: transparency and efficiency of

[32] The differentiation is evidenced by the European Data Portal Maturity reports that compare the evolution of Member States, available at https://data.europa.eu/en/impact-studies/open-data-maturity.

[33] Directive 2019/1024 ("Open Data Directive"), Preamble, Recital 17.

policy making, and increased awareness and participation of citizens (European Commission 2018d, pp. 5–7).

The focus of the proposal was the provision of real-time access to dynamic data via adequate technical means, the reduction of restrictions on the re-use of high-value public data, including financial barriers, data generated in the context of the provision of certain services of general economic interest by public undertakings and by publicly funded research, new forms of exclusive arrangements, the use of exceptions to the principle of charging the marginal cost, and the relationship between the directive and certain related legal instruments (European Commission 2018c, p. 5).

3.2 *The "Open Data Directive"*

Directive 2003/98 was repealed by Directive 2019/1024 on open data and the re-use of public-sector information (the "Open Data Directive"). The "Open Data Directive" is the final step in the path to ensure that public sector information is available for re-use. It is part of a global reform implemented to create a European data space (the "2018 Data Package").

The purpose of Directive 2019/1024 is "to bring the legislative framework up to date with the advances in digital technologies and to further stimulate digital innovation, especially with regard to artificial intelligence" (Preamble, Recital 3). According to the new Directive "[t]he rules originally adopted in 2003, and amended in 2013, no longer keep pace with those rapid changes, and as a result, the economic and social opportunities offered by the re-use of public data risk being missed" (Preamble, Recital 10). The Directive recognises the need to support public bodies, including European bodies, in modernising their digital capacities (Preamble, Recital 8).

Several principles are recalled: liability of re-users;[34] fair competition;[35] non-discrimination;[36] proportionality;[37] transparency;[38] accountability.[39]

[34] Preamble, Recital 44.

[35] Preamble, Recital 47. Any conditions on re-use cannot restrict competition (Article 8 (1, § 2)).

[36] Article 11. If conditions for re-use should be non-discriminatory for comparable categories of re-use, the prohibition of discrimination should not, for example, prevent the exchange of information between public sector bodies free of charge for the exercise of public tasks, whilst other parties are charged for re-use of the same documents. A differentiated charging policy for commercial and non-commercial re-use is legitimate (Preamble, Recital 46). Licencing conditions should be non-discriminatory (Article 8).

[37] Preamble, Recital 32.

[38] Article 7 (1) and (2). Any charges should be pre-defined and published or indicated at the outset. Transparency is also present regarding licences (Article 8 (2)) and a condition in exclusive arrangements (Articles 12(2) and 12 (3 §2)).

[39] Means of redress should be available (Article 7 (3)).

Despite being called the "Open Data Directive" and stating that access to information is a fundamental right,[40] this Directive does not implement a straightforward "open data" policy. The intervention stays in line with the previous "low intensity" regulation, mixing "hard" and "soft" obligations and recommendations (European Commission 2018c, pp. 7–8). The Directive is still a minimum harmonisation directive following the "incremental" approach[41] and simply goes one step further in the prescriptive path. Although limited, it establishes a comprehensive binding regime for public data that is at the core of a broader framework with a differentiated normative reach.

Access to documents[42] of public sector bodies at every level, related to political or administrative activities, is regarded as "a fundamental instrument for extending the right to knowledge, which is a basic principle of democracy" (Preamble, Recital 43).

The articulation with the database *sui generis* right is clarified:[43] the "Open Data Directive" derogates that right and public bodies that fall within the scope of the directive cannot refuse the re-use of database information that is publicly available. The Directive encourages Member States "to promote the creation of data based on the principle of «open by design and by default», regarding all documents falling within the scope of this Directive".[44] This approach serves as a handbook and can guide Member States when they are exercising their competences, namely regarding which documents will be accessible and any restrictions imposed. Access to documents within the scope of the Directive remains in the realm of Member States[45] and they can restrict or refuse access as enshrined in national law or according to the exceptions of the directive.[46] Article 1 (2) lays down a long list of exclusions.[47]

---

[40] Preamble, Recital 5.

[41] This approach looked more feasible than "the higher intensity regulatory intervention scenario" (European Commission 2018c, p. 8).

[42] "Document" covers any representation of acts, facts or information—and any compilation of such acts, facts or information—whatever its medium (paper, or electronic form or as a sound, visual or audio-visual recording), but not computer programmes. Member States may extend the application of Directive 2019/1024 to computer programmes" (Preamble, Recital 30).

[43] Article 1 (6).

[44] Article 5 (2).

[45] Article 1 (3) states "[t]his Directive builds on, and is without prejudice to, Union and national access regimes."

[46] Preamble (23). Article 8 (1) admits conditions on re-use only insofar as they are "objective, proportionate, non-discriminatory and justified on grounds of a public interest objective."

[47] According to that provision, the directive does not apply to "a) documents the supply of which is an activity falling outside the scope of the public task of the public sector bodies concerned as defined by law or by other binding rules in the Member State, or, in the absence of such rules, as defined in accordance with common administrative practice in the Member State in question, provided that the scope of the public tasks is transparent and subject to review; (b) documents held by public undertakings: (i) produced outside the scope of the provision of services in the general interest as defined by law or other binding rules in the Member State; (ii) related to activities

When documents are available for general access, the Directive lays down that these may be re-used by any type of users, such as business, other public sector bodies or public undertakings, researchers and individuals.[48] This general principle is not universally applicable, either because it is accepted that there are documents which can only be accessed by those demonstrating a particular interest,[49] or because it does not apply to one of the new categories of documents covered. The directive recognises the sensitivity of critical infrastructure and essential services.[50]

In addition to public sector bodies, Directive 2019/1024 introduces two new categories that fall within its scope: 1) public undertakings and 2) public research organisations and publicly funded research data.

Directive 2019/1024 applies to public undertakings acting in the areas defined in Directive 2014/25/EU on procurement (the water, energy, transport and postal services sectors), acting as public service operators, acting as air carriers fulfilling public service obligations, and acting as community shipowners fulfilling public service obligations,[51] with regard to data produced as part of the provision of services in the general interest.[52] The Directive encourages Member States to go further and "to apply the requirements of this Directive to private undertakings, in

directly exposed to competition and therefore, pursuant to Article 34 of Directive 2014/25/EU, not subject to procurement rules; (c) documents for which third parties hold intellectual property rights; (d) documents, such as sensitive data, which are excluded from access by virtue of the access regimes in the Member State, including on grounds of: (i) the protection of national security (namely, State security), defence, or public security; (ii) statistical confidentiality; (iii) commercial confidentiality (including business, professional or company secrets); (e) documents access to which is excluded or restricted on grounds of sensitive critical infrastructure protection related information as defined in point (d) of Article 2 of Directive 2008/114/EC; (f) documents access to which is restricted by virtue of the access regimes in the Member States, including cases whereby citizens or legal entities have to prove a particular interest to obtain access to documents; (g) logos, crests and insignia; (h) documents, access to which is excluded or restricted by virtue of the access regimes on grounds of protection of personal data, and parts of documents accessible by virtue of those regimes which contain personal data the re-use of which has been defined by law as being incompatible with the law concerning the protection of individuals with regard to the processing of personal data or as undermining the protection of privacy and the integrity of the individual, in particular in accordance with Union or national law regarding the protection of personal data; (i) documents held by public service broadcasters and their subsidiaries, and by other bodies or their subsidiaries for the fulfilment of a public service broadcasting remit; (j) documents held by cultural establishments other than libraries, including university libraries, museums and archives; (k) documents held by educational establishments of secondary level and below, and, in the case of all other educational establishments, documents other than those referred to in point (c) of paragraph 1; (l) documents other than those referred to in point (c) of paragraph 1 held by research performing organisations and research funding organisations, including organisations established for the transfer of research results."

[48] Article 3 (1).

[49] Article 1 (2) f).

[50] Article 1 (2) e).

[51] Article 1 (1) b).

[52] Article 1 (2) b) i). This provision excludes documents related to activities directly exposed to competition and therefore not subject to procurement rules.

particular those that provide services of general interest".[53] However, unlike the situation with public sector bodies, the rules do not create an obligation to make information available for re-use. If information is made available for re-use, the rules laid down in Chapters III and IV of the Directive apply,[54] but the administrative burden is lightened (the procedural rules and time limits for responding to requests do not apply and there are exceptions to the obligation to use certain technical means if these are too burdensome).[55]

Public research organisations and publicly funded research data (e.g. the results of experiments, measurements, statistics, observations resulting from fieldwork, survey results, interview recordings and images, but also meta-data, specifications and other digital objects) is the second new category covered by the "Open Data Directive".[56] These are subject to a mandatory policy of open access and re-use,[57] according to the "FAIR principle" and the "open by default" principle, except for publications in scientific journals.[58] To prevent costs and other burdens, the obligations only apply to research data that has already been made publicly available through an institutional or subject-based repository.[59]

The most relevant innovation in the "Open Data Directive" is the focus on dynamic data, high-value datasets, and the availability of datasets through open API.[60] The Directive requires public sector bodies and public undertakings to make dynamic data available for re-use immediately after collection, via suitable APIs and, where relevant, as a bulk download.[61]

Some of this dynamic data is part of a new category of data identified by the 2019 Directive: high-value datasets, i.e. data "with important benefits for society, the environment and the economy".[62] The Directive immediately lists six of these datasets (Annex 1): geospatial; earth observation and environment; meteorological; statistics; companies and company ownership; and mobility. Others may be defined by

[53] Preamble, Recital 19.

[54] Article 3 (2).

[55] Article 4 (6).

[56] Article 1 (1) c).

[57] Article 10 (2). Open access enhances quality, reduces unnecessary duplication of research, speeds up scientific progress, combats scientific fraud, and "it can overall favour economic growth and innovation" (Preamble, Recital 27).

[58] Publications in scientific journals are still excluded because of difficulties related to intellectual property rights.

[59] Article 10 (2).

[60] API should follow the principles of availability, stability, maintenance over lifecycle, uniformity of use and standards, user-friendliness as well as security (Preamble, Recital 32).

[61] Article 5 (5) and 5 (7). If that imposes a disproportionate effort, "those dynamic data shall be made available for re-use within a time frame or with temporary technical restrictions that do not unduly impair the exploitation of their economic and social potential" (Article 5 (6)).

[62] Article 2 (10).

the Commission in a delegated act.[63] High-value datasets should be provided via APIs and, where relevant, as bulk download.[64] Every type of document (written texts, databases, audio files, film fragments) containing information on these matters is covered. Given their importance to the economy and society, these must be available free of charge in machine readable formats.[65] Charges may apply related to the exercise of public authority, in particular certifying the authenticity or veracity of documents,[66] or to ensure fair competition regarding specific high-value datasets held by public undertakings.[67] A two-year transitional period of exemption from the free-of-charge rule may be applied to public sector bodies that are required to generate revenue to cover a substantial part of their costs relating to the performance of their public tasks and that would otherwise suffer a substantial impact on their budgets.[68] High-value datasets made available by libraries, including university libraries, museums and archives are not subject to the free-of-charge rule.[69]

Free-of-charge re-use becomes the rule.[70] It applies without exception to the re-use of publicly funded research data.[71] High-value datasets are also to be made available for re-use free of charge subject to Article 14 (3, 4 and 5).[72] The costs incurred for the reproduction, provision and dissemination of documents as well as for anonymisation of personal data[73] and measures taken to protect commercially confidential information may be charged.[74] Some exceptions are set out: a) public sector bodies that are required to generate revenue to cover a substantial part of their costs relating to the performance of their public tasks; (b) libraries, including university libraries, museums and archives; (c) public undertakings.[75] These institutions may exceptionally recover other costs related to "a reasonable return on investment"[76] (a value of 5% above the ECB's fixed interest rate is deemed adequate).[77] For cultural public bodies, the reasonable return can be benchmarked against the prices charged by similar private entities.[78] Finally, cross-subsidies are

[63] Article 13. The Commission adopted the Implementing Regulation (EU) 2023/138 of 21 December 2022 laying down a list of specific high-value datasets and the arrangements for their publication and re-use. It does not include new datasets.

[64] Article 14 (1).

[65] Article 14 (1).

[66] Preamble, Recital 69.

[67] Article 14 (3).

[68] Article 14 (5).

[69] Article 14 (4).

[70] Article 6 (1).

[71] Article 6 (6) b).

[72] Article 6 (6) a).

[73] For instance, anonymisation has a cost and doubts were raised as to its inclusion.

[74] Article 6 (1).

[75] Article 6 (2).

[76] Article 6 (4) and (5).

[77] Article 2 (16).

[78] Preamble, Recital 38.

forbidden within a public body that performs public tasks and commercial activities; if data resulting from the performance of those public tasks is re-used for the body's commercial activities the same conditions applied to others must apply.[79]

Exclusive arrangements and licencing are better dealt with, especially considering new forms of exclusive arrangements.[80] The Directive lays down conditions and offers solutions, such as digital standard licences.[81] Article 12 (1) sets out a prohibition on exclusive arrangements. The digitisation of cultural resources is not subject to this prohibition[82] and an exclusive right is permitted "for the provision of a service in the public interest", subject to regular review and at least every three years.[83] Exclusive arrangements already in force before 17 July 2013 or 16 July 2019 must be terminated at the end of the contract or at the very latest by 2043 or 2049, respectively.[84]

Directive 2019/1024 regulates intensively procedural issues, including redress. It also establishes a comprehensive set of operational obligations for national authorities and for the bodies covered by the directive: the setting up of arrangements to facilitate the search for documents available for re-use, including cross-linguistic search (*e.g.* online in machine readable format; asset lists of main documents with relevant metadata; portal sites linked to those lists).[85] The processing of requests is subject to a comprehensive regime set out in Article 4, including deadlines for responding to requests.[86] Public undertakings, educational establishments, research performing organisations and research funding organisations are exempt from these obligations. Article 5 emphasises the importance of providing access through electronic means, in formats that are open, machine-readable, accessible, findable and re-usable, together with their metadata, unless this would involve disproportionate effort, going beyond a simple operation. Means of redress must be put in place, including an impartial review body.[87]

The "Open Data Directive" is the culmination of the progressive path started with the "PSI Directive". Access to public data is not guaranteed but it is promoted and enforced according to the "FRAND" principles (Fair, Reasonable and Non-discriminatory). There is a decisive prescriptive advance, mainly relating to procedures. Even though Member States retain the competence to decide which documents should be available for public access, preserving their autonomy with regard to public interest, the Directive establishes an extensive and comprehensive regulatory

[79] Article 11 (2).

[80] Preamble, Recital 4.

[81] Article 8 (2).

[82] Article 12 (2, §2). These exclusive rights shall in general not exceed 10 years. A copy has to be provided to the public body (Article 12 (3)).

[83] Article 12 (2).

[84] Article 12 (5).

[85] Article 9.

[86] Article 4 (2) sets a deadline of 20 days for the delivery of a document or to finalise a licence.

[87] Article 4 (4).

framework that limits and constrains that competence. The extended scope of the entities and documents covered and, especially, the focus on dynamic data and high-value data, an update that is crucial to keep up with the "4th industrial revolution", are of the utmost importance. Nevertheless, there is a serious concern that, because of technical requirements and costs, public sector bodies will decide not to make data available, since access is not mandatory.

The implementation deadline for Member States was 17 July 2021.[88] The Directive's impact is not yet clear and depends on its articulation with the extensive "Data package", which has been in preparation since 2017 with the aim of building a "European data space".

4 Building Global and Sectoral European Data Spaces

4.1 Policy Framework for a Global European Data Space

Data can be regarded as the new production factor, at least as important as capital or labour. It is important to strengthen European competitiveness in the digital sector. A global and comprehensive policy on access and sharing encompassing all types of data is necessary.

Free movement of personal data within the EU is in force. All the necessary safeguards have been put in place by the GDPR and Member States cannot impose restrictive measures to protect that data. Access to and re-use of public data has been enhanced. It is necessary to go further and build a global European data space together with a European data governance framework, the focus of which will be data sharing between businesses and between businesses and public bodies across borders. Most of the data that moves across the internal market and is exchanged is non-personal data, generated by people or by machines. This type of data is more important to businesses and the impact of restrictions on flows is significant (Frontier Economics 2022). There cannot be a truly European data space without considering, alongside access to and re-use of public data, the flow of non-personal data created, processed, and aggregated at every level, whether public or private.

Since 2014, the European Commission has published several policy documents on data. The Communication *Towards a thriving data-driven economy* (European Commission 2014, p. 12) proposes two strands for action: European public-private partnerships, involving the Commission, Member States and the industry to build a data community; building framework conditions through the fostering of open access and support to large-scale technical infrastructures (*e.g.* 5G networks; supercomputing facilities). It recalled that "data location requirements (…) form a barrier to a single market for cloud computing and big data". The 2015 Communication *A*

[88] All Member States communicated implementing measures although some are pre-existing acts. This raises doubts on the adequacy of these measures.

Digital Single Market Strategy for Europe exposed the negative effects of a fragmented data market (European Commission 2015b, p. 14). In 2017, the Commission published the Communication *Building a European data economy* (European Commission 2017b) accompanied by the *Staff Working Document on the free flow of data and emerging issues of the European data economy* (European Commission 2017c).

Even though it is still an emerging market (European Commission 2018a, p. 14), an awareness emerged on the need of regulation to unlock the potential and to respond to the risks of this new data-driven economy. The Commission stated that "the lack of a legal environment adapted to the trade of data within the EU may contribute to insufficient access to large datasets, possible entry barriers to new market entrants, and stifling effects on innovation" and focused its attention on unjustified restrictions on the free movement of data, such as "requirements imposed by public authorities on the location of data for storage or processing purposes" (European Commission 2017b, p. 3). These requirements hinder the internal market freedoms (European Commission 2017b, p. 5), increase the burdens on companies, and may be labelled as "data protectionism". It is necessary to prevent the move towards a "splinternet" based on maps of nation-states (Malcomson 2016). On the other hand, the EU intends to guarantee the strengthening of the "open strategic autonomy of the Union".[89] This concept combines a liberal perspective of data flows with "sovereignty" concerns that emerged in Europe in the light of the absolute dominance of non-European enterprises in this sector.

Restrictions on the free flow of data result from legal or administrative requirements to store private and public data locally, irrespective of its sensitivity or purpose (*e.g.* regulatory, fiscal, privacy, security). Certain data, such as data related to critical infrastructure, may reasonably be subject to location requirements,[90] but the general principle arising from the TFEU and secondary legislation[91] is the "free movement of data within the EU" (European Commission 2017b, p. 7). An analysis of 50 localisation requirements in 21 Member States revealed a global trend of increasing data localisation (European Commission 2017c, pp. 5–6).

Restrictions are also placed by companies, especially the technology giants that hold large quantities of data (European Commission 2017c, p. 15). There is no common legal framework, certainty is lacking and there is a risk of increased divergence between Member States (European Commission 2017b, pp. 9–11; 2017c, pp. 22–25). Portability issues, especially for business and non-personal data, have also received attention (European Commission 2017b, p. 15).

In 2018, the European Commission provided a thorough analysis of the European data economy. It identified two broad groups of legal barriers: contractual (*e.g.* 'data ownership' and restrictions on access to and (re-)use of data) and non-contractual

[89] Recital 1 of the Preamble of Regulation 2022/868 ("Data Governance Act").

[90] Localisation and security are not necessarily linked.

[91] For instance, the GDPR rules, Directive 2000/31/EC (the E-commerce Directive), Directive 2006/123/EC (the Services Directive) and, as regards draft technical regulations and draft rules on Information Society Services, Directive 2015/1535 (the Transparency Directive).

(*e.g.* extra-contractual liability) (European Commission 2018a, pp. 15 and 176). Other barriers were highlighted, such as the lack of skills or the unequal bargaining power between stakeholders. The removal of these barriers is considered fundamental to grasp the economic potential of data. At the same time, the Commission stressed the need to prevent risks to consumers, citizens, or the public interest. It put forward as the best choices several policy options and recommended the adoption of horizontal non-legislative measures, such as awareness-raising measures, sharing of best practices, funding research etc., that are either sector-specific, cross-sectoral or general (pp. 13, 15 and 177). Following this approach, the Commission published the Communication *Towards a common European data space* (European Commission 2018e), a guide on data sharing between businesses and between businesses and the public sector (European Commission 2018f), and updated the Recommendation on access to and preservation of scientific information (European Commission 2018g).

In 2020, the Commission published the *European Strategy for Data*[92] ("ESD") (European Commission 2020a) intended to enable the data economy for the coming five years. This document lays down the overarching vision of the Commission and the policy roadmap to make the EU "the most attractive, most secure and most dynamic data-agile economy in the world – empowering Europe with data to improve decisions and better the lives of all of its citizens" (European Commission 2020a, p. 25).

The potential benefits to be derived from the data economy are highlighted with a recommendation that data should become universally available while protecting the interests of the individual in accordance with European values, fundamental rights and rules (European Commission 2020a, pp. 1 and 4). Governance structures for handling data are identified as a policy objective in order to create a "single European data space" which is both secure and open. This data space should "ensure that: (i) data can flow within the EU and across sectors; (ii) European rules and values, in particular personal data protection, consumer protection legislation and competition law, are fully respected; (iii) the rules for access to and use of data are fair, practical and clear, and there are clear and trustworthy data governance mechanisms in place; (iv) there is an open, but assertive approach to international data flows, based on European values" (European Commission 2020a, p. 5).

The Commission highlights several issues. One is the importance of an active industrial policy and funding to improve technologies and infrastructures to support the creation of European data pools enabling Big Data analytics and machine learning. A global approach should be accompanied by sector specific approaches in areas such as manufacturing, agriculture, health and mobility, which are labelled as "strategic" areas. Another issue is the multi-level relevance of data re-use: G2B (public sector/government-held data to business to foster innovation in products and services); B2B (private and business-held data to business); B2G (private and business-held data to government to inform public policies); G2G (public sector/government-to-government). Each of these levels has specific shortcomings and

[92] This document is part of a "three pack" also including the Communication "Shaping Europe's Digital Future" and the "White Paper on AI".

challenges, such as market imbalances, interoperability, governance organisation, respect for fundamental rights or cybersecurity (European Commission 2020a, pp. 6–11).

The programme is built on four pillars: A. A cross-sectoral governance framework for data access and use; B. Enablers: Investments in data and strengthening Europe's capabilities and infrastructures for hosting, processing and using data, interoperability; C. Competences: Empowering individuals, investing in skills and in SMEs; D. Common European data spaces in strategic sectors and domains of public interest.

In Pillar A, to prevent the stifling of innovation, the Commission states that it abstains "from overly detailed, heavy-handed ex ante regulation, and will prefer an agile approach to governance that favours experimentation (such as regulatory sandboxes), iteration, and differentiation". The governance priorities are "to support decisions on what data can be used in which situations, facilitate cross-border data use, and prioritise interoperability requirements and standards within and across sectors", to make more high-quality public sector data available for re-use,[93] to provide incentives for horizontal data sharing across sectors (for instance, related to co-generated IoT data) on a voluntary basis and based on stakeholder horizontal guidelines, and to approach liability issues. Competition is a concern, and the Commission states its commitment to reviewing the existing self-regulatory framework for cloud provider switching (SWIPO) and to following the work of the Observatory of the Online Platforms Economy over "Big Tech" companies. The Commission also admits the possibility of adopting legislation "to address more systemic issues (…) to ensure that markets stay open and fair", and pledges to lead this move through the EU Open Data Portal[94] and the European Open Science Cloud (European Commission 2020a, pp. 12–15).

In Pillar B, the aim is to build an environment that supports data-driven innovation and strengthens the EU's technological sovereignty, in co-ordination with the Member States. The EU will invest funds and focus on next-generation infrastructures for data processing, standard setting, tool development and best practices collection on how to deal with personal data (especially pseudonymisation).[95] The approach to be adopted will be soft, horizontal and coordinated, involving Member States and stakeholders.[96] One of the instruments involved is the *Multi-Country*

[93] The Annex of the Implementing Regulation 2023/138 includes a list of High value Datasets and the arrangements for their re-use in the following areas: Geospatial, Earth observation and environment, Meteorological, Statistics, Companies and company ownership, Mobility.

[94] In 2021, the portal data.europa.eu (https://data.europa.eu/en) consolidated the *EU Open Data Portal* and the *European Data Portal*.

[95] Within the strategic EU investments in new technologies and as part of its industrial strategy, the Commission mentions a "High Impact Project on European data spaces and federated cloud infrastructures" to implement in the period 2021–2027.

[96] The Commission spoke of *Memoranda of Understanding* with Member States on cloud federation and of an EU (self-)regulatory cloud rulebook. On 15 October 2020, all Member States signed the *Declaration on European Cloud*. In 2021, the *European Alliance on Industrial Data and Cloud* was set up by the *Declaration of the European Alliance for Industrial Data, Edge and Cloud*. The

Project (MCP) in European Common Data Infrastructure and Services, which combines investments from the EU budget, Member States and industry, building on the Recovery and Resilience Facility and other EU funding (European Commission 2020a, pp. 16–20).

In Pillar C, the Commission recognises the need to empower individuals with digital skills and literacy. It admits the possible development of safe "personal data spaces" by way of secure and universally usable digital identities or by granting neutral broker status to providers of personal data spaces. Certain concerns are noted, for example, the effectiveness of the portability right enshrined in Article 20 of the GDPR and the control over who can access and use machine-generated data related to individuals, such as that generated from smart devices and home appliances. Capacity building for SMEs and start-ups through a favourable regulatory approach and funding programmes is also mentioned (European Commission 2020a, pp. 20–21).

Pillar D aims, through common data spaces, to increase the availability of large pools of data in strategic economic sectors and domains of public interest where the use of data will have systemic impact on the entire ecosystem and on citizens. The Commission states that it will support the creation of nine common European data spaces, in addition to the European Open Science Cloud already in existence. This list of nine comprises a Common European industrial (manufacturing) data space; a Common European Green Deal data space; a Common European mobility data space; a Common European health data space; a Common European financial data space; a Common European energy data space; a Common European agriculture data space; Common European data spaces for public administration; and a Common European skills data space. Others may follow in other sectors (European Commission 2020a, pp. 22–23[97]) and in 2024 there are initiatives in 14 sectors (https://digital-strategy.ec.europa.eu/pt/policies/data-spaces).

Finally, the Commission outlines its desire for the EU to lead international cooperation and shape data standards in accordance with European rules and values, an approach labelled as "open but assertive" (European Commission 2020a, pp. 23–24). One problematic area it wishes to address are foreign extraterritorial jurisdictional claims to grant access to EU-generated data stored outside the EU, and even in the EU, without a guarantee of respect for Union rules.

The aim of the "ESD" is to build a European Data Space through the establishment of general enhancing conditions and the development of sectoral European data spaces with infrastructure and governance frameworks to facilitate data pooling and sharing. These data spaces must follow certain design principles: data

Declaration is continuously open to the adherence of industry, national and local public authorities, civil society and other stakeholders that are relevant to the data processing value chain. See https://ec.europa.eu/eusurvey/runner/EU-Cloud-Alliance. Nonetheless, this venture is now seen as a failure. See https://ainowinstitute.org/publications/xi-why-europes-cloud-ambitions-have-failed. Amazon Web Services (AWS), Microsoft Azure, and Google Cloud Platform (GCP) dominate around 62% share of the world cloud storage (Statista, 2025).

[97] The Appendix details the objectives and the initiatives to be taken.

control of the data subject/holder; appropriate governance; respect for EU rules and values; reliable technical infrastructure; interconnection and interoperability through the development of standards; openness to all relevant actors.

In February 2022, the Commission published an overview of the common European data spaces that are being developed in various sectors or domains (European Commission 2022a). The document analyses the ten sectoral common European data spaces provided for in the "European Data Strategy" and other common European data spaces, in the media sector (launched in December 2020), and for cultural heritage (launched in November 2021). It also acknowledges the developments in course in other sectors, such as tourism and construction. A second review was presented in the Commission Staff Working Document on Common European Data Spaces, SWD(2024) 21 final, Brussels, 24.01.2024, published in January 2024.

4.2 *The "Free Flow Regulation"*

In 2017, the Commission published the Proposal for a Regulation on a framework for the free flow of non-personal data in the European Union (European Commission 2017d). It was accompanied by a working document (European Commission 2017e).

The objectives were to improve the mobility of non-personal data across the internal market, and to foster portability for professional users of data storage and processing services, while keeping a balance with the needs of regulatory controls and audit by the supervisory authorities (European Commission 2017d, p. 2). The proposal envisaged a positive effect on competition and innovation in data storage or other processing services, making it easier to enter new markets, particularly for new and small service providers, as well as the promotion of cross-border and cross-sector use of data storage or other processing services and the development of the data market. It also sought to create new opportunities for European citizens, businesses and public administrations (European Commission 2017d, p. 8), through a uniform general legal framework in order to ensure certainty and build trust, with a mix of prescriptive rules and self-regulatory measures facilitated by the Commission.

Regulation 2018/1807 on a framework for the free flow of non-personal data in the European Union (the "Free Flow Regulation") was enacted on 14 November 2018 and has been in force since 28 May 2019. With the GDPR, the "Open Data Directive" and the "Free Flow Regulation", there is now almost complete freedom of movement for data in the EU.[98]

[98] The articulation between these acts is important since often personal and non-personal data are present simultaneously in datasets, whether public or private. The Commission was mandated by Regulation 2018/1807 to publish informative guidance on how to handle data sets composed of both personal and non-personal data (Preamble, Recital 37). That was done on 29 May 2019 through the Communication "Guidance on the Regulation on a framework for the free flow of non-personal data in the EU", COM(2019)250 (European Commission 2019).

The "Free Flow Regulation" outlines two types of obstacles to data mobility and the internal market: "data localisation requirements put in place by Member States' authorities and vendor lock-in practices in the private sector".[99] Data localisation requirements encompass different restrictions, resulting from the obligation to locate or process data in a specific territory or to use technological facilities that are certified or approved within a specific Member State, and constitute a restriction on the freedom to provide services or on freedom of establishment. Some public policy reasons may justify such rules.[100] Regarding the second obstacle, although freedom of contract applies to data location and processing, there can be vendor lock-in effects. The legality of such State or contract rules is not clear and there are demands for regulatory intervention to guarantee a level playing field in the EU. The fact that the general rules of the Treaty apply, as well as secondary legislation, does not prevent legal uncertainty that case-by-case decisions by the ECJ cannot remedy. A uniform framework is necessary,[101] but this should involve a flexible principle-based approach and self-regulation.[102]

The main objective is "the free flow of data other than personal data within the Union".[103] This category of data is defined by exclusion: non-personal data is data other than personal data as defined by the GDPR,[104] and encompasses two categories of data: sensor-generated data from devices not related to persons (*e.g.* sensors to measure weather conditions); data that was personal but has been anonymised and is no longer attributable to a specific person.[105]

The Regulation limits its own scope. It does not apply to activities which are not covered by Union law.[106] The purpose of this clarification is to assert the respect for Member States' competences according to Article 4 (2) TEU. The Regulation encourages[107] but does not require State authorities to outsource data processing activities to the private sector. Where they do so, they are subject to the regulation.[108]

It covers electronic processing in EU territory of non-personal data relating to natural persons or public or private legal persons, residing or established in the Union, regardless of whether the processing is done by that same person or provided

[99] Preamble, Recital 2.

[100] The Regulation mentions internal and external public security, referring to the meaning of that concept in the case-law of the ECJ (Preamble, Recital 19). Data location is often seen as a "proxy for data security", which does not correspond to reality (Preamble, Recital 33).

[101] Preamble, Recital 7.

[102] Preamble, Recital 11. There are no technical details.

[103] Article 1.

[104] Article 2(1) and Article 3(1).

[105] Anonymisation is a difficult task and demands state-of-the-art techniques to prevent re-identification. On this, see Article 29 Data Protection Working Party (2014, p. 9).

[106] Article 2 (3).

[107] Preamble, Recital 14.

[108] Article 2 (3, § 2).

as a service by a third person, established in the Union or otherwise.[109] On the other hand, there is no uniform regime vis-à-vis third countries and no claim of extraterritorial scope. The Regulation does not apply to the processing of data outside the EU and to localisation requirements related to that processing. It does not rule out any Member States' restrictions on the free flow of data to any territory outside the EU.[110]

The rules of the "GDPR" are upheld.[111] Notwithstanding, mixed datasets, composed of personal and non-personal data, raise difficult issues regarding clarity. Article 2 (2) lays down the general rule: the Regulation applies to the non-personal data part of the dataset; if personal and non-personal data are inextricably linked, the GDPR applies to the whole mixed dataset.[112]

Regulation 2018/1807 lays down the general principle of free movement of non-personal data within the Union.[113] The arrangements put in place give effect to this principle in a twin-track approach. The first is directed at Member States, while the second is directed at private operators.

According to Article 4 (1), localisation requirements on data are prohibited. These requirements are "any obligation, prohibition, condition, limit or other requirement provided for in the laws, regulations or administrative provisions of a Member State or resulting from general and consistent administrative practices in a Member State and in bodies governed by public law, including in the field of public procurement (…) which imposes the processing of data in the territory of a specific Member State or hinders the processing of data in any other Member State".[114] A data owner or holder may contract a data processing service at any location within the Union and can move his/her/its data to any location within the Union.

Some localisation requirements are lawful and exempt from the general prohibition. Member States can impose these for public security reasons, subject to proportionality. The concept of "public security" is defined according to the case law.[115] Such measures must be enshrined in a general legal act and publicised via an online information point.[116] Existing location requirements which did not comply with

---

[109] Article 2 (1).

[110] Article 1.

[111] The "GDPR" lays down the conditions for the transfer of personal data to third countries.

[112] For criticism see Graef et al. (2018). If only the GDPR applies, intellectual property rights and trade secrets may ultimately be unprotected (Baloup 2022). The "Data Governance Act" and the "Data Act" seek to overcome that shortcoming.

[113] Article 4.

[114] Article 3 (5). Directive 2014/24/EU on procurement is upheld.

[115] Preamble (19). See judgment of the Court of Justice of 23 November 2010, *Land Baden-Württemberg v Tsakouridis*, C-145/09, ECLI:EU:C:2010:708, paragraph 43; judgment of 4 April 2017, *Sahar Fahimian v Bundesrepublik Deutschland*, C-544/15, ECLI:EU:C:2017:225, paragraph 39; judgment of the Court of Justice of 22 December 2008, *Commission of the European Communities v Republic of Austria*, C-161/07, ECLI:EU:C:2008:759, paragraph 35 and case law referred to therein; judgment of 26 March 2009, *Commission of the European Communities v Italian Republic*, C-326/07, ECLI:EC:C:2009:193, paragraph 70 and case law referred to therein.

[116] Article 4 (4).

these conditions had to be repealed by 30 May 2021.[117] The Regulation puts in place a preventive control, in accordance with Directive 2015/1535, for new measures of Member States that introduce or change localisation requirements.[118]

The second path to secure the free flow of data is the enhancement of non-personal data portability. The objective is to reduce the risks of vendor lock-in practices in the cloud market and to facilitate competition between cloud service providers. Lock-in practices may result from specific data formats or contractual arrangements. In this respect, the Regulation limits itself to "soft rules" that encourage the Commission to facilitate the adoption of codes of conduct and the exchange of best practices by the data industry, namely open standards.

The right to portability[119] of the personal data subject means that data controllers have a duty to transfer the personal data to the data subject or to another controller in a structured, commonly used and machine-readable format, according to the will of the data subject. There is no similar right under the "Free Flow Regulation". Non-personal data portability will be subject to private contractual arrangements following the adoption of expected voluntary, self-regulatory codes of conduct. Transparency and interoperability are the main principles in this regard[120] and a "soft" data porting principle aims to ensure that users, consumers and enterprises face no difficulties in choosing a data service provider and moving their data anywhere in the EU.

To fulfil that purpose SWIPO (*Switching Cloud Service Providers and Porting Data*) was created and has published the *Code of Conduct for Infrastructure as a Service* (IaaS) (SWIPO AISBL 2020a) and the *Code of Conduct for Software as a Service* (SaaS) (SWIPO AISBL 2020b), with best practices and information requirements to ensure that cloud service providers supply their customers with sufficiently detailed, clear and transparent information before a cloud service agreement is entered into. SWIPO AISBL, a multi-stakeholder association that now brings together 23 members from the industry, oversees the maintenance and development of these codes of conduct. More recently, SWIPO has created a Body for Complaints and a Body of Appeals and the respective procedures for complaints and appeals (SWIPO AISBL 2021).

Supervision and control by States for legitimate purposes (*e.g.* fiscal) is not overlooked. The authorities of Member States are entitled to obtain access to data "for the performance of their official duties in accordance with Union or national law" even if the storage and processing is done in another Member State.[121] If there is not voluntary cooperation from the service provider, the Member State authorities can use existing European or international cooperation mechanisms or, in the absence of

[117] Article 4 (3).

[118] Article 4 (2).

[119] Regarding the "right to portability", see Graef et al. (2019).

[120] Article 6 (1).

[121] Article 5 (1).

these, the procedure laid down in Article 7 of the Regulation consisting of a platform of contact points between the Member States and the Commission.[122]

The Regulation has been in force since 18 December 2018 and its rules have applied since 18 June 2019. Member States must designate a "Single information point" and a "Single information contact". Some have not (until 20 June 2025).[123]

To provide clarification on some of the difficult issues, such as anonymisation of personal data, mixed datasets, or localisation requirements, Article 8 (3) requires the Commission to publish informative guidance, which it did in the Communication *Guidance on the Regulation on a framework for the free flow of non-personal data in the European Union* (European Commission 2019).

Regarding the complex issue of re-identification of anonymised personal data and the interaction between non-personal and personal data, if there is any possibility, directly or indirectly, of relating any data to a natural person, making that person identifiable, such data must be considered personal and the GDPR applies (p. 7).[124]

In mixed datasets, personal and non-personal data can be considered "inextricably linked" for technical or economic reasons, such as significant costs or the decrease in value of the dataset resulting from the separation of the two types of data (p. 10).[125] There is no obligation to separate personal and non-personal data but not doing so means the GDPR rules will apply to the whole dataset.

The Communication expands on the definition of localisation requirements and distinguishes between direct and indirect requirements. Examples of the former are the obligation to store data in a specific geographic location or to comply with unique national technical requirements. Indirect localisation requirements "may include requirements to use technological facilities that are certified or approved within a specific Member State or other requirements that have the effect of making it more difficult to process data outside of a specific geographic area or territory within the European Union" (pp. 11–12) and an analysis of the specific circumstances of the case will be necessary. The Communication offers some enlightening examples (pp. 14–15). It also brings clarity on public security reasons that may justify localisation requirements (pp. 12–13). Public security covers internal and

[122] If necessary, in the case of abuse of rights, Member State authorities may take interim measures, including temporary re-localisation requirements, pursuant to Article 5 (4, § 2).

[123] See https://europa.eu/youreurope/business/running-business/developing-business/free-flow-non-personal-data/index_en.htm.

[124] For instance, data in a quality report on a production line, because it can be related to specific workers, or a legal person name which is the same as that of the natural person that is its owner. On this issue, see judgment of the Court of Justice of 9 November 2010 in joint cases *Volker und Markus Schecke GbR* and *Hartmut Eifert* v Land Hessen, C-92/09 and C-93/09, ECLI:EU:C:2010:662, paragraph 52; judgment of the Court of Justice of 19 October 2016, *Patrick Breyer v. Bundesrepublik Deutschland*, C 582/14, ECLI:EU:C:2016:779.

[125] Health datasets are an example of mixed datasets. A Draft Code of Conduct on privacy for mobile health applications was published (https://digital-strategy.ec.europa.eu/en/library/code-conduct-privacy-mhealth-apps-has-been-finalised). The importance of health datasets for medical research and for health policy purposes requires creative solutions to ensure GDPR compliance, such as "data altruism".

external security but "presupposes the existence of a genuine and sufficiently serious threat affecting one of the fundamental interests of society, such as a threat to the functioning of institutions and essential public services and the survival of the population, as well as the risk of a serious disturbance to foreign relations or the peaceful coexistence of nations, or a risk to military interests".

The Communication also provides some clarification on the free flow of personal data governed by the GDPR, which is not without controversy. The protection of personal data cannot be a reason for restrictions on the free flow of such data, including sensitive genetic data, and biometric and health data. Other reasons shall be assessed in the light of the freedoms, principles and rules of the internal market and EU law.[126]

Finally, the Communication indicates the criteria which should inform the codes of conduct to be adopted (p. 17) regarding non-personal data and personal data (pp. 19–21)[127] and it clarifies the scope of portability in the "Free Flow Regulation" and the GDPR (pp. 18–19). In the former, portability relates to business-to-business interactions between a professional user (regarding its own data but also to personal and non-personal data of natural persons that is in the possession of that professional user) and a service provider that falls within the scope of Article 6, and the application of the GDPR is not excluded, namely regarding mixed datasets.

4.3 The "Data Governance Act"

Following the proposal of the European Commission (European Commission 2020b), Regulation 2022/868 on European data governance was enacted on 30 May 2022 and has been in force since 23 June 2022 ("Data Governance Act", "DGA").

This Regulation intends to build a "European way of data governance", to overcome legal fragmentation and to put in place institutional and technological requirements to ensure a "human-centric, trustworthy and secure data society and

[126] Such as Directive 2006/123/EC and Directive 2000/31/EC and the future Digital Market Act and Digital Services Act. See judgment of the Court of Justice of 19 June 2008, *Commission of the European Communities v Grand Duchy of Luxemburg*, C-319/06, ECLI:EU:C:2008:350, paragraphs 90–91 (the Court considered that an obligation to keep available and retain certain documents in a particular Member State constitutes a restriction on the freedom to provide services; a justification that it is 'generally easier for the authorities to perform their supervisory tasks' is not sufficient).

[127] The European Data Protection Board published its *Guidelines 1/2019 on Codes of Conduct and Monitoring Bodies under the General Data Protection Regulation*, available online at: https://edpb.europa.eu/our-work-tools/our-documents/guidelines/guidelines-12019-codes-conduct-and-monitoring-bodies-under_en. Several sectoral codes of conduct were adopted, namely the *EU Cloud Code of Conduct* (https://eucoc.cloud/en/home), the *Code of Conduct of the Cloud Infrastructure Services Providers in Europe (CISPE)* (https://cispe.cloud/code-of-conduct/), and the *Cloud Security Alliance's Code of Conduct for GDPR Compliance* (available at https://cloudsecurityalliance.org/privacy/gdpr/).

economy",[128] reducing the digital divide and promoting inclusiveness for all Union citizens, especially women, and enabling the capacities of SMEs and start-ups.[129] The main objectives of the European data policy are "data access neutrality", "data portability", "interoperability" and "avoiding lock-in effects".[130]

It supplements the "Open Data Directive", the "Free Flow Regulation", and the GDPR. It lays down "hard" and "soft" rules outlining the conditions for the re-use of data held by public sector bodies associated with their public tasks that was not considered in the "Open Data Directive":[131] personal data not covered by Directive 2019/1024 and data protected on the grounds of commercial and statistical confidentiality and the protection of intellectual property rights of third parties,[132] without prejudice to the legislation that protects such data.[133] Public sector bodies are encouraged to facilitate re-use of data protected by copyright.

The regulation enshrines the prohibition of exclusive arrangements with a possible derogation, if necessary, for the provision of a service or the supply of a product in the general interest "that would not otherwise be possible".[134]

An important rule to ensure wider access to data is the prohibition on public bodies of exercising the *sui generis* right over databases as provided for in Article 7 (1) of Directive 96/9/EC to prevent or restrict re-use of data.[135]

There is a single rule on the request procedure, and it imposes a deadline of two months for public sector bodies to grant or refuse re-use.[136] The Regulation enshrines a right to redress with review from an independent administrative or judicial body.[137]

The aim is to enhance availability of data without hampering legally protected rights and interests. Justified and objective conditions for re-use can be imposed, subject to publicity, non-discrimination, transparency, and proportionality.[138] If consent from the data subject or data holder is necessary, the public sector body shall use its best efforts to provide assistance in obtaining that consent.[139] Notwithstanding, the protected nature of the data must be preserved.[140] This can be done through

---

[128] Recital 3.

[129] Recital 2.

[130] Recital 2.

[131] Article 1 (1) a).

[132] Article 3 (1).

[133] Besides the GDPR, Regulation 2016/943 on the lawful acquisition, use or disclosure of trade secrets. At the level of primary law, Article 8 and Article 17 of the Charter (right to property).

[134] Article 4 (points 1, 2). The granting of the exclusive right to re-use data is subject to the principles of transparency, equal treatment and non-discrimination and limited to 12 months (points 3, 4 and 5). There is a transitional period for existing arrangements (point 6).

[135] Article 5 (7).

[136] Article 9 (1). If the request is exceptionally complex and extensive that period may be extended by up to 30 days.

[137] Article 9 (2).

[138] Article 5 (1), (2).

[139] Article 5 (6).

[140] Article 5 (3).

anonymisation and prohibition of re-identification in the case of personal data and a method of disclosure control, such as aggregation or modification, for other protected data.[141] Another possibility is to impose access and re-use in a secure processing environment[142] or within the physical premises of the public sector body.[143]

Although this is a particularly important step in structuring a "European data space", it continues to follow the limited and incremental approach. There is no imperative on public sector bodies to make access available and the Act respects any conditions laid down in Union and national law.[144] Moreover, the scope of exclusions is extensive: data held by public undertakings, public service broadcasters, cultural and educational establishments; data protected for reasons of public security, defence or national security.[145] Member States may decide to extend its application to public or private undertakings that exercise public sector duties or provide services of general interest. The Regulation does not apply to the exchange of data within the exercise of public duties between public sector bodies and the exchange of data between researchers for non-commercial research purposes, including across the Union, with third countries or international organisations.

The concerns of public bodies regarding the financial costs related to compliance with the requirements and the conditions to preserve the rights and interests of data subjects or data holders leads to the absence of a "free of charge principle".[146] Nevertheless, fees must correspond to the costs borne to preserve legally protected rights and interests and the costs of reproduction and dissemination. These costs must be transparent, non-discriminatory, proportionate and objectively justified, and they must not restrict competition. There should be a special consideration for SMEs and start-ups, civil society and educational establishments with free of charge or discounted fees.[147]

The most significant innovation in building a trustworthy European data space is the creation of new types of organisations for the provision of data services: the "Data Intermediation Services Provider" and the "Data Altruism Organisation". These organisations are expected to promote data availability while improving transparency, control and trust for data subjects and data holders.[148]

---

[141] A confidentiality obligation is referred to in Article 5 (5).

[142] Following the model of Regulation 557/2013 as regards access to confidential data for scientific purposes.

[143] Article 5 (3). The last possibility is permitted only if remote access "cannot be allowed without jeopardising the rights and interests of third parties", and there is a strict obligation on the public body to impose conditions to preserve the integrity of the protection of the data, including the right to verify the process, the means and results and to prohibit the use of results that may have that jeopardising effect (Article 5 (4)).

[144] Article 1 (2).

[145] Article 3 (2).

[146] Article 6 regulates fees.

[147] Article 6 (4).

[148] Recital 5.

"Data intermediation services providers" connect public and private data subjects/holders and data users and facilitate the pooling and sharing of data, including through the creation of platforms, databases and data cooperatives,[149] and can also offer additional services, such as temporary storage, conversion, curation, anonymisation, etc. A specific category of intermediation services intends to enhance the control that data subjects have over their data, assisting them in exercising their rights, including through the offer of a "personal data space" to safely process their data. Intermediation services provision must be fair, transparent and non-discriminatory, and is subject to several other conditions set out in Article 12. Data intermediation services providers should be neutral and not use the data exchange for any other purpose. These new organisations may be market data places brokers or data orchestrators of data pools and may become the hub of sector and cross-sectoral data spaces.

Before providing their services, "data intermediation services providers" are required to submit a notification to the competent authority of the Member State where their main establishment is located (or their legal representative for third country providers)[150] and they may subsequently provide those services across the EU under the monitoring and supervision of that authority,[151] which include the power to require postponement of commencement of the service provision, its suspension, or the cessation of any infringement, with the potential imposition of financial penalties.[152] A label "data intermediation services provider recognised in the Union" may be used and a *logo* was created by Commission Implementing Regulation (EU) 2023/1622 of 9 August 2023.[153] A harmonised regulatory framework and voluntary codes of conduct, together with the development of standards for intermediation services, should contribute to a "European way of data governance",[154] separating data provision, data intermediation and data use.

The other particularly interesting innovation is the category of non-profit "Data altruism organisations". Member States must facilitate their establishment through organisational and technical arrangements.[155] These add to organisational and technical tools and initiatives put in place by Member States to increase informed consent for the sharing of data (with compensation limited to the costs incurred with the sharing) by data subjects/holders, especially in general interest domains such as health care, mobility, etc.

[149] Article 10. Article 12 sets the conditions to prevent conflicts of interest.

[150] Article 11. The information to provide in the notification is laid down in point 6.

[151] Assistance and cooperation from competent authorities of other Member States is enshrined in Article 14 (7).

[152] Article 34 sets outs the principles and criteria that Member States must respect when they approve the penalties applicable to infringements. These should be effective, proportionate and dissuasive.

[153] Article 11 (9). Until 26 June 2025 there were 24 registered organisations in six Member States. See https://digital-strategy.ec.europa.eu/en/policies/data-intermediary-services.

[154] Recital 32.

[155] Article 16.

Registered "Data altruism organisations"[156] could establish trans-European data repositories and data pools and provide a secure processing environment. They must provide tools for obtaining consent and permission to process the data made available by data subjects/holders and for easy withdrawal of that consent/permission.[157] The right balance between the right of withdrawal and the altruistic purpose demanding some stability and predictability is difficult. The label "Data altruism organisation recognised in the Union"[158] and the common *logo*[159], approved in 2023, can improve trust and therefore increase the consent of data subjects/holders to allow the re-use of personal and non-personal data for purposes of common interest. The registration of a data altruism organisation is subject to several requirements:[160] it has to be a recognised non-profit legal person with general interest objectives according to national law; it has to be independent from any for-profit entities (therefore not applicable to enterprise associations); it has to carry out its data altruistic activities through a structure that is separate from its other possible activities; it cannot use the data for objectives other than those of common interest for which the data subject or data holder allow the processing.[161]

Transparency requirements are extremely important in "Data altruism organisations".[162] There is a detailed duty to inform data subjects/holders regarding the objectives of common interest and legitimate purpose for processing and the location of processing in a third country.[163] The competent authority for the registration of "Data altruistic organisations" shall monitor and supervise compliance with the requirements laid down in the regulation[164] and shall have the power to require the cessation of any infringement, to withdraw the right to use the label "Data

[156] Registration and its conditions are ruled under Article 19. Member States must put in place a public national registry of recognised data altruism organisations established or with their main establishment in their territory. Entities not established in the Union must designate a legal representative, pursuant to Article 19 (3). The registration is valid in all Member States (point 5). Until the 26 June 2024 only one was registered (in Spain). See https://digital-strategy.ec.europa.eu/en/policies/data-altruism-organisations.

[157] Article 21 (3).

[158] Article 17 (2).

[159] The label and the logo are established in line with the procedure referred to in Article 33 (2). They have been approved by the Commission Implementing Regulation (EU) 2023/1622 of 9 August 2023 on the design of common logos to identify data intermediation services providers and data altruism organisations recognised in the Union (see https://digital-strategy.ec.europa.eu/en/library/logos-data-intermediaries-and-data-altruism-organisations-recognised-union).

[160] Articles 18, 20 and 21.

[161] Article 21 (2). Until 26 June 2025 only one Data altruism organisation was registered, in Spain. See https://digital-strategy.ec.europa.eu/en/policies/data-altruism-organisations. It seems the mood is not for altruism, even if people and corporations are daily offering their data for free to digital platforms. The complexity of the regime may help to explain the failure.

[162] Articles 20 and 21 require records and annual activity reports to be kept.

[163] Article 21 (1) and (6).

[164] Article 24.

altruism organisation recognised by the Union" and to remove the organisation from the national register.[165]

A European consent form for altruistic purposes should be developed.[166] A delegated act of the Commission should propose a rulebook with information, technical and security requirements, communication roadmaps and interoperability standards.[167] The procedures of notification and registration should take place online and in a cross-border manner, through the single digital gateway established pursuant to Regulation 2018/1724. These procedures are added to Annex II of that regulation.

The last important focus is the flow of data to third countries. The "DGA" explicitly states that it intends to strengthen "the open strategic autonomy of the Union".[168] The world of data is global, yet there are no general international rules on data, only "soft" initiatives or bilateral agreements. Following on from the GDPR, the EU began building a framework for non-personal data in 2018 through bilateral agreements and a unilateral assessment through "Adequacy Decisions". The "Free Flow Regulation" did not lay down rules on international transfers of data. The "DGA" refers to respect for international agreements on the protection of the category of data encompassed under the regulation, such as TRIPS.[169]

"Open" means admitting international free flow of data, although in line with European values and fundamental rights[170] and subject to public policy exceptions or restrictions or the necessary conditions to respect the rights and interests of data subjects/holders, such as IP rights and trade secrets. "Strategic autonomy" in the EU stands for "sovereignty",[171] both at policy level and regarding the data subject/holder, meaning "independence and freedom to choose".

The conditions for data transfer to third countries are quite strict and are laid down in Article 5 (points 9 to 14) and Article 31. The international transfer of non-personal data protected by IP and trade secrets by a re-user of public sector data is subject to rules similar to those used for personal data. The re-user must inform the public body of that intention and the purpose of the transfer when making the request and it may be necessary to have permission from the data subject/holder.[172] "Data intermediation services providers" must provide information to data subjects/

---

[165] Article 24 (4).

[166] Article 25.

[167] Article 22. The initiative.

[168] Recital 1. On the importance of this act for the international transfer of non-personal data, see Baloup (2021, 2022).

[169] Article 3 (3) a).

[170] Recital 62 refers especially to the right to privacy, the protection of personal data, the freedom to conduct a business, the right to property and the integration of persons with disabilities (regarding the latter, the Regulation highlights the standard "Design for all in ICT").

[171] The Digital Assembly of 2022, co-organised by the European Commission and the French Presidency, focused on EU sovereignty and autonomy (https://digital-strategy.ec.europa.eu/en/events/digital-assembly-2022-closer-look-digital-future).

[172] Article 5 (9).

holders if data re-use is to take place in a third country and tools to give or withdraw the consent or permission.

The Commission may adopt implementing acts establishing model contractual clauses or "Adequacy Decisions"[173] that confirm the existence in a third country of an equivalent protection system.[174] If there is no "Adequacy Decision"[175] regarding legal, supervisory and enforcement arrangements of that third country, the re-user must commit to respecting intellectual property rights and confidentiality obligations after the transfer and to accepting the jurisdiction of the courts of the Member State of the public sector body.[176] This is a "soft" extraterritorial claim of EU law. This requirement could constitute a severe constraint on the industry but with the dissemination of edge computing processing and analytics, transfer loses relevance.

Certain data categories, to be determined in a delegated act of the Commission, such as safety and public health data or other types of highly sensitive data (where there is a risk of re-identification of non-personal, anonymised data), will be subject to special conditions and restrictions on international transfer to third countries.[177]

If the requirements set out in Article 5 (10), (12) and (13) are not met, there cannot be any international transfer of data to third countries.[178] The Union is thus attempting to infuse the "European way" and expects the so-called "Brussels effect" to result from deployment of its normative power. For some authors, the conditions imposed may conflict with international treaty obligations.[179]

There is some concern regarding third country rules that allow governmental access to non-personal data no matter where it is stored (extraterritorial claims).[180] Such access should be based on an international agreement or include the provision

---

[173] For a critical view of this "Adequacy system", see Baloup (2021, 2022).

[174] Article 5 (11) (12). The Commission has adopted several "Adequacy Decisions" related to personal data (https://ec.europa.eu/info/law/law-topic/data-protection/international-dimension-data-protection/adequacy-decisions_en). The EDPB published recommendations on international personal data transfers: https://edpb.europa.eu/sites/default/files/files/file1/edpb_recommendations_202002_europeanessentialguaranteessurveillance_en.pdf; https://edpb.europa.eu/system/files/2021-06/edpb_recommendations_202001vo.2.0_supplementarymeasurestransferstools_en.pdf (on these, see Christakis 2020).

[175] These are enshrined in Article 5 (12) and the adoption procedure is laid down in Article 33 (3).

[176] Article 5 (10).

[177] Article 5 (13). These delegated acts are enacted in accordance with the procedure laid down in Article 32.

[178] Article 5 (14).

[179] On this, see Baloup (2021, 2022).

[180] The transatlantic transfer of data has raised numerous objections (see the "Schrems judgments"). A new agreement in principle on a new *Trans-Atlantic Data Privacy Framework* was announced on 25 March 2022. In October 2022, President Biden issued Executive Order (EO) 14086 to provide stronger protection of privacy and civil liberties, including a redress mechanism. To facilitate the transfers of data the US Commerce Department launched the Data Privacy Framework. On 10 July 2023, the European Commission adopted an adequacy decision for the EU-U.S.

of specific safeguards.[181] The same applies to third country court decisions.[182] If this is not possible, the consent of the rights owner is required ("accountability system").

The "DGA" provides for multi-level governance of the European data space with the Commission and the European Data Innovation Board[183] at its centre. Member States can create independent general and/or sectoral "competent authorities" with technical capabilities, the role of which is to support public sector bodies, or which have competence to grant or refuse re-use.[184] Information about available data resources, the conditions for re-use and the criteria for granting exclusive arrangements must be made public at a single information point (connected to possible sectoral information points) that is also competent to receive requests.[185] The Commission will establish a European information point where it will be possible to search available information in national information points[186] and a public register of all data intermediation services providers based on the information notified by Member States.[187] A similar network of national competent authorities is to be established for data intermediation services providers and data altruism organisations, and these authorities will be legally distinct from and functionally independent of those providers and organisations.[188]

In addition, articulation with national and European data protection and supervisory authorities is necessary.[189] The European Data Innovation Board[190] itself is a multi-level expert group, with representatives from the competent authorities for data intermediation services and the competent authorities for the registration of data altruism organisations of all Member States, the European Data Protection Board, the European Data Protection Supervisor, ENISA, the Commission, the EU SME Envoy and other expert representatives. The Board's role is to advise and assist the Commission in the coordination of national policies and practices, to support stakeholders of the industry in adhering to the European Interoperability Framework principles and other standardisation frameworks, thus contributing to the development of common European data spaces, and to facilitate cooperation between Member States and competent authorities. The Commission has competence to approve the necessary implementing acts, through its delegated powers (Article 290 TFEU) and executive powers (Article 291 TFEU).

---

[181] The "DGA" includes an assessment of the remedy system, one sort of "rule of law assessment" (on this, see Baloup 2022).

[182] Article 31 (3). The interpretation of these rules will not be immune to judicial controversy before the CJEU.

[183] Articles 29 and 30.

[184] Article 7.

[185] Article 8 (1), (2) and (3).

[186] Article 8 (4).

[187] Article 11 (10) and (14).

[188] Articles 13, 19 (5), 23, and 26.

[189] Article 13 (3).

[190] Article 29 (1).

Natural and legal persons have the right to bring individual or collective complaints against "Data intermediation services providers" or "Data altruism organisations"[191] and the right to an effective judicial remedy regarding decisions of the competent authorities, before national courts.[192] Member States are required to adopt the necessary framework, including penalties for infringement of the Regulation.[193]

The "DGA" applies since 24 September 2023 (for "Data intermediation services providers" the provisions laid down will apply from 24 September 2025, the year in which an assessment of the Regulation will be carried out).

Finally, on 13 December 2023 the Data Act (Regulation (EU) 2023/2854) was enacted harmonising rules on fair access to and use of data, especially through guidelines and principles for B2B and B2G sharing. This is "the second major horizontal legislative initiative after the "Data Governance Act" (European Commission 2022b, p. 40).[194] This act will complete the general framework on data.[195]

5 Conclusion

The EU has put in place a comprehensive framework for every type of data, establishing the basis for a European data space, in general, and sector-specific data spaces, which are human-centred, free, non-discriminatory, fair, competitive and sovereign. The data governance ecosystem is multi-level and complex, but also limited, soft and differentiated. Several common principles and rules are laid down. Yet, access to public sector held data is not mandatory. Contractual freedom and fairness are guaranteed through soft enhancing principles. The general regulatory and governance framework is almost complete. With the enactment of the "Data Act", a positive legislative and policy option would be to bring together all the legislation enacted since 2018 in one "European Data Code". This would help citizens and enterprises to be fully aware of their rights and duties to be able to better exercise them. An assessment of the framework's adequacy and results can only come after it has passed the test of application and enforcement. For now, the results are not bright.

---

[191] Article 27. If the competent authority fails to act, a judicial or administrative review must be guaranteed, pursuant to Article 28 (3).

[192] Article 28.

[193] Article 34.

[194] COM (2022) 45 final, 23.02.2022, p. 40.

[195] The "Data Act" was adopted on 13 December 2023 (Regulation (EU) 2023/2854 of the European Parliament and of the Council on harmonised rules on fair access to and use of data). This is not analysed here.

References

Article 29 Data Protection Working Party (2014) Opinion 05/2014 on anonymisation techniques, WP216. https://ec.europa.eu/justice/article-29/documentation/opinion-recommendation/files/2014/wp216_en.pdf. Accessed 30 Sept 2024

Baloup J (2021) The data governance act: new rules for international transfers of non-personal data held by the public sector, European law blog. https://www.law.kuleuven.be/citip/blog/the-data-governance-act-new-rules-for-international-transfers-of-non-personal-data-held-by-the-public-sector/. Accessed 20 Sept 2024

Baloup J (2022) The data act or the final piece to create a comprehensive legal framework for international transfers of data, European law blog, 14 June 2022. https://www.openlegalblogarchive.org/2022/06/14/the-data-act-or-the-final-piece-to-create-a-comprehensive-legal-framework-for-international-transfers-of-data/. Accessed 20 Sept 2024

Benhamou Y (2020) Big data and the law: a holistic analysis based on a three-step approach-mapping property-like rights, their exceptions and licensing practices. Rev Suisse Droit Aff Marché Financ 4:393–418. https://archive-ouverte.unige.ch/unige:145046. Accessed 27 Sept 2024

Bughin BJ, Windhagen FE, Smit AS, Mischke ZJ, Sjatil PE, Gürich HB, McKinsey Global Institute (2022) Innovation in Europe: changing the game to regain a competitive edge. https://www.mckinsey.com/~/media/mckinsey/featured%20insights/innovation/reviving%20innovation%20in%20europe/mgi-innovation-in-europe-discussion-paper-oct2019-vf.ashx. Accessed 27 Sept 2024

Cantazariti M (2021) Algorithmic law: law production by data or data production by law? In: Micklitz H-W, Pollicino O, Reichman A, Simoncini A, Sartor G, De Gregorio G (eds) Constitutional challenges in the algorithmic society. Cambridge University Press, Cambridge, pp 78–92. https://cadmus.eui.eu/bitstream/handle/1814/74296/Constitutional_Challenges_in_the_Algorithmic_Society.pdf?sequence=3&isAllowed=y. Accessed 27 Sept 2024

Capgemini (2020) Analytical report on EU law applicable to sharing of non-personal data support centre for data sharing. DG CONNECT SMART 2018/1009. https://eudatasharing.eu/sites/default/files/2020-02/EN_AR%20on%20EU%20law%20applicable%20to%20sharing%20of%20non-personal%20data.pdf. Accessed 27 June 2022

Carroll SR, Garba I, Figueroa-Rodríguez OL, Holbrook J, Lovett R, Materechera S, Parsons M, Raseroka K, Rodriguez-Lonebear D, Rowe R (2020) The CARE principles for indigenous data governance. Data Sci J 19:43. https://datascience.codata.org/articles/10.5334/dsj-2020-043. Accessed 27 Sept 2024

Christakis T (2020) "Schrems III"? First thoughts on the EDPB post-schrems II recommendations on international data transfers, European law blog. https://www.europeanlawblog.eu/pub/schrems-iii-first-thoughts-on-the-edpb-post-schrems-ii-recommendations-on-international-data-transfers-part-1/release/1, https://www.europeanlawblog.eu/pub/schrems-iii-first-thoughts-on-the-edpb-post-schrems-ii-recommendations-on-international-data-transfers-part-2/release/1, https://www.europeanlawblog.eu/pub/schrems-iii-first-thoughts-on-the-edpb-post-schrems-ii-recommendations-on-international-data-transfers-part-3/release/1. Accessed 20 Sept 2024

Cohen J (2020) Between truth and power: the legal construction of information capitalism. Oxford University Press, Oxford

Cukier K (2020) Data, data everywhere: a special report on managing information. 394, 3–5. The Economist, London, England. https://www.economist.com/special-report/2010/02/27/data-data-everywhere. Accessed 27 Sept 2024

DAMA International (2017) DAMA-DMBOK: data management body of knowledge, 2nd edn. Technics Publications, New Jersey

Daskal J (2015) The un-territoriality of data. Yale Law J 125:326–398. https://www.yalelawjournal.org/article/the-un-territoriality-of-data. Accessed 27 Sept 2024

Demchenko Y, Los W, de Laat C (2018) Data as economic goods: definitions, properties, challenges, enabling technologies for future data markets. ITU J ICT Discov 2:11. https://pure.uva.nl/ws/files/58458207/ITU2018_12.pdf. Accessed 27 Sept 2024
European Commission (1998) Public sector information: a key resource for Europe: Green Paper on public sector information in the information society, COM(1998) 585 final. European Commission, Brussels. http://aei.pitt.edu/1168/1/public_sector_information_gp_COM_98_585.pdf. Accessed 27 Sept 2024
European Commission (2011) Communication from the Commission to the European Parliament, the Council, the European Economic and Social Committee and the Committee of the Regions. Open data. An engine for innovation, growth and transparent governance, COM(2011) 882 final. European Commission, Brussels. https://eur-lex.europa.eu/LexUriServ/LexUriServ.do?uri=COM:2011:0882:FIN:EN:PDF. Accessed 27 Sept 2024
European Commission (2013) Public sector information group main page. https://digital-strategy.ec.europa.eu/en/library/public-sector-information-group-main-page. Accessed 27 Sept 2024
European Commission (2014) Communication from the Commission to the European Parliament, the Council, the European Economic and Social Committee and the Committee of the Regions towards a thriving data-driven economy, COM(2014) 442 final. European Commission, Brussels. https://eur-lex.europa.eu/legal-content/EN/TXT/PDF/?uri=CELEX:52014DC0442&from=EN. Accessed 27 Sept 2024
European Commission (2015a) Creating value through open data: study on the impact of re-use of public data resources. European Commission, Brussels. https://data.europa.eu/sites/default/files/edp_creating_value_through_open_data_0.pdf. Accessed 27 Sept 2024
European Commission (2015b) Communication from the commission to the European Parliament, the Council, the European Economic and Social Committee and the Committee of the Regions a digital single market strategy for Europe, COM(2015) 192 final. European Commission, Brussels. https://eur-lex.europa.eu/legal-content/EN/TXT/?uri=celex%3A52015DC0192. Accessed 27 Sept 2024
European Commission (2017a) Communication from the Commission to the European Parliament, the Council, the European Economic and Social Committee and the Committee of the Regions on the mid-term review on the implementation of the digital single market strategy. A connected digital single market for all, COM(2017) 228 final. European Commission, Brussels. https://eur-lex.europa.eu/legal-content/EN/TXT/?uri=COM%3A2017%3A228%3AFIN. Accessed 27 Sept 2024
European Commission (2017b) Communication from the Commission to the European Parliament, the Council, the European Economic and Social committee and the Committee of the Regions "Building a European data economy", COM(2017) 9 final. European Commission, Brussels. https://eur-lex.europa.eu/legal-content/EN/TXT/?uri=COM%3A2017%3A9%3AFIN. Accessed 27 June 2022
European Commission (2017c) Commission staff working document on the free flow of data and emerging issues of the European data economy accompanying the document communication building a European data economy, SWD(2017) 2 final. European Commission, Brussels. https://eur-lex.europa.eu/legal-content/EN/TXT/?uri=CELEX%3A52017SC0002. Accessed 27 Sept 2024
European Commission (2017d) Proposal for a regulation of the European Parliament and of the Council on a framework for the free flow of non-personal data in the European Union, COM(2017) 495 final. European Commission, Brussels. https://eur-lex.europa.eu/legal-content/EN/TXT/?uri=COM%3A2017%3A495%3AFIN. Accessed 27 Sept 2024
European Commission (2017e) Commission staff working document impact assessment accompanying the document proposal for a regulation of the European Parliament and of the 7Council on a framework for the free flow of non-personal data in the European Union, SWD(2017) 304 final – impact assessment. European Commission, Brussels. https://eur-lex.europa.eu/legal-content/EN/TXT/?uri=SWD:2017:304:FIN. Accessed 27 Sept 2024

European Commission (2018a) Study on emerging issues of data ownership, interoperability, (re-) usability and access to data, and liability. Final Report. European Commission, Brussels. https://op.europa.eu/en/publication-detail/-/publication/74cca30c-4833-11e8-be1d-01aa75ed71a1/language-en. Accessed 27 Sept 2024
European Commission (2018b) Commission staff working document evaluation accompanying the document proposal for a directive of the European Parliament and of the Council on the re-use of public sector information, SWD(2018) 145 final. European Commission, Brussels. https://eur-lex.europa.eu/legal-content/EN/TXT/?uri=SWD%3A2018%3A145%3AFIN. Accessed 27 Sept 2024
European Commission (2018c) Proposal for a directive of the European Parliament and of the Council on the re-use of public sector information (recast), COM(2018) 234 final. European Commission, Brussels. https://eur-lex.europa.eu/legal-content/EN/TXT/?uri=CELEX%3A52018PC0234. Accessed 27 Sept 2024
European Commission (2018d) Commission staff working document impact assessment accompanying the document proposal for a directive of the European Parliament and of the Council on the re-use of public sector information, SWD(2018) 127 final. European Commission, Brussels. https://eur-lex.europa.eu/LexUriServ/LexUriServ.do?uri=SWD:2018:0127:FIN:EN:PDF. Accessed 27 Sept 2024
European Commission (2018e) Communication from the Commission to the European Parliament, the Council, the European Economic and Social Committee and the Committee of the Regions "Towards a Common European Data Space", COM/2018/232 final. European Commission, Brussels. https://eur-lex.europa.eu/legal-content/en/TXT/?uri=CELEX%3A52018DC0232. Accessed 27 Sept 2024
European Commission (2018f) Commission staff working document guidance on sharing private sector data in the European data economy accompanying the document communication from the commission to the European Parliament, the Council, the European Economic and Social Committee and the Committee of the Regions "towards a common European data space", SWD(2018) 125 final. European Commission, Brussels. https://eur-lex.europa.eu/legal-content/EN/TXT/?uri=CELEX%3A52018SC0125. Accessed 27 Sept 2024
European Commission (2018g) Commission recommendation (EU) 2018/790 of 25 April 2018 on access to and preservation of scientific information. European Commission, Brussels. https://eur-lex.europa.eu/eli/reco/2018/790/oj. Accessed 27 Sept 2024
European Commission (2019) Communication from the Commission to the European Parliament and the Council. Guidance on the regulation on a framework for the free flow of non-personal data in the European Union, COM 2019(250) final. European Commission, Brussels. https://eur-lex.europa.eu/legal-content/EN/TXT/PDF/?uri=CELEX:52019DC0250&rid=2. Accessed 27 Sept 2024
European Commission (2020a) Communication from the Commission to the European Parliament, the Council, the European Economic and Social Committee and the Committee of the Regions. A European Strategy for Data, COM(2020) 66 final. European Commission, Brussels. https://eur-lex.europa.eu/legal-content/EN/TXT/?uri=CELEX%3A52020DC0066. Accessed 27 Sept 2024
European Commission (2020b) Proposal for a regulation of the European Parliament and of the Council on European data governance, COM (2020) 767 final. European Commission, Brussels. https://eur-lex.europa.eu/legal-content/EN/TXT/?uri=celex%3A52020PC0767. Accessed 27 Sept 2024
European Commission (2021) Proposal for a decision of the European Parliament and of the Council establishing the 2030 policy programme "path to the digital decade", COM(2021) 574 final. European Commission, Brussels. https://eur-lex.europa.eu/legal-content/EN/TXT/?uri=CELEX%3A52021PC0574. Accessed 27 Sept 2024
European Commission (2022a) Commission staff working document on Common European Data Spaces, SWD(2022) 45 final. European Commission, Brussels. https://data.consilium.europa.eu/doc/document/ST-6532-2022-INIT/en/pdf. Accessed 27 Sept 2024

European Commission (2022b) Proposal for a regulation of the European Parliament and of the Council on harmonised rules on fair access to and use of data (Data Act), COM (2022)68 final. European Commission, Brussels. https://eur-lex.europa.eu/legal-content/EN/TXT/?uri=COM%3A2022%3A68%3AFIN. Acessed 27 Sept 2024

European Parliament, Directorate-General for Internal Policies of the Union, Blackman C, Forge S (2017) Data flows – future scenarios. In-depth analysis for the ITRE committee. European Commission, Brussels. https://data.europa.eu/doi/10.2861/91583. Accessed 27 Sept 2024

Frontier Economics (2022) Beyond personal data: the cost of data flow restrictions to EU companies. Frontier Economics, London, UK. https://research.ccianet.org/reports/beyond-personal-data-cost-data-flow-restrictions-eu-companies/. Accessed 27 Sept 2024

G8 (2013) G8 Open Data Charter. https://assets.publishing.service.gov.uk/media/5a7c1dd340f0b61a825d68e7/Open_Data_Charter.pdf. Accessed 27 Sept 2024

Graef I, Gellert R, Husovec M (2018) Towards a holistic regulatory approach for the European data economy: why the illusive notion of non-personal data is counterproductive to data innovation. TILEC discussion paper DP 2018-028. https://www.researchgate.net/publication/328060880_Towards_a_Holistic_Regulatory_Approach_for_the_European_Data_Economy_Why_the_Illusive_Notion_of_Non-Personal_Data_is_Counterproductive_to_Data_Innovation. Accessed 27 Sept 2024

Graef I, Husovec M, Boom J (2019) Spill-overs in data governance: the relationship between the GDPR's right to data portability and EU sector-specific data access regimes. TILEC discussion paper DP 2019-005. https://www.researchgate.net/publication/332479221_Spill-Overs_in_Data_Governance_The_Relationship_Between_the_GDPR's_Right_to_Data_Portability_and_EU_Sector-Specific_Data_Access_Regimes. Accessed 27 Sept 2024

Hummel P, Braun M, Augsberg S, Dabrock P (2018) Sovereignty and data sharing. ITU J ICT Discov 2. https://www.researchgate.net/publication/330555591_Sovereignty_and_Data_Sharing. Accessed 27 Sept 2024

Malcomson S (2016) Splinternet: how geopolitics and commerce are fragmenting the world wide web. OR Books, New York, NY

Manyika J, Chui M, Brown B, Bughin J, Dobbs R, Roxburgh C, Byers AH, McKinsey Global Institute (2011) Big data: the next frontier for innovation, competition, and productivity. https://www.mckinsey.com/capabilities/mckinsey-digital/our-insights/big-data-the-next-frontier-for-innovation. Accessed 20 Sept 2024

Moody D, Walsh P (1999) Measuring the value of information: an asset valuation approach. Paper presented at the 7th European Conference on Information Systems (ECIS'99), Copenhagen Business School, Frederiksberg, Denmark, 23–25 June 1999 (it can be requested to the Author at ResearchGate)

National Institute of Standards and Technology (2015) Big data interoperability framework: volume 1, definitions. NIST, Gaithersburg, MD. https://nvlpubs.nist.gov/nistpubs/SpecialPublications/NIST.SP.1500-1r2.pdf. Accessed 27 Sept 2024

OECD (2022) Recommendation of the Council on Enhancing Access to and Sharing of Data, OECD/LEGAL/0463. https://legalinstruments.oecd.org/en/instruments/OECD-LEGAL-0463. Accessed 27 Sept 2024

Open Knowledge Foundation (n.d.) Defining open in open data, open content and open knowledge. https://opendefinition.org/. Accessed 27 Sept 2024

Pollicino O, De Gregorio G (2021) Constitutional law in the algorithmic society. In: Micklitz H-W, Pollicino O, Reichman A, Simoncini A, Sartor G, De Gregorio G (eds) Constitutional challenges in the algorithmic society. Cambridge University Press, Cambridge, pp 3–24. https://www.cambridge.org/core/books/constitutional-challenges-in-the-algorithmic-society/831B39F76C7870B330052D852D598F98. Accessed 27 Sept 2024

SIIA Policy (2013) Data-driven innovation – a guide for policymakers: understanding and enabling the economic and social value of data, SIIA White Paper. Software & Information Industry Association, Washington, DC (it can be requested to MEMBERSHIP@SIIA.NET)

Somaini L (2020) Regulating the dynamic concept of non-personal data in the EU: from ownership to portability. Eur Data Prot Law Rev 6:84–93. https://edpl.lexxion.eu/article/EDPL/2020/1/10. Accessed 27 Sept 2024

SWIPO AISBL (2020a) Code of conduct for data portability and cloud service switching for infrastructure as a service (IaaS) cloud services. SWIPO AISBL, Brussels. https://swipo.eu/wp--content/uploads/2020/07/SWIPO-IaaS-Code-of-Conduct.pdf. Accessed 27 Sept 2024

SWIPO AISBL (2020b) Code of conduct. Switching and portability of data related to software as a service (SaaS). SWIPO AISBL, Brussels. https://swipo.eu/wp-content/uploads/2020/07/SWIPO-SaaS-Code-of-Conduct.pdf. Accessed 27 Sept 2024

SWIPO AISBL (2021) Version 3 approved by GA8 on 3 December 2021 appeals and complaints procedures. SWIPO AISBL, Brussels. https://swipo.eu/wp-content/uploads/2021/12/SWIPO_AISBL_GA8_Complaints-and-Appeals_V3_Approved-by-GA8-on-03.12.2021.pdf. Accessed 27 Sept 2024

UN Statistical Commission (2017) UN's Cape Town Global Action Plan for Sustainable Development Data. https://unstats.un.org/sdgs/hlg/Cape_Town_Global_Action_Plan_for_Sustainable_Development_Data.pdf. Accessed 27 Sept 2024

UNESCO (2021) UNESCO recommendation on open science. UNESCO, Paris, France

United Nations Development Group Data Privacy (2017) Data Privacy, Ethics and Protection Guidance Note on Big Data for Achievement of the 2030 Agenda. https://unsdg.un.org/sites/default/files/UNDG_BigData_final_web.pdf. Accessed 27 Sept 2022

United Nations Secretariat (2019) Frontier technology quarterly: data economy: radical transformation or dystopia?. Department of Economic and Social Affairs, Economic Analysis and Policy Division. United Nations Secretariat, New York. https://www.un.org/development/desa/dpad/publication/frontier-technology-quarterly-january-2019/. Accessed 27 Sept 2024

Wilkinson MD, Dumontier M, Aalbersberg IJ et al (2016) The FAIR guiding principles for scientific data management and stewardship. Sci Data 3:160018. https://www.nature.com/articles/sdata201618. Accessed 27 Sept 2022

Woods AK (2018) Litigating data sovereignty. Yale Law J 128:328–406. https://www.yalelawjournal.org/pdf/Woods_i233nhrp.pdf. Accessed 27 Jun 2024

Zuboff S (2019) The age of surveillance capitalism: the fight for a human future at the new frontier of power. Public Affairs, New York

Graça Enes Faculty of Law of the University of Porto, Portugal. CIJ Researcher, Coordinator of the Jean Monnet Module "A Digital Europe for Citizens. Constitutional and Policymaking Challenges" (Project ID: 101085671; Call: ERASMUS-JMO-2022-HEI-TCH-RSCH; ERASMUS2027; EACEA).

Should Merger Control Rules Apply to the Granting of Special or Exclusive Rights by a Member State to an Undertaking? A Contribution to Tighten a Loose Knot

José Luís da Cruz Vilaça and Rita Leandro Vasconcelos

1 Introduction

One of the most paradigmatic objectives of the European Union ("EU") is the establishment of an internal market, including a "*system ensuring that competition is not distorted*". This is enshrined in Article 3(3) of the Treaty on European Union ("TEU"), and supplemented by Protocol No 27 on the Internal Market and Competition.[1] The EU is based on a highly competitive social market economy and the activities of the Member States and the EU are conducted in accordance with the principle of an open market economy with free competition, as set out in Article 119 of the Treaty on the Functioning of the European Union ("TFEU"). The EU is also neutral on the issue of property ownership. According to Article 345 TFEU, the "*Treaties shall in no way prejudice the rules in Member States governing the system of property ownership*". Nevertheless, the activities of Member States may interfere

[1] Protocols to the treaties form an integral part thereof (Article 51 TEU).

José Luís da Cruz Vilaça is Partner at Antas da Cunha Ecija, Former Judge at the CJEU and Advocate General at the Court of Justice of the European Union.
Rita Leandro Vasconcelos is Partner at Pérez-Llorca, Lisbon, Portugal. Visiting Professor at Universidade Católica Portuguesa, School of Law, Lisbon, Portugal.

J. L. da Cruz Vilaça (✉)
Antas da Cunha Ecija, Lisbon, Portugal
e-mail: jvilaca@adcecija.pt

R. Leandro Vasconcelos
Universidade Católica Portuguesa, Faculty of Law, Lisbon, Portugal

Pérez-Llorca, Lisbon, Portugal
e-mail: rvasconcelos@perezllorca.com

I. Quadros, M. Gorjão-Henriques (eds.), *Revisiting the Liberal Constitutional Features of the European Union*, https://doi.org/10.1007/978-3-031-95717-8_12

with EU objectives. For this reason, Member States cannot, as a matter of principle, introduce distortions of competition without scrutiny.[2] This is why Member States have obligations under competition rules, such as the control of special or exclusive rights and State aid, enshrined in Articles 106 to 109 TFEU.

Notwithstanding the large amount of case-law of the Court of Justice of the European Union[3] concerning the application of competition law to Member States and the interplay between Article 106 TFEU and competition rules, there still remain some unresolved issues. In Portugal, this is the case with the following question: how to treat the granting of a concession from the point of view of Regulation (EC) No 139/2004 ("EU Merger Regulation")[4] and the national merger control rules, in particular Articles 36 *et seq.* of Law No. 19/2012, of 8 May (the "Portuguese Competition Act").[5]

We may find decisions from the European Commission ("Commission")[6] and the Portuguese Competition Authority ("*Autoridade da Concorrência*"),[7] as well as legal literature (Gonçalves 2012, p. 259; Rodrigues 2014, p. 219), arguing that the granting of a concession would qualify as a concentration between undertakings when it involves the transfer of assets engaged in an economic activity. In our opinion, this interpretation needs to be very carefully articulated with EU primary law.

In this article we will first set the scene with a brief analysis of the concepts of concentration and concession. We will then discuss the complexities involved in applying the competition rules, in particular the merger control rules, to the act of granting a concession by a public authority. Finally, we will present our views on the proper interaction between the grant of special or exclusive rights and the merger control rules.

---

[2] See, for example, Craig and de Búrca (2020, p. 1149).

[3] The term Court of Justice of the European Union covers both EU courts: the Court of Justice and the General Court.

[4] Council Regulation (EC) No. 139/2004 of 20 January 2004 on the control of concentrations between undertakings, OJ L 24, 29.1.2004, p. 1.

[5] Law No. 19/2012, of 8 May, published in the Official Gazette No. 89/2012, series I of 8.5.2012, and amended by Law No. 89/2012, published in the Official Gazette, series I of 8.5.2012, Law No. 107/2018, of 5 June, published in the Official Gazette, series I of 5.6.2018, Decree-law No. 236/2021, of 7 December, published in the Official Gazette, series I of 7.12.2021, and Law No. 17/2022, of 17 August, published in the Official Gazette, series I of 17.8.2022.

[6] For example, Commission Decision of 20.9.2007, M.4797 – *Govia/West Midlands Passenger Rail Franchise*; Commission Decision of 18.3.2015, M.7483 – *Abellio Transport/Scotrail;* Commission Decision of 27.1.2016, Case M.7897 – *Arriva Rail North/Northern Franchise;* and Commission Decision of 5.5.2017, M.8441 – *Firstgroup / MTR Corporation / South Western Rail Franchise*.

[7] For example, decision of 6.7.2021, CCent. 25/2021 – *SCML/SG HCV*, para 30; decision of 9.11.2021, Ccent/2021/49 – *Transdev Interior / Concessão*, para 46; decision of 11.4.2022, Ccent/2021/36 – *JCDecaux / Concessão de Publicidade Exterior em Lisboa*; decision of 24.8.2022, Ccent/2022/33 – *Mota-Engil / Concessão do Hospital de Lisboa Oriental*, para 3; and decision of 22.11.2022, Ccent/2022/48 – *Concessão de Serviço Público de Transporte Rodoviário de Passageiros na RAM*, para 6.

2 A Concentration as a Change of Control Over an Undertaking and the Purpose of Merger Control

The first question to be answered is what constitutes a concentration[8] within the meaning of the EU Merger Regulation and the Portuguese Competition Act, and how this compares with the scope of Article 106(1) TFEU.

The EU rules on merger control are not included in the Treaty. They are contained in the EU Merger Regulation,[9] which has both Article 103 and Article 352 TFEU as its legal basis. According to Article 3(1) of the EU Merger Regulation, "*a concentration shall be deemed to arise where a change of control on a lasting basis results from: (a) the merger of two or more previously independent undertakings or parts of undertakings, or (b) the acquisition, by one or more persons already controlling at least one undertaking, or by one or more undertakings, whether by purchase of securities or assets, by contract or by any other means, of direct or indirect control of the whole or parts of one or more other undertakings*".

The definition of concentration given by the Court of Justice is very similar to that in the EU Merger Regulation. In *Ernst & Young*, the Court of Justice summarised decades of case-law and decision practice by stating that "*a concentration is deemed to arise where a change of control on a lasting basis results from the merger of two or more previously independent undertakings or parts of undertakings, or the acquisition, by one or more persons already controlling at least one undertaking, or by one or more undertakings of direct or indirect control of the whole or parts of one or more other undertakings, that control being constituted by the possibility, conferred by rights, contracts or any other means, of exercising decisive influence on an undertaking*".[10]

The Commission's Consolidated Jurisdictional Notice explains the concept of control—as enshrined in Article 3(2) of the EU Merger Regulation—as the possibility of exercising decisive influence on an undertaking.[11] The General Court defines the power to control, in the context of the EU Merger Regulation, as "*the possibility of exercising decisive influence on an undertaking, in particular where the undertaking with that power is able to impose choices on the other in relation to its strategic decisions*".[12] It is not necessary to demonstrate that such influence is or will be

[8] We will use the expressions "concentration" and "merger" interchangeably.

[9] The current EU Merger Regulation was preceded by Council Regulation (EEC) No. 4064/89 of 21 December 1989 on the control of concentrations between undertakings, OJ L 395, 30.12.1989, pp. 1–12. Before the adoption of such framework, Article 102 TFEU was invoked to catch mergers by undertakings in a dominant position. See judgment of 21.2.1973, *Europemballage Corporation and Continental Can Company v Commission*, 6/72, EU:C:1973:22.

[10] Judgment of 31.5.2018, *Ernst & Young*, C-633/16, EU:C:2018:23, para 45. See, also, Craig and de Búrca (2020, p. 1125).

[11] See, also, opinion of Advocate General Collins, delivered on 27.4.2023, *Altice Group Lux v European Commission*, C-746/21 P, EU:C:2023361, paras 35 and 64.

[12] See judgment of 6.7.2010, *Aer Lingus Group v Commission*, T-411/07, EU:T:2010:281, para 63; and judgments of 9.11.2023, EU:C:2023:836, *Altice v Commission*, para 140; and of 22.9.2021, *Altice Europe v Commission*, T-425/18, EU:T:2021:607, para 84.

exercised. Nonetheless, the possibility of exercising that influence must be effective.[13]

The object of control is usually understood as "*one or more, or also parts of, undertakings which constitute legal entities, or the assets of such entities, or only some of these assets. The acquisition of control over assets can only be considered a concentration if those assets constitute the whole or a part of an undertaking, i.e. a business with a market presence, to which a market turnover can be clearly attributed*".[14] The idea that granting a concession can be treated as a concentration is likely derived from this definition.

A key element in the definition of a concentration is therefore the transfer of control between two undertakings over pre-existing assets which are capable of constituting a business with a market presence and to which a turnover can be clearly attributed (Cunha 2005, pp. 75–83; Pais 2006, p. 79; Da Fonseca and Ferreira 2009, pp. 44–71; Rodrigues 2012, pp. 50–51; Boyce and Lyle-Smythe 2018, p. 595; Whish and Bailey 2021, pp. 876–880). Indeed, as the Court of Justice rightly held in the *Austria Asphalt* case, the essential element of the concept of concentration is the change in the control of an undertaking.[15] Consequently, not every single transaction will be considered a concentration under the EU Merger Regulation.

It does not follow, however, that all actions by undertakings which do not amount to a concentration are beyond the control of the Commission or the competent national competition authorities.[16] Articles 101 and 102 TFEU (and their implementing regulation, Regulation 1/2003[17]) continue to apply to the actions of undertakings which, without constituting a concentration within the meaning of the EU Merger Regulation or national competition rules, may nevertheless infringe those articles.[18]

Similarly, the Court of Justice stated that Article 102 TFEU continues to apply to the actions of undertakings which, despite constituting a concentration within the meaning of the EU Merger Regulation or national merger control rules, fall below the jurisdictional thresholds for *ex ante* control.[19] Indeed, the EU Merger Regulation forms part of a body of law designed to implement Articles 101 and 102 TFEU and

[13] See judgment of 23.2.2006, *Cementbouw Handel & Industrie v Commission*, T-282/02, EU:T:2006:64, para 58.

[14] Consolidated Jurisdictional Notice, paras 16 and 24.

[15] Judgment of 7.9.2017, *Austria Asphalt*, C-248/16, EU:C:2017:643, para 26. The case concerned the transfer of control of a joint venture, but its conclusions on the importance of change of control are fully applicable to joint or sole control.

[16] Case C-248/16, *Austria Asphalt*, para 30.

[17] Council Regulation (EC) No 1/2003 of 16 December 2002 on the implementation of the rules on competition laid down in Articles 81 and 82 of the Treaty, OJ L 1, 4.1.2003, 1–25.

[18] Case C-248/16, *Austria Asphalt*, para 33.

[19] Judgment of 16.3.2023, *Towercast*, C-449/21, EU:C:2023:207, paras 30–53.

to establish a system of control to ensure that competition in the EU internal market is not distorted.[20]

The purpose of the EU Merger Regulation (and its predecessor, Regulation No 4064/89[21]) is to provide *ex ante* control by requiring certain proposed concentrations—those that meet the thresholds set out in the Regulation[22]—to be assessed before they are implemented.[23] Such concentrations should not be implemented until the Commission has taken a decision either declaring them compatible with the internal market (in some cases subject to the acceptance of remedies proposed by the parties) or declaring them incompatible with the internal market.[24] In the latter case, the parties are not allowed to implement the concentration.[25]

The concept of concentration enshrined in Article 36(1) of the Portuguese Competition Act[26] mirrors the EU concept and should be interpreted in conformity with it (Vilaça 2013, pp. 288–289). Indeed, such an obligation to interpret national law in conformity with EU law (conform interpretation) has been shaped by the case-law of the Court of Justice as one of the tools to ensure the *effet utile* of EU law in national legal systems.[27] This has been recognised by the Portuguese legislator. According to the latest version of the law, the Portuguese Competition Act is to be interpreted in accordance with EU law in the light of the jurisprudence of the Court of Justice.[28] The procedure for authorising or prohibiting a concentration is also inspired by the EU method.

---

[20] Case C-449/21, *Towercast*, para 39.

[21] Council Regulation (EEC) No 4064/89 of 21 December 1989 on the control of concentrations between undertakings, OJ L 395, 30.12.1989, 1–12.

[22] Articles 1(2) and 1(3) of the EU Merger Regulation. This is without prejudice to the application of Articles 4, 9 and 22 of the EU Merger Regulation, where the circumstances of the case so justify.

[23] Recital 5 of the EU Merger Regulation. See, Case C-449/21, *Towercast*, para 36; Case C-633/16, *Ernst & Young*, para 41; and Case C-248/16, *Austria Asphalt*, para 21. Gonçalves (2012, p. 250).

[24] Articles 2(2) and (3), 6, 7 and 8 of the EU Merger Regulation.

[25] Articles 2(3), 7(1) and 8(3) of the EU Merger Regulation.

[26] It should be noted that the EU Merger Regulation sets forth a system of "one stop shop", whereby a concentration subject to that Regulation should not be reviewed by national competition authorities (Articles 21(1)(3) of the EU Merger Regulation).

[27] See, *inter alia*, judgment of 10.4.1984, *Von Colson and Kamann v Land Nordrhein-Westfalen*, 14/83, EU:C:1984:153, para 26; judgment of 4.2.1988, *Murphy v An Bord Telecom Eireann*, 157/86, EU:C:1988:62, para 11; judgment of 13.11.1990, *Marleasing v Comercial Internacional de Alimentación*, 106/89, EU:C:1990:395, para 8; judgment of 14.7.1994, *Faccini Dori v Recreb*, 91/92, EU:C:1994:292, para 26; judgment of 5.10.2004, *Pfeiffer and Others*, joined cases C-397/01–C-403/01, EU:C:2004:584, para 113; judgment of 4.7.2006, *Adeneler and Others*, C-212/04, EU:C:2006:443, para 108; and judgment of 24.1.2012, *Dominguez*, C-282/10, para 24.

[28] Article 2(3) of the Portuguese Competition Act. This was already acknowledged in practice. In this sense, see, also, Case C-633/16, *Ernst & Young*, para 33.

Concentrations that meet the jurisdictional criteria[29] cannot be implemented until the Portuguese Competition Authority has taken a positive decision, which may include modifications resulting from proposed remedies.[30]

However, the Portuguese Competition Act innovates in relation to the EU Merger Regulation, as it sets out specific rules on the interplay between the merger control procedure and public procurement. Indeed, Article 37(2) and (3) provides that a concentration resulting from a public procurement procedure must be notified after the final award and before its implementation. The relationship between the two procedures should be determined by the contracting authority on a case-by-case basis.[31]

3 A Concession as a Special or Exclusive Right

Concessions are a form of partnership between public and private players. They usually take the form of an agreement—subject to specific rules—to provide different kinds of public services, such as transport, water supply, waste disposal and energy, or to develop, operate and maintain an infrastructure such as toll roads and ports.[32] The concession holder has the right to operate the infrastructure and provide services directly to the public, subject to applicable regulations and the specific provisions of the concession agreement, under the supervision of the grantor. Concessions are subject to public procurement rules, and competition usually occurs when the tender is contested by several bidders ("competition for the market") (OECD 2017, p. 1).

The term concession is not defined in the Treaty. For some time, there was some uncertainty about the concept of concession. Initially, the main concern was to distinguish between public works or service concessions and public works or service contracts (Bogdanowicz 2020, pp. 3–4).[33] The main difference between these two concepts was the origin of the consideration received by the concessionaire. In the case of a public contract, this consideration was paid by the contracting authority, whereas in the case of a concession contract, it derived mainly from a direct rela-

[29] Article 37 of the Portuguese Competition Act.

[30] Articles 40, 41(3) and (4), 50(1) and (2), 51 and 53(1) of the Portuguese Competition Act. The substantive test also mirrors the one set out in the EU legislation. See Cunha (2005, pp. 55–59), Da Fonseca and Ferreira (2009, pp. 145,152–153), Silva (2018, pp. 209–210, 217–218).

[31] For a critical appraisal of the law, see Rodrigues (2012, pp. 55–59).

[32] See, Macmillan (2019, p. 4). On the concept of concession see Neergaard (2005, pp. 149–181).

[33] The Commission issued a proposal to establish a legal framework for service contracts, where it proposed to include public service concessions, but it was not followed by the EU legislator. See Proposal 91/C 23/01 of 13 December 1990 for a Council Directive relating to the coordination of procedures on the award of public service contracts (OJ 1991 C 23, 1) and its amended proposal 91/C 250/05 of 28 August 1991 for a Council Directive relating to the coordination of procedures on the award of public service contracts (OJ 1991 C 250, 4). See, also, order of the Court of 30.5.2002, *Buchhändler-Vereinigung*, C-358/00, EU:C:2002: 317, paras 23 to 25.

tionship with the users and was linked to the right of exploitation (Bogdanowicz 2020, p. 4). However, doubts remained as to the meaning and scope of the exploitation right and whether a payment by the contracting authority as a partial payment to the concessionaire was compatible with the existence of a concession (Bogdanowicz 2020, p. 5).

Initially, the case-law of the Court of Justice followed the principle described above.[34] Slowly, the ideas and the law began to evolve. In 2000, the Commission published its interpretative communication on concessions under Community law,[35] in which it identified the transfer of the risk of exploitation to the concession holder as the key element for the concept of concession.[36] The definitive shift would come later, when the Court of Justice moved away from the focus on the source of the remuneration to attach greater importance to the transfer of the operating risk to the concessionaire.[37]

Finally, a general legal framework for concession contracts was adopted, based on the concept developed by the Court of Justice. According to Directive 2014/23/EU,[38] a concession is a contract for pecuniary interest whereby a contracting authority or a public entity entrusts one or more economic operators with the execution of works, or the provision and the management of services, the consideration for which consists either solely in the right to exploit the works or services that are the subject of the contract or in that right together with payment. It is in the nature of a concession that most of the risk is transferred to the concessionaire.[39]

It is not the purpose of this article to develop a general theory of concessions. It is more specific than that. It seems clear that concessions, like any act of a Member State laying down the conditions governing economic activities, are subject to the Treaties, to applicable secondary legislation, and also to the principles emerging from the case-law of the Court of Justice, notably non-discrimination, transparency,

---

[34] See, for example, judgment of 10.11.1998, *Gemeinde Arnhem and Gemeente Rheden v BFI Holding*, C-360/96, EU:C:1998:525, para 25; and judgment of 7.12.2000, *Telaustria and Telefonadress*, C-324/98, EU:C:2000:669, paras 30, 43 and 58.

[35] Communication from the Commission – Commission interpretative communication on concessions under Community law, OJ C 121, 24.4.2000, 2–13.

[36] Commission interpretative communication on concessions under Community law, p. 3.

[37] Judgment of 13.11.2008, *Commission v Italy*, C-437/07, EU:C:2008:624, paras 27 to 31. This criterion has been consolidated in subsequent rulings which help to define the nature and extent of the risk to be borne by the concession holder. Judgment of 11.6.2009, *Hans & Christophorus Oymanns*, C-300/07, EU:C:2009:358, paras 71 and 74; judgment of 10.9.2009, *Eurawasser*, C-206/08, EU:C:2009:540, paras 53 to 77; judgment of 15.10.2009, *Acoset*, C-196/08, EU:C:2009:628, paras 37 to 45; judgment of 10.3.2011, *Privater Rettungsdienst und Krankentransport Stadler*, C-274/09, EU:C:2011:130, paras 21 to 48; judgment of 10.11.2011, *Norma-A and Dekom*, C-348/10, EU:C:2011:721, paras 44 to 59; and judgment of 21.5.2015, *Kansaneläkelaitos*, C-269/14, EU:C:2015:329, paras 31 to 41.

[38] Directive 2014/23/EU of the European Parliament and of the Council of 26 February 2014 on the award of concession contracts, OJ L 94, 28.3.2014, 1–64.

[39] Opinion of Advocate General Sharpston, delivered on 21.3.2019, *European Commission v Italian Republic*, C-526/17, EU:C:2019:244, para 85.

and proportionality.[40] The selection procedure for participation in a concession contract,[41] based on the principle of competition ,[42] is important in this respect, and aims to ensure fair competition between bidders. However, the Directive does not address the issue of merger control.[43] The aim of this article is, therefore, to determine whether the award of a concession is subject to European or national merger control rules, or whether it is excluded by application of Article 106 TFEU.

At this point, it is important to stress that, as concessions are usually of long duration and often of an exclusive nature, they normally concern activities of such a nature and purpose that they may be subject to special or exclusive rights.[44]

4 The Complex Application of the Competition Rules to the Act of Granting a Concession

EU law makes a distinction between the competition rules applicable to private or public undertakings (namely the rules on restrictive agreements and concerted practices, and on abuses of a dominant position, set out in Articles 101 and 102 TFEU, as well as the rules on merger control established in the EU Merger Regulation) and those applicable to Member States (namely, the rules on the control of special or exclusive rights and of State aid set out in Articles 106(1) and 107 to 109 TFEU).[45] It is argued that this difference is fundamental in determining the rules applicable to the granting of a concession.

---

[40] Commission interpretative communication on concessions under Community law, p. 6.

[41] Title II of Directive 2014/23/EU.

[42] For example, recital (73) of Directive 2014/23/EU. This is actually one of the primary goals of public tenders. In this regard, see Odudu and Sanchez-Graells (2023, p. 601).

[43] Article 38(7)(e) of Directive 2014/23/UE provides for the possibility of exclusion of a bidder, on grounds of competition concerns, when the contracting authority has reasons to believe that the undertaking has entered into agreements that distort competition.

[44] Commission interpretative communication on concessions under Community law, p. 4. See opinion of Advocate General Da Cruz Vilaça, delivered on 11.2.1988, *Corinne Bodson v Pompes Funèbres des Régions Libérées*, 30/87, para 71. See Rodrigues (2013, p. 454) and Graells (2009, p. 45).

[45] To these can be added the rules under which Member States may establish State monopolies of a commercial character, as set out in Article 37 TFEU.

4.1 The Purpose of Article 106(1) TFEU

Article 106(1) TFEU contains a prohibition addressed to the Member States.[46] According to this provision "*[i]n the case of public undertakings and undertakings to which Member States grant special or exclusive rights, Member States shall neither enact nor maintain in force any measure contrary to the rules contained in the Treaties, in particular to*" the rules on competition (Articles 101 to 109 TFEU).

The rule contained in Article 106(1) TFEU is closely related to Article 4(3) TEU, which enshrines the principle of sincere cooperation, since they both aim at ensuring compliance with the Treaty rules by the Member States.[47] Moreover, the Treaty is widely understood (Craig and de Búrca 2020, p. 1153) to favour the normal application of competition principles. The purpose of Article 106(1) TFEU is, therefore, to prevent measures taken by Member States in respect of undertakings with which they maintain special relations of proximity—public undertakings and undertakings to which they have granted special or exclusive rights—from undermining the *effet utile* of the rules contained in the Treaties (Brisimi 2016, pp. 157–159).

4.2 The Elements of Article 106(1) TFEU

When considering the application of Article 106(1) TFEU, it is necessary to clarify the meaning of its terms, in particular the terms "public undertakings", "undertaking to which Member States grant special or exclusive rights" and "State measure".

The Court of Justice has adopted a functional and broad approach in the interpretation of this provision. Firstly, it defined the concept of "undertaking"—a concept of EU law—as an entity engaged in an economic activity, regardless of its legal status and the way in which it is financed.[48] The concept of "entity" has also been interpreted broadly: it includes natural and legal persons, as well as State bodies and other public entities.[49] The second element of the definition of undertaking—"an

[46] Judgment of 23.4.1991, *Höfner and Elser v Macrotron*, C-41/90, EU:C:1991:161, para 16; and judgment of 19.5.1993, *Corbeau*, C-320/91, EU:C:1993:198, paras 10–12. See Opinion of Advocate General Da Cruz Vilaça, 30/87, *Corinne Bodson v Pompes Funèbres des Régions Libérées*, para 64. Whish and Bailey (2021, p. 232), Colino (2019, pp. 497–498).

[47] Judgment of 16.11.1977, *INNO v ATAB*, 13/77, EU:C:1977:185, paras 30–38 and 42.

[48] Case C-41/90, *Höfner and Elser v Macrotron*, para 21; judgment of 18.6.1998, *Commission v Italy*, C-35/96, EU:C:1998:303, para 36; judgment of 25.10.2001, *Ambulanz Glöckner*, C-475/99, EU:C:2001:577, para 19; judgment of 17.2.1993, *Poucet and Pistre v AGF and Cancava*, joined cases C-159 and C-160/91, EU:C:1993:63, paras 17–19; judgment of 16.3.2004, *AOK Bundesverband and o.*, joined cases C-264/01, C-306/01, C-354/01 and C-355/01, para 46; and judgment of 15.7.2015, *Socitrel and Companhia Previdente v Commission*, T-413/10, EU:T:2015:500, para 197.

[49] See judgment of 16.6.1987, *Commission v Italy*, 118/85, EU:C:1987:283, para 16. See, also, Jones et al. (2023, p. 609), Sierra (2014, p. 813) and Gonçalves (2012, p. 259).

economic activity"—covers any activity consisting in offering goods and services on a given market[50] as long as it is not based on the principle of solidarity.[51] Secondly, the Court clarified that "public undertakings" are those subject to the dominant influence of public authorities of a Member State.[52] Finally, the Court made it clear that undertakings to which the State has granted special or exclusive rights (sometimes called privileged undertakings) may be public or private.[53]

An "exclusive right" has been defined as the right granted by a State measure to an undertaking to engage in an economic activity on an exclusive basis.[54] Special rights refer to the granting of other types of legal or regulatory advantages.[55] Although there is a difference between exclusive and special rights—since not all special rights confer exclusivity—, the case-law of the Court of Justice does not make a distinction between them. The Court of Justice's definition is that a special or exclusive right—the definition applies to both (Silva 2018, p. 215)—confers protection on a limited number of undertakings and may substantially affect the ability of other undertakings to exercise the economic activity in question in the same geographical area under substantially equivalent conditions.[56] The crux of this notion is that the right is conferred on "a limited number of undertakings".

Finally, Article 106(1) TFEU applies to measures of the Member States[57] directed towards those categories of undertakings; these include legislative acts, administrative orders, the exercise of shareholders' rights or even non-binding recommendations (Sierra 2014, p. 813; Holmes and Gregory 2018, p. 981; Whish and Bailey

[50] Judgment of 12.9.2000, *Pavlov and Others*, joined cases C-180/98 to C-184/98, EU:C:2000:428, para 75; see, also, to that effect, Case 118/85, *Commission v Italy*, para 7, and Case C-41/90 *Höfner and Elser v Macrotron*, para 21.

[51] Joined cases C-159 and C-160/91, *Poucet and Pistre*, paras 17–19.

[52] Judgment of 6.7.1982, *French Republic, Italian Republic and United Kingdom of Great Britain and Northern Ireland v Commission of the European Communities. Public undertakings - Transparency of financial relations with the State*, joined cases 188-190/80, EU:C:1982:257, para 25. This definition may be found in Commission Directive 2006/111/EC of 16 November 2006 on the transparency of financial relations between Member States and public undertakings as well as on financial transparency within certain undertakings, OJ L 318, 17.11.2006, p. 17–25, Article 2(b). See, also, Craig and de Búrca (2020, p. 1152) and Sierra (2014, p. 817).

[53] Lang (1985, p. 817). See the judgment of 5.9.2013, *SOA*, C-327/12, EU:C:2013:530, para 32.

[54] Case C-203/96, *Chemische Afvalstoffen Dusseldorp and o. v Minister van Volkshuisvesting, Ruimtelijke Ordening en Milieubeheer*, para 58; case C-30/87, *Bodson v Pompes funèbres des régions libérées,* para 33; and judgment of 4.3.2020, *CSTP Azienda della Mobilità v Commission,* C-587/18 P, EU:C:2020:150, para 7; See, notwithstanding, judgment of 23.5.2000, *Sydhavnens Sten & Grus*, C-209/98, EU:C:2000:279, para 54, where the Court of Justice considered the allocation of licenses to three companies as an exclusive right.

[55] Judgment of 1.7.2008, *MOTOE,* C-49/07 EU:C:2008:376, para 43.

[56] Case C-475/99, *Ambulanz Glöckner*, para 24; Case C-327/12, *SOA*, para 41; and opinion of Advocate General Francis Jacobs delivered on 17.5.2001, *Ambulanz Glöckner*, C-475/99, EU:C:2001:284, paras 83–89.

[57] See, inter alia, judgment of 17.5.1994, *Corsica Ferries Italia Srl*, C-18/93, EU:C:1994:195, paras 42 and 43.

2021, p. 236).[58] It is longstanding case-law of the Court of Justice that Article 106(1) TFEU applies both to the original granting of an exclusive right and to the subsequent measures granted to either a public undertaking or an undertaking to which a Member State has previously granted an exclusive or special right.[59] Therefore, the granting of a concession, may be considered, by its very nature, a State measure.[60]

4.3 The Functioning of Article 106(1) TFEU

The granting of a special or exclusive right under Article 106(1) TFEU entails a prohibition on Member States taking "*any measure contrary to the provisions of the Treaties*". As an expression of the principle of sincere cooperation enshrined in Article 4(3) TEU, Article 106 TFEU is therefore only applicable in conjunction with other provisions of the Treaty, which together have direct effect.[61] Although potentially applicable in conjunction with any provision of the Treaties—for example, the rules on free movement[62]—Article 106(1) TFEU refers explicitly to the competition rules set out in Articles 101 to 109 TFEU.[63] This is because the granting of special or exclusive rights almost always has an impact on the market position of the privileged undertakings and on the ability of their competitors to carry on the economic activity in question, in the same territory, under substantially equivalent

[58] Provided that the measure is capable of influencing and frustrating the objectives of the Union. See judgment of 24.11.1982, *Commission v Ireland ("Buy Irish")*, C-249/81, EU:C:1982:402, para 28.

[59] See judgment of 19.3.1991, *France v Commission*, 202/88, EU:C:1991:120, para 22; case C-179/90, *Merci convenzionali Porto di Genova v Siderurgica Gabrielli,* para 24; case C-323/93, *Centre d'insémination de la Crespelle v Coopérative de la Mayenne*, paras 15–22; Case C-203/96, *Dusseldorp*, paras 60–63; judgment of 5.6.2019, *Poste Italiane*, C-434/19, EU:C:2021:162, para 78; and judgment of 2.3.2023, *Bursa Română de Mărfuri*, C-394/21, EU:C:2023:146, para 37. See, in the doctrine, Sierra (2014, p. 822).

[60] Case 30/87, *Bodson v Pompes funèbres des regions libérées*, para 33. Commission Interpretative Communication on Concessions under Community law, section 2.4., p. 5.

[61] Judgment of 30.4.1974, *Sacchi*, 155/73, EU:C:1974:40, para 18; Case C-179/90, *Merci Convenzionali Porto di Genova v Siderurgica Gabrielli*, para 23; judgment of 17.7.1997, *GT-Link A/S v De Danske Statsbaner ("DSB")*, C-242/95, EU:C:1997:376, para 57; and judgment of 27.3.2019, *Pawlak*, C-545/17, EU:C:2019:260, para 44. See, also, judgment of 19.4.2007, *Asociación Nacional de Empresas Forestales ("Asemfo") v Transformación Agraria SA ("Tragsa") and O.*, C-295/05, ECLI:EU:C:2007:227, para 40, where it can be read: "*It follows from the clear terms of Article [106](1) [TFUE] that it has no independent effect in the sense that it must be read in conjunction with the relevant rules of the Treaty*".

[62] Case C-179/90, *Merci Convenzionali Porto di Genova v Siderurgica Gabrielli*, para 24; Case C-323/93, *Centre d'insémination de la Crespelle v Coopérative de la Mayenne*, para 29; and Case C-545/17, *Pawlak*, para 44.

[63] Together with the prohibition of discrimination on the grounds of nationality in Article 18 TFEU, they constitute one of the foundations of the internal market which they seek to realise.

conditions.[64] It may therefore be the case that the granting of a concession is likely to create or strengthen a dominant position.

The Court of Justice has ruled that the fact that a dominant position is created due to the granting of a special or exclusive right does not in itself constitute an infringement of Article 102 TFEU[65] (just as the acquisition of a dominant position does not in itself constitute an abuse of dominance). It is the manner in which the right is exercised that may give rise to such a breach.

For the rule to apply, the causal link between the State measure and the infringement by the undertaking does not have to be very strong. In older cases, the Court seemed to suggest that a State measure would only infringe Articles 106(1) and 102 TFEU if it would inevitably lead to an abuse of a dominant position by the undertaking to which a special or an exclusive right had been granted.[66] In more recent case-law, however, the Court of Justice has adopted a less strict approach: an infringement may be found if the measure leads (or is likely to lead) an undertaking to abuse a dominant position;[67] such abuse does not actually need to occur, the mere risk of it occurring is sufficient.[68] The precise threshold (high or low) for finding an infringement is likely to depend on the facts of the case. As Advocate General Fennelly put it in his opinion in *Raso*: "*I do not think that any general test can be enunciated for determining in advance the existence of such a link. Instead, in each individual case when guiding national courts, it will be necessary to assess the impact of impugned national rules in the economic and factual circumstances in which they operate*".[69]

Examples of the application of Article 106(1) in conjunction with Article 102 TFEU include the inability to satisfy demand for a particular service,[70] the extension

[64] Case C-475/99, *Ambulanz Glöckner*, para 24; Case C-327/12, *SOA*, para 41. See, also, Opinion of Advocate General Jacobs in case C-475/99, *Ambulanz Glöckner*, para 87.

[65] Case 155/73, *Sacchi*, para 14; case C-41/90, *Höfner and Elser v Macrotron*, para 29; case C-179/90, *Merci Convenzionali Porto di Genova v Siderurgica Gabrielli*, para 16; judgment of 30.3.2006, *Servizi Ausilliari Dottori Commercialisti*, C-451/03, EU:C:2006:208, para 23; judgment of 2.7.2015, *Gullota*, C-497/12, EU:C:2015:168, para 23; and case C-553/12 P, *Commission v DEI*, para 46. See, also, Lenaerts et al. (2021, p. 290); Lianos et al. (2019, p. 8).

[66] Case C-41/90, *Höfner and Elser*, para 29; Case C-323/93, *Centre d'insémination de la Crespelle v Coopérative de la Mayenne*, para 18; and case C-202/88, *France v Commission*, para 22.

[67] See, for example, judgment of 18.6.1991, *ERT v DEP*, C-260/89, EU:C:1991:254, para 12; judgment of 10.2.2000, *Deutsche Post*, joined cases C-147/97 and C-148/97, EU:C:2000:74, para 48; judgment of 12.2.1998, *Raso and O.*, C-163/96, EU:C:1998:54, para 27; Case C-209/98, *Sydhavnens Sten & Grus*, para 66; joined cases C-180/98 and C-184/98, *Pavlov*, para 127; and judgment of 17.7.2014, *Commission v DEI*, C-553/12, EU:C:2014:2083, paras 23 and 47.

[68] Case C-49/07, *MOTOE*, para 50. See, also, Case C-553/12 P, *Commission v DEI*, para 42.

[69] Opinion of Advocate General Fennelly, delivered on 9.10.1997, *Raso and O.*, C-163/96, EU:C:1997:477, para 65.

[70] For example, case C-41/90, *Höfner and Elser v Macrotron*, para 31; and order of the Court of 30.6.2016, *Slovenská Posta v Commission*, C-293/15 P, EU:C:2016:511, paras 34–36.

of dominance to neighbouring markets,[71] the creation of a conflict of interest,[72] the creation of inequality of opportunities[73] or discrimination[74] between economic operators as a result of the State measure (Whish and Bailey 2021, pp. 237–242; Jones et al. 2023, pp. 611–631).

However, it is important to recall that Article 106(1) is a measure addressed to the Member States. Therefore, the real conceptual issue in the application of Article 106(1) TFEU is to determine how, and in what circumstances, a Member State may itself infringe the Treaties.[75] As will be discussed below, this will inevitably affect the possibility of applying the EU Merger Regulation to the granting of a concession.

The wording of Article 106(1) TFEU, its interpretation by the Court of Justice, and the comments of legal scholars[76] reflect the delicate interplay between the application of competition principles and the economic and social policies pursued by Member States when granting special or exclusive rights (Whish and Bailey 2021, pp. 222–223). As clearly stated by Advocate General Da Cruz Vilaça in *Bodson*, "*there is nothing in the Treaty to prevent a Member State, for considerations of public interest, of a non-economic nature, from removing some [...] services from the field of competition by conferring on one or more establishments or undertakings holding concessions an exclusive right to provide them*".[77]

The following sections build on these concepts and ideas and analyse how the application of the EU Merger Regulation to concessions may be challenging.

---

[71] Judgment of 13.12.1991, *RTT v GB-Inno-BM*, 18/88, EU:C:1991:474, para 18; and case C-553/12 P, *Commission v DEI*, paras 58–59.

[72] See case C-49/07, *MOTOE*, paras 48 et seq.

[73] See case C-553/12 P, *Commission v DEI*, paras 43 and 44; and judgment of 22.5.2003, *Connect Austria*, C-462/99, EU:C:2003:297, paras 83 and 84.

[74] Case C-179/90, *Merci Convenzionali Porto di Genova v Siderurgica Gabrielli*, paras 18–20; judgment of 6.9.2006, *Portugal v Commission*, C-163/99, EU:C:2001:189, paras 66 and 73.

[75] Opinion of Advocate General Da Cruz Vilaça, 30/87, *Bodson v Pompes Funèbres des Régions Libérées*, para 91. Lenaerts et al. (2021), p. 237. Of course, the undertakings themselves must also comply with competition rules.

[76] Case C-553/12 P, *Commission v DEI*, para 23; and Case C-394/21, *Bursa Română de Mărfuri*, para 37. In the doctrine, Colomo (2022, pp. 385–386).

[77] Case C-155/73, *Sacchi*, para 14. Opinion of Advocate General Da Cruz Vilaça, 30/87, *Bodson v Pompes Funèbres des Régions Libérées*, para 73.

5 Inconsistencies in the Application of Merger Control Rules to the Act of Granting a Concession

Concessions have become a popular instrument for Member States to ensure the execution of works or the provision and management of services through a contract with economic operators.[78] As such contracts usually involve the transfer of rights to economic operators, and given that these economic operators are typically undertakings from a competition law perspective, we currently find a growing number of decisions by the Commission[79] and the Portuguese Competition Authority analysing the granting of a concession from a merger control perspective.[80]

However, there are clear difficulties in the application of merger control rules to a situation where a Member State (or an entity within a Member State, such as a municipality) grants a concession. This is the case even where such an activity has previously been performed by an economic operator and the right to develop such activity is awarded (by means of the concession agreement) to another economic operator. For the purposes of this article, this situation will be referred to as "the act of granting a concession" or simply "the granting of a concession".

5.1 Article 106(1) TFEU Should Take Precedence Over the EU Merger Regulation and the National Merger Control Rules

The argument put forward in favour of considering the act of granting a concession to be a concentration focuses on the existence of a pre-existing economic activity at the time the concession is granted and is based on the idea that the concession is the instrument by which the assets associated with that economic activity are transferred.

The Commission's practice can be illustrated by case M.7483—*Abellio Transport/Scotrail*.[81] This case concerned the award by the Scottish Ministers, to Abellio Scotrail, following a competitive tendering procedure, of the right to provide rail passenger services on the rail network in Scotland for a period of seven years, extendable to 10 years. The Commission concluded that the concession (franchise) constituted a business with a market presence, with which a turnover was associated.[82] Therefore, its transfer resulted in a "change of control on a lasting

[78] See, for example, Maduro (2023, p. 34). See Commission interpretative communication on concessions under Community law, para 4.

[79] See footnote 6.

[80] See footnote 7. See, also, from the Spanish Comisión Nacional de los Mercados y de la Competencia, decision of 11.4.2022, C/1248/21: *Sercomisa / Mediterranea Pitiusa*; and decision of 16.11.2017, C/0898/17, *Meridiam/COPCISA/COMSA/Cedinsa*.

[81] Case M.7483 – *Abellio Transport / Scotrail*, paras 5–9.

[82] See also Case M.8441 – *Firstgroup / MTR Corporation / South Western Rail Franchise*, para 10: "*The Franchise constitutes a business with a market presence to which a turnover can be clearly attributed under para 24 of the Commission Jurisdictional Notice*".

basis" and the act of granting the concession was therefore considered to be a concentration.

The reasons for this decision can be summarised as follows. First, the concession (or franchise) would generate revenue through a direct contract between the concession holder and the passengers, and such revenue would be retained by the former. Second, the concession holder would bear the commercial risks of operating the concession (it would use significant assets, such as staff and leased rail vehicles). Third, the concession holder would make commercial decisions and influence strategic decisions relating to the concession.

Another example is Case M.4797—*Govia/West Midlands Passenger Rail Franchise*,[83] where the Commission's final decision stated that "*[t]he proposed concentration concerns the award of the West Midlands Passenger Rail Franchise*".[84] Another decision with similar characteristics, in Case M.7897—*Arriva Rail North/Northern Franchise.*[85] finds that the award of a franchise to a single undertaking is an acquisition of control.[86]

All these cases originate from the same (former) Member State, the United Kingdom, and take place in the same sector, rail transport.[87] Notwithstanding, the Commission did accept this concept of concentration and justified it with reference to paragraph 24 of the Commission's Consolidated Jurisdictional notice without including Article 106 TFEU in the equation. What is remarkable, however, is that, to the best of our knowledge, the granting of concessions for the use of public resources such as water, communication frequencies[88] or energy is not being reviewed under the EU Merger Regulation.

Several examples can also be cited from the recent practice of the Portuguese Competition Authority.[89] For this purpose, we will highlight Ccent. 36/2021—*JCDecaux / Concessão de Publicidade Exterior em Lisboa*,[90] in which the Portuguese Competition Authority decided that the concession of a right to use the public domain amounted to a concentration. Its reasoning can be summarised in

[83] Commission's decision of 20.9.2007, Case M.4797, *Govia/West Midlands Passenger Rail Franchise*.

[84] Case M.4797, *Govia/West Midlands Passenger Rail Franchise*, para 9.

[85] Case M.7897, *Arriva Rail North/Northern Franchise*.

[86] Case M.7897, *Arriva Rail North/Northern Franchise*, para 11.

[87] This is not surprising, given that Section 66(3) of the Railways Act 1993 provides that the award of a rail franchise constitutes an acquisition of control of an "enterprise" for the purposes of the merger control provisions of the UK Enterprise Act 2002. According to the UK's Competition and Markets Authority, this rule also applies where the winning bid meets the EU jurisdictional thresholds (Competition and Markets Authority (CMA) 2018, p. 6) See Section 66(3) Railways Act 1993, available at https://www.legislation.gov.uk/ukpga/1993/43/section/66.

[88] We note that there was no notification to the European Commission or the *Autoridade da Concorrência* following the auction of the 5G licences in Portugal. Nevertheless, some of the winning entities were strong players in the market.

[89] See footnote 7.

[90] Case Ccent. 36/2021 – *JCDecaux / Concessão de Publicidade Exterior em Lisboa.*

the following main points. Starting from the concept of concentration, the Portuguese Competition Authority analyses whether the object of the concession can constitute a set of assets with a market presence to which a turnover can be clearly attributed. The key is to determine whether this set of assets is, *per se*, capable of allowing the pursuit of an economic activity.[91] The decision then analyses whether, in this particular case, the change of control can take place through the granting of concession contracts, following public procurement procedures.[92] According to this thesis, a concession may amount to a concentration if an economic activity is already being pursued at the time it is granted.[93] This seems to be in line with the Commission's practice with regard to the transfer of assets (although not specifically through the granting of a concession), as can be seen in paragraphs 18, 19 and 24 of the Consolidated Jurisdictional Notice.

However, in our view, this thesis fails to take full account of Article 106(1) TFEU. First, such application is at odds with the rationale of that provision, which is to preserve the freedom of Member States to define and pursue their own economic policies (see Article 5(1) TFEU and Articles 120 et seq. TFEU), within the limits set by the Treaties (notably competition rules).

Second, it would be inconsistent with the general scheme of the competition rules applicable to undertakings as set out in the TFEU, in their articulation with the EU merger control rules. In fact, to the extent that the EU Merger Regulation is part of a legislative whole, intended to implement Articles 101 and 102 TFEU, it is included in the section of the Treaty on competition rules applicable to undertakings.[94] As the Court recently held in *Towercast*, the operation and general scheme of the protection afforded by EU law against potential distortions of competition arising from concentrations provide some support to the view that, for reasons of legal certainty, the mechanism for prior control of concentrations provided for in Article 3 of the EU Merger Regulation is applied with priority over a pure and simple application of Articles 101 and 102 TFEU.[95] However, in the same judgment the Court of Justice also ruled that such a mechanism cannot prevent a competition authority from reviewing a concentration in the light of Article 102 TFEU, as some concentrations may escape *ex ante* control, e.g. by reason of not reaching the thresholds set

[91] This can be contentious, as occurred in the Case Ccent/2021/36, *JCDecaux / Concessão de Publicidade Exterior em Lisboa*, where the set of assets consisted mainly of a right of use of the public domain. It was doubtful whether those assets had the capacity of contributing, *per se*, to the development of such economic activity.

[92] Case Ccent. 36/2021 – *JCDecaux / Concessão de Publicidade Exterior em Lisboa*, paras 27, 28, 35.

[93] This understanding results clearly from the decision of 24.8.2022, Ccent. 33/2022 – *Mota-Engil / Concessão do Hospital de Lisboa Oriental*, where, in paras 12 to 15, the Portuguese Competition Authority explains that an *ex novo* concession is not a concentration, because there is no change in control over a pre-existing economic activity.

[94] Case C-248/16, *Austria Asphalt*, para 31; case C-633/16, *Ernst & Young*, para 55; and case C-449/21, *Towercast*, para 39.

[95] Case C-449/21, *Towercast*, para 40.

in the regulation.[96] A different interpretation would be tantamount to "*ruling out the direct applicability of a provision of primary law* [in this case, Article 102 TFEU] *by reason of the adoption of a piece of secondary legislation covering certain types of conduct of undertakings on the market.*"[97]

It would therefore be inconsistent with the whole scheme of competition protection in the EU to apply the EU Merger Regulation—or a concept of concentration based on its provisions—to the granting of an exclusive or special right[98] instead of Article 106(1) TFEU in conjunction with another primary law provision, such as Article 101 or Article 102 TFEU.

This follows from the principle of hierarchy of norms (and the principle derived from it that *lex superior derogate legi inferiori*),[99] as well as from the need to interpret secondary law in accordance with the rules of the Treaties. Indeed, a provision of secondary law cannot limit the scope or direct applicability of a provision of primary law. On the contrary, it must comply with the requirements of the latter and, if necessary, be interpreted restrictively.[100]

A fortiori, national legislation, such as the Portuguese Competition Act, cannot jeopardise the direct applicability of the Treaty provisions. The principle of primacy of EU law establishes the supremacy of EU law over the law of the Member States[101] and obliges all Member State authorities to give full effect to EU provisions. Therefore, the law of the Member States may not undermine the effects attached to those provisions within the territory of those States.[102] National competition authorities are ultimately obliged to disapply national legislation which contravenes those provisions.

---

[96] Case C-449/21, *Towercast*, paras 40 and 41.

[97] Case C-449/21, *Towercast*, para 42.

[98] Case 30/87, *Bodson v SA Pompes funèbres des régions libérées*, para 18.

[99] Judgment of 26.6.2012, *Poland v Commission*, C-335/09 P, EU:C:2012:385, para 127.

[100] In the words of Advocate General Kokott, "*particular importance is to be attached to the latter's status of primary law and its direct applicability*" (Opinion delivered on 13.10.2022, *Towercast*, C-449/21, EU:C:2022:777, para 28). See also Judgment of 20.1.2021, *Commission v Printeos*, C-301/19 P, EU:C:2021:39, paras 70 et seq.

[101] Judgment of 15.7.1964, *Costa v E.N.E.L.*, 6/64, EU:C:1964:66, pp. 1159 and 1160; and judgment of 24.6.2019, *Popławski,* C-573/17, EU:C:2019:530, para 52.

[102] Case C-573/17, Popławski, para 53. In other words, the primacy of EU law means that provisions of EU law should always take precedence over conflicting national legal rules, whose provisions may only apply in matters not covered by Union law. See Lenaerts et al. (2021, p. 632), Vilaça (2013, pp. 284–285).

5.2 *The Application of Merger Control Rules to the Act of Granting a Concession is at Odds with the Concept of Concentration itself*

Even from the sole point of view of the concept of concentration in the EU Merger Regulation and the Portuguese Competition Act (see Sect. 2) the thesis criticised here has obvious shortcomings.

Let us first consider the point of view of the parties (subjective element). Competition rules apply to undertakings, which are entities engaged in an economic activity. The Court of Justice has had occasion to clarify that activities which fulfil a social function based on the principle of solidarity do not normally constitute an economic activity.[103] Conversely, if the activity is profit-oriented and based on the principle of capitalisation, it is considered to be an economic activity.[104] The State itself or a public body may act as an undertaking.[105] To the extent that a public body performs an economic activity that can be separated from the exercise of its public powers, that body acts as an undertaking in relation to that activity. On the contrary, if that economic activity cannot be separated from the exercise of its public powers, all the activities carried out by that entity remain connected with the exercise of public powers.[106]

According to the case-law of the Court of Justice, activities carried out on the basis of public procurement are not considered economic for that reason alone. This depends on the subsequent use of the goods or services purchased.[107] *A fortiori*, the same applies to the act of granting a concession. In this case, the Member State is allowing or promoting the provision of a certain economic activity in the public interest, rather than engaging in an economic activity itself or acquiring the product from that activity on the market for its own needs.[108]

Looking at the concept of concentration in the light of these considerations, it becomes clear that this concept is not well suited to concessions. Indeed, the concept of concentration between undertakings is based on a change of control. It is well known that the seller is not an undertaking concerned for the purposes of

[103] See joined cases C-159 and C-160/91, *Poucet and Pistre*, paras 17–19; and judgment of 16.3.2004, *AOK-Bundesverband and Others*, joined cases C-264/01, C-306/01, C-354/01 and C-355/01, EU:C:2004:150, paras 51–55.

[104] Case C-41/90, *Höfner and Elser v Macrotron*, paras 17 and 21–23; case C-35/96, *Commission v Italy*, paras 36 and 37; and judgment of 19.2.2002, *Wouters and Others*, C-309/99, EU:C:2002:98, paras 47–49.

[105] Judgment of 20.3.1985, *Italy v Commission*, 41/83, EU:C:1985:120, paras 16 to 20. See also judgment of 12.7.2012, *Compass-Datenbank*, C-138/11, EU:C:012:449, para 35.

[106] Judgment of 26.3.2009, *Selex Sistemi Integrati* v *Commission*, C-113/07 P, EU:C:2009:191, para 72 et seq. See also case C-138/11, *Compass-Datenbank*, para 38.

[107] Case C-113/07 P, *Selex Sistemi Integrati v Commission*, para 102; judgment of 11.7.2006, *FENIN v Commission*, C-205/03 P, EU:C:2006:453, para 26; and case C-49/07, *MOTOE*, para 25. See, albeit criticising the approach, Graells (2009), p. 32 et seq.

[108] For a somewhat similar argument, see Drijber and Stergiou (2009, p. 843).

triggering the thresholds for filing a notification under the EU Merger Regulation[109] or the Portuguese Competition Act.[110] These are the acquirer and the target and this is where the concentration lies. However, if the target is an activity granted by means of a concession, the classification of such an act as a concentration would necessarily confer the character of an undertaking on the grantor, since an economic activity can only be transferred if it exists in the first place.

Secondly, the question must be analysed from an objective and a substantive point of view, i.e. what is the object of the transfer (operated by means of a concession) and how does this transfer affect the structure of the market? Of course, the subject matter of a concession can cover a wide variety of rights, licences, and assets. It is not our intention to limit the scope of this article to a single type of concession, as we believe that all concessions should receive the same legal treatment.

Once again, the key point is that, since the public body is not acting as an undertaking[111] (its action is limited to granting the right to develop a certain business or to carry out a certain activity or to provide a certain service), it is not transferring an activity to another undertaking but exercising its prerogative of public power to grant to a concessionaire the right to carry on that activity in the public interest. Therefore, there is no transfer of control of an undertaking, or part of it, from one undertaking to another, which is a key element of the concept of concentration between undertakings.[112]

From the point of view of the concession holder, the granting of a concession is also more akin to organic growth than to a structural change in the market resulting from a change in control, since in most cases the former will have to set up an entirely new business in terms of assets, equipment, technology and workforce.

In the same vein, in cases where the concession is not being granted for the first time, it cannot be argued that there is an indirect transfer of control over an undertaking between the previous and the current concession holder. Firstly, there is no direct relationship between these undertakings. Secondly, this would create an unjustified difference of treatment between pre-existing and *ex novo* concessions. Article 106(1) TFEU, and the Treaty in general, gives Member States significant margin for manoeuvre in defining their economic policy. The Member States' freedom should not be different depending on whether the concession is granted for the first time or subsequently, or whether or not there are material assets of a certain

[109] Article 5(2) of the EU Merger Regulation. See, also, Commission Consolidated Jurisdictional Notice, para 136.

[110] Article 37 of the Portuguese Competition Act.

[111] See, for example, case C-205/03 P, *FENIN v Commission*, para 26.

[112] In the judgment of 11.7.2024, *Società Italiana Imprese Balneari v Comune di Rosignano Marittimo et al.*, C-598/22, EU:C:2024:597, para 58, the Court of Justice stated that, in the situation at stake, "*the renewal of a concession for the occupation of State-owned land takes the form of a succession of two titles of occupation of State-owned land and not in the continuation or extension of the first*". This case was not directly related to the subject of this article. Nevertheless, it shows that, when interpreting the case law as a whole, we are obliged to conclude that one concession does not spill over into another as if they were one and the same entity/activity.

importance which are transferred with the concession and which might indicate that a turnover could be associated with them.

It is true that some case-law seems to undermine this idea. In case T-696/17, *Havenbedrifj Antwerpen*, the General Court held that the activity of providing port infrastructure, access to port infrastructure or land available to third parties for providing services to port users in return for port fees or concession fees is an economic activity carried out by the port.[113] However, we maintain that the correct interpretation of Article 106(1) TFEU is the one put forward above. As clarified in that same judgment, "*the concept of economic activity is an objective concept which derives from matters of fact, in particular the existence of a market for the services concerned, and does not depend on national choices or assessments*".[114] It is crystal clear that the activity of granting concessions for the provision of certain services in general is not, by itself, economic. Nevertheless, there may be situations where the State itself is engaged in economic activities, such as port management. A case-by-case analysis will be required, as may be seen in Sect. 6.

5.3 Article 106(1) TFEU and the Merger Control Rules Do Not Work in the Same Way

The application of the EU Merger Regulation to the act of granting a concession may pose other difficulties. Since the adoption of the first cases on the application of Articles 106(1) and 102 TFEU, the Court of Justice has made it clear that the creation of a dominant position—even a monopoly—through the granting of an exclusive right is not forbidden.[115] When Advocate General Jacobs proposed a definition of special or exclusive rights, he clarified that this "*serves only the purpose of determining the scope of application*" of Article 106(1) TFEU, since "*[t]he separate and further question whether those rights are legitimate is to be determined according to the Treaty provisions to which Article [106(1)] refers*", in particular Articles 101 to 109 TFEU, which are precisely the competition rules[116] (see Sect. 4.3 above).

This normative requirement is reinforced by considering the practical consequences of applying either the EU Merger Regulation or national merger control rules to the act of granting concessions, as will be shown in the following paragraphs.

---

[113] Judgment of 20.10.2019, *Havenbedrijf Antwerpen and Maatschappij van de Brugse Zeehavenv Commission*, T-696/17, EU:T:019:652, paras 62, 63 and 82.

[114] Case T-696/17, *Havenbedrijf Antwerpen and Maatschappij van de Brugse Zeehavenv Commission*, para 98.

[115] See footnote 65 above.

[116] Opinion of Advocate General Jacobs in case C-475/99, *Ambulanz Glöckner*, para 88.

First of all, the EU Merger Regulation no longer requires[117] the Commission to declare a merger incompatible with the common (or the internal) market if it gives rise to a dominant position, but rather if it creates a significant impediment to effective competition. Nevertheless, the creation of a dominant position can result in a significant impediment to effective competition. Article 2(3) of the Merger Regulation provides that "*a concentration which would significantly impede effective competition [...], in particular as a result of the creation or strengthening of a dominant position, shall be declared incompatible with the common market*".[118] Moreover, the case-law of the Court of Justice and the practice of the Commission tend to apply the test as before.[119] Indeed, the Commission guidelines on horizontal mergers make it clear that the creation of a dominant position will only be exceptionally allowed if it is offset by efficiencies.[120] Portuguese legislation mirrors the EU solution (Article 41(4) of the Portuguese Competition Act).

While merger control rules apply *ex ante*, Article 106 in conjunction with Article 102 TFEU apply *ex post*, after an infringement has been identified (Graells 2009, p. 24). Thus, the EU Merger Regulation would prohibit *ex ante* something that is not forbidden by the joint application of Articles 106 and 102 TFEU, i.e. the acquisition of a dominant position.[121] Even if it is not prohibited, the concentration may be subject to remedies in order to secure clearance,[122] thereby undermining the *effet utile* of Article 106.

Furthermore, in most concession cases, there is an open tender, which aims to ensure transparency and fair competition between bidders. The winning bid should be the one that best serves the public interest.[123] This also helps to demonstrate that merger control is difficult to reconcile with the concession granting procedures, which already have to take competition concerns into account, in particular by applying rules ensuring transparency and equal treatment.[124]

Moreover, as mentioned above, it follows from Articles 5(1) and 119 TFEU that Member States are competent to define their economic policies and to regulate economic activities within the limits laid down in the Treaties, including coordination

[117] Unlike the current Regulation No 139/2004, Regulation (EEC) No 4064/89 provided that a concentration with a Community dimension which created or strengthened a dominant position as a result of which effective competition in the common market or in a substantial part of it would be significantly impeded, should be declared incompatible with the common market (the "dominance criterion").

[118] See also Guidelines on the assessment of horizontal mergers under the Council Regulation on the control of concentrations between undertakings (2004/C 31/03), 5 February 2004, para 13.

[119] Case C-248/16, *Austria Asphalt*, para 21. See, also, Riesenkampff (2003–2004, p. 716).

[120] Guidelines on the assessment of horizontal mergers under the Council Regulation on the control of concentrations between undertakings (2004/C 31/03), 5.2.2004, p. 5, paras 76–78.

[121] Case C-497/12, *Gullotta*, para 23; case C-351/12, *SOA*, para 83; and case C-394/21, *Bursa Română de Mărfuri*, para 37.

[122] See Article 6(2) of the EU Merger Regulation and Article 23(1) of the Portuguese Competition Act.

[123] Article 41(1) of Directive 2014/23/EU.

[124] Articles 30(2) and 35 of Directive 2014/23/EU. Odudu and Sanchez-Graells (2023, pp. 599 and 601); Rodrigues (2014, p. 216).

between them and respect for the principle of an open market economy with free competition.[125] Article 106(1) safeguards this competence while guaranteeing that competition rules are not circumvented. Making the act of granting a concession subject to the EU Merger Regulation, cumulatively or in lieu of Article 106(1) TFEU, would undermine Member States' rights and competences under the Treaties. This would mean that in some cases—where the merger is prohibited or approved subject to remedies—the Member State will be prevented from granting special or exclusive rights, notwithstanding the absence of an infringement of Article 106(1) in conjunction with Article 101 or 102 TFEU.

There is yet another difficulty in applying the EU Merger Regulation to concessions. Article 106 TFEU, in conjunction with other Treaty rules, notably Articles 101 and 102, triggers application of its own control mechanisms, under the supervision of the Court of Justice, in order to prevent any abuse of market power obtained through the granting of special or exclusive rights.

To accept otherwise would be tantamount to subjecting the control of Member States' compliance with Article 106(1) TFEU to rules and mechanisms specific to the competition rules applicable to undertakings, in particular those on the control of concentrations. Indeed, the control of Member States' obligations is generally ensured by infringement procedures provided for in Articles 258 to 260 TFEU as well as by the procedural mechanisms specific to State aid. It is not appropriate to subject Member States to the powers of investigation, inquiry, and sanction granted to the Commission (or, within their respective competences, to the national competition authorities) by Regulation 1/2003 and the EU Merger Regulation unless they are acting strictly as undertakings. This is not the case where a public body acts only as a grantor of a concession. Subjecting concessions to merger control rules would mean that the transfer from the State to an undertaking of the power to exercise an economic activity (in the public interest) has to comply with two standards: those of Article 106(1) TFEU and those of the merger control rules, whereas, in the case of two private parties, only the standard of merger control would apply. This outcome could disrupt the institutional balance within the EU and between the latter and the Member States, by transferring the judicial control of Member States' obligations to the administrative procedure of the EU Merger Regulation or the national competition authorities.

[125] Case C-155/73, *Sacchi*, para 14. Opinion of Advocate General Da Cruz Vilaça, 30/87, *Bodson v Pompes Funèbres des Régions Libérées*, para 73. For an argument similar to this one, see Jones et al. (2023, p. 604).

6 The Right Balance Between the Grant of Special and Exclusive Rights and the Merger Control Regime

Having established the difficulties of articulation between merger control rules and the granting of a concession, it remains to be clarified to what extent the EU Merger Regulation or national merger control rules[126] may apply to these cases.

Article 106(1) TFEU does not preclude the independent application of competition rules to undertakings which have been granted special or exclusive rights.[127] Nothing said above contradicts this idea and nowhere in this article is it suggested that concessions—and in particular concession holders—are immune from competition law. The prohibition of restrictive practices laid down in Articles 101 and 102 TFEU and Articles 9 to 13 of the Portuguese Competition Act applies autonomously to the conduct of undertakings that have been granted special or exclusive rights, just as it does to any other undertaking (Holmes and Gregory 2018, p. 987; Silva 2018, p. 217). This will only not be the case if the conditions of the Article 106(2) exception apply. However, this matter falls outside the scope of this article.

In this context, the EU Merger Regulation and the national merger control rules continue to apply to transactions involving undertakings with special or exclusive rights, notably concession holders. The purpose of this article is not to create exceptions to the EU Merger Regulation and the national merger control rules, in particular those set out in the Portuguese Competition Act, as they are generally understood and applied, but simply to provide a more correct articulation of these rules with the obligations arising from Article 106(1) TFEU.

Building on the considerations outlined above, there are essentially two possible scenarios in which merger control rules apply to concessions: cases where the Member State itself (or an entity within the State) has previously performed the economic activity which is the object of the concession; and cases of concentrations indirectly involving concessions (e.g., a merger or acquisition involving the concession holder, and joint ventures set up to bid for the award of the concession).

6.1 Cases in Which the State Acts as an Undertaking

As to the first scenario, where the Member State itself carries on the activity that will be the object of the concession, the Member State itself (or an entity within it) should be considered an undertaking, under the terms described in Sect. 2. In this case, the change in control over assets to which a turnover may be attributed shall be deemed a concentration, regardless of the instrument implementing it. It is

[126] Article 21(3) of the EU Merger Regulation introduces the principle of "one-stop shop", whereby no Member State shall apply its national legislation on competition to any concentration that has an EU dimension.

[127] Case C-41/90, *Höfner and Elser v macrotron*, para 26.

important, however, to clarify that merger control rules may only be applicable in those cases where the State or the public entity is previously acting under the principle of capitalisation. i.e., the public entity must be previously acting as an undertaking itself. In cases where an activity is being pursued under the principle of solidarity and is then transferred to an undertaking, merger control rules cannot apply for the reasons stated above.

A number of examples can be found in the decision-making practice of the Portuguese Competition Authority.[128] For this purpose, decision Ccent. 78/2007—*Galp/TGLS*[129] (probably the first in which this issue was discussed before the Portuguese Competition Authority) should be highlighted. It is noteworthy that the Portuguese Competition Authority stated that "*(...) the commercial operation of the TGLS – until then carried out by [the grantor] – will now be the responsibility of the notifying undertaking. In this sense, the latter will acquire rights of use or enjoyment over all or part of the undertaking's assets (...), thereby exercising a decisive influence over its commercial activity and, as a result, constituting a change of a structural and lasting nature that could constitute a concentration (...)*".[130] Although other arguments were put forward by the Authority to justify the application of the Portuguese merger control rules to the situation, this was, in our view, the most compelling.

[128] Commission decision of 5.5.2017, M.8441 – *Firstgroup / MTR Corporation / South Western Rail Franchise*, paras 1 and 10. In the Portuguese Competition Authority's practice, see, decision of 28.8.2015, Ccent. 33/2015 – *CTSA / Metropolitano de Lisboa / CARRIS*, paras 35–42 (in this case, not only was the activity being carried on by public undertakings, but there was also joint control); decision of 27.11.2015, Ccent. 48/2015 – *STCP*Alsa/STCP*, para 16. Both cases regarded concessions or sub-concessions of urban public transportation, where public undertakings were previously carrying on the activity at stake. See, for the port sector, Ccent. 18/2018 – *ALB/Área Logística Bobadela, S.A.*, para 4; and for the electricity sector decision of 27 June 2008, Ccent. 6/2008 – *EDP/EDIA*, paras 81, 118 and 123. In these cases, the activities were being carried on by public entities prior to the award of the concession.

[129] Decision of the Portuguese Competition Authority of 26 June 2008, Ccent. 78/2007 – *Galp/TGLS*.

[130] Ccent. 78/2007 – *Galp/TGLS*, para 20 (iv). The translation is ours.

6.2 Cases in Which Concessions Are Indirectly Involved

A change of control over an undertaking with special or exclusive rights is one way for a merger to indirectly involve a concession.[131] In that situation, the importance of those rights for competition assessment cannot fail to be assessed in the substantive analysis, but this does not imply a judgment on their granting.[132]

A concentration may also involve a concession where a joint venture is set up to bid for the award.[133] The creation of this new entity between two formerly independent undertakings can qualify as a concentration, given that, once the concession is awarded, the joint venture will most likely perform, on a lasting basis, all the functions of an autonomous entity.[134]

7 Conclusions and Proposals

The articulation between the award of concessions and merger control is a long and tortuous one. Although the best interpretation to protect the full effect of Article 106(1) TFEU and the Member State's right to organise economic activities within its territory (subject to the provisions of the Treaties) is to consider that the granting of a concession should not be subject to merger control, we are witnessing a growing tendency among competition authorities and some legal scholars in the opposite direction. As can be seen in some decisions of the Commission and the Portuguese Competition Authority, the authorities tend to focus on the idea that the activity associated with a concession has the characteristics of a business operating on a market to which a turnover may be attributed rather than on the instrument that grants the right to carry on that activity.

---

[131] For example, Commission Decision of 22.9.2006, case M.4249 – *Abertis/Autostrade*, paras 4 and 6; Commission decision of 10.6.2013, M.6862 – *Vinci/Aeroportos de Portugal*, paras 3, 4 and 8; Commission Decision of 6.6.2018, M.8694 – *Hochtief/Abertis*, paras 11 et seq., 21 and 22. In the Portuguese practice, see, among many, decision of 25.6.2007, Ccent. 31/2007 – *MEAS/Multiterminal*, para 1; decision of 7.10.2016, Ccent. 36/2016 – *Lusovia/Ativos do Grupo Ascendi*, paras 6–9; decision of 31.1.2018, Ccent. 3/2018 – *ROADIS/AEO*, para 1.

[132] See, for example, case M.6862 – *Vinci/Aeroportos de Portugal*, paras 27–30.

[133] For example, Commission decision of 24.9.2007, M.4806 – DSB/FIRST/ÖRESUNDS TÅG, para 6; Commission Decision of 29.3.2021, M.10119 – *Deme Concessions/CDC/Région Occitanie/Port-La Nouvelle*, para 1; Commission Decision of 1.3.2019, M.9083 – *Saba Portugal / Egis Portugal / Viseu Car Park Assets*, para 1. In the Portuguese practice, see, decision of 28.3.2014, Ccent. 7/2014 – *Global Liman*Grupo Sousa e outros*NewCo / Terminal de. Cruzeiros de Lisboa*, paras 10–20 (in this case, the AdC decided that there was no joint control and, therefore, concluded that the transaction did not amount to a concentration); decision of 24.3.2015, Ccent. 42/2014 – *ETE*ETF/TML*, paras 1, 8, 10 and 12.

[134] Commission Consolidated Jurisdictional Notice, para 105. This will require a case-by-case analysis of its full-functionality.

In our view, the real issue is not the object of the transfer—and whether it qualifies as a set of assets to which a turnover can be clearly attributed—but rather the nature of that transfer. In other words, the act of granting a concession should not be analysed from the perspective of whether it is a concentration under the EU Merger Regulation or under the national competition rules. The correct perspective is, firstly, to determine whether the Member State (or entity within the Member State) is acting as an undertaking. Only in the latter case do the EU Merger Regulation or the national merger control rules apply.

This is a formal but necessary distinction that must not be blurred. It is necessary to distinguish between rules that apply to undertakings and those that apply to Member States, with all the consequences that this entails, in particular with regard to infringements of these rules.

There are, however, situations where the State itself carries on the economic activity linked to the concession to be awarded and others in which a concentration is indirectly involved. These cases do not escape merger control, although such control must be applied with caution.

In its Article 37(2), final part, and (3), the Portuguese Competition Act attempts to establish a link between the public procurement procedure in general (which usually precedes the granting of a concession) and the merger control procedure. According to these provisions, in order to achieve procedural coordination, the awarding authority should anticipate the possibility of merger control and coordinate its own public procurement procedure with the merger control procedure. Although some degree of coordination seems necessary, the legislator's choice is not satisfactory. Firstly, the powers of the awarding authority are limited, since in cases where the concession has the substantive value of a concentration it is not within the discretion of an administrative authority to override the notification obligations set out in the EU Merger Regulation and the Portuguese Competition Act. Moreover, and most importantly, it does not resolve the issue of the application of merger control rules to the act of granting concessions. In fact, we argue that the possibilities of applying Article 37(2), final part, and (3) to concessions are limited to those already developed in this article, i.e. when the State acts as an undertaking or when concessions are indirectly involved in a merger.

The problem that the Portuguese Competition Act seeks to avoid by introducing these rules is the risk of the awarding authority creating an unsustainable situation in a market subject to public procurement. This kind of flexible and *a la carte* approach may hinder the uniform application of EU law and does not contribute to the creation of a level playing field in the internal market.

Rather, it is desirable to require contracting authorities to design their concession tenders and contracts in such a way as to optimise competition for the market, by embedding the principle of competition in their public procurement procedures. The transparency rules in the Concessions Directive[135] already aim to ensure the largest possible number of bidders and to ensure effective competition between

[135] Articles 3, 30, 31, 33 and 41 of Directive 2014/23/EU.

them during the procedure. The duration of the concession is another key element of the tender. According to the Concessions Directive,[136] the duration should not exceed the minimum number of years necessary for the concessionaire to reasonably recoup the investment made to carry out the works or services and to obtain a return on the capital invested under normal operating conditions. Such a rule aims at ensuring effective competition in the form of competition for the market. Finally, the Directive provides that the contracting authority must check for signs of collusion and exclude bids on this basis.[137]

However, there is still room for improvement. In particular, information is key to increase the number of participants. It is essential that authorities design tenders in such a way that potential bidders can reasonably estimate costs and value.[138] In the case of a concession that is being awarded for a subsequent time, the information to be provided to the potential bidders should be complete, transparent and clear so that no information advantage benefits the incumbent (OECD 2017, p. 5). Particular attention should be paid to the size or scope of the concession in order to try to maintain some competition in the market, either horizontally, if it is possible to divide it into lots, or vertically, by differentiating activities and separating those where competition is possible from those where it is not (Rodrigues 2014, p. 222; OECD 2017, pp. 2–3). The tender should be designed in a neutral way, in particular from a technological point of view. Finally, the contracting authority can include competition in the market considerations[139] in the award criteria when selecting the winning bid. Involvement of the national competition authorities in the design and preparation of the tenders (with the possibility of referral to the Commission in cases where trade between Member States is affected) would be advisable.

All of the above shows that, although they converge in their objectives, we are dealing with two different blocks of legislation, based on different regulatory principles, whose spheres of application complement each other but make it essential to respect the different entities' competences inherent in each. In short, Article 106 TFEU would be devoid of purpose if the Commission or any national competition authority could freely choose any other set of EU law provisions (more precisely the rules on merger control) to replace or neutralise the full application of that article in its own sphere of application.

In conclusion, for the reasons set out above, making concessions subject to merger control rules does not seem the best approach. It is preferable to introduce more competition considerations into EU public procurement law and to provide legal principles that contracting authorities should take into account when designing their own tenders (just as they have to take into account possible violations of competition law or State aid rules in the selection criteria), rather than to mix two

[136] Article 18(2) of Directive 2014/23/EU.

[137] Article 38(7)(e) of Directive 2014/23/EU.

[138] See Autoridade da Concorrência (2020, p. 2). Although this guidance is directed to a specific sector, some general conclusions can be drawn.

[139] Together with careful attention to the rules on State aid.

different types of procedures, which may lead to opposite results. This would allow both the benefits of competition and the pursuit of other legitimate public interests of Member States, without undermining the effectiveness of Article 106(1) TFEU.

Acknowledgments The authors would like to thank Francisco Costa-Cabral for his input and Inês Domingues Alves for her invaluable support in preparing this article.

References

Autoridade da Concorrência (2020) Recomendação de boas práticas no âmbito das concessões de exploração publicitária de mobiliário urbano. https://www.concorrencia.pt/sites/default/files/processos_e_decisoes/epr/2020/2020%2520-%2520Recomenda%C3%A7%C3%A3o%2520de%2520boas%2520pr%C3%A1ticas%2520no%2520%C3%A2mbito%2520das%2520concess%C3%B5es%2520de%2520explora%C3%A7%C3%A3o%2520publicit%C3%A1ria%2520de%2520mobili%C3%A1rio%2520urbano.pdf. Accessed 27 Sept 2024

Bogdanowicz P (2020) Regulation of PPP and concessions in European Union law – different but equal? In: Public-private partnerships and concessions in the EU. Edward Elgar Publishing, Cheltenham, UK, pp 1–16

Boyce J, Lyle-Smythe A (2018) Merger control. In: Bailey D, John LE (eds) Bellamy & child European Union law of competition. Oxford University Press, Oxford

Brisimi V (2016) The interface between competition and the internal market – market separation under article 102 TFEU. Hart Publishing, Oxford and Portland, Oregon

Colino SM (2019) Competition law of the EU and UK. Oxford University Press, Oxford

Colomo PI (2022) Will article 106 TFEU case law transform EU competition law? J Eur Compet Law Pract 13:385–386

Competition and Markets Authority (CMA) (2018) Guide rail franchises: a guide for potential bidders. https://assets.publishing.service.gov.uk/media/5aaa772140f0b66b5fb4bbc0/revised_rail_franchise_qa.pdf. Acessed 28 Sept 2023

Craig P, de Búrca G (2020) EU law: text, cases and materials. Oxford University Press, Oxford

Cunha C (2005) Controlo das concentrações de empresas. Almedina, Coimbra

Da Fonseca MR, Ferreira LDN (2009) O procedimento de controlo das operações de concentração de empresas em portugal – a prática decisória da autoridade da concorrência à luz da Lei n.° 18/2003, de 11 de junho. Almedina, Coimbra

Drijber BJ, Stergiou H (2009) Public procurement law and internal market law. Common Mark Law Rev 46:805–846

Gonçalves PC (2012) Controlo de concentração de empresas no direito português (uma visão jus-administrativista). Rev Concorr Regul 7/8:245–310

Graells AS (2009) Distortions of competition generated by the public (power) buyer: a perceived gap in EC competition law and proposals to bridge it. https://papers.ssrn.com/sol3/papers.cfm?abstract_id=1458949. Accessed 20 Sept 2024

Holmes Q, Gregory D (2018) The competition rules and acts of member states. In: Bailey D, John LE (eds) Bellamy & child European union law of competition. Oxford University Press, Oxford, pp 971–1010

Jones A, Sufrin B, Dunne N (2023) EU competition law: text, cases and materials. Oxford University Press, Oxford

Lang JT (1985) Community antitrust law and government measures relating to public and privileged enterprises: article 90 EEC Treaty. In: Hawk B (ed) 1984 Fordham Corporate Law Institute, pp 543–581

Lenaerts K, Van Nuffel P, Corthaut T (2021) EU constitutional law. Oxford University Press, Oxford

Lianos L, Korah V, Siciliani P (2019) Competition law, analyses, cases and materials. Oxford University Press, Oxford
Macmillan R (2019) Competition for the market: enforcement issues with concession contracts. https://one.oecd.org/document/DAF/COMP/GF(2019)12/en/pdf. Accessed 27 Sept 2024
Maduro MP (2023) Ensuring market and state accountability – the private-public distinction in the EU internal market. In: Andriychuk O (ed) Antitrust and the bounds of power – 25 years on. Hart Publishing, Oxford, pp 33–50
Neergaard U (2005) The concept of concession in EU public procurement versus EU competition law and national law. In: Nielsen R, Treumer S (eds) The new EU public procurement directives. Djof, Copenhagen, pp 149–181
Odudu O, Sanchez-Graells A (2023) EU law on State aid and public procurement. In: Barnard C, Peers S (eds) European Union Law. Oxford University Press, Oxford, pp 583–602
OECD (2017) Competition policy and concessions. OECD, Paris
Pais SO (2006) O novo regime de controlo das concentrações de empresas na Lei n.° 18/2003. In: Marques MML, Soares AG (eds) Concorrência – Estudos, Almedina, Coimbra, pp 71–101
Riesenkampff A (2003–2004) New E.C. Merger control test under article 2 of the merger control regulationn, the symposium on European competition law. Northwest J Int Law Bus 24:715
Rodrigues NC (2012) A adjudicação de concessões na nova lei da concorrência. Rev Contratos Públicos 5:47–68
Rodrigues NC (2013) A contratação pública como instrumento de política de concorrência. Almedina, Coimbra
Rodrigues NC (2014) O Princípio da concorrência nas novas Diretivas sobre contratação pública. Rev Concorr Regul 19:214–224
Sierra BLJ (2014) Article 106 – exclusive or special rights and other anti-competitive state measures. In: Faull J, Nikpay A (eds) The EU law of competition. Oxford University Press, Oxford, pp 809–879
Silva MM (2018) Direito da Concorrência – uma introdução jurisprudencial. AAFDL, Almedina, Coimbra, Lisboa
Vilaça JLDC (2013) Le principe de l'effet utile du droit de l'Union dans la jurisprudence de la Cour. In: Rosas A, Livits E, Bots Y (eds) The court of justice and the construction of europe: analyses and perspectives on sixty years of case-law -la cour de justice et la construction de l'Europe: analyses et perspectives de soixante ans de jurisprudence. T.M.C. Asser Press, The Hague, The Netherlands, pp 279–306
Whish R, Bailey D (2021) Competition law. Oxford University Press, Oxford

José Luís da Cruz Vilaça Partner at Antas da Cunha Ecija. Former Judge at the CJEU and Advocate General at the Court of Justice of European Union.

Rita Leandro Vasconcelos Partner at Pérez-Llorca, Lisbon, Portugal. Visiting Professor at Universidade Católica Portuguesa, School of Law, Lisbon, Portugal.

Data Retention in Portugal: Big Brother Is (No Longer) Watching

Francisco Pereira Coutinho

1 Introduction

The usually placid waters of the Portuguese legal order were shaken in mid-April 2022 by a judicial ruling with the potential to trigger a tsunami of criminal conviction reversals that is already provoking a backlash in the investigation and repression of serious criminal offences committed online (Caixinha 2022). Several provisions of the so-called "Data Retention Law" (Law 32/2008), originally adopted to transpose the contentious "Data Retention Directive" (Directive 2006/24/EC), were declared unconstitutional by the Portuguese Constitutional Court (PCC), as they breach the rights to privacy, data protection and to an effective legal remedy, as interpreted in accordance with the Charter of Fundamental Rights of the European Union ("Charter").[1] The ruling caused shockwaves across the political spectrum and triggered a constitutional crisis (of sorts) (Delgado 2022; Violante 2022), with both the President of the Republic (Carmo 2022a) and the Prime Minister (Carmo 2022b) hinting on media outlets at the need for a mooted constitutional amendment in a

[1] Decision 268/2022, 828/19, 19 April 2022.

The analysis of the PCC's case law on data retention develops an article published in *Diritti Comparati* (Coutinho 2022). Direct quotes from doctrinal, legal and judicial sources in Portuguese were translated by the author. Judicial rulings referred to with no indication of source should be presumed to have originated from the Court of Justice (of the European Union).

F. P. Coutinho (✉)
NOVA School of Law, CEDIS – Research & Development Centre on Law and Society, Lisbon, Portugal
e-mail: fpereiracoutinho@novalaw.unl.pt

I. Quadros, M. Gorjão-Henriques (eds.), *Revisiting the Liberal Constitutional Features of the European Union*, https://doi.org/10.1007/978-3-031-95717-8_13

field pre-empted by EU law. The Attorney-General went as far as to request the annulment of the ruling (Gustavo 2022), an unprecedented claim promptly dismissed by the PCC on procedural and material grounds.[2]

Eight years into the data retention saga, initiated with the landmark *Digital Rights Ireland* ruling of the Court of Justice that annulled the Data Retention Directive,[3] this chapter seeks to ascertain why it took so long to remove this national law, which stemmed from what was once accurately described as the "the most privacy-invasive instrument ever adopted by the EU in terms of scale and the number of people it affects" (European Data Protection Supervisor 2010), from the statute book. I will begin by discussing the impact that a general and indiscriminate (blanket) retention of metadata has on fundamental rights (Sect. 1), which will be followed by an analysis of the relevance of metadata for law enforcement and intelligence authorities (Sect. 2). My attention will then shift to an analysis of the lifespan of the Data Retention Directive, from its conception to its demise, and further attempts at resurrection in light of the case law of the Court of Justice (Sect. 3). I will finish by addressing how the implementation of the Data Retention Directive unfolded in the Portuguese legal order, focusing on the behaviour of key stakeholders in the legislative, executive, and judicial branches (Sect. 4).

2 A CCTV Camera for Inside One's Head

Metadata are "data about data". In the context of electronic communications services in the EU, they refer to data generated by natural persons ("data subjects") through the use of landline phones, fax, mobile phones and the internet, namely traffic data—i.e. "data processed for the purpose of the conveyance of a communication on an electronic communications network or for the billing thereof"—and location data—i.e. "data processed in an electronic communications network, indicating the geographic position of the terminal equipment of a user of a publicly available electronic communications service" [Article 2(b)(c) of the "E-privacy Directive" (Directive 2002/58/EC)].[4] They include, *inter alia*, calling telephone numbers, numbers called, as well as web (URL), IP and email addresses.

[2] Decision 382/2022, 828/19, 13 May 2022.

[3] C-293/12 and C-594/12, 8 April 2014, ECLI:EU:C:2014:238.

[4] The following definition of "electronic communication metadata" is included in Article 3(4)(c) of the proposal for an "E-privacy Regulation" (COM/2017/010 final): "(D)ata processed in an electronic communications network for the purposes of transmitting, distributing or exchanging electronic communications content; including data used to trace and identify the source and destination of a communication, data on the location of the device generated in the context of providing electronic communications services, and the date, time, duration and the type of communication".

Metadata are personal data whenever they can be used to trace and identify persons involved in electronic communications.[5] If that is the case, they can only be collected for specified, explicit and legitimate purposes (purpose limitation principle) (Article 5 (1)(b) GDPR) and must be kept in a form which permits identification of data subjects for no longer than is necessary (storage limitation principle) (Article 5 (1)(e) GDPR). Except when technically necessary for the conveyance of a communication, their storage and access by providers of publicly available electronic communications services or of public communications networks ("service providers") is in principle prohibited without the consent of the data subjects concerned (confidentiality of communications principle) (Article 5 of the E-privacy Directive). Retention of traffic data is allowed solely for billing (i.e. for the benefit of the data subject/consumer) or for marketing purposes (when the data subject has given consent) (Article 6 of the E-privacy Directive), while location data "may only be processed when they are made anonymous, or with the consent of the users or subscribers (of electronic communication systems) to the extent and for the duration necessary for the provision of a value-added service" (Article 9 of the E-privacy Directive). In other words, unless consent is given by the data subject, metadata must be erased or anonymised by service providers after they are no longer needed for interconnection or billing purposes.[6]

Legal safeguards limiting data retention are necessary because metadata, taken as a whole, can tell you a lot about a person's private life. Who has that person been in touch with, and how often? Where is she and where has she been? What are her interests and habits? Metadata retention is like having a CCTV (Close-Circuit Television) camera installed inside one's head (Bowden 2001, p. 4). As smartphones became ubiquitous—84% of the Portuguese population had one in 2020 –,[7] the

---

[5] Discovering whether metadata are personal data is often tricky. In *Breyer,* C-582/14, 19 October 2016, ECLI:EU:C:2016:779, §49, a dynamic IP address was considered personal data when registered by an online media service provider, where the latter has the legal means which enable it to identify the data subject with additional data which the internet service provider has about that person. According to Article 4(1) of the General Data Protection Regulation ("GDPR") (Regulation (EU) 2016/679) "personal data means any information relating to an identified or identifiable natural person". An identifiable natural person is one who can be identified, directly or indirectly, in particular by reference to an identifier such as a name, an identification number, location data, or an online identifier.

[6] *Tele2 Sverige*, C-203/15 and C-698/15, 21 December 2016, ECLI:EU:C:2016:970, §86. According to the Article 29 Data Protection Working Party (2003, §§2.6.–2.8. and 4.2), the principle of proportionality requires that, in the cases where the bill has been paid by the data subject/consumer and is not being challenged, the storage period of metadata should have a maximum duration of three to six months, and can only include traffic data that are adequate, relevant and not excessive for billing purposes. This implies that if there is no billing for certain types of communications, the corresponding metadata cannot be retained. In the Portuguese legal order, the six-month limitation period for electronic communication billings enshrined in Article 10 (1) of Law 23/96, concerning public services, sets the outside temporal limit during which data may be stored by service providers when a bill is not being challenged or payment is not pursued.

[7] See https://www.marktest.com/wap/a/n/id~2700.aspx.

compilation of a detailed profile of almost the entire population is no longer in the realm of sci-fi.[8]

It is thus simply wrong to disregard the privacy-encroaching potential of metadata *vis-à-vis* content data and classify the interference with fundamental rights stemming from data retention as "very low" (Gouveia 2022). A general and indiscriminate retention of metadata by service providers—and its further access by law enforcement and intelligence agencies—entails a particularly serious interference with the right to privacy and the other rights (e.g. respect for communications) laid down in Article 7 of the Charter, and also with the right to data protection enshrined in Article 8 of the Charter.[9] Furthermore, the mere knowledge that data are being retained and may subsequently be used to establish patterns of individuals' behaviour without the data subjects being informed has a "chilling effect" on the exercise of other fundamental rights.[10] Not only is people's willingness to gather together in support of common beliefs on political, religious, cultural and other matters curtailed, but free speech is also deterred, which is particularly problematic for whistleblowers and for persons whose communications are subject to obligations of professional secrecy.[11] The effects of even a "vague"[12] or "diffuse"[13] feeling of constant surveillance may arguably be considered as an interference with the constitutional rights to freedom of expression (Article 11 of the Charter) and to freedom of association (Article 12 of the Charter).

[8] See *Digital Rights Ireland*, C-293/12 and C-594/12, cit., para. 27 ("(Metadata) (…) may allow very precise conclusions to be drawn concerning the private lives of the persons whose data has been retained, such as the habits of everyday life, permanent or temporary places of residence, daily or other movements, the activities carried out, the social relationships of those persons and the social environments frequented by them"), and *Quadrature du Net*, C-511/18, C-512/18 and C-520/18, 6 October 2020, ECLI:EU:C:2020:791, § 117 ("(Metadata) may reveal information on a significant number of aspects of the private life of the persons concerned, including sensitive information such as sexual orientation, political opinions, religious, philosophical, societal or other beliefs and state of health").

[9] *Digital Rights Ireland*, C-293/12 and C-594/12, cit., §§ 32-37, and *Tele2 Sverige*, C-203/15 and C-698/15, cit., §100.

[10] The "chilling effect" doctrine on the exercise of fundamental rights was recognised by the European Court of Human Rights in *Altuğ Taner Akçam v. Turkey*, 27520/07, 25 October 2011, §81 (freedom of expression) and by the United States Supreme Court in *NAACP v. Alabama*, 357 U.S. 499 (1958), at 462 (freedom of association).

[11] *Quadrature du Net*, C-511/18, C-512/18 and C-520/18, cit., § 118.

[12] Opinion of Advocate General Cruz Villalón delivered on 12 December 2013, *Digital Rights Ireland*, 8 April 2014, C-293/12 and C-594/12, ECLI:EU:C:2013:845, §§ 52 and 72.

[13] German Federal Constitutional Court, *Data Retention,* 2 March 2010, 1 BvR 256/08, 263/08, and 586/08, *BVerfGE* 125, at 260, §212.

3 Big Brother Is Watching

The potential relevance of the swarm of metadata generated by the dissemination of electronic communications in the unravelling of serious crime, and particularly for detecting and dismantling terrorist and organised crime networks, has not gone unnoticed.[14] Law enforcement and intelligence authorities soon realised that, besides trawling metadata to identify potential criminals, they could very easily "delve into the past" of any citizen by examining metadata tracing the history of communications made by persons well before they were suspected of being connected with a felony. Since access required storage, two models of data retention programmes were lawfully pursued.[15] The most problematic, considering the prohibition of unfettered large-scale exploratory or general surveillance,[16] was the "telephone record programme" developed in the United States of America by the National Security Agency under Section 215 of the "Patriot Act" (2001). The programme was based on the unrestricted collection from telecommunication operators ("telcos") of metadata covering five years of telephone calls made by whole of the American population, and the subsequent trawling of that metadata for terrorist suspects (Privacy and Civil Liberties Oversight Board 2014, pp. 8–10).[17] The other model avoided the costs of building large State-run data storage facilities by simply providing public authorities with access on a case-by-case basis to metadata collected and retained by service providers, while at the same time obliging the latter to screen their networks in search of links that might constitute a terrorist threat.[18]

In the EU, Article 14(1) of the "Telecommunication Privacy Directive" (Directive 97/66/EC) already allowed for restrictions to the principle of confidentiality resulting from proportional measures aimed at safeguarding national security and/or the enforcement of criminal law. However, the explicit green light for the adoption of national data retention programmes preventing the deletion of data no longer needed for billing purposes, and also obliging service providers to transmit that data, giving the public authorities access to it and/or screening metadata on behalf of the

---

[14] See Council of the European Union (2002a, §5): "(B)ecause of the significant growth in the possibilities afforded by electronic communications, data relating to the use of electronic communications is now a particularly important and useful tool in the investigation and prosecution of crime, in particular organised crime".

[15] I will not deal with the unlawful programmes for mass surveillance of personal data developed by Western intelligence agencies revealed after the Snowden scandal. For a thorough assessment of those surveillance practices in some Member States, see Bigo et al. (2013).

[16] European Court of Human Rights, *Klass and Others v. Germany*, 5029/71, 6 September 1978, §51.

[17] This data retention programme was restricted by the US Congress in 2015 ("Freedom Act") and, particularly, in 2020 ("Safeguarding American's Private Records Act").

[18] See Article L. 851-3 (I) of the French Internal Security Code: "(F)or the sole purpose of preventing terrorism, (telcos and ISPs) may be required to implement on their networks automated data processing practices designed (…) to detect links that might constitute a terrorist threat".

authorities, was given by the so-called "data retention amendment" introduced in Article 15 (1) of the E-privacy Directive.

The E-privacy "data retention amendment", which states that Member States "may, *inter alia*, adopt legislative measures providing for the retention of data for a limited period", was adopted in the aftermath of the terrorist attacks in the United States of America on 11 September 2001. Its origin relates directly to a Council meeting of 20 September 2001 that mandated the Commission "to submit proposals for ensuring that law enforcement authorities are able to investigate criminal acts involving the use of electronic communications systems and to take legal measures against their perpetrators" (Council of the European Union 2001, §4), and to the implementation of the international obligation stemming from the Security Council's Resolution 1373 adopted a week later, which requires States to "take the necessary steps to prevent the commission of terrorist attacks" (Security Council 2001, §2(b)).

Terrorism became the trump card to restrict fundamental rights by obliging service providers to store metadata for periods longer than needed for technical or commercial purposes, so that public authorities could be granted access to them.[19] Mandatory blanket retention of metadata was adopted mainly, but by no means exclusively, as a counterterrorism measure in Belgium (retention for 1 year), the Czech Republic (1 year), Denmark (one year), Luxembourg (1 year), France (1 year), Ireland (3 years), Italy (up to 4 years) and Spain (1 year).[20]

Securitization gained decisive traction after mass terrorism arrived in Europe with the Atocha train station bombing attacks that killed 193 people on 11 March 2004 in Madrid (Ray 2022a). "Deeply shocked", the European Council declared that acts of terrorism were attacks against the values on which the Union is founded, and further instructed the Council to establish common rules on the retention of metadata by service providers (European Council 2004, p. 4). One month later, France, Ireland, Sweden and the United Kingdom submitted a proposal for a framework decision that foresaw the blanket storing of metadata between 12 and 36 months "to meet the needs of the security, intelligence and law enforcement agencies in the fight against modern criminals including terrorists" (Council of the

[19] *Ireland v Parliament and Council*, C-301/06, 10 February 2009, ECLI:EU:C:2009:68, § 67: "The evidence submitted to the Court confirms that, following the terrorist attacks [of 11 September 2001 in New York (United States), 11 March 2004 in Madrid (Spain) and 7 July 2005 in London (United Kingdom)], several Member States, realising that data relating to electronic communications constitute an effective means for the detection and prevention of crimes, including terrorism, adopted measures pursuant to Article 15(1) of Directive 2002/58 with a view to imposing obligations on service providers concerning the retention of such data".

[20] See, respectively, Article 14 of the Law on Cybercrime, of 28 November 2000 (Belgium), Act 127/2005 (Electronic Communications Act) (Czech Republic), Act 378 of 6 June 2002 (Anti-Terrorism Act), which extended the scope of Section 786 of the Administration of Justice Act (Denmark), Privacy and Electronic Communications Act, of 30 May 2005 (Luxembourg), Article 29 of the Law on Everyday Security, of 15 November 2001 (France), Secret direction of the Irish Government of April 2002 adopted under Section 110(1) of the Postal and Telecommunications Services Act, 1983 (Ireland), Section 132 of the Data Protection Code (Decree-Law of 30 June 2003, 196) (Italy), and Article 12(1) of the Information Society and Electronic Services Law (Law 34/2002) (Spain).

European Union 2004a, p. 6). The proposal was particularly relevant for the British and Irish Governments, which were struggling to gain Parliamentary approval for legislation requiring service providers to retain data (McIntyre 2008, pp. 329–330; Jones and Hayes 2013, p. 10).

In addition to avoiding national parliaments, a "third-pillar" framework decision under Title VI of the EU Treaty also allowed national governments to bypass the will of the European Parliament, although this body did have to be consulted. Not surprisingly, given the emphatic stance it took on 6 September 2001 that "a general data retention principle must be forbidden" (European Parliament 2001, §I), the European Parliament rejected the legislative initiative (European Parliament 2005a), endorsing the report of the Committee on Civil Liberties, Justice and Home Affairs, which questioned the proportionality of blanket data retention and the legal basis chosen by the Council to pursue it (European Parliament 2005b). The argument that regulating obligations imposed on service providers necessarily fall within European Community competence and, therefore, had to be approved by the Council in tandem with the European Parliament, based on a Commission proposal for a directive, was also supported by the Council's own legal service (Legal Service of the Council of the European Union 2005), and eventually led to the data retention framework proposal being abandoned.[21]

EU-wide blanket data retention would possibly have reached a political dead-end had it not been for the terrorist attacks that killed 56 people in London on 7 July 2005 (Ray 2022b). The United Kingdom held the Presidency of the Council at the time and used the attacks as a justification for the urgent adoption of the directive on data retention proposed by the Commission on 21 September 2005 (Jones and Hayes 2013, p. 9). The Council's call was quickly answered by the European Parliament, which adopted the proposal on 14 December 2005 in a single reading (European Parliament 2005c). Responsiveness to the public's growing security concerns probably explain the European Parliament's transformation into a "responsible legislator" (Servent 2013, p. 982) at the expense of "selling out" its traditional civil liberties principles regarding data protection (Peers 2005, pp. 7–8). The fastest legislative procedure in the history of the EU ended on 15 March 2006 (Hornung and Schnabel 2009, p. 120), following the Council's qualified majority approval, with Ireland and Slovakia voting against (Council of the European Union 2006a, p. 4).

---

[21] See the minutes of the 12 October 2005 meeting of the Council of the European Union (2005), where a majority of delegations expressed their openness to the idea of adopting a directive on data retention.

4 Lifetime of the Most Privacy-Invasive Legislative Instrument Ever Adopted by the EU

4.1 A Securitarian DNA that Reflects a Controversial Conception and Birth

The European legislator justified the compression of fundamental rights arising from data retention with the overarching threat to public and national security posed by terrorism:

> Because retention of data has proved to be such a necessary and effective investigative tool for law enforcement in several Member States, and in particular concerning serious matters such as organised crime and terrorism, it is necessary to ensure that retained data are made available to law enforcement authorities for a certain period, subject to the conditions provided for in this Directive. The adoption of an instrument on data retention that complies with the requirements of Article 8 (right to privacy) of the (European Convention of Human Rights) is therefore a necessary measure (Recital 9 of the Data Retention Directive).

The idea that data retention is a *necessary* and *effective* counterterrorism law enforcement instrument is at best wishful thinking. An official report from 2014 on the pervasive NSA telephone metadata retention programme found not "a single instance involving a threat to the United States in which the (…) program made a concrete difference in the outcome of a counterterrorism investigation", or "an instance in which the program directly contributed to the discovery of a previously unknown terrorist plot or the disruption of a terrorist attack" (Privacy and Civil Liberties Oversight Board 2014, p. 146). In *Tele 2 Sverige*, the most persuasive evidence in this regard provided to the Court of Justice was the statement from the French Government that access to the communications data of the persons involved in the terrorist attacks of 2015 in France was "extremely useful" in discovering the authors of those attacks and their accomplices.[22]

The Data Retention Directive was clearly the offspring of a securitarian zeitgeist. After stating the overall importance of metadata "for the investigation, detection, and prosecution of criminal offences, as demonstrated by research and the practical experience of several Member States" (Recital 11),[23] the Directive determined that

---

[22] Opinion of Advocate General Saugmandsgaard Øe delivered on 19 July 2016, *Tele2 Sverige*, C-203/15 and C-698/15, ECLI:EU:C:2016:572, §183.

[23] This statement convinced neither the Article 29 Data Protection Working Party (2005, pp. 5–6), which considered that the necessity for "unprecedented, continued, pervasive monitoring of all kinds of communication and movement of the totality of citizens in their daily life" was not based on "crystal-clear evidence", nor the European Data Protection Supervisor (2011, §75), which advised the Commission to "invest in collecting further practical evidence from the Member States in order to demonstrate the necessity of data retention as a measure under EU law" before presenting a revised version of the Directive. This debate is still not settled, with a comparative statistical study of the European Parliament requested by a Pirate Party MEP finding in January 2020 no direct impact of data retention on crime clearance rates across Member States (European Parliament Research Service 2020, p. 3).

metadata should be available to law enforcement authorities dealing with "serious crime" (Article 1 (1)). Purpose creep naturally ensued, with several Member States failing to elaborate on the concept or allowing data to be accessed and used to prevent and combat crime generally or for national security purposes (European Commission 2011, pp. 6, 8), thereby ignoring the Council's urge for Member States to have due regard to the crimes listed in Article 2(2) of the Framework Decision on the European Arrest Warrant and crime involving telecommunication (Council of the European Union 2006b, p. 2).

Service providers were to be obliged to collect and store metadata necessary to trace and identify the source of a communication and its destination, to identify the date, time, duration and type of a communication, to identify the users' communication equipment, and to establish the location of mobile communication equipment (Article 5 of the Data Retention Directive). The retention could not cover content data of electronic communications, including information consulted using an electronic communications network (Article 1 (2) *in fine* of the Data Retention Directive). Member States were given leeway to decide on whether to reimburse storage costs and to set the length of the retention period within a temporal window of 6 months to 2 years (Article 6 of the Data Retention Directive). Access to data or the use thereof by the police or judicial authorities was also left to be defined by national law (Recital 25 and Article 4 of the Data Retention Directive), which had also to ensure service providers' respect for data security.[24]

Preventive blanket data retention had long been pursued by law enforcement and intelligence agencies as an alternative to the less intrusive targeted surveillance of data preservation ("quick freeze")—i.e. the conservation of specific data relating to specified individuals in certain cases. "Quick freeze" was considered insufficient to trace the source of illegal content, such as racist and xenophobic material and child pornography or the source of attacks against information systems, or to identify those involved in using electronic communications networks for the purpose of organised crime and terrorism (Council of the European Union 2004b, Recitals 5 and 6). While data preservation allows access to metadata generated by communications made *after* someone has been identified as a suspect of a crime, with data retention law enforcement authorities can go "back in time" (European Commission 2015, p. 12) by examining metadata generated by someone *before* that person has been identified as being potentially connected, even indirectly or remotely, with a

[24]Article 7 of the Data Retention Directive, which refers to the following data security principles with respect to data retained: (a) the retained data shall be of the same quality and subject to the same security and protection as those data on the network; (b) the data shall be subject to appropriate technical and organisational measures to protect the data against accidental or unlawful destruction, accidental loss or alteration, or unauthorised or unlawful storage, processing, access or disclosure; (c) the data shall be subject to appropriate technical and organisational measures to ensure that they can be accessed by specially authorised personnel only; and (d) the data, except those that have been accessed and preserved, shall be destroyed at the end of the period of retention. Compliance with data security by service providers had to be supervised by "one or more public authorities" in accordance with Article 9 of the Data Retention Directive.

crime.[25] According to the Cybercrime Office of the Portuguese Public Prosecution Service (European Commission 2015, p. 4), this is the reason why:

> (D)ata retention must be indiscriminate, on the one hand, and include every citizen, on the other. When data are collected and retained it is not possible to know if they may be needed in the future as evidence of a crime. Only after a crime has been committed will data previously obtained through general and indiscriminate retention have value as evidence. When there is already a suspect under investigation, other instruments can be used to gather information relating to that person that may be necessary (e.g. the interception of communications). It is precisely when evidence of the facts has not been obtained in advance or a suspect has not been identified that it is useful to access retained data– the latter may actually be the only means of discovering who committed a particular crime. However, at that moment, such data must have already been retained and stored (all data regarding every citizen). This explains why data retention (…) is only useful if the data regard every citizen, indiscriminately.

4.2 The Troubles of Infancy

The transposition of the Data Retention Directive proved troublesome, unsurprisingly. The deadline of 15 September 2007 was generally ignored. The European Commission sent letters of formal notice under the 258 TFEU infringement procedure, informing of default and requesting action, to Austria, Bulgaria, Cyprus, Estonia, Finland, Greece, Hungary, Ireland, Italy, Lithuania, Luxembourg, Malta, the Netherlands, Poland, Portugal, Romania, Slovenia, Slovakia, and Sweden.[26] Reasoned opinions followed on 18 September 2008 targeting Austria, Greece, Ireland, Lithuania, the Netherlands, Poland, Romania, and Sweden.[27] Judicial actions were brought in May and June 2009 against Austria, Greece, Ireland, the Netherlands and Sweden, in August 2010 against Luxembourg, and in July 2012 against Germany.[28] The Court of Justice declared an infringement by Austria,

[25] Opinion of Advocate General Saugmandsgaard Øe, *Tele2 Sverige*, C-203/15 and C-698/15, cit., §§179–180.

[26] The letters were sent on 27 November 2007 in infringements procedures 2007/1036, 2007/1045, 2007/1051, 2007/1078, 2007/1092, 2007/1071, 2007/1083, 2007/1108, 2007/1116, 2007/1126, 2007/1133, 2007/1139, 2007/1149, 2007/1153, 2007/1159, 2007/1168, 2007/1178, 2007/1187, 2007/1193 and 2007/1181. Formal notices were afterwards sent to Belgium on 16 September 2012 (infringement procedure 2012/2152), to the Czech Republic on 25 November 2011 (infringement procedure 2011/1143), and to Germany on 16 June 2011 (infringement procedure 2011/2091).

[27] Reasoned opinions were afterwards also sent to Belgium (30 May 2013), the Czech Republic (22 March 2012), Germany (27 November 2011 and 22 March 2012), Luxembourg (20 November 2009), and again to Romania (27 October 2011 and 22 March 2012).

[28] In cases C-189/09 (Commission v Austria), C-211/09 (Commission v Greece), C-202/09 (Commission v Ireland), C-192/09 (Commission v Netherlands), C-185/09 (Commission v Sweden), C-394/10 (Commission v Luxembourg), and C-329/12(Commission v Germany).

Greece, Ireland, and Sweden.[29] Only Sweden ended up being fined € 3 million, in May 2013.[30]

Delays in transposition stemmed from staunch political resistance to data retention.[31] Constitutional judicial challenges to national law implementing the directive followed suit in Austria (Anderl and Klammer 2021, pp. 44–48), Belgium (Van de Heyning 2021, p. 61), Bulgaria (Kashumov 2021, pp. 76–77), Cyprus (Kombos and Shaelou 2019, pp. 1412–1414), the Czech Republic (Polčák 2021, pp. 104–107), Germany (Albers 2021, pp. 120–121), Ireland (Fennelly 2021, pp. 140–141), Poland (Podkowik and Zubik 2021, pp. 160–162) Romania (Şandru 2021, pp. 191–198), Slovakia (Gera and Husovec 2021, pp. 206–209), and Slovenia (Toplak 2021, pp. 221–222). A couple of judicial decisions stand out.

On 8 October 2009, the Constitutional Court of Romania struck down Law 298/2008—a.k.a. "Big Brother Law" (Şandru 2021, p. 192)—considering that the obligation it imposed on service providers to proceed to an open-ended collection of metadata for law enforcement purposes was a disproportionate infringement of the right to privacy (Article 26 of the Constitution), the right to secrecy of correspondence (Article 28 of the Constitution), and freedom of expression (Article 30(1) of the Constitution) (Zubik et al. 2021). This was tantamount to indirectly declaring the Data Retention Directive itself unconstitutional (Şandru 2021, p. 192). The Romanian court unfortunately failed to appropriately qualify the issue at hand as a problem of European constitutional law—i.e. on the compatibility with the Charter of national law implementing EU law (Article 51(1) of the Charter)—that required a request for a preliminary ruling on validity to be submitted to the Court of Justice under Article 267(3) TFEU. Some of the arguments the Constitutional Court of Romania used on the inadmissibility of blanket data retention would, however, resonate years later in Luxembourg. It argued that any obligation to retain data is an exception to the principle of confidentiality of communications. Blanket retention of metadata is inadmissible precisely because it transforms the exception into an absolute rule. Its indiscriminate nature is, moreover, "likely to overturn the presumption of innocence and to transform *a priori* all users of electronic communications services or public communications networks into persons suspected of committing terrorist offences or serious crimes" (Zubik et al. 2021, pp. 354–355).

A few months later, several provisions of the German data retention legislation received the same fate as the Romanian legislation, in a mass complaint case

[29] In cases *Commission v Austria*, C-189/09, 29 July 2010, ECLI:EU:C:2010:455, §22, *Commission v Greece*, C-211/09, 26 November 2009, ECLI:EU:C:2009:737, §10, *Commission v Ireland*, C-192/09, 26 November 2009, ECLI:EU:C:2009:736, §14, and *Commission v Sweden*, C-185/09, 4 February 2010, ECLI:EU:C:2010:59, §12.

[30] *Commission v Sweden*, C-270/11, 30 May 2013, ECLI:EU:C:2013:339, §60. On 16 April 2014, the Commissioner Cecilia Mallström pledged in the European Parliament to return the fine to Sweden after the *Digital Rights Ireland* ruling of the Court of Justice invalidating the Data Retention Directive (European Parliament 2014).

[31] That was the case in Austria (*Commission v Austria*, C-189/09, cit., §4), Germany (Grimm et al. 2019, pp. 459, 477), and Sweden (*Commission v Sweden*, C-270/11, cit., §33).

triggered by around 34,000 citizens at the Federal Constitutional Court. However, unlike their Romanian counterparts, the German judges ruled that the blanket data storage obligation stemming from the Directive was not unconstitutional. It was considered an exceptional but otherwise proportional restriction of fundamental rights. This conclusion was based on the arguments that the preventive retention of data: (i) was imposed on multiple private service providers and not on public authorities, which could only retrieve and use the data under strict conditions; (ii) did not include the content of telephone conversations and emails or websites visited online; (iii) was limited to six months;[32] and (iv) was a response to pressing social needs created by the development of new technologies—e.g. the repression of serious criminal offences perpetrated online that would escape detection if metadata were deleted.[33] A preliminary reference to the Court of Justice was not necessary because the Federal Constitutional Court only purported to review national law implementing the directive in respect of matters left to the discretion of the national legislator, namely the level of data security, storage requirements, and the procedures governing access and use of data by public authorities.[34] Given the severe level of encroachment on fundamental rights of the possible use of metadata, which according to the court allows for the creation of meaningful personal and mobility profiles of virtually every citizen,[35] the principle of proportionality in the narrow sense required preventive blanket data retention to follow high standards of data security and to subject data access and use by public authorities to strict procedural and substantive requirements[36]—e.g. the retrieval and transmission of data had to be limited to situations where it was necessary "to ward off dangers to the life, limb or freedom of a person, to the existence or the security of the Federation or of a *Land* or to ward off a danger to public safety",[37] and required, in principle, prior judicial review[38] and prior notification of the data subjects concerned.[39] As neither those standards nor the said requirements were generally met in the German legislation on

[32] This was considered a very long storage period "at the upper limit of what (could) be justified from the point of view of proportionality" (*Data Retention*, 2 March 2010, cit., §215 bb)).

[33] *Data Retention*, 2 March 2010, cit., §§213 b), 214 aa), 215 bb), 216 cc) and 218. This conclusion, argues Albers (2021, pp. 126-127), is hardly reconcilable with the prohibition of preventive storage of personal data for indefinite or not yet definable purposes—itself a corollary of the principle of limitation of purpose which requires data to be necessary for the respective purposes—adopted in the *Census* judgment of 15 December 1983 (1 BvR 209/83 et al., *BVerfGE* 65, at 46-47), as it admits the constitutionality of a bulk retention of data that will necessarily determine that a vast majority of the data retained will prove unnecessary.

[34] Articles 4, 7 and 8 of the Data Retention Directive. In *Ireland v Parliament and Council*, C-301/06, cit., §83, the Court of Justice clarified that the aim of the Directive was not to harmonise the issue of access to data by the competent national law enforcement authorities or that relating to the use and exchange of those data between those authorities.

[35] *Data Retention*, 2 March 2010, cit., §211.

[36] Idem, §§220 and 225–231.

[37] Idem, §231.

[38] Idem §§247 aa) and 249.

[39] Idem, §243 bb).

data retention, the Court declared a breach of the inviolability of the secrecy of telecommunication foreseen in Article 10 of the Basic Law.[40]

4.3 Demise

Ireland immediately sought the annulment of the Directive at the Court of Justice, arguing that data retention had to be dealt with under a "third pillar" legal basis where Member States hold veto power.[41] The Luxembourg court rejected the claim considering that the Directive essentially regulated operations of service providers in the internal market independent of the implementation of any police and judicial cooperation in criminal matters, as it harmonised neither the issue of access to data by public authorities nor that relating to the use and exchange of data between authorities.[42]

Ireland's annulment request related solely to the choice of legal basis and not to any possible infringement of fundamental rights.[43] The Court of Justice was again able to avoid reviewing a possible interference of data retention with the exercise of fundamental rights when Austria claimed that its delay in transposing the Directive stemmed from doubts as to whether it respected the right to privacy enshrined in Articles 8 of the ECHR and the Charter.[44] The Court promptly dismissed the argument, considering it should have been raised in an action for annulment and not, as was the case, as a means of defence in an infringement action.[45] The assurance in Recital 22 of the Directive of "full compliance with citizens' fundamental rights" was later invoked in another infringement action to measure the degree of seriousness of the breach of EU law imputed on Member States for not transposing the directive.[46]

Yet it was only a matter of time until the national courts questioned the Court of Justice directly on the compatibility of the Directive with the exercise of fundamental rights protected by the Charter, under the Article 267 TFEU procedure. Preliminary references in this regard were submitted by the Irish High Court and the Austrian Constitutional Court during 2012. On 8 April 2014, the Court of Justice declared the Data Retention Directive invalid due to breach of Articles 7 and 8 of the Charter.[47]

---

[40] Idem, §§292.

[41] Ireland contented that the only legal basis on which the measures contained in Directive 2006/24 could be validly founded was Title VI of the EU Treaty ("TEU"), namely Articles 30 TEU, 31(1)(c) TEU and 34(2)(b) TEU (*Ireland v Parliament and Council*, C-301/06, cit., §28).

[42] Ireland v Parliament and Council, C-301/06, cit., §§83–85.

[43] Idem, §57.

[44] *Commission v Austria*, C-189/09, cit., §10–11.

[45] Idem, §15.

[46] *Commission v Sweden*, C-270/11, cit., §48–49.

[47] *Digital Rights Ireland*, C-293/12 and C-594/12, cit., §69.

Digital Rights Ireland is a landmark ruling that effectively bans securitarian legal instruments based on a preventive general and indiscriminate retention of metadata. The Court of Justice had no qualms in classifying the retention of data mandated by the Directive as a "wide-ranging and particularly serious" interference with the rights to privacy and data protection of virtually the entire European population.[48] The fact that data were retained and could subsequently be used without data subjects being informed was considered likely to generate in their minds the feeling that their private lives were under constant surveillance.[49] The judicial review of the discretion of the legislator in this domain had to be strict, considering the extent and seriousness of the interference.[50] The Court salomonically conceded that the data retention obligations stemming from the Directive were a "valuable tool" in attaining the objective, in the general interest, of contributing to the fight against serious crime in order to ensure public security, and breached neither the essence of the right to privacy, as the content of communications as such was not stored, nor the essence of the right to data protection, as service providers had to respect certain principles of data protection and data security.[51]

However, the storage of data in bulk required by the Directive failed the test of proportionality as it was not limited to what was strictly necessary. The breach of the principle of proportionality derived directly from the general and indiscriminate nature of the retention, which covered all persons and all means of electronic communication, as well as all metadata "without any differentiation, limitation or exception being made in the light of the objective of fighting against serious crime".[52] This meant it affected even persons for whom there was no "evidence capable of suggesting that their conduct might have a link, even an indirect or remote one, with serious crime", as well as persons whose communications were subject to the obligation of professional secrecy.[53] A proportional measure required retained data to have at least some indirect link to a threat to public security. That would be the case of targeted retention surveillance measures focused on collecting data pertaining either "to a particular period and/or a particular geographical zone and/or to a circle of particular persons likely to be involved, in one way or another, in a serious crime", or "to persons who could, for other reasons, contribute, by the retention of their data, to the prevention, detection or prosecution of serious offences".[54] Such a data retention measure should also, contrary to that laid down by the Directive, distinguish between the categories of retained data and their "possible usefulness for the purposes of the objective pursued or according to the persons concerned",[55] and

[48] Idem, §§37, 56 and 65.

[49] *Digital Rights Ireland*, C-293/12 and C-594/12, cit., §37.

[50] Idem, §§47–48.

[51] Idem, §§ 39–50.

[52] Idem, §57.

[53] Idem, §58.

[54] Idem, §59.

[55] Idem, §63.

adopt a particularly high level of protection and security to ensure effective protection of the retained data against the risk of abuse and against any unlawful access and use of that data.[56] Service providers should, *inter alia*, be obliged to retain data in the EU and to irreversibly destroy data at the end of the data retention period.[57]

Surprisingly, given that issues of access to data were outside the scope of the Directive,[58] the Court also lambasted the European legislator for not setting any substantive and procedural conditions on access to the retained data and their subsequent use. Unrestricted access by public authorities would be tantamount to unlawful exploratory or general surveillance (Article 29 Working Party 1999, p. 8). Therefore, access to the retained data required a prior review carried out by a court or by an independent administrative body. Furthermore, access to data or the use thereof had to be strictly restricted to a limited number of persons involved in preventing and detecting precisely defined serious offences or in conducting criminal prosecutions relating thereto.[59]

4.4 Attempts at Resurrection

Digital Rights Ireland relieved Member States from implementing the Directive at a time when most of them had already duly introduced data retention into their domestic legal orders.[60] The ruling of the Court of Justice retroactively eliminated the effects of the Directive from the legal system of the EU (Türk 2009, pp. 228–229),[61] but had no effect on the *formal* validity of the corresponding implementing national law, as the latter stemmed from *domestic* sources of law.[62] For that

---

[56] Idem, §66–68.

[57] Idem, §67–68.

[58] *Ireland v Parliament and Council*, C-301/06, cit., §83, and Recital 25 and Article 4 of the Data Retention Directive.

[59] *Digital Rights Ireland*, C-293/12 and C-594/12, cit., §§61–62.

[60] The exceptions being Germany and the Czech Republic after the *Data Retention* judgments of the Federal Constitutional Court of Germany of 2 March 2010, cit., and of the Constitutional Court of the Czech Republic of 22 March 2011, Pl. ÚS 24/10 (Albers 2021, p. 131; Polčák 2021, pp. 114–115).

[61] *FMC*, C-212/94, 8 February 1996, ECLI:EU:C:1996:40, §55 ("(A) judgment of the Court in proceedings for a preliminary ruling declaring a (EU) act to be invalid takes effect, like a judgment annulling an act, from the date on which the act entered into force, with all the consequences which that entails"), and, by analogy, Court of First Instance, *Corus UK* Ltd, T-171/99, 10 October 2001, ECLI:EU:T:2001:249, §50 ("(A) judgment of annulment (…) takes effect *ex tunc* and thus has the effect of retroactively eliminating the annulled measure from the legal system").

[62] Portuguese Constitutional Court, 420/2017, 13 July 2017, §10: "(T)he declaration of invalidity of a directive has no automatic consequence on the validity of a transposing Portuguese legal act. This act (…) stems from an autonomous source of validity and legitimacy". See also Bobek (2017, p. 164): "National law can only be invalidated by the national institutions and EU law by the EU institutions".

reason, between June 2014 and June 2015 legislation transposing the Directive was judicially rendered inoperative in the Netherlands,[63] and revoked by constitutional courts in Austria, Belgium, Bulgaria, Poland, Romania, Slovenia, and Slovakia.[64] In most Member States, however, legislation providing for a general and indiscriminate retention of metadata remained untouched. Since Member States were expressly authorised to adopt data retention as an exception to the principle of confidentiality (Article 15(1) of the E-privacy Directive), could such legislation still be enforced?

As national law on data retention falls within the scope of Article 15(1) of the E-privacy Directive,[65] and thus implements EU law within the meaning of Article 51(1) of the Charter,[66] a negative answer looked straightforward in light of the principle of primacy: since the Directive was held to be incompatible with Articles 7 and 8 of the Charter, then it followed that implementing national legislation with the very same provisions also breached the Charter, and consequently had to be rendered inapplicable in the domestic legal realm.[67]

A positive answer was, however, voiced based on the idea that the *Digital Rights Ireland* ruling could not be interpreted as establishing a ban on the adoption of a blanket data retention legal scheme. National law adopted to implement the Data Retention Directive was not structurally incompatible with the Charter and was lawful if accompanied by appropriate procedural and substantive safeguards.[68] The argument was far-fetched, but it was even used by Advocate General Øe in response to preliminary references submitted by British and Swedish courts in the *Tele2 Sverige* case.[69]

The remaining doubts on the lawfulness of blanket data retention were resolved by the Court of Justice on 21 December 2016. Article 15(1) of the E-privacy Directive requires data retention to be an exception to the principle of

[63] By a decision of 11 March 2015 of a District Court of The Hague considering the Data Retention Act 2009 to be manifestly incompatible with EU law (Besselink and Claes 2019, p. 203).

[64] Constitutional Court of Austria, 27 June 2014, G 47/2012; Constitutional Court of Slovenia, 3 July 2014, U-I-65/13; Romanian Constitutional Court, 8 July 2014, 440; Constitutional Tribunal of the Republic of Poland, 30 July 2014, K 23/11; Constitutional Court of Bulgaria, 12 March 2015, 8/2014; Constitutional Court of Slovakia, 29 April 2015, PL. ÚS 10/2014; Constitutional Court of Belgium, 11 June 2015, 84/2015.

[65] *Tele2 Sverige*, C-203/15 and C-698/15, cit., §§65–81.

[66] *Fransson*, C-617/10, 26 February 2013, ECLI:EU:C:2013:105, §§20–21.

[67] *Simmenthal*, 106/77, 9 March 1978, EU:C:1978:49, §17.

[68] See: in Cyprus, several rulings of the Supreme Court discussed by Markou (2021, pp. 90-94); in Denmark, a memorandum of the Danish Ministry for Justice dated 2 June 2014, quoted by Krunke and Baumbach (2019, pp. 297-298); in Estonia, a decision from the Supreme Court of 23 February 2015, quoted by Ernits et al. (2019, p. 927); in Finland, an opinion from the Constitutional Law Committee of Parliament dated April 2014, quoted by Ojanen and Salminen (2019, p. 318); in Sweden, the special report from the Swedish Ministry for Justice "Datalagring, EU-rätten och svensk rätt, Ds 2014:23", 13 June 2014, quoted in *Tele2 Sverige*, C-203/15 and C-698/15, cit., §46; in the United Kingdom, the ruling of the English High Court in *Davis & Ors v. SSHD*, 17 July 2015, CO/3665/2014, CO/3667/2014, CO/3794/2014, §89.

[69] *Tele2 Sverige*, C-203/15 and C-698/15, cit., §205.

confidentiality which can only be pursued with the objective of fighting serious crime.[70] National law implementing the Data Retention Directive transforms the exception into a rule as it provides for a "general and indiscriminate" retention of metadata.[71] It therefore exceeds the limits of what is strictly necessary and is not justified as required by Article 15(1) of the E-Privacy Directive, read in the light of Articles 7, 8, 11 and 52(1) of the Charter.[72] These provisions do not, however, preclude Member States from adopting legislation permitting, as a preventive measure, the *targeted* retention of metadata provided that such retention is limited to what is strictly necessary in terms of the categories of data to be retained, the means of communication affected, the persons concerned, and the retention period adopted.[73] Such retention of data is admissible only when there is "objective evidence which makes it possible to identify a public whose data is likely to reveal a link, at least an indirect one, with serious criminal offences", namely when national authorities consider that "there exists, in one or more geographical areas, a high risk of preparation for or commission of such offences".[74] Given the seriousness of the interference with fundamental rights it entails, national legislation authorising preventive targeted data retention relating to specific circles of people or geographical locations must establish stringent safeguards concerning access to the retained data and the protection and security of that data. Beyond the requirements laid down in *Digital Rights Ireland*, the Court declared that access should be restricted to cases that deal with serious crime and, as a general rule, should only be granted "to the data of individuals suspected of planning, committing or having committed a serious crime or of being implicated in one way or another in such a crime".[75] Moreover, the principle of transparency requires national authorities that have been granted access to "notify the persons affected, under the applicable national procedures, as soon as that notification is no longer liable to jeopardise the investigations being undertaken by those authorities" so that such persons can exercise their right to a legal remedy.[76]

[70] Idem, cit., §§102–104.

[71] Idem, §97 and 104.

[72] Idem, §107.

[73] Idem, §108.

[74] Idem, §111. In *La Quadrature du Net*, C-511/18, C-512/18 and C-520/18, cit., §150, the Court added that those areas may include places "vulnerable to the commission of serious criminal offences, such as places or infrastructure which regularly receive a very high volume of visitors, or strategic locations, such as airports, stations or tollbooth areas", while in *Commissioner of An Garda Síochána*, C-140/20, cit., §80, it admitted that Member States could pursue targeted data retention derived from the use of average crime rate statistics in a geographical area, without public authorities necessarily having specific indications as to the preparation or commission, in the areas concerned, of acts of serious crime.

[75] *Tele2 Sverige*, C-203/15 and C-698/15, cit., §§115 and 119. The Court also acknowledged that access to the data of other persons might also be granted where there is objective evidence from which it can be deduced that that data might, in a specific case, make an effective contribution to combating terrorist activities (idem, §119).

[76] Idem, §121.

The *Tele2* ban on blanket data retention was tweaked in *La Quadrature du Net*, where the Court of Justice admitted the lawfulness of national legislation providing for precautionary, general, and indiscriminate retention of data for a limited period of time in order to safeguard national security in the face of a serious threat that is shown to be genuine and present or foreseeable.[77] The court of Luxembourg also accepted that the following categories of traffic data could be retained in bulk: (i) IP addresses, with the objective of safeguarding national security, combating serious crime and preventing serious threats to public security;[78] (ii) data relating to the civil identity of subscribers and registered users of electronic communications ("users' civil identity data") with the objective of safeguarding national security, combating crime and safeguarding public security.[79] Any national measure had to ensure that the retention of data complies with the applicable substantive and procedural conditions and that the persons concerned have effective safeguards against the risk of abuse and unlawful access.[80]

5 Data Retention in Portugal: Chronicle of a Fate (Long) Foretold

5.1 Primacy

The EU Treaties created their own legal system which "became an integral part of the legal systems of the Member States and which their courts are bound to apply".[81] The judicial catchphrase is arguably the most important in the history of legal integration in Europe. It basically means that, contrary to public international law, EU law is directly applicable (enforceable) in each Member State. The "justiciability" stemming from the direct effect of EU provisions opens up the possibility of normative conflicts with national law. But how should national judicial and administrative bodies deal with vertical conflicts in a federal polity such as the EU? According to the principle of primacy, prevalence must always be given to the application of EU law:

> (B)odies called upon, within the exercise of their respective powers, to apply EU law are obliged to adopt all the measures necessary to ensure that EU law is fully effective, disap-

[77] *La Quadrature du Net,* C-511/18, C-512/18 and C-520/18, cit., §137. Such a retention, however, could not be "systematic in nature" (idem, §138).

[78] Idem, cit., §168. The Court accepted the argument that where an offence is committed online, inter alia, in cases involving particularly serious child pornography offences, IP addresses retained in bulk might be the only means of investigation enabling the person to whom that address was assigned at the time of the commission of the offence to be identified (Idem, §154).

[79] Idem, cit., §168. See also *Ministerio Fiscal*, C-207/16, 2 October 2018, ECLI:EU:C:2018:788, paras. 59–61.

[80] *La Quadrature du Net,* C-511/18, C-512/18 and C-520/18, cit., §168.

[81] *Costa v ENEL*, 6/64, 15 July 1964, ECLI:EU:C:1964:66, at 593.

> plying if need be any national provisions or national case-law that are contrary to EU law. This means that those bodies, in order to ensure that EU law is fully effective, must neither request nor await the prior setting aside of such a provision or such case-law by legislative or other constitutional means.[82]

The legal status of the Portuguese Data Retention Law was not in doubt after the *Digital Rights Ireland* ruling of the Court of Justice. It could not be applied as it breached the Charter by imposing a general and indiscriminate retention of data (Guerra and Calvão 2015, pp. 79–80; Ramalho and Coimbra 2015, pp. 1038–1039; Silveira and Freitas 2017, pp. 52–53; Coutinho and Piçarra 2019, p. 616). In light of the ongoing and widespread enforcement of the Data Retention Law in the Portuguese legal order, the principle of sincere cooperation required an intervention by the legislative, executive or judicial branch. The resilience of this law is a testimony to a delusional legislator, an absent data protection supervisor, and an erratic Constitutional Court.

5.2 A Delusional Legislator

The Portuguese Government initially took an ambivalent stance on data retention. While advocating the adoption of EU-wide legislation on the matter (Council of the European Union 2002b, pp. 20–22), domestically it dithered even in following through with international obligations regarding the (much) less privacy-intrusive alternative of "quick-freeze" data preservation.[83] Unsurprisingly, it voted for the Data Retention Directive (Council of the European Union 2006a, p. 4), and diligently approved a draft bill on its implementation less than a fortnight before the transposition deadline.[84] But the endorsement of preventive blanket data retention was half-hearted. In *Digital Rights Ireland*, written observations were submitted to the Court of Justice questioning whether the measure was adequate in terms of attaining the objective of fighting serious crime, since there were several methods of electronic communication which fell outside the scope of the Directive, or which allowed anonymous communication.[85]

The draft bill on data retention sailed through Parliament. The only opposition came from the far-left parties, which were not shy in portraying the measure as an unprecedented attack on civil liberties stemming from a "European securitarian paranoia on the loose" (Filipe 2008, pp. 22–23). The Government counterargued

---

[82] *Minister for Justice and Equality*, C-378/17, 4 December 2018, ECLI:EU:C:2018:979, §50.

[83] See Article 12 of the Cybercrime Law (Law 109/2009), which implements Article 16 of the Convention on Cybercrime of the Council of Europe, ETS 105 (entry into force 1 July 2004). The Portuguese Government signed the Convention on 23 November 2001, but only approved a Draft Bill on its object on 14 May 2009.

[84] Draft Bill 161/X/3, approved by the Council of Ministers on 6 September 2007.

[85] *Digital Rights Ireland*, C-293/12 and C-594/12, cit., §50.

that "special safeguards" "fully" protected the right to privacy (Silveira 2008, pp. 19–20).

So strong were the safeguards that the Portuguese Data Retention Law was even considered "a special case of legality" and an "example" for other national laws (Portela and Cruz-Cunha 2010, pp. 3, 10). Unfortunately, the Portuguese Government firmly believed this legal myth to be true. After informing the Council that no legislative action was needed following the *Tele2* ruling (Council of the European Union 2017, p. 10), the Government ignored recommendations to the contrary submitted by the data protection authority (Comissão Nacional de Proteção de Dados, 2017b) and by the Ombudsman (2019) urging the limitation of the scope of the data retention legal framework, and instead promoted its expansion by allowing access to data retained in bulk in cases of fraud and counterfeiting of non-cash means of payment.[86]

The delusion was not justified. After *Tele2*, no doubts remained as to the unlawfulness of the obligation imposed on service providers to retain *all* metadata of *all* data subjects for *all* means of electronic communication with the intent to make this data accessible for the purpose of the investigation, detection and prosecution of serious crime.[87] National law, such as the Portuguese, providing for a general and indiscriminate retention of data exceeded, by default, the limits of what was strictly necessary, thereby breaching Articles 7, 8, 11 and 52(1) of the Charter.[88] The nature of the safeguards introduced by the national legislator was irrelevant to assess the validity of such a serious interference with fundamental rights.[89]

In any event, the "special safeguards" introduced by the Portuguese legislator, such as making access to retained data subject to prior judicial review (Article 3(2) and 9 of Law 32/2008), would always fall very short of what was necessary to effectively protect the data subjects in question against any unlawful access to and use of their data. Firstly, as service providers were not required to retain data within the EU, there was no guarantee that the protection and security requirements for the retained data would be controlled by an independent data protection authority.[90]

[86] Article 4 of Law 19/2021, which amends Article 2(g) of Law 32/2008.

[87] *Tele2 Sverige*, C-203/15 and C-698/15, cit., §112.

[88] Idem, §107.

[89] The Court of Justice addressed this issue directly in *Commissioner of An Garda Síochána*, C-140/20, cit., §47: "(N)ational legislation ensuring full respect for the conditions established by the case-law interpreting Directive 2002/58 as regards access to retained data cannot, by its very nature, be capable of either limiting or even remedying the serious interference, which results from the general retention of those data provided for under that national legislation, with the rights guaranteed by Articles 5 and 6 of that directive and by the fundamental rights to which those articles give specific effect".

[90] *Digital Rights Ireland*, C-293/12 and C-594/12, cit., §68, and *Tele2 Sverige*, C-203/15 and C-698/15, cit., §§122-3. This was not a "minor issue" (Ramalho and Coimbra 2015, at 1038) given that retained data could even have been transferred to a third country (the United States of America) where the legislation authorises public authorities to have unrestricted access to those data while not providing for any possibility for an individual to pursue legal remedies in order to have access to personal data relating to them, or to obtain the rectification or erasure of such data (*Schrems I*, C-362/14, 6 October 2015, ECLI:EU:C:2015:650, §§93–95).

Secondly, data subjects' rights, under Articles 7 and 8 of the Charter, to request access to their personal data and, where appropriate, to have the latter rectified or erased, and, under Article 47(§1) of the Charter, to avail themselves of an effective remedy before a tribunal, were restricted because public authorities that had been granted access to the retained data were not obliged to notify the persons affected.[91] Thirdly, service providers were not obliged to implement technical measures providing for the *irreversible* destruction of the data at the end of the data retention period.[92] Fourthly, no objective criterion was established limiting the *number of persons* authorised to access and subsequently use the retained data.[93] Fifthly, data security concerning the transmission of retained data to law enforcement authorities was impaired by the non-binding nature of the electronic application created for that specific purpose by Ordinance 469/2009.[94]

Finally, proportionality was compromised by the fact that the Data Retention Law established a single period of retention without any distinction being made between the categories of data to be retained based on their possible usefulness for the purposes of fighting serious crime or according to the persons concerned.[95]

The principle of sincere cooperation enshrined in Article 4(3)(§2) TUE obliged the Portuguese legislator to take appropriate measures to ensure fulfilment of the obligations arising out of the Treaties, which meant revising the legal framework on data retention in line with the Charter, as interpreted in the case law of the Court of Justice. Its sole intervention extending public authorities' access to data retained under the Data Retention Law only amplified the seriousness of the infringement of EU law.

5.3 *An Absent Supervisor*

The *Comissão Nacional de Proteção de Dados* is an independent supervisory authority established by the Portuguese State to review the level of data protection guaranteed by EU law in the Portuguese legal order (Article 3 of Law 58/2019). That control is expressly required by Article 8(3) of the Charter and constitutes an essential element of the right to data protection.[96] National data protection authorities are different to other domestic administrative bodies because they derive directly from EU primary law and, consequently, their tasks and powers are determined by EU secondary law (Articles 55 to 59 GDPR). They form a "European composite

---

[91] *Tele2 Sverige*, C-203/15 and C-698/15, cit., §121.

[92] *Digital Rights Ireland*, C-293/12 and C-594/12, cit., §67, and *Tele2 Sverige*, C-203/15 and C-698/15, cit., §122.

[93] *Digital Rights Ireland*, C-293/12 and C-594/12, cit., §62.

[94] *Privacy International*, C-623/17, 6 October 2020, ECLI:EU:C:2020:790, §68. This IT application was still not being used in 2017 (Comissão Nacional de Proteção de Dados 2017b, p. 9).

[95] *Digital Rights Ireland*, C-293/12 and C-594/12, cit., §63.

[96] *Tele2 Sverige*, C-203/15 and C-698/15, cit., §123.

administration" through their participation in the European Data Protection Board, as well as in the complex administrative procedures of cooperation and consistency (Articles 60–62, 63–67, and 68 (3) GDPR). Data protection authorities are thus hybrid bodies: they are national public entities established under national law that perform tasks of a European agency (Hijmans 2016, pp. 309–311; Coutinho 2020, pp. 16–17). For that reason, they must act with "complete independence", remaining free from external influence, whether direct or indirect, and neither seeking nor taking instructions from anybody (Article 52(1) and (2) GDPR).

Called upon to comment on draft versions of the Data Retention Law, the Portuguese data protection authority proposed several amendments, which were duly incorporated by the Government. The most relevant was arguably the proposal to reduce the retention period from two years to one year to follow the standard set in many Member States, some of which had recently suffered terrorist attacks (Comissão Nacional de Proteção de Dados 2007a, p. 3; Silveira 2008, pp. 20–21). Harmonisation was not, however, a criterion that could be considered objective to establish a period of retention limited to what was strictly necessary.[97] Given that Portugal fortunately never experienced severe security threats, the retention period should have been "as short as possible" (Article 29 Data Protection Working Party 2005, p. 6), which meant six months.

Another important contribution concerned the need for the law to specify the purpose of retaining data. The data protection authority accurately stated that the definition of purpose is crucial (Comissão Nacional de Proteção de Dados 2007b, pp. 3–4). The problem is that it never turned these words into action by using its corrective powers, under Article 58(2) GDPR, to check and sanction the unlawful access by law enforcement authorities (public prosecutors and criminal police) to data retained by service providers for billing purposes.

A practice was adopted to deliberately circumvent the limitation of access to retained data to cases related to serious crime listed in Article 2(1)(g) of the Data Retention Law. The list was considered "very restrictive" as it did not include many of the offences set out in Article 187(1) of the Code of Criminal Procedure and in Article 11 of the Cybercrime Law, such as slander, smuggling or generally any cybercrime (Pinho 2018, pp. 169–170). As metadata were deemed "essential evidence" (Pinho 2018, p. 169), access to data retained by service providers for billing purposes was sought following two legal pathways: (i) traffic and location data were accessed after judicial authorisation under Article 189(2) of the Code of Criminal Procedure in cases related to criminal offences listed in Article 187(1) of the Code of Criminal Procedure; (ii) IP addresses and users' civil identity data were accessed *without* prior judicial review in cases related to *any* crime in accordance with Articles 11 and 14 of the Cybercrime Law (Cybercrime Office (Public Prosecution Service) 2016, p. 7).[98]

---

[97] *Digital Rights Ireland*, C-293/12 and C-594/12, cit., §62.

[98] In *Prokuratuur*, C-746/18, 2 March 2021, ECLI:EU:C:2021:152, §57, the Court of Justice declared that the Estonian public prosecution service could not be considered an "independent

The practice breaches the principle of specificity which requires data retention and subsequent access to be solely related to billing. Further exceptions to the principle of confidentiality can only be admitted under Article 15(1) of the E-Privacy Directive, read in the light of Articles 7, 8, 11 and 52(1) of the Charter, as interpreted by the case law of the Court of Justice. Blanket retention of metadata is admissible in very specific circumstances (serious threat to national security) or for specific metadata (IP addresses and users' civil identity data), and only for criminal law and/or national security purposes that have to be clearly and precisely laid down in law, which has also to establish strict safeguards concerning access and data protection and security. Neither those purposes nor those safeguards are set out in Law 41/2004, which implements the E-Privacy Directive.[99] That did not stop the Public Prosecution Service from declaring, after the annulment of the Data Retention Law by the Constitutional Court, that it will persist in its blatant breach of EU law by requesting IP addresses from service providers under Article 14(1) and (4) of the Cybercrime Law (Cybercrime Office (Public Prosecution Service) 2022, pp. 2–3)—an odd announcement given that IP addresses are *traffic data* which are not necessary for billing purposes, and thus cannot be retained by service providers in accordance with Article 6 of Law 41/2004.[100]

The national data protection authority also remained silent after the seminal *Digital Rights* constitutional ruling of the Court of Justice of 8 April 2014. It took more than fourteen months for it to elliptically declare that the "legitimacy" of data retention under Law 32/2008 was yet to be determined in the Portuguese legal order (Comissão Nacional de Proteção de Dados 2015, p. 10). Right after the *Tele2* ruling, it went further by stating that the lack of proportionality of blanket data retention "endangers the 'validity' of the law implementing the Directive and, therefore, compromises its constitutionality", thereby predicting the inevitability of a Constitutional Court's decision (Comissão Nacional de Proteção de Dados 2017a, pp. 20–21). A few weeks later, the authority requested Parliament to amend the Data Retention Law (Comissão Nacional de Proteção de Dados 2017b). In the absence of any foreseeable action from the legislative branch, it invoked the principle of primacy to declare it would no longer enforce its sanctioning powers under the Data Retention Law (Comissão Nacional de Proteção de Dados 2017c, p. 3). This basically meant that service providers no longer had any incentive to fulfil their obligations to ensure a "particularly high level of protection and security" of the retained data, as no independent supervisory authority was ensuring compliance with data protection (Ombudsman 2019, p. 15). This problem was solved on 7 June 2022 when the data protection authority used its powers under Article 58(2)(d) of the GDPR, and ordered service providers to delete, in 72 hours, data retained in

administrative body" for the purpose of carrying out the prior review to which access by the competent national authorities to retained data must be subject.

[99] Pinho (2018, p. 171): "(T)he fact that the storage of data for billing purposes (…) is not procured for the investigation, detection, and prosecution of criminal offences means that this processing does not include the safeguards applicable to that specific purpose".

[100] Pinho (2018, p. 171) and *La Quadrature du Net,* C-511/18, C-512/18 and C-520/18, cit., §154.

accordance with Law 32/2008 (Comissão Nacional de Proteção de Dados 2022a). The following week, with a staggering 2933-day delay,[101] service providers duly announced they had deleted the data (De Sousa 2022).

The national data protection authority's justification for its decision to order the deletion of retained data was the need to comply with the Constitutional Court ruling of 19 April 2022. It stated that the declaration of unconstitutionality annulled the Data Retention Law and, consequently, rendered application of its provisions impossible in the Portuguese legal order (Comissão Nacional de Proteção de Dados 2022a). The problem is that, as the data protection authority *expressly* recognised in July 2017 (Comissão Nacional de Proteção de Dados 2017c), the Data Retention Law breached the Charter and was *already* inapplicable in the Portuguese legal order, which begs the question why the deletion of data was not ordered right after the *Digital Rights Ireland* and *Tele2 Sverige* rulings. The national data protection authority thus failed miserably by standing idly by and passively observing a serious breach of the fundamental rights of almost the entire Portuguese population for more than eight years.

5.4 An Erratic Constitutional Court

The "*Simmenthal* mandate" obliges national courts to apply EU law in its entirety to cases within their jurisdiction and to protect rights which individuals derive from it, setting aside, if necessary, any conflicting provision of national law (Claes 2006, p. 108). Portuguese courts were thus obliged to apply the Charter and refuse any request to access data retained by service providers under the Data Retention Law made after the *Digital Rights* ruling of the Court of Justice.

On 16 October 2016, this mandate was sidestepped in a child pornography case by a judge in a lower criminal court in Lisbon, who invoked the Portuguese Constitution to deny access to civil identity data of the subscriber or user of electronic communication systems to whom an IP address was allocated at the time of a communication. Instead of dismissing the appeal submitted by the Public Prosecution Service, arguing this was a question regarding the application of EU law to be decided by ordinary courts with the assistance of the Court of Justice,[102] the PCC

[101] Service providers were obliged to destroy the database created under the Data Retention Law for the simple reason that the processing of those data was not necessary for compliance with an *applicable* legal obligation to which they were subject (Article 6(1)(c) GDPR). In the absence of any other *lawful basis* for processing, the storage of data in breach of the principle of lawfulness was liable to be sanctioned. See, however, Ramalho and Coimbra (2015, p. 1040), who reject such liability, claiming that service providers were not obliged to disapply national law breaching EU law and could thus continue to enforce a law which the authors themselves consider to be in a state of "latency" (Ramalho and Coimbra 2015, p. 1042).

[102] See, among others, Decision 466/2003, 125/02, 14 October 2003, Decision 46/04, 885/03, 19 January 2004, Decision 598/04, 685/03, 12 October 2004, and Decision 569/2016, 238/16, 19 October 2016, which refused to qualify the compatibility between national law and EU primary

surprisingly decided to uphold the lawfulness of blanket retention and further use of users' civil identity data in Decision 410/2017.

Neglecting the fact that any legal provisions imposing data retention on service providers necessarily fall within the scope of Article 15 (1) of the E-Privacy Directive and must meet the requirements of the Charter as interpreted by the Court of Justice, the PCC declared it was not bound by the latter's case law and would follow an autonomous hermeneutic path based on national, European, and international fundamental rights parameters.[103] This path had the Court identifying users' civil identity data and IP addresses as basic data when they are, according to the Court of Justice, traffic data,[104] and, in a blatant breach of its obligation to submit a preliminary reference in accordance with Article 267 (3) TFEU, it implicitly considered that such metadata could be retained in bulk, a matter the Luxembourg court only dealt with in L*a Quadrature du Net*.[105] Most importantly, the decision allowed the PCC to bypass the *Tele2 Sverige* ruling, which it quotes but ostensibly ignores, by not reviewing the nature of the general and indiscriminate retention of data enforced by the Data Retention Law or the latter's safeguards protecting the data subjects in question against the risk of abuse and unlawful access. The Court satisfied itself with a reference to pre-*Tele2 Sverige* soft law guidelines from the Public Prosecution Service's Cybercrime Office that claim that the strictness of the safeguards included in the Data Retention Law sheltered it from any problems of constitutionality (Cybercrime Office 2015, p. 3). The PCC then undertook a "specific" constitutional review, where it concluded that the provision granting law enforcement authorities access to users' civil identity data is a proportional restriction to the right to privacy.[106]

The ruling empowered the unfettered judicial application of provisions manifestly in breach of EU constitutional law. On 28 November 2018, the Lisbon Civil Court of Appeal, after quoting the decision of the PCC at length to conclude on the applicability of the Data Retention Law, quashed a first instance court ruling that rejected granting access to civil identity data retained for billing purposes under Article 14(1) and (4) of the Cybercrime law, arguing that such a possibility was

law as a question of constitutionality subject to review by the PCC, referring to Da Costa (1998, p. 1371): "(T)he incompatibility between provisions of domestic law and (EU law) should not be assimilated to a category or a dogmatic concept whose utilization or application (…) would mean withdrawing from ordinary courts the final decision of that question within their jurisdiction".

[103] Decision 410/2017, §10.

[104] See, regarding users' civil identity data, *Ministerio Fiscal*, C-207/16, cit., §42 ("(I)t is apparent from recital 15 of Directive 2002/58 that traffic data may include, inter alia, the name and address of the person sending a communication or using a connection to carry out a communication. Data relating to (…) identity (…) can also prove necessary in order to bill for the electronic communications services provided and therefore form part of traffic data as defined in subparagraph (b) of the second paragraph of Article 2 of the directive"), and concerning IP Addresses, *Quadrature du Net*, C-511/18, C-512/18 and C-520/18, cit., §152.

[105] Decision 410/2017, §11.

[106] Idem, §§12-14. See also Violante (2021, pp. 183–184).

forfeited after the *Digital Rights Ireland* ruling.[107] It was against this bleak legal background that the Ombudsman, following an application in December 2017 from a privacy advocacy group (D3 2017), requested the PCC to conduct an abstract constitutional review of the Data Retention Law in an exceptionally well-reasoned legal opinion delivered on 16 September 2019 (Ombudsman 2021).

When reviewing the Data Retention Law, the PCC essentially had two options. It could have dismissed the case, arguing that it could not address the constitutionality of provisions which were inapplicable in the Portuguese legal order, as they manifestly breached the Charter. Such a constitutional review could theoretically be observed as hypothetical, similarly to the review of legal provisions revoked before entering into force. The PCC wisely pursued a different path. Even if the Data Retention Law provisions were inapplicable in the domestic realm, they *organically* stemmed from a national source of law the formal validity of which could never be affected by a ruling of the Court of Justice. EU law, the PCC states, quoting the Spanish Constitutional Court's Declaration 1/2004 on the Constitutional Treaty, has *primacy* but not *supremacy* over national law (i.e. it trumps but does not revoke national law).[108] That meant that the contested provisions on data retention could only be revoked by the Portuguese Parliament or by the PCC in an abstract review procedure. Given that the Data Retention Law was being profusely applied in the Portuguese legal order (including by the PCC), the question could not be said to be (*factually*) hypothetical. Under the duty of sincere cooperation, the PCC was then obliged to do everything within its means to secure the uniform application of EU law in the Portuguese legal order. It followed this obligation by interpreting the relevant fundamental rights provisions of the Portuguese Constitution in accordance with the Charter, as interpreted by the Court of Justice—I fail to understand the criticism of six justices in a concurring vote on the use of the principle of consistent interpretation instead of the direct application of the Charter in a case that revolved exclusively around the technical revocation of inapplicable provisions of national law breaching EU constitutional law and, *a fortiori*, the Portuguese Constitution. The hermeneutic path taken by the PCC mimics that of other Constitutional Courts also dealing with data retention,[109] and is perfectly aligned with the obligation to apply EU law provisions in the *conditions prescribed* by EU law (Article 8 (4) of the Portuguese Constitution), which is based on the pluralistic constitutional assumption of the existence of a systemic compatibility between fundamental rights protection in the Portuguese and European constitutional orders.[110] Such a path obviously

[107] Tribunal da Relação de Lisboa, 28 November 2018, 8617/17.8T9LSB-A.L1-3, at 3.3. and 3.4.

[108] Decision 268/2022, cit., §8.1.

[109] That was the case of the Belgium Constitutional Court (Popelier and Van de Heyning 2019, p. 1249), the Slovak Constitutional Court (Vikarská and Bobek 2019, p. 868), and the Slovenian Constitutional Court (Bardutzky 2019, p. 714).

[110] As Violante (2022, p. 5) accurately remarked, the principle of consistent interpretation allowed the PCC to "link the national standard of protection with the European parameter, leading to a fully congruent standard of fundamental rights protection through the application of the national constitutional provisions".

precluded the possibility of a decision limiting the ruling's effects under Article 282 of the Constitution, including those concerning *res judicata*, as the PCC expressly acknowledged by invoking, in response to the Attorney General's ruling annulment request,[111] the *Commissioner of An Garda Síochána* ruling of the Court of Justice.[112] In a nutshell, the PCC limited itself to certifying the obituary of provisions which (legally) were already dead in the water.

The 19 April 2022 ruling is arguably the most compelling ever adopted by the PCC concerning the relation between EU and national constitutional law. It is an 11 to 1 decision which, without ever admitting it, in effect reverses its previous case law solving the conundrum posed by the unlawful resilience of the Portuguese data retention legal framework. The Court recognises the regulation of data retention as falling within the scope of the Charter, and thus subject to a constitutional review within the parameters set by the (ever abundant) Court of Justice's case law on data retention.[113] The Data Retention Law was found to have two major structural flaws—both missed by the July 2017 ruling of the PCC. Firstly, by not requiring metadata to be retained in the EU it jeopardises the effectiveness of data protection authorities' powers under the GDPR.[114] Secondly, by not creating an obligation for data subjects to be notified that their data are being shared with public authorities, it effectively impairs access to legal remedies for unlawful access to personal data.[115] Although these flaws would be enough to strike down the metadata law *in totum*, the PCC also reviewed the proportionality of data retention, only admitting, in line with the Luxembourg court, the bulk retention of users' civil identity data, and, in cases concerning serious criminal offences, such as child pornography, the blanket retention of IP addresses.[116]

Astonishingly, the ruling is not centred on the crux of the constitutional problem posed by the enforcement of a general and indiscriminate retention of data of almost the entire Portuguese population. The PCC opted to focus its review primarily on an assessment of the safeguards concerning access, data protection and data security set out in the Data Retention Law, arguing that *in theory* the strictness of these safeguards could allow for a broader scope of the restriction on fundamental rights entailed by data storage.[117] This assumption was at the heart of its ruling in 2017, but is at odds with the case law of the Court of Justice, which made it crystal clear that a blanket retention of data such as that envisaged in Portugal is, *by itself*, a "very far-reaching" and "particularly serious" unlawful interference with fundamental rights, it being irrelevant whether the retained data has been used subsequently, since access to such data is a separate interference with fundamental rights and thus

[111] Decision 382/2022, cit., §4.
[112] C-140/20, 5 April 2022, §128.
[113] Decision 268/2022, cit., §8.2.
[114] Idem, §16.
[115] Idem, §19.
[116] Idem, §17.1–17.4.
[117] Decision 268/2022, cit., §14.

requires a separate justification.[118] The assumption was also immaterial to the case at hand; even if the Data Retention Law, as the PCC wrongly assumed in Decision 410/17, included minimum safeguards effectively protecting data subjects against the risk of abuse and unlawful access, it would still have to be declared unconstitutional as it provided for continuous and systematic retention of data.

Throughout its judgment, the PCC is always at pains to articulate its reasoning with its previous case law on data retention. This explains why it decided to embark on a thorough review of the admissibility of specific bulk retention of users' civil identity data and static and dynamic IP addresses—the latter of which it now conceptually acknowledges may well qualify as traffic data—in order to conclude that the retention of these metadata for one year would not be, *in itself*, unconstitutional, *if* the legislator had laid down the obligation for data to be stored in the EU.[119] The proportionality balancing carried out in Decision 410/17 is, according to the PCC, perfectly aligned with that of the Court of Justice.[120] *Alas*, this is a bold statement not reconcilable with the fact that, concerning IP addresses, the retention period exceeded what was strictly necessary in light of the objective pursued,[121] and not enough conditions and safeguards were established concerning the use of that specific data regarding communications made and activities carried out online, particularly via tracking.[122]

I am also not convinced by the fundamental rights review undertaken by the PCC concerning the blanket retention of traffic and location data. This measure was found to breach the right to privacy and the right to data protection after failing the proportionality test.[123] According to the Court of Justice, while these rights are not absolute and must be considered in relation to their function in society,[124] the sensitive nature of the information that traffic and location data may provide, determines that the confidentiality of that data is *essential* for the right to respect for private life.[125] Should it not then follow that systematic retention of metadata breaches the essence of the right to privacy? In *Tele2 Sverige*, the Court stated that it did not. Although it classified the interference with fundamental rights stemming from national legislation implementing the Data Retention Directive as "very far-reaching" and "particularly serious", it dismissed any breach of the essence of the

---

[118] *Tele2 Sverige*, C-203/15 and C-698/15, cit., §100, and *La Quadrature du Net*, C-511/18, C-512/18 and C-520/18, cit., §§115–119 and 140–141.

[119] Decision 268/2022, cit., §17.4.

[120] Idem, §17.3.

[121] By way of comparison, Article 113(b) of the German Law on Telecommunications establishes a 10-week maximum period of retention.

[122] According to the Court of Justice, *La Quadrature du Net*, C-511/18, C-512/18 and C-520/18, cit., §§153 and 156, IP addresses "may be used, among other things, to track an Internet user's complete clickstream and, therefore, his or her entire online activity", and thus enable a detailed profile of the internet user to be produced.

[123] Decision 268/2022, cit., §18.

[124] *Schrems II*, C-311/18, 16 July 2020, EU:C:2020:559, §172.

[125] *La Quadrature du Net*, C-511/18, C-512/18 and C-520/18, cit., §142.

right to privacy, arguing that the content of the communications was not stored.[126] However, the Luxembourg court contradictorily recognised that the retained data was a means of establishing a profile of the individuals concerned, which was information "no less sensitive, having regard to the right to privacy, than the actual content of communications".[127] The idea that the bulk storage of metadata is necessarily less intrusive than the acquisition of content was also rejected by the European Court of Human Rights in *Big Brother Watch*.[128] If, as former National Security Agency general counsel Stewart Baker reportedly stated, "metadata absolutely tells you everything about somebody's life", meaning that if law enforcement and intelligence authorities have enough metadata they "don't really need content" (Cole 2014), then there is no reason to distinguish between the bulk retention of metadata *vis-à-vis* content data when considering its adverse effects on the essence of the right to privacy. It is my contention that the Court of Justice and the PCC failed by not declaring that a general and indiscriminate retention of data of the whole population envisaged in the Data Retention Directive and in the Data Retention Law must be regarded as compromising the essence of the fundamental right to respect for private life, as guaranteed by Article 7 of the Charter; the Luxembourg court should have followed the reasoning taken in *Schrems* regarding legislation permitting public authorities to have access on a generalised basis to the content of electronic communications.[129]

6 Conclusion

In Decisions 403/2015 and 464/2019, the PCC blocked successive legislative attempts to grant intelligence agencies access to metadata retained in bulk by service providers. But is it reasonable to believe that metadata have not been accessed *unlawfully* by intelligence agencies over the past two decades? There is no doubt that was the case of law enforcement authorities concerning data retained under Laws 41/2004 and 32/2008. A passive European Commission, which has been ignoring pledges to launch infringement procedures against Member States whose laws implementing the Data Retention Directive have not been repealed (European Parliament 2020, §32), combined with a systemic failure of all relevant national stakeholders in the executive, legislative and judicial branches allowed general and indiscriminate retention of data to continue in the Portuguese legal order until April 2022.

[126] *Tele2 Sverige*, C-203/15 and C-698/15, cit., §§100–101.

[127] Idem, §99.

[128] *Big Brother Watch and Others v. United Kingdom*, 25 May 2021, 58170/13, 62322/14 and 24960/15, §363.

[129] *Schrems I*, C-362/14, cit., §94.

The ink on the PCC's ruling was barely dry when the Government proposed an amendment to Law 41/2004 granting access to law enforcement authorities to metadata retained for billing purposes, while obliging service providers to retain data not necessary for that specific purpose (e.g. IP addresses).[130] This was a clumsy attempt to square the circle by covertly transforming the purpose of a database created for consumer law purposes (Comissão Nacional de Proteção de Dados 2022b, §47). If approved, it would most certainly not have survived a preventive constitutional review submitted by the President of the Republic. The PCC will surely check every securitarian drift that would otherwise impair the effectiveness of EU law by upholding the fundamental right of data subjects to expect that their communication and data relating thereto will remain anonymous.[131]

Acknowledgments I would like to thank Graça Canto Moniz, Mateus Correia de Carvalho, Marta Marinho and Teresa Violante for their comments and bibliographical suggestions. The usual disclaimers apply.

References

Albers M (2021) Data retention in Germany. In: Zubik M, Podkowik J, Rybski R (eds) European constitutional courts towards data retention laws. Springer, Cham, Switzerland, pp 117–136

Anderl A, Klammer A (2021) Data retention in Austria. In: Zubik M, Podkowik J, Rybski R (eds) European constitutional courts towards data retention laws. Springer, Cham, Switzerland, pp 39–52

Article 29 Data Protection Working Party (2003) Opinion 1/2003 on the storage of data for billing purposes, 29 January 2003

Article 29 Data Protection Working Party (2005) Opinion 4/2005 on the proposal for a directive of the European Parliament and of the council on the retention of data processed in connection with the provision of public electronic communication services and amending directive 2002/58/EC (COM (2005)438 final of 21.09.2005), 21 October 2005, at 5-6

Article 29 Working Party (1999) Recommendation 2/99 on the respect of privacy in the context of interception of telecommunications, adopted on 3 May 1999

Bardutzky S (2019) The future mandate of the constitution of Slovenia: a potent tradition under strain. In: Albi A, Bardutzki S (eds) National constitutions in European and global governance: democracy, rights, the rule of law: national reports. Asser Press, The Hague, Netherlands, pp 687–744

Besselink L, Claes M (2019) The Netherlands: the pragmatics of a flexible, Europeanised constitution. In: Albi A, Bardutzki S (eds) National constitutions in European and global governance: democracy, rights, the rule of law. Asser Press, The Hague, Netherlands, pp 179–220

Bigo D, Hernanz N, Jeandesboz J, Parkin J, Ragazzi F, Scherrer A (2013) National programmes for mass surveillance of personal data in EU member states and their compatibility with EU law. Doctoral dissertation, Parliament Européen

---

[130] Draft Bill 11/XV/1, approved by the Council of Ministers on 26 May 2022.

[131] A parliamentary attempt to reintroduce preventive data retention through the adoption of amendments to the Data Retention Law was quashed by the PCC in Decision 300/2023, judgement of 4 December 2023, Case 1130/2023. A subsequent parliamentary attempt to enforce data retention in Portugal led to the adoption of Law 18/2024, of 5 February (not yet reviewed by the PCC).

Bobek M (2017) The effects of EU law in the national legal systems. In: Barnard C, Peers S (eds) European Union law. Oxford University Press, Oxford, UK, pp 143–176
Bowden C (2001) Closed circuit television for inside your head: blanket traffic data retention and the emergency anti-terrorism legislation. Duke Law Technol Rev 1:1–7
Caixinha C (2022) Preso por pornografia de menores libertado ao abrigo dos metadados, RR, 10 June 2022. https://rr.sapo.pt/noticia/pais/2022/06/10/preso-por-pornografia-de-menores-libertado-ao-abrigo-dos-metadados/287941/. Accessed 5 Apr 2024
Carmo C (2022a) Marcelo admite alterações à Constituição por causa da lei dos metadados: "O problema é que não há revisões pontuais, TSF, 11 May 2022. https://www.tsf.pt/portugal/politica/o-problema-e-que-nao-ha-revisoes-pontuais-marcelo-admite-alterar-constituicao-por-causa-da-lei-dos-metadados-14847184.html/. Accessed 5 Apr 2024
Carmo C (2022b) Costa admite revisão constitucional, mas que pode ser "cirúrgica" por causa dos metadados, TSF, 11 May 2022. https://www.tsf.pt/portugal/politica/o-prCosta%20admite%20revis%C3%A3o%20constitucional,%20mas%20que%20pode%20ser%20%22cir%C3%BArgica%22%20por%20causa%20dos%20metadadosoblema-e-que-nao-ha-revisoes-pontuais-marcelo-admite-alterar-constituicao-por-causa-da-lei-dos-metadados-14847184.html/. Accessed 5 Apr 2024
Claes M (2006) The national courts' mandate in the European Constitution. Hart Publishing, Portland, OR
Cole D (2014) We kill people based on metadata, New York Review of Books, 10 May 2014. https://www.nybooks.com/online/2014/05/10/we-kill-people-based-metadata/. Accessed 5 Apr 2024
Comissão Nacional de Proteção de Dados (2007a) Opinion 47/07, of 29 August
Comissão Nacional de Proteção de Dados (2007b) Opinion 38/07, of 16 July
Comissão Nacional de Proteção de Dados (2015) Opinion 51/2015, of 16 June
Comissão Nacional de Proteção de Dados (2017a) Opinion 24/2017, of 18 April
Comissão Nacional de Proteção de Dados (2017b) Deliberation 641/2017, of 9 May
Comissão Nacional de Proteção de Dados (2017c) Deliberation 1008/2017, of 18 July
Comissão Nacional de Proteção de Dados (2022a) CNPD ordena eliminação dos dados das comunicações conservados ao abrigo de norma declara constitutional, 9 June 2022
Comissão Nacional de Proteção de Dados (2022b) Opinion 50/2022, of 21 June
Council of the European Union (2001) Extraordinary council meeting – justice, Home Affairs and Civil Protection, C/01/327, 12019/01 (Presse 327), 20 September 2001
Council of the European Union (2002a) 2477th council meeting, 15691/02 (Presse 404), 19 December 2002
Council of the European Union (2002b) Answer to questionnaire on traffic data retention, 14107/02, 20 November 2002, Brussels, published in Statewatch, 12, 6, November-December 2002
Council of the European Union (2004a) Explanatory memorandum – framework decision on the retention of communications data, 8958/04 ADD 1, 28 April 2004
Council of the European Union (2004b) Draft framework decision on the retention of data processed and stored in connection with the provision of publicly available electronic communications services or data on public communications networks for the purpose of prevention, investigation, detection and prosecution of crime and criminal offences including terrorism, 8958/04, 28 April 2004
Council of the European Union (2005) Combating crime: prevention of crime, criminal offences and terrorism, retention of data processed on public communications networks. Framework decision. Initiative France, Ireland, Sweden, and United Kingdom, (2004/0813(CNS))
Council of the European Union (2006a) 2709ème session du Conseil de l'Union européenne (Justice et affaires interieures), tenue à Bruxelles, le 21 février 2006, 6598/06 ADD 1, 27 February 2006
Council of the European Union (2006b) Proposal for a directive of the European Parliament and of the council on the retention of data processed in connection with the provision of pub-

lic electronic communication services and amending Directive 2002/58/EC [First reading]–Statements, Doc. 5777/06 ADD 1, 10 February 2006
Council of the European Union (2017) Retention of electronic communication data, 6726/1/17 REV 1, 7 March 2017
Coutinho FP (2020) A independência da comissão nacional de Proteção de dados (The independence of the Portuguese data protection authority), Anuário da Proteção de Dados. https://ssrn.com/abstract=3647602. Accessed 5 Apr 2024
Coutinho FP (2022) Better late than never: blanket data retention struck down at last by the Portuguese constitutional court, Diritti Comparati, 24 June 2022 Accessed 5 April 2024
Coutinho FP, Piçarra N (2019) Portugal: the impact of European integration and the economic crisis on the identity of the constitution. In: Albi A, Bardutzki S (eds) National constitutions in European and global governance: democracy, rights, the rule of law. Asser Press, Tha Hague, Netherlands, pp 591–640
Cybercrime Office (Public Prosecution Service) (2015) Retenção de dados de tráfego e Lei n° 32/2008, de 17 de Julho", Nota Prática n° 7, 30 December 2015
Cybercrime Office (Public Prosecution Service) (2016) Pedido de dados a operadores de comunicações", Nota Prática n° 8, 18 February 2016
Cybercrime Office (Public Prosecution Service) (2022) Nota informativa: retenção de dados de tráfego – acórdão do tribunal constitucional", 17 May 2022
D3 (2017) Press release: D3 pede à provedora de Justiça que leve metadados ao constitucional", 27 November 2017
Da Costa JMC (1998) O tribunal constitucional Português e o tribunal de justiça das comunidades Europeias. In: Varela A et al (eds) Ab uno ad omnes. 75 anos da Coimbra Editora (1920-1995). Coimbra Editora, Coimbra, Portugal, pp 1363–1380
De Sousa FA (2022) Nos, Vodafone e Altice garantem cumprimento da lei de metadados, Eco, 12 June 2022. https://eco.sapo.pt/2022/06/12/vodafone-e-altice-garantem-cumprimento-da-lei-de-metadados/. Accessed 5 Apr 2024
Delgado MM (2022) The EU law of a Portuguese institutional crisis: the data retention ruling of the Portuguese constitutional court, EU Law Live, 23 May 2022. https://eulawlive.com/the-eu-law-of-a-portuguese-institutional-crisis-the-data-retention-ruling-of-the-portuguese-constitutional-court-by-miguel-mota-delgado/. Accessed 5 Apr 2024
Ernits M, Ginter C, Laos S, Allikmets M, Tupay PK, Värk R, Laurand A (2019) The constitution of Estonia: the unexpected challenges of unlimited primacy of EU law. In: Albi A, Bardutzki S (eds) National constitutions in European and global governance: democracy, rights, the rule of law. Asser Press, The Hague, Netherlands, pp 887–950
European Commission (2011) Evaluation report on the data retention directive (Directive 2006/24/EC), COM/2011/0225 final
European Commission (2015) Annex to the proposal for a directive of the European Parliament and of the council on the retention of data processed in connection with the provision of public electronic communication services and amending Directive 2002/58/EC, SEC (2005) 1131, 21 September 2015
European Council (2004) Declaration on combating terrorism, Brussels, 25 March 2004
European Data Protection Supervisor (2010) "Moment of truth" for the data retention directive: EDPS demands clear evidence of necessity, Communique de Presse, EDPS/10/17, 3 December 2010
European Data Protection Supervisor (2011) Opinion of the European data protection supervisor on the evaluation report from the commission to the council and the European Parliament on the data retention directive (Directive 2006/24/EC), 2011/C 279/01, 31 May 2011, §75
European Parliament (2001) Recommendation of the European Parliament on the strategy for creating a safer information society by improving the security of information infrastructures and combating computer related crime (2001/2070(COS)), adopted on 6 September 2001, A5-0284/2001

European Parliament (2005a) European Parliament legislative resolution on the initiative by the French Republic, Ireland, the Kingdom of Sweden and the United Kingdom for a draft framework decision on the retention of data processed and stored in connection with the provision of publicly available electronic communications services or data on public communications networks for the purpose of prevention, investigation, detection and prosecution of crime and criminal offences including terrorism, adopted on 27 September 2005 (8958/2004 – C6-0198/2004 – 2004/0813(CNS))

European Parliament (2005b) Report of the committee on civil liberties, justice and home affairs on the initiative by the French Republic, Ireland, the Kingdom of Sweden and the United Kingdom for a draft framework decision on the retention of data processed and stored in connection with the provision of publicly available electronic communications services or data on public communications networks for the purpose of prevention, investigation, detection and prosecution of crime and criminal offences including terrorism, adopted on 31 May 2005 (8958/2004 – C6-0198/2004 – 2004/0813(CNS))

European Parliament (2005c) European Parliament legislative resolution on the proposal for a directive of the European Parliament and of the council on the retention of data processed in connection with the provision of public electronic communication services and amending Directive 2002/58/EC (COM(2005)0438 – C6-0293/2005 – 2005/0182(COD)), adopted on 14 December 2005

European Parliament (2014) European Court of Justice judgment of 8 April concerning data retention (C 293/12 and C 594/12), Debates, 16 April 2014

European Parliament (2020) Resolution of 26 November 2020 on the situation of fundamental rights in the European Union - Annual report for the years 2018-2019 (2019/2199(INI))

European Parliament Research Service (2020) General data retention/Effects on crime, 27 January 2020

Fennelly D (2021) Data retention in Ireland. In: Zubik M, Podkowik J, Rybski R (eds) European constitutional courts towards data retention laws. Springer, Cham, Switzerland, pp 137–154

Filipe AMCP (2008) Diário da Assembleia da República, I, 31, 5 January 2008, 19–26

Gera M, Husovec M (2021) Data retention in Slovakia. In: Zubik M, Podkowik J, Rybski R (eds) European constitutional courts towards data retention laws. Springer, Cham, Switzerland, pp 203–217

Gouveia JB (2022) Erros de todos, boa fortuna de alguns, ódio ardente institucional, Diário de Notícias, 5 May 2022. https://www.dn.pt/opiniao/erros-de-todos-boa-fortuna-de-alguns-odio-ardente-institucional-14857442.html/. Accessed 5 April 2024

Grimm D, Wendel M, Reinbacher T (2019) European constitutionalism and the German basic law. In: Albi A, Bardutzki S (eds) National constitutions in European and global governance: democracy, rights, the rule of law. Asser Press, The Hague, Netherlands, pp 407–492

Guerra C, Calvão F (2015) Anotação, Forum de Proteção de Dados, 1 July 2015, 79–82

Gustavo R (2022) Procuradoria pede anulação do acórdão do constitucional sobre os metadados. E apresentou dois motivos para o fazer, Expresso, 9 May 2022. https://expresso.pt/sociedade/2022-05-09-Procuradoria-pede-anulacao-do-acordao-do-Constitucional-sobre-os-metadados.-E-apresentou-dois-motivos-para-o-fazer-f37c2671. Accessed 5 Apr 2024

Hijmans H (2016) The European Union as a constitutional guardian of internet privacy and data protection. PhD thesis, University of Amsterdam

Hornung G, Schnabel C (2009) Data protection in Germany II: recent decisions on online-searching of computers, automatic number plate recognition and data retention. Comput Law Secur Rev 25:115–122

Jones C, Hayes B (2013) The EU data retention directive: a case study in the legitimacy and effectiveness of EU counter-terrorism policy. Statewatch. https://www.statewatch.org/media/documents/news/2013/dec/secile-data-retention-directive-in-europe-a-case-study.pdf. Accessed 5 Apr 2024

Kashumov A (2021) Data retention in Bulgaria. In: Zubik M, Podkowik J, Rybski R (eds) European constitutional courts towards data retention laws. Springer, Cham, Switzerland, pp 75–83

Kombos C, Shaelou SL (2019) The Cypriot constitution under the impact of EU law: an asymmetrical formation. In: Albi A, Bardutzki S (eds) National constitutions in European and global governance: democracy, rights, the rule of law. Asser Press, The Hague, Netherlands, pp 1373–1432

Krunke H, Baumbach T (2019) The role of the Danish constitution in European and transnational governance. In: Albi A, Bardutzki S (eds) National constitutions in European and global governance: democracy, rights, the rule of law. Asser Press, The Hague, Netherlands, pp 269–315

Legal Service of the Council of the European Union (2005) Projet de décision-cadre sur la rétention de données traitées et stockées en rapport avec la fourniture de services de communications électroniques accessibles au public ou de données transmises via des réseaux de communications publics, aux fins de la prévention, la recherche, la détection et la poursuite de délits et d'infractions pénales, y compris du terrorisme - Base juridique, 7688/05, 5 April 2005

Markou C (2021) Data retention in Cyprus in the light of EU data retention law. In: Zubik M, Podkowik J, Rybski R (eds) European constitutional courts towards data retention laws. Springer, Cham, Switzerland, pp 85–99

McIntyre TJ (2008) Data retention in Ireland: privacy, policy and proportionality. Comput Law Secur Rev 24:326–334

Ojanen T, Salminen J (2019) Finland: European integration and international human rights treaties as sources of domestic constitutional change and dynamism. In: Albi A, Bardutzki S (eds) National constitutions in European and global governance: democracy, rights, the rule of law. Asser Press, The Hague, Netherlands, pp 359–404

Ombudsman (2019) Recommendation 1/B/2019, of 22 January

Ombudsman (2021) Lei n.° 26/2020. Provedora de Justiça requer a fiscalização do Tribunal Constitucional, 16 September 2021

Peers S (2005) The European parliament and data retention: chronicle of a 'sell-out' foretold? Statewatch Analysis, 1 December 2005. https://www.statewatch.org/news/2005/december/eu-statewatch-analysis-the-european-parliament-and-data-retention-chronicle-of-a-sell-out-foretold/. Accessed 5 Apr 2024

Pinho C (2018) Lei de retenção de dados de comunicações eletrónicas: aposentar ou reformar? Rev Minist Público 154:167–192

Podkowik J, Zubik M (2021) Data retention in Poland. In: Zubik M, Podkowik J, Rybski R (eds) European constitutional courts towards data retention laws. Springer, Cham, Switzerland, pp 155–173

Polčák R (2021) Data retention in the Czech Republic. In: Zubik M, Podkowik J, Rybski R (eds) European constitutional courts towards data retention laws. Springer, Cham, Switzerland, pp 101–116

Popelier P, Van de Heyning C (2019) The Belgian constitution: the efficacy approach to European and global governance. In: Albi A, Bardutzki S (eds) National constitutions in European and global governance: democracy, rights, the rule of law. Asser Press, The Hague, Netherlands, pp 1225–1270

Portela I, Cruz-Cunha MM (2010) What about the balance between law enforcement and data protection? In: Portela I, Cruz-Cunha MM (eds) Information communication technology law, protection and access rights: global approaches and issues. IGI Global, Pennsylvania, PA, pp 1–18

Privacy and Civil Liberties Oversight Board (2014) Report on the telephone records program conducted under section 215 of the USA Patriot Act and on the operations of the foreign intelligence surveillance court, 23 January 2014

Ramalho DS, Coimbra JD (2015) A declaração de invalidade da Diretiva 2006/24/CE: presente e futuro da regulação sobre conservação de dados de tráfego para fins de investigação, deteção e repressão de crimes graves. O Direito 147:997–1045

Ray M (2022a) Madrid train bombings of 2004, Encyclopedia Britannica, 4 March 2022. https://www.britannica.com/event/Madrid-train-bombings-of-2004. Accessed 5 Apr 2024

Ray M (2022b) London bombings of 2005, Encyclopedia Britannica, 30 June 2022. https://www.britannica.com/event/London-bombings-of-2005. Accessed 5 Apr 2024

Şandru S (2021) Data retention in Romania. In: Zubik M, Podkowik J, Rybski R (eds) European constitutional courts towards data retention laws. Springer, Cham, Switzerland, pp 189–202
Security Council (2001) S/RES/1373 (28 September 2001)
Servent AR (2013) Holding the European parliament responsible: policy shift in the data retention directive from consultation to codecision. J Eur Public Policy 20:972–987
Silveira A, Freitas PMF (2017) The recent jurisprudence of the CJEU on personal data retention: implications for criminal investigation in Portugal. UNIO – EU Law J 3:45–56
Silveira JT (2008) Diário da assembleia da República, I, 31, 5 January 2008, at 19-26
Toplak J (2021) Data retention in Slovenia. In: Zubik M, Podkowik J, Rybski R (eds) European constitutional courts towards data retention laws. Springer, Cham, Switzerland, pp 219–225
Türk AH (2009) Judicial review in EU law. Edward Elgar Publishing, Cheltenham, UK and Northampton, MA
Van de Heyning C (2021) Data retention in Belgium. In: Zubik M, Podkowik J, Rybski R (eds) European constitutional courts towards data retention laws. Springer, Cham, Switzerland, pp 53–74
Vikarská Z, Bobek M (2019) Slovakia: between Euro-optimism and Euro-concerns. In: Albi A, Bardutzki S (eds) National constitutions in European and global governance: democracy, rights, the rule of law. Asser Press, The Hague, Netherlands, pp 835–886
Violante T (2021) Data retention in Portugal. In: Zubik M, Podkowik J, Rybski R (eds) European constitutional courts towards data retention laws. Springer, Cham, Switzerland, pp 175–187
Violante T (2022) How the data retention legislation led to a national constitutional crisis in Portugal, Verfassungsblog, 9 June 2022. https://verfassungsblog.de/how-the-data-retention-legislation-led-to-a-national-constitutional-crisis-in-portugal/. Accessed 5 Apr 2024
Zubik M, Podkowik J, Rybski R (2021) The constitutional court of Romania: judgment of 8 October 2009, Ref. No. 1258/2009. In: Zubik M, Podkowik J, Rybski R (eds) European constitutional courts towards data retention law. Springer, Cham, Switzerland, pp 350–356

Francisco Pereira Coutinho NOVA School of Law, Lisbon, Portugal. Member of CEDIS—I & D Research Centre for Law and Society.

On the Verge of Autonomy

The First Portuguese Constitutional Court Ruling on Supremacy of EU Law: The Wait Is Finally Over

Patrícia Fragoso Martins

1 Introduction

After decades of waiting, and following a rather long discussion between its members,[1] in July 2020 the Portuguese Constitutional Court finally delivered its first ruling on the scope of supremacy of European Union (EU) law in light of the national Constitution. It is a decision of the plenary formation of the Court taken unanimously and drafted by the Constitutional Court Justice José António Teles Pereira.[2]

The purpose of the Court was to fix a general and forward-looking criterion that would allow it, as well as ordinary courts and judicial actors, to interpret and litigate on the basis of Article 8(4) of the Portuguese Constitution.[3] According to the latter provision, the "provisions of the treaties that govern the European Union and the norms issued by its institutions in the exercise of their respective competences are applicable in Portuguese internal law in accordance with Union law and with respect for the fundamental principles of a democratic state based on the rule of law". Article 8(4) is included in a set of norms dealing with the application of international law in the domestic legal system. It was introduced in the Constitution to allow for the ratification of the Constitutional Treaty of the EU of 2004. Although

[1] Acknowledged in the ruling itself, para. 1.5.

[2] Judgment no. 422/2020, of 15 July 2020, Proc. no. 528/17. Full English version available at: https://www.tribunalconstitucional.pt/tc/en/acordaos/20200422.html.

[3] Para. 2.7.

P. F. Martins (✉)
Universidade Católica Portuguesa, Faculty of Law, Católica Research Centre for the Future of Law, Lisbon, Portugal
e-mail: pfmartins@ucp.pt

I. Quadros, M. Gorjão-Henriques (eds.), *Revisiting the Liberal Constitutional Features of the European Union*, https://doi.org/10.1007/978-3-031-95717-8_14

the latter was eventually abandoned, the norm remained in the Portuguese Constitution. However, up until 2020 the Constitutional Court had issued no decision on its interpretation. Hence the importance of judgment no. 422/2020: this was truly the first time the Portuguese Constitutional Court addressed the issue of supremacy in the Portuguese legal order, clarifying the scope and meaning of Article 8(4), and in doing so drawing on the judicial dialogues of other Member States with the Court of Justice of the EU (CJEU) and fixing a principle that governs the separation of jurisdiction between the national constitutional authority and the European courts.

The purpose of this contribution is to present a brief critical analysis of the decision, which arrives more than 15 years after the adoption of Article 8(4) and 35 years after Portuguese accession to the European Communities. The subject is of renewed importance in current times, notably in light of the *Weiss*[4] judgment handed down by the German Constitutional Court and, more recently, the sequel from the Polish Constitutional Tribunal.[5] Remarkably, the pandemic has been rich in terms of constitutional dialogues in the EU that deserve a closer look.

2 The Case

The facts of the case which gave rise to the decision are not particularly exciting, as the norms invoked by the applicant dealt with a particularly complex and technical matter of EU law.

The case began in the civil judicial courts, in Lisbon, where the applicant moved an action against the "*Instituto de Financiamento da Agricultura e Pescas*" (hereinafter "IFAP", which is the public institute responsible for validating and paying public national and European funds to companies operating in the agricultural, rural development and fisheries sectors and other similar sectors) and a bank. The applicant—*Cruz&Companhia*—was a commercial company engaged in the marketing of wine, spirits and derivatives thereof, including production, storage and purchase for resale. In the course of its business, it had exported wine to Angola at a lower price than it would have obtained if it had sold it on the EU market. It therefore applied for export refunds, giving a bank guarantee in the approximate amount of € 230,000. In the case at hand, the applicant argued that the security in question had expired in the meantime.

The financing operation took place pursuant to Commission Regulation (EEC) No. 2220/85 of 22 July 1985 laying down common detailed rules for the application

[4] Judgment of 5 May 2020, 2 BvR 859/15, 2 BvR 1651/15, 2 BvR 2006/15, 2 BvR 980/16 available at: https://www.bundesverfassungsgericht.de/SharedDocs/Entscheidungen/EN/2020/05/rs20200505_2bvr085915en.html.

[5] Case K 3/21 available at: https://trybunal.gov.pl/en/hearings/judgments/art/11662-ocena-zgodnosci-z-konstytucja-rp-wybranych-przepisow-traktatu-o-unii-europejskiej.

of the system of securities for agricultural products.[6] The latter set out a system that is commonly referred to as "export refunds", which corresponds to a subsidy that compensates exporting companies for the difference between the price of the products in the internal market and the price abroad. The constitution of a security was a pre-condition to benefit from the advance payment of the subsidy in relation to the export process.[7] The security was designed to guarantee the repayment of the advance where it appeared subsequently that the refund should not have been paid. Moreover, the market operator would only be entitled to the refund in definitive terms at the end of the process and the security would be released at that time. In particular, under Article 19 of the said regulation securities would be released when: (a) final entitlement to the sum granted as advance has been established, or (b) the sum granted, plus any addition provided for in the specific regulation, has been repaid. The right to benefit from the subsidies was conditional upon the exported products being of "sound and fair marketable quality". It further followed from the wording of Article 4(1) of Regulation No. 3665/87[8] that the refund was to be paid only upon proof being furnished that the products for which the export declaration was accepted had, within 60 days from the date of such acceptance of the export declaration, left the customs territory of the EU. Hence, Article 13 of the latter regulation established that no refund would be granted on products which were not of sound and fair marketable quality, or on products intended for human consumption whose characteristics or condition excluded or substantially impaired their use for that purpose.

The applicant argued in the case that by the time the bank guarantee was activated by IFAP, it had already expired. However, it lost the case in the court of first instance. Consequently, the company appealed to the Lisbon Court of Appeals ("*Tribunal da Relação*"), which considered the issue of when exactly operators are definitively entitled to the refund and when the security must be released and can no longer be activated. In this context, the applicant drew the court's attention to a case pending before the CJEU where a preliminary question had already been raised by the Lisbon Court of Appeals. It argued therein that the right to the refund was definitely acquired with proof of clearance of those goods through customs in the importing third country, in so far as a different understanding would create unjustified discrimination between importers who had benefited from advance refunds and

[6] *OJ L 205, 3.8.1985, p. 5-11.* The act has meanwhile been repealed by Commission Implementing Regulation (EU) No. 282/2012 of 28 March 2012 laying down common detailed rules for the application of the system of securities for agricultural products (*OJ L 92, 30.3.2012, p. 4-14*), which in turn was later repealed by Commission Delegated Regulation (EU) No 907/2014 of 11 March 2014 supplementing Regulation (EU) No. 1306/2013 of the European Parliament and of the Council with regard to paying agencies and other bodies, financial management, clearance of accounts, securities and use of euro (*OJ L 255, 28.8.2014, p. 18-58*).

[7] Pursuant to Article 4 of the Regulation "a security shall be given by or on behalf of the party responsible for paying the sum of money due if an obligation is not met".

[8] Commission Regulation (EEC) No. 3665/87 of 27 November 1987 laying down common detailed rules for the application of the system of export refunds on agricultural products, *OJ L 351, 14.12.1987, p. 1-33, meanwhile repealed and replaced as well.*

those who had benefited from the normal regime of export subsidies. In this context, in the case *sub judice*, the Court of Appeals decided not to make a preliminary reference to the CJEU but instead wait for the decision on the case pending before that European Court.

The latter was the case of *Cruz&Companhia*,[9] in which the Lisbon Court of Appeals had addressed the CJEU asking for clarification of the export refunds scheme. In this case, the applicant applied in June 1995 to the "*Instituto Nacional de Intervenção e Garantia Agrícola*" (hereinafter "INGA") for advance payment of the refund. It submitted, for that purpose, the documents concerning acceptance of the export declaration, proof that the products had left the customs territory of the EU within 60 days following that acceptance, and a bank guarantee drawn up at a bank on 14 June 1995, for an amount equal to the amount of the advance payment on the refund, plus 15%. That month, the refund was paid to *Cruz&Companhia*. After completing the export, *Cruz&Companhia* submitted to INGA the documents relating to the export, namely, the invoices, certificate, declaration of composition of the goods, the selected sample and the import declaration document. Furthermore, the goods entered the third country of destination and were cleared through customs. However, INGA never returned the bank guarantee to *Cruz&Companhia*. Years later, following an inspection to check the regularity of the wine exports carried out by the same company, INGA ordered, by a decision of 29 July 2004, the repayment of the sum received by *Cruz&Companhia* by way of export refund, within 30 days, subject to the penalty of triggering the mechanisms required for enforcement of the bank guarantee. The company decided not to pay the sum claimed, and instead it brought an action before the administrative courts, where it lost its case. Hence, it initiated civil proceedings against IFAP (the body which replaced INGA) seeking a declaration that the subject-matter of the bank guarantee was extinguished on 31 August 1995, the date on which the documents proving that the goods had entered Angola were submitted, and that, in those circumstances, the enforcement of the guarantee by IFAP was unlawful.[10] In those circumstances, the Lisbon Court of Appeals decided to stay proceedings and refer three questions to the CJEU for a preliminary ruling. In essence, these questions referred to "whether Article 19(1)(a) of Regulation No. 2220/85 must be interpreted as meaning that the guarantee furnished by an exporter to ensure the repayment of the advance received by way of export refund must be considered to be extinguished where it is established that the exporter submitted the acceptance of the export declaration, proof that the goods left the customs territory of the European Union within a maximum period of 60 days after that acceptance, and the proof of clearance of those goods through customs in the importing third country".[11]

To that question the CJEU provided a negative and straightforward answer:

---

[9] Judgment of 11 December 2014, *Cruz & Companhia*, Case C-128/13, ECLI:EU:C:2014:2432.

[10] See paras. 15–25.

[11] Para. 27.

> Article 19(1)(a) of Regulation No. 2220/85 must be interpreted as meaning that the guarantee furnished by an exporter to ensure the repayment of the advance received by way of export refund must not be considered to be extinguished even where it is established that the exporter submitted the acceptance of the export declaration, proof that the products left the customs territory of the European Union within a maximum period of 60 days after that acceptance, and the proof of clearance of those products through customs in the importing third country, if the other conditions for the grant of the refund, in particular the condition of sound and fair marketable quality of the products exported, provided for in Article 13 of Regulation No. 3665/87, are not satisfied.[12]

As the Lisbon Court of Appeals had asked for a clarification on the scope of the ruling, the CJEU added in *Cruz&Companhia II,*[13] that "the guarantee furnished by an exporter to ensure the repayment of the advance received by way of export refund may be implemented where, following an inspection carried out after the actual export and customs clearance of the products in question, it is established that one of the other conditions for the grant of that refund, in particular the condition of sound and fair marketable quality of the products exported, provided for in Article 13 of Commission Regulation (EEC) No. 3665/87 (...) is not satisfied".

In this light, subsequently, in the case that reached the Constitutional Court, the Lisbon Court of Appeals applied the previous ruling of the CJEU and dismissed the case. The applicant then appealed to the Supreme Court where it again argued on the basis of discrimination in particular in light of Article 13 of the national Constitution which provides for the principle of equality. The Supreme Court disregarded the appellant's arguments and considered that the issue was sufficiently solved by the case-law of the CJEU and no question of unjustified discrimination arose in the case. In particular, the Court considered that there was a relevant material distinction between operators who benefited from advance payments and those who did not. The question of knowing when the security must be released only arises with reference to exporters who have requested advance payments. Other exporters are in a completely different situation as they have not benefited from advanced funds, and therefore no question on securities arises in relation to them. Therefore, according to the Supreme Court there had not been any breach of the principle of equality in the case.

It was against the Supreme Court's decision that the applicant appealed to the Constitutional Court. It is worth remembering that in Portugal, access by individuals to the Constitutional Court is based on an appeals system, through the so-called "diffuse and concrete constitutional review mechanism". Pursuant to Article 280(1) of the Portuguese Constitution, an appeal may be made to the Constitutional Court against court decisions that either refuse the application of any norm on the grounds of its unconstitutionality or that apply a norm whose unconstitutionality has been raised during the proceedings. Furthermore, Article 70 of the Law of the Constitutional Court[14] provides for the cases where constitutional appeals in judicial

---

[12] Para. 42.

[13] Order of 23 October 2015, *Cruz & Companhia*, Case C-152/15, ECLI:EU:C:2015:740.

[14] Law no. 28/82, of 15 November.

cases are possible. Under Article 70(1)(b) of said statute, individuals may lodge an appeal against decisions of ordinary courts applying a rule the unconstitutionality of which has been raised during the proceedings.[15] This appeal may only be lodged by the party that raised the question of unconstitutionality. Article 72(2)(b) provides that, besides the Public Prosecutor's Office, persons who, in accordance with the law governing the case in which the decision was passed, have standing to file an appeal, may appeal to the Constitutional Court.[16]

3 The Constitutional Court Ruling: *Acte Éclairé* and the Jurisdictional Rule Included in Article 8(4) of the National Constitution

Pursuant to Article 76 of the Law of the Constitutional Court, it is for the court that issued the decision which is the object of appeal to examine the admission of the respective appeal. It was in this light that the Constitutional Court interpreted Article 8(4) of the Constitution. In fact, the court began by highlighting that the appeal in question involved a norm of secondary EU law, notably Article 19(1)(b) of Regulation no. 2220/85 in the interpretation followed by the Supreme Court, which in turn followed the interpretation fixed by the CJEU in *Cruz&Companhia*. The argument before the Constitutional Court was that the Supreme Court's decision disregarded the breach of the principle of equality as protected by the national Constitution. The question thus raised was whether a legal norm as interpreted by the CJEU was in conformity with internal constitutional rules, in particular Article 13 of the national Constitution.

In this sense, the case is akin to *Internationale Handelsgesellschaft*,[17] the famous case of March 1970 that motivated the constitutional dialogue between the CJEU and the German Constitutional Court and led to the handing down of *Solange I*.[18] As is well known, in the latter case, the *Verwaltungsgericht Frankfurt-am-Main* referred two questions to the CJEU on the validity of the system of export licences and of the deposit attaching to them provided for by several European regulations, which according to the referring court were invalid, notably for breach of certain structural

[15] Pursuant to Article 72(2) of the Law on the Constitutional Court, the appeals envisaged in Article 70(1) *b)* and *f)* may only be filed by the party that has raised the question of unconstitutionality or illegality in a way that is procedurally appropriate before the court that gave the decision appealed against in terms of the latter being obliged to know it.

[16] Also, the appeals envisaged in sub-paragraphs *b)* and *f)* only apply to decisions that admit no ordinary appeal because the law does not provide for this, or because all those available to the case have been exhausted, except those aimed at standardising jurisprudence.

[17] Judgment of 17 December 1970, *Internationale Handelsgesellschaft mbH/Einfuhrund Vorratsstelle für Getreide und Futtermittel*, Case 11/70, ECR 1970 p. 1125, ECLI:EU:C:1970:114.

[18] Judgment of 29 May 1974 – AZ. 2 BvL 52/71.

principles enshrined in the national constitutional law.[19] In short, in this type of cases, the validity of EU law is questioned under national constitutional standards.[20]

In this context, the Portuguese Constitutional Court considered that in order to reply to the central issue of the appeal it had to previously determine whether it had jurisdiction to hear the case, *i.e.* whether it had competence to issue a decision on the validity of a piece of EU law in light of the national Constitution. The normative framework to answer that question was provided by Article 8(4) of the Constitution, which establishes that, as a rule, EU law applies in the domestic legal system according to the rules and principles established at the European level, leaving aside – as a limit and/or exception – the cases where EU law compromises the fundamental principles of a "democratic state based on the rule of law". The decision was thus focused on this preliminary jurisdictional question, although the merits of the case were also taken into consideration indirectly in the judgment. In the words of the Constitutional Court, although Article 8(4) of the Constitution "does not strictly correspond to a rule of jurisdiction, it nevertheless conveys, in very different terms, spheres of jurisdictional scope relating to the intervention of this Court, in the sense that they give rise, according to their distinct positioning within the rule in question, to decisions on whether or not to hear the appeal based on the distinct *scopes of jurisdiction* coexisting therein".[21]

In this regard, recalling the terms of the proceedings and the application of Regulation no. 2220/85 under the jurisprudence of the CJEU, the Portuguese Court reached the conclusion that under EU law, Article 19(1)(b) had become *acte éclairé*, pursuant to the *Cilfit*[22] judgment. In this sense, the case raised the issue of whether the Constitutional Court could second-guess a decision of the CJEU.

At this point, the Court embarked on a rather long exercise of evoking the history of the principle of supremacy of EU law from when it was initially affirmed by the CJEU in *Van Gend en Loos*[23] and *Costa/ENEL*.[24] Here, the Court specifically mentioned certain constitutional dialogues, in particular those between the German and Italian Constitutional Courts and the CJEU, and referred to national and international literature on the scope of the principle of supremacy.[25]

---

[19] As stated in *Internationale*, para.2: "More particularly, the system of deposits runs counter to the principles of freedom of action and of disposition, of economic liberty and of proportionality arising in particular from articles 2(1) and 14 of the Basic Law. The obligation to import or export resulting from the issue of the licences, together with the deposit attaching thereto, constitutes an excessive intervention in the freedom of disposition in trade, as the objective of the regulations could have been attained by methods of intervention having less serious consequences".

[20] *Infra* Sects. 4.3 and 4.4.

[21] Para. 2.3.

[22] Judgment of 29 February 1984, *Cilfit*, Case 77/83, ECR 1984 p. 1257, ECLI:EU:C:1984:91.

[23] Judgment of 5 February 1963, *Van Gend en Loos/Administratie der Belastingen*, Case 26/62, ECR 1963 p. 1, ECLI:EU:C:1963:1.

[24] Judgment of 15 July 1964, *Costa/E.N.E.L.*, Case 6-64, ECR 1964 p. 585, ECLI:EU:C:1964:66.

[25] *Infra* Sect. 4.3.

Somewhat surprisingly and in a rather extended fashion, the Constitutional Court drew attention to the difference between actions for infringements brought under Articles 258-260 TFEU and systemic infringements that may constitute the object of Article 7 TEU proceedings, referring to the CJEU's rulings in *LM*[26] and *Aranyosi and Căldăraru.*[27] These references have, however, little or no consequences either for the case at hand or for the final definition of the normative criterion underlying Article 8(4) of the national Constitution. It may be assumed that these references were included in the judgment mostly due to considerations of context, given the timing of the decision. As is well known, shortly before the ruling was delivered, the German Constitutional Court had issued a controversial judgment rejecting the authority of the CJEU, and in particular compliance with the latter's decision on the validity of the European Central Bank programme adopted in 2018, which allowed for the purchase of assets in secondary markets.[28] Indeed, the German Constitutional Court has maintained an intense dialogue with the CJEU since the 1970s on the scope of the supremacy of EU law, the absolute and unconditional nature of which it firmly opposes. On several occasions it has threatened to overrule EU rules on constitutional grounds, and in 2020 it made it clear that it will not only "bark", but is willing to actually "bite" whenever the CJEU acts *ultra vires*. The latter ruling was criticised by several scholars who highlighted the "precedent effect" of the decision. In fact, by rejecting the authority of a CJEU ruling, the German Constitutional Court was paving the way for other episodes of disobedience by other Member States of the EU who were involved in the "rule of law fight",[29] as was the case of Poland and Hungary, against which Article 7 TEU was triggered in 2017 and 2018 respectively. The decision of the Polish Constitutional Court of October 2021[30] may well be seen as a sequel—and a very serious one—of that movie.

[26] Judgment of 25 July 2018, *Minister for Justice and Equality (Deficiencies in the system of justice)*, Case C-216/18 PPU, ECLI:EU:C:2018:586.

[27] Judgment of 5 April 2016, *Aranyosi and Căldăraru*, Joined Cases C-404/15 and C-659/15 PPU, ECLI:EU:C:2016:198.

[28] *Supra* note 4.

[29] See opinions at https://esthinktank.com/2020/06/21/the-eu-in-danger-what-the-german-constitutional-courts-weiss-ruling-might-mean-for-europe/; https://verfassungsblog.de/some-preliminary-remarks-on-the-pspp-decision-of-the-german-constitutional-court/.

[30] The Polish case escalated with the delivery of the already famous judgment of the Polish Constitutional Tribunal of October 2021 where the latter refused to comply with the decision of the CJEU on the rules of appointment of judges for the Supreme Court. *Supra* note 5. See also: https://europeanlawblog.eu/2021/10/21/polands-constitutional-tribunal-on-the-status-of-eu-law-the-polish-gover.comnment-got-all-the-answers-it-needed-from-a-court-it-controls/. In March 2021, the CJEU considered that the successive amendments to the Polish Law on the National Council of the Judiciary which have the effect of removing effective judicial review of that Council's decisions proposing to the President of the Republic candidates for the office of judge at the Supreme Court are liable to infringe EU law. See Judgment of 2 March 2021, *A.B. and others (Nomination des juges à la Cour suprême - Recours)*, Case C-824/18, ECLI:EU:C:2021:153.

In any case, after these historical and contextual references, the Portuguese Constitutional Court dedicated significant attention to the regime of Articles 7 and 8 of the national Constitution, and its combined application.

According to Article 7(5), Portugal is committed to reinforcing the European identity and to strengthening the European states' actions in favour of democracy, peace, economic progress and justice in the relations between peoples. Furthermore, pursuant to Article 7(6), subject to reciprocity and with respect for the fundamental principles of a democratic state based on the rule of law and for the principle of subsidiarity, and with a view to the achievement of the economic, social and territorial cohesion of an area of freedom, security and justice and the definition and implementation of a common external, security and defence policy, Portugal may agree to the exercise jointly, in cooperation or by the Union's institutions, of the powers needed to construct and deepen the EU. For its part, Article 8 sets out the rules and principles that govern the relationship between international and European law and the constitutional legal order.

In the understanding of the Court, these provisions are complementary and consequential: whereas Article 7 provides for the constitutional foundations of membership of the EU, Article 8 establishes the legal consequences of that political choice.[31] Article 8 provides thus for a fundamental principle of constitutional law that shapes the system of sources of law in Portugal. The Court explained the history of both legal provisions, highlighting that although Article 8 was introduced to justify ratification of the Constitutional Treaty, it survived beyond that original vocation and subsists as a fundamental principle of the Portuguese constitutional legal order. The Court further noted the influence of the positions assumed in *Frontini*[32] and *Solange II*[33] in the drafting of Article 8. Moreover, citing the ruling of the German Constitutional Court on the Lisbon Treaty,[34] the Court drew attention to the fact that the legal foundation of the EU legal order is the informed consent of Member States who retain the competence to decide on the scope of competences of the Union—the so-called *Kompetenz-kompetenz*—associated with the notion of sovereignty.

It is against this background that the Court claimed for itself the judicial *Kompetenz-kompetenz* and fixed the interpretation of Article 8(4), therein identifying two levels of intervention by the constitutional jurisdiction. Firstly, regarding the first part of the provision, there is a general limitation imposed on the jurisdiction of the Court in assessing the constitutionality of EU law norms. EU law is, thus, under Article 8(4) first sentence, immune to *regular* constitutional review, and the provisions of the Constitution providing for control of constitutionality of all norms

[31] Para. 2.6.1.

[32] Judgment no. 183/1973, of 27.12.1973.

[33] Judgment of 22 October 1986, Az: 2 BvR 197/83.

[34] Judgment of 30 June 2009, 2 BvE 2/08.

applicable in the domestic legal order—in particular Article 277[35]—are in this respect derogated. Secondly, functioning as a "counter-limitation", the last part of the provision re-establishes the role of the constitutional jurisdiction in so far as a potential breach of the principles of a democratic state based on the rule of law are at stake. Here, the jurisdiction of the Court is reopened. The Court acknowledged that the space for this intervention is quantitively reduced, in particular concerning the protection of fundamental rights. However, at this level, it introduced the notion of constitutional identity of the Republic, considering that the elements that compose this identity limit in of themselves the possibility of Portugal agreeing "to the exercise jointly, in cooperation or by the Union's institutions, of the powers needed to construct and deepen the European Union".[36] Here, the Court affirmed that the competence to decide its own competence falls in this domain. Therefore, not only the competence to decide on the respect for the said principles but also the competence to decide the scope of its own jurisdiction must remain with the Constitutional Court.

In the definition of the exact line that separates parts one and two of Article 8(4), the Court rejected the need to identify a list of subject-matters that are either immune or always subject to national constitutional review. On the contrary, the "border zone" implied in Articles 7(6) and 8(4) must be understood under a general criterion that guides the interpreter for future cases. In this regard, the Court acknowledged that in general, the European legal order already provides and protects – notably through the jurisdiction of the CJEU - the fundamental values of a democratic state based on the rule of law. Hence, there is, as a rule, equivalent protection of the same parametric values at the European and national levels.[37] By contrast, when the case involves issues of national identity, only the Constitutional Court is in a position to act as guardian of those values. With regard to these issues the CJEU cannot ensure, by definition, an equivalent level of protection. As such, in a rather sophisticated formula, the Court established that:

> … the refusal to apply – and, logically, access by the national constitutional jurisdiction – a rule of EUL (i.e., the activation of the counter-limit that underlies the final part of Article 8(4)) presupposes an incompatibility with a fundamental principle of a democratic state based on the rule of law that, in this context (including, therefore, the CJEU case law), does not have a parameter materially equivalent to that recognised in the Constitution of the Portuguese Republic, namely by incorporating the **constitutional identity of the Republic**, since such a principle necessarily applies to the agreement on the **"[…] exercise jointly, in cooperation or by the Union's institutions, of the powers needed to construct and deepen the European Union"**. It follows – and this corresponds to the second alternative that can be interpreted in Article 8(4) – that whenever the assessment of a rule of EUL is at issue with respect to a (fundamental) principle of a democratic state based on the rule of law that, within the scope of EUL, has a parameter functionally equivalent to the one recognised

[35] According to Article 277(1) norms that contravene the provisions of the Constitution or the principles enshrined therein are unconstitutional.

[36] Paras. 2.6.2.2 and 2.6.3.

[37] Para. 2.6.4.

> in the Portuguese Constitution, the Constitutional Court should not assess the compatibility of the rule with the latter and should issue a decision refusing to take cognisance.[38]

This is thus "the constitutional criterion" that governs the competence of the Constitutional Court under Article 8(4) as a reflex of the constitutional and political decision taken pursuant to Article 7(6). The application of this formula requires a comparative exercise: *i.e.*, to identify the legal principle or norm at stake, locate its position in the European legal order and determine whether it matches the level of protection ensured within the domestic constitutional system.

4 Critical Remarks

Despite the considerably long extension of the judgment and the effort noted therein to cover the fundamentals of the principle of supremacy of EU law, there are some relevant shortcomings in the decision that are worth pointing out.

4.1 Primacy as "Applicative Preference"

Firstly, not surprisingly, the Court refers to supremacy as a kind of "decisional rule"[39] that determines preference for EU law to the detriment of national law. Such a rule is exhausted by the results it implies, without requiring a hierarchical foundation typical of monist systems. Hence, EU law prevails not because it is *lex superior* but most of all because it is "materially competent" to rule the subject matter of the case. As such EU law does not determine the invalidity of national law, which remains fully valid needing only to be set aside in the cases at hand. In the Court's words:

> The fact is that primacy, the principle established by the Court of Justice in the 1960s, even in its later guises, namely in the *Internationale Handelsgesellschaft* Ruling (1970), which we will refer to in greater detail below, despite sometimes being identified by the noun *superiority* (referring to EUL in its relationship with national law), thereby conveying a less precise semantic slant, "[...] *does not* [*presuppose*] *a typical relationship of infra- and supra-ordination between norms* [, *not being applicable*] *as a requirement of hierarchical prevalence* [*: the*] *EU rule prevails over the national rule not because it is superior to it, but because it is materially competent to resolve the specific dispute.* [...] [*The*] *relationship between European Union law and the law of Member States is built on the principle of conferral and by reference to the principle of collaboration or functional complementarity between autonomous legal systems*" (Maria Luísa Duarte, *Direito Internacional Público e ordem jurídica global do século XXI*, 2nd reprint, Lisbon, 2019, p. 339). Moreover, the expression *superiority*, being inferable from the noun *pre-eminence*, which was the one actually used by the Court of Justice in the *Costa v Enel* Ruling [*preminenza* in Italian, the

[38] Para. 2.7.

[39] Para. 2.3.2.1.

> language of the case: "[*l*]*a preminenza del diritto comunitario trova conferma* [...]"; *precedence*, in the English version; *prééminence*, in French, the expression presumably chosen by the rapporteur, Robert Lecourt: "[...] *attendu que la prééminence du droit communautaire est confirmée* [...]"; *primacía*, in Spanish; *Vorrang*, in German; *primado*, in the Portuguese translation], did not correspond (neither *superiority* nor even *supremacy*) symptomatically to the noun chosen to identify the intended idea, *pre-eminence* providing synonymy, common to the various languages being applied, with expressions (such as *primacy* and *preponderance*) which more accurately capture the exact meaning of the idea intended to be asserted: EUL, directly projecting onto the legal orders of the Member States, by its very essence and purpose as result of the Treaties, needs to prevail over (to set aside, to *bypass*) domestic law in competing or conflicting situations to avoid stultifying to the point of total ineffectiveness, and cannot, ultimately, within its own domain, be supplanted by domestic law, applying the latter to its own detriment. In other words, the conflict created at that level between domestic norms and EUL is generated by an *actual competition* between valid rules (valid in their own terms for their own field), essentially consisting in an *apparent competition*, whose *antinomy* is overcome based on a *criterion of speciality*, which the principle of primacy insists on resolving by applying the European norm.[40]

In this light, the Court highlighted that supremacy of EU law is different from the supremacy that exists in federal systems.[41] Within the latter, federal courts may assess the compatibility of state law with federal law, which is not possible for the CJEU (at least directly).[42] In fact, the CJEU does not have competence to assess the validity of national rules.[43] Also, whereas in federal systems the unity of the legal order is ensured by the supremacy of federal law and the federal judiciary, primacy of EU law is entirely dependent on the preference given to it by national courts. Hence, as the EU is not a federation of states, the relationship between EU law and national law cannot be understood in strict hierarchical terms. In this sense, according to the Portuguese Constitutional Court, primacy of EU law lies somewhere between supremacy of federal law and classical guarantees of international law. As a consequence, supremacy of EU law determines the mere disapplication of conflicting national law.

There is some truth in the analysis provided by the Constitutional Court. Since *Simmenthal*,[44] it is clear that as a matter of EU law, conflicting national rules need only to be set aside in specific cases, their validity remaining, in principle, intact. The words in *Simmenthal* are famous:

> ... in accordance with the principle of the precedence of Community law, the relationship between provisions of the Treaty and directly applicable measures of the institutions on the one hand and the national law of the Member States on the other is such that those provisions

[40] Para. 2.3.2.1.

[41] Para. 2.3.2.3.

[42] Indirectly the CJEU controls the admissibility of national law in infringement proceedings and preliminary rulings on interpretation.

[43] Notwithstanding, the Court mentioned the case of *Rimšēvičs/Latvia*, where the CJEU actually invalidated a piece of national law. See Judgment of 26 February 2019, *Rimšēvičs/Latvia*, Joined Cases C-202/18 and C-238/18, ECLI:EU:C:2019:139.

[44] Judgment of 9 March 1978, *Amministrazione delle finanze dello Stato/Simmenthal*, Case 106/77, ECR 1978, p. 629.

> and measures not only by their entry into force *render automatically inapplicable any conflicting provision* of current national law but - in so far as they are an integral part of, and take precedence in, the legal order applicable in the territory of each of the Member States - also preclude the valid adoption of new national legislative measures to the extent to which they would be incompatible with community provisions.[45]

Also, it is true that such affirmation is associated in the CJEU's case-law with the limited field of application of EU law, *i.e.*, where the EU exercises its competences. In the same case, the CJEU further stated that:

> Indeed any recognition that national legislative measures *which encroach upon the field within which the Community exercises its legislative power* or which are otherwise incompatible with the provisions of Community law had any legal effect would amount to a corresponding denial of the effectiveness of obligations undertaken unconditionally and irrevocably by Member States pursuant to the Treaty and would thus imperil the very foundations of the Community.[46]

Thus, when in a later case the Commission tried to infer from *Simmenthal* that EU law precludes the valid adoption of new national legislative measures which would be incompatible with EU law provisions, with the result that said provision should be treated as non-existent, the CJEU clarified that that was not the case:

> ... in *Simmenthal*, the Court held that every national court must, in a case within its jurisdiction, apply Community law in its entirety and protect rights which the latter confers on individuals, setting aside any provision of national law which may conflict with it, whether prior or subsequent to the Community rule (*Simmenthal*, paragraphs 21 and 24). That case-law has been reaffirmed on numerous occasions (see, in particular, *Debus*, cited above, paragraph 32; Case C-158/91 *Levy* [1993] ECR I-4287, paragraph 9; and Case C-347/96 *Solred v Administración General del Estado* [1998] ECR I-937, paragraph 30).

It cannot therefore, contrary to the Commission's contention, be inferred from the judgment in *Simmenthal* that the incompatibility with Community law of a subsequently adopted rule of national law *has the effect of rendering that rule of national law non-existent. Faced with such a situation, the national court is, however, obliged to disapply that rule*, provided always that this obligation does not restrict the power of the competent national courts to apply, from among the various procedures available under national law, those which are appropriate for protecting the individual rights conferred by Community law (see Case 34/67 *Lück v Hauptzollamt Köln-Rheinau* [1968] ECR 245)".[47]

Without prejudice, the affirmation of the Portuguese Constitutional Court referring to the great difference between the primacy of EU law and that of federal law ignores several important rules and principles.

Firstly, and still according to *Simmenthal*, it is for Member States to determine the terms and conditions under which supremacy operates at the national level. It is within the national procedural framework that national courts must draw all the

[45] Para. 17.

[46] Para. 18.

[47] Judgment of 22 October 1998, *Ministero delle Finanze/IN.CO.GE.'90 and others*, Joined Cases C-10/97 to C-22/97, ECR 1998 p. I-6307, ECLI:EU:C:1998:498, paras. 20–21.

consequences of the principle of supremacy, meaning that nothing precludes national judges from declaring, as a matter of national law, a domestic norm or act to be invalid for breach of EU law rules and principles.[48]

Secondly, although it is undeniable that the EU does not translate into a "perfect federal model"—whatever the latter's features might be—, it is also undisputable that the EU legal order has a federal nature. As is well known, the essence of federalism lies with the division of competences between federate units and the federal Union, both at the internal and external level. In this respect, it is clear, at the outset, that the EU rests on a transfer of competences from the Member States to the EU, early and emblematically upheld in *Costa/ENEL*.[49] The existence of conferred powers is the basis of all federal models. As such, the EU, as a federation, may only act - as a rule and regularly—within the scope of competences that have been transferred to it by the Member States. The Treaty states twice that the competences that have not been transferred to the Union remain within the Member States.[50]

Without prejudice, it is also well known that the separation of powers between the EU and its Member States is far from clear-cut. Throughout the several amendments to the Treaties not only have Member States increasingly transferred competences to the Union, but they have done so with a considerable degree of variation and flexibility. Hence, since its inception, the Union has acquired all types of competences—currently designated as exclusive, shared, support, and complementary, among others[51]—all of them entailing different legal consequences from the point of view of their relationship with Member States' law. As a consequence, it is not always clear whether a certain subject-matter falls within the scope of competences of the Union in such a way that supremacy unequivocally operates. On the contrary,

[48] *Ibidem*. Notably, the CJEU added that: "22. It remains to be considered whether non-application, as the result of a judgment given by the Court, of national legislation which introduced a levy contrary to Community law has the result of depriving that levy retroactively of its character as a charge and thereby divesting of its fiscal nature the legal relationship established when that charge was levied between the national tax authority and the companies liable to pay it. (…) 26. Thus, the obligation on the national court to ensure that a domestic charge levied in breach of Community law is refunded must, subject to compliance with the two conditions laid down by the Court in its case-law, be discharged in accordance with the provisions of its national law. It follows that the detailed rules for repayment which are to apply and the classification, for that purpose, of the legal relationship established when that charge was levied between the tax authorities of a Member State and particular companies in that State are matters which fall to be determined under national law".

[49] Cf. para. 8: "By creating a Community of unlimited duration, having its own institutions, its own personality, its own legal capacity and capacity of representation on the international plane and, more particularly, real powers stemming from a limitation of sovereignty or a transfer of powers from the states to the Community, the Member States have limited their sovereign rights, albeit within limited fields, and have thus created a body of law which binds both their nationals and themselves".

[50] Pursuant to Articles 4 and 5 TEU, the limits of Union competences are governed by the principle of conferral. Under the principle of conferral, the Union shall act only within the limits of the competences conferred upon it by the Member States in the Treaties to attain the objectives set out therein. Competences not conferred upon the Union in the Treaties remain with the Member States.

[51] See Articles 2–6 TFEU.

not only do the several heads of EU competence often overlap with each other, but more significantly the line that separates Union intervention from Member States' competences is frequently blurred and uncertain.

Additionally, both Article 352 TFEU and the doctrine of implied powers developed in the CJEU's jurisprudence have contributed to "muddying the waters" even further. Pursuant to Article 352 TFEU, the Union may deliberate to expand the scope of its competences, if an action by the Union proves necessary, "within the framework of the policies defined in the Treaties, to attain one of the objectives set out in the Treaties, and the Treaties have not provided the necessary powers". Clearly the operation of Article 352 TFEU is subject to strict procedural and substantive limitations,[52] yet, its potential to expand Union intervention in an uncertain and unpredictable way is undeniable.

Furthermore, according to CJEU case-law, "where an Article of the EEC Treaty (...) confers a specific task on the Commission it must be accepted, if that provision is not to be rendered wholly ineffective, that it confers on the Commission necessarily and *per se* the powers which are indispensable in order to carry out that task".[53] The existence of implied powers of the EU has had particularly drastic consequences at the external level, with the CJEU concluding often that Member States are precluded from concluding international treaties, in as much as such competence has been implicitly granted to the Union either in exclusive or shared terms.[54] This jurisprudence has contributed significantly to the federalisation of the EU at the external level. Indeed, by acknowledging that the Union replaces the Member States in the international realm, the CJEU is effectively not only contributing to expanding the competences of the EU but also to reinforcing the federal features of the European constitutional model. Even when the CJEU concludes that the Union merely has a shared external competence that must be exercised in articulation with the Member States, cases demonstrate once again that the line separating Union intervention from Member State action is far from clear.[55]

Thirdly, also in an effort to identify strict separate circles of intervention reserved to Union law and Member States' laws, the Constitutional Court pointed to Article 51(1) of the Charter of Fundamental Rights, pursuant to which EU law binds the

---

[52] The Council must act unanimously on a proposal from the Commission and after obtaining the consent of the European Parliament. The Commission shall draw national Parliaments' attention to proposals based on this Article. Measures based on Article 352 TFEU must not entail harmonisation of Member States' laws or regulations in cases where the Treaties exclude such harmonisation, cannot serve as a basis for attaining objectives pertaining to the common foreign and security policy, and must respect the limits set out in Article 40 § 2 TEU.

[53] Judgment of 9 July 1987, *Germany, France, Netherlands, Denmark and United Kingdom/Commission*, Joined Cases 281, 283, 284, 285 and 287/85, ECR 1987 p. 3203), ECLI:EU:C:1987:351, para. 28.

[54] Judgment of 31 March 1971, *Commission/Council (ERTA)*, Case 22/70, ECR 1971 p. 263; Opinion 1/03 (New Lugano Convention), of 7 February 2006, ECR 2006 p. I-1145, ECLI:EU:C:2006:81; See also Articles 216 TFEU and Article 3(2) TEU.

[55] See *e.g.* Opinion 2/91, of 19 March 1993 (ECR 1993 p. I-1061) and Opinion 1/94, of 15 November 1994 (ECR 1994 p. I-5267).

Member States "only when they are implementing Union law". Although in itself that affirmation is true, it seems to ignore the case-law of the CJEU that has contributed to the so-called "incorporation of the Charter" (Eeckhout 2002, pp. 945–994) and the acknowledgement that the latter can be invoked against the Member States in a significant number of fields and cases.[56]

Moreover, the Portuguese Constitutional Court failed to consider the scope of Article 53 of the Charter and the CJEU's understanding in this respect. In particular, in *Melloni*[57] the CJEU affirmed that although Article 53 of the Charter confirms that, where an EU legal act calls for national implementing measures, national authorities and courts remain free to apply national standards of protection of fundamental rights, "the level of protection provided for by the Charter, as interpreted by the Court, and the primacy, unity and effectiveness of EU law"[58] cannot ever be compromised.

The difficulty in understanding the division of powers between the EU and Member States in strict terms, as well as the consequences of applying Article 53 of the Charter, can easily be illustrated by the case of *Åkerberg Fransson,*[59] where the CJEU introduced the notion of a "situation where action of the Member States is not entirely determined by European Union law".[60] In this case, several national governments and the European Commission disputed the admissibility of the questions referred for a preliminary ruling, arguing that the CJEU would have jurisdiction to answer them only if the tax penalties imposed on Mr. Åkerberg Fransson and the criminal proceedings brought against him that were the subject-matter of the main proceedings arose from the implementation of EU law. As that was not the case, in accordance with Article 51(1) of the Charter, those penalties and proceedings could not come under the *ne bis in idem* principle secured by Article 50 of the Charter. While coming to the opposite conclusion on the merits,[61] the CJEU highlighted its previous case-law according to which fundamental rights guaranteed in the legal order of the EU are applicable in all situations governed by EU law, but not outside such situations. Hence, the CJEU once again affirmed that it has no power to examine the compatibility with the Charter of national legislation lying outside the scope of EU law. However, that said,:

[56] See *e.g.*, Judgment of 13 July 1989, *Wachauf/Bundesamt für Ernährung und Forstwirtschaft*, Case 5/88, ECR 1989 p. 2609, ECLI:EU:C:1989:321; Judgment of 18 June 1991, *ERT/DEP*, Case C-260/89, ECR 1991 p. I-2925; Judgment of 12 June 2003, *Schmidberger*, Case C-112/00, ECR 2003 p. I-5659. ECLI:EU:C:2003:333.

[57] Judgment of 26 February 2013, *Melloni,* Case C-399/11, ECLI:EU:C:2013:107.

[58] Para. 60. See, *inter alia*, Besselink (2014, pp. 531–552); Cavallone (2014, pp. 19–40).

[59] Judgment of 26 February 2013, *Åkerberg Fransson*, Case C-617/10, ECLI:EU:C:2013:105.

[60] Para. 29.

[61] Para. 27: "It follows that tax penalties and criminal proceedings for tax evasion, such as those to which the defendant in the main proceedings has been or is subject because the information concerning VAT that was provided was false, constitute implementation of Articles 2, 250(1) and 273 of Directive 2006/112 (previously Articles 2 and 22 of the Sixth Directive) and of Article 325 TFEU and, therefore, of European Union law, for the purposes of Article 51(1) of the Charter".

> ...where a court of a Member State is called upon to review whether fundamental rights are complied with by a national provision or measure which, *in a situation where action of the Member States is not entirely determined by European Union law*, implements the latter for the purposes of Article 51(1) of the Charter, national authorities and courts remain free to apply national standards of protection of fundamental rights, *provided that the level of protection provided for by the Charter, as interpreted by the Court, and the primacy, unity and effectiveness of European Union law are not thereby compromised* (see, in relation to the latter aspect, Case C-399/11 *Melloni* [2013] ECR, paragraph 60).[62]

As a final difficulty, understanding the supremacy of EU law as limited to the latter's field of application further ignores the cases where the CJEU has made clear that even when exercising national competences Member States must respect fundamental principles of EU law. This is the position that has been taken, for instance, in the case-law on European citizenship.[63] And it could be argued that the recent decision in *Associação Sindical dos Juízes Portugueses*[64] extended this possibility without limitation, in so far as the CJEU disregarded any link whatsoever to the scope of application of EU law when it affirmed the need for national jurisdictional systems to respect the values enshrined in Article 2 TEU.

All in all, although the doctrine of "applicative preference" finds its roots in the jurisprudence of the CJEU, there are other lines in recent case-law that reveal the need to further consider the issue of supremacy beyond the idea that it only operates with limited scope within the field of conferred powers. Not only should the latter not be understood "with a ruler and a square" but also, more importantly, requirements of effectiveness of EU law seem to reach much further than EU competences actually do. In this regard, the federal nature of the EU legal order cannot be denied and it is far more complex than other potentially comparable systems, leading to important consequences in terms of the supremacy of EU law.

4.2 Disregard for Les Verts

The second critical remark regarding the Portuguese Constitutional Court ruling relates to a specific paragraph of the decision that mentions the case of *Les Verts*.[65] Indeed, while referring to constitutional conflicts the Court re-called paragraph 23 of *Les Verts*, where the CJEU stated that "the European Economic Community is a community based on the rule of law, inasmuch as neither its Member States nor its

---

[62] Para. 29.

[63] Judgment of 12 September 2006, *Eman and Sevinger*, Case C-300/04, ECR 2006 p. I-8055 ECLI:EU:C:2006:545, on the scope of the right to vote for European Parliament elections; and Judgment of 2 March 2010, *Rottmann*, Case C-135/08, ECR 2010 p. I-1449, ECLI:EU:C:2010:104, on loss of citizenship.

[64] Judgment of 27 February 2018, *Associação Sindical dos Juízes Portugueses*, Case C-64/16, ECLI:EU:C:2018:117.

[65] Judgment of 23 April 1986, *Les Verts/Parliament*, Case 294/83, ECR 1986 p. 1339, ECLI:EU:C:1986:166.

institutions can avoid a review of the question whether the measures adopted by them are in conformity with the basic constitutional charter, the Treaty".[66] Surprisingly, though, the Constitutional Court affirmed that that statement does not go beyond that specific case, which involved the need to acknowledge constitutional review of acts of the European Parliament.[67] This claim is puzzling as it seems to ignore the importance of *Les Verts* in the process of constitutionalising the EU and the subsequent and consistent case-law of the CJEU on the constitutional nature of the Union.

In fact, the importance of *Les Verts* must not be underestimated. This was the first time that the CJEU expressly drew attention to the constitutional nature of the Treaty and it was thus a pivotal decision. The ruling emerged as a consequence of the *dicta* in *Van Gend* and *Costa*, according to which the Treaties created a new legal order that is independent of those of the Member States and of international law.

The famous statement would later be repeated in subsequent judgments[68] and Opinions of the Court,[69] as well as Opinions of several Advocate-Generals,[70] and would become one of the most important and controversial ideas regarding the nature of European integration.[71] It has been noted that by stating that the Treaties are the basic constitutional charter of the Community, the CJEU came close to the idea of Chief Justice Marshall of the U.S. Supreme Court in *McCulloch v. Maryland* when he proclaimed that "we must never forget that it is a constitution we are expounding".[72] Also, what the CJEU stated in *Les Verts* goes to the heart of EU constitutionalism as reflected in Article 16 of the Declaration of the Rights of Man and of the Citizen, approved by the National Assembly of France, in August 1789: "A society in which the observance of the law is not assured, nor the separation of powers defined, has no constitution at all".

The Portuguese Constitutional Court's disregard for the importance of *Les Verts* within the debate on the supremacy of EU law is even more perplexing if we consider that this ruling is of paramount importance for the very reasoning adopted by the Constitutional Court in its interpretation of Article 8(4) of the national Constitution, in particular its first part. It is precisely because the Union is also

[66] Para. 23.

[67] See Para. 2.4.1.

[68] *E.g.*, Judgment of 23 March 1993, *Weber/Parliament*, Case C-314/91, ECR 1993 p. I-1093, ECLI:EU:C:1993:109, para. 8; Judgment of 10 July 2003, *Commission/EIB*, Case C-15/00, ECR 2003 p. I-7281, ECLI:EU:C:2003:396, para. 75; Judgment of 21 September 2005, *Yusuf and Al Barakaat International Foundation/Council and Commission*, Case T-306/01, ECR 2005 p. II-3533, ECLI:EU:T:2005:331, para. 260.

[69] See *e.g.*, Opinion 1/91, of 14 December 1991 (ECR 1991 p. I-6079), paras. 20–21.

[70] See *e.g.*, Opinions of AG Ruiz-Jarabo Colomer in *Ismeri Europa/Court of Auditors*, Case C-315/99 P, ECR 2001 p. I-5281, ECLI:EU:C:2001:391, para. 39 and *Portugal/Commission*, Case C-249/02, ECR 2004 p. I-10717, ECLI:EU:C:2004:704, para. 40; and Opinion of AG Maduro in *Spain/Eurojust*, Case C-160/03, ECR 2005 p. I-2077, ECLI:EU:C:2005:168, para. 15.

[71] See, *inter alia*, Weiler (1999, pp. 10–101); Craig (2001, pp. 125–150); Dashwood (2004, pp. 355–381); Jacobs (2004, pp. 303–316); Lenaerts and Gerard (2004, pp. 289–322).

[72] *McCulloch v. Maryland*, 17 US (4 Wheat.) 316, 407 (1819). See Lenaerts (2010, p. 298).

based on the rule of law that the Court concludes and assumes that constitutional guarantees are regularly, and as a rule, protected at the level of the Union in an equivalent manner to their protection in the Portuguese Constitution. Hence, it is regrettable that the Constitutional Court did not take the chance to explain its understanding of EU constitutionalism in a decision dealing precisely with one of the fundamental principles of constitutional orders: that of respect for constitutional guarantees. This was, thus, a missed opportunity to develop and explain the place of the Portuguese Constitution - and its dialogue with the European Constitution - within the European constitutional compound.

4.3 *Main Absences: Constitutional Dialogues and Variations post-*Solange II

On a positive note, the Constitutional Court judgment stressed that even when the case-law of the CJEU points to an absolute and unconditional approach to precedence of EU law, the jurisprudential practice shows a more relative and complex picture of the application of the principle, highlighting the existence of important constitutional dialogues between European and national courts.

However, although it attempted to present the background of the most important judicial dialogues in the EU, the Court failed to give due consideration to core decisions by national courts, especially after *Solange II*.[73] Thus, the decision devotes significant attention to the context and history of the Italian decision in *Frontini*[74]—in dialogue with *Costa*[75]—and of the German *Solange I*[76] and *Solange II* in dialogue with *International Handelsgesellschaft*.[77] There is also a brief reference to the judgments of the German Constitutional Court in the *Bananas* case,[78] the Maastricht Treaty,[79] the Treaty of Lisbon[80] and more recently in *Gauweiler*.[81] However, not only are the latter references limited but they mostly fail to address the novelties of these decisions and their contributions to the European constitutional debate.

Additionally, there is no articulated mention of the argument introduced in the German Maastricht judgment on the doctrine of *ultra vires* exercise of competences,

[73] *Supra* note 33. Also pointing out this shortcoming, see Medeiros (2021, pp. 113–114).

[74] Judgment no. 183/1973 of the Italian Constitutional Court.

[75] See paras. 2.3.1.2, 2.5.1, and 2.6.2.

[76] *Supra* note 18.

[77] See para. 2.3.3.2.

[78] Judgment of 7 June 2000, 2 Bvl 1/97.

[79] Judgment of 12 October 1993 - 2 BvR 2134/92, 2 BvR 2159/92. See para. 2.4. of the Portuguese Constitutional Court judgment.

[80] *Supra* note 34.

[81] Judgment of 21 June 2016 2 BvR 2728/13, 2 BvE 13/13, 2 BvR 2731/13, 2 BvR 2730/13, 2 BvR 2729/13.

i.e., the idea that the EU must act within the strict limits defined by the Member States in the Treaties and that the legislative *Kompetenz-kompetenz* remains within the States. This decision is particularly relevant in so far as it introduced the argument on the scope of application of the principle of supremacy, and justified later decisions such as the one recently issued in *Weiss*[82] (which somewhat surprisingly is also ignored in the decision of the Portuguese Constitutional Court, although it had only been handed down two months earlier).[83]

In the set of rulings cited by the Court, particular attention is dedicated to the *Taricco* saga.[84] The rulings of both the *Corte Costituzionale* and the CJEU in the two *Taricco* cases are of indisputable importance. The cases involved an issue of the compatibility of national law with EU norms and constituted an important occasion to explore further the relationship between the European and the Italian constitutional legal orders. In particular, in the first *Taricco* case, the referring judge questioned the CJEU on whether the limitation period provided for in the Italian criminal code was compatible with several EU law provisions, notably Articles 101, 107 and 119 TFEU, and Article 158 of Council Directive 2006/112/EC of 28 November 2006[85] (and as such Article 325 TFEU). To these questions the CJEU replied, *inter alia*, that:

> …in the event that the national court concludes that the national provisions at issue do not satisfy the requirement of EU law that measures to counter VAT evasion be effective and dissuasive, that court would have to ensure that EU law is given full effect, if need be by disapplying those provisions and thereby neutralising the consequence referred to in paragraph 46 above, without having to request or await the prior repeal of those articles by way of legislation or any other constitutional procedure.[86]

In fact, considering that paragraphs (1) and (2) of Article 325 TFEU "impose on Member States a precise obligation as to the result to be achieved that is not subject to any condition regarding application of the rule (…) which they lay down",[87] they have the effect, in accordance with the principle of the precedence of EU law, of rendering automatically inapplicable, merely by their entry into force, any conflicting provision of national law.

Following this judgment, the *Corte Costituzionale* expressed doubts as to whether this approach was compatible with the overriding principles of the Italian constitutional order and with observance of the inalienable rights of the individual.

---

[82] *Supra* note 4.

[83] Noting also the lack of reference to the constitutional jurisprudence of Eastern and Central European constitutional courts, see Medeiros (2021, p. 114).

[84] Judgment of 8 September 2015, *Taricco and others,* Case C-105/14, ECLI:EU:C:2015:555; Judgment of 5 December 2017, *M.A.S. and M.B.*, Case C-42/17, ECLI:EU:C:2017:936. See, *inter alia*, Bonelli (2018)BONELLI: 2018: pp. 357–373; Di Marco (2018)DI MARCO: 2018: pp. 843–855; GALLO: 2017: pp. 249–277 Gallo (2017).

[85] Council Directive 2006/112/EC of 28 November 2006 on the common system of value added tax, OJ L 347, 11.12.2006, pp. 1–118.

[86] Para. 49.

[87] Paras. 51–52.

In particular, according to the Italian Constitutional Court, such an approach would be liable to interfere with the principle that offences and penalties must be defined by law, which requires that rules of criminal law are precisely determined and cannot be retroactive (*nullum crime sine lege*). The Court then decided to ask the CJEU for further clarification. In its second *Taricco* judgment,[88] the CJEU would mitigate its *Taricco I* decision and considered that "if the national court were … to come to the view that the obligation to disapply the provisions of the Criminal Code at issue conflicts with the principle that offences and penalties must be defined by law, it would not be obliged to comply with that obligation, even if compliance with the obligation allowed a national situation incompatible with EU law to be remedied (…). It [would] then be for the national legislature to take the necessary measures…".[89]

The *Taricco* cases constitute an exemplary dialogue between a national constitutional court and the CJEU, providing proof of the space that national constitutional standards can be afforded under EU law. However, for the purposes of the Portuguese case, *Taricco* is not the ideal *simile* as it does not involve an analogous situation to the one decided by the Constitutional Court. *Taricco* originated from a situation very different from the one at stake in the Portuguese case. In fact, the latter did not involve a possible conflict between national legal rules and EU law, but instead the alleged incompatibility of a norm of EU law with national constitutional rules, *i.e.*, the validity of EU law in of itself. Hence, whereas *Taricco*-type cases involve a challenge to an act of a Member State, the Portuguese case involved a challenge to an act adopted by the Union. In this sense, the latter is much closer to cases like *Melloni,*[90] where the CJEU had to clarify the scope of precedence of EU law in situations where the validity of EU law was questioned under national constitutional standards. Indeed, in *Melloni*, the Spanish Constitutional Court not only had doubts on whether Article 4a(1) of Framework Decision 2002/584/JHA[91] was compatible with the requirements deriving from the right to an effective judicial remedy and to a fair trial, provided for in the Charter of Fundamental Rights of the EU, but it also questioned the CJEU as to whether Article 53 of the Charter allows a Member State to afford those rights a greater level of protection than that deriving from EU law, in order to avoid an interpretation which restricts or adversely affects a fundamental right recognised by the constitution of said Member State. Therefore, *Melloni* was precisely a case where an act of the EU was possibly incompatible with the national constitution, much like that being argued in the Portuguese case.

In this light, it is somewhat troubling that there is no mention of *Mellon*i in the judgment of the Portuguese Constitutional Court. This absence is all the more relevant as its inclusion would have allowed the Court to make a distinction between

---

[88] Judgment of 5 December 2017, *M.A.S. and M.B.*, Case C-42/17, ECLI:EU:C:2017:936. See Maesa (2018, pp. 50–56).

[89] Para. 61.

[90] *Supra* note 58.

[91] Council Framework Decision of 13 June 2002 on the European arrest warrant and the surrender procedures between Member States (2002/584/JHA) OJ L 190, 18.7.2002, pp. 1–20.

two types of supremacy cases that emerge subtly from the foundational precedents: *Costa* vs. *Internationale*. On close examination, these cases reveal an important difference, which is that one thing is to question the admissibility of national law in the light of EU law, while another is to question the validity of EU law under national rules and principles. In *Costa*, the admissibility of the law providing for the nationalisation of electricity in Italy was questioned in light of the Treaties. On the other hand, in *Internationale* a set of European regulations were challenged under the German Constitution. It is true that in both scenarios one is discussing the same fundamental question, i.e. whether EU law trumps national law in all cases regardless of the legal nature of the normative instruments at stake. However, it is quite different to affirm that national law cannot as such override EU law, or that EU law takes precedence over national constitutions. It is thus not surprising that in *Costa*-type cases—of which *Taricco* is also an example—the CJEU has allowed Member States some leeway in providing for the protection of fundamental interests enshrined in the national constitutions. This has happened in several cases, mostly situations involving conflicts between market freedoms and fundamental rights. Hence, for instance, in *Schimdberger,*[92] Austria was allowed to authorise a demonstration of an environmental association interrupting circulation on the Brenner motorway, as freedom of expression as protected by the national constitutional order would trump free movement of goods. In *Omega Spielhalen,*[93] Germany was authorised to prohibit the commercial exploitation of games involving the simulation of acts of violence against persons, in particular the representation of acts of homicide, as such prohibition "corresponded to the level of protection of human dignity which the national constitution seeks to guarantee in the territory of the Federal Republic of Germany".[94] In another case, Lithuania was allowed to maintain in force national legislation aiming to protect the national language.[95] Several other cases can be pointed to where the CJEU has been willing to acknowledge the importance of national constitutional values and interests, granting national courts a wide margin of appreciation (Martins 2017, pp. 133–150).

By contrast, in cases where the validity of EU law is at stake, the CJEU has resisted any attempt by national courts to enforce domestic standards, in particular those included in national constitutions. This was evident in *Internationale,* in the 1970s, but is also clear under the more recent *Melloni* judgment. Pursuant to the latter, although Article 53 of the Charter confirms that, where an EU legal act calls for national implementing measures, national authorities and courts remain free to apply national standards of protection of fundamental rights, the level of protection provided for by the Charter, as interpreted by the CJEU, and the primacy, unity and

[92] Judgment of 12 June 2003, *Schmidberger,* Case C-112/00, ECR 2003 p. I-5659, ECLI:EU:C:2003:333.

[93] Judgment of 14 October 2004, *Omega,* Case C-36/02, ECR 2004 p. I-9609, ECLI:EU:C:2004:614.

[94] Para. 39.

[95] Judgment of 12 May 2011, *Runevič-Vardyn and Wardyn,* Case C-391/09, ECR 2011 p. I-3787, ECLI:EU:C:2011:291.

effectiveness of EU law, cannot be compromised in any way.[96] Bearing this distinction in mind, and considering that the Portuguese case clearly falls in the second of these two categories of cases, the Constitutional Court could have been expected to engage in some kind of dialogue with this jurisprudence.

Lastly, another important failing in the Portuguese judgment is the reference to Article 4(2) TEU. This provision is mentioned only once,[97] when the Court refers to the counter-limit to the constitutional jurisdiction as being embodied in the constitutional identity of the Republic (herein including subject matters that in of themselves can only be effectively protected by the Constitutional Court). Within this ambit, it would have been interesting to explore further the meaning of Article 4(2) TEU and its interaction with the constitutional criterion provided for in the Court's ruling. Indeed, while imposing, as a matter of EU law, respect "for national identities, inherent in their fundamental political and constitutional structures", Article 4(2) TEU constitutes, since the Lisbon Treaty entered into force, an unescapable normative point of reference in the discussion on the nature of European constitutionalism and, as such, on the scope of the principle of supremacy of EU law. In fact, in this discussion, one must not forget that, at the outset, the Treaties themselves determine the need to "as a matter of EU law, respect the constitutional identity claimed by Member States, and if necessary, provide for exceptions and derogations" (Claes 2013, p. 122).

4.4 Conceptual Confusion: From **Cilfit** *to* **Foto-Frost**

After establishing the normative criterion that governs the application of Article 8(4) of the national constitution, the Constitutional Court concluded that there was no breach of the principle of equality in the case *sub judice* that would justify exercising jurisdiction to review the constitutionality of the contested EU regulation.

To reach that conclusion, the Court applied the analytical framework it had just fixed. As such, it began by identifying the existence of an equivalent protection at EU level of the constitutional guarantee invoked by the applicant, notably the principle of equality enshrined in Article 13 of the national Constitution. Here, as relevant normative provisions equivalent to Article 13, the Court mentioned Article 2 TEU, Articles 18 and 19 TFEU, and Article 21(1) of the Charter of Fundamental Rights (together with Article 6(1) TEU). With regard to the interpretation of these provisions by the CJEU, the decision cited the *Karlssom* case,[98] which involved a dispute of allegedly unequal attribution of milk quotas. In this case, the CJEU

[96] Para 60 of *Melloni*. See also Judgment of 6 March 2014, *Siragusa,* Case C-206/13) ECLI:EU:C:2014:126, para. 32.

[97] Para. 2.6.

[98] Judgment of 13 April 2000, *Karlsson and others,* Case C-292/97, ECR 2000 p. I-2737, ECLI:EU:C:2000:202.

acknowledged the principle of equality as a general principle of EU law, affirming that:

> The second subparagraph of Article 40(3) of the Treaty, which prohibits all discrimination in the context of the common agricultural policy, *is merely a specific expression of the general principle of equal treatment*, which requires that comparable situations not be treated differently and different situations not be treated alike unless such treatment is objectively justified (Case 203/86 *Spain v Council* [1988] ECR 4563, paragraph 25, and Case C-15/95 *EARL de Kerlast* [1997] ECR I-1961, paragraph 35).[99]

Afterwards, the Constitutional Court considered that the case at hand did not imply any of the suspected classifications forbidden by Article 13[100] and it did not involve any form of arbitrary discrimination. That was supported, at the outset, by the ruling of the CJEU in *Cruz&Companhia*. Nonetheless, at this point the Court entered in conceptual confusion, by affirming that while both *acte éclairé* and *acte clair* existed in the case, there was no possibility of addressing the CJEU through a preliminary reference on the validity of Article 19(1)(a) of the regulation at stake. According to the Constitutional Court that would amount to requesting the CJEU to interpret an interpretation that had already been fixed by the same court. Hence, in light of the exceptions to the obligation to refer provided for in *Cilfit,*[101] the Court considered that no such reference was justified.

Regardless of how sound the decision might be, these statements demonstrate confusion between, on the one hand, questions of interpretation and, on the other hand, questions on the validity of EU law. As is well known, in *Cilfit*, the CJEU provided for three situations where a court or tribunal of a Member State deciding without the possibility of an appeal is exempted from referring preliminary questions to Luxembourg (for the purposes of Article 267 § 3 TFEU). Within this ambit, the CJEU affirmed that Article 267 TFEU:

> … is to be interpreted as meaning that a court or tribunal against whose decisions there is no judicial remedy under national law is required, where a question of Community law is raised before it, to comply with its obligation to bring the matter before the Court of Justice, unless it has established that the question raised is irrelevant or that the Community provision in question has already been interpreted by the Court or that the correct application of Community law is so obvious as to leave no scope for any reasonable doubt.[102]

The CJEU justified the three scenarios on the basis of several considerations. Firstly, it acknowledged the same margin of leeway that is granted to national courts under Article 267 § 2 TFEU. Secondly, recalling *Da Costa,*[103] it considered that a refer-

---

[99] Para. 39.

[100] Article 13 of the national constitution provides that all citizens possess the same social dignity and are equal before the law, and that no one may be privileged, favoured, prejudiced, deprived of any right or exempted from any duty for reasons of ancestry, sex, race, language, territory of origin, religion, political or ideological beliefs, education, economic situation, social circumstances or sexual orientation.

[101] *Supra* note 22.

[102] Para. 21.

[103] Judgment of 27 March 1963, *Da Costa en Schaake NV and others/Administratie der Belastingen,* Joined Cases 28 to 30/62, ECR 1963 p. 31.

ence does not make sense when such interpretation has already been given by the CJEU, notably when the question raised is materially identical to a question which has already been the subject of a preliminary ruling in a similar case, or where previous decisions of the CJEU have already dealt with the point of law in question (*acte éclairé*). Lastly, it considered that when the correct application of EU law is "so obvious as to leave no scope for any reasonable doubt" as to the manner in which the question raised is to be resolved, a preliminary ruling should not be mandatory (*acte clair*). On this point, the CJEU was particularly strict when fixing the conditions for establishing the existence of *acte clair* for the purposes of Article 267 TFEU.[104]

In its ruling, the Portuguese Constitutional Court invoked the second and third *Cilfit* scenarios, arguing that the CJEU had already clarified the interpretation of the regulation at stake in its previous ruling in *Cruz&Companhia*, and that there was therefore no doubt as to the interpretation to be given to the provision. However, whereas *Cilfit* is relevant with regard to questions of interpretation of EU law, no such question arose before the Constitutional Court in the case. The latter involved, on the contrary, a question on the validity of EU law. This distinction further adds to the one identified above:[105] on the one hand, cases where acts of Member States are questioned in the light of EU law may give rise to questions on the interpretation of EU law, and the *Cilfit* criteria apply; on the other hand, when the invalidity of EU measures is at stake, *Foto-Frost*[106] applies instead (Craig 2010, pp. 185–191; Edward 2010, pp. 173–184).

As we know, in *Foto-Frost* the CJEU established its exclusive jurisdiction to decide on questions of validity of EU law. In this type of cases, the order in *Foto-frost* is clear: when in doubt, national courts must refer all questions on the validity of EU law. The CJEU distinguished two possibilities therein:

---

[104] Paras. 16–20 in *Cilfit:* "16. Before it comes to the conclusion that such is the case, the national court or tribunal must be convinced that the matter is equally obvious to the courts of the other Member States and to the Court of Justice. Only if those conditions are satisfied, may the national court or tribunal refrain from submitting the question to the Court of Justice and take upon itself the responsibility for resolving it. 17. However, the existence of such a possibility must be assessed on the basis of the characteristic features of Community law and the particular difficulties to which its interpretation gives rise. 18. To begin with, it must be borne in mind that Community legislation is drafted in several languages and that the different language versions are all equally authentic. An interpretation of a provision of Community law thus involves a comparison of the different language versions. 19. It must also be borne in mind, even where the different language versions are entirely in accord with one another, that Community law uses terminology which is peculiar to it. Furthermore, it must be emphasized that legal concepts do not necessarily have the same meaning in Community law and in the law of the various Member States. 20. Finally, every provision of Community law must be placed in its context and interpreted in the light of the provisions of Community law as a whole, regard being had to the objectives thereof and to its state of evolution at the date on which the provision in question is to be applied".

[105] *Supra* Sect. 4.3.

[106] Judgment of 22 October 1987, *Foto-Frost/Hauptzollamt Lübeck-Ost*, Case 314/85, ECR 1987 p. 4199, ECLI:EU:C:1987:452.

(a) when those courts consider that the grounds put before them by the parties in support of invalidity are unfounded, they may reject them, concluding that the measure is completely valid;
(b) on the other hand, those courts do not have the power to declare acts of the EU institutions invalid as "divergences between courts in the Member States as to the validity of Community acts would be liable to place in jeopardy the very unity of the Community legal order and detract from the fundamental requirement of legal certainty".[107]

Hence, under *Foto-Frost*, when confronted with a question of validity of EU law, it is clear that national courts have jurisdiction to assess the issue. If they conclude that there are not sufficient grounds to consider the act invalid, they must simply apply the provision at stake. The reasoning underlying the judgment is simple: "by taking that action they are not calling into question the existence of the Union measure".[108]

This implies that neither *acte clair* or *éclairé* according to *Cilfit* applies in the context of questions on validity, which the Court has already made clear.[109] As Advocate-General Bobek has recently put it:

> … the text of the Treaty does not distinguish between questions of interpretation and questions of validity in terms of the scope of the obligation to refer. However, as regards questions on validity, the Court has stated that all national courts, that is to say not only those of last instance, are under an unreserved obligation to refer to the Court such questions. National courts have no jurisdiction themselves to determine the validity of acts of the EU institutions. The requirement of uniformity is particularly essential where the validity of an EU act is in question. Differences between courts of the Member States as to the validity of EU acts would be liable to jeopardise the essential unity of the EU legal order and undermine the fundamental requirement of legal certainty.
>
> Such considerations place questions concerning the validity of EU law acts on a different and separate track. Crucially, since the reason for the categorical duty on all national courts to refer any issue of validity to the Court of Justice is different from the reasons for the duty to refer questions of interpretation, the same is true as regards their exceptions. The CILFIT exceptions are not applicable to the duty to refer a question on validity.[110]

---

[107] Para. 20.

[108] Para. 19.

[109] See Judgment of 6 December 2005, *Gaston Schul Douane-expediteur*, Case C-461/03, EU:C:2005:742, paras. 20 to 25: "20. Firstly, even in cases which at first sight are similar, careful examination may show that a provision whose validity is in question is not comparable to a provision which has already been declared invalid because, for instance, it has a different legal or factual context, as the case may be. (…) 25. It follows from all the foregoing considerations that the answer to the first question must be that the third paragraph of Article 234 EC requires a court or tribunal of a Member State against whose decisions there is no judicial remedy under national law to seek a ruling from the Court of Justice on a question relating to the validity of the provisions of a regulation even where the Court has already declared invalid analogous provisions of another comparable regulation".

[110] Opinion in *Consorzio Italian Management e Catania Multiservizi and Catania Multiservizi*, Case C-561/19, paras. 44–45. The CJEU did not take up the proposal of the Advocate-General, which adds to the Opinion of former Advocate General Jacobs in the *Wiener* case (Judgment of 20 November 1997, *Wiener/Hauptzollamt Emmerich*, Case C-338/95, ECR 1997 p. I-6495, ECLI:EU:C:1997:552).

In this light, it is clear that the question raised before the Constitutional Court was not the same as the one decided by the CJEU in *Cruz&Companhia*. The latter involved a question on the interpretation, rather than the validity, of the contested regulation. They are undoubtedly twin cases in so far as they involved highly similar facts. However, they gave rise to two different legal questions from the point of view of EU law. In *Cruz&Companhia*, the CJEU clarified the scope and meaning of Article 19(1)(a) of the regulation, whereas in the case decided by the Constitutional Court, the applicant argued the invalidity of said regulation when applied as such to the case. Consequently, as the latter case did not involve the same issue of interpretation of the regulation but instead a question of alleged invalidity of the regime therein established, the Constitutional Court should have justified its decision not to refer the question to the CJEU on the basis of *Foto-Frost* alone, arguing that the grounds invoked by the applicant were insufficient to call into question the validity of said piece of legislation.

It could be argued that the Constitutional Court intended to base its decision solely on the existence of precedent. However, even if the existence of a valid and sufficient precedent to decide the case could be admitted, regarding questions on the validity of EU law, the legal basis for such an assessment would be the judgment of the CJEU in *ICC.*[111] and not *Cilfit.*

The CJEU was silent in this regard. It can be argued that the Court presumably assumed that no genuine issue of validity arose in the case. As a matter of fact, the Court considered that the arguments put forward by the applicant were vague and lacking purpose. According to the ruling, it is not enough to invoke in the abstract and in an unsubstantiated manner a breach of a constitutional principle as a kind of "open sesame" to gain access to the constitutional jurisdiction. Mere empty and artificial invoking of constitutional norms cannot justify triggering the jurisdiction by the Constitutional Court. Such a decision would frustrate and trivialise the rule enshrined in Article 8(4) of the national constitution.[112] As such, it would be super-

[111] Judgment of 13 May 1981, *International Chemical Corporation/Amministrazione delle fianze dello Stato*, Case 66/80, ECR 1981 p. 1191. In this case, the CJEU established that: "although a judgment of the Court given under Article 177 of the Treaty declaring an act of an institution, in particular a Council or Commission regulation, to be void is directly addressed only to the national court which brought the matter before the Court, it is sufficient reason for any other national court to regard that act as void for the purposes of a judgment which it has to give. That assertion does not however mean that national courts are deprived of the power given to them by Article 177 of the Treaty and it rests with those courts to decide whether there is a need to raise once again a question which has already been settled by the Court where the Court has previously declared an act of a Community institution to be void. There may be such a need in particular if questions arise as to the grounds, the scope and possibly the consequences of the invalidity established earlier" (cf. paras. 13–14).

[112] See para. 2.7.1.2: "However, this abstract correspondence – almost only arising from the recitation of the principle, as if it were a kind of "*Open Sesame!*"—is not enough to satisfy the final clause of Article 8(4) of the CRP and does not in itself provide access to the national constitutional jurisdiction (the triggering of its competence). In effect, it amounts to the mere invocation of questions of unconstitutionality whose construction is undisguisedly artificial, not effectively corresponding to the essential substantial aspect justifying the reactivation of, contrary to what is overwhelmingly predominant in said paragraph 4, the jurisdictional reach of the Court, by involv-

fluous to address the CJEU again, submitting the question on the validity of the regulation.

In short, when deciding that there was no need to refer a question to the CJEU, the Constitutional Court confused the *Cilfit* and *Foto-Frost* scenarios. It is clear that *Cilfit* exceptions do not apply to the *Foto-frost* obligation. No *acte éclairé* or *acte clair* applies to questions on validity. When confronted with any doubts on the validity of a EU norm or act, national courts must address the CJEU. If there are no doubts in that regard, they must simply apply EU law, without the need to make a preliminary reference. In any case, should the national court get it wrong, Member States can always be held liable for breaches of EU law committed by the judiciary, either within an action for infringement,[113] or an action for damages initiated by individuals in national courts.[114]

5 Concluding Observations

It is probably too soon to estimate what impact the Portuguese Constitutional Court ruling will have on future cases. As the system of constitutional review in Portugal is a mixed one, combining abstract and concentrated review by the Portuguese Constitutional Court with concrete and diffuse review by the ordinary courts, the current ruling will prove decisive for future litigation.

Not surprisingly, the case was immediately cited in the subsequent case on tax on imported vehicles,[115] where the Constitutional Court made its first preliminary reference to the CJEU on the interpretation of Article 110 TFEU, in a case involving unequal taxation of vehicles acquired in other Member States of the Union.[116] More recently, it was also taken into consideration in the judgment where the Constitutional Court ruled on the unconstitutionality of the national law transposing Directive

ing the possibility of disapplying EUL in the internal order, in the terms defined by said EUL. Such situations, due to their notorious inconsistency, should be ruled out – i.e., assumed by the Constitutional Court to be outside its competence in this area. The appraisal of such questions would distort the meaning of the constitutional rule, through the trivialisation of what it intended to prevent in overwhelmingly expressive terms. Any other position – even if related to the mere appearance of a procedural requirement – would undermine the meaning of the constitutional decision underlying the construction of that rule".

[113] Judgment of 4 October 2018, *Commission/France (Advance payment)*, Case C-416/17, ECLI:EU:C:2018:811.

[114] Judgment of 30 September 2003, *Köbler*, Case C-224/01, ECR 2003 p. I-10239, ECLI:EU:C:2003:513 and Judgment of 9 September 2015, *Ferreira da Silva e Brito and others*, Case C-160/14, ECLI:EU:C:2015:565.

[115] Judgment no. 711/2020, 9 December 2020, Proc. 173/2020.

[116] The reference runs parallel to the action for infringement initiated by the Commission in April 2020 (Judgment of 2 September 2021, *Commission/Portugal (Taxe sur les véhicules)*, Case C-169/20, ECLI:EU:C:2021:679).

2006/24/EC of the European Parliament and of the Council of 15 March 2006[117] on the retention of data generated or processed in connection with the provision of publicly available electronic communications services or of public communications networks.[118] In the latter judgment the Court considered that the criterion established in its previous judgment applies equally to cases involving the invalidity of EU law itself and situations where the compatibility of national law with EU law is at stake. It is yet to be seen how other courts will apply the criterion devised in judgment 422/2020 to future cases.

In parallel, scholars also need time to assess the soundness of the Court's judgment. Medeiros has already pointed out, for instance, the difficulties surrounding constitutional protection of social rights in Portugal. In fact, although it is in principle uncontroversial to affirm the existence of an equivalent level of protection of fundamental rights in the EU when compared with the Portuguese constitutional order, this may well not be true with regard to the protection of social rights (Medeiros 2021, pp. 120–121): "it is well known that the Portuguese Constitution, besides associating a significant set of public policies with social rights, did not simply reject a Constitution without social rights or with a deficit in this category of fundamental rights, but rather opted to extend fundamental rights claims of a social nature far beyond the universe of basic social rights" (Medeiros 2021). As such, it is not evident that the counter-limits of Article 8(4) associated with the notion of constitutional identity necessarily have a limited field of operation in this respect.

For what it is worth, judgment no. 422/2020 inaugurates a new stage in the Constitutional Court's jurisprudence. It not only represents the first, much awaited decision on the scope of the principle of supremacy in the Portuguese legal order, but it also has the declared intention of having fixed a general criterion intended to be applied in future cases.

References

Besselink L (2014) The parameters of constitutional conflict after Melloni. Eur Law Rev 39:531–552

Bonelli M (2018) The Taricco saga and the consolidation of judicial dialogue in the European Union. Maastricht J Eur Comp Law 25:357–373

Cavallone G (2014) European arrest warrant and fundamental rights in decisions rendered in absentia: the extent of Union law in the case C-399/11 Melloni v. Ministerio Fiscal. Eur Crim Law Rev 4:19–40

Claes M (2013) National identity: trump card or up for negotiation? In: Arnaiz AS, Llivina CA (eds) National identity and European integration. Intersentia, Cambridge, pp 109–139

Craig P (2001) Constitutions, constitutionalism, and the European union. Eur Law J 7:125–150

[117] Judgment no. 268/2022, of 19 April 2022, Proc. 829/19.

[118] OJ L 105, 13.4.2006, pp. 54–63.

Craig P (2010) The classics of EU law revisited: CILFIT and foto-frost. In: Maduro M, Azoulai L (eds) The past and future of EU law: the classics of EU law revisited on the 50th anniversary of the Rome treaty. Hart Publishing, Oxford/Portland, Oregon, pp 185–191

Dashwood A (2004) The relationship between the Member States and the European union/ European community. Common Mark Law Rev 41:355–381

Di Marco R (2018) The 'path towards European integration' of the Italian constitutional court: the primacy of EU law in the light of the judgment no. 269/17. Eur Pap 3:843–855

Edward D (2010) CILFIT and foto-frost in their historical and procedural context. In: Maduro M, Azoulai L (eds) The past and future of EU law: the classics of EU law revisited on the 50th anniversary of the Rome treaty. Hart Publishing, Oxford/Portland, Oregon, pp 173–184

Eeckhout P (2002) The EU charter of fundamental rights and the federal question. Common Mark Law Rev 39:945–994

Gallo D (2017) Controlimiti, identità nazionale e i rapporti di forza tra primato ed effetto diretto nella saga Taricco. Il Diritto dell'Unione Europea 2:249–277

Jacobs F (2004) The evolution of the European legal order. Common Mark Law Rev 41:303–316

Lenaerts K (2010) The basic constitutional charter of a community based on the rule of law. In: Maduro M, Azoulai L (eds) The past and future of EU law: the classics of EU law revisited on the 50th anniversary of the Rome treaty. Hart Publishing, Oxford/Portland, Oregon, pp 295–315

Lenaerts K, Gerard D (2004) The structure of the union according to the constitution for Europe: the emperor is getting dressed. Eur Law Rev 29:289–322

Maesa CDF (2018) Effectiveness and primacy of EU Law v. Higher national protection of fundamental rights and national identity. Eur Crim Law Assoc Forum 1:50–56

Martins PF (2017) A Europa e a Constituição: o lugar das constituições nacionais no modelo constitucional Europeu. In: Vaz MA, Botelho CS, Terrinha LH, Coutinho P (eds) Jornadas nos quarenta anos da Constituição da República Portuguesa: impacto e evolução. UCE, Porto, pp 133–150

Medeiros R (2021) The primacy of European union law over the Portuguese constitution according to the constitutional court – comment on constitutional court judgment no. 422/2020. Catól Law Rev 5:111–124

Weiler JHH (1999) The constitution of Europe: "do the new clothes have an Emperor?" and other essays on European integration. Cambridge University Press, Cambridge

Patrícia Fragoso Martins Universidade Católica Portuguesa, Lisbon School of Law, Portugal. Researcher at the Católica Research Centre for the Future of Law.

The Charter of Fundamental Rights of the European Union and Constitutional Judicial Review of National Rules

Afonso Patrão

1 The Issue

If the Constitutional Court is asked to review the constitutionality of *national* rules which prove to be incompatible with EU Law, we may consider the consequences of this for constitutional judicial review. There is some debate surrounding which conduct the Constitutional Court should adopt when reviewing *national rules* contrary to the Charter of Fundamental Rights of the European Union (CFREU) and within its scope, mainly whether it should declare those rules unconstitutional.

The Charter embodies a catalogue of fundamental rights, drafted in the image of national constitutions, which binds the *European Union itself*, so as to guarantee that the ceding of national competences to the European institutions does not decrease citizens' protection.[1] Yet, because it is not (usually) the European Union

[1] Cf. Article 6(1) of the Treaty on European Union (TEU) and Article 51(1) of the CFREU. *See* Canotilho (2008, p. 139), Oliveira (2018, p. 20), Vitorino (2002, p. 24).

Afonso Patrão is Judge at the Portuguese Constitutional Court.

A. Patrão (✉)
Univ Coimbra, UCILeR - University of Coimbra Institute for Legal Research, Faculty of Law, Coimbra, Portugal

Portuguese Constitutional Court, Lisbon, Portugal
e-mail: apatrao@fd.uc.pt

I. Quadros, M. Gorjão-Henriques (eds.), *Revisiting the Liberal Constitutional Features of the European Union*, https://doi.org/10.1007/978-3-031-95717-8_15

that implements its own legal acts—but rather national authorities[2]—the CFREU is also binding on Member States *when implementing EU law* (Article 51 CFREU).[3]

In this context—considering that the CFREU (as primary law of the European Union) is (i) a *yardstick for considering the validity of European secondary law*[4] and (ii) that it binds Member States *when implementing EU law*—it is important to understand the legal effect of the Charter in constitutional review.

Should the Constitutional Court declare that such national rules are unconstitutional? What relevance should be given to the Charter in constitutional judicial review?

2 The Principle of Autonomy and Primacy of EU Law

The Portuguese Constitution states that European Union law shall be applied in the internal order *under the conditions laid down by EU law*. Except for the final part of Article 8(4) of the Constitution, it is EU law that governs its relationship with the national legal order[5] To that extent, consequences of the collision of national rules and rules of EU law must be sought first and foremost in the European legal order itself.

EU law, even when incorporated into the domestic legal order, retains its *autonomy,* and its own mechanisms for interpretation, monitoring and application (Isaac and Blanquet 2001, p. 143; Soares 2002, p. 775; Tillotson and Foster 2003, p. 78;

---

[2] Cf. Article 291 of the Treaty on the Functioning of the European Union (TFEU). Cf. Peers and Costa (2012, p. 441), Paris (2017, p. 793), Mendes (2013, p. 29).

[3] The case-law of the Court of Justice of the European Union (CJEU) allows us to identify three situations that correspond to the assumption that the Charter applies to Member States *"when implementing Union law"* (Art. 51 CFREU): the action of the Member States in the application of the Charter (Art. 51 CFREU) and the action of the national courts in the application of the Charter (Art. 52 CFREU).The action of the States as agents of the Union, enforcing its rules—namely by implementing directives (i); the action of the States in areas in which the Community rules confer discretion to national authorities, *e.g. by* admitting derogations to rules from a European source (ii); national legislative activity in areas that are already subject to Community regulation (iii). (cf. Canotilho (2008, p. 140), Lenaerts (2012, pp. 378, 380, 385), De Visser (2014, p. 45), Oliveira (2018, pp. 34, 40), Sarmiento (2013, p. 1276)).

[4] Cf. Article 6 of the Treaty on European Union (TEU). *See* Gorjão-Henriques (2019, p. 271), Machado (2018, p. 207), (Campos et al. 2014, p. 287), Patrão (2008, p. 141), Isaac and Blanquet (2001, p. 147), Simon (2001, p. 309), Tillotson and Foster (2003, p. 67), Bieber and Salomé (1996, p. 913).

[5] See Article 8(4) of the Constitution. The constitutional rule accepts the application of European law as determined *by it,* without making a dogmatic choice as to the relationship between the legal orders. In fact, the provision may be based on a monist conception, accepting the mode of relationship postulated by that legal order, or on a dualist understanding, since it is the national Constitution itself which authorises, and in a conditioned manner, the internal normative force of European Union law.

Cf. Ramos (1999a, p. 101).

Steiner et al. 2006, p. 72; Martins 2017, p. 340). Therefore, European norms do not revoke national legal rules and neither is the validity of the European legal order affected if it contradicts rules of a given national constitution.

The *principle of autonomy* of EU law is reflected both in the identification of the court responsible for assessing the validity of its rules and in the consequences of a normative conflict between rules deriving from *autonomous* legal orders.

Regarding jurisdictional competence, the autonomy of EU law implies the Court of Justice is the competent authority to assess its validity,[6] according to *its own standards:* European rules are not nullified by contradicting provisions of domestic law (even domestic constitutional law).[7] This is understandable, since making European rules *prima facie* immune to constitutionality control is the only solution compatible with the uniform application of EU law.[8]

Similarly, and symmetrically, it is the responsibility of the national courts to control the validity (in material, formal and organic terms) of domestic law, even when its content implements EU law obligations. In fact, because the European Court of Justice (ECJ) has no federal character, its jurisdictional remedies are restricted to European acts.[9]

Another aspect of the autonomy of EU law is the fact that in relations between European law and national law, the *"pyramid paradigm"* has been set aside: a conflict with EU law does not lead to the nullity or repeal of national rules. The *network paradigm* has been adopted, in which no point is privileged over another, and no

---

[6] Indeed, by virtue of the principle of autonomy, the Court of Justice is the competent body to assess the invalidity of European law by reference to its own standards (cf. CJEU judgment of 22 October 1987, *Foto-Frost,* proc. 314/85, paragraph 15; CJEU judgment of 6 October 2015, *Schrems,* proc. C362/14-, paragraph 61). Cf. Paris (2017, p. 793), Claes (2006, p. 103, 464), Mengozzi (2016, p. 840).

[7] Judgment of 17 December 1970, Internationale Handelsgesellschaft, Case 11/70, paragraph 3: "Recourse to the legal rules or concepts of national law in order to judge the validity of measures adopted by the institutions of the community would have an adverse effect on the uniformity and efficacy of Community law. The validity of such measures can only be judged in the light of community law. In fact, the law stemming from the treaty, an independent source of law, cannot because of its very nature be overridden by rules of national law, however framed, without being deprived of its character as community law and without the legal basis of the community itself being called in question. Therefore the validity of a community measure or its effect within a member state cannot be affected by allegations that it runs counter to either fundamental rights as formulated by the constitution of that state or the principles of a national constitutional structure".

Thus, the invocation either of offences to fundamental rights enshrined in national constitutions or of structuring principles of the national constitution cannot affect the validity or effectiveness of a Union norm or act (cf. Martins (2013, p. 79)).

[8] Cf. Maduro (2003, p. 534) (*"the claim for uniform application of EU law is safeguarded by the national constitutional courts' explicit or implicit recognition that they will not review the validity of specific EU legal acts in light of national constitutional law"*), and therefore a certain immunity of directly applicable European norms from constitutionality review is accepted (Claes 2006, pp. 559–560; Paris 2017, pp. 793). On the cases in which this model could be questioned, see our study Patrão and Canotilho (2019, p. 30ff).

[9] Cf. Articles 263 and 267 of TFEU; Gorjão-Henriques (2019, p. 415), Moreira (2016, p. 913).

point is unequivocally subordinate to another (Ramos 1999b, p. 231; Piçarra 2006; Dougan 2019, p. 1460).

In fact, in an expression that has been used repeatedly since *Simmenthal,* a contradiction between European and national rules is solved by *disapplying* the national rules in the specific case, without the latter being deemed invalid.[10] Disapplication is required regardless of the source of the conflicting rules, i.e. regardless of whether the European norm is contained in primary law (such as the CFREU) or secondary law (such as a directive or regulation), or of whether the national rule is contained in a regulatory act, a legislative act or even in the Constitution.[11]

Primacy of EU law—rooted in the *full effectiveness* of the European legal order (Claes 2006, p. 132; De Witte 2021, p. 192)—is thus understood as a *collision rule* (leading to the preferential application of EU law) and not as a strict rule of normative supremacy (causing the nullification of domestic law).[12] Disapplication is, in

[10] ECJ judgment of 15.07.1964, Costa c. ENEL, proc. 6/64; ECJ judgment of 9.3.1978, Simmenthal, proc. 106/77, para. 21 ("every national court must, in a case within its jurisdiction, apply community law in its entirety and protect rights which the latter confers on individuals and must accordingly *set aside any provision of national law* which may conflict with it, whether prior or subsequent to the community rule"); ECJ judgment of 5.10.10.2010, Elchinov, Case C-173/09, paragraph 31 ("a national court which is called upon, within the exercise of its jurisdiction, to apply provisions of European Union law is under a duty to give full effect to those provisions, if necessary *refusing of its own motion to apply* any conflicting provision of national legislation"); ECJ judgment of 19.11.11.2009, Krzysztof Filipiak, Case C-314-08, paragraph 82 ("Pursuant to the principle of the primacy of Community law, a conflict between a provision of national law and a directly applicable provision of the Treaty is to be resolved by a national court applying Community law, if necessary by *refusing to apply* the conflicting national provision, and *not by a declaration that the national provision is invalid*", adding that "the incompatibility with Community law of a subsequently adopted rule of national law *does not have the effect of rendering that rule of national law non-existent*. Faced with such a situation, the national court is *obliged to disapply* that rule" (point 83) [emphasis added].

[11] Thus, *any* rules of EU law, regardless of whether they appear in treaties (*see e.g.* ECJ judgments of 4.02.1988, *Murphy* v. *Bord Telecom Eireann,* proc. 157/86, para. 11; and of 6.09.2012, *Philips Electronics, proc.* C-18/11, no. 40), of the CDFUE (judgment of 20.12.2017 *Protect Natur-, Arten- und Landschaftsschutz Umweltorganisation,* Case C-664/15) or of acts of secondary legislation (judgment of 06.03.2014, *Napoli,* proc. C-595/12). This primacy exists over *all* national law, the Court of Justice having declared its applicative preference also as regards rules with a constitutional source (Judgment of 17 December 1970, *Internationale Handelsgesellschaft, proc.* 11/70, paragraph 3).

[12] Canotilho and Moreira (2007) See the judgments of the Court of Justice cited in footnote 10, with particular clarity in the Judgment of the ECJ of 19.11.2009, *Krzysztof Filipiak, Case* C-314-08, paragraphs 82 and 83. *See* De Witte (2021, p. 206) (*"there remains a distinction between* invalidity *and* non-application, *and the Court of Justice only requires the latter"*) and p. 208; Dougan (2019, p. 1463) (*"the basic mechanism by which primacy resolves any direct and actionable conflict of norms is indeed through the practical disapplication of the relevant national measures. In particular, the principle of primacy does not have the effect of rendering incompatible national measures void or otherwise requiring such acts to be treated as invalid as a matter of either Union or domestic law"*) and p. 1466 (*"the principle of primacy is virtually inseparable, if not altogether indistinguishable, from its remedy of disapplication"*); Steiner et al. (2006, p. 75) (*"The finding that a provision of national law is 'inapplicable' because of its incompatibility with Community law does not, however, result on its annulment, or even prevent its application in situations falling outside*

any case, the *ultima ratio* solution,[13] to be used only when consistent interpretation proves to be impossible,[14] when the European norm has direct effect[15]—and to the

the scope of Community law"); Gorjão-Henriques (2012, p. 321), Canotilho (2008, pp. 82, 177), de Quadros (2013, p. 317), Maduro (2001, p. 145), Duarte (1995, pp. 701–702), Amaral and Piçarra (2009, pp. 33, 64–66), Martins (2006, p. 22).

It was for this reason that the Spanish Constitutional Court dissociated the concepts of *primacy* and *supremacy,* in Declaration no. 1/2004, of 13 December 2004: *"La proclamación de la primacía del Derecho de la Unión por el art. I-6 del Tratado no contradice la supremacía de la Constitución. Primacía y supremacía son categorías que se desenvuelven en órdenes diferenciados. Aquélla, en el de la aplicación de normas válidas; ésta, en el de los procedimientos de normación. La supremacía se sustenta en el carácter jerárquico superior de una norma y, por ello, es fuente de validez de las que le están infraordenadas, con la consecuencia, pues, de la invalidez de éstas si contravien lo dispuesto imperativamente en aquélla. La primacía, en cambio, no se sustenta necesariamente en la jerarquía, sino en la distinción entre ámbitos de aplicación de diferentes normas, en principio válidas, de las cuales, sin embargo, una o unas de ellas tienen capacidad de desplazar a otras en virtud de su aplicación preferente o prevalente debida a diferentes razones. Toda supremacía implica, en principio, primacía (de ahí su utilización en ocasiones equivalente, así en nuestra Declaración 1/1992, FJ 1), salvo que la misma norma suprema haya previsto, en algún ámbito, su propio desplazamiento o inaplicación. La supremacía de la Constitución es, pues, compatible con regímenes de aplicación que otorguen preferencia aplicativa a normas de otro Ordenamiento diferente del nacional siempre que la propia Constitución lo haya así dispuesto, que es lo que ocurre exactamente con la previsión contenida en su art. 93".*

[13] Cf. Dougan (2019, p. 1462): *"the Court insists that primacy and disapplication should be treated only as a legal tool of last resort".* This is consistent with the idea that *"prior to disapplying a domestic provision as contrary to EU law, national courts are obliged to ask the CJEU for a preliminary ruling"* (Lacchi 2015, p. 1676).

[14] It is well known that *consistent interpretation with EU law* takes precedence over the primacy principle: if it is possible to eliminate the conflict of rules by giving national rules a meaning compatible with European rules, the former will not be disapplied. Cf. Judgment of 24.01.2012, *Maribel Dominguez, proc.* 282/10, no. 23 (*"It should be stated at the outset that the question whether a national provision must be disapplied in as much as it conflicts with European Union law arises only if no compatible interpretation of that provision proves possible"*); Judgment of 11.01.01.2007, *ITC, proc.* C-208/05, no. 69; Judgment of 24.05.2012, *Amia, proc.* C-97/11, no. 27; Judgment of 9.10.2013, *Spedition Welter, proc,* C-306/12, no. 28; CJEU judgment of 19.06.2019, *Poplawski,* proc. 573/17, nos. 57 and 58. On the principle of consistent interpretation, see our comments *infra,* chapter V.

[15] This is a requirement that goes back to the origins of the construction of the principle of primacy and has been constantly reaffirmed by European jurisprudence. Cf. CJEU judgment of 19.06.2019, *Poplawski,* Case 573/17, paragraph 68: *"a national court's obligation to disapply a provision of its national law which is contrary to a provision of EU law, if it stems from the primacy afforded to the latter provision, is nevertheless dependent on the direct effect of that provision in the dispute pending before that court. Therefore,* ***a national court is not required, solely on the basis of EU law, to disapply a provision of its national law which is contrary to a provision of EU law if the latter provision does not have direct effect****"* [emphasis added]. Otherwise, the application of national law is maintained and the person concerned is protected by the other mechanisms of effectiveness of Union law—such as State liability and infringement proceedings: *'if the relevant provisions of Union law fail to cross the threshold of cognizability required for direct effect, national law will retain its domestic priority (regardless of any abstract state of incompatibility with Union law). The only remaining avenue of legal redress for disappointed intended beneficiaries of the relevant Union provisions is to seek reparation from the Member State pursuant to the Francovich case law'* (Dougan 2019, p. 1463). Cf. also Lenaerts and Corthaut (2006, p. 290).

strict extent of the incompatibility with the European rule.[16] Consequently, the addressee of the primacy is the *national judge*,[17] who is responsible for guaranteeing its legal effect.

Thus, the consequences of collision with primary EU law (such as the CFREU) are different for *organically European rules* (i.e. adopted by the institutions) and *national rules*. The former are invalidated and therefore prone to annulment by the ECJ; the latter are *disapplied* by national bodies and their lawfulness is not affected.[18]

This model departs from the typical federal archetype (Schütze 2006, p. 1029; Martins 2013, p. 66; de Quadros 2013, p. 515; Dougan 2019, p. 1461) and embodies one of the specific features of European integration.

Moreover, by accepting that different authorities - with diverse sources of legitimacy - exercise powers in the same territory, it may give rise to discussion on the dogmatic roots of the relationship between legal orders. Although *primacy* of EU law can be fully explained in the light of a *pluralist* conception of constitutionalism (MacCormick 1993, p. 8, 1995, p. 264; Pernice 1999, p. 707; Kumm 2005, pp. 267-268; Walker 2009, p. 19, 2016, p. 33ff; Bogdandy and Schill 2011, p. 1420; Maduro 2012, p. 68; Jaklic 2014, p. 81), the legal effect of primacy is also coherent with a monist position (which would explain the weakening of the internal rule deriving from the European norm), and a dualist conception, according to which it is possible for a national constitution to accept and recognise the claims of a non-national legal order (Medeiros 2015, p. 283).

Before a constitutional judicial review of internal norms, it is important to determine the relevance of their contradiction with EU law for a constitutional court. Because collision between national and European rules does not render the former invalid (the remedy, instead, being their *non-application*), EU law will necessarily have different effects for the ordinary courts—which deal with the case—and for

[16] Given the principle of *effectiveness* that underlies the primacy principle, the duty of disapplication is restricted to the limited scope of normative incompatibility. To that extent, the national rule *can be applied* outside the field of influence of EU law; and the duty of disapplication ceases if the incompatible European rule is, in the meantime, revoked. Cf. De Witte (2021, p. 206), Claes (2006, p. 455), Schütze (2006, p. 1032), Dougan (2019, p. 1463).

[17] Cf. Ramos (1999b, p. 230), Martins (2013, p. 57), Gorjão-Henriques (2012, p. 321), de Quadros (2013, p. 517), Maduro (2001) This is, moreover, a *protagonism* attributed to the jurisdictional power, in the normative system - as highlighted in Medeiros (2015, p. 116).

The deep-rooted expression that it is the "national judge" who is the addressee of the principle of primacy should be understood as referring to the bodies applying the law—and not only the judicial authorities. In fact, the Court of Justice has already concluded that the obligation of disapplication applies to the Administration and State agencies, *before any judicial intervention*—see Judgment of 22.06.1989, *Fratelli Costanzo,* proc. Judgment of 09.09.2003, *CIF,* proc. C-198/01, paragraph 49; Judgment of 12.01.2010, *Petersen, proc.* C-341/08, paragraph 80; Judgment of 14.10.2010, *Fuß, proc.* C-243/09, paragraph 61; Judgment of 04.12.2018, *Commissioner of An Garda, proc.* C378/17-, paragraph 38. Cf. Claes (2006, pp. 99, 266).

[18] Lenaerts (2012, p. 376) (*"EU legislation found to be in breach of an Article of the Charter is to be held void and national law falling within the scope of EU law that contravenes the Charter must be set aside"*).

the Constitutional Court, which is responsible for confirming that the national rules are in line with the Constitution.

Ordinary courts—which are guaranteed a *direct* relationship with the ECJ through the preliminary reference procedure,[19] when faced with national and European rules that prove to be incompatible, use the remedy of *disapplication* of the national norm in that specific case.[20] The duty to disapply exists even if the Constitutional Court has deferred the effects of the unconstitutionality of the internal rule, since primacy *does not depend on* the judgments of the national courts.[21]

As for the Constitutional Court—equally bound to ensure the *full effectiveness* of EU law—because it is called upon to assess the validity of legal rules, it must give a different role to EU law. In fact, the remedy of disapplication by the common courts may prevent the intervention of the Constitutional Courts: if ordinary courts disapply national rules contradicting European law, the effectiveness of EU law is guaranteed without submitting the national rule to constitutionality control.[22] This justifies the decisions of national constitutional courts *not to assess* the compatibility of national rules with European rules[23] and may explain the rarity of occasions when the constitutional courts do interact with the ECJ (Bobek 2012, pp. 285, 297; Paris 2017, pp. 794–795).

[19] In fact, the reference in the *Simmenthal* Judgment (cit. 12) is precisely intended to confer on the *ordinary* courts the power to give effect to the rule of European law *without any constraint*—in that regard, cf. De Witte (2021, p. 205), and Dani (2017, p. 194), Costa (1998, p. 1369). We shall return to this question below.

[20] Cf. Brito (2003, p. 312), Paris (2017, p. 798) (*"a conflict between domestic legislation and EU law does not amount to a conflict between a sub-constitutional law and the constitution, but only between two sub-constitutional norms. Solving this conflict is, in accordance with the principle of primacy, the business of ordinary courts. If needed, they can request the CJEU's help through a preliminary reference"*); Komarek (2017, p. 825) (*"The action must come from ordinary courts, which should be much more constrained in challenging the separation of both kinds of legality. This will ultimately preserve not only constitutional courts' place in constitutional democracies, but also the authority of ordinary courts"*).

[21] Cf. inter alia, ECJ judgment of 19.11.2009, Krzysztof Filipiak, case C-314/08, paragraph 84 ("the deferral by the Trybunał Konstytucyjny of the date on which the provisions at issue will lose their binding force does not prevent the referring court from respecting the principle of the primacy of Community law and from declining to apply those provisions in the proceedings before it, if the court holds those provisions to be contrary to Community law"); ECJ judgment of 8.09.09.2010, Winner Wetten, Case C-409/06, paragraph 69 ("by reason of the primacy of directly-applicable Union law, national legislation [...]cannot continue to apply during a transitional period"); ECJ judgment of 5 April 2022, Commissioner of An Garda Síochána, Case C-140/20, paragraphs 119-126 and 128. Cf. Bobek (2012, p. 295), Komarek (2013, p. 421), Komarek (2014, p. 527).

[22] Cf. De Witte (2021, p. 213) (*"By doing so, the constitutional courts allow the other courts to ensure compliance with EU law even when this involves setting aside an act of parliament, which ordinary courts would normally not be allowed to do in a system of centralized constitutional review"*); Paris (2017, p. 802) (*"according to the CJEU's constant jurisprudence, the principle of primacy requires ordinary courts to set aside domestic laws that are inconsistent with EU law. Consequently, ordinary courts will never have to apply a statute that conflicts with EU law in a concrete case. Hence, in practical terms, the principle of primacy inhibits the referral of a conflict between a statute and EU law to the Italian Constitutional Court"*); Claes (2006, pp. 387ff, 464).

[23] Cf. the analysis of this jurisprudence in Chapter IV, footnote no. 31.

3 EU Law as a Yardstick in Constitutional Judicial Review?

Although primacy does not involve the annulment of internal rules, nothing prevents national constitutional systems from establishing the *unconstitutionality* of domestic rules that are incompatible with EU law: while *disapplication* is the *minimum* effect prescribed by the European legal order, Member States are not forbidden to *nullify* national rules that are contrary to European norms.[24]

In fact, making EU law a yardstick for constitutional judicial review would promote legal certainty and even *maximise* the effectiveness of EU law: if a Constitutional Court removes a national rule from the legal system, the likelihood of an ordinary court applying it ceases to exist.[25]

This effect may be achieved by accepting EU law as constitutional law (*e.g.*, recognising such effect on the basis of Article 7 of the Portuguese Constitution) and arguing that national rules that are incompatible with EU law should be understood as violating the constitutional rule which accepts European Union rules (*e.g.*, Article 8(4) of the Portuguese Constitution). According to this reasoning, since national standards cannot be applied in the normative area occupied by European norms, the yardstick for judicial review must be replaced by the EU standards, which take precedence over national standards.

The idea is not entirely new. Indeed, it has been considered with regard to whether general international law—automatically integrated under Article 8(1) of the Portuguese Constitution—could be a yardstick for constitutional judicial review (Almeida 1987, point 1.4). Moreover, it is coherent with a *monist* concept of constitutionalism, since the unity of the system may imply that the very *validity* of any national rule contradicting external principles is at issue (Pernice 2009). This is basically Vital Moreira's position—although he recognises that the solution requires a constitutional amendment (Moreira 2016, p. 913)—and it seems to find support in Ana Maria Guerra Martins' writings (Martins 2000, p. 343). Similarly, this solution is found in one of the first decisions of the Italian Constitutional Court on the matter (1975), which considered that *"il contrasto con i principi enunciati dagli artt. 189 e 177 del Trattato istitutivo della C.e.e., che comporta violazione dell'art. 11 della nostra Costituzione, in base al quale l'Italia ha aderito alla Comunità consentendo,*

---

[24] Cf. Dougan (2019, pp. 1463-1464): *"Of course, each Member State can decide for itself that provisions of national law which are found to be incompatible with its Treaty obligations should be rendered or capable of being declared invalid for the purposes of the domestic legal system; or to provide for itself that the remedy of disapplication (or optional finding of invalidity) should extend to situations which strictly speaking fall either outwith the scope of Union law or beyond the extent of national law's actual incompatibility with the Treaties. But those are essentially national choices"*. This is therefore an exclusively national choice and is in no way determined by ECJ case law—cf. Orator (2015, pp. 1439–1440), Claes (2006, pp. 109, 456–457).

[25] Cf. Paris (2017, p. 815): *"The additional guarantee that constitutional courts can provide by nullifying statutes with general effect might then improve the effectiveness of the primacy of EU law. In particular, it can reduce the legal uncertainty that is inherent in the potential conflict between domestic legislation and EU law"*.

in condizioni di parità con gli altri Stati, le limitazioni di sovranità richieste per la sua istituzione".[26]

Moreover, this theory may be a plausible explanation for the judgment of the Austrian Constitutional Court of 14.03.2012 which, in what is called *"activist judicial constitutionalization"* (Orator 2015, p. 1447), invoked norms of the CFREU (but not of the other sources of European Union law) as a yardstick for a constitutional complaint, admitting the possibility of doing so in the context of *judicial review*.[27]

This ruling is somewhat removed from the *Recht auf Vergessen I* and *Recht auf Vergessen II* decisions of the German Federal Constitutional Court,[28] which reject

[26] Setenza no. 232/1975 of the *Corte Costituzionale of* 22 October 1975, no. 8.

[27] Ruling of the Austrian Constitutional Court of 14.03.2012 (U 466/11.18; U 1836/11-13 - VfSlg 19.632/2012). In this decision, on the subject of a *constitutional complaint* (and not *judicial review* of *national norms*) the Austrian Court recalled its entire case-law to the effect that it was impossible to invoke European norms as a yardstick (§§22-24) and expressly modified it, deciding on the viability of invoking the fundamental rights of the Charter as a standard (§35 – *"Der Verfassungsgerichtshof kommt daher zum Ergebnis, dass auf Grund der innerstaatlichen Rechtslage der Äquivalenzgrundsatz zur Folge hat, dass auch die von der Grundrechte-Charta garantierten Rechte vor dem Verfassungsgerichtshof als verfassungsgesetzlich gewährleistete Rechte gemäß Art.144 bzw."*). Now, although this was a constitutional complaint, the Court has stated that it may act in the same way in judicial review, under Articles 139 and 140 of the Austrian Constitution: *"Art. 144a B-VG geltend gemacht werden können und sie im Anwendungsbereich der Grundrechte-Charta einen Prüfungsmaßstab in Verfahren der generellen Normenkontrolle, insbesondere nach Art. 139 und Art. 140 B-VG bilden"*.

The fact that the Austrian Constitutional Court has limited the invocation to the Charter—expressly excluding all the other EU law—implies the conclusion that there was a ***partial*** *constitutionalisation* of the European Union law, limited to the CFREU, it being the *only one* (both in the European and Austrian framework) that has accepted the fundamental rights of the CFREU as a standard of normative constitutionality—cf. De Witte (2021, p. 213) (*"The Austrian constitutional court decided, in 2012, to include the EU Charter of Rights [but not the rest of EU law] among the standards of constitutional review"*); Orator (2015, p. 1429) (*"The Austrian* Verfassungsgerichtshof *[Constitutional Court] substantially extended the applicable yardstick, according to which the constitutionality of ordinary laws and administrative action may be assessed, to certain Charter rights"*), as an *exception to* the value attributed to the other sources of European Union law—cf. Paris (2017, pp. 800, 806), and the case-law cited therein.

[28] Contrary to that decided by the Austrian court, the decisions of the German Federal Constitutional Court do not invoke European law as a yardstick of *normative* control, only admitting its *direct* relevance when assessing the *concrete case*, in the light of constitutional complaints addressed to decisions of other courts—cf. Wendel (2020, p. 157), Komarek (2013, p. 422), Komarek (2014, p. 528).

In its judgment of 6.11.2019 - 1 BvR 16/13 [*Recht auf Vergessen I*], the German Federal Constitutional Court ruled that the control of fundamental rights takes place primarily by attention to the national constitution (§45 – *"Auch soweit Unionsgrundrechte danach gemäß Art. 51 Abs. 1 Satz 1 GRCh zu 45 denen des Grundgesetzes hinzutreten, übt das Bundesverfassungsgericht seine Prüfungskompetenz primär am Maßstab des Grundgesetzes aus"*) by interpreting national fundamental rights in line with the Charter (§48). Direct invocation of the Charter's norms has been admitted only in cases where it is impossible to guarantee the European level of protection by interpreting national standards and, exclusively in the field of *constitutional complaint* (when the Court *does not assess the validity of any national rules*) (§63 – *"Eine Prüfung allein am Maßstab*

directly invoking the Charter as a criterion of normative control, limiting its application to the areas of *constitutional amparo* or *complaint.* Unlike the 2012 Austrian decision, the German Federal Judge did not accept that national norms should be reviewed with reference to EU law, stating that the latter should only be directly used in *complementary* instruments for the protection of fundamental rights conferred by the ordinary courts.[29] In such judicial remedies, considering that ordinary courts *give primacy* to CFREU norms when these are in conflict with national rules, the intervention of the German Federal Constitutional Court regarding *decisions of other courts [or public authorities]* will use the *same standards.*[30]

---

der deutschen Grundrechte ist dann nicht ausreichend, wenn konkrete und hinreichende Anhaltspunkte vorliegen, dass hierdurch das grundrechtliche Schutzniveau des Unionsrechts ausnahmsweise nicht gewährleistet ist. Insoweit ist dann eine Prüfung innerstaatlichen Rechts, das der Durchführung des Unionsrechts dient, auch unmittelbar an den Grundrechten der Charta geboten". Therefore the conclusion was that the constitutional complaint in question should be assessed on *the basis of the national constitution* (§74).

In its Judgment of 6.11.2019 - 1 BvR 276/17 - *[Recht auf Vergessen II],* the Court admitted the invocation of the Charter as a yardstick for *national judicial decisions* (and not of norms), *restricted to the figure of the constitutional complaint* when the norms applicable to the dispute are *fully covered by European Union law* (§33: *"Der Rechtsstreit richtet sich nach Regelungen, die durch das Unionsrecht vollständig vereinheitlicht sind und bei deren Anwendung deshalb grundsätzlich alleindie Charta der Grundrechte der Europäischen Union anwendbar ist"*). That is why it was laid down that the European standard should only be applied to *decisions of* national bodies implementing European law: *"Maßstab für die konkretisierende Anwendung von vollvereinheitlichtem Unionsrecht durch innerstaatliche* ***Behörden*** *und* ***Gerichte*** *ist die Grundrechtecharta"* (§46, emphasis added). This action was expressly separated from *judicial review,* where the case-law of the BvG even maintains that it is possible to review the validity of European norms themselves by reference to the German Constitution (§§51 ff.). On the cases in which the German Court reserves the power to control—exceptionally—the constitutionality of European norms, cf. Patrão and Canotilho (2019, p. 20), and Witte (1995, p. 158).

[29] Judgment of 6.11.2019 - 1 BvR 276/17 - [Recht auf Vergessen II] §63: "Die Verfassungsbeschwerde ergänzt den fachgerichtlichen Rechtsschutz bewusst um eine eigene verfassungsgerichtliche Kontrolle".

[30] Judgment of 6.11.2019 - 1 BvR 276/17 - [Recht auf Vergessen II]: "*Von einer vollständigen Vereinheitlichung ist erst recht für die aktuelle Rechtslage unter Geltung der Datenschutz-Grundverordnung auszugehen,* ***die im Falle einer Aufhebung und Zurückverweisen der angegriffenen Entscheidung auch vom Oberlandesgericht zu beachten wäre***" (§41, emphasis added), implying that the level of protection in question is guaranteed by the catalogue of fundamental rights that constrain European rules with prevalent application (Paragraph 42 – "*Bei der Anwendung unionsrechtlich vollständig vereinheitlichter Regelungen sind grundsätzlich nicht die deutschen Grundrechte, sondern allein die Unionsgrundrechte maßgeblich; das Unionsrecht hat hier gegenüber den Grundrechten des Grundgesetzes Anwendungsvorrang*"). Cf. Wendel (2020, p. 159).

It is this speciality which justifies the fact that *only in systems with an appeal for protection* or a *constitutional complaint* have the Constitutional Courts assumed control of the obligation to ask for a preliminary ruling—cf. Lacchi (2015, p. 1665): *"The* conditio sine qua non *for this practice is that, in the Member States under analysis, when other legal remedies are exhausted, individuals may file a complaint, under certain circumstances, before those Constitutional Courts"*); Paris (2017, p. 807).

4 Separating Compatibility with EU Law and Constitutional Judicial Review

The idea of using EU law as a yardstick for constitutional judicial review has always been rejected by the majority of constitutional courts,[31] including the Portuguese Constitutional Court.[32] According to most legal theorists, contradiction between

---

[31] In essence, "What unites the jurisprudence of the constitutional courts examined so far is the fundamental contention that a violation of EU law as such does not amount to a violation of the constitution", and therefore "In principle, constitutional courts do not use EU law as a yardstick for constitutional review. They consider their task to be that of upholding the constitution, not EU law" (Paris 2017, pp. 801 and 798 respectively).

As regards the German Federal Constitutional Court, see, among many others, the decision of 13 September 2005 (2 BvF 2/03), §145, where the BVerfG refers the problem of the compatibility with the Treaty of the rule to be reviewed to the normal jurisdiction of the Court of Justice.

As for the Czech Constitutional Court, see, among others, Judgment of 27.03.2008 (reiterating established case law) Pl.ÚS 56/05, *Squeeze-out,* no. 48: *"Here we cannot but state what the Constitutional Court has already stated several times (in particular, judgements Pl. ÚS 50/04, no. 154/2006 Coll. and Pl. ÚS 36/05, no. 67/2007 Coll.). The reference point for review of the constitutionality of statutes under Art. 87 par. 1 let. a) and Art. 88 par. 2 of the Constitution of the CR is the constitutional order. The Constitutional Court does not have jurisdiction, in such proceedings, to review whether domestic law is consistent with community law. The application of community law as directly applicable law (see decision of the European court of Justice, matter 106/77, Amministrazione delle Finanze dello Stato v Simmenthal SpA. Reference a preliminary ruling: Pretura di Susa - Italy. The non-use of a statute that is inconsistent with the law of the Community, known to the domestic court as Simmenthal II, available in the Collection of Decisions, vol. 1978, p. 629, e.g. at eur-lex.europa.eu) is in the jurisdiction of the ordinary courts, which, in cases of doubt about the application of the law, have the opportunity, or obligation, to turn to the European Court of Justice with a preliminary issue under Art. 234 of the TEC"* (official translation); and Judgment of 21.02.2006 Pl.ÚS 19/04, paragraph 29.

As for the Spanish Constitutional Court, cf. decision no. 28/1991, which expressly rejects the thesis of *indirect unconstitutionality* in paragraphs 4 to 6.

In France, *see* the *Conseil Constitutionnel*'s consistent case-law, since decision 74-54 DC of 15 January 1975, paragraph 5, and reiterated in decisions 89-268 DC of 29 December 1989, paragraph 85; no. 91-293 DC of 23 July 1991, paragraph 5; 98-405 DC of 29 December 1998, paragraph 22 - and which remained even after the constitutional amendment of 2008 (cf. decision 2010-605 DC of 12 May 2010, paragraph 16; and No. 2014-694 of 28 May 2014, paragraph 2: *"Le moyen tiré du défaut de compatibilité d'une disposition législative aux engagements internationaux et européens de la France ne saurait être regardé comme un grief d'inconstitutionnalité; que l'examen d'un tel grief fondé sur les traités ou le droit de l'Union européenne relève de la compétence des juridictions administratives et judiciaires".*

This is also the traditional case-law of the Austrian Constitutional Court (VfSlg. 14.886/1997, 15.189/1998, 15.215/1998, 15.753/2000, 15.810/2000 and 18.266/2007), although—as seen above, note no. 39—the Court has admitted the possibility of invoking the rules of the CFREU *for normative control* (but no longer of the other sources of EU law).

[32] Cf. Ramos (2017, p. 53). Cf. Ruling no. 326/98, when the appellant invoked the transgression of a norm of a directive as generating violation of Article 8 of the Constitution: the Constitutional Court concluded that the review of constitutionality does not cover *"situations in which such a violation arises indirectly"*, requiring that *"a certain norm, whose unconstitutionality was questioned, directly or, if you like, immediately violates a norm or principle contained in the Fundamental Law"*; in Ruling no.621/98, refusing to attribute to the rule under review a defect of

national and European rules does not render the former *unconstitutional* (Piçarra 1992, p. 43; Duarte 1995, p. 702; Costa 1998, pp. 1371–1372; Miranda 2002–2003, p. 19; Araújo et al. 2003, p. 268; Medeiros 2015, p. 319).

In fact, because EU law retains its autonomy, such conflict is solved by *disapplying* the national rule—with the possible involvement of the ECJ by way of a preliminary ruling, *without any infringement of the Constitution being assessed.*[33] This ensures coherence of the EU legal order and allows the harmonisation of the jurisdictions of the national constitutional courts and the ECJ (Brito 2003, p. 311).

There are two reasons why this is so.

Firstly, European law must be applied uniformly. If conflicts with European rules were to be converted into a constitutionality issue, the effects of this would depend on the system of judicial review in a given Member State. In countries where the ordinary judge is not allowed to address constitutionality rules, this would undermine primacy of EU law, since instead of acting *by its very nature,* primacy would be effective through the (non-uniform) system for constitutional judicial review of those Member States (Piçarra 1992, p. 45; Schütze 2006, p. 1031).

Such a consequence could jeopardise the prerogatives of the ECJ regarding conflicts between national and European rules if ordinary courts were to be forbidden to make preliminary references in order to set aside (by their own authority) national law. In fact, the very operation of primacy of EU law entails giving *ordinary courts the* power and duty—even in systems which do not allow them to undertake judicial review—to *set aside* national rules and consult the ECJ on the matter in question. This is what ensures the uniform application of European law and thus relieves the

---

unconstitutionality due to its contradiction with European rules, because *"the confrontation between rules of domestic law and Community rules has a specific jurisdictional mechanism (the preliminary ruling procedure, which is usually known as a 'preliminary reference')", and therefore "the "qualification of the incompatibility of domestic law with Community law as a situation of 'unconstitutionality' that it falls to the Constitutional Court to assess" should be rejected"*; in Ruling no. 93/2001, with regard to the invocation of violation of Article 8 of the Constitution due to the contradiction of national rules with European Union law, the Constitutional Court concluded that *"the Community legal order, globally received by Portuguese law, by means of a clause in the constitutional text itself - Article 8(2) - comprises a judicial body. This would make it incongruous for another body of the same or similar type, such as the Constitutional Court, to intervene at a domestic level for the same purpose";* and, more recently, in Ruling no. 268/2022 (although in that case *the Constitutional Court was the only body that could be called upon to intervene at a domestic level).* More recently, in Ruling 268/2022 (although there were divergent explanations of vote), it was concluded that *"the demonstration of the contradiction between the norms in question and European Union law does not allow us to conclude that they are unconstitutional".*

[33] Cf. Paris (2017, p. 798).

This issue must not be confused with the consideration, nowadays supported by the case-law of several constitutional courts, that violation of the obligation to ask a preliminary question may imply a breach of *the Constitution*—namely by violating the right to effective judicial protection. The issue at stake here is whether the right to effective judicial protection (in our case, enshrined in Article 20 of the Constitution) includes the right to call on the ECJ to interpret EU law, given its jurisdiction. Obviously, this case-law is restricted to systems of *constitutional complaint,* questioning directly before the constitutional court the decisions of ordinary courts—cf. Lacchi (2015, p. 1666).

constitutional courts of such task (Claes 2006, p. 102; Bobek 2012, p. 294; Paris 2017, p. 794). This very concern led the Italian Constitutional Court to change its case-law as early as 1984, refraining from turning contradiction with EU law into an issue of constitutionality and thus referring the problem to the ordinary courts.[34]

It should also be noted that the Court of Justice, in case *A. and B.*, expressed its discomfort with the 2012 decision of the Austrian Constitutional Court, in which the latter decided to consider national rules in the light of the CFREU. The conformity of that decision with EU law is subject to the guarantee that *ordinary courts retain the power to enforce primacy of EU law* by ensuring the full effectiveness of EU law *before* (or *independently of*) the intervention of the Constitutional Court.[35] Hence the concern of the ECJ with regard to making a conflict with EU law a constitutionality issue (De Visser 2015, p. 1326; Paris 2017, p. 813), which the *Mecanarte*[36] and *Melki and Abdeli* judgments[37] had already criticised.

[34] The jurisprudential inversion was expressed, in Sentenza n. 170/1984, Nos. 8 and 9: "*Compete al giudice rimettente accertare se gli invocati regolamenti e principi dell'ordinamento comunitario consentano, e a qual titolo, che il regime del prelievo agricolo, sotto il profilo dedotto nella presente controversia, sia fatto retroagire soltanto fino alla data di pubblicazione della pronunzia interpretativa della Corte del Lussemburgo, sopra richiamata*". Nevertheless, the Italian Constitutional Court appears to continue to accept the invocation of European Union law in abstract review proceedings (Sentenza of 10 November 1994, no. 384/1994; Sentenza of 30 March 1995, no. 94/1995).

[35] Judgment of the Court of Justice (Fifth Chamber) of 11 September 2014, *A v B* and Others., *proc.* C-112/13, para. 46. According to the EU judge, the assumption of such responsibility by the Austrian Constitutional Court is compatible with EU law only *"provided that those ordinary courts may: - at any time during the proceedings which they consider appropriate, even after the conclusion of the incidental procedure for the general review of laws, refer to the Court of Justice any question referred for a preliminary ruling which they consider necessary; - take any measure necessary in order to ensure provisional judicial protection of rights conferred by the legal order of the Union; and - not apply, on completion of that incidental procedure, the national legislative provision at issue if they consider it to be contrary to Union law"*. Therefore, the Constitutional Court cannot *block* access to European jurisdiction by ordinary courts, which are responsible for ensuring the primacy of EU law (cf. Bobek 2012, p. 295; De Visser 2015, p. 1330).

[36] Cf. Bobek (2012, p. 295), Komarek (2013, p. 438). As is well known, in the *Mecanarte* case the Court was asked whether, if the incompatibility with Union law was comparable to *unconstitutionality,* it was unnecessary to ask a question for a preliminary ruling. The Court made it very clear that *"the effectiveness of Community law would be in jeopardy if the existence of an obligation to refer a matter to a constitutional court could prevent a national court hearing a case governed by Community law from exercising the right conferred on it by Article 177 of the EEC Treaty to refer to the Court of Justice questions concerning the interpretation or validity of Community law in order to enable it to decide whether or not a provision of domestic law was compatible with Community law"*. Judgment of 27 June 1991, *Mecanarte, Case* C-348/89, paragraph 45.

[37] In this judgment, the ECJ stressed that this *direct relationship* cannot be conditional: if the fact that a certain rule is contrary to both European rules (leading to its disapplication) and the Constitution (leading to its invalidity) is invoked, EU law requires that the national court ask for a preliminary ruling *even if the national system establishes some kind of priority* for *reviewing constitutionality*—cf. CJEU judgment of 22.06.2010, *Melki* and *Abdeli,* joined cases C-188/10 and 189/10, paragraphs 42ff.

Secondly, it is impossible to declare unconstitutionality (on the basis of a contradiction between national and European rules) by reference to constitutional statutes which *accept EU law* (such as Article 8(4) of the Portuguese Constitution). In fact, given the nature of the principle of primacy, a national rule that is in conflict with EU law *does not breach the rules of the Constitution which accept EU law,* since those provisions accept primacy as a *rule of collision* addressed to *the judge of the specific case,* who must, in obedience, *set it aside* and give precedence to the European rule. In other words, a contradiction between domestic rules and European law *does not offend* the Constitution rules which accept EU law. On the contrary, it *calls upon them*: by accepting the primacy of EU law, the Constitution agrees to the *setting aside* of the national rule (Piçarra 1992, p. 48).

5 Consistent Interpretation as a Guarantee of the *Effectiveness of* EU Law

Effectiveness of European Union law—which is the *European mandate to* national courts[38]—is not achieved *only* by primacy, direct effect or direct applicability.[39] Indeed, a very important (perhaps *the most important*) part of the full effectiveness of European law relies on the *principle of consistent interpretation,* which is particularly appropriate for a *non-hierarchical* system of sources of law.[40]

Accordingly, the fact that European Union law is not used as a direct yardstick for the validity of national rules does not mean constitutional jurisdictions are dissociated from EU law or that there is no possibility of dialogue between national constitutional courts and the ECJ.[41] On the contrary, EU law is vital in constitutional

[38] Cf. Claes (2006, p. 27) (*"The national judges are under a Community obligation to ensure the full effect of Community law and effective judicial protection of the rights which individuals derive from Community law"*); Kumm (2005, p. 299), Bossuyt and Verrijdt (2011, p. 384) (*"The Court obliges all domestic judges to immediately take all action required in order to guarantee EU law's full effect"*).

[39] There is no doubt that the principle of *effectiveness of* EU law underpins *direct effect* and the *primacy* of European rules. Cf. De Witte (2021, p. 208), Claes (2006, p. 45).

[40] Cf. Agnieszka (2017, p. 52), Bossuyt and Verrijdt (2011, p. 389), who stress that *"effectiveness can be obtained using several techniques"*.

In the words of Maduro (2010, p. 846): *"this situation does require a conception of the law which is no longer dependent on a classical, hierarchical understanding and construction of the law and the constancy of supremacy. It is I have called of "counterpunctual law". Similar to what happens in music where you can have different melodies, one can have different mechanisms of recognising the supremacy of EU law that can be perfectly compatible with one another so long as they lead to the same result. Thus, to take full advantage of this idea of legal and constitutional pluralism we need to conceive forms of reducing or managing the potential conflict between legal orders and promoting communication between them"*.

[41] The rarity of dialogue between the constitutional courts and the ECJ can be explained by the role played by the *ordinary courts* which, when faced with a conflict between national and European

judicial review,[42] affecting it indirectly: *"the narrator is still the national Constitution but the script has changed*" (Betlem 2002, p. 398; Maduro 2012, p. 75; Paris 2017, p. 796).

In fact, *under EU law,* the meaning to be given to national rules (from any source) must take European law into account. Consistent interpretation dates back to the 1970s—when the ECJ established an obligation on national courts to interpret national law so as to give full effect to the provisions of directives which could not have direct effect.[43] The concept has since developed into a general principle for interpreting national law (all national law) in order to ensure the full effectiveness of European Union law. The principle lays down that national courts are required to interpret domestic law, so far as possible, in conformity with EU law: *'This obligation to interpret national law in conformity with European Union law is inherent in the system of the Treaty on the Functioning of the European Union, since it permits national courts, for the matters within their jurisdiction, to ensure the full effectiveness of European Union law when they determine the disputes before them*'.[44] Its limits are set by *the European legal order itself*: it *'is limited by general principles of law and it cannot serve as the basis for an interpretation of national law contra legem*'.[45]

In essence, within the obligation on national authorities to take measures to ensure the full effectiveness of Union law—based on the *principle of sincere cooperation*, enshrined in Article 4(3) TFEU—there is a duty to interpret national law in conformity with EU law.[46] This is therefore a legal effect of European law which, according to the Court of Justice itself, *prevents* the implementation of primacy of

legislation, refer the matter directly to the Community judicature and apply the principle of primacy. Cf. Bobek (2012, pp. 285, 297), Paris (2017, pp. 794–795).

[42] See Opinion of Advocate General Kokott in Case C-169/08, *Presidente del Consiglio dei Ministri v. Regione autonoma della Sardegna,* paragraph 23: *"Even without such express incorporation, [of* European law as a yardstick for constitutional judicial review], *Community law may be relevant to the decision in constitutional law disputes where, for example, the purported effects of a Community law measure are at issue in constitutional law proceedings or where the scope left by a Community law measure for the national legislature is open to review by a constitutional court".*

[43] Cf. judgments of the CJEU *Mazzalai*, 20.05.1976, proc. 111/75; *Von Colson,* 10.04.1984, proc. 14/83; *Marleasing*, 13.11.1990, proc. 106/89. Cf. de Quadros (2013, p. 564), Dougan (2019, p. 1462), Tridimas (2001, p. 329), Lenaerts and Corthaut (2006, p. 292), Drake (2005, p. 331).

[44] Cf. CJEU judgment of 24.01.2012, *Maribel Dominguez*, proc. C-282/10, no. 25.

[45] See, among many others, CJEU judgments of 24.01.2012, *Maribel Dominguez, proc.* C-282/10, paragraph 25; *Maria Pupino, of* 16.06.2005, proc. C-105/03, paragraphs 44 and 47; *Adeneler, of* 04.07.2006, proc. C-212/04, paragraph 110; *Impact,* of 15.04.2008, proc. C-268/06, paragraph 100; and *Angelidaki, of* 23.04.2009, procs. C-378/07 to C-380/07, paragraph 199; of 11.01.2007, *ITC, proc.* C-208/05, paragraph 68: judgment of 9.10.2013, *Spedition Welter, proc,* C-306/12, paragraph 29. On the limits of consistent interpretation, *see* Lenaerts and Corthaut (2006, p. 295), Betlem (2002, p. 406).

[46] Pais (2013). In the same vein, cf. de Quadros (2013, p. 564), Dani (2017, p. 204), Lanceiro (2010, p. 273), Dougan (2007, p. 945), Lenaerts and Corthaut (2006, p. 293), Betlem (2002, p. 399).

European Union law.[47] National courts are bound, when determining the meaning of rules of national law, to give full effect to European law and, within the margin allowed by domestic rules of interpretation, to choose the interpretation best suited to European rules.[48] And it is their duty, where appropriate, to establish the questions to be referred for a preliminary ruling in order to determine the precise meaning to be given to EU rules.[49]

In fact, where there are multiple sources of law which are conditioned by each other and interpreted by different judicial actors—often with exclusive, but partial, powers of interpretation of the overall normative system—legal interpretation is no longer possible without considering the interactive horizon of the converging legal orders and the actions of each of the judicial bodies.

Miguel Poiares Maduro terms this *counterpoint* interpretation: the aim is to harmonise standards, interpreting them harmoniously and avoiding regulatory conflict.[50] Effectiveness of EU law can be achieved by *aligning standards*, resulting in the simultaneous protection of national and European yardsticks (Claes 2006, pp. 142, 145 and 464; Dougan 2007, p. 946).

---

[47] Cf. judgment of 24.01.2012, Maribel Dominguez, proc. 282/10, para. 23 ("It should be stated at the outset that the question whether a national provision must be disapplied in as much as it conflicts with European Union law arises only if no compatible interpretation of that provision proves possible"); judgment of 11.01.01.2007, ITC, proc. C-208/05, para. 69; Judgment of 9.10.2013, Spedition Welter, proc, C-306/12, para. 28; CJEU judgment of 19.06.2019, Poplawski, proc. 573/17, paras. 57 and 58.

In essence, "the preferred means of resolving that tension is through the duty of consistent interpretation: national law must, as far as possible, be construed so as to comply with the Member State's obligations under the Treaties. Only if such consistent interpretation proves impossible (for example, when faced with a simple contra legem incompatibility between Union and national legislation) does the domestic court need to reconstruct and address the relationship between Union and national law in potentially more abrasive terms" (cf. Dougan (2019, p. 1462)). Also, Lenaerts and Corthaut (2006, p. 314); Moniz (2012, p. 289).

[48] To that extent, as stated in the Murphy judgment of 4 February 1988, Case 157/86, "it is for the national court to interpret and apply domestic law in accordance with the requirements of Community law, in so far as it is given discretion under domestic law". This implies, therefore, that 'the interpreter and enforcer of the law must, even where he is required to apply only national law, give an interpretation of national law which conforms to the meaning, scheme and wording of European rules' (cf. Gorjão-Henriques (2019, p. 393)).

[49] Cf. Judgment of the CJEU of 14.12. 2000, *Fazenda Pública c. Câmara Municipal do Porto*, proc. C-446/98, no. 48.

[50] Cf. Maduro (2003, p. 523): "*Counterpoint is the musical method of harmonising different melodies that are not in a hierarchical relationship* inter se. (…) *In law we too have to learn how to manage the non-hierarchical relationship between different legal orders and institutions and to discover how to gain from the diversity and choices thereby offered us without generating conflicts that ultimately will destroy those legal orders and the values they sustain*". As the author illustrates (Maduro 2010, p. 835), "*in spite of their claims to ultimate authority and legal sovereignty, both the EU and national legal orders make more or less explicit concessions towards the claim of authority of the other legal order. They make the necessary adjustments to their respective claims in order to prevent an actual collision. EU law has introduced substantive constitutional changes such as fundamental rights in order to accommodate the claims made by national constitutions. National constitutions have been interpreted in a manner that tends to prevent the review of specific EU acts*".

6 Consistent Interpretation and the *Constitutional Protection Network*

The principle of consistent interpretation plays a decisive role in the protection of fundamental rights. The autonomy of national and European legal orders (retaining their own referrals of validity and a specific jurisdictional structure) does not mean that the judicial activity of national constitutional courts is indifferent to European values and rules (Ramos 2007, p. 808; Medeiros 2015, pp. 331, 348). On the contrary, constitutional courts should take European standards into consideration when establishing the meaning of *national rules*—including constitutional rules—within the field of application of EU law,[51] ensuring its effectiveness.

In fact, in the context of the protection of fundamental rights, there is a predisposition towards alignment between European and national legal orders. This is recognised by most constitutional courts[52] and by the ECJ—when it admits the application of national catalogues to address the European level of protection.[53]

This harmonising is the result of the influence the different sources have on each other (Martins and Roque 2014, p. 44).

On the one hand, the European legal order takes the national catalogues as a reference—*"Fundamental rights, as guaranteed by the European Convention for the Protection of Human Rights and Fundamental Freedoms and* ***as they result from the constitutional traditions common to the Member States****, shall constitute general principles of the Union's law"*.[54] Furthermore, the EU is bound by the Charter of Fundamental Rights of the European Union, which contains a catalogue

[51] In the words of Maduro (2003, p. 529): *"Any national court must take into account the interpretations of the same European rules and legal principles made by other national courts. This requires them to fit any 'national interpretation' of EU law with the interpretations given by other national courts and the European Court of Justice. It is this that will guarantee both vertical and horizontal coherence of the European legal order"*.

[52] Cf, the case-law of the German Federal Constitutional Court, both in its *Solange* case-law and, most recently, in its judgment of 6.11.2019 - 1 BvR 16/13 [*Recht auf Vergessen I*]), §55: *"kann sich das Bundesverfassungsgericht auf die Vermutung stützen, dass durch eine Prüfung am Maßstab der Grundrechte des Grundgesetzes das Schutzniveau der Charta, wie sie vom Europäischen Gerichtshof ausgelegt wird, in der Regel mitgewährleistet ist"*).

Likewise, see Sentenza 20/2019 of the Italian Corte Costituzionale: *"i principi e i diritti enunciati nella CDFUE intersecano in larga misura i principi e i diritti garantiti dalla Costituzione italiana (e dalle altre Costituzioni nazionali degli Stati membri), e che la prima costituisce pertanto "parte del diritto dell'Unione dotata di caratteri peculiari in ragione del suo contenuto di impronta tipicamente costituzionale"*.

In Portugal, the same happened in Constitutional Court Ruling no. 268/2022, paragraph 8.2.

[53] CJEU judgment of 26 February 2013, Melloni, C-399/11, paragraph 60: "national authorities and courts remain free to apply national standards of protection of fundamental rights, provided that the level of protection provided for by the Charter, as interpreted by the Court, and the primacy, unity and effectiveness of EU law are not thereby compromised". Cf. Wendel (2020, p. 160).

[54] Cf. Article 6(3) TEU. Emphasis added.

of fundamental rights drawn up in the image of the national constitutions: the *"constitutional traditions common to the Member States"* constitute a standard for interpreting the Charter itself (Article 53 CFREU) (de Quadros 2005, p. 691; Martins 2011, p. 135).

On the other hand, the principle of the highest level of protection of fundamental rights (Article 53 CFREU) will not only act as a rule of collision, but also as an *interpretative standard,* requiring that international catalogues of fundamental rights be considered when applying internal constitutional rules (Kumm 2005, p. 289; Canotilho 2008, pp. 173 and 183-184; Komarek 2013, p. 446). Therefore, when national authorities implement EU law (Article 51(1) of the CFREU), the meaning to be given to *national* fundamental rights shall privilege harmony with the binding European standards, which are, themselves, the result of inter-constitutional dialogue.[55]

In fact, uniform application of EU law would be jeopardised if yardsticks did not match each other, with the establishment of a different level of protection (*maxime,* a lower level) than that given by the CFREU.[56] The many sources of protection of fundamental rights—together with the diversity of jurisdictional bodies—implies a *practical alignment* between yardsticks. This articulation is also exercised by national constitutions, moulding the content of the rights contained in them to the European standards.[57]

To that extent, not only can it be concluded that the fundamental rights of the Constitution guarantee, in *principle,* those of the Charter (Claes 2006, p. 685; Amaral and Piçarra 2009, p. 25; Maduro 2010, p. 847; Lenaerts 2012, p. 397; Moreira 2014, p. 191; Dani 2017, p. 792; Wendel 2020, p. 158), but also that the essence of the relationship between the European constitutional order and the national constitutional order is 'interactive' rather than hierarchical.[58]

---

[55] This is what the German Federal Constitutional Court emphasises in its judgment of 6.11.2019 - 1 BvR 16/13 [*Recht auf Vergessen I],* stressing that the fundamental protection has evolved in a joint direction and is the result of two-way dialogue between European and national sources: *"Die Einstellung des Zeitfaktors in die Beurteilung der verfassungsmäßigen Anforderungen an die Verbreitung von Informationen stellt sich als Teil einer Entwicklung im Austausch der europäischen Grundrechtsentwicklung dar".*

[56] Cf. CJEU Judgments of 26 February 2013, *Melloni,* C-399/11, paragraph 60 and *Âkerberg Fransson,* C-617/10, paragraph 29. cf. Wendel (2020, p. 160).

[57] This is especially clear in the amendments of Article 35 of the Portuguese Constitution. Cf. Castro (2016, p. 65), Calvão (2017, p. 89).

[58] Cf. Amaral (2005, p. 423). This is the idea expressed by MacCormick (1995, p. 264) (*"the most appropriate analysis of the relations of legal systems is pluralistic rather than monistic, and interactive rather than hierarchical"*), and Pernice (2009, p. 383) (*"In the view of multilevel constitutionalism, this is to be expected because there is no hierarchy between the two components of the European legal system. Rather, the relationship is pluralistic and cooperative"*).

This common acquis—which, in principle, prevents *total irreconcilability of* the rights enshrined in the different sets of catalogues—allows *consistent interpretation* to ensure the full effectiveness of European Union law, when the content of the rights is not totally identical.

It is in the interpretation of *constitutional standards* that EU law (and more specifically the Charter of Fundamental Rights of the European Union) should intervene—rather than as an autonomous yardstick—when the Constitutional Court is asked to review *national* rules (Agnieszka 2017, p. 52). The Constitutional Court is responsible for guaranteeing alignment between standards *"by seeking to interpret the constitution according to Community law"*,[59] *(if necessary)* asking preliminary questions to obtain the exact meaning of the European standard (Ramos 2003, p. 376, Ramos 2008, p. 248) and accepting the jurisdiction of the Court of Justice.[60] Interpretation of constitutional yardsticks considers *European rules*, even with regard to the conditions of *restriction of* fundamental rights (Coutinho 2020, p. 34, n91).

In essence, although the yardstick used by national constitutional courts when assessing the *unconstitutionality* of rules of domestic law is the *Constitution,* its interpretation is not limited to the national horizon as its exclusive frame of reference (Betlem 2002, p. 398; Ramos 2007, p. 29; Maduro 2012, p. 74; Paris 2017, p. 796). This ensures coherence between autonomous legal orders and the effectiveness of EU law.[61]

---

[59] Cf. Ramos (2000, p. 8). Also, cf. Kumm (2005, p. 300) (*"this conception can be applied to the interpretation of constitutions in all Member States and the European legal order"*); MacCormick (1995, p. 265) (*"National Courts ought not to interpret laws or constitutions without regard to the resolution of their compatriots to take full part in European Union and European Community"*); Gorjão-Henriques (2012, p. 369).

[60] Cf. Maduro (2010, p. 847) (*"They have to accept that the protection of the fundamental values of their legal order may be better achieved by another institution or that the respect owed to the identity of another legal order should lead them to defer to that jurisdiction. This requires courts to both develop instruments for institutional comparison and to set the limits for jurisdictional deference at the level of systemic identity"*).

[61] Cf. Paris (2017, p. 796) (*"By reviewing domestic acts in light of EU law, they accept the task of guaranteeing not only the domestic order's compliance with the constitution, but also compliance with EU law. Yet formally, they remain subject to a single master, the constitution"*); Maduro (2003, p. 524) (*"These principles guarantee that the European legal order will both fulfil the aims involved in its pluralist conception and guarantee the harmony between the diversity of legal discourses and forms of European power that such a pluralist conception entails"*).

This is the approach followed by most constitutional courts,[62] as is clearly stated in the words of the Portuguese,[63] German,[64] Italian,[65] Spanish,[66] Czech,[67] Polish[68] and Latvian constitutional courts.[69] There is an obligation for national courts to frame their decisions *in European terms,* ensuring alignment between the national

---

[62] Cf. Violante (2022, p. 4), Maduro (2012, p. 75).

Even the Austrian Constitutional Court, which seems to accept the Charter as a yardstick for judicial review in its Judgment of 14.03.2014 (cf. *supra,* note no. 27), does not fail to postulate this *consistent interpretation* of the various standards: *'Der Verfassungsgerichtshof schließt daraus, dass die sich aus den nationalen Verfassungen, völkerrechtlichen Verträgen und der Grundrechte-Charta ergebenden Grundrechte möglichst kohärent auszulegen sind'* (§46).

[63] See Judgment 268/2022.

[64] BVerfG judgment of 6.11.2019 - 1 BvR 16/13 [Recht auf Vergessen I], §60: "*Der Einbettung des Grundgesetzes wie auch der Charta in gemeinsame europäische Grundrechtsüberlieferungen entspricht es vielmehr, dass auch die Grundrechte des Grundgesetzes im Lichte der Charta auszulegen sind*".

[65] Cf. Sentenza 20/2019: "*principi e diritti fondamentali enunciati dalla CDFUE intersecano, come meglio si chiarirà, principi e diritti fondamentali garantiti dalla Costituzione*".

[66] Cf. Ruling of the Spanish Constitutional Court no. 26/2014, in the case that gave rise to the Melloni Judgment: "*Tanto la interpretación dada por el Tribunal Europeo de Derechos Humanos del derecho a un proceso equitativo recogido en el artículo 6 del Convenio europeo como la realizada por el Tribunal de Justicia de la Unión Europea de los derechos a la tutela judicial efectiva, a un proceso equitativo y de defensa recogidos en los arts. 47 y 48.2 de la Carta, coincidentes en buena medida, operan, en el caso que nos ocupa, como criterios hermenéuticos que nos permiten delimitar la parte de lo que hemos denominado contenido absoluto del derecho a un proceso con todas las garantías, que es la que despliega eficacia ad extra; esto es, la que permite delimitar aquellas facultades y garantías cuyo desconocimiento por las autoridades extranjeras puede dar lugar a una vulneración indirecta en caso de que acuerde la entrega por los poderes públicos españoles*".

[67] Cf. judgment of 27 March 2008 Pl.ÚS 56/05, Squeeze-out, no. 48: "An obligation arises from Art. 1 par. 2 of the Constitution of the CR for the Constitutional Court, as a state body, of the Czech Republic, to make an interpretation of the constitutional order consistent with European law (see also judgment file no. Pl. ÚS 66/04, no. 434/2006 Coll., in relation to European Union law) in those areas where community law and the legal order of the Czech Republic meet (the undertaking of loyalty under Art. 10 of the TEC)" [official translation]. Cf. Kühn (2019, p. 801).

[68] Cf. analysis of the case-law of the Polish Constitutional Court by Agnieszka (2017, p. 53ff), and Biernat and Kawczyńska (2019, p. 755).

[69] Cf. Krūma and Statkus (2019, p. 988): *"It should be noted that the general approach adopted by the Constitutional Court is one of consistent interpretation. The practice of consistent interpretation has great potential to secure compliance with European and international obligations".*

and European legal orders[70] and guaranteeing that the level of protection afforded by the CFREU is not compromised.[71]

This goes well beyond merely alluding to the European text as a persuasive argument: rather, the Charter is called upon as a standard of protection that must be achieved—insofar as this is *possible*[72]—by using the national constitutional catalogue. Fundamental rights enshrined in national and European sources are not mutually *exclusive* or *conflicting,* and coherence can be sought without redirecting the monitoring standards to only one of these catalogues.[73]

---

[70] Cf. Maduro (2003, p. 534) (*"Uniformity would be further safeguarded, even in light of higher discretionary powers being granted to national courts, by the obligation imposed on national courts to frame their decisions in universal terms and to secure the consistency between any such national decision and the European legal order as a whole"*); De Witte (2021, p. 222) (*"one should accept that there are inherently different viewpoints, that the search for a perfect hierarchical ordering between legal norms and across legal systems may therefore be futile, and that the relationship between the EU and national legal orders is, and remains, a 'heterarchical' one"*). It is what might be called *cooperative duties* (in the expression of Besson (2004, p. 170)) or a *"sophisticated set of EU-member state inter-systemic bridging mechanisms centred around the preliminary reference procedure, which - in a prime example of the management of overlapping autonomies - allows each system virtually seamlessly to claim a persuasive sovereign pedigree for that same corpus"* (Walker 2002, p. 347).

[71] CJEU judgments of 26 February 2013, *Melloni,* C-399/11, paragraph 60 and *Âkerberg Fransson,* C-617/10, paragraph 29. It is in this sense that the German Federal Constitutional Court used its mandate to interpret the Constitution by reference to the Charter: Ruling BVerfG of 6.11.11.2019 - 1 BvR 16/13 (*Recht auf Vergessen I),* §48 (*"Allerdings ist dabei dafür Sorge zu tragen, dass das Schutzniveau der Charta, wie sie vom Gerichtshof ausgelegt wird, nicht beeinträchtigt wird (...). Dies ist bei der verfassungsgerichtlichen Kontrolle am Maßstab der Grundrechte zu berücksichtigen"*) and §62, determining that interpretation as *far as possible* (*"Eine europa- und Völkerrechtsfreundliche Auslegung, die andere überstaatliche Grundrechtskataloge berücksichtigt und sich von deren Interpretation inspirieren lässt, bedeutet nicht, dass unter Nutzung des offenen Wortenlauts der Grundrechte jede Interpretation internationaler oder europäischer Entscheidungsinstanzen und Gerichte zu übernehmen ist"*).

[72] Cf. the limits of the principle of consistent interpretation, explained above. Cf. Kühn (2019, p. 802).

[73] Cf. Wendel (2020, p. 160) (*"Das BVerfG geht einen großen Schritt auf den EuGH zu, wenn es nun den europäischen Grundrechtspluralismus im Sinne eines weitreichenden Neben- und Miteinanders von nationaler und europäischer Grundrechtsordnung anerkennt und sein Bemühen um deren wechselseitige Exklusivität aufgibt"*) and p. 163 (*"Soweit ein Gericht den Rekurs auf die ausländische Rechtsprechung zum Bestandteil der eigenen Entscheidungsgründe macht, braucht die gerichtlich praktizierte Verfassungsvergleichung nicht auf die Rolle eines hermeneutischen Hilfsmittels oder den Hinweis auf eine externe Fachautorität beschränkt bleiben, sondern kann ihrerseits performativ zu einem transnationalen Prozess der Herausbildung gemeineuropäischen Verfassungsrechts beitragen. Im Grundrechtsbereich ist dies von besonderer Bedeutung"*); Lenaerts (2012, p. 376), Bossuyt and Verrijdt (2011, p. 384).

This understanding is not only about ensuring the effectiveness of EU law.[74] In fact, it aids the *legitimacy* of European integration - especially by defining its constitutional limits.

This solution fits in particularly well with constitutional pluralism (Amaral 2005, p. 424), which is the best way to explain the interaction between autonomous legal orders integrated in the same interdependent and non-hierarchical system. The legitimacy of that system is guaranteed by means of a stable balance between the various levels, which—mutually and reciprocally—accept its authority (MacCormick 1993, p. 10, MacCormick 1995, p. 264; Pernice 1999, p. 707; Walker 2002, p. 337, Walker 2009, p. 19, Walker 2016, pp. 342, 345, and 354; Besson 2004, p. 177; Kumm 2005, pp. 267–268; Bogdandy and Schill 2011, p. 1420; Maduro 2012, pp. 70, 72; Jaklic 2014, p. 81).[75] This also explains the national identity clause of the TEU (Article 4(2)), which legitimises the action of national courts *with their own standards*, as well as the conditions associated with the standards of *European integration* of several national constitutions (subordinating European integration to compliance with constitutional principles — as in Article 7(6) of the Portuguese Constitution),[76] or the principle of the highest level of protection of Article 53 of the CFREU.[77]

In fact, multi-level articulation means there is no need to decide *who has the last word*, since harmonious interpretation of national and European yardsticks (associated with inter-jurisdictional dialogue between national constitutional courts and the ECJ) leads to a *coherent* response from the different jurisdictions:[78] the opening

[74] In essence, "strong interpretative use of the Charter could achieve similar results (even amounting to a judicially created assumption of equivalent meaning between national human rights protection and the Charter, parallel to the one the Charter itself makes with respect to the ECHR in Article 52 (3))"—cf. Bobek (2012, p. 305), footnote 35.

[75] In the opposite direction, criticising the foundations of constitutional pluralism, *see* Cruz (2018, p. 42ff).

[76] Cf. Bogdandy and Schill (2011, p. 1419) (*"this provision endorses a pluralistic vision of the relationship between EU law and domestic constitutional law. Article 4(2) should be seen as integrating the thrust of the jurisprudence of numerous domestic constitutional courts on the relationship between EU law and national constitutional law. The revised identity clause in article 4(2) TEU not only demands the respect for national constitutional identity, but can be understood as permitting domestic constitutional courts to invoke, under certain limited circumstances, constitutional limits to the primacy of EU law"*) and p. 1421 (*"It transpires, for example, in structural safeguard clauses in domestic constitutions final stop the most explicit one is article 23(1)(1) of the German constitution which requires that Germany's participation in the EU take place in accordance with its core constitutional principles"*).

[77] Cf. Lenaerts (2012, p. 399): *"In accordance with such a reading, Article 53 of the Charter would be an expression of constitutional pluralism"*.

[78] Cf. Walker (2016, p. 338): *"Rather than endorsing one over the other, the coherence of each on its own terms may be acknowledged, including the open-ended capacity of each to absorb the other in its own normative terms. On this detached view, what we are left with when confronting the EU legal configuration is quite unexceptional. It is merely a multiplicity of particular legal systems adjacently positioned, each claiming for its own purposes an exclusive and exhaustive jurisdiction even at the outer boundaries of it normative capacity-a feature of legal-institutional life with which, from the very diversity of sovereign statehood, the world has long been familiar"*. Basically, *"one of the purposes of constitutional pluralism is precisely to legitimate leaving that question*

of national constitutions to the Charter involves genuine participation of national constitutional courts in the European system of fundamental rights.[79]

However, this response does not mean that constitutional pluralism is accepted, since it is explained within monist or dualist systems.[80] In fact, the purpose of assigning such a role to constitutional courts is not to highlight the roots of authority of European constitutionalism, but rather to explain its relationship with other legal orders.[81]

Firstly, this is because even within a monist system—which would imply the invalidity of national rules contrary to European rules[82]—EU law expressly allows the use of national standards, provided that their interpretation leads to the European level of protection,[83] and dualist systems also accept the viability of *recognising* rules of other legal orders and their claims to authority.[84]

---

open and that, at an empirical level, the fact that the question remains open is a simple description of the constitutional status quo in Europe and only serves to reinforce the value of constitutional pluralism since its articulation of techniques of accommodation of the competing constitutional claims helps decreasing the number of times that the question will pose itself" (cf. Maduro (2012, p. 73)). Also, cf. Kumm (2005, p. 286), Jaklic (2014, p. 52 and 150), Botelho (2020) §20.

[79] Cf. Wendel (2020, p. 162), citing the German Federal Constitutional Court Judgment of 6.11.2019 - 1 BvR 276/17 - [*Recht auf Vergessen II*], §55 ("*Die Permeabilität bzw. Öffnung des Grundgesetzes meint unter diesem Blickwinkel gerade "nicht einen Rückzug der deutschen Staatsgewalt aus der Verantwortung für die der Union übertragenen Materien, sondern sieht vielmehr eine Mitwirkung der Bundesrepublik an deren Entfaltung vor*"); and Maduro (2003, p. 523).

[80] Cf. Claes (2006, p. 116): "*This is true both in dualist and in monist systems. In the context of Community law, consistent interpretation was used as a technique to give effect to Community law in the domestic legal orders by national courts even before the Court of Justice made it part of their Community law mandate, and thus made it compulsory*".

[81] Cf. Maduro (2012, p. 68), Pernice (2009, p. 372), Kumm (2005) This does not mean that this answer ends up constituting a form of limitation and legitimation of power and, to this extent, it is a meaningful answer. Cf. Medeiros (2015, p. 279).

[82] It is debatable whether the epistemological unity of law of monism necessarily implies the nullity of national norms (Medeiros 2015, p. 266). In any case, it seems to be the sanction of *nullity* that informs the words of Kelsen (1928, p. 149): "*Nur wenn man sich auf einen rein staatsrechtlichen Standpunkt stellt und von der Geltung des Völkerrechtes absieht, kann die - nur vom Standpunkt des Völkerrechts diesem zuwiderlaufende, die völkerrechtliche Delegation verletzende und daher ebenso yölkerrechtswidrige wie völkerrechtlich nichtige - staatliche Rechtsnorm gültig sein*".

[83] CJEU judgment of 26 February 2013, *Melloni*, C-399/11, no. 60. Cf. Paris (2017, p. 812): "*the principle of equivalence does not mandate constitutional courts to use EU law as a standard for constitutional review*".

[84] Specifically regarding the compatibility with a dualist system, see the considerations of Medeiros (2015, pp. 282, 328, 348) stressing nothing prevents *relations of recognition* between legal systems and that there is a *European commitment* that implies them, even as a *duty*; and Ribeiro (2019, pp. 206–207) stressing it is consistent with "moderate dualism" to make a *cosmopolitan commitment*, which includes the *duty to consider* other systems' claims to authority.

Secondly, even though the dogmatic conception may influence the way constitutional courts evaluate EU law,[85] consistent interpretation makes it possible to *avoid* conflicts which—in a monist system—would dismiss the national norm.

Interpretation in line with European Union law within constitutional judicial review of national rules is methodologically compatible with a dualist, monist or pluralist approach, since—within its limits—it *prevents* normative conflicts and allows national constitutional courts to guarantee the *network of constitutional protection* (Medeiros 2015, p. 365).

7 Conclusions

The main consequence of the CFREU in constitutional judicial review of *national rules* lies in the obligation of constitutional courts to interpret their own constitutional standards in line with European rules, avoiding normative conflict through the coherent and pluralistic articulation of the yardsticks.[86] Within the hermeneutical limits of national law, fundamental rights guaranteed by the European catalogue (within its scope of application) can be protected by national catalogues (Wendel 2020, p. 161), without this necessarily implying their replacement as a yardstick.

It is in this way, and not through the hierarchical supremacy that one legal order has over the other, that the *network of constitutional protection* (Machado 2018, p. 79) is safeguarded, allowing national constitutional courts to promote a coherent standard of protection of fundamental rights when asked to review national rules. Principles of *effectiveness* and *sincere cooperation* are not restricted to primacy.[87]

References

Agnieszka S (2017) The obligation to interpret national law in accordance with the European Union law in the jurisprudence of polish constitutional court – focus on limits. Eur J Public Matters 1:51–62

Almeida LND (1987) A justiça constitucional no quadro das funções do Estado vista à luz das espécies, conteúdo e efeitos das decisões sobre a constitucionalidade das normas jurídicas. Rev Minist Público 8:7SS

---

[85] Cf. Claes (2006, p. 56), Higgins (2009, p. 927). It will have, at least, influence in questions regarding the source of legitimacy of the European legal order (cf. Kumm (2005, p. 266)) and regarding which legal system will be used to find the norms regulating the internal relevance of European law (cf. Medeiros (2015, p. 264)).

[86] Cf. Lenaerts (2012, p. 376): "*the Charter also serves as an aid to interpretation, since both EU secondary law and national law falling within the scope of EU law must be interpreted in light of the Charter*".

[87] Cf. Steiner et al. (2006, p. 7): "*The obligation on Member states to ensure the full effectiveness of Community law requires national courts not only to 'disapply' the offending national law but also to supply a remedy which is not available under national law*".

Amaral DFD, Piçarra N (2009) O tratado de Lisboa e o princípio do primado do direito da União Europeia: uma evolução na continuidade. Rev Direito Público 1:9–56
Amaral ML (2005) A forma da República — Uma introdução ao estudo do direito constitucional. Coimbra Editora, Coimbra
Araújo A, Brito MND, Costa JPCD (2003) As relações entre os tribunais constitucionais e as outras jurisdições nacionais, incluindo a interferência, nesta matéria, da acção das jurisdições Europeias. In: Estudos em homenagem ao Conselheiro José Manuel Cardoso da Costa. Coimbra Editora, Coimbra, pp 203–273
Besson S (2004) Sovereignity in conflict. Eur Integr Online Pap 8:131–190
Betlem G (2002) The doctrine of consistent interpretation: managing legal uncertainty. Oxf J Leg Stud 22:397–418
Bieber R, Salomé I (1996) Hierarchy of norms in European law. Common Mark Law Rev 33:909–932
Biernat S, Kawczyńska M (2019) The role of the polish constitution (Pre-2016): development of a liberal democracy in the European and international context. In: Albi A, Bardutzky S (eds) National constitutions in European and global governance: democracy, rights, the rule of law: national reports. T.M.C. Asser Press, The Hague, pp 745–793
Bobek M (2012) The impact of the European mandate of ordinary courts on the position of constitutional courts. In: Claes M, De Visser M, Popelier P, Van De Heyning C (eds) Constitutional conversations in Europe. Internsentia, Cambridge, pp 285–308
Bogdandy AV, Schill SW (2011) Overcoming absolute primacy: Respect for national identity under the Lisbon treaty. Common Mark Law Rev 48:1417–1453
Bossuyt M, Verrijdt W (2011) The full effect of EU law and of constitutional review in belgium and france after the Melki judgment. Eur Const Law Rev 7:355–391
Botelho CS (2020) Transnational constitutional law. In: Max planck encyclopedia of comparative constitutional law [MPECCoL]
Brito MH (2003) Relações entre a ordem jurídica comunitária e a ordem jurídica nacional: desenvolvimentos recentes em direito Português. In: Estudos em homenagem ao Conselheiro José Manuel Cardoso da Costa. Coimbra Editora, Coimbra, pp 301–317
Calvão FU (2017) O direito fundamental à proteção dos dados pessoais e a privacidade 40 anos depois. In: Vaz MA, Botelho CS, Terrinha LH, Coutinho P (eds) Jornadas nos quarenta anos da constituição da República Portuguesa - impacto e evolução. Universidade Católica Editora, Porto, pp 85–101
Campos JMD, Campos JLMD, Pereira AP (2014) Manual de Direito Europeu. Coimbra Editora, Coimbra
Canotilho JJG, Moreira V (2007) Constituição da República Portuguesa anotada. Coimbra Editora, Coimbra
Canotilho M (2008) O princípio do nível mais elevado de protecção em matéria de direitos fundamentais. Faculdade de Direito da Universidade de Coimbra, Coimbra
Castro CSE (2016) 40 anos de utilização da informática - o artigo 35.° da constituição fa República Portuguesa. E-Publica 3:42–66
Claes M (2006) The national courts' mandate in the European constitution. Hart Publishing, Oxford
Costa JMCD (1998) O tribunal constitucional Português e o tribunal de justiça das comunidades Europeias. In: Ab Vno ad Omnes — 75 anos da Coimbra editora. Coimbra Editora, Coimbra, pp 1363–1380
Coutinho FP (2020) A independência da comissão nacional de proteção de dados. Anu Prot Dados:9–48
Cruz JB (2018) What's left of the law of integration? Decay and resistance in European Union law. Oxford University Press, Oxford
Dani M (2017) National constitutional courts in supranational litigation: a contextual analysis. Eur Law J 23:189–212
de Quadros F (2005) Constituição Europeia e constituições nacionais. O Direito 137:687–698
de Quadros F (2013) Direito da União Europeia. Almedina, Coimbra
De Visser M (2014) National constitutional courts, the court of justice and the protection of fundamental rights in a post-charter landscape. Hum Rights Rev 15:39–51

De Visser M (2015) Juggling centralized constitutional review and EU primacy in the domestic enforcement of the Charter: A.V.B. Common Mark Law Rev 52:1309–1337
De Witte B (2021) Direct effect, primacy, and the nature of the legal order. In: The evolution of EU law, 3rd edn. Oxford University Press, Oxford, pp 187–227
Dougan M (2007) When worlds collide — competing visions of the relationship between direct effect and supremacy. Common Mark Law Rev 44:931–963
Dougan M (2019) Primacy and the remedy of disapplication. Common Mark Law Rev 56:1459–1507
Drake S (2005) Twenty years after Von Colson: the impact of 'indirect effect' on the protection of the individual's community rights. Eur Law Rev 30:329–348
Duarte ML (1995) O tratado da União Europeia e a garantia da constituição. In: Estudos em memória do Professor Doutor João de Castro Mendes. Lex, Lisboa, pp 665–715
Gorjão-Henriques M (2012) Compreensões e pré-compreensões sobre o primado na aplicação do direito da União: breves notas jurídico-constitucionais relativamente ao Tratado de Lisboa. In: Dias JDF, Canotilho JG, Costa JFDF (eds) Ars Iudicandi: estudos em homenagem ao Prof. Doutor António Castanheira Neves — studia iuridica. Coimbra Editora — Boletim da Faculdade de Direito da Universidade de Coimbra, Coimbra, pp 317–371
Gorjão-Henriques M (2019) Direito da união. Almedina, Coimbra
Higgins R (2009) Dualism in the face of a changing legal culture. In: Themes and theories. Oxford University Press, Oxford, pp 926–938
Isaac G, Blanquet M (2001) Droit communautaire général. Armand Colin, Paris
Jaklic K (2014) Constitutional pluralism in the EU. Oxford University Press, Oxford
Kelsen H (1928) Das problem der souveränität und die theorie des völkerrechts: beitrag zu einer reinen rechtslehre. Mohr, Tübingen
Komarek J (2013) The place of constitutional courts in the EU. Eur Const Law Rev 9:420–450
Komarek J (2014) National constitutional courts in the European constitutional democracy. Int J Const Law 12:525–544
Komarek J (2017) National constitutional courts in the European constitutional democracy: a rejoinder I-con debate. Int J Const Law 15:815–825
Krūma K, Statkus S (2019) The constitution of latvia – a bridge between traditions and modernity. In: Albi A, Bardutzky S (eds) National constitutions in European and global governance: democracy, rights, the rule of law: national reports. T.M.C. Asser Press, The Hague, pp 951–995
Kühn Z (2019) The Czech Republic: from a euro-friendly approach of the constitutional court to proclaiming a court of justice judgment ultra vires. In: Albi A, Bardutzky S (eds) National constitutions in European and global governance: democracy, rights, the rule of law: national reports. T.M.C. Asser Press, The Hague, pp 795–833
Kumm M (2005) The jurisprudence of constitutional conflict: constitutional supremacy in europe before and after the constitutional treaty. Eur Law J 11:262–307
Lacchi C (2015) Review by constitutional courts of the obligation of national courts of last instance to refer a preliminary question to the court of justice of the EU. Ger Law J 16:1663–1700
Lanceiro RT (2010) O tratado de Lisboa e o princípio da cooperação leal. Cad Direito 5:265–299
Lenaerts K (2012) Exploring the limits of the EU Charter of Fundamental Rights. Eur Const Law Rev 8:375–403
Lenaerts K, Corthaut T (2006) Of birds and hedges: the role of primacy in invoking norms of EU law. Eur Law Rev 31(3):287–315
MacCormick N (1993) Beyond the sovereign state. Mod Law Rev 56:1–18
MacCormick N (1995) The Maastricht-Urteil: sovereignty now. Eur Law J 1:259–266
Machado J (2018) Direito da União Europeia. Gestlegal, Coimbra
Maduro MP (2001) O superavit democrático Europeu. Anál Soc 36:119–152
Maduro MP (2003) Contrapunctual law: Europe's constitutional pluralism in action. In: Walker N (ed) Sovereignty in transition. Hart Publishing, London, pp 501–538
Maduro MP (2010) Interpreting European law — judicial adjudication in a context of constitutional pluralism. In: Miranda J, Cordeiro AM, Ferreira EP, Nogueira JD (eds) Estudos em homenagem ao professor doutor paulo de pitta e cunha. Almedina, Coimbra, pp 833–850

Maduro MP (2012) Three claims of constitutional pluralism. In: Avbelj M, Komárek J (eds) Constitutional pluralism in the European Union and beyond. Hart Publishing, London, pp 67–84
Martins AMG (2000) A natureza jurídica da revisão do tratado da União Europeia. Lex, Lisboa
Martins AMG, Roque MP (2014) A tutela multinível dos direitos fundamentais — A posição do Tribunal Constitucional Português. In: XVI conferência trilateral dos tribunais constitucionais Espanhol, Italiano e Português Lisboa, pp 1–59
Martins PF (2006) O princípio do primado do direito comunitário sobre as normas constitucionais dos Estados-Membros. Principia, Cascais
Martins PF (2011) Um supremo tribunal para a União? Reflexões sobre o lugar do TJCE na arquitectura judiciária Europeia. In: Estudos dedicados ao professor Doutor Luís Alberto Carvalho Fernandes. Universidade Católica Editora, Lisboa, pp 99–156
Martins PF (2013) Princípio do primado do direito da união. In: Pais SO (ed) Princípios fundamentais de direito da união Europeia — uma abordagem jurisprudencial. Almedina, Coimbra, pp 41–91
Martins PF (2017) Princípio do primado do direito da UE. In: Brandão AP, Coutinho FP, Camisão I, Abreu JC (eds) Enciclopédia da União Europeia. Petrony, Lisboa, pp 339–342
Medeiros R (2015) A constituição Portuguesa num contexto global. Universidade Católica Editora, Lisboa
Mendes J (2013) Delegated and implementing rule making: proceduralisation and constitutional design. Eur Law J 19:22–41
Mengozzi P (2016) A European partnership of courts. Judicial dialogue between the EU court of justice and national constitutional courts. In: Estudos em homenagem ao conselheiro presidente Rui Moura Ramos. Tribunal Constitucional, Lisboa, pp 827–845
Miranda J (2002–2003) A constituição Europeia e a ordem jurídica Portuguesa. O Direito 134:9–29
Moniz AR (2012) A recusa de aplicação de regulamentos pela administração com fundamento em invalidade. Almedina, Coimbra
Moreira V (2014) Introdução à carta dos direitos fundamentais da União Europeia. In: Respublica Europeia — estudos de direito constitucional da União Europeia. Coimbra Editora, Coimbra, pp 169–194
Moreira V (2016) A CRP e a União Europeia. In: Estudos em homenagem ao conselheiro presidente rui moura ramos. Tribunal Constitucional, Lisboa, pp 869–926
Oliveira ASPD (2018) A Carta dos Direitos Fundamentais da União Europeia. Principia, Lisboa
Orator A (2015) The decision of the Austrian *Verfassungsgerichtshof* on the EU charter of fundamental rights: an instrument of leverage or rearguard action? Ger Law J 16:1429–1448
Pais SO (2013) Princípio da interpretação conforme. In: Pais SO (ed) Princípios fundamentais de direito da união Europeia — Uma abordagem jurisprudencial. Almedina, Coimbra, pp 93–107
Paris D (2017) Constitutional courts as European Union courts: the current and potential use of EU law as a yardstick for constitutional review. Maastricht J Eur Comp Law 24:792–821
Patrão A (2008) O direito derivado da União Europeia à luz do tratado de Lisboa. Temas Integr 26:139–167
Patrão A, Canotilho M (2019) A admissibilidade dos recursos de fiscalização concreta da constitucionalidade de normas de regulamentos da União Europeia. In: Estudos em homenagem ao conselheiro presidente Joaquim de Sousa Ribeiro. Almedina, Lisboa, pp 11–38
Peers S, Costa M (2012) Accountability for delegated and implementing acts after the treaty of Lisbon. Eur Law J 18:427–460
Pernice I (1999) Multilevel constitutionalism and the treaty of Amsterdam: European constitution-making revisited? Common Mark Law Rev 36:703–750
Pernice I (2009) The treaty of Lisbon: multilevel constitutionalism in action. Columbia J Eur Law 15:349–408
Piçarra N (1992) Comentário ao Acórdão *Mecanarte* — Cobrança *a posteriori* dos direitos aduaneiros. Colect Anot Jurisprud Comunitária 4:21–50
Piçarra N (2006) A justiça constitucional da União Europeia. In: Estudos jurídicos e económicos em homenagem ao Prof. Doutor António Sousa Franco. Coimbra Editora, Coimbra, pp 467–501

Ramos RM (1999a) As comunidades Europeias—enquadramento normativo-institucional. In: Das comunidades à União Europeia—estudos de direito comunitário. Coimbra Editora, Coimbra, pp 7–102
Ramos RM (1999b) Reenvio prejudicial e relacionamento entre ordens jurídicas na construção comunitária. Coimbra Editora, Coimbra
Ramos RM (2000) The adaptation of the Portuguese constitutional order to community law. Bol Fac Direito Univ Coimbra 76:1–12
Ramos RM (2003) O Tratado que estabelece uma constituição para a Europa e a posição dos tribunais constitucionais dos estados-membros no sistema jurídico e jurisdicional da União Europeia. In: Estudos em homenagem ao Conselheiro José Manuel Cardoso da Costa. Coimbra Editora, Coimbra, pp 365–395
Ramos RM (2007) O tribunal constitucional Português e as normas de outros ordenamentos jurídicos. In: Estudos em memória do conselheiro luís nunes de Almeida. Coimbra Editora — Tribunal Constitucional, Coimbra, pp 781–826
Ramos RM (2008) Constituição Europeia e constituição da República Portuguesa. Rev Legis Jurisprud 137:239–248
Ramos RM (2017) O constitucionalismo Português na europeização. In: Olhar o constitucionalismo Português nos 40 anos da constituição de 1976. Instituto Jurídico, Coimbra, pp 27–60
Ribeiro GDA (2019) Recensão a *A Constituição num contexto global,* de Rui Medeiros. Catól Law Rev 3:200–209
Sarmiento D (2013) Who's afraid of the Charter? The court of justice, national courts and the new framework of fundamental rights protection in Europe. Common Mark Law Rev 50:1267–1304
Schütze R (2006) Supremacy without pre-emption? The very slowly emergent doctrine of community pre-emption. Common Mark Law Rev 43:1023–1048
Simon D (2001) Le système juridique communautaire. Presses universitaires de France, Paris
Soares AG (2002) Os princípios gerais de direito na ordem jurídica comunitária. In: Ramos RM (ed) Estudos em homenagem à professora doutora Isabel de Magalhães Collaço. Almedina, Coimbra, pp 757–778
Steiner J, Woods L, Twigg-Flesner C, Steiner J (2006) EU law. Oxford University Press, Oxford
Tillotson J, Foster NG (2003) Text, cases, and materials on European Union law. Cavendish Pub, London
Tridimas T (2001) Black, white, and shades of grey: horizontality of directives revisited. Yearb Eur Law 21:327–354
Violante T (2022) How the Data Retention Legislation Led to a National Constitutional Crisis in Portugal, VerfBlog, 2022/6/09, https://verfassungsblog.de/how-the-data-retention-legislation-led-to-a-national-constitutional-crisis-in-portugal/, https://doi.org/10.17176/20220610-032725-0. Accessed 1 February 2024
Vitorino A (2002) Carta dos direitos fundamentais da União Europeia. Principia, São João do Estoril
Walker N (2002) The idea of constitutional pluralism. Mod Law Rev 65:317–359
Walker N (2009) Multilevel constitutionalism: looking beyond the German debate. LSE 'Europe Quest Discuss Pap Ser 1–31 http://eprints.lse.ac.uk/53361/1/__Libfile_repository_Content_European%20Institute_LEQS%20Discussion%20Papera_LEQSPaper8Walker.pdf. Accessed 27 Sept 2024
Walker N (2016) Constitutional pluralism revisited. Eur Law J 22:333–355
Wendel M (2020) Das Bundesverfassungsgericht als garant der unionsgrundrechte. Juristen Ztg (JZ) 75:157–168
Witte BD (1995) Sovereignty and European integration: the weight of legal tradition. Maastricht J Eur Comp Law 2:145–173

Afonso Patrão Portuguese Constitutional Court. Universidade de Coimbra, Faculty of Law, Coimbra, Portugal.

A "Principle of Exclusive Competence of the Court for the Definitive Interpretation of EU Law"? Is There Anybody in There? I'll Need Some Information, First!

Miguel Gorjão-Henriques

1 Introduction

The Lisbon treaty echoed a structural reform in the EU legal order, implementing in the *modified* EU—the 1992/93 *quasi*-entity that replaced and succeeded to the European Community and its legal order (Article 1, § 3 *in fine* TEU)—a *soi-disant* version of the treaty establishing a constitution for Europe, with the adaptations decided by the June 2007 European Council.[1] At the time, it was noted that "the constitutional concept, which consisted in repealing all existing Treaties and replacing them by a single text called 'Constitution', is abandoned. The Reform Treaty

[1] Of 21 and 22 June 2007. In its Annex I "IGC Mandate", among other adaptations, it reads that "3. The TEU and the Treaty on the Functioning of the Union will not have a constitutional character. The terminology used throughout the Treaties will reflect this change: the term "Constitution" will not be used, the "Union Minister for Foreign Affairs" will be called High Representative of the Union for Foreign Affairs and Security Policy and the denominations "law" and "framework law" will be abandoned (…). Likewise, there will be no article in the amended Treaties mentioning the symbols of the EU such as the flag, the anthem or the motto. Concerning the primacy of EU law, the IGC will adopt a Declaration recalling the existing case law of the EU Court of Justice. 4. As far as the content of the amendments to the existing Treaties is concerned, the innovations resulting from the 2004 IGC will be integrated into the TEU and the Treaty on the Functioning of the Union, as specified in this mandate. Modifications to these innovations introduced as a result of the consultations held with the member States over the past six months are clearly indicated below" (available at https://data.consilium.europa.eu/doc/document/ST-11177-2007-REV-1/en/pdf, last accessed on 3.12.2023). See, in particular, Declarations 1, 17, 52 and 53 annexed to the Treaty of Lisbon. On the different interpretation methods of Declarations, particularly after the Lisbon treaty, see Lattanzi (2022).

M. Gorjão-Henriques (✉)
Univ Coimbra, Faculty of Law, Coimbra, Portugal
e-mail: mgh@fd.uc.pt

I. Quadros, M. Gorjão-Henriques (eds.), *Revisiting the Liberal Constitutional Features of the European Union*, https://doi.org/10.1007/978-3-031-95717-8_16

will introduce into the existing Treaties, which remain in force, the innovations resulting from the 2004 IGC, as set out below in a detailed fashion".

In the aftermath of the Lisbon Treaty, the EU not only kept its autonomy and legal personality under the "same" Maastricht Treaty (TEU) and enhanced these, even though other changes in the EU legal order were extremely significant. Although the Court of Justice itself (hereinafter, ECJ or Court[2]), in Opinion 2/2013, recognised that the European Union "is, under international law, precluded by its very nature from being considered a State",[3] the fact is that, following the amendments by the Lisbon Treaty, a *newer legal order* seems to be forged under the Courts' case-law.

The roots are clear, from the perspective of the reform treaty. The EU internalizes the role that up until the Lisbon Treaty—notwithstanding the respect for fundamental rights by the EC/EU—was assured, almost exclusively, by the Council of Europe and the ECHR system, at western European level, and particularly at least until the fall of the Berlin wall and the 2004 enlargement. The Lisbon treaty, mainly through Article 2 TEU, mirrors Article 2 of the Council of Europe's Treaty of London (1949) and, combined with Article 19 TEU, supersedes with thunder the former discussions at EC level.[4] A specific EU competence on fundamental rights (i.e. Article 6 TEU), the accession to the ECHR and the incorporation of a specific and extended bill of rights into EU primary law (the Charter of Fundamental Rights of the EU, "Charter") are clear signs, but another one is the precise focus on principles of rule of law and democracy (in this case, both representative—see Article 10 TEU—and participatory—see *inter alia*, Articles 11 TEU or 24 TFEU). However, these must be read in conjunction with Article 19 TEU, which excels the mere fact of the traditional *diktat* according to which it is up to "the Court of Justice and the [former] Court of First Instance, each within its jurisdiction, ensure that in the interpretation and application of this Treaty the law is observed". Article 19 (1), second paragraph, TEU states that "Member States shall provide remedies sufficient to ensure effective legal protection in the fields covered by Union law", one of the most disputed

[2] The reference to Court/ECJ refers specifically to the Court of Justice and not to the EU institution Court of Justice of the European Union (CJEU—Articles 13 and 19 (1) § 1 TEU), which includes, in addition to the ECJ, the General Court and the specialized courts (currently there are none of the latter).

[3] Opinion 2/13, *cit.*, point 156, further developing all the "constitutional features" of the EU legal order in the subsequent paragraphs, 157–177. The potential "state-building process" of the EU is, however, the direct object of our reflections but, here, just an *obiter dicta*.

[4] For an overview of such discussions around the time of the Convention and to demonstrate how the ECJ case-law has moved forward since Lisbon, see Lenaerts and Van Nuffel (1999, pp. 539–550, in particular p. 546), where it is proposed, as a solution to prevent member States from being "squeezed between the primacy of Community law, on the one hand, and obligations under the ECHR, on the other" that "that problem could be resolved by allowing the Court of Justice and the Court of First Instance to make references for preliminary rulings to the European Court of Human Rights".

and invoked provisions of EU law since the *K.* case (C-475/16) and, of course, *Associação Sindical dos Juízes Portugueses*.[5]

The EU came close to a "constituent event"[6] of having a formal Constitution—instead of a *de facto*, *in fieri* or even transforming constitution –, a bill of rights Charter transparently included in the treaties themselves and all the symbols of statehood, including an express primacy clause, even without calling into question the main *sui generis* characteristics of the EU institutional system of democracy (bluntly reinforced) and institutional equilibrium.[7]

On its side, the Court has managed to drastically enhance its role in promoting European integration[8] and a common fundamental rights plateau, not only in relation to the respect for EU values by EU institutions, bodies, offices and agencies, but also by the member States, not only when member States apply EU law (as one might deduce from Article 51 of the Charter) but also insofar as they *may* apply EU law, as the fully-fledged debate and case-law on the independence of the judiciary highlights.[9]

One sign of this *revolution* is the dramatic push in the Court of Justice of the European Union (CJEU) case-law towards the enforcement of the Charter, from the post-Nice/pre-Lisbon period to the post-Lisbon phase (1.12.2009[10]). In fact, hardly

[5] Judgment of the Court (Grand Chamber) of 27 February 2018, *Associação Sindical dos Juízes Portugueses v. Tribunal de Contas*, case C-64/16, EU:C:2018:117. The doctrine is immense on the topic. For a recent overview in the Portuguese doctrine, see Duarte (2023) and Gorjão-Henriques (2025).

[6] Borrowing the words of Da Cruz Vilaça and Piçarra (2014, p. 46). On the subject-matter of constituent power in the EU, see the discussion in Conway (2013, pp. 100–106).

[7] It is not surprising, therefore, to find recurring voices and projects of institutional reform and mechanisms that ensure that constitutional pluralism is not a vain expression used merely to justify unilateral supremacy, reforming the CJEU. On this subject, in the Portuguese legal writing, see Da Cruz Vilaça and Piçarra (2014, pp. 48–54), which continues to be relevant; and the various projects involving Joseph H. H. Weiler, which even date back to the last millennium (in the 1990's, critically, e.g. Da Cruz Vilaça and Piçarra (2014, p. 49, n. 14); more recently, a new initiative has been documented, now with Sarmiento (2023); or the Costa et al. (2023).

[8] Bredimas (1978), apud Conway (2013, p. 116); or Lecourt (2008, pp. 240, 271).

[9] But even before—see, for previous case-law (post-Lisbon), at least since *Åklagaren v Hans Åkerberg Fransson*, case C-617/10, EU:C:2013:280, Sofia Oliveira Pais, *Estudos*, *cit.*, in particular pages 168–172. The author concludes that also in the *Melloni* case (C-399/11) the solution (imposing an unconditional direct effect of an EU rule over a national constitutional provision, as interpreted nationally, ensuring a higher level of protection of fundamental rights) does not seem problematic, since both legal orders consistently ensure fundamental rights (in our view, this is arguably also an interpretation that may be said to derive from—and have been assumed by—the Portuguese Constitutional Court in its judgment 422/2020, which seems also to follow in fact, in our view, the longstanding solution upheld in Portugal by Piçarra (1991, pp. 88–89). As we know, *Melloni*, the '*Taricco saga*' and other cases (e.g. *Weiss*) have been a source of several instances of 'dialogue' between the constitutional courts and the ECJ (see, in the Portuguese legal writing, De Mesquita (2022, pp. 310-335); Jorge and Burns (2021). Arguably with a different perspective, but in an earlier text, Duarte (2017, pp. 145–146).

[10] Regarding the impact of the Charter prior to the Lisbon Treaty in the Portuguese legal writing, Moreira (2014, p. 190). As we know, the Court's attitude was stricter than that of several advocate

ever was the Charter invoked by the Court in judgments or decisions in the pre-Lisbon period as a source on its own merits, although it was proclaimed by the democratic EU institutions (European Parliament, Council and European Commission) and indeed by the European Council at Nice on 7 December 2000. Only in cases reported by Alan Rosas and Cunha Rodrigues was the Charter invoked for material fundamental rights. Alan Rosas, rapporteur in two of those cases (C-540/03 and C-244/06), recognised the autonomous value of the Charter regarding the fundamental right of protection of children, despite it as not being a mandatory legal act (see C-540/03, points 36 and 58). However, in all other cases, the Court merely used the Charter as confirmation of its earlier case-law (see cases C-432/05,[11] C-303/05, C-438/05, C-341/05, C-244/06, C-402/05 P, C-47/07 P, C-35/07 P and C-12/08) and, remarkably, almost entirely to reinforce the principle of effective judicial protection (from mid-2008 on, Article 47 of the Charter was the only rule invoked). In other cases, including, but not limited to, *Promusicae*, the Court interpreted the reference to the Charter as grounds for allowing the Court to make reference to <u>other</u> EC rules (see, points 42 and 46) and, even though paragraph 2 of the preamble of Directive 2002/5/EC made express reference to the Charter, the Court carefully avoided departing from a strict interpretation of what was then binding EC law.[12]

Clearly, the main reason for this may be the fact that the Charter was not legally binding. However, it does not explain why the same attitude was not to be found in the advocate general's conclusions or even in the First Instance Court case-law in the same period. These arguably divergent trends merely show the impact of the entry into force of the Lisbon Treaty. And as Juha Raitio has stressed, regarding the perspective of post-Lisbon case-law: "the more the Court would be inclined to apply various fundamental rights and rely on Charter rights the more teleological the Court rulings become" (Raitio 2013, p. 209).

The CJEU has always remained central in the definition and enforcement of the EU constitutional attributes.[13] In the European integration process, from the very first decade the Court affirmed the autonomy and specific characteristics of the (now) EU legal order, even when only economic communities existed, construing a

---

generals and of the Court of First Instance, during that period. There were few cases in which the Court made any specific reference to the Charter, even as an interpretative tool. We have identified no more than 11 cases. On the issue of whether the Court should be considered an institution for the sake of the Charter (and later, Article II-111 of the 2004 Constitution), see Picod (2005, pp. 647; and 1, 394–395).

[11] A highly significant judgment of the Court (Grand Chamber) of 13 March 2007, *Unibet (London) Ltd and Unibet (International) Ltd v Justitiekanslern*, case C-342/05, EU:C:2007:163, on the principle of judicial protection.

[12] Making no further reference to the Charter – Judgment of Court (Grand Chamber) of 29 January 2008, case C-275/06, EU:C:2008:54. This may be exemplified also in the *Schmidberger* case, also contrasting the progressive view of AG Jacobs with that of the Court (judgment of 12 June 2003, *Eugene Schmidberger v. Republik Österreich*, case C-112/00, EU:C:2003:333).

[13] There is a vast amount of legal writing on the subject—see the collection of essays in Rosas et al. (2013).

set of principles that, even today, it is hard to find expressly in the wording of the treaties (a sort of *bible*), but which constitutes, with the CJEU case-law, the *tradition* that springs from the original goals and purposes of European integration, thus harmoniously uniting the member States and the EU citizens.

The definition of the EU legal order as autonomous is undisputed. Using a classic summary from a renowned Portuguese scholar and former CFI judge, the EU legal order is "*autonomous because, although integrated in the Public International law in wider terms, it is characterised not only by different methods of formation (or, at least sources of law that have a different scope to that which general public international law recognises for them) but also by significant differences in its application*".[14] The autonomy of the EU legal order is, of course, a consequence of the constitutional build-up of the Treaties and the scope of the EU goals (see Article 2 TEU), but also of the fact that the European Union forms and expresses its will through procedures and institutional means that are largely independent of the member States (through the institutions provided for in Article 13 TEU), with a set of formal sources of law (see Article 288 TFEU). The EU legal order is construed as including a set of principles (effectiveness or *effet utile*, in its various forms: direct effect, primacy,[15] uniform application, loyal cooperation (Lanceiro 2019), conform interpretation, state liability for infringement of EU law, etc.) that are ultimately assured by the constitutional role of the Court of Justice.[16]

The autonomy of the EU legal order has also been evident at other times during the Union's history. One may recall the particularly extensive discussions in the 1990s on whether there were material limits to the revision of the Treaties, or even the recurrent affirmation of the—for now—abandoned[17] principle of the *acquis communautaire* that would prevent, *inter alia*, the renationalisation of powers or any pushback in the integration process.

Another example is the increasingly frequent intervention of the Court on the limits of the international decision-making process of EU institutions and member States or on the differences between traditional international treaties and the EU construction, as paradigmatically summarised in Opinion 1/91 on the EEA: "In contrast, the EEC Treaty, albeit concluded in the form of an international agreement, none the less constitutes the constitutional charter of a community based on the rule of law. The Community treaties established a new legal order for the benefit of

---

[14] Free translation of this classical quotation of 1994, Ramos (1995, p. 100).

[15] In other words, prevalence of primacy of application. On the fundamental principles of EU law as formulated by the ECJ, in the Portuguese legal writing, Pais (2011).

[16] According to the CJEU case-law, preservation of the EU legal order's autonomy supposes that its competences are not changed – Opinion 1/91 (negative) on the EEA Treaty, points 61–65, and Opinion 1/92 of 10 April 1992, EU:C:1992:189 points 32–41 (as the Court stated, although in this case referring to the field of competition, "the Community may accept rules (...) provided that those rules do not change the nature of the powers of the Community and of its institutions as conceived in the Treaty").

[17] At least for shared competences (see Article 2 TFEU; see also 48 (2) TEU). In Portugal, Maria Luísa Duarte links these modifications to the reinforcement of the contractual basis of European integration (Duarte 2021, p. 139).

which the States have limited their sovereign rights and the subjects of which comprise not only Member States but also their nationals. The essential characteristics of the Community legal order which has thus been established are in particular its primacy over the law of the Member States and the direct effect of a whole series of provisions (see, in particular, the judgment in Case 26/62 *Van Gend en Loos* [1963] ECR 1). The essential characteristics of the Community legal order which has thus been established are in particular its primacy over the law of the Member States and the direct effect of a whole series of provisions which are applicable to their nationals and to the Member States themselves".

The autonomy of the EU legal order has been affirmed *vis-à-vis* Public International Law[18] and the internal legal orders of the member States. Primary and secondary EU law have an identity of their own. Even when subject to incorporation under national law (e.g. the implementation required by EU Directives), the norms and legal commands keep their international, *rectius* European Union, nature, and thus both legal orders are "*coexistent and interpenetrated, although independent*" (De Morais 1998, p. 374). And this is also, in a sense, a condition for the legality of EU acts or even member States' acts in the international and EU (and even national) sphere. In the first sense one may recall the ways in which the Court has been seen to use its consultative powers (currently laid down in Article 218 (11) TFEU) to sustain the autonomy of the EU legal order (or previously, of the EEC or EC legal order) vis-à-vis the ECHR and the Council of Europe (see Opinions 2/94 or 2/13[19]). Also, it is not uncommon to see the Court decide upon the limits of the powers of members States and/or of the EU to enter into international agreements by force of which an organ external to the EU would have the competence to interpret EU law to the detriment of the preliminary ruling procedure (Article 267 TFEU) or, in a more general wording, in *Slowakische Republik c. Achmea BV*,[20] of the obligations laid down—with direct effect—in Article 19 (1), second paragraph, TEU.[21] Long gone is the interpretation that this paragraph "in terms of content, (…) does not

[18] Although it is not subtracted from it, as occurs with the States, at least given the "Archimedes principle"—David (1999, p. 5).

[19] Opinion of the Court (Grand Chamber) of 18 February 2014, EU:C:2014:2454.

[20] Judgment of the Court (Grand Chamber) of 6 March 2018, Slovak *Republic v. Achmea BV*, case C-284/16, EU:C:2018:158, points 34–38 and 54–59.

[21] Such being justified by the Court (Grand Chamber) judgment of 26 October 2021, *Republiken Polen v. PL Holdings*, case C-109/20, EU:C:2021: 875, point 52, in which the Court recalled that "Lastly, it follows both from the judgment of 6 March 2018, *Achmea* (C-284/16, EU:C:2018:158), and from the principles of the primacy of EU law and of sincere cooperation, not only that the member States cannot undertake to remove from the judicial system of the European Union disputes which may concern the application and interpretation of EU law, but also that, where such a dispute is brought before an arbitration body on the basis of an undertaking which is contrary to EU law, they are required to challenge, before that arbitration body or before the court with jurisdiction, the validity of the arbitration clause or the *ad hoc* arbitration agreement on the basis of which the dispute was brought before that arbitration body".

seem to add anything new, merely reiterating the general principle of effective judicial protection developed by the ECJ in its case law".[22]

We turn our attention to a recent and (in a certain way) subtle modification of the wording—and therefore the perception—that the Court is transmitting by declaring in several recent judgments its exclusive competence to deliver a "definitive interpretation" of EU law. The role the CJEU assumes under Article 19 (1) TEU is well known, arising both *in written form* [in the wording of the treaties or of secondary legislation] and *in the form of Tradition* [the Court's own case-law], and providing the Court with a specific authority that, nevertheless, ought to be accepted with harmony at member State level in order to prevent a paradigm shift in the future,[23] be it as an example of constitutional pluralism or even counterpoint law (Maduro 2023), or in the form of a systematic coherent approach, as reaffirmed in *W.S.* regarding the relationship between the Charter and the ECtHR case-law.[24]

The fact is that in *Melloni* and in a growing number of cases since Lisbon (for a recent case, see *European Commission v. Kingdom of Spain*[25]), the Court declared that a member State may be found in breach of principles laid down in the ECJ case-law, without invoking any primary law rule that ought to be considered infringed. The evolution of the principles implicated in the idea of *effet utile* (including primacy, direct effect, State liability and other dimensions of the effectiveness or uniformity principle, as it has been more commonly referred to recently) and their application in situations where the CJEU case-law erodes the role of constitutional or supreme national Courts—or even of the legislator or of the Constitution of the member State—may give rise to some thoughts on how balance can be achieved without risking annihilating the effectiveness of, and the adherence of the European peoples and legal systems to the European integration process. It is my contention that the Court should also hold dear the idea that the European *depositum fidei* only makes sense if it serves the treaties and the plan for underlying the peace and progress program enshrined therein—including the *2004 motu* proclaimed in *Lisbon* by

---

[22] Arnull (2013, p. 767). The same can arguably be said—although not disputed and addressed here—of Declaration 1 on the Charter annexed to the Lisbon Treaty.

[23] Speaking of dialogue and peaceful coexistence (Pais 2017, p. 98).

[24] Point 123: "(...) in so far as the Charter sets out rights corresponding to rights guaranteed under the ECHR, Article 52(3) of the Charter is intended to ensure the necessary consistency between the rights contained in the Charter and the corresponding rights guaranteed under the ECHR, without thereby adversely affecting the autonomy of EU law. According to the Explanations relating to the Charter of Fundamental Rights (OJ 2007 C 303, p. 17), the second paragraph of Article 47 of the Charter corresponds to Article 6(1) ECHR. The Court must, therefore, ensure that the interpretation which it gives to the second paragraph of Article 47 of the Charter safeguards a level of protection which does not fall below the level of protection established in Article 6(1) ECHR, as interpreted by the European Court of Human Rights (see, to that effect, judgments of 29 July 2019, *Gambino and Hyka*, C-38/18, EU:C:2019:628, paragraph 39 and the case-law cited, and of 26 March 2020, Review *Simpson* v *Council* and *HG* v *Commission*, C-542/18 RX-II and C-543/18 RX-II, EU:C:2020:232, paragraph 72)".

[25] See judgment of the Court (Grand Chamber) of 28 June 2022, *European Commission v. Kingdom of Spain*, case C-278/20, EU:C:2022:503 – for a critical reading, Feilhès (2022).

16 member States, unity in diversity—and if the teachings and directives are received with *docility*. The contrary would amount to autarchy, an expression that "refers to a government in which a single [entity] exercises absolute control over all citizens and every aspect of their lives" and "attempts to be completely self-reliant".[26] Additionally, the Court should ensure that it is not being abused by national Courts or the public or private parties involved in order to circumvent national rules or rulings.[27] As the well-known adage says, "with great power comes great responsibility".

2 The Concept of "Definitive Interpretation" in the ECJ Case-Law

It is in this light that we consider a current trend of cases in the Court that introduce a new *diktat* rarely seen in earlier case-law and which, in our view, should be limited to its rightful place, in order not to create a new yardstick that would do more harm than good to the solidity and development of the Court's constitutional role under Article 19 (1) TEU.[28] In some recent cases, the ECJ has referred to itself as the one being responsible for the "definitive interpretation" of EC/EU law. It is true that in the past the CJEU established its sole and exclusive competence to declare the illegality of an ECSC/EC/EU rule (following the disputed but established *Foto-Frost* doctrine[29]), and also that it has consistently stated since the late 1950's that no national rules may oppose European rules without calling into question the nature

[26] https://definitions.uslegal.com/a/autarchy/, last accessed on 28.9.2022. The French report to the 2023 Sofia FIDE Congress recalls a series of criticisms that the EU and its judiciary face – Loïc Azoulai/Sébastien Platon, "France", in particular pp. 311–313 (available at https://cic.events/fide/fide-publications-vol-1.pdf, last consulted on 30.11.2023).

[27] In an extension of the abuse of EU law concepts—on the issue of abuse of EU law, which increasingly may also be assumed by national public authorities, such as regulators or public prosecutors' offices, and with further reading recommendations, Markus (2023).

[28] Turning principles into even more than "*normes hypothétiques fondamentales («Grundnorm»), par essence non discutées, de nature à légitimer d'autres normes. L'antécédent prend ici bien la forme d'un postulat, c'est-à-dire d'un a priori théorique, qui permet de consolider l'édifice normatif qui, pour le dire simplement, repose sur la validation de chaque norme par la référence à une autre norme*", in a Kelsen applied way—Bergé (2022, p. 1867).

[29] Judgment of the Court of 22 October 1987, *Foto-Frost v. Hauptzollamt Lübeck-Ost*, case 314/85, EU:C:1987:452. It is impossible and inappropriate to include, as in almost any other matter, an overview of the extensive legal writing and case-law regarding this "*contra-legem* interpretation of Article 267 TFEU"—Martins (2017, p. 583).

of the Union and the purposes of European integration, although the methodology used has evolved greatly from the separation method adopted in *Stork*[30] or *Leonesio*.[31]

However, in the area of interpretation of (what is now) EU law, the CJEU has traditionally presented the dual nature and functioning of Article 267 TFEU: on one hand a dialogue between two courts; on the other hand, a contribution sought or needed to ensure the uniform application of EU law. Nevertheless, the fact that the Court replies to the referring national court, providing it (and all judicial bodies within the EU, e.g. all the member States' courts, but also administration, and even legislative powers) with a binding interpretation of the EU rule at stake, does not mean that it is granting itself the power to determine the definitive interpretation of an EU rule once and for all cases. Of course, departing from established case-law would imply the possibility or even the need for a new preliminary reference by the national court, following, *inter alia*, *Cilfit*[32] or the developments in *Consorzio Italian Management*.[33] This having been said, except in the case of last instance courts or tribunals, it cannot be excluded that the same court or other courts in the same or in different member States, not being bound to make a mandatory preliminary reference, may adopt their own sovereign interpretation of EU law, although they may have the option (as said, in such a case, a duty for last instance courts or tribunals) to refer a question to the ECJ on the interpretation of the exact same EU rule and, frequently, on whether the reading provided in the past remains untouched, considering the national rules with which they should relate to in the national case.

In recent case-law, the Court has reminded national courts (and all other interested parties in its case-law) of its competence to provide the "definitive interpretation" of EU law. This expression has only emerged in the context of affirming the Court's jurisdiction (since *Hermès*[34]) in relation to other types of specific international courts, such as the Benelux Court (*Parfums Christian Dior* et al. *vs. Evora BV*[35]), or other entities that may or may not be considered as such, for the purposes

[30] Judgment of the Court of 4 February 1959, *Friedrich Stork & Cie v. High Authority of the ECSC*, case 1/58, point 4, EU:C:1959:4. Although rightly abandoned by the Court, the General Court still resorted to the *Stork formula* as late as 28 May 2013 in *Mohamed Trabelsi and others v. Council*, case T-187/11, EU:T:2013:273, point 61.

[31] Judgment of the Court of 17 May 1972, *Orsolina Leonesio v Ministero dell'agricoltura e foreste*, case 93/71, EU:C:1972:39, point 24. More focused on the direct effect of certain EU rules, due to their lack of conditionality, see judgment of the Court of 19 December 2019, *Coöperatieve Producentenorganisatie en Beheersgroep Texel UA v. Minister van Landbouw, Natuur en Voedselkwaliteit*, case C-386/18, EU:C:2019:1122.

[32] There is a vast amount of legal writing on Cilfit—see the contributions of David Edward, Paul Craig, Daniel Sarmiento and Alec Stone Sweet in Maduro and Azoulai (2010, pp. 173–210).

[33] Judgment of the Court (Grand Chamber) of 6 October 2021, *Consorzio Italian Management and Catania Multiservizi SpA v Rete Ferroviaria Italiana SpA*, case C-561/19, EU:C:2021:799.

[34] Judgment of the Court of 16 June 1998, *Hermès International (a partnership limited by shares) v FHT Marketing Choice BV*, case C-53/96, EU:C:1998:292.

[35] Case C-337/95, EU: C: 1997: 517. Linked to the idea of ensuring the uniform interpretation of Community law, the Court made reference to the equivalent role of the Benelux Court, since "the Benelux Court has the task of ensuring that the legal rules common to the three Benelux States are

of Article 267 TFEU, such as the *Collège juridictionnel de la Région de Bruxelles-Capitale* (in *De Coster*, but see, mainly, the extensive conclusions of AG Ruiz Járabo-Colomer, case C-17/00), the Complaints Board of the European Schools (in *Miles*[36]) or arbitral tribunals in investment treaties (in *Achmea*[37]).

Notwithstanding the incidental use of the expression by AG Mengozzi in the *Melli Bank Case* (C-380/09 P)—in the context of an annulment action –, the turning point was, of course, Opinion 2/2013. Although Opinion 1/09 marked a significant moment in the early post-Lisbon days, the Court did not actually use or affirm the principle or the expression in that Opinion,[38] although it did assume that, on one hand, the "guardians" of the EU legal order are both the CJEU and the national member States' "courts and tribunals" and that such a conclusion results from Article 19 (1) TEU (point 66). As the current case-law of the Court states, the very existence of effective judicial review designed to ensure compliance with provisions of EU law is inherent to the existence of the rule of law, and Article 19 TEU gives concrete expression to the value of the rule of law stated in Article 2 TEU and entrusts the responsibility for ensuring the full application of EU law in all member States and effective judicial protection of the rights of individuals under that law to national courts and tribunals and to the Court, *while the Court has exclusive jurisdiction to give the definitive interpretation of that law*. The EU judicial system is therefore a complete system of legal remedies and procedures designed to ensure review of the legality of acts of the institutions, bodies, offices and agencies of the European Union. The tasks attributed to the national courts and to the Court of Justice, respectively, are indispensable to the preservation of the very nature of the law established by the Treaties ("inherent in the system of the treaties on which the European Union is based").

Of course, the emphasis added highlights that the issue at stake was the relationship between the CJEU and other international courts, whether it be the European and Community Patents Court (Opinion 1/09[39]), the European Court of Human Rights (ECtHR) (Opinion 2/13) or the Energy Charter Treaty dispute settlement system (ECT), and in all these cases there were no doubts that both courts qualified as a "court or tribunal of Member States" (under the *Parfums Christian Dior* case-law). However, the ECJ's use of the phrase "definitive interpretation" departed from its traditional use—and, as a matter of fact, from the dissenting view of AG Juliane

---

applied uniformly and (…) the procedure before it is a step in the proceedings before the national courts leading to definitive interpretations of common Benelux legal rules" (points 22–23).

[36] C-196/09, EU:C:2010:777 and EU:C:2011:388, point 41. The Court declined its jurisdiction to rule on a reference for a preliminary ruling from said organ, since, even though it seems to be considered a "court or tribunal", it is not a "court or Tribunal of a member State", and, therefore, falls outside the scope of Article 267 TFEU. The Court committed any development in this area to a change in the treaties, in the wake of *Unión de Pequeños Agricultores (UPA)* case-law (point 45).

[37] C-284/16, EU:C:2018:158, point 48.

[38] EU:C:2011:123, Opinion 1/09.

[39] Opinion of the Court (Full Court) of 8 March 2011, EU:C:2011:123.

Kokkot[40]—in order to establish its primacy so as to ensure the uniform interpretation of EU law:

> 245. The interpretation of a provision of EU law, including of secondary law, requires, in principle, a decision of the Court of Justice where that provision is open to more than one plausible interpretation.
>
> 246. **If the Court of Justice were not allowed to provide the definitive interpretation of secondary law**, and if the ECtHR, in considering whether that law is consistent with the ECHR, had itself to provide a particular interpretation from among the plausible options, there would most certainly be a breach of **the principle that the Court of Justice has exclusive jurisdiction over the definitive interpretation of EU law**.
>
> 247. Accordingly, limiting the scope of the prior involvement procedure, in the case of secondary law, solely to questions of validity adversely affects the competences of the EU and the powers of the Court of Justice in that it **does not allow the Court to provide a definitive interpretation of secondary law in the light of the rights guaranteed by the ECHR**.

We contend that this type of language shall not be interpreted literally and did not intend to undermine the system of cooperation laid down in Article 267 TFEU or the dialogue between national courts or tribunals and the Court, as in fact clearly results from the settled case-law (e.g. Opinion 1/09[41]). As a matter of fact, the point was to ensure the autonomy and specific characteristics of the EU legal order and the specific nature of the ECJ's role dating from the 1950 Schuman Declaration, and impose a prior involvement mechanism that would allow the Court to exercise the "principle of the exclusive jurisdiction of the Court over the definitive interpretation of EU law" (CETA Courts, Opinion 1/17, § 43) that, according to the Belgian government, was affirmed in § 246 of Opinion 2/13.

This is quite possible, at least formally. In the *CSUE c. KF* judgment of 25 June 2020 (case C-14/19 P[42]), the Court used the expression not only in the context of the obligation of member States to ensure effective judicial remedies in all areas covered by EU law (combining Article 2 and, as a "concrete expression" of the principle of the rule of law, Article 19 (1), § 2), but also with regard to a similar obligation

---

[40] Opinion Procedure 2/13, view delivered on 13 June 2014. Although AG Kokott's conclusion was the opposite of that of the Court, one of the conditions for compatibility was the requirement that "the prior involvement of the Court of Justice of the European Union pursuant to Article 3(6) of the draft agreement extends to all legal issues relating to the interpretation, in conformity with the ECHR, of EU primary law and EU secondary law".

[41] Points 84–85: "The system set up by Article 267 TFEU therefore establishes between the Court of Justice and the national courts direct cooperation as part of which the latter are closely involved in the correct application and uniform interpretation of European Union law and also in the protection of individual rights conferred by that legal order. It follows from all of the foregoing that the tasks attributed to the national courts and to the Court of Justice respectively are indispensable to the preservation of the very nature of the law established by the Treaties". It is worth noting that the negative opinion of the Court was based on the fact that the appeals system therein established would prevent national courts from interpreting EU law and from making preliminary references to the Court.

[42] Judgment of the Court (Second Chamber) of 25 June 2020 *European Union Satellite Centre v KF*, case C-14/19 P, EU:C:2020:492.

of the EU institutions,[43] justifying this position with the following expressive statement: "as is apparent from Article 2 TEU, the Union is founded, *inter alia*, on the values of equality and the rule of law. The very existence of effective judicial review designed to ensure compliance with provisions of EU law is inherent in the existence of the rule of law (judgment of 19 July 2016, *H* v *Council and Others*, C-455/14 P, EU:C:2016:569, paragraph 41)". Since then we have seen the same principle be successively asserted, for example in *Euro Box Promotion* et al. (case C-357/19 et al.[44]), where the Court went a little further in explaining the object of this interpretative task: "in the exercise of that jurisdiction, it is ultimately for the Court to clarify the scope of the principle of the primacy of EU law in the light of the relevant provisions of that law; that scope cannot turn on the interpretation of provisions of national law or on the interpretation of provisions of EU law by a national court which is at odds with that of the Court. To that end, the preliminary-ruling procedure provided for in Article 267 TFEU, which is the keystone of the judicial system established by the Treaties, sets up a dialogue between one court and another, specifically between the Court of Justice and the courts of the member States, having the object of securing the uniform interpretation of EU law, thereby serving to ensure its consistency, its full effect and its autonomy as well as, ultimately, the particular nature of the law established by the Treaties". This doctrine has thus become settled case-law, decided by an Order, for example in *FX and Others*.[45]

Hence, its true meaning lies in the sharing of powers between the ECJ and national courts as set out by AG Hogan in point 92 of his conclusions in *Randstad*

---

[43] As the Court stated, "the judicial system of the European Union is therefore a complete system of legal remedies and procedures designed to ensure review of the legality of acts of the institutions, bodies, offices and agencies of the European Union (see, to that effect, Opinion 1/09 of 8 March 2011, EU:C:2011:123, point 70). The tasks attributed to the national courts and to the Court of Justice, respectively, are indispensable to the preservation of the very nature of the law established by the Treaties (Opinion 1/09 of 8 March 2011, EU:C:2011:123, point 85). It follows that, although, in the present case, the 'specific conditions and arrangements' referred to in the fifth paragraph of Article 263 TFEU do indeed allow a body, office or agency of the European Union to draw up internal terms and conditions which are prerequisites to legal proceedings and govern, inter alia, the operation of a self-monitoring mechanism or the course of an out-of-court settlement, as the General Court stated in paragraph 107 of the judgment under appeal, those conditions and arrangements cannot, contrary to what SatCen contends, be interpreted as allowing an institution of the European Union to shield disputes involving the interpretation or application of EU law from the jurisdiction of both the courts of the member States and the EU courts".

[44] Judgment of 21 December 2021 of the Grand Chamber, *Euro Box Promotion* et al., joined cases C-357/19, C-379/19, C-547/19, C-811/19 and C-840/19, point 254 (EU:C:2021:1034). The Court cites in this judgment its previous judgment delivered two months earlier, in *Republic of Moldova vs. Komstroy LLC* (of 21 September 2021, case C-741/19), but this case is aligned with the *Christian Dior Parfums* doctrine (although the Grand Chamber of the Court cites it in its judgment of 22 February 2022, *RS*, in case C-430/21, point 72, EU:C:2022:99, and in Opinion 1/20 of 16 June 2022, point 47).

[45] Order of the Court of 7 November 2022, case C-859/19, EU:C:2022:878, point 133. In the same sense, see the opinion of AG Collins delivered on 15 December 2022 in *European Commission v. Poland*, case C-204/21, EU:C:2022:991, point 60.

Italy: "Indeed, since it is for the national courts to apply EU law, the first task of interpretation necessarily falls to them. As previously stated by the Court, national courts, in collaboration with the Court of Justice, fulfil a duty entrusted to them both of ensuring that in the interpretation and application of the Treaties the law is observed. It follows from the judicial system established by the Treaties – and in particular Article 4(3) TEU, Article 19(1) TEU and Article 267 TFEU (…) – that the Court does not have a monopoly on the interpretation of EU law but rather has exclusive jurisdiction to give the *definitive* interpretation of that law", within the "dialogue" established under the preliminary reference mechanism,[46] which is argued *à outrance*, as recently reaffirmed in the case-law (*CI*[47]).

It is not possible to arrive at a general principle that calls into question this reasoning and gives the "principle" an interpretation that would harm the integrity of the preliminary ruling mechanism and the development of the EU legal order, as we were recently reminded by the Court in its broad statement in *Confédération paysanne and others*, on 7 February 2023[48]:

> Moreover, even if, as the Fédération française des producteurs d'oléagineux et de protéagineux puts forward, the solution to the dispute in the main proceedings can been inferred from the judgment of 25 July 2018, *Confédération paysanne and Others* (C-528/16, EU:C:2018:583), and does not give room for any reasonable doubt, those circumstances are not such as to show the inadmissibility of the request for a preliminary ruling. Those circumstances are, at best, capable of exempting the referring court from its obligation under the third paragraph of Article 267 TFEU to make a reference.
>
> First, even when there is case-law of the Court resolving the point of law at issue, national courts and tribunals retain the broadest power to bring a matter before the Court if they consider it appropriate to do so, and the fact that the provisions whose interpretation is sought have already been interpreted by the Court does not deprive the Court of jurisdiction to give a further ruling (see, to that effect, judgments of 27 March 1963, *Da Costa and Others*, (…), *Cilfit and Others*, (…), *Consorzio Italian Management and Catania Multiservizi*). Second, a national court is in no way prohibited from referring questions to the Court for a preliminary ruling which, in the opinion of one of the parties to the main proceedings, leaves no room for reasonable doubt (see, to that effect, judgments of 1 December 2011, *Painer*, C-145/10, EU:C:2011:798, paragraphs 64 and 65, and of 24 February 2022, *Viva Telecom Bulgaria*, C-257/20, EU:C:2022:125, paragraph 42)

Furthermore, aside from establishing "self-standing precedents" where "precedent has incrementally come to assume a central role of the EU legal system", and even

---

[46] Opinion delivered on 9 September 2021, *Randstad Italia SpA v. Umana SpA and others*, case C-497/20, EU:C:2021:725.

[47] Judgment of the Court (Grand Chamber) of 24 July 2023, *Criminal procedures against C.I and others*, case 107/23 PPU, EU:C:2023:606.

[48] Judgment of the Court (Grand Chamber), *Confédération paysanne and others v. Premier Ministre and other*, Case C-688/21, EU:C:2023:75, point 35. Reaffirmed in the Ordonnance of the ECJ *Groupama Asigurari SA*, case C-310/23, n.° 19 (no English version available), although in this latter cases the Court focused on the restatement of the "motives": ("*une juridiction nationale, qui éprouve des doutes quant à l'interprétation des motifs d'un arrêt de la Cour rendu à la suite d'une demande de décision préjudicielle introduite par une autre juridiction nationale, peut saisir la Cour de questions préjudicielles concernant l'interprétation de ces motifs*").

"a large body of 'common law' of the EU legal order" (G. Beck), there are several cases in which the Court contradicted or differentiated[49] new cases from previous case-law, maybe due, in fact, to the "absence of a formal doctrine of *ratio decidendi*" (*idem*). Some examples may be found in cases such as *Keck and Mithouard*[50] or, even more recently, in cases related to the penalty payment under Article 260 (3) TFEU.[51]

Therefore, contrary to AG Michal Bobek's spirited reference[52] to US Justice Jackson's opinion in *Brown v. Allen*, it cannot be said under the EU system that 'We are not final because we are infallible, but we are infallible only because we are final'. Thankfully, the "rule of precedent" (*atypical precedent*: Duarte 2017, p. 384[53]) does not play the same role in the US and in the Luxembourg CJEU, since the Court usually replies *in abstract,*[54] and so Article 267 TFEU defends us from dogma and infallibility, both national and European.[55] However, the move towards

---

[49] On the topic of reinterpretation and differentiation as a means to adapt and determine a more precise interpretation of EU law, see, inter alia, Beck (2012, pp. 257–258) (although including *Mangold*, which arguably in our view may under no circumstances be considered a reversal of previous ECJ case-law) or 345–347.

[50] Judgment of the Court (Grand Chamber) of 24 November 1993, *Criminal proceedings against Bernard Keck and Daniel Mithouard*, joined cases C-267/91 and C-268/91, EU:C:1993:905, point 16.

[51] Cases V-543/17 vs. C-549/19 and C-550/18. Other cases of alleged reversal of the Court's case—law are invoked. This is argued by AG Michal Bobek in *E v. Bezirkshauptmannschaft Hartberg-Fürstenfeld* (opinion delivered on 23 September 2021, note 57; and judgment of the Grand Chamber of 8 March 2022, case C-205/20, EU:C:2022:168, point 88), claiming derogation from the *Link-Logistic* doctrine (judgment of the Court of 4 October 2018, *Dooel Uvoz-Izvoz Skopje Link Logistic N&N v. Budapest Rendőrfőkapitánya*, case C-384/17, EU:C:2018:810, points 51–56). In our view, this is not the case. To simplify, there is one major difference between the two Directives and their rules on proportionality. Whilst in *Link-Logistic* the member State did not implement the Directive, in *E* the Member State implemented the Directive, although in a disproportionate manner, as the Court found. In this particular, although it could seem *de facto* disturbing the distinction (that exceeds our purpose) between unconditionality and the recognition that member States may exert "a certain discretion" when adopting national rules to comply with it, as long as they respect the limits to procedural autonomy (effectiveness and equivalence) case-law that unconditional rules may leave some "*margin of manoeuvre*" for member States (see, for instance, the *Randstad Italia* judgment of 21 December 2021, case C-497/20, EU:C:2021:1037, points 52–57).

[52] Opinion delivered on 23 September 2021, *NE v Bezirkshauptmannschaft Hartberg-Fürstenfeld*, case C-205/20, note 57.

[53] S 384; see also Martins (1988) and Coutinho (2013, pp. 197–198 and 399–402) (on how the national courts perceived the authority of 267 TFEU judgments).

[54] See, for recent cases, Judgment of the Court (Ninth Chamber) of 25 October 2018, *'Roche Lietuva' UAB*, case C-413/17, point 43, EU:C:2018:865; Order of the Court of 1 March 2022, *K.M.*, case C-493/21, point 24, EU:C:2022:191.

[55] Natascha hopefully has reached 33 years in 2023 and the right to a new preliminary reference remains valid (Pertek 2001, pp. 157–161) even if the clarifications by the Court will be dealt with in the form of an Order (e.g. C-493/21). And this is also true for the dominant Portuguese constitutional doctrine, although there is a trend to limit it (see Machado 2022, p. 738); Martins (2017,

an EU *Marbury v. Madison* (heard at an EU law public event in 2023[56]) seems closer, and even (indirectly) affirmed (in *W.Ż.*).[57]

References

Arnull A (2013) Article 19. (The court of justice of the European Union) (Ex-articles 220-224 EC). In: Blanke HJ, Mangiameli S (eds) The treaty on European Union (TEU): a commentary. Springer, Cham, pp 759–783

Beck G (2012) The legal reasoning of the court of justice of the European Union. Hart Publishing, Oxford

Bergé JS (2022) Que faire de nos a priori en droit? Jalons pour une recherche antécédente. Recl Dalloz Sirey 198:1865–1871

Bredimas A (1978) Methods of interpretation and community law. North-Holland Publishing, London

Conway G (2013) The limits of legal reasoning and the European court of justice. Cambridge University Press, Cambridge

Costa O, Schwarzer D, Berès P, Gressani G, Marti G, Mayer F, Nguyen T, Von Ondarza N, Russack S, Tekin F, Vallée S, Verger C (2023) Report of the Franco-German working group on EU institutional reform: sailing on high seas: reforming and enlarging the EU for the 21st century, Paris-Berlin, 18 September 2023. https://www.auswaertiges-amt.de/blob/2617206/4d0e0010ffcd8c0079e21329bbbb3332/230919-rfaa-deu-fra-bericht-data.pdf. Accessed 30 Nov 2023

p. 598) follows the traditional position set out, *inter alia*, in the classic Pierre Pescatore comment to Article 177 EEC (Pescatore 1992).

[56] In all the ECJ doctrine, it appears that only in the conclusions of AG Tamara Ćapeta delivered on 17 November 2022, *Changmao Biochemical Engineering Co. Ltd v. European Commission*, case C-123/21 P, there is a reference to the 1803 US Supreme Court case *Marbury v. Madison* (24.2.1803, available at https://tile.loc.gov/storage-services/service/ll/usrep/usrep005/usrep005137/usrep005137.pdf, see in particular pages 176–180: "It is emphatically the province and duty of the judicial department to say what the law is"). AG Tamara Ćapeta's Opinion draws on the American case to remind us that it is up to the Court to "say what the law is" (para. 35), which is a bizarre quote from the US case, anyway, considering the perennial words of Article 19 (1), paragraph 1, and its earlier versions.

[57] Judgment of the Court (Grand Chamber) of 21 October 2021, *W.Ż.*, case C-487/19, EU:C:2021:789. points 71 and 155–161 (and dispositive). In the judgment of the Court (Grand Chamber) of 13 July 2023, *Criminal proceedings against YP and Others*, Joined Cases C-615/20 and C-671/20, EU:C:2023:562, point 64, it was recalled that it "is also apparent from settled case-law that, even in the absence of national legislative measures having brought to an end a failure to fulfil obligations established by the Court, it is for the national courts to take all measures to facilitate the full application of EU law in accordance with the *dicta* in the judgment establishing a failure to fulfil obligations. Moreover, those courts are required, under the principle of sincere cooperation laid down in Article 4(3) TEU, to **nullify** the unlawful consequences of an infringement of EU law (emphasis added). Although the Court cited earlier case-law for this *dicta* (namely judgment of the Court (Third Chamber) of 10 March 2022, *"Grossmania" Mezőgazdasági Termelő és Szolgáltató Kft v Vas Megyei Kormányhivatal*, case C- 117/20, EU:C: point 63, combined with 38, where the reference to national courts should "facilitate"), the fact is that this former case said that "**Member States**" were to nullify and gave some discretion in how they could do so, thus not departing from traditional and settled case-law. Anyway, for this topic, a recent *aperçu* may be found in Dougan (2022); and Gorjão-Henriques (2020).

Coutinho FP (2013) Os tribunais nacionais na ordem jurídica da União Europeia – o caso Português. Coimbra Editora, Coimbra, Portugal

Da Cruz Vilaça J, Piçarra N (2014) Are there substantive limits to the amendment of the treaties. In: Da Cruz Vilaça J (ed) EU law and integration: twenty years of judicial application of EU law. Hart Publishing, Oxford, pp 13–43

David E (1999) Le droit international applicable aux organisations internationales. In: Dony M, Walsche AD (eds) Mélanges en hommage à Michel Waelbroeck. Bruylant, Bruxelles, Belgium, pp 3–22

De Mesquita MJR (2022) Introdução ao contencioso da União Europeia. Almedina, Coimbra, Portugal

De Morais CB (1998) As Leis Reforçadas – as leis reforçadas pelo procedimento no âmbito dos critérios estruturantes das relações entre actos legislativos. Coimbra Editora, Coimbra, Portugal

Dougan M (2022) The primacy of union law over incompatible national measures: beyond disapplication and towards a remedy of nullity? Common Mark Law Rev 59:1301–1332

Duarte ML (2017) Direito do contencioso da União Europeia. AAFDL Editora, Lisboa, Portugal

Duarte ML (2021) Direito da União Europeia – lições desenvolvidas. AAFDL Editora, Lisboa, Portugal

Duarte RA (2023) A crise do estado de direito na União Europeia e o papel do TJUE. Almedina, Coimbra, Portugal

Feilhès L (2022) Responsabilité de l'État et autonomie procédurale: les nouvelles (im)précisions sur les principes d'équivalence et d'effectivité. Rev Aff Eur 2022(3):551–570

Gorjão-Henriques M (2020) The EU jurisdictional structure and the enforcement of EU law: notes from the past to the future. Temas Integração, 40:289–336

Gorjão-Henriques M (2025) Direito da União Europeia, 10th ed., Almedina, Coimbra

Jorge T, Burns T (2021) Duelo de Titãs. O conflito entre o tribunal constitucional federal Alemão e o tribunal de justiça da União Europeia à luz do pluralismo constitucional. Themis Rev Direito 20-21:185–249

Lanceiro RTL (2019) O princípio da cooperação leal e a administração – a europeização do procedimento de acto administrativo. PhD thesis, AAFDL

Lattanzi S (2022) L'evoluzione delle tecniche di interpretazione del diritto dell'Unione: tra tendenze passate e sviluppi recenti. Dirit Dell'Unione Eur 2022/2:361–390

Lecourt R (2008) L'Europe des juges. Bruylant, Bruxelles, Belgium

Lenaerts K, Van Nuffel P (1999) Constitutional law of the European Union. Sweet & Maxwell, London, UK

Machado JEM (2022) Direito da União Europeia. Coimbra Editora, Coimbra, Portugal

Maduro MP (2023) General report on topic 1 ("Mutual trust, mutual recognition and the rule of law") to the Sofia 2023 Fide Congress. https://cic.events/fide/fide-publications-vol-1.pdf. Accessed 3 Dec 2023

Maduro MP, Azoulai L (2010) The past and future of EU law – the classics of EU revisited on the 50th anniversary of the Rome Treaty. Hart Publishing, Oxford, UK

Markus J (2023) Abuse of EU law revisited: an analytical perspective. Eur Public Law 28:351–372

Martins AMG (1988) Efeitos dos acórdão prejudiciais do Artigo 177.° do TR (CEE). AAFDL Editora, Lisboa, Portugal

Martins AMG (2017) Manual de direito da União Europeia. Almedina, Coimbra, Portugal

Moreira V (2014) "Respublica" Europeia - Estudos de direito constitucional da União Europeia. Coimbra Editora, Coimbra, Portugal

Pais SO (2011) Princípios fundamentais de direito da União Europeia. Almedina, Coimbra, Portugal

Pais SO (2017) Estudos de direito da União Europeia. Almedina, Coimbra, Portugal

Pertek J (2001) La pratique du renvoi préjudiciel en droit communautaire. Litec, Paris, France

Pescatore P (1992) Article 177 CEE. In: Constantinesco V, Jacques JP, Robert K, Simon D (eds) Traite instituant la CEE - Commentaire article par article. Economica, Paris, France, p 1120

Piçarra N (1991) O tribunal de justiça das comunidades Europeias como juiz legal e o processo do artigo 177.° do Tratado CEE. AAFDL Editora, Lisboa, Portugal

Picod F (2005) Treaty establishing a constitution for Europe, volume 2, part II, the Charter of fundamental rights of the Union, article by article commentary (and, to a certain extent, “Article I-29”). Bruylant, Brussels, Belgium, Tome 1, pp 394–395

Raitio J (2013) The expectation of legal certainty and horizontal effect of EU law. In: Bernitz U, Groussot X, Schulyok F (eds) General principles of EU law and European private law. Wolters Kluwer, Alphen aan den Rijn, Netherlands, pp 199–211

Ramos RM (1995) Das comunidades à União - Estudos. Coimbra Editora, Coimbra, Portugal

Rosas A, Livits E, Bots Y (2013) The court of justice and the construction of Europe: analyses and perspectives on sixty years of case-law. Asser Press/Springer Verlag, The Hague/Berlin

Sarmiento D (2023) The comeback of the mixed chamber: institutional reform and competence creep in an enlarged Union. https://verfassungsblog.de/the-comeback-of-the-mixed-chamber/. Accessed 30 Nov 2023

Miguel Gorjão-Henriques Universidade de Coimbra, Faculty of Law, Coimbra, Portugal, Lawyer.

The manufacturer's authorised representative in the EU is Springer Nature Customer Service Centre GmbH, Europaplatz 3, 69115 Heidelberg, Germany. If you have any concerns regarding our products, please contact ProductSafety@springernature.com

Printed and bound by CPI Group (UK) Ltd, Croydon, CR0 4YY
30/09/2026
02225590-0017